Fodor's

VIENNA & THE
BEST OF AUSTRIA

D0601160

Welcome to Austria

From Vienna to the Alps, Austria celebrates the elegance of the past yet also embraces the pleasures of contemporary culture and the outdoors. Sophisticated Vienna buzzes with former imperial palaces and striking modern structures, traditional coffeehouses and chic locavore restaurants. Beyond the capital, you can hike the Salzkammergut with its cool blue lakes, ski the fashionable slopes of Innsbruck, or soak in the enduring charms of Salzburg's classical music scene. As you plan your upcoming travels to Austria, please confirm that places are still open and let us know when we need to make updates by writing to us at this address: editors@fodors.com.

TOP REASONS TO GO

★ **Vienna:** Baroque and art nouveau architecture, cool boutiques and concert halls.

★ **Scenery:** Stunning views of alpine passes, the Danube Valley, and lowland vineyards.

★ **Music:** The land of Mozart and Strauss entertains fans with performances galore.

★ **Historic Palaces:** From Mirabell to Schönbrunn, Austria flaunts its imperial past.

★ **Museums:** The Kunsthistorisches, MuseumsQuartier, and Museum der Moderne, for a start.

★ **Skiing:** Posh resorts and world-class runs at Kitzbühel, St. Anton, and more.

Contents

MAPS

EXPERIENCE VIENNA AND THE BEST OF AUSTRIA

12 ULTIMATE EXPERIENCES

Austria offers terrific experiences that should be on every traveler's list. Here are Fodor's top picks for a memorable trip.

1 Schönbrunn Palace

Play royalty for a day in Vienna by visiting the summer residence of the Habsburgs with its elegant gardens, fountains, fake Roman ruins, a hilltop café, and Europe's oldest zoo. *(Ch.7)*

2 Sachertorte

Indulge in a slice of Sachertorte, a dense chocolate cake layered with apricot jam. It was invented in the early 19th century by one of Austria's court confectioners.

3 Grossglockner High Alpine Highway

In the Alps, you can ascend to Austria's tallest peak and view the Pasterze glacier from 12,470 feet. See it while you can; it shrinks 30 feet every year. *(Ch. 10)*

4 Heurigen

Visit a wine tavern where owners serve new wines from their own vineyards. In September, sample Sturm, a drink made from the first pressing of the grapes. *(Ch. 7)*

5 Thermal Spas

Soak in hot springs at one of several thermal spas that dot small towns throughout Austria. Then brag that you've experienced the country's unofficial leisure sport. *(Ch. 10)*

6 The Ringstrasse

Streetcars travel full circle along Vienna's best-known avenue, lined with monumental buildings that recall the city's imperial splendor. *(Ch. 3)*

7 The Salzkammergut

Enjoy a hike in this rural paradise in Upper Austria with 76 lakes and the Dachstein Mountain range. The opening scenes from The Sound of Music were filmed here. *(Ch. 11)*

8 The Viennese Ball

As many as 400 black-tie balls are held every year during Vienna's Fasching, or carnival season, which lasts from New Year's Eve through Mardi Gras. *(Ch. 2)*

9 Hofbibliothek

Browse the stacks at Vienna's National Library, a cathedral of books and one of the world's most ornate Baroque libraries. *(Ch. 3)*

10 MAK Museum

In Vienna, this gorgeous collection of Austrian art objects and contemporary works also includes a fascinating display devoted to the Wiener Werkstätte. *(Ch. 5)*

11 Kitzbühel

This 16th-century village with a medieval town center has carved out a reputation as one of Europe's most fashionable winter ski resorts. *(Ch. 13)*

12 Fortress Hohensalzburg

Evening classical music concerts take place in the prince's chamber of this mighty castle overlooking Salzburg's skyline. *(Ch. 9)*

WHAT'S WHERE

1 Vienna. Vienna mixes old-world charm with elements of a modern metropolis. The city's neighborhoods offer a journey thick with history and architecture, and the famous coffeehouses are havens for an age-old coffee-drinking ritual.

2 Sidetrips from Vienna. Vienna is surrounded with enticing options such as hiking in the Vienna Woods and exploring the nearby towns of Marchegg and Carnuntum. The famously blue Danube courses through Austria past medieval abbeys, fanciful Baroque monasteries, verdant pastures, and compact riverside villages. A convenient base is Linz, Austria's third-largest city, and probably its most underrated.

3 Salzburg. Salzburg is an elegant city with a rich musical heritage that also draws visitors for its museums and architecture, the von Trapp family history, old-fashioned cafés, and glorious fountains.

4 The Eastern Alps. Farther south and into the Alps, panoramic little towns, spas, and an array of sports highlight this section of Austria. No road in Europe matches the Grossglockner High Alpine Highway, the most spectacular pass through the Alps.

5 Salzkammergut. The Salzkammergut stretches across three states—from Salzburg through Styria to Upper Austria—and includes Austria's Lake District. Hallstatt is touted as one of the world's prettiest lakeside villages.

6 Carinthia and Graz. Carinthia is the country's sunniest (and southernmost) province. Here you'll find the Austrian Riviera, a blend of mountains, valleys, and placid blue-green lakes with lovely resorts, while Graz, the capital of Styria, is the country's second-largest city.

7 Innsbruck, Tyrol, and Vorarlberg. The Tyrol is a region graced with cosmopolitan cities and monuments, but with the glorious Alps playing the stellar role, Nature steals every scene. Nearby, Vorarlberg's big draw is its powdery skiing regions.

What to Eat and Drink in Austria

WIENER SCHNITZEL

No city is more synonymous with a dish than Vienna (Wien in German) and Wiener Schnitzel—thin breaded cutlets served with a lemon slice and sprig of parsley. By Austrian law, a Wiener Schnitzel must be veal. Breaded cutlets from chicken and pork are sold under different names.

SAUSAGE

Sausages of all varieties can be found at the ever-present *Wurstelstand. Burenwurst* is a pork sausage similar to kielbasa. *Bosna* is a wurst served with onions. For those who like smoked meat, there's the *Waldviertler*, which is smoked wurst, and the more elaborate *Beinwurst*, made of smoked pork, a selection of herbs, and wine. *Bockwurst* is a pork sausage, and *Weisswurst* is a veal sausage, boiled, and often eaten for breakfast. The *Nürnberger* is a small spicy pork wurst, and the *Blutwurst* is a sausage with congealed blood. Other varieties include the paprika-spiced *Debreziner* and the cheese-filled *Käsekrainer.*

POTATO GOULASH

Goulash has origins in Hungary as a beefy stew, but the local take on it is heavy on potatoes and onions instead. Many recipes include slices of sausage so be sure to double check if eating meat is an issue.

KÄSESPÄTZLE

A variation on macaroni and cheese has strips of egg pasta called *Spätzle* layered with onions and grated cheese, then pan fried to a golden brown and topped with fried onions. For vegetarians this may be the best option in many eateries.

TAFELSPITZ

The "tip of meat for the table" was Emperor Franz Josef I's favorite dish. Slices of beef boiled with root vegetables are accented by apples, potatoes, horseradish, and sour cream. You'll find Emperor Franz Josef's favorite meal on the menu in most restaurants in Vienna. Plachutta is especially famous for its Tafelspitz presentation.

SELCHFLEISCH

Chunks of smoked pork boiled in broth are mixed together with sauerkraut or steamed cabbage and served with dumplings. This rather heavy meal will warm you up on a chilly day.

TIROLER GRÖSTL

Bacon bits, potatoes, and onions fried in a pan and usually topped with a fried egg help to keep skiers and hikers going in the Alpine regions. It has its origins in using up leftovers from Sunday dinner.

BEER

While Austrian wines, particularly whites, are now recognized by wine experts around the world for their excellent quality, Austria is definitely beer territory. One of the most popular types is *Märzenbier*, a hoppy amber-colored brew traditionally made in March and served in the summer. Also look for the cloudy *Weissbier* (wheat beer) common to the Salzburg area. *Radler*, a mix of beer and lemonade is a popular summertime refreshment in Austria.

Adrienne Pitts/Shutter

COFFEE

Don't ask for Viennese coffee, say *Kaffee mit schlagobers* to get the hot caffeinated beverage with whipped cream. Ask for a *Maria Theresa* and your coffee will come with a shot of orange liquer inside. The most common coffee drink is the *Melange*, the Austrian version of the cappuccino featuring steamed milk and milk foam. The *Kapuziner* is a coffee with a splash of sweet cream (not a cappuccino, despite the similar-sounding name.) The *Schwarzer Mokka* is a straight espresso.

POWIDLTASCHERL

Crescent-shaped potato-flour dumplings filled plum jam are rolled in toasted bread crumbs and sprinkled with sugar. Austrian composer Hermann Leopoldi liked them so much he wrote a humorous song about them.

SACHERTORTE

The famous chocolate cake with a layer of apricot jam and dark chocolate icing is so synonymous with Vienna that it was featured as a lyric in a Beatles song. Developed in the 19th century, the Hotel Sacher lays claim to the "original" recipe, supposedly known only to a few individuals and kept under lock and key.

APFELSTRUDEL

A Viennese culinary innovation that spread across Europe, the cinnamon-flavored apple strudel is often served with a dollop of cream and is the perfect accompaniment for an after-dinner coffee. The oldest known recipe is stored in Vienna's City Hall Library.

LINZER TORTE

The famous Austrian torte with a lattice design made of pastry, cinnamon, hazelnuts, and red currant jam, dates to the 17th century and is named for the city of Linz, the capital of upper Austria. The dish is traditionally served at Christmastime but typically available year-round for visitors. Note: The finer the grid on top, the more expert the patissier.

WHITE WINE

The center of wine production in Austria is found in northern and eastern Lower Austria, in Burgenland, in Styria, and on the hilly terraces overlooking Vienna. The most popular white variety is Grüner Veltliner, followed by Riesling, Sauvignon Blanc, and Pinot Blanc (often labeled as Weissburgunder). Wineries to look for include Wieninger, Bründlmayer, and Umathum.

Best Museums in Vienna

AZ W—ARCHITEKTURZENTRUM WIEN

The national architecture center houses a permanent show on the country's built environment from the 1850s onward, and temporary exhibits on urban planning and similar themes. It's one of the world's leading institutions in its field.

LEOPOLD MUSEUM

Fans of early 20th century Austrian art will find the largest collection of works by Egon Schiele plus pieces by Gustav Klimt, Oskar Kokoschka, and Richard Gerstl that explore Art Nouveau and Expressionism.

KUNSTHISTORISCHES MUSEUM WIEN

The domed Museum of Fine Art was built in the late 1800s to open the vast imperial collections to the public. All the big names from Michelangelo to Rubens plus a few modern masters are represented.

BELVEDERE

Prince Eugene of Savoy's summer palace complex sits in a sculpted park. The upper and lower palaces have the largest collection of works by Gustav Klimt as well as Art Nouveau, French Impressionism, and Baroque masterpieces. There is also a modern pavilion for contemporary art and events.

KUNSTHALLE WIEN

The Art Hall of Vienna focuses on contemporary art and social change, with works by both established and rising stars. It began in a makeshift metal container but now is in the neo-Classical winter riding arena of the Imperial Mews.

ALBERTINA

Duke Albert of Saxony-Teschen, the son-in-law of Empress Maria Theresia, began collecting prints and drawings in 1776. The collection comprises more than a million prints and 60,000 drawings, and includes masterpieces by Schiele, Cézanne, Klimt, Kokoschka, Picasso, Rauschenberg, and more.

ALBERTINA MODERN

Vienna's €50 million new venue for post-1945 art is an offspring of the world-famous Albertina set in the newly renovated Künstlerhaus. The in-house collection includes the works of such renowned Austrians as Arnulf Rainer and Maria Lassnig, as well as art by leading international artists, including Anselm Kiefer, Damien Hirst, Andy Warhol, and Cindy Sherman.

MAK

Design, architecture, and contemporary art meet at the Museum für angewandte Kuns (Museum of Applied Art), whose roots go back to the 1860s. Be sure to check out the gift shop for cool design objects and the stylish restaurant.

SISI MUSEUM

Sisi is the nickname of Empress Elisabeth of Austria, who was the Princess Diana of the late 19th century. She remains the idol of many young women, and her personal possessions can be seen in the Hofburg Imperial Palace.

BANK AUSTRIA KUNSTFORUM WIEN

Don't let the name put you off, the exhibits at the Art Forum are about post-war art, not banking. Recently, they have also put the spotlight on contemporary artists. The remodeled former bank building sees a quarter of a million visitors per year.

JÜDISCHES MUSEUM WIEN

The Jewish Museum Vienna offers a poignant overview of the history of the Jewish people in Austria. There are two sites (one ticket): the main venue, the Palais Eskeles, is the former townhouse of a noble Jewish family. The Judenplatz facility features the foundations of a 15th century synagogue and the medieval Jewish ghetto, as well as Rachel Whiteread's impressive monument to the 65,000 Austrian Jews who were exterminated during the Holocaust.

MUMOK

The acronym comes from Museum moderner Kunst, or Museum of Modern Art. Inside there are works by Warhol, Picasso, Jasper Johns, and Roy Lichtenstein. The core of the collection comes from industrialist Peter Ludwig.

Under the Radar Vienna

NASCHMARKT

Vienna's largest market is best visited on a food tour to visit the market's best small vendors and enjoy tastings while dodging the crowds. There's a flea market on Saturday.

RUEFF DANCE SCHOOL

Learn how to waltz in the city where it was invented over 150 years ago. Lessons are available in English and German (no reservations necessary if part of a pair) and are tailored to the student's experience level. Advanced dancers can join practice sessions held several evenings a week. Casual clothing is fine, but smooth-soled shoes are a must.

GÜRTEL

Nightclubs and bars thrive in the Jungenstil arches under the Stadtbahn railway, where the noise of electronic dance music won't be an issue at night. Gürtel means belt, and refers to the busy adjacent street.

THE THIRD MAN MUSEUM

The post-war decade in Vienna is seen through exhibits related the famous 1948 film "The Third Man," which starred Orson Welles as a black marketeer. There are scripts, props, books, posters, and other memorabilia including personal items from Welles.

TÜRKENSCHANZPARK
The site of Turkish military encampment during sieges of the 1600s is now one of Vienna's prettiest parks, known for its undulating landscape and rare botanical plants. A brick tower provides lovely city views. Meandering paths lead you to ponds, streams, monuments, fountains, a playground, and a cafe and restaurant with a large terrace.

KURPARK OBERLAA
Flowers and lakes dot this sprawling urban park on a sloping hill in Favoriten. There's a flower maze, a Japanese garden, a Baroque fountain, and a petting zoo, and the famous Oberlaa café and its cake shop are particularly popular attractions.

CENTRAL CEMETERY
One of the world's largest cemeteries, you can find the tombs of composers Beethoven, Schubert, and Johann Strauss Jr., as well as a monument for Mozart, among many other famous people.

Das Rote Wien Waschsalon

JUSTIZCAFE
This rooftop restaurant sits atop the Renaissance-style Palace of Justice and offers unrestricted 360-degree views of Vienna's top attractions. Most of the patrons are judges and lawyers but—shhh!—it is also open to the general public. Food and beverages are above standard and reasonably priced.

DAS ROTE WIEN WASCHSALON
Red Vienna in the Laundry Room is located in the Karl-Marx-Hof in the 19th District, a 1,300-apartment complex that extends over two-thirds of a mile and spans four tram stops. The former laundry room is now a museum that explores the history of the city of Vienna and the mark left on it by social democracy.

SIGMUND FREUD MUSEUM
The newly renovated apartments where Freud, the founder of modern psychology, lived for almost half a century trace his life though photographs. You can see his private rooms, waiting room, antique collection, and visit his original practice space.

What to Buy in Vienna

FÜRST MOZARTKUGEL
If you're sweet on Wolfgang Amadeus Mozart, you'll be nuts for these pistachio marzipan and nougat–filled chocolates, with a foil wrapper sporting the composer's likeness. Rival brands, each using a different portrait of Mozart, claim to be the original, but the blue-and-silver wrapped ones made by Fürst came first (appropriately).

FREY WILLE
This enamel jewelry manufacturer was founded in the early 1950s in Vienna and is known for its colorful, hand-decorated designs. Shop for bracelets, watches, earrings, and pendants in the flagship store in Stephensplatz.

LEATHER GOODS
Austria's long tradition creating quality leather goods and footwear makes for quality, bespoke souvenirs. Designers to look for include traditional Viennese establishments R. Horn and Albert Pattermann, and contemporary local brands Ina Kent, Eva Blut, and Susanne Kitz. For shoes, Rudolf Scheer has been crafting bespoke shoes by hand since 1816 and for seven generations.

LOBMEYR GLASS
Family owned J. & L. Lobmeyr has been in Vienna since 1823, supplying chandeliers to many palaces and opera houses and all manner of glassware to upper class and noble families. Today they are known for hand-blown and etched stemware, vases, and decorative pieces.

HAND-MADE CHOCOLATES AND PRALINES
Chocolatey treats are an art form in Vienna. Textured balls with soft centers, pink hearts with drizzled stripes, and whimsical shapes in a variety of colors are handmade daily in small shops throughout Vienna. Look for Zotter, Xocolat, and Heindl.

SVAROVSKI CRYSTAL
Internationally renowned precision-cut crystal maker Svarovski has its headquarters and museum in Wattens, near Innsbruck, and three stories filled with sparkling jewelry, watches, figurines, lighting, phone cases, and more on Kärntner Strasse in Vienna.

SNOW GLOBES
An effort by Austrian surgical supplier Erwin Perzy to improve hospital lighting with water-filled globes and reflective particles led to the creation of the first snow globes. Today, they are a favorite souvenir for travelers and still made by the third generation of the Perzy family. You'll find the biggest selection at the Perzy snow globe museum in Vienna or at Christmas Markets. Look for globes with holiday themes and Austrian landmarks.

DIRNDL DRESS
The traditional peasant dress of Austria, the drindl, has a frilly blouse, colorful bodice, and waist apron. For a quality, traditional dirndl and other traditional folkwear, head to the flagship Gössl store in Salzburg where you can find a museum and avail of a tailor, or look for their stores in Vienna.

AUSTRIAN FASHIONS
Austria's fashion capital is home to style-conscious locals and flagship stores of international and local designers. Local brands to look for include JCH Juergen Christian Hoerl, Lena Hoschek, Jutta Pregenzer, and Michel Meyer. Ferrari Zöchling offers limited-edition designs and collaborations with Austrian designers while Mühlbauer Hutmanufaktur has been handcrafting hats for more than 100 years.

What to Watch and Read

THE THIRD MAN
BY GRAHAM GREEN
Grahame Green wrote the novel as well as the screenplay for director Carol Reed's famed 1949 film. Both capture Vienna just after World War II, a divided city trying to recover its normalcy. A man's search for his childhood friend leads to an investigation into a suspicious funeral, and some dark secrets. In the film, Orson Welles steals the show in a brief role.

THE MAN WITHOUT QUALITIES
BY ROBERT MUSIL
A meandering philosophical story captures the mood of the end of the Austro-Hungarian Empire. At more than 1,000 pages, the unfinished novel, published in three parts between 1930 and 1943, is considered a modern masterpiece. The plot centers on a mathematician named Ulrich and his search for meaning. The same author's 1906 semi-autobiographical debut novel *The Confusions of Young Törless*, about life in a boarding school, is also worth checking out and a more manageable 176 pages.

THE SEVEN-PER-CENT SOLUTION
BY NICHOLAS MEYER
A bit of fun finds Sherlock Holmes going to Vienna in 1891 to seek Sigmund Freud's medical help for his cocaine problem. But a kidnapping piques Holmes' curiosity, and he pursues the case across Austria. The stakes are high, as somehow all of this is tied to someone trying the embroil Europe in a large war. Meyer also wrote the screenplay for the 1976 film adaptation, which features Laurence Olivier in a supporting role.

THE PIANO TEACHER
BY ELFRIEDE JELINEK
Nobel Prize–winning author Elfriede Jelinek's best-known work is *The Piano Teacher,* published in 1983 and adapted into a French-language film in 2001. The novel tracks the strange relationship of a controlling, elderly mother and her adult daughter, who teaches piano at the Vienna Conservatory. The daughter attempts a relationship with a student, but the result is awkward to say the least.

THE PAINTED KISS
BY ELIZABETH HICKEY
Painter Gustav Klimt shows Vienna's wild side to his naive young model Emilie Floge, who posed for the famous painting The Kiss. Floge would eventually become the painter's mistress in an on-again off-again affair. Much of the story is speculative as little is known about Floge's real life aside from a basic outline.

THE GOALIE'S ANXIETY AT THE
PENALTY KICK BY PETER HANDKE
A former football player is fired from his construction job in an insignificant town, and subsequently commits a murder for no reason. He feels completely disconcerted from his actions, but follows the case in the papers. The avant-garde 1970 novel was a milestone of post-war European literature. Director Wim Wenders made a 1972 film adaptation. Handke won the Nobel Prize for Literature in 2019.

WHEN NIETZSCHE WEPT
BY IRVIN D. YALOM
Philosopher Friedrich Nietzsche meets Dr. Josef Breuer, an early psychologist, in Vienna in 1882. The meeting, which in reality didn't actually happen, provides the opportunity to explore philosophy, history, and romantic desire. Notable figures such as Sigmund Freud and Richard Wagner get shout outs as the story progresses. The discussion helps Nietzsche to formulate his ideas for *Thus Spoke Zarathustra*.

OLD MASTERS: A COMEDY BY THOMAS BERNHARD

An elderly music critic spends the morning of every other day in a museum sitting on a bench in front of Italian painter Tintoretto's *White-bearded Man*. One day a man, Atzbacher, meets the critic and arranges another meeting on the next day. The novel is split between that Atzbacher's speculations about the man and their following conversation. Thomas Bernhard is one of the most important German-language authors of the late 20th century. Other notable works include *Wittgenstein's Nephew*, *Correction,* and *The Loser.*

SOUND OF MUSIC DIRECTED BY ROBERT WISE

The adventures of the singing von Trapp family provides the basis for this beloved musical, which won five Academy Awards and was for a time the top grossing film ever. Julie Andrews stars as a prospective nun who is sent to be the governess of some over-disciplined children. She teaches them the joys of singing and enjoying the outdoors. All the time, World War II looms on the horizon. The story is adapted from Maria von Trapp's 1949 memoir *The Story of the Trapp Family Singers.*

AMADEUS DIRECTED BY MILOŠ FORMAN

In this widely regarded film, *Amadeus* shows the supposed rivalry between Mozart and Austrian court composer Salieri. Tom Hulce, who has since given up acting and turned to producing, gave an unforgettable performance as the talented but juvenile Mozart. Salieri, played by F. Murray Abraham, can't accept that his own mediocre works will be forgotten while Mozart's will live forever. While set in 18th century Vienna, filming actually took place in Prague. The film won eight Academy Awards.

BEFORE SUNRISE DIRECTED BY RICHARD LINKLATER

An American tourist played by Ethan Hawke meets a French woman played by Julie Delpy on a train, and they decide to explore Vienna together. Popular landmarks form the backdrop as they fall in love. The plot is very thin, but the sincere acting and well-defined characters have made it a favorite date film. It is followed by two sequels, set in Paris and a Greek Island.

COLONEL REDL BY ISTVÁN SZABÓ

A West German–Hungarian–Austrian co-production from 1985 looks at the true story of Colonel Alfred Redl, played by Klaus Maria Brandauer. The officer's stellar career in counter-intelligence gets derailed by rumors about his sexual orientation in the days before World War I. Redl was also closely involved in Archduke Franz Ferdinand's plot to overthrow Emperor Franz Josef I. Director Szabó and Brandauer collaborated again on the 1988 Austrian co-production *Hanussen,* about a clairvoyant in the days before World War II.

SISSI DIRECTED BY ERNST MARISCHKA

The first of a trilogy of films about Empress Elisabeth of Austria, known popularly as Sissi (or more commonly Sisi), came out in 1955 with Romy Schneider, then 16 years old, in the lead role. The films are still massively popular with young girls, while young adults have turned them into a drinking game, taking a sip every time Sissi's name is said. The plot is an entirely fanciful account of how the real-life Bavarian princess met her future husband, Austrian Emperor Franz Josef I.

Vienna and Austria Today

Almost two-thirds of Austria is covered by mountains, making Vienna, which qualifies as a region, a bit distinct from the rest of the country. Over one in five Austrians live in Vienna, making the rest of the country rather sparsely populated by comparison. Graz, the second-largest city in Austria, has been growing rapidly into a smart city and tech hub, due to the number of students and young grads there.

STILL WINNING ON LIVING

According to an annual index compiled by The Economist Intelligence Unit (EIU), the Austrian capital was named the most liveable city in the world in 2019 and 2020, and has consistently ranked in the top five since 2015. On the EIU's index, which ranks 140 cities on 30 factors bunched into five categories—stability, health care, culture and environment, education, and infrastructure—Vienna scores a near-perfect 99.1 out of 100. The Mercer Quality of Life Index, focused on professional relocation, has ranked Vienna at number one for 10 years in a row for many of the same reasons. You don't have to be a local to benefit from the clean air, low crime rate, and cheap, reliable public transport that comes with this ranking.

BUT THE SUBWAY SMELLS LIKE A SUBWAY

Like many cities, Vienna has been promoting public transit to reduce pollution from vehicles and reduce traffic congestion. And like all major cities, at peak times, the metro here can get crowded and a little stale, especially when the temperatures pick up. During the summer of 2019, Wiener Linien, the company that runs the city's U-Bahn subway system, conducted an experiment to infuse the underground air with pleasing scents to improve ride quality. Green tea, grapefruit, sandalwood, and melon were piped through the train system for several months but the public turned up their noses to the perfumed trains, preferring an au naturale commute.

MUSIC

Austria is synonymous with classical music almost to the point of obsession; therefore, changes in the musical landscape often take time. After more than 500 years in existence, the famed Vienna Boys' Choir only received their first theater all to themselves in 2012: the 400-seat MuTh (Music & Theater) concert hall, where classical enthusiasts can hear this world-renowned choir, founded in 1498 by Holy Roman Emperor Maximillian I, perform music by Mozart, Schubert, and more. The theater mixes Baroque and contemporary architecture enriched with distinctive seating and panels to create some of the best acoustics in Vienna. In addition to calling on MuTh, classical devotees can listen to music (free in many cases) at Vienna's often overlooked University of Music and Performing Arts, where students from across the globe come to study.

Perhaps more than any other genre except for Austria's beloved classical, electronic music has grabbed national—and, increasingly, international—attention. Since the 1990s when Austrian duo Kruder & Dorfmeister began popularizing downtempo, which is more mellow than house or trance, Vienna has been the unofficial international capital of the cozy groove genre; visitors will find it playing in clubs, bars, and cafés throughout the city. Popular techno lounges frequently change up their playlists to keep things fresh for eager crowds, while more and more outdoor parties like the aptly named Kein Sonntag ohne Techno (No Sunday Without Techno) dot the city's new musical terrain. Record stores are also filled with electronic music produced by small labels, which have helped fuel the movement. Beyond Vienna, the Ars Electronica Festival, held every September in the northern city of Linz, focuses on digital culture with the final day devoted to electronic music, while the southeastern city of Graz—a UNESCO World Heritage Site—hosts the urban electronic arts and music Springfestival in May, drawing international crowds that bear witness to the growing popularity of electronica.

A CHANGING SKYLINE

Vienna may be known for its opulent and imposing imperial palaces and its Gothic, Romanesque, Art Nouveau, and Jugendstil residential buildings and stores, but a bold and innovative new Vienna has been emerging over the past decade, with assertive statements of modern architecture expanding on the somewhat conservative skyscrapers of the 2000s. The city's tallest building, the DC Tower opened in 2014 and features a cascading façade that reflects the neighboring Danube river. The sister DC Tower 2 will be the city's fourth-tallest building and is scheduled to be completed by the end of 2023.

Schools, hotels, restaurants, and malls across Vienna are now shifting to a more modern or even post-modern look. The Hotel Topazz by BWM Architekten und Partner, completed in 2012, boasts elliptical windows and a gemlike polished facade. Completed in 2013, the Library and Learning Centre University of Economics Vienna by Zaha Hadid Architects is a sharp futuristic polygonal block that juts out over a plaza, with an interior reminiscent of a sci-fi spaceship. The Steirereck Restaurant, expanded in 2014, uses mirror-covered wooden pavilions with large windows to reflect the surrounding park and create a unique experience inside and out. Italian star architect, Renzo Piano's Parkapartments am Belvedere, completed in 2018, thrust high into the sky on daring-looking stilts to dominate the skyline from afar. The sleek and modern Wien Mitte The Mall, Vienna's largest shopping center, is just minutes from St. Stephen's Cathedral in the heart of the city and its generously dimensioned urban figure marks present-day Vienna in direct dialogue with the historic core.

FOOD

The modern sustainable food movement commonly called "farm-to-table" didn't begin in Austria, but it may as well have. The country's small size, distinct seasons, aversion to processed food, and varied growing areas from mountains to vineyards to grassy flatlands provide the perfect setting for getting food quickly from its source, something that has been normal practice in Austria since the years immediately following World War II, when the country struggled to provide enough food within its borders for its citizens. Only recently has farm-to-table been promoted as such. Austrian farms and vineyards have been known to practice "biodynamic agriculture," a holistic approach that treats the farm as an entire organism, a concept developed by Austrian thinker Rudolf Steiner. Austria is considered one of the pioneers of organic farming with one-fifth of the agricultural land in the country being farmed organically, the highest percentage in the European Union. The country also has more organic farmers than all of the other EU countries together. Many restaurants have gotten into the habit of publishing the source of each ingredient, both to appease picky diners and excite foodies, with products derived from organic farming and humane animal keeping.

Austrian cuisine, like that of some of its neighbors, has long been heavy on the *Wiener Schnitzel* (breaded and deep fried veal), *Tafelsptiz* (boiled beef in broth), *Leberknödel* (spiced, boiled beef-liver), and *Fiedermaus* (pork), but it's not all meat and potatoes here. An influx of immigrants and more environmentally aware younger generations means the restaurant scene has become more inventive in recent years and many of the new entries focus on vegan or vegetarian food, sustainable practices, and less traditional experiences.

MODERN COFFEE CULTURE

Since 2011, the traditional Viennese coffeehouse culture has been classified an intangible cultural heritage by UNESCO. Traditional coffeehouses are local institutions and lingering in one for an afternoon is an essential experience on a visit to Vienna. That said, the art of coffee hasn't stood still in Vienna. Modern iterations of the typical Viennese cafe are popping up constantly to enrich the tradition with contemporary style and innovation. While traditional cafes focus on the culture of taking coffee, these new cafes focus more on the art of coffee-making. Specialty cafes to look for include Gebrüder Gepp, a combination cafe, cake shop, and hairdresser (with a focus on sustainability) run by three brothers—each with his own specialty. The pretty Balthazar Kaffee Bar in the 2nd District run by Otto Bayer, a former star chef from Tyrol, offers everything from slowly filtered to finely aerated flat whites. Perhaps, old meets new best in Supersense on Vienna's Praterstrasse, the mother of all concept coffeeshops. You'll find great coffee, eclectic furnishings and decor, live music, art shows, and more, all in a stunning building styled after a Venetian palace.

WHAT'S NEW?

Vienna's latest addition to the museum scene, the Albertina Modern opened its doors in March 2020. The Albertina Modern, an annex of the world-famous Albertina a few blocks away, occupies the fully refurbished Künstlerhaus on Karlsplatz. The Künstlerhaus was built in 1868, and underwent a three-year renovation to bring it back to its original glory inside and out. Murals and period terrazzo flooring were restored to create a magnificent space worthy of the most important collections of Austrian art after 1945.

The Sigmund Freud Museum reopened in late 2020 after 18 months of renovations. The building, where the famed psychiatrist worked and created his most famous works for almost half a century, has been expanded to include all of Freud's private rooms as well as his original consultation room for the first time.

Vienna International Airport is undergoing a €500 million expansion and facelift. Pre-COVID-19, the airport was handling a record 31.7 million passengers, making it one of Europe's busiest airports. Works include a Southern Enlargement project, scheduled for completion in 2023, which will offer passengers a more luxurious experience and more space to linger, shop, and eat. In the long term, another runway is planned though that has met with opposition from locals.

TRAVEL SMART

Updated by
Patti McCracken

★ **CAPITAL:** Vienna	☎ **COUNTRY CODE:** 43	⏱ **TIME:** Six hours ahead of New York
👥 **POPULATION:** 8.8 million	⚠ **EMERGENCIES:** 112	✈ **AIRPORT:** VIE
💬 **LANGUAGE:** German	🚗 **DRIVING:** On the right	🌐 **WEB RESOURCES:** www.austria.info www.tiscover.com www.wien.info
$ **CURRENCY:** Euro	⚡ **ELECTRICITY:** 230v/50 cycles; electrical plugs have two round prongs	

Know Before You Go

Austrians revel in quality of life – in fact, they've won many awards for it. With its wealth of cultural offerings, delicious food, and incredible sights, it's really not that hard to be a very happy visitor here, either, but we rounded up a few tips to be sure you do make time for coffee and don't honk your car horn.

YOU MIGHT WANT TO STAY

For the 10th year running, Vienna was dubbed the Most Livable City in 2019, topping the list of 231 world capitals. The survey looks at a host of factors, ranging from public transportation, to education, to infrastructure to recreation, to crime rate. The Viennese are rightfully proud of this achievement, but might be Viennese enough to frown at it when mentioned, and go on to cite a laundry list of things that could be better.

SPRECHEN SIE ENGLISCH?

German is the official language in Austria. You may want to learn a few words before you visit— Austrians are usually delighted if you make even a small effort. You'll hear a round of *Grüss Gott*, the informal hello, every time you step into a cafe or pub, and you'll be sent off with an *Auf Wiedersehen*, or a *Tschüs*, the informal word for goodbye. In larger cities and most resorts you will usually have no problem finding people who speak English. Note that all public announcements on trams, subways, and buses are in German. Train announcements are usually given in English as well, but if you have any questions, try to get answers before boarding.

GET YOUR COFFEE TO STAY

While it is not against the law to visit Vienna and drink coffee in Starbucks (yes, they're here), it may be a sin, or at least silly. Coffee is not mere fuel to Austrians, it is a cultural experience. In fact, in November 2011, the Viennese coffeehouse culture was officially included in the UNESCO National Inventory of Intangible Cultural Heritage. Per UNESCO, "The coffee houses are a place where time and space are consumed, but only the coffee is found on the bill." Order a mélange (served with half-steamed milk and milk froth, and with whipped cream unless you tell them no) or a Grösser Brauner (large brown), which comes closest to what you might think of as an ordinary coffee. Sip slowly and soak up the atmosphere.

DON'T SMOKE

Smoking is still surprisingly common in Austria, and so it is no surprise that efforts to implement smoking bans were met with resistance. In late 2019, a smoking ban finally made it illegal to smoke inside pubs, restaurants, public transport, and all the expected places. So if you want to smoke, you will need to nip outside.

DO DRIVE

There are so many amazing day trips at Vienna's doorstep that you may consider renting a car for part, or the duration, of your visit. In most European cities, this would be a terrible idea but driving is a lot less stressful in Vienna than it is in most other large cities. There's not as much congestion (okay, it's a city so there's congestion, just not as much), and Austrians are rule followers. Also, no one will honk, because it's against the law. If you get on the Autobahn, be sure to have a toll sticker, which is called a Vignette. You can buy them at gas stations, post offices, or online.

TAKE PUBLIC TRANSIT

While driving is not an unpleasant experience in Vienna, you should also know that the city has one of the best public transportation systems in the world. The trains, trams, and buses are clean and reliable, and you are generally going to get where you are going faster if you take public transportation. Even getting from the airport to the city center is simple with the City Airport Train that connects through to

Wien Mitte. Download the WienierLinien app to help route your journeys. The 1 tram follows almost the whole inner-city circle so it's a good way to access many points of interest along the western part of the inner city, from the big-ticket museums to the cobbled pedestrian streets with quaint boutiques. It's like a Get On Get Off tour without the tour-bus vibe.

ALPINE WATER IS ON TAP

Before you leave your hotel in the morning, fill a reusable bottle with water from the tap and bring it with you. Vienna's water supply couldn't be fresher or cleaner — it comes from an Alpine stream, taking about 36 hours to wind into the city water network (no pumps, thanks to gravity), under the strictest guidance and robustly exceeding federal standards of drinking water. In summer, water stations are added around the city to help keep you cool and hydrated.

WINE ON TAP

Vienna is the only major city in the world that produces significant amounts of wine within city limits. Vienna has 1,574 acres of vineyard and more than 600 producers in the greater metropolitan area. Most wine made in Vienna is white—the famous Gruener Veltliner as well as Rieslings and blends, but there are some decent reds (Zweigelt, Blaufränkisch) too. The best way to enjoy local wine is by taking a "Heuriger hike" (Heuriger means wine tavern) in the 19th district, to wander

between small historic wine taverns and taste wine by the glass. If you are looking to avoid other wine-loving tourists, head to the more local-feeling Stammersdorf and Jedlersdorfer in the 21st district.

TIPPING

While it's customary to round up to the nearest euro, you do not need to tip generously, or at all, in Austria. Hotels tend to include a service charge in their rates and your concierge is tipped only if you've made a special request. The cleaning service is tipped only if you stay for more than a few days. Restaurants will usually add 10 percent gratuity, so tipping is not required and is seen as a little gauche. Note, because waiters don't rely on tips for their income you may notice a gruff nonchalance in their service style. Waiters here train for years in service and hospitality schools and they deal with annoying tourists all day long, so be as polite and friendly as possible, even if they are "rude" in the beginning. Viennese waiters warm up once you settle in, if you have the right (not demanding or entitled) attitude.

(UN)DRESS CODE

Austrians are big fans of FKK—freikörperkultur, or Free Body Culture—which means they like to get naked. You won't find them naked in the streets, but you will find them naked at the beach. Most saunas and steamrooms are unisex and do not allow bathing suits. Towels are mandatory.

DON'T GET HEATED ABOUT THE A.C.

Europe never developed the love affair with the air conditioner that America did, so don't expect to find it cranked. Austrians believe A.C. is bad for the health and the environment (they have a point on both counts) and many of those beautiful old buildings are not equipped to handle HVAC systems. Best to spend your energy observing how they have adapted, rather than raising your temperature at the poor hotel clerk. Plus, the windows usually open.

GET OUT OF VIENNA

The charming provinces are there for the taking and you really need to take advantage. Forty miles west of Vienna is the Wachau Valley, a picturesque stretch of the Danube between Krems and Melk. It is a significant wine region, and home to Dürnstein castle, where England's King Richard the Lionheart was held for ransom. Forty miles east of Vienna is Carnuntum, an archaeologist's dream, and the Middle Ages walled town of Hainburg, where composer Josef Haydn lived as a boy.

Getting Here and Around

Air

Flying time from New York to Vienna is eight hours; it's nine hours from Washington, D.C., and two hours from London.

Austria's major air gateway is Vienna's Schwechat Airport, on the southeast outskirts of the city. Salzburg Airport is Austria's second-largest airport, just west of the center. Just south of Graz, in Thalerhof, is the Graz Airport. Two other airports you might consider, depending on where in Austria you intend to travel, are Bratislava's M. R. Stefanik International airport in neighboring Slovakia, and Munich Airport International in Germany, not far from Salzburg. Bratislava is about 80 km (50 miles) east of Vienna and is the hub for Ryanair, a budget carrier with low-cost connections to several European cities. Frequent buses can take you from Bratislava airport to central Vienna in about an hour. Consider Munich if your primary destination is western Austria, Salzburg, or Innsbruck.

GROUND TRANSPORTATION AND TRANSFERS

The City Airport Train (CAT) provides service from Schwechat to downtown Vienna for €21 round-trip (€12 one way). Tickets are available at the CAT counter in the arrivals hall; the trip takes about 15 minutes. Travel into the city on the local S-Bahn takes about 25 minutes and costs €4.20 (ticket machines are on the platforms). City bus No. 2 runs every 10 minutes between both the city center and Salzburg's main train station and the airport; transfers cost €2.40. A taxi ride from the airport will be about €20. Schwechat Airport's website has information for all ground transfers.

FLIGHTS

Budget airlines, including Ryanair and Lauda, offer low-cost flights from major cities around Europe. These airlines are not normally recommended for connecting with transatlantic flights because of the hassle of changing airports, but they provide a low- cost way of getting around within Europe. German charter carrier Condor has flights between Vienna and Las Vegas, and Canadian charter airline Air Transat (⊕ *www.airtransat.ca*), offers flights from Montreal and Toronto to Vienna.

Within Austria, Austrian Airlines and its subsidiary, Tyrolean Airways, offer service from Vienna to Linz, Salzburg, Klagenfurt, and Innsbruck; they also provide routes to and from points outside Austria.

Bicycle

Cycling is a growing part of Austrian culture, especially as it goes more green. Twenty percent of Salzburg residents cycle their commute rather than drive or use public transportation. Citybike is a nationwide bike-sharing facility that you'll find in both small towns and big cities. The first hour is free, after a €1 deposit, second hour €2, third hour €3, and the price is capped at the fourth hour at €4. Credit card only.

Boat

For leisurely travel between Vienna and Linz, or eastward across the border into Slovakia or Hungary, consider taking a Danube boat. **DDSG Blue Danube Schifffahrt** offers a diverse selection of pleasant cruises, including trips to Melk Abbey and Dürnstein in the Wachau, a grand tour of Vienna's architectural sights from the river, and a dinner cruise, with Johann Strauss waltzes as background music. **Brandner Schifffart** offers the same kind of cruises between Krems and Melk, in the heart of the Danube Valley. ■**TIP➔ As soon as you get on board, give the steward a tip for a deck chair and ask them to place it where you will get the best views. Be sure to book cabins in advance.**

For cruises up and down the Danube, the DDSG Blue Danube Steamship Company departs and arrives at Reichsbrücke near Vienna's Mexikoplatz. The DDSG has a port on the right side of the Reichsbrücke bridge. There is no pier number, but you board at Handelskai 265. Boat trips from Vienna to the Wachau run daily from May to September. The price is €26.50 one way and €31 round-trip. There are other daily cruises within the Wachau, such as from Melk to Krems. Other cruises—to Budapest, for instance—operate from April to early November. The website has dozens of options and timetables in English. For cruises from Krems to Melk, contact Brandner Schifffahrt.

Bus

Austria has an extensive national network of buses run by the national postal and railroad services. Where Austrian trains don't go, buses do, and you'll find the railroad and post-office buses (bright yellow for easy recognition) in the towns and villages carrying passengers as well as mail. You can get tickets on the bus, and in the off-season there is no problem getting a seat; on routes to favored ski areas, though, reservations are essential during holiday periods. Bookings can be handled at the ticket office (there's one in most towns with bus service) or by travel agents. In most communities bus routes begin and end at or near the train station,

making transfers easy. Increasingly, coordination of bus service with railroads means that many of the discounts and special tickets available for trains also apply to buses. Buses run like clockwork, typically departing and arriving on time, even, astonishingly, in mountainous regions and during bad weather. Most operators on the information lines speak English and, impressively, many of the drivers do, too.

Car

Vienna is 300 km (187 miles) east of Salzburg, 200 km (125 miles) north of Graz. Main routes leading into the city are the A1 Westautobahn from Germany, Salzburg, and Linz and the A2 Südautobahn from Graz and points south. Rental cars can be arranged at the airport or in town.

On highways from points south or west or from Vienna's airport, "Zentrum" signs clearly mark the route to the center of Vienna. From there, however, finding your way to your hotel is a challenge, because traffic planners have limited traffic in the city core. Traffic congestion within Vienna is not as bad as in some places, but driving to in-town destinations generally takes longer than does public transportation.

The entire 1st through 9th Districts, and most of the rest of the city, are limited-parking zones and require a Parkschein, a prepaid-parking chit that can be purchased at tobacconists (AustriaTabak), gas stations, and, oddly, from cigarette machines. They must be filled out and displayed on the dash. They are required from 8 am to 10 pm, and a maximum parking time of two hours is permitted. You can park for 15 minutes free of charge, but you must get a purple "gratis" chit to display on your

Getting Here and Around

dash.. ■ TIP→ If you will be using a car in Vienna, you will want to download two apps, HandyParke and ParkNow to simplify the Parkschein puzzle and pay through your phone.

GASOLINE

Gasoline and diesel are readily available, but on Sunday stations in the more out-of-the-way areas may be closed. Stations carry only unleaded (*bleifrei*) gas, both regular and premium (super), and diesel. If you're in the mountains in winter with a diesel, and there is a cold snap (with temperatures threatening to drop below -4°F [-20°C]), add a few liters of gasoline to your diesel, about 1:4 parts, to prevent it from freezing. Gasoline prices are the same throughout the country, slightly lower at discount and self-service stations. Expect to pay about €1.38 per liter for regular gasoline and slightly less for diesel. If you are driving to Italy, fill up before crossing the border, because gas in Italy is even more expensive. Oil in Austria is expensive, retailing at €14 or more per liter. If need be, purchase oil, windshield wipers, and other paraphernalia at big hardware stores.

CAR RENTAL

If your plans are to see Vienna and one or two other urban destinations, you're better off taking the train, which is affordable and hassle free. If you rent a car, bear in mind the cost of gas is more than twice what you'll pay in the U.S., and you'll still have tolls to pay. On the other hand, if you decide to travel by car, you'll be happy to know the roads are mostly very well maintained, even in rural districts and mountainous regions. Bear in mind that if you're traveling in winter, by law your car needs to be fitted with winter tires, and you should also carry snow chains. And note that even in summer you can come across sudden winterlike conditions on the high mountain passes.

If you want to to drive an automatic, you will have to arrange ahead of time. Most cars on the road in Austria are manual transmission. Rental rates in Vienna begin at about €80 per day and €100 per weekend for an economy car with manual transmission. This includes a 21% tax on car rentals. Rates are more expensive in winter months, when a surcharge for winter tires may be added. Renting a car is cheaper in Germany, but make sure the rental agency knows you are driving into Austria and ask for the car to be equipped with a vignette, a toll sticker for Austria's autobahn. The answer will usually be that you have to buy your own vignette, which you can get from any service station. Get your sticker before driving to Austria.

The age requirement for renting a car in Austria is generally 19, and you must have had a valid driver's license for one year. There is no extra charge to drive over the border into Italy, Switzerland, or Germany, but there may be some restrictions for taking a rental into Slovakia, Slovenia, Hungary, the Czech Republic, or Poland. If you're planning on traveling east, it's best to let the agency know beforehand.

In Austria, an International Driver's Permit (IDP; $20) is required. These international permits are universally recognized and can be obtained in person or by mail from AAA (⊕ *www.aaa.com*). A translation of your license is an alternative acceptable option, and that can be obtained at one of the two Austrian automobile clubs: ÖAMTC or ARBÖ.

ROAD CONDITIONS

Roads in Austria are excellent and well maintained—perhaps a bit too well maintained, judging by the frequently encountered construction zones on the autobahns. Secondary roads may be narrow and winding. Remember that in winter you will need snow tires and sometimes chains, even on well-traveled roads. It's wise to check with the automobile clubs for weather conditions, because mountain roads are often blocked, and ice and fog are hazards.

ROADSIDE EMERGENCIES

If you break down along the autobahn, a small arrow on the guardrail will direct you to the nearest emergency (orange-color) phones that exist along all highways. Austria's two automobile clubs, ÖAMTC and ARBÖ, operate motorist service patrols. Both clubs charge nonmembers for emergency service. Call 120 for ÖAMTC: and 123 for ARBÖ. No area or other code is needed for either number.

RULES OF THE ROAD

Tourists from EU countries may bring their own cars into Austria with no documentation other than the normal registration papers and their regular driver's license. A Green Card, the international certificate of insurance, is recommended for EU drivers and compulsory for others. All cars must carry a first-aid kit (including rubber gloves, a red warning triangle, and a yellow neon jacket to use in case of accident or breakdown). These are available at gas stations, automotive supply stores, and most large hardware stores.

The minimum driving age in Austria is 18, and children under 12 must ride in the back seat; smaller children require a car seat. Note that all passengers must use seat belts.

Drive on the right side of the road in Austria. Unmarked crossings, particularly in residential areas, are common, so exercise caution at intersections. Trams always have the right-of-way. No turns are allowed on red.

When it comes to drinking and driving, the maximum blood-alcohol content allowed is 0.5 parts per thousand, which in real terms means very little to drink. Remember when driving in Europe that the police can stop you anywhere at any time for no particular reason.

Unless otherwise marked, the speed limit on autobahns is 130 kph (80 mph), although this is not always strictly enforced. On other highways and roads the limit is 100 kph (62 mph), 80 kph (49 mph) for RVs or cars pulling a trailer weighing more than 750 kilos (about 1,650 pounds). In built-up areas a 50-kph (31 mph) limit applies and is likely to be taken seriously. In some towns special 30-kph (20-mph) limits apply. Speeding is monitored by radar camera, rarely by highway patrol. If you're pulled over for speeding, it's because you're viewed as driving recklessly. Fines are payable on the spot and can be heavy.

■ TIP➜ If you're going to travel Austria's highways, make absolutely sure your car is equipped with the Autobahnvignette, which can be purchased at gas stations, tobacconists and online via the ASFINAG website. Minimum fine for being vignette-less: €120. Bear in mind that the vignette does not cover all tolls: tunnels, mountain passes, and some valleys, such as the Kaunertal in Tyrol or the Tauplitzalm in Styria, will be additional costs.

Ⓜ Public Transit

Overseen by Wiener Linien, Vienna's public transportation system is fast, clean, safe, and easy to use. Vienna's subway system, called the U-Bahn, services the core of the inner city. Several apps are available to ease travel, offering timetables, ticket purchase, information

Getting Here and Around

about service disruptions, and more. Visit ⊕ *www.wien.gv.at/english/transporta-tion-urbanplanning/public-transport/* for a list and links.

Five subway lines, whose stations are prominently marked with blue "U" signs, crisscross the city. Track the main lines of the U-Bahn system by their color codes on subway maps: U1 is red; U2 purple, U3 orange, U4 green, and U6 brown. The last subway runs at about 12:30 am.

Streetcars (*Strassenbahnen*) run from about 5:15 am until about midnight. Where streetcars don't run, buses— *Autobusse*—do. Should you miss the last streetcar or bus, special night buses with an "N" designation operate at half-hour intervals over several key routes; the starting (and transfer) points are the Opera House and Schwedenplatz. These night-owl buses accept all normal tickets.

Tickets are valid for all public transpor-tation—buses, trams, and the subway. Although there are ticket machines on trams and buses, there is a surcharge of €2.60. You'll need to punch your ticket before entering the boarding area at U-Bahn stops, but for buses and trams you punch it on board. If you're caught without a ticket you'll pay a sad price for it.

Buy single tickets for €2.20 from dispens-ers on the streetcar or bus, from ticket machines in subway stations, or online at ⊕ *shop.wienerlinien.at*. At tobacco shops, newsstands, or U-Bahn offices you can buy a 24-hour ticket for €8, 48-hour for €14.10, a three-day ticket for €17.10, and a *Wochenkarte* (week card), valid Monday to Sunday, can be had for the same price as the three-day pass. Lower fares are offered for seniors, and kids under six travel free; children under 15 travel free on Sunday and public holidays.

The Vienna Card, in addition to providing an array of deep discounts at sites, can also be used on all public transportation. You can buy them for periods of 24 hours, 48 hours, or 72 hours, with prices starting from €17.

🚗 Ride-Sharing

Bolt and **Uber** offer the same free plat-form, in which you book ahead with a credit card, and message the driver to set meeting and drop-off points. Bolt uses only electric vehicles, in keeping with Austria's green habits.

🚕 Taxi

Taxis in Vienna are relatively reasonable. The initial charge is €2.50, and about 5% more from 11 pm until 6 am. They also may charge for each piece of luggage in the trunk. It's customary to round up the fare to cover the tip. Several companies offer chauffeured limousines.

🚆 Train

Austrian train service is excellent: it's fast and, for Western Europe, relatively inexpensive, particularly if you take advantage of discount fares. Trains on the mountainous routes are slow, but no slower than driving, and the scenery is gorgeous. Many of the remote rail routes will give you a look at traditional Austria, complete with Alpine cabins tacked onto mountainsides and a back-drop of snowcapped peaks.

The IC (InterCity) or EC (EuroCity) trains are fastest. EN trains have sleeping facilities. The EC trains usually have a dining car with fairly good food. The trains originating in Budapest have good Hungarian cooking. Otherwise, there is usually a fellow with a cart serving snacks and hot and cold drinks.

The difference between *erste Klasse* (first class), and *zweite Klasse* (second class) on Austrian trains is mainly a matter of space. First- and second-class sleepers and couchettes (six to a compartment) are available on international runs, as well as on long trips within Austria. Women traveling alone may book special compartments on night trains or long-distance rides (ask for a *Damenabteil*). If you have a car but would rather watch the scenery than the traffic, you can put your car on a train in Vienna and accompany it to Salzburg, Innsbruck, Feldkirch, or Villach: you relax in a compartment or sleeper for the trip, and the car is unloaded when you arrive.

Allow yourself plenty of time to purchase your ticket before boarding the train. IC and EC tickets are also valid on D (express), E (*Eilzug*; semi-fast), and local trains. For information, unless you speak German fairly well, it's a good idea to have your hotel call for you. You may also ask for an operator who speaks English. You can reserve a seat for €3.50 (€3 online) up until four hours before departure. Be sure to do this on the main-line trains (Vienna–Innsbruck, Salzburg–Klagenfurt, Vienna–Graz, for example) at peak holiday times.

For train schedules from the Austrian rail service, the ÖBB, ask at your hotel, stop in at the train station and look for large posters labeled "*Abfahrt*" (departures) and "*Ankunft*" (arrivals), or log on to the website. In the Abfahrt listing you'll find the departure time in the main left-hand block of the listing and, under the train name, details of where it stops en route and the time of each arrival. There is also information about connecting trains and buses, with departure details. Working days are symbolized by two crossed hammers, which means that the same schedule might not apply on weekends or holidays. A little rocking horse sign means that a special playpen has been set up on the train for children.

There's a wide choice of rail routes to Austria, but check services first; long-distance passenger service across the continent is undergoing considerable reduction. There is regular service from London's St. Pancras station to Vienna via Brussels and Frankfurt; the fastest journey time is 13 hours, 55 minutes. An alternative is to travel via Paris, where you can change to an overnight train to Salzburg and Vienna. Be sure to leave plenty of time between connections to change stations. First- and second-class sleepers and second-class couchettes are available as far as Innsbruck. Although rail fares from London to these destinations tend to be much more expensive than air fares, the advantages are that you'll see a lot more of the countryside en route and you'll travel from city center to city center.

A few years ago, Vienna's railroad system completed an extensive and much-needed overhaul. The former Südbahnhof station was converted into the city's main train station, Hauptbahnhof Wien (or Vienna Central Station) for national and international travel.

Essentials

🍴 Dining

When dining out, you'll get the best value at simpler restaurants. Most post *Speisekarten* (menus with daily specials) with prices outside. If you begin with the *Würstelstand* (sausage vendor) on the street, the next category would be the *Imbissstube,* for simple, quick snacks. Many meat stores serve soups and a daily special at noon. Many cafés also offer lunch. *Gasthäuser* are simple restaurants or country inns. Austrian hotels have some of the best restaurants in the country, often with outstanding chefs. Some Austrian chain restaurants offer excellent value for the money, such as the schnitzel chains Wienerwald and Schnitzelhaus and the excellent seafood chain Nordsee. With migration from Turkey and Northern Africa on the rise, and an influx of Balkan immigrants, thousands of small kebab restaurants have set up shop all over Austria. Many more vegan and vegetarian restaurants are popping up, with surprisingly tasty fare. In Vienna some restaurants go on serving until 1 and 2 am; a tiny number also through the night. The rest of Austria is more conservative.

■ TIP➔ **In all restaurants be aware that the basket of bread put on your table isn't free.** Most of the older-style Viennese restaurants charge €0.70–€1.25 for each roll that is eaten, but more and more establishments are beginning to charge a per-person cover charge—anywhere from €1.50 to €5—which includes all the bread you want, plus usually an herb spread and butter. Tap water (*Leitungswasser*) in Austria comes straight from the Alps and is some of the purest in the world. Be aware, however, that a few restaurants in touristy areas are beginning to charge for tap water.

Restaurant reviews have been shortened. For full information, visit Fodors.com.

TIPPING

In Austria, tipping is customary. In cafés, bistros, and other less expensive eateries, the Viennese usually round up to the nearest euro. If they are very happy with the service in a fancier restaurant, they will give the waiter anywhere from €1 to €3. They never tip 15% to 20% of the total bill, as is customary in the United States. Tipping so much can be insulting to the waitstaff.

COSTS

Prices in the reviews are the average cost of a main course at dinner or, if dinner is not served, at lunch.

What it Costs on Euros			
$	$$	$$$	$$$$
AT DINNER			
under €18	€18–€23	€24–€31	over €31

WINES, BEER, AND SPIRITS

Austrian wines range from unpretentious *Heurigen* whites to world-class varietals. Look for the light, fruity white *Grüner Veltliner,* intensely fragrant golden *Traminer,* full-bodied red *Blaufränkischer,* and the lighter red *Zweigelt.* Sparkling wine is called *Sekt,* some of the best coming from the Kamptal region northwest of Vienna. Some of the best sweet dessert wines in the world (*Spätlesen*) come from Burgenland. Austrian beer rivals that of Germany for quality. Each area has its own brewery and local beer, to which people are loyal. A specialty unique to Austria is the dark, sweet Dunkles beer. Look for Kaiser Doppelmalz in Vienna, as well as Gössler. They even have a cycler's cider brew called Rädler. Schnapps is an after-dinner tradition in Austria; many restaurants offer several varieties, and it is not uncommon for the management to offer a complimentary schnapps at the end of a meal. One of the most popular types is nicknamed a "little Willy," made from the William pear.

Health

Travel in Austria poses no specific or unusual health risks. The tap water is safe to drink—in fact, Austrians are obsessed about water quality, and Austria has some of the purest in the world. The only potential risk worth mentioning is tick-bite encephalitis, which is only a concern if you're planning to do extensive cycling or hiking in the backcountry.

COVID-19

COVID-19 brought all travel to a virtual standstill in 2020, and interruptions to travel have continued into 2021. Although the illness is mild in most people, some experience severe and even life-threatening complications. Once travel started up again, albeit slowly and cautiously, travelers were asked to be particularly careful about hygiene and to avoid any unnecessary travel, especially if they are sick.

Older adults, especially those over 65, have a greater chance of having severe complications from COVID-19. The same is true for people with weaker immune systems or those living with some types of medical conditions, including diabetes, asthma, heart disease, cancer, HIV/AIDS, kidney disease, and liver disease. Starting two weeks before a trip, anyone planning to travel should be on the lookout for some of the following symptoms: cough, fever, chills, trouble breathing, muscle pain, sore throat, new loss of smell or taste. If you experience any of these symptoms, you should not travel at all.

And to protect yourself during travel, do your best to avoid contact with people showing symptoms. Wash your hands often with soap and water. Limit your time in public places, and, when you are out and about, wear a face mask that covers your nose and mouth. Indeed, a mask may be required in some places, such as on an airplane or in a confined space like a theater, where you share the space with a lot of people. You may wish to bring extra supplies, such as disinfecting wipes, hand sanitizer (12-ounce bottles were allowed in carry-on luggage at this writing), and a first-aid kit with a thermometer.

Given how abruptly travel was curtailed at the onset of COVID-19, it is wise to consider protecting yourself by purchasing a travel insurance policy that will reimburse you for any cancellation costs related to COVID-19. Not all travel insurance policies protect against pandemic-related cancellations, so always read the fine print.

OVER-THE-COUNTER REMEDIES

You must buy over-the-counter remedies in an *Apotheke (app-oh-take-uh)*, and most personnel speak enough English to understand what you need. Try using the generic name for a drug, rather than its brand name. Some of the medications sold over the counter in the USA, because of higher potency, are not available in Austria without a prescription. Natural remedies, including some homeopathic and herbal medicines, are a routine part of the health care system in Austria.

SHOTS AND MEDICATIONS

No special shots are required before visiting Austria, but if you will be cycling or hiking through the eastern or southeastern parts of the country, get inoculated against encephalitis; it can be carried by ticks.

Essentials

Lodging

Starting at the lower end, you can find a room in a private house or on a farm, or dormitory space in a youth hostel. Next come the simpler pensions, many of them identified as *Frühstückspensionen* (bed-and-breakfasts). *Gasthäuser* are simpler country inns. Fancier pensions in cities can often cost as much as hotels; the difference lies in the services they offer. Most pensions, for example, do not staff the front desk around the clock. Among the hotels, you can find accommodations ranging from the most modest, with a shower and toilet down the hall, to the most elegant, with every possible amenity. Increasingly, more and more hotels in the lower to middle price range are including breakfast with the basic room charge, but check when booking. Room rates for hotels in the rural countryside can often include breakfast and one other meal. The cheaper option in Austria will usually still bring high standards. Most village *Gasthöfe* take great pride in providing sparkling cleanliness and a warm welcome—and you'll often find they have spacious rooms of great character.

These German words might come in handy when booking a room: air-conditioning (*Klimaanlage*); private bath (*Privatbad*); bathtub (*Badewanne*); shower (*Dusche*); double bed (*Doppelbett*); twin beds (*Einzelbetten*).

All hotels listed *in this guide* have private bath unless otherwise noted. *Hotel reviews have been shortened. For full information, visti Fodors.com.*

HOTELS IN VIENNA

The luxury hotel market has surged in Vienna in recent years, bringing top rivals to the revered landmark lodgings that have dominated the city for well over a century. The grand old five-star dames of the Ringstrasse still stand supreme with their gilt mirrors, red velvet, and crystal-chandelier opulence. The service tends toward impeccable.

For those with more modest requirements and purses, ample rooms are available in less costly but no less alluring hotels. A number of new hotels have opened in this category as well, making for an array of affordable and enticing choices.

If you have only a short time to spend in Vienna, you'll probably choose to stay in the inner city (the 1st District, or 1010 postal code), to be within walking distance of the most important sights, restaurants, and shops. Outside the 1st District, though, there are many other delightful neighborhoods in which to rest your head. The "Biedermeier" quarter of Spittelberg, in the 7th District of Neubau, has cobblestone streets, rows of 19th-century houses, a wonderful array of art galleries and restaurants, and, increasingly, some good hotel options. Just to its east is the fabulous MuseumsQuartier, an area that has some very nice hotel finds. Schwedenplatz is the area fronted by the Danube Canal—a neighborhood that is one of the most happening in the city, although just a stroll from the centuries-old lanes around Fleischmarkt. Other sweet hotel options can be found in the 8th District of Josefstadt, an area noted for antiques shops, good local restaurants, bars, and theater.

Because of the Christmas markets, the weeks leading up to the holidays are a popular time to visit, as is the week around New Year's (*Silvester*), with its orchestral concerts. Summer months are not as busy, perhaps because the opera is not in season. You'll find good bargains at this time of year, especially in August. Vienna also hosts a number of conventions in April, May, and September, causing hotel prices to rise and vacancy rates to drop. Air-conditioning is customary in the top-category hotels only, so don't be surprised if you have to do without. On the plus side, nights are generally cool.

In Vienna in particular, reservations are a necessity—rooms fill up quickly, so book as far in advance as possible. WienTourismus (⊕ www.wien.info/en/travel-info), the Viennese Tourist Board, lets you reserve accommodations in all categories online.

APARTMENT AND HOUSE RENTALS
For rental apartments in Vienna, check out ⊕ www.apartment.at or ⊕ www.net-land.at/wien. Airbnb is legal and thriving in Austria ⊕ www.airbnb.com.

CASTLES
The Castle in An Other Country (formerly known as Castle Hotels and Mansions) is an association of castles and palaces that have been converted into hotels. The quality of the accommodations varies with the property, but many have been beautifully restored and can be a memorable alternative to standard hotels. The website is in English ⊕ www.experiencecharacter.com and has plenty of photos. The association also lists a smattering of castles in the Czech Republic, Hungary, Slovenia, Croatia, and Italy.

COSTS
Prices in the reviews are the average cost of a standard double room during high season.

What it Costs in Euros

$	$$	$$$	$$$$
FOR TWO PEOPLE			
under €120	€120–€170	€171–€270	over €270

Online Booking Resources

Interhome	800/882–6864	⊕ www.inter-home.us
Villas and Apartments Abroad	212/213–6435	⊕ www.vaanyc.com
Villas International	415/499–9490 or 800/221–2260	⊕ www.villasintl.com

Ⓢ Money

Austria is a member of the European Union (EU) and its currency is the euro.

Although fees charged for ATM transactions may be higher abroad than at home, Cirrus and Plus exchange rates are excellent, because they are based on wholesale rates offered only by major banks. Otherwise, the most favorable rates are through a bank. You won't do as well at exchange booths in airports or train and bus stations, in hotels, in restaurants, or in stores, although you may find their hours more convenient than the banks'.

🎭 Performing Arts

SCHEDULES AND SEASONS
A monthly printed program, the *Wien-Programm,* distributed by the city tourist board and available at any travel agency or hotel, gives an overview of what's going on in the worlds of opera, concerts, jazz, theater, and galleries, and similar information is posted on billboards and advertising columns around the city.

The film schedules in the daily newspapers *Der Standard* and *Die Presse* list foreign-language film showings; *Der Falter,* a weekly paper issued every

Essentials

Wednesday, publishes a comprehensive listing of events and films, while *OmU* lists showings for films in their original language with German subtitles.

BALLS

The city's ball culture is carefully nurtured, and almost everybody between the ages of 16 and 19 attends a dancing school (some even learn to waltz as part of the official high school curriculum). On your strolls through the inner city, peek in at Elmayer's on Bräunerstrasse to see young couples practice the quadrille for the next Carnival extravaganza.

Ever since the 19th-century Congress of Vienna—when pundits joked "The city dances, but it never gets anything done"—Viennese extravagance and gaiety have been world-famous. Fasching, the season of Carnival, was given over to court balls, opera balls, masked balls, chambermaids' and bakers' balls, and a hundred other gatherings, many held within the glittering interiors of Baroque theaters and palaces. White-gloved women and men in white tie would glide over marble floors to heavenly melodies. They still do. Now, as in the days of Franz Josef, Vienna's old three-quarter-time rhythm strikes up anew at the stroke of the clock on New Year's Day and continues through Carnival, or Fasching.

During the Ball Season, as many as 40 balls may be held in a single evening. Many events are organized by a professional group, including the Hofburg New Year's Ball, Philharmonikerball (Ball of the Philharmonic Orchestra), Kaffeesiederball (Coffee Brewers' Ball), the Zuckerbaeckerball (Confectioners' Ball), or the Opernball (Opera Ball). The invitation reads *"Frack mit Dekorationen,"* which means that ball gowns and tails are usually required for most events (you can always get your tux from a rental agency) and women mustn't wear white (reserved for debutantes). But there's something for everyone these days, including the "Ball of Bad Taste" or "Wallflower Ball." The zaniest might be the Life Ball, sponsored by a charity raising funds for people with HIV. After your gala evening, finish off the morning with a *Katerfrühstuck*—hangover breakfast—of goulash soup.

Among the 400 balls that are held each winter, the majority are open to the public. Ticket prices vary widely, and can go as high as €600. Starting at 8 or 9 pm, these "full dress" events last until 3 or 4 am.

DANCE

Dance performances at the Staatsoper and Volksoper feature both classic and contemporary choreography. Dancers from both houses belong to the Vienna State Ballet under the direction of Manuel Legris, former star of the Paris Ballet.

FILM

Vienna has a thriving film culture, with many viewers seeking original rather than German-dubbed versions of English-language films. If you're here in late October, make sure to check out Europe's oldest film festival, the Viennale ⊕ *www.viennale.at/en*, which draws crowds of nearly 100,000 to the city's historic movie palaces and showcases films by national and international directors.

MUSIC

Vienna is one of the world's foremost music centers. Contemporary music gets its due, but it's the classics—the works of Beethoven, Brahms, Haydn, Mozart, Strauss, and Schubert—that draw the Viennese public and make tickets to the Wiener Philharmoniker the hottest of commodities. Vienna is home to four full symphony orchestras: the great Wiener Philharmoniker (Vienna Philharmonic), the outstanding Wiener Symphoniker (Vienna

Symphony), the broadcasting service's ORF Symphony Orchestra, and the Niederösterreichische Tonkünstler. There are also hundreds of smaller groups, from world-renowned trios to chamber orchestras.

Although the well-known mid-May to mid-June Wiener Festwochen (Vienna Festival) signals the official end of the concert season, the rest of the summer brims with musical performances, particularly in the Theater an der Wien.

OPERA AND OPERETTA
Austria's handling of political scandals has led some to call it an "operetta state." It's small wonder that this antiquated art form is still cherished in musical theaters such as the Volksoper, albeit in a tongue-in-cheek manner. Although the Viennese officially boast of opera productions at the Staatsoper, many not so secretly prefer light-hearted operettas and cabarets. Expect grand opera with all the attendant pomp and circumstance at the Staatsoper. In addition to offering operas that are just as satisfying as those at the Staatsoper, the Volksoper strikes just the right balance between operetta, musicals, and dance performances.

THEATER
Opera and classical music get all the attention, but theater is also very popular among the Viennese. Tickets to the Burgtheater, one of the world's top German-language theaters, can be hard to come by so plan ahead.

🛍 Shopping
Outside the city center, shops are generally open weekdays from 9 am to 6 pm and on Saturday from 9 am to noon. On the busy shopping thoroughfares, most shops stay open until 8 pm during the week and 5 or 6 pm on Saturday. *Stores are closed on Sunday and public holidays.* In the 7th District of Neubau, the boutiques often don't open until 11 am.

SHOPPING DISTRICTS
The Kärntner Strasse, Graben, and Kohlmarkt—the latter is home to the so-called Goldenes Quartier (Golden Quarter)—are pedestrian areas in the Inner City that claim to have the best shops in Vienna. For some items, such as jewelry, they're probably some of the best anywhere. The side streets in this area have shops selling antiques, art, clocks, jewelry, and period furniture. A collection of attractive small boutiques can also be found in the Palais Ferstel passage at Freyung 2 in the 1st District.

Gumpendorferstrasse, in the 6th District, and the nearby 7th District, Neubau, are two of the hippest shopping destinations in town, with small boutiques, trendy hairstylists, and great eateries. On Neubaugasse, Kirchengasse, Lindengasse, and the quaint Mondscheingasse, fashionistas find unique clothing, jewelry, and footwear in lovely little boutiques. Also in the 7th District, on Spittelberggasse between Burggasse and Siebensterngasse, are small galleries and handicraft shops. In competition for the top neighborhood of them all is Praterstrasse in the 2nd District. From the city center toward the Praterstern U station, great boutiques, cafés, and restaurants have popped up.

Vienna's Naschmarkt (between Linke and Rechte Wienzeile, starting at Getreidemarkt) is one of Europe's great and most colorful food and produce markets. Stalls open at 6 am, and the pace is lively until about 6 pm. Saturday is the big day, though, when farmers come into the city to sell at the back end of the market. Also on Saturday is a huge flea market at the Kettenbrückengasse end. The Naschmarkt is closed Sunday. Christmas is

Essentials

the time for the tinselly Christkindlmarkt (Rathausplatz in front of City Hall). In protest of its commercialization, smaller markets specializing in handicrafts have sprung up on such traditional spots as Am Hof, the Freyung, and in front of the Schönbrunn and Belvedere palaces.

$ Taxes

The Value Added Tax (V.A.T.) in Austria is 20% generally, but this is reduced to 10% on food and clothing and certain tourism services. If you're not an EU resident, and you are planning to take your purchases with you when you leave Austria (export them), you can get a refund. Wine and spirits are heavily taxed—nearly half of the sale price goes to taxes. For every contract signed in Austria (for example, car-rental agreements), you pay an extra 1% tax to the government, so tax on a rental car is 21%.

When making a purchase of more than €75 , ask the sales clerk to fill out a Global Blue tax free form, and staple the receipt to it. Some stores will give the refund on-site, but are not required to. As you're leaving the country (or the EU if you're visiting multiple EU countries), have the form stamped like any customs form by customs officials. After you're through passport control, take the form to a refund-service counter for an on-the-spot refund (which is usually the quickest and easiest option), or mail it to the address on the form (or the envelope with it) after you arrive home. You receive the total refund stated on the form, but the processing time can be long, especially if you request a credit-card adjustment.

Global Refund is a Europe-wide service with 225,000 affiliated stores and more than 700 refund counters at major airports and border crossings. Its refund

form, called a Tax Free Check, is the most common across the European continent. The service issues refunds in the form of cash, check, or credit-card adjustment.

Tours

SPECIAL-INTEREST TOURS
BIKING
The Austrian national tourist information website, ⊕ www.austria.info, includes excellent sections on hotels that welcome cyclists, as well as some of the better-known tours and routes.

You can no longer rent a bike at train stations in Austria. The cost of renting a bike (21-gear) from a local agency is around €31 a day. Tourist offices have details (in German), including maps and hints for trip planning and mealtime and overnight stops that cater especially to cyclists. Ask for the booklet "Radtouren in Österreich" or go to the website ⊕ www.radtouren.at. There's also a brochure in English: "Biking Austria—On the Trail of Mozart" that provides details in English on the cycle route through the High Tauern mountains in Salzburg Province and neighboring regions in Bavaria (⊕ www.mozartradweg.com).

E-bikes are becoming increasingly popular and are widely available for rent.

ECOTOURS
Austria is a popular vacation spot for those who want to experience nature—many rural hotels offer idyllic bases for hiking in the mountains or lake areas. The concept of the *Urlaub am Bauernhof* (farm vacation), where families can stay on a working farm and children can help take care of farm animals, is increasingly popular throughout Austria. There are numerous outfitters that can provide information on basic as well as specialty farms, such as organic farms or farms for

children, for people with disabilities, or for horseback riders.

HIKING AND MOUNTAIN CLIMBING

With more than 50,000 km (about 35,000 miles) of well-maintained mountain paths through Europe's largest reserve of unspoiled landscape, the country is a hiker's paradise. Three long-distance routes traverse Austria, including the E-6 from the Baltic, cutting across mid-Austria via the Wachau valley region of the Danube and on to the Adriatic. Wherever you are in Austria, you will find shorter hiking trails requiring varying degrees of ability. Routes are well marked, and maps are readily available from bookstores, the Österreichische Alpenverein (ÖAV: Austrian Alpine Club), and the automobile clubs.

If you're a newcomer to mountain climbing or want to improve your skill, schools in Salzburg province will take you on. Ask the ÖAV for addresses. All organize courses and guided tours for beginners as well as for more advanced climbers.

Tourist offices have details on hiking holidays; serious climbers can write directly to ÖAV for more information. Membership in the club (€55, about $74) will give you a 30%–50% reduction on the regular fees for overnights in the 275 mountain refuges it operates in Austria and for huts operated by other mountain organizations in Europe. Membership also includes accident insurance for vacations of up to six weeks. Memberships for young people up to age 25 and for senior citizens have a reduced price.

U.S. Embassy/Consulate

Most foreign governments have embassies in Vienna (some also have consular offices in other Austrian cities), and most offer consular services in the embassy building.

When to Go

High Season: May, June, and September are busy and expensive but offer major festivals and better weather. July and August are the hottest months in the east (less so to the west) but this is also when most Viennese take their own vacations.

Low Season: Late January and February are the best times for airfares and hotel deals—and to escape the crowds. But unless you are skiing, winter offers the least appealing weather. Snowfall, icy winds, and freezing temperatures can cause travel disruptions (more so in the mountainous west than in the dryer east).

Value Season: October is gorgeous, with temperate weather, good hotel deals, and lots of cultural events. By November temperatures start to drop. Late March and April are good months to visit, before the masses arrive and when snows are nearly gone and springtime activities are abuzz.

Visitor Information

The main center for information is the Vienna City Tourist Office, open daily 9–7 and centrally located on Albertinaplatz between the Hofburg and Kärntnerstrasse. Ask about a Vienna Card, which combines the use of public transportation and more than 210 steep discounts at museums, galleries, theaters, concert halls, as well as bars, cafés, and restaurants. The cards are also available at hotels and train stations.

Great Itineraries

Vienna to Vorarlberg

This itinerary travels the country from end to end, hitting the heights and seeing the sights—all in a one-week to 14-day trip.

DAYS 1–3: VIENNA

Austria's glorious past is evident everywhere, but especially where this tour begins, in Vienna. Get to know the city by trolley with a sightseeing tour of the Ringstrasse. Take in the Kunsthistoriches Museum, where the incredible details of the famous Brueghel paintings could keep you fascinated for hours, and then walk along Kärntnerstrasse, the city's Fifth Avenue, to magnificent St. Stephen's Cathedral, and spend an afternoon in one of the city's cozy coffeehouses. Devote a half day to Schönbrunn Palace, and set aside an evening for a visit to a jovial *Heurige* wine tavern. You should also keep an afternoon open for a slice of Sachertorte, the famous Viennese chocolate cake with layers separated by apricot jam, at the Hotel Sacher Wien, where it was invented. Be sure to visit the Judenplatz Museum, built over the remains of a 13th-century synagogue, for exhibits about life in Vienna from medieval times through World War II. Finally, make a stop at Spanische Reitschule (Spanish Riding School) to watch the stark white Lippizzaner horses who will dance their way into your heart.

DAY 4: DANUBE RIVER FROM VIENNA TO LINZ

To zoom from Vienna to Linz by autobahn would be to miss out on one of Austria's most treasured sights, the blue Danube. To tour some quaint wine villages, follow the "Austrian Romantic Road" (Route 3), along the north bank of the river, instead of the speedier A1 autobahn. Cross to the south side of the Danube to the breathtaking Baroque abbey at Melk, and along the way visit the 1,000-year-old town of Krems and picture-perfect towns of Spitz and Dürnstein, in the heart of the Wachau wine region.

DAYS 5 AND 6: LINZ

Fast-forward into Austria's future with a stop in progressive Linz, the country's third-largest city. Linz is a busy port on the Danube and an important center for trade and business. Techno-music geeks will enjoy the Ars Electronica Museum; others can wander the beautifully restored medieval courtyards of the Altstadt (Old Town). For great views, ride the city's Pöstlingbergbahn, the world's steepest mountain railway, or opt for a Danube steamer cruise to Enns. Be sure to take time to visit the Schlossmuseum Linz (Linz Castle Museum), built in the 1400s, with a vast collection of art and weaponry.

Tips

There is frequent train service between the major cities in this itinerary. Side trips into the countryside are possible by bus or train. Trains leave every half hour from the Westbahnhof in Vienna, arriving in Linz in about 90 minutes. From Linz it is one hour to the Salzburg Hauptbahnhof and another two hours to the Innsbruck terminal, then another 2½ hours to Bregenz.

For a more romantic kickoff, travel by Blue Danube Schifffahrt/DDSG riverboat from Vienna to Linz (departs from Vienna three times a day between mid-April and September).

DAYS 7 AND 8: SALZKAMMERGUT

For Austria in all its Hollywood splendor, head to the idyllic Salzkammergut, better known as the Lake District, where *The Sound of Music* was filmed. The town of Bad Ischl—famous for its operetta festival and pastries—makes a good base. Travel south on Route 145 to Hallstatt, one of Austria's most photographed lakeside villages. Return to Bad Ischl, then head west to St. Wolfgang for swimming and sailing.

DAYS 9 AND 10: SALZBURG

This is a city made for pedestrians, with an abundance of churches, palaces, mansions, and—as befits the birthplace of Mozart—music festivals. Stroll through the old city center with its wrought-iron shop signs, tour the medieval Fortress Hohensalzburg, and relax in the Mirabell Gardens (where the von Trapp children "Do-Re-Mi"-ed). Children of all ages will adore the famed Marionettentheater.

DAYS 11 AND 12: INNSBRUCK AND TYROL

Tour Innsbruck's treasures—including the famous Golden Roof mansion and the Hofburg—but do as the Tyroleans do and spend time reveling in the high-mountain majesty. After all, Innsbruck is the only major city in the Alps. For a splendid panorama, take the cable railway to the Hafelekar, high above the Inn Valley. For a trip through the quaint villages around Innsbruck, ride the Stubaitalbahn, a charming old-time train, or head by bus to the Stubai Glacier for year-round skiing. You can also take the train to Wattens, 30 minutes away, to visit Swarovski Kristalwelten (Crystal World), a kind of Disneyland for crystalware that adjoins the company's headquarters.

DAYS 13 AND 14: BREGENZ

Taking the Arlberg Pass (or the much more scenic Silvretta High Alpine Road), head to the city of Bregenz, capital of Vorarlberg. Bregenz owes its character as much to neighboring Switzerland and Germany as to Austria, and is most appealing in summer, when sun worshippers crowd the shores of Lake Constance to enjoy an opera festival set on the world's largest outdoor floating stage. Take a lake excursion and explore Bregenz's medieval streets.

The Mountains of Austria

This is a trip where Alpine glory is all around you: meadows and forests set against a backdrop of towering craggy peaks, and gentle wooded rambles that lead to clear mountain lakes and storybook castles. Let go of your worries and let the natural beauty of the countryside work its magic.

Great Itineraries

DAYS 1 AND 2: BAD ISCHL/ ST. WOLFGANG

The villages and lakes of the Salzkammergut region extend south from Salzburg. Base yourself in Bad Ischl, a first-class spa in the heart of the Lake District and a favorite of Austrian Emperor Franz Josef a century ago. A walk through the village passes several locations that honor Austria's operetta tradition and composers such as Franz Lehar. From there, head west to St. Wolfgang, one of the most photo-friendly villages in Austria. For the most scenic surroundings, park in nearby Strobl and hop one of the lake ferries to the pedestrian-only village, where you can marvel at the 16th-century Michael Pacher altarpiece in the parish church and take the railway up the 5,800-foot Schaftberg peak for gasp-inducing vistas.

DAY 3: HALLSTATT

Set on fjordlike Hallstättersee, this jewel is an optical illusion perched between water and mountain—a tight grouping of terraced fishermen's cottages and churches offering, at first glance, no apparent reason why it doesn't tumble into the lake. On a sunny day the views of the lake and village, considered the oldest settlement in Austria, are spectacular, and on a misty morning they are even more so. Consider a canoe outing, or tour the Hallstatt salt mine, the oldest in the world and a UNESCO World Heritage Site.

DAY 4: WERFEN

Take in the birds-of-prey show at the formidable Burg Hohenwerfen, a castle built in the 11th century; tour the Eisriesenwelt ("World of the Ice Giants"), the largest collection of ice caves in Europe; and cap the day with dinner at Obauer, one of Austria's finest restaurants.

Tips

Although it is much simpler to travel this route by car, it can also be undertaken using public transportation (note that many trains do not run on Sunday). Trains link Salzburg, Bad Ischl, Hallstatt, and Kitzbühel; travel to St. Wolfgang by postbus. From Hallstatt, hop the train to Bad Aussee and on to Irdning, where you may have to change trains to Bischofshofen before reaching Zell am See. Travel to and from Heiligenblut by bus.

DAY 5: ZELL AM SEE

Southwest of Werfen, the charming lake resort of Zell am See is nestled under the 6,000-foot Schmittenhöhe mountain. Ride the cable car from the center of town for a bird's-eye view, then take the narrow-gauge Pinzgauer railroad through the Salzach river valley to famous Krimmler waterfalls.

DAY 6: HEILIGENBLUT

Head skyward over the dizzying Grossglockner High Alpine Highway to one of Austria's loveliest villages, Heiligenblut, which fans out across the upper Möll Valley with fabulous views of the Grossglockner, at 12,470 feet the highest mountain in Austria.

DAY 7: KITZBÜHEL

Travel to the glamorous resort town of Kitzbühel for a bit of window-shopping and celebrity spotting, or avoid the crowds to explore nearby Kufstein and its 13th-century mountaintop fortress. On the road headed west, the sunny valley has plenty of snow in winter and golf in summer. End your trip in Innsbruck, 91 km (57 miles) west.

On the Calendar

January

Hofburg New Year's Ball. Vienna's Ball Season kicks off on New Year's Eve with this glittering—and expensive—event (formerly known as Kaiserball), held in the elegant rooms of the Hofburg. ☎ *01/58736–66214* ⊕ *www.hofburg.com.*

Wiener Philharmoniker. The New Year in Vienna is greeted with a concert by the Vienna Philharmonic. Reserve at leat one year in advance. ☎ *01/505–6525* ⊕ *www.musikverein.at.*

February

Fasching. In February, Fasching (or Fasnacht, as it's called in the western part of the country), is the Carnival period before Lent and it can get wild, with huge processions of costumed figures and the occasional unwilling participation by spectators.

Wiener Opernball (*Vienna Opera Ball*). Perhaps the year's biggest society event, the Vienna Opera Ball is held the Thursday before Ash Wednesday at the magnificent Staatsoper. ☎ *01/5144–42250.*

March

Oestermarkt (*Easter Market*). Easter markets start to pop up in plazas throughout Austria about two to three weeks before Easter (usually late March to April). While less elaborate than Christmas markets, Easter markets are a great resource for quality arts and crafts, local cuisine, and of course, a wide variety of decorative eggs. ⊕ *www.austria.info.*

April

Steiermarkdorf. In April, the province of Styria, known for its dishes involving pumpkinseed oil, showcases its culinary skills in Rathausplatz during the Styrian Spring Festival. ⊕ *www.steiermarkdorf.at.*

May

Genuss Festival. Taking place over a weekend in May, the Vienna Food Festival is held in the Stadtpark on the Ringstrasse. The event aims at preserving Austria's rich and varied culinary traditions by highlighting delicacies from different regions. Food producers from all over the country present their creations, from poppy-seed oil to ox sausage. ⊠ *Vienna.*

Wiener Festwochen. This festival of theater, music, film, and exhibitions takes over Vienna from mid-May to mid-June. ☎ *01/589–220* ⊕ *www.festwochen.at.*

June

Donauinselfest (Danube Island Festival). Held in late June, this is Europe's largest open-air music fest, attracting 3 million visitors each year. Entrance is free. In 2020, coronavirus altered the map and the schedule for this beloved festival. It took place over eighty days and was in all of the city, not just the Danube Island. Check before you visit to confirm if the festival has been restored to its original structure. It may operate on a modified plan for the coming years, ⊠ *Donauinsel, Vienna* ⊕ *www.donauinselfest.at.*

On the Calendar

July and August

Bregenz Festival. A highlight of this monthlong music and arts festival (held mid-July to mid-August) is the floating stage on the lake. ⊕ *www.bregenzerfestspiele.com/en.*

Salzburg Festival. From Opera's elite flock to Salzburg from mid-July through August for six weeks of opera, concerts, and stage plays in one of the world's premiere events of the art form. ⊕ *www.salzburgerfestspiele.at.*

Waldviertelpur. At the end of August, Austria's northernmost region of Waldviertel draws many visitors to Vienna's Heldenplatz for this festival celebrating their regional culture. Servers wearing traditional dirndls serve dumplings to the sounds of brass music. ⊕ *www.waldviertelpur.at.*

September

Volksoper. The opera season runs from September through June. If you can't get into the Philharmonic concert, try for one of the performances of the Franz Lehar operetta *Die lustige Witwe,* or another light delight. ☎ *01/5144–43670* ⊕ *www.volksoper.at.*

October

Long Night of the Museums. More than 100 museums in Vienna and other parts of Austria open their doors from 6 pm until 1 the next morning in a cultural free-for-all that attracts thousands each year. Comfortable shoes not included. ⊕ *www.wien.info.*

National Day. Marking the day in 1955 when Austria declared its neutrality, the city takes a day off to take a tour of the parliament, see a free museum or two, or to check out the military's giant display on Heldenplatz in the center of Vienna.

December

Christkindlmarkt (Christmas Market). In Vienna the biggest Christmas market goes up in mid-November in the plaza in front of the city's Rathaus (town hall); there are more than 30 smaller ones dotted around town, including outside Schönbrunn and the Belvedere Palace, in the Spittelberg Quarter on the Freyung square, and in front of Karlkirche on Karlsplatz.

Silent Night Celebration. On Christmas Eve, join locals to celebrate at the chapel in the village of Obendorf, near Salzburg, where the timeless Christmas song was written in 1818. ⊕ *www.visit-salzburg.net/surroundings/silentnightchapel.htm.*

Contacts

Air

AIRPORTS Graz Airport (GRZ). ☎ *0316/2902–172* ⊕ *www.flughafen-graz. at.* **M. R. Stefanik Airport (Bratislava, BTS).** ☎ *044/702–402–0722 from outside of Slovakia* ⊕ *bts.aero.* **Salzburg Airport (SZG).** ☎ *0662/85800* ⊕ *www.salzburg-airport. com.* **Vienna International Airport (Schwechat Airport). (***VIE***).** ☎ *01/70070* ⊕ *www. viennaairport.com.*

AIRLINES Austrian Airlines. ☎ *800/843–0002, 05/1766–1000 within Austria* ⊕ *www.austrian. com.*

AIRPORT TRANSPORTATION CONTACTS Airport Driver. ☎ *01/22822* ⊕ *www.airportdriver.at.* **S-Bahn.** ⊕ *www.schnell-bahn-wien.at.* **Vienna Airport Lines.** ☎ *01/7007–32300* ⊕ *www.postbus.at.* **Vienna Bus.** ☎ *01/7909–100* ⊕ *www.wienerlinien. at.* **Vienna International Airport (Schwechat). (***VIE***).** ☎ *01/7007–22233 for flight information* ⊕ *www. viennaairport.at.*

ⓞ Boat

CRUISE LINES Brandner Schifffahrt. ☎ *07433/259–021* ⊕ *www.brandner.at.* **DDSG/Blue Danube Schifffahrt.** ☎ *01/58880* ⊕ *www. ddsg-blue-danube.at.*

ⓑ Bus

CONTACTS Blaguss Reisen. ☎ *01/610900* ⊕ *www. blaguss.at/en.* **Columbus.** ☎ *01/534–110* ⊕ *www. columbus-reisen.at.* **Dr. Richard Reisebusse.** ☎ *01/331–00–335* ⊕ *www. richard.at.* **Post und Bahn.** ☎ *05/1717 customer service for postbuses and trains* ⊕ *www.postbus.at, www.oebb.at.*

⚠ Emergencies

Ambulance. ☎ *144.* **Fire.** ☎ *122.* **Police.** ☎ *133.*

ROADSIDE EMERGENCY SERVICES ARBÖ. ☎ *01/891–21–0* ⊕ *www.arboe.at.* **ÖAMTC.** ☎ *0810/120–120* ⊕ *www. oeamtc.at.*

ⓛ Lodging

CASTLES The Castle in An Other Country. ✎ *hello@ experiencecharacter.com* ⊕ *www.experiencecharacter.com.*

Performing Arts

TICKETS Albertinaplatz Tourist Information. ✉ *Albertinaplatz, corner of Maysedergasse, 1st District.* **Bundestheaterkassen.** ✉ *Operngasse 2, 1st District* ☎ *01/514–44–7810* ⊕ *www.bundestheater. at.* **Vienna Ticket.** ⊕ *www. viennaticket.at.*

ⓜ Public Transportation

Wiener Linien. ☎ *01/790–9100* ⊕ *www.wienerlinien.at.*

Taxi

31300 Taxi. ☎ *01/31300.* **40100 Taxi.** ☎ *01/40100.* **60160 Taxi.** ☎ *01/60160.*

Contacts

Tours

BIKING Austria Radreisen.
☎ 07712/5511–0 ⊕ www.
austria-radreisen.at. **Back-roads.** ☎ 800/462–2848
⊕ www.backroads.com.
Butterfield & Robinson.
☎ 866/551–9090 from the
U.S., 800/678–1477 from
other countries ⊕ www.
butterfield.com. **Euro-Bike
Tours.** ☎ 833/968–0491
⊕ www.eurobike.at/
en. **Mountain Bike Hotels.**
☎ 0810/101818 ⊕ www.
austria.info. **Pedal Power.**
☎ 01/729–7234 ⊕ www.
pedalpower.at. **VBT
(Vermont Biking Tours).**
☎ 800/245–3868 ⊕ www.
vbt.com.

BUDGET Cosmos.
☎ 800/276–1241 ⊕ www.
cosmos.com.

**ECOTOURS Austrian Tourist
Board.** ☎ 212/575–7723
in the U.S., 416/967–3381
in Canada ⊕ www.austria.
info. **Naturidyll Hotels.**
☎ 01/867–3660–16,
0800/80–18–400 reserva-tions ⊕ www.naturidyll.at.

FARM VACATIONS Farm-house Holidays in Austria.
⊕ www.farmholidays.com.
Tirol/Das Land der Berge.
☎ 664/88727494 ⊕ www.
tirol.co.

**FIRST-CLASS Brendan
Tours.** ☎ 800/687–1002
⊕ www.brendanvaca-tions.com. **Trafalgar Tours.**
☎ 866/513–1995 ⊕ www.
trafalgartours.com.

HIKING Inn Travel. ☎ 44
1653/617001 from
outside U.K. ⊕ www.
inntravel.co.uk. **Öster-reichischer Alpenverein.**
☎ 0512/59547 ⊕ www.
alpenverein.at.

SUPER-DELUXE Abercrom-bie & Kent. ☎ 800/554–7016 ⊕ www.abercrom-biekent.com. **Travcoa.**
☎ 888/979–4044 ⊕ www.
theluxurytravelgroup.com/
travcoa.

🚆 Train

CONTACTS ÖBB (Österre-ichische Bundesbahnen).
☎ 05/1717 ⊕ www.oebb.
at.

**VIENNA TRAIN STATIONS
Central Train Station (Wien
Hauptbahnhof).** ☎ 05/1717
⊕ www.hauptbahn-hof-wien.at. **Franz-Josef
Bahnhof.** ✉ Julius-Tandler-Platz 3, 9th District/Alser-grund. **Meidling Bahnhof.**
✉ Eichenstrasse 27, 12th
District/Meidling. **West-bahnhof.** ✉ Europaplatz 2,
15th District/Rudolfsheim–Fünfhaus. **Wien-Mitte.**
✉ Landstrasser Haupt-strasse 1c, 3rd District/
Landstrasse ☎ 01/05711.
Wien Praterstern Bahnhof.
✉ Lassallestrasse, 2nd
District/Leopoldstadt
☎ 05/1717 ÖEBB.

🇺🇸 U.S. Embassy/ Consulate

**EMBASSIES Consulate of
the U.S./Passport Division.**
✉ Parkring 12a, 1st Dis-trict ☎ 01/313–3975–35,
01/313–390 for after-hours
emergencies ⊕ at.usem-bassy.gov. **Embassy of the
United States.** ✉ Boltzman-ngasse 16, 9th District/
Alsergrund ☎ 01/31–339–0
⊕ at.usembassy.gov.

📍 Visitor Information

Austria Tourist Office.
⊕ www.austria.info . **Vien-na City Tourist Office.** ✉ Am
Albertinaplatz 1, at May-sedergasse, 1st District
☎ 01/24555 ⊕ www.wien.
info. **MuseumsQuartier.**
⊕ www.mqw.at. **Salzburg.**
⊕ salzburg.info.

INNERE STADT

DISTRICT 1

Updated by
Caroline Sieg

 Sights
★★★★★

 Restaurants
★★★★★

 Hotels
★★★★★

 Shopping
★★★★★

 Nightlife
★☆☆☆☆

NEIGHBORHOOD SNAPSHOT

TOP EXPERIENCES

■ **The Albertina and Albertina Modern:** Take in masterpieces from Dürer, Rubens, Schiele, Cézanne, Klimt, Kokoschka, Picasso, and Rauschenberg, before exploring the Albertina's new modern art outpost just minutes away.

■ **Stephansdom:** Vienna's most famous landmark is also Austria's most important Gothic building and it holds a series of treasures which you can see on a tour.

■ **Spanish Riding School:** Catch the famous Lippizaner horses trotting in style and elegance at a show or their morning rehearsal.

■ **Wiener Staatsoper:** Enjoying a performance at the Vienna State Opera is a feast for the ears and the eyes, too. Non-opera fans can take a guided tour behind the scenes.

■ **Cafe Hop:** You could spend a week, or a lifetime, lingering in the exquisite quintessential Viennese coffeehouses to be found in this part of the city.

■ **Sala Terrena:** Experience Mozart played by a chamber group in historic costumes in the ornate jewel box setting that once hosted the master himself.

QUICK BITES

■ **Würstelstand am Hohen Markt.** Beloved sausage stand serving wurst, wine, beer, and bubbly. ⊠ *Hoher Markt, corner of Marc-Aurel-Strasse, Innere Stadt* Ⓜ *U1/U4 Schwedenplatz.*

■ **Pizza Bizi.** Casual pizza joint where you can pick up a slice as well as a takeout salad or pasta dish. ⊠ *Rotenturmstrasse 4, Innere Stadt* ⊕ *www.pizzabizi.at* Ⓜ *U1/U3 Stephansplatz.*

■ **Cin Cin Buffet.** Despite the word buffet in its name, this is a very Italian cafe servining strong java, cocktails, and wine alongside a display case of marinated anchovies, peppers, and a hearty selection of small pizzas and paninis. ⊠ *Schottenbastei 2, Innere Stadt* ⊕ *cincinbuffet.at* Ⓜ *U2 Schottentor.*

PLANNING YOUR TIME

During the week, this area is filled with a lively mix of visitors sightseeing, locals heading to their offices, and shoppers hitting the large and small shopping areas. It gets busier with shoppers on Saturday, and quieter on Sunday when shops are closed (so it's the perfect time to meander). Evenings are calm when restaurants and bars remain open but all else is closed.

GETTING HERE

Trams run right around the entire Innere Stadt, and easy ways to get here on the subway include the central Stephansplatz subway stop, right next to St. Stephens Cathedral, the major interchanges at Karlsplatz, at the edge of the area by the Opera House, and Schwedenplatz on the other end next to the Danube canal.

For more than eight centuries, the commanding Stephansdom cathedral has remained the nucleus around which the city has grown. Vienna of the Middle Ages is encapsulated behind it, and you could easily spend half a day or more just prowling the endless cobbled lanes and passageways extending from the cathedral square.

Stephansplatz is the logical starting point from which to explore Vienna's past and present. Streets here are named after medieval trades: Bäckerstrasse was the street of the bakers, and weavers peddled their wares on Wollzeile. Legend has it that several Knights Templar were murdered in Blutgasse, or "Blood Alley." The compact area bounded roughly by the back side of the Hofburg palace complex and Staatsoper, the Kohlmarkt, the Graben, and Kärntnerstrasse belongs to the oldest core of the city. Remains of the Roman city are just below the present-day surface. This was and still is the city's commercial heart, dense with shops and markets for various commodities.

Today, the Kohlmarkt and Graben in particular offer the choicest luxury shops. The area is marvelous for its visual treats, from the decorated squares to the varied art-drenched architecture to shop windows. The evening view down Kohlmarkt from the Graben is an inspiring classic, and the gilded dome of Michael's Gate, illuminated at night, shines its light into the palace complex, creating a glittering backdrop. Sights in this area range from the sacred—the Baroque Peterskirche—to the more profane pleasures of Demel, Vienna's beloved pastry shop, and the modernist masterwork of the Looshaus.

A walk through the Imperial Palace, called the Hofburg, brings you back to the days when Vienna was the capital of a mighty empire. You can still find in Viennese shops vintage postcards and prints that show the revered and bewhiskered Emperor Franz Josef leaving his Hofburg palace for a drive in his carriage. Today you can walk in his footsteps, gaze at the old tin bath the emperor kept under his simple iron bedstead, marvel at his bejeweled christening robe, and, along the way, feast your eyes on great works of art, impressive armor, and some of the finest Baroque interiors in Europe.

Until 1918 the Hofburg was the home of the Hapsburgs, rulers of the Austro-Hungarian Empire. Now it is a vast smorgasbord of sightseeing attractions, including the Imperial Apartments, two imperial treasuries, six museums, the National Library, and the famous Winter Riding School. One of the latest Hofburg attractions is a museum devoted to "Sisi," the beloved Empress Elisabeth, wife of Franz

Josef, whose beauty was the talk of Europe and whose tragic assassination (the murder weapon is one of the various exhibits) was mourned by all. The entire complex takes a minimum of a full day to explore in detail.

Sights

★ Albertina Modern

MUSEUM | Vienna's newest—and hottest—museum opened in 2020 in the Künstlerverein, a neo-classical palace and iconic Viennese building, just steps away from the opera house and its sister museum, the famed Albertina Museum. Exhibits focus on modern and contemporary art, and the permanent collection features works by famous Austrians like Maria Lassnig and Arnulf Rainer, and leading international artists, including Damien Hirst, Andy Warhol, Anselm Kiefer, and Cindy Sherman. ⊠ *Karlsplatz 5, 1st District* ☎ *01/534–830* ⊕ *www.albertina.at/albertina-modern* ⊠ *€12; €23 Albertina Modern and Albertina* Ⓜ *Karlsplatz.*

★ Albertina Museum

MUSEUM | One of the largest of the Habsburg residences, the Albertina rests on one of the last remaining fortresses of the Old City. The must-see collection of nearly 65,000 drawings and almost a million prints is one of the most prized graphic collections in the world. All the Old Masters are showcased here: Leonardo da Vinci, Michelangelo, Raphael, Rembrandt. The Batliner Collection includes excellent examples of French and German Impressionism and Russian avant-garde. The mansion's early-19th-century salons—all gilt boiserie and mirrors—provide a jewel-box setting. The excellent Do & Co restaurant, with a patio long enough for an empress's promenade, offers splendid vistas of the historical center, and the Burggarten is the perfect place to take a break. ⊠ *Augustinerstrasse 1, 1st District* ☎ *01/534–830* ⊕ *www.albertina.at* ⊠ *€16.90; €23 Albertina and Albertina Modern* Ⓜ *U3/Herrengasse.*

Am Hof

PLAZA | In the Middle Ages, the ruling Babenberg family built its castle on what is today's Vienna's oldest square, the Am Hof (which translates to "at court"). The **Mariansäule**—or Maria's column—was erected in 1667 to mark victory in the Thirty Years' War. The onetime Civic Armory at the northwest corner has been used as a fire station since 1685 (the high-spirited facade, with its Habsburg eagle, was "Baroqued" in 1731). The complex includes a firefighting museum that's open on Sunday morning. Presiding over the east side of the square is the noted **Kirche Am Hof,** formerly a Jesuit monastery and now a Croatian church. At No.13 is the fairly stolid 17th-century **Palais Collalto,** famous as the setting for Mozart's first public engagement at the age of six. In Bognergasse, to the right of the church, is the **Engel Apotheke** (pharmacy) at No. 9, with a Jugendstil mosaic depicting winged women collecting the elixir of life in outstretched chalices. At the turn of the 20th century, the inner city was dotted with storefronts decorated in a similar manner; today this is the sole survivor. A fantastic permanent light installation became a fixture on the Am Hof in 2017; every day, for an hour at sundown, you can witness Olafur Eliasson's "Yellow Fog" transform the square into a supernatural wonder.

From March through November, there is an art and antiques market every Friday and Saturday from 10 to 5. Am Hof also hosts one of Vienna's celebrated Christmas Markets as well as an Easter Market. ⊠ *Am Hof, 1st District* Ⓜ *U3/ Herrengasse.*

Augustinerkirche (*Augustinian Church*)

RELIGIOUS SITE | Built during the 14th century and presenting the most unified Gothic interior in the city, the church is something of a fraud—the interior dates from the late 18th century, not the early 14th—though the view from the entrance doorway is stunning: a soaring harmony of vertical piers, ribbed vaults, and hanging chandeliers that makes Vienna's other Gothic interiors look earthbound by comparison. Napoléon was wed here, as were Emperor Franz Josef and his beloved Sisi. Note on the right the magnificent **Tomb of the Archduchess Maria-Christina,** sculpted by the great Antonio Canova in 1805, with mourning figures trooping into a pyramid. The imposing Baroque organ sounds as heavenly as it looks, and the Sunday-morning high mass (frequently with works by Mozart or Haydn) sung here at 11 can be the highlight of a trip. To the right of the main altar, in the small Loreto Chapel, stand silver urns containing some 54 hearts of Hapsburg rulers. This rather morbid sight is viewable after mass on Sunday or by appointment. ⊠ *Josefsplatz, 1st District* ☎ *01/533–7099* Ⓜ *U3/Herrengasse.*

Burggarten

CITY PARK | The intimate Burggarten in back of the Neue Burg is a quiet oasis that includes a statue of a contemplative Franz Josef and an elegant statue of Mozart, moved here from the Albertinaplatz after the war, when the city's charred ruins were being rebuilt. Today the park is a favored time-out spot for the Viennese; an alluring backdrop is formed by the striking former greenhouses, now the gorgeous Palmenhaus restaurant and the **Schmetterlinghaus.** Enchantment awaits you at Vienna's unique Butterfly House. Inside are towering tropical trees, waterfalls, a butterfly nursery, and more than 150 species on display (usually 400 winged jewels are in residence). The park also has entrances on Hanuschgasse and Goethegasse. ⊠ *Opernring, 1st District* ⊕ *www.schmetterlinghaus.at* ⊠ *€7* Ⓜ *U2/MuseumsQuartier; Tram: 1, 2, and D/Burgring.*

Burgtheater (*National Theater*)

ARTS VENUE | One of the most important theaters in the German-speaking world, the Burgtheater was built between 1874 and 1888 in the Italian Renaissance style, replacing the old court theater at Michaelerplatz. Emperor Franz Josef's mistress, Katherina Schratt, was once a star performer here, and famous Austrian and German actors still stride across this stage. The opulent interior, with its 60-foot relief *Worshippers of Bacchus* by Rudolf Wyer and lobby ceiling frescoes by Ernst and Gustav Klimt, makes it well worth a visit. ⊠ *Dr. Karl Lueger-Ring 2, 1st District* ☎ *01/514–4441–40* ⊕ *www.burgtheater.at* ⊠ *From €7.50* Ⓜ *Tram: 1, 2, and D/Burgtheater, Rathaus.*

Collection of Historical Musical Instruments

MUSEUM | See pianos that belonged to Brahms, Schumann, and Mahler, along with collections of a variety of ancient and antique instruments in this Neue Burg museum. Also here is Anton Karas' zither, on which he played "The Third Man" theme. ⊠ *Neue Burg, Heldenplatz, 1st District* ⊕ *www.khm.at/en* ⊠ *€12 includes Imperial Armory and the Weltmuseum Wien* Ⓜ *U2/MuseumsQuartier.*

Dominikanerkirche (*St. Maria Rotunda*)

RELIGIOUS SITE | The Postgasse, to the east of Schönlaterngasse, introduces this unexpected visitor from Rome, built in the 1630s, some 50 years before the Viennese Baroque building boom. Its facade is modeled after the Roman churches of the 16th century. The interior illustrates why the Baroque style came to be considered the height of bad taste during the 19th century (and it still has many detractors today). "Sculpt 'til you drop" seems to have been the motto here, and the viewer's eye is given no respite. This sort of Roman architectural orgy never really gained a foothold in Vienna, and when the great Viennese architects did pull out all the decorative stops at the Belvedere Palace, they did it in a very different style and with far greater success. ⊠ *Postgasse 4, 1st District* ☎ *01/512–9174* ⊕ *www.erzdioeze-ese-wien.at/Wien-Maria-Rotunda* Ⓜ *U3/Stubentor/Dr.-Karl-Lueger-Platz.*

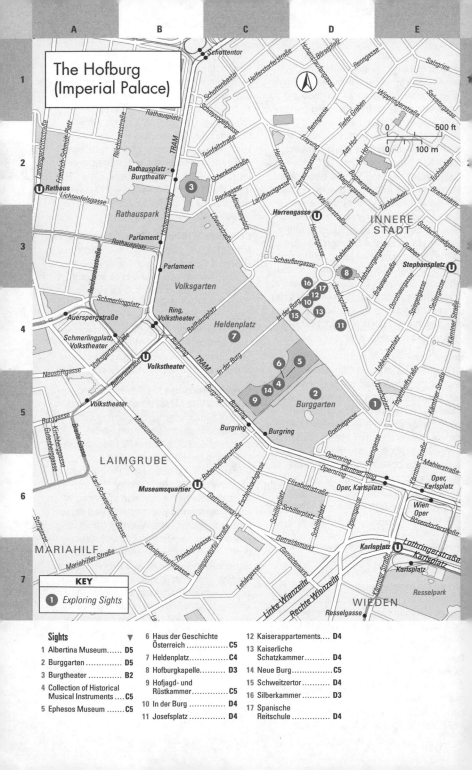

The Hofburg (Imperial Palace)

KEY

1 *Exploring Sights*

Sights ▼

1	Albertina Museum...... **D5**
2	Burggarten **D5**
3	Burgtheater **B2**
4	Collection of Historical Musical Instruments **C5**
5	Ephesos Museum **C5**
6	Haus der Geschichte Österreich **C5**
7	Heldenplatz............... **C4**
8	Hofburgkapelle.......... **D3**
9	Hofjagd- und Rüstkammer.............. **C5**
10	In der Burg **D4**
11	Josefsplatz **D4**
12	Kaiserappartements.... **D4**
13	Kaiserliche Schatzkammer........... **D4**
14	Neue Burg............... **C5**
15	Schweitzertor **D4**
16	Silberkammer **D3**
17	Spanische Reitschule **D4**

Ephesos Museum

MUSEUM | The tiny Ephesus Museum contains a small but exceptional collection of Roman antiquities unearthed by Austrian archaeologists in Turkey at the turn of the 20th century. ✉ *Neue Burg, Heldenplatz, 1st District* ⊕ *www.khm. at/en/visit/collections/ephesos-museum* 🎫 *€8, includes Haus der Geschichte Österreich* ⊗ *Closed Mon.* Ⓜ *Tram: 1, 2, and D/Burgring.*

Freyung

PLAZA | This square, whose name means "freeing"—so called, according to lore, because for many centuries monks at the adjacent Schottenkirche had the privilege of offering sanctuary for three days to anyone on the lam. In the center of the square stands the allegorical **Austria Fountain** (1845), notable because its Bavarian designer, Ludwig Schwanthaler, had the statues cast in Munich and then supposedly filled them with cigars to be smuggled into Vienna for black-market sale. Around the sides of the square are some of Vienna's greatest patrician residences, including the Ferstel, Harrach, and Kinsky palaces.

The Schottenhof, the shaded courtyard at Freyung 6, typifies the change that came over Viennese architecture during the Biedermeier era (1815–1848). The Viennese, according to the traditional view, were so relieved to be rid of the upheavals of the Napoleonic Wars that they accepted without protest the iron-handed repression of Prince Metternich, chancellor of Austria. Restraint also ruled in architecture; Baroque license was rejected in favor of a new and historically "correct" style that was far more controlled and reserved. Kornhäusel led the way in establishing this trend in Vienna; his Schottenhof facade is all sober organization and frank repetition. But in its marriage of strong and delicate forces it still pulls off the great Viennese-waltz

trick of successfully merging seemingly antithetical characteristics. ✉ *Am Hof and Herrengasse, 1st District* Ⓜ *U3/ Herrengasse.*

Globe Museum

MUSEUM | Across the street from the Café Central, the beautifully renovated Palais Mollard has a rare collection of more than 240 terrestrial and celestial globes on display in its second-floor museum—the only one of its kind in the world open to the public. The oldest is a globe of the Earth dating from 1536, produced by Gemma Frisius, a Belgian doctor and cosmographer. On the ground floor is a small but fascinating Esperanto museum, which explores the history of Esperanto and other planned languages. Both museums are run by the Austrian National Library. ✉ *Herrengasse 9, 1st District* ☎ *01/534–10–710* ⊕ *www.onb. ac.at/museen/globenmuseum* 🎫 *€5, includes Esperanto museum* ⊗ *Closed Mon. Oct.–Mar.* Ⓜ *U3/Herrengasse.*

The Graben

NEIGHBORHOOD | One of Vienna's major crossroads, the Graben's unusual width gives it the presence and weight of a city square. Its shape is due to the Romans, who chose this spot for the city's southwestern moat (Graben literally means "moat" or "ditch"). The Graben's centerpiece is the effulgently Baroque **Pestsäule,** or Plague Column. Erected by Emperor Leopold I between 1687 and 1693 as thanks to God for delivering the city from a particularly virulent plague, today the representation looks more like a host of cherubs doing their best to cope with the icing of a wedding cake wilting under a hot sun. Protestants may be disappointed to learn that the foul figure of the Pest also stands for the heretic plunging away from the "true faith" into the depths of hell. ✉ *Between Kärntnerstrasse and Kohlmarkt, 1st District* Ⓜ *U1 or U3/Stephansplatz.*

Mozart, Mozart, Mozart!

The composer Wolfgang Amadeus Mozart (1756–91) crammed a prodigious number of compositions into the last 10 years of his life, many of which he spent in Vienna. Here, he experienced many of the high points of his life, both personal and artistic. He wed his beloved Constanze Weber (with whom he would have six children) at St. Stephen's Cathedral in August 1782, and led the premieres of several of his greatest operas. But knowing his troubled relations with his home city of Salzburg makes his Vienna sojourn even more poignant.

From the beginning of Mozart's career, his father, frustrated in his own musical ambitions at the archbishopric in Salzburg, looked beyond the boundaries of the Austro-Hungarian Empire to promote the boy's fame. At the age of six, his son caused a sensation in the royal courts of Europe with his skills as an instrumentalist and impromptu composer. As Mozart grew up, however, his virtuosity lost its power to amaze and he was forced to make his way as an "ordinary" musician, which then meant finding a position at court. Not much more successful in Salzburg than his father had been, he was never able to rise beyond the level of organist. In disgust, he relocated to Vienna, where despite the popularity of his operas he was able to obtain only an unpaid appointment as assistant Kapellmeister at St. Stephen's mere months before his death. By then, patronage subscriptions had been taken up in Hungary and the Netherlands that would have paid him handsomely. But it was too late. Whatever the story behind his untimely death, the fact remains that he was not given the state funeral he deserved, and he was buried in an unmarked grave (as were most Viennese at the time) after a sparsely attended funeral.

Only the flint hearted can stand in Vienna's Währingerstrasse and look at the windows behind which Mozart wrote those last three symphonies in just six weeks in the summer of 1788 and not be touched. For this was the time when the Mozart fortunes had slumped to their lowest. "If you, my best of friends, forsake me, I am unhappily and innocently lost with my poor sick wife and my child," he wrote. And if one is inclined to accuse Mozart's fellow countrymen of neglect, they seem to have made up for it with a vengeance. Visitors to Vienna and Salzburg cannot escape the barrage of Mozart candies, wine, beer, coffee mugs, T-shirts, and baseball caps. Mozart, always one to appreciate a joke, would surely see the irony in the belated veneration. Today, places with which he is associated are all reverently marked with memorial plaques.

Haas-Haus

BUILDING | Designed by the late Hans Hollein, one of Austria's best-known contemporary architects, who died in 2014, the Haas-Haus is one of Vienna's more controversial buildings. The modern lines contrast sharply with the venerable walls of St. Stephen's just across the way, which can be seen in the mirrored facade of the Haas-Haus. ✉ *Stephansplatz 12, 1st District* Ⓜ *U1 or U3/Stephansplatz.*

Haus der Geschichte Österreich (*House of Austrian History*)

MUSEUM | One of Vienna's newest museums is also Austria's first museum of contemporary history, which explores what it means to be Austrian today through the lense of culture and events since the founding of the democratic republic in 1918. Exhibits tackle themes from the growth of fascism, Nazi occupation, post-WWII development, inequality, immigration, and the highs and lows of this coutnry's recent history. You'll find everything from original footage of Vienna after the end of the the first world war, displays on the growth of fascism and the complicity of locals, the dress that Conchita Wurst, Austria's most famous drag queen wore when she won the 2014 Eurovision Song Contest for Austria, as well as the infamous USB stick with "Ibiza" footage that brought down the Austrian government in 2019. ⊠ *The Neue Burg, Heldenplatz, 1st District* ☎ *01/534–10805* ⊕ *www.hdgoe.at* ⊠ *€8 includes the Ephesos Museum* ⊗ *Closed Mon.* Ⓜ *Tram: 1, 2, and D/Burgring.*

★ **Haus der Musik** (*House of Music*)

MUSEUM | FAMILY | You could spend an entire day at this ultra-high-tech museum, housed on several floors of an early-19th-century palace near Schwarzenbergplatz. This is a highly interactive experience; in "Facing Mozart," visitors animate a Mozart portrait using a technology called facetracking. Assuming the role of virtual conductor, you can conduct the Vienna Philharmonic (or a video projection of it, anyway) and have the orchestra follow your every command; the conductor's baton is hooked to a computer, which allows you to have full control over the simulated orchestra. For added fun, the stairs at the beginning of the tour are musical; each step produces a note. Other exhibits trace the evolution of sound (from primitive noises to the music of the classical masters) and illustrate the mechanics of the human ear (you can even measure your own frequency threshold). ⊠ *Seilerstätte 30, 1st District* ☎ *01/513–4850* ⊕ *www.hdm. at* ⊠ *€14* Ⓜ *U1, U2, or U4/Karlsplatz, then Tram D/Schwarzenbergplatz.*

Heiligenkreuzerhof (*Holy Cross Court*)

PLAZA | Off the narrow streets and alleys behind the Stephansdom is this peaceful spot, approximately ½ km (¼ mile) from the cathedral. The beautiful Baroque courtyard has the distinct feeling of a retreat into the 18th century. ⊠ *Schönlaterngasse 5, 1st District* Ⓜ *U1 or U3/Stephansplatz.*

Heldenplatz

PLAZA | The Neue Burg was never completed and so the Heldenplatz was left without a discernible shape, but the space is punctuated by two superb equestrian statues depicting Archduke Karl and Prince Eugene of Savoy. The older section on the north includes the offices of the federal president. ⊠ *Hofburg, 1st District* Ⓜ *Tram: 1, 2, and D/ Burgring.*

Himmelpfortgasse

HISTORIC SITE | The maze of tiny streets surrounding Himmelpfortgasse (literally, "Gates of Heaven Street") conjures up the Vienna of the 19th century. The most impressive house on the street is the Ministry of Finance. The rear of the Steffl department store on Rauhensteingasse now marks the site of the house in which Mozart died in 1791. There's a commemorative plaque that once identified the street-side site. ⊠ *Himmelpfortgasse 6, 1st District* Ⓜ *U1 or U3/Stephansplatz.*

Hofburgkapelle (*Chapel of the Imperial Palace*)

RELIGIOUS SITE | Fittingly, this is the main venue for the beloved Vienna Boys' Choir, since the group has its roots in the Hofmusikkapelle choir founded by Emperor Maximilian I five centuries ago (Haydn and Schubert were both participants as young boys). The choir sings mass here at 9:15 on Sunday from mid-September to June. Be aware that

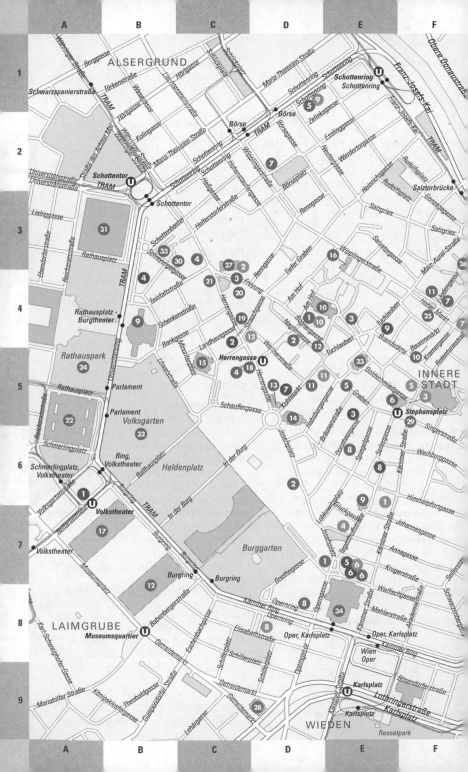

Sights ▼

1 Am Hof **D4**
2 Augustinerkirche **D6**
3 Freyung **C4**
4 Globe Museum **C5**
5 The Graben **E5**
6 Haas-Haus. **E5**
7 Hoher Markt. **F4**
8 Jüdisches Museum
  Wien. **E6**
9 Kaisergruft. **E6**
10 Kirche am Hof **D4**
11 Kohlmarkt. **D5**
12 Kunsthistorisches
  Museum **B8**
13 Looshaus. **D5**
14 Michaelerplatz. **D5**
15 Minoritenkirche. **C5**
16 Museum Judenplatz **E3**
17 Naturhistorisches
  Museum **A7**
18 Österreiche
  Nationalbibliothek **C5**
19 Palais Ferstel. **C4**
20 Palais Harrach **C4**
21 Palais Kinsky **C4**
22 Parlament. **A5**
23 Peterskirche. **E5**
24 Rathaus **A5**
25 Römermuseum. **F4**
26 Ruprechtskirche. **F3**
27 Schottenkirche. **C3**
28 Secession Building. **D9**
29 Stock-im-Eisen. **F5**
30 Third Man Portal. **B3**
31 Universität Wien. **B3**
32 Volksgarten. **B6**
33 Wien Museum Beethoven
  Pasqualatihaus **B3**
34 Wiener Staatsoper **E8**

Restaurants ▼

1 DO & CO Albertina **D7**
2 Esterházykeller. **D4**
3 Gösser Bierklinik. **E4**
4 Melker Stiftskeller **C3**
5 Restaurant Edvard **D1**
6 Restaurant Grüne Bar... **E7**
7 Restaurant Hansen **D2**
8 Veggiezz **D8**
9 Vestibül **B4**
10 Wrenkh Restaurant and
  Cooking Salon. **F4**
11 Würstelstand am
  Hohen Markt **F4**
12 Zum Schwarzen
  Kameel. **D4**

Quick Bites ▼

1 Cafe Bellaria **A6**
2 Café Central **C4**
3 Café Hawelka **E5**
4 Café Landtmann **B4**
5 Café Mozart **E7**
6 Café Sacher **E7**
7 Demel **D5**
8 Oberlaa **E6**
9 Veganista **E4**

Hotels ▼

1 Ambassador. **E6**
2 Benediktushaus. **C3**
3 Do & Co Hotel **F5**
4 The Guesthouse **E7**
5 Hotel Am
  Stephansplatz. **F5**
6 Hotel Sacher Wien **E7**
7 Hotel Topazz Lamee **F4**
8 Le Méridien Vienna. **D8**
9 Palais Hansen
  Kempinski Vienna. **D1**
10 Park Hyatt Vienna **D4**
11 Pension Nossek. **E5**
12 Radisson Blu Style
  Hotel. **C4**

you *hear* the choirboys but don't see them; soprano and alto voices peal forth from a gallery behind the seating area. ⊠ *Hofburg, Schweizer Hof, 1st District* ☎ *01/533–9927* ⊕ *www.hofmusikkapelle. gv.at* Ⓜ *U3/Herrengasse.*

Hofjagd- und Rüstkammer (*Imperial Armory*)

MUSEUM | Home to one of the most extensive arms and armor collections in the world the Imperial Armory houses the armor and ornamental weapons of almost all western European princes from the 15th to the early 20th centuries on display. It's located within the Neue Burg museum complex, and you can enter at the triumphal arch set into the middle of the curved portion of the facade. ⊠ *Neue Burg, Heldenplatz, 1st District* ⊕ *www.hofjagd-ruestkammer. at* ☜ *€16, includes admission to the Weltmuseum Wien and the Collection of Historic Musical Instruments* ☉ *Closed Mon. and Tues.* Ⓜ *U2/MuseumsQuartier.*

Hoher Markt

PLAZA | Crowds gather at noon each day to see the huge mechanical Anker Clock strike the hour. That's when the full panoply of mechanical figures of Austrian historical personages parades by; see if you can spot Marcus Aurelius, Joseph Haydn, and Maria Theresa. The Anker Clock (named for the Anker Insurance Company, which financed it) took six years (1911–1917) to build. It managed to survive the World War II artillery fire that badly damaged much of the square. The graceless buildings erected around the square since 1945 do little to show off the square's lovely Baroque centerpiece, the St. Joseph Fountain (portraying the marriage of Joseph and Mary), designed in 1729 by Joseph Emanuel Fischer von Erlach, son of the great Johann Bernhard Fischer von Erlach. ⊠ *1st District* Ⓜ *U1 or U4/Schwedenplatz.*

In der Burg

PLAZA | This prominent courtyard of the Hofburg complex focuses on a statue of Francis II and the noted **Schweizertor** gateway. Note the **clock** on the far upper wall at the north end of the courtyard: it tells time by a sundial, also gives the time mechanically, and even, above the clockface, indicates the phase of the moon. ⊠ *1st District* ✛ *Off Löwelstrasse* Ⓜ *U3/Herrengasse.*

Josefsplatz

PLAZA | Many consider this Vienna's loveliest courtyard and, indeed, the beautifully restored imperial style adorning the roof of the buildings forming Josefsplatz is one of the few visual demonstrations of Austria's onetime widespread power and influence. The square's namesake is represented in the equestrian **statue of Emperor Josef II** (1807) in the center. ⊠ *Herrengasse, 1st District* Ⓜ *U3/ Herrengasse.*

Jüdisches Museum Wien (*Jewish Museum of Vienna*)

MUSEUM | The former Eskeles Palace, once an elegant private residence, now houses the Jewish Museum of Vienna. Permanent exhibits tell of the momentous role Viennese Jews have played in everything from music and medicine to art and philosophy, both in Austria and in the world at large. A permanent exhibition called "Our City" shows Jewish life in Vienna up to the present day. The museum complex includes a café and bookstore. ⊠ *Dorotheergasse 11, 1st District* ☎ *01/535–0431* ⊕ *www. jmw.at* ☜ *€12 includes admission to the Judenplatz Museum* ☉ *Closed Sat.* Ⓜ *U1 or U3/Stephansplatz.*

Kaiserappartements (*Imperial Apartments*)

CASTLE/PALACE | From the spectacular portal gate of the Michaelertor—you can't miss the four gigantic statues of Hercules and his labors—you climb the marble Kaiserstiege (Emperor's Staircase) to begin a tour of a long, repetitive

Vienna's Hofburg Quarter

A walk through the Imperial Palace, called the Hofburg, brings you back to the days when Vienna was the capital of a mighty empire. You can still find in Viennese shops vintage postcards and prints that show the revered and bewhiskered Emperor Franz Josef leaving his Hofburg palace for a drive in his carriage. Today you can walk in his footsteps, gaze at the old tin bath the emperor kept under his simple iron bedstead, marvel at his bejeweled christening robe, and, along the way, feast your eyes on great works of art, impressive armor, and some of the finest Baroque interiors in Europe.

Until 1918 the Hofburg was the home of the Hapsburgs, rulers of the Austro-Hungarian Empire. Now it is a vast smorgasbord of sightseeing attractions, including the Imperial Apartments, two imperial treasuries, six museums, the National Library, and the famous Winter Riding School. One of the latest Hofburg attractions is a museum devoted to "Sisi," the beloved Empress Elisabeth, wife of Franz Josef, whose beauty was the talk of Europe and whose tragic assassination (the murder weapon is one of the various exhibits) was mourned by all. The entire complex takes a minimum of a full day to explore in detail.

■TIP➔ If your time is limited (or if you want to save most of the interior sightseeing for a rainy day), omit all the museums mentioned below except for the Imperial Apartments and the Schatzkammer. An excellent multilingual, full-color booklet, describing the palace in detail, is for sale at most ticket counters within the complex; it gives a complete list of attractions, and maps out the palace's complicated ground plan and building history wing by wing.

Vienna took its imperial role seriously, as evidenced by the sprawling Hofburg complex, which is still today the seat of government. While the buildings cover a considerable area, the treasures lie within, discreet. Franz Josef was beneficent—witness the broad Ringstrasse he ordained and the panoply of museums and public buildings it hosts. With few exceptions (Vienna City Hall and the Votive Church), rooflines are on an even level, creating an ensemble effect that helps integrate the palace complex and its parks into the urban landscape without overwhelming it. Diplomats still bustle in and out of high-level international meetings along the elegant halls. Horse-drawn carriages still traverse the Ring and the roadway that cuts through the complex. Ignore the cars and tour buses, and you can easily imagine yourself in a Vienna of a hundred or more years ago.

Architecturally, the Hofburg—like St. Stephen's—is far from refined. It grew up over a period of 700 years (its earliest mention in court documents is from 1279, at the very beginning of Hapsburg rule), and its spasmodic, haphazard growth kept it from attaining a unified identity. But many individual buildings are fine, and the National Library is a tour de force. ■TIP➔ Want to see it all without breaking the bank? A €36 Sisi Ticket includes admission to the Kaiserappartements, the Silberkammer, the Imperial Furniture Depot, Vienna Furniture Museum, and a Grand Tour of the Schönbrunn Palace.

3

Innere Stadt

Imagine the lives of Emperor Franz Josef and Empress Elisabeth as you wander through their apartments and back in time to the latter half of the 19th century.

suite of 18 conventionally luxurious state rooms. The red-and-gold decoration (19th-century imitation of 18th-century Rococo) tries to look regal, but much like the empire itself in its latter days, it's only going through the motions, and ends up looking merely official. Still, these are the rooms where the ruling family of the Hapsburg empire ate, slept, and dealt with family tragedy—in the emperor's study on January 30, 1889, Emperor Franz Josef was told about the tragic death of his only son, Crown Prince Rudolf, who had shot himself and his soulmate, 17-year-old Baroness Vetsera, at the hunting lodge at Mayerling. Among the few signs of life are Emperor Franz Josef's spartan, iron field bed, on which he slept every night, and Empress Elisabeth's wooden gymnastics equipment (obsessed with her looks, Sisi suffered from anorexia and was fanatically devoted to exercise). In the Sisi Museum, part of the regular tour, five rooms display many of her treasured possessions, including her jewels, the gown she wore the night before her marriage, her

dressing gown, and the opulent court salon railroad car she used. There is also a death mask made after her assassination by an anarchist in Geneva in 1898, as well as the murder weapon that killed her: a wooden-handled file. ⌂ *Hofburg, Schweizer Hof, 1st District* ☎ *01/533–7570* ⊕ *www.hofburg-wien.at* ⌁ *€15, includes admission to Silberkammer; €18 for a guided tour* Ⓜ *U3/Herrengasse.*

Kaisergruft (*Imperial Burial Vault*)

MEMORIAL | On the southwest corner of the Neuer Markt, the Kapuzinerkirche, or Capuchin Church, is home to one of the more intriguing sights in Vienna: the Kaisergruft, or Imperial Burial Vault. The crypts contain the partial remains of some 140 Hapsburgs (most of the hearts are in the Augustinerkirche and the entrails in St. Stephen's) plus one non-Hapsburg governess ("She was always with us in life," said Maria Theresa, "why not in death?"). Perhaps starting with their tombs is the wrong way to approach the Hapsburgs in Vienna, but on the upside, at least it gives you a chance to get their names in sequence, as they lie in rows, their pewter coffins ranging from the simplest explosions of funerary conceit—with decorations of skulls, snakes, and other morbid symbols—to the huge and distinguished tomb of Maria Theresa and her husband. Designed while the couple still lived, their monument shows the empress in bed with her husband—awaking to the Last Judgment as if it were just another morning, while the remains of her son (the ascetic Josef II) lie in a simple copper casket at the foot of the bed. In 2011, 98-year-old Otto Hapsburg, the eldest son of the last emperor, was laid to rest here with as much pomp as was permissible in a republic. ✉ *Tegetthofstrasse 2, 1st District* ☎ *01/512–6853* 🖵 *€7.50* Ⓜ *U1, U3/ Stephansplatz; U1, U4/Karlsplatz.*

★ **Kaiserliche Schatzkammer** (*Imperial Treasury*)

MUSEUM | The entrance to the Schatzkammer, with its 1,000 years of treasures, is tucked away at ground level behind the staircase to the Hofburgkapelle. The elegant display is a welcome antidote to the rather staid Imperial Apartments, and the crowns and relics glow in their surroundings. Here you'll find such marvels as the Holy Lance (reputedly the lance that pierced Jesus's side), the Imperial Crown (a sacred symbol of sovereignty once stolen on Hitler's orders), and the Saber of Charlemagne. Don't miss the Burgundian Treasure, connected with that most romantic of medieval orders of chivalry, the Order of the Golden Fleece. ✉ *Hofburg, Schweizer Hof, 1st District* ☎ *01/525–240* ⊕ *www.kaiserliche-schatzkammer.at* 🖵 *€12* ⊙ *Closed Tues.* Ⓜ *U3/Herrengasse.*

Kärntner Strasse

STORE/MALL | Vienna's leading central shopping street is much maligned—too commercial, too crowded, too many tasteless signs—but when the daytime tourist crowds dissolve, the Viennese arrive regularly for their evening promenade, and it is easy to see why. The street comes alive with outdoor cafés, wonderfully decorated shop windows, buskers, and well-dressed citizens walking their small, manicured dogs. Despite tourists, it has an energy that the more tasteful Graben and the impeccable Kohlmarkt lack. ✉ *1st District* Ⓜ *U1, U4/ Karlsplatz, or U1, U3/Stephansplatz.*

Kirche Am Hof

RELIGIOUS SITE | On the east side of the Am Hof, the Church of the Nine Choirs of Angels is identified by its sprawling Baroque facade designed by Carlo Carlone in 1662. The interior is sombre, but the checkerboard marble floor lightens things up and may remind you of Dutch churches. ✉ *Am Hof 1, 1st District* Ⓜ *U3/ Herrengasse.*

Kohlmarkt

STORE/MALL | Aside from its classic view of the domed entryway to the imperial palace complex of the Hofburg, the Kohlmarkt is best known as Vienna's most elegant shopping street, and fronts the area being refashioned the Goldenes Quartier (Golden Quarter). All the big brand names are represented here: Gucci, Louis Vuitton, Tiffany, Chanel, and Armani, to name a few. The shops, not the buildings, are remarkable, although there is an entertaining odd-couple pairing: No. 11 (early 18th century) and No. 9 (early 20th century). The mixture of architectural styles is similar to that of the Graben, but the general atmosphere is low-key, as if the street were consciously deferring to the showstopper dome at the west end. The composers Haydn and Chopin lived in houses on the street. ✉ *Between Graben and Michaelerplatz, 1st District* Ⓜ *U3/Herrengasse.*

★ **Kunsthistorisches Museum** (*Museum of Fine Art*)

MUSEUM | Even if you're planning on a short stay in Vienna, don't miss one of the greatest art collections in the world at the Kunsthistorisches Museum. Its collections of Old Master paintings reveal the royal taste and style of many members of the mighty House of Hapsburg, which ruled over the greater part of the Western world in the 16th and 17th centuries. The collection stands in the same class with the Louvre, the Prado, and the Vatican. The museum is most famous for the largest collection of paintings under one roof by the Netherlandish 16th-century master Pieter Brueghel the Elder—many art historians say that seeing his sublime *Hunters in the Snow* is worth a trip to Vienna. The Flemish wing also includes masterful works by Rogier van der Weyden, Holbein, Rembrandt, and Vermeer, while the Italian wing features Titian, Giorgione, Raphael, and Caravaggio. One level down is the remarkable Kunstkammer, displaying priceless objects created for the Hapsburg emperors. ⊠ *Maria-Theresien-Platz, 1st District* ☎ *01/525–240* ⊕ *www.khm.at* ⊠ *€16* ⊗ *Closed Mon. in Sept.–May* Ⓜ *U2/MuseumsQuartier; U2 or U3/Volkstheater*.

Looshaus

HOUSE | In 1911 Adolf Loos built the Looshaus on imposing Michaelerplatz, facing the Imperial Palace, and it was considered nothing less than an architectural declaration of war. After 200 years of Baroque and neo-Baroque exuberance, the first generation of 20th-century architects had had enough. Loos led the revolt; *Ornament and Crime* was the title of his famous manifesto, in which he inveighed against the conventional architectural wisdom of the 19th century. He advocated buildings that were plain, honest, and functional. The city was scandalized by Looshaus. Emperor Franz Josef, who lived across the road, was so offended that he ordered the curtains of his windows to remain permanently shut. Today the building has lost its power to shock, and the facade seems quite innocuous. The interior remains a breathtaking surprise; the building now houses a bank, and you can go inside to see the stylish chambers and staircase. To really get up close and personal with Loos, head to the splendor of his Loos American Bar, about six blocks east at No. 10 Kärntnerdurchgang. ⊠ *Michaelerplatz 3, 1st District* Ⓜ *U3/Herrengasse*.

Michaelerplatz

PLAZA | One of Vienna's most historic squares, this small plaza is now the site of an excavation that took place from 1989–1991. Some remarkable Roman ruins were discovered, including what some believe was a brothel for soldiers. The excavations are a latter-day distraction from the Michaelerplatz's most noted claim to fame—the eloquent entryway to the palace complex of the Hofburg.

Mozart's *Requiem* debuted in the **Michaelerkirche** on December 10, 1791. More people stop in today due to a discovery American soldiers made in 1945, when they forced open the crypt doors, which had been sealed for 150 years. Found lying undisturbed for centuries were the mummified remains of former wealthy parishioners of the church—even the finery and buckled shoes worn at their burial had been preserved by the perfect temperatures contained within the crypt. ⊠ *Herrengasse, Reitschulgasse, and Schauflergasse, 1st District* ☎ *0676/503–4164* Ⓜ *U3/Herrengasse*.

Minoritenkirche (*Minorite Church*)

RELIGIOUS SITE | Minoritenplatz is named after its centerpiece, the Minoritenkirche, a Gothic affair with a strange stump of a tower, built mostly in the 14th century. The front is brutally ugly, but the back is a wonderful, if predominantly 19th-century, surprise. The interior contains an impressive and gigantic mosaic reproduction of Leonardo da Vinci's *Last Supper*, commissioned by Napoléon in 1806 and later purchased by Emperor Franz Josef. ⊠ *Minoritenplatz 2A, 1st District* ☎ *01/533–4162* Ⓜ *U3/Herrengasse*.

★ Mozarthaus

MUSEUM | This is Mozart's only still-existing abode in Vienna. Equipped with an excellent audio guide and starting out on the third floor of the building, you can hear about Mozart's time in Vienna: where he lived and performed, who his friends and supporters were, and his passion for expensive attire. The second floor deals with Mozart's operatic works. The first floor focuses on the 2½ years that Mozart lived here, when he wrote dozens of piano concertos, as well as *The Marriage of Figaro* and the six quartets dedicated to Joseph Haydn (who once called on Mozart here, saying to Mozart's father, "Your son is the greatest composer that I know in person or by name"). For two weeks in April 1787, Mozart taught a pupil who would become famous in his own right, the 16-year-old Beethoven. ■**TIP→ You can purchase a combined ticket for Mozarthaus Vienna and Haus der Musik for €18.** ⊠ *Domgasse 5, 1st District* ☎ *01/512–1791* ⊕ *www.mozarthausvienna.at* ⊠ *€11* Ⓜ *U1 or U3/Stephansplatz.*

Museum Judenplatz

MUSEUM | In what was once the old Jewish ghetto, construction workers discovered the fascinating remains of a 13th-century synagogue while digging for a new parking garage. Simon Wiesenthal (a former Vienna resident) helped to turn it into a museum dedicated to the Austrian Jews who died in World War II. Marking the outside is a concrete cube whose surfaces are casts of library shelves, signifying a love of learning. Downstairs are three exhibition rooms devoted to medieval Jewish life and the synagogue excavations. Also in Judenplatz is a statue of the 18th-century playwright Gotthold Ephraim Lessing, erected after World War II. ⊠ *Judenplatz 8, 1st District* ☎ *01/535–0431* ⊕ *www.jmw.at/museum-judenplatz* ⊠ *€12 includes admission to Jewish Museum of Vienna* ⊙ *Closed Sat.*

Naturhistorisches Museum (*Natural History Museum*)

MUSEUM | **FAMILY** | The palatial 19th-century museum, twin of the celebrated Kunsthistorisches Museum, is the home of the *Venus of Willendorf,* a tiny statuette (actually, a replica—the original is in a vault) thought to be some 20,000 years old. This symbol of the Stone Age was originally unearthed in the Wachau Valley, not far

from Melk. The reconstructed dinosaur skeletons draw the most attention, especially among kids. Also not to be missed is the Meteorite Room, which holds the largest and oldest collection of meteorites on the planet. A 3-D simulator allows you to stage a powerful meteor strike. The digital planetarium, with its state-of-the-art Fulldome technology, offers shows several times a day on biology, astronomy, prehistory, and the deep sea. ⊠ *Maria-Theresien-Platz, 1st District* ☎ *01/52177* ⊕ *www.nhm-wien.ac.at* ⊠ *€12* ⊙ *Closed Tues.* Ⓜ *U2 or U3/Volkstheater.*

Neue Burg

CASTLE/PALACE | Standing today as a symbol of architectural overconfidence, the Neue Burg was designed for Emperor Franz Josef in 1869 as a "new château" that was part of a much larger scheme meant to make the Hofburg rival the Louvre, if not Versailles. The German architect Gottfried Semper planned a twin of the present Neue Burg on the opposite side of the Heldenplatz, with arches connecting the two with the other pair of twins on the Ringstrasse, the Kunsthistorisches Museum (Museum of Art History) and the Naturhistorisches Museum (Museum of Natural History). But World War I intervened, and with the empire's collapse the Neue Burg became the last in a long series of failed attempts to bring architectural order to the Hofburg. Today the Neue Burg houses four specialty museums: the **Imperial Armor Collection,** the **Collection of Historical Musical Instruments,** the **Ephesus Museum,** and the **Ethnological Museum.** For details on these museums, see separate listings. ⊠ *Heldenplatz, 1st District* ☎ *01/525–240* ⊕ *www.khm.at* Ⓜ *U2/MuseumsQuartier.*

★ Osterreichische Nationalbibliothek (*Austrian National Library*)

LIBRARY | This is one of the grandest Baroque libraries in the world, a cathedral of books. Its centerpiece is the spectacular Prunksaal—the Grand Hall—which probably contains more book treasures

Formerly the court library to the Hapsburgs, the Österreische Nationalbibliothek is a breathtaking baroque masterpiece.

than any comparable collection outside the Vatican. The main entrance to the ornate reading room is in the left corner of Josefsplatz. Designed by Fischer von Erlach the Elder just before his death in 1723 and completed by his son, the Grand Hall is full-blown high Baroque, with trompe-l'oeil ceiling frescoes by Daniel Gran. Twice a year, special exhibits highlight some of the finest and rarest tomes, well documented in German and English. From 1782 Mozart performed regularly at the Sunday matinees of Baron Gottfried van Swieten, who lived here in a suite of rooms. Four years later the baron founded the Society of Associated Cavaliers, which held oratorio performances with Mozart conducting. Across the street at Palais Palffy, Mozart reportedly first performed *The Marriage of Figaro*. ⊠ *Josefsplatz 1, 1st District* ☎ *01/534–100* ⊕ *www.onb.ac.at* ⊠ *€8* ⊗ *Closed Sun.* Ⓜ *U3/Herrengasse.*

Palais Ferstel

CASTLE/PALACE | Not really a palace, this commercial complex dating from 1856 is named for its architect, Heinrich Ferstel. The facade is Italianate, harking back in its 19th-century way to the Florentine palazzi of the early Renaissance. The interior is unashamedly eclectic: vaguely Romanesque in feel and Gothic in decoration, with a bit of Renaissance or Baroque sculpted detail thrown in for good measure. Such eclecticism is sometimes dismissed as derivative, but here the architectural details are so respectfully and inventively combined that the interior is a pleasure to explore. The 19th-century stock-exchange rooms upstairs are now gloriously restored and used for conferences, concerts, and balls. ⊠ *Freyung 2, 1st District* ⊕ *www.palaisevents.at* Ⓜ *U3/Herrengasse.*

Palais Harrach

HOUSE | Mozart and his sister Nannerl performed here as children for Count Ferdinand during their first visit to Vienna in 1762. The palace, next door to Palais Ferstel, was altered after 1845 and severely damaged during World War II. Some of the state rooms have lost their historical luster, but the Marble Room, set with gilt boiseries, and the Red Gallery, topped with a spectacular ceiling painting, provide grand settings for receptions. ⊠ *Freyung 3, 1st District* Ⓜ *U3/Herrengasse.*

Palais Kinsky

CASTLE/PALACE | Just one of the architectural treasures that comprise the urban set piece of the Freyung, the Palais Kinsky is the square's best-known palace, and is one of the most sophisticated pieces of Baroque architecture in the whole city. Built between 1713 and 1716 by Hildebrandt—and returned to its former glory in the 1990s—it now houses Wiener Kunst Auktionen, a public auction business offering artwork and antiques. If there's an auction viewing, try to see the palace's spectacular 18th-century staircase, all marble goddesses and crowned with a trompe-l'oeil ceiling painted by Marcantonio Chiarini. ⊠ *Freyung 4, 1st District* ☎ *01/532–4200* ⊕ *www.palaisevents.at* Ⓜ *U3/Herrengasse.*

Parlament (*Parliament*)

GOVERNMENT BUILDING | Reminiscent of an ancient Greek temple, this sprawling building is the seat of the country's elected representative assembly. An embracing, heroic ramp on either side of the main structure is lined with carved marble figures of ancient Greek and Roman historians. Its centerpiece is the Pallas-Athene-Brunnen, a fountain designed by Theophil Hansen that is crowned by the Greek goddess of wisdom and surrounded by water nymphs symbolizing the executive and legislative powers governing the country. Interior renovations are scheduled well into 2021.

⊠ *Dr. Karl Renner-Ring 3, 1st District* ☎ *01/401–1024–00* ⊕ *www.parlament. gv.at* Ⓜ *Trams 1, 2, or D/Stadiongasse, Parlament.*

Peterskirche (*St. Peter's Church*)

RELIGIOUS SITE | One of Vienna's most well-known churches, St. Peter's Church stands on what was once the site of a church built in the latter half of the 4th century, making this spot the oldest Christian sacred site in the city. A few centuries later, Charlemagne built another church here, and finally St. Peter's Church was constructed between 1702 and 1708 by Lucas von Hildebrandt, who also built the Belvedere Palace. The facade has angled towers, graceful turrets (said to have been inspired by the tents of the Turks during the siege of 1683), and an unusually fine entrance portal. Inside, the Baroque decoration is elaborate, with some fine touches (particularly the glass-crowned galleries high on the walls on either side of the altar and the amazing tableau of the martyrdom of St. John Nepomuk). Just before Christmas each year the basement crypt is filled with a display of nativity scenes. The church is shoehorned into tiny Petersplatz, just off the Graben. ⊠ *Petersplatz, 1st District* ⊕ *www.peterskirche.at* Ⓜ *U1 or U3/Stephansplatz.*

Rathaus (*City Hall*)

GOVERNMENT BUILDING | Designed by Friedrich Schmidt and resembling a Gothic fantasy castle with its many spires and turrets, the Rathaus took more than 10 years to build and was completed in 1883. The facade holds a lavish display of standard-bearers brandishing the coats of arms of the city of Vienna and the monarchy. Nearly 10 acres of regally landscaped park grace the front of the building, and the area is usually brimming with activity. In winter it's the scene of the most famous Christmas markets in Vienna (which includes an ice-skating rink!). After the New Year, the ice-skating rink continues and is expanded. In summer,

3

Innere Stadt

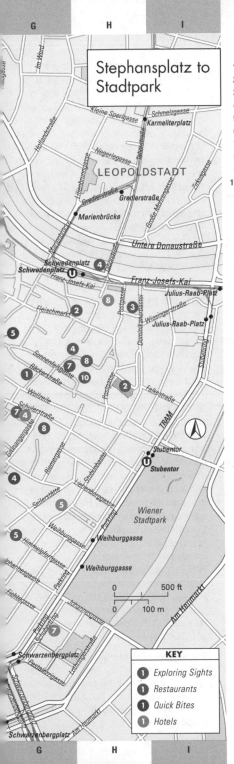

Stephansplatz to Stadtpark

Sights ▼

1 Albertina Modern **F9**
2 Dominikanerkirche **H5**
3 Haus der Musik **F7**
4 Heiligenkreuzerhof **G5**
5 Himmelpfortgasse **G7**
6 Kärntnerstrasse **E7**
7 Mozarthaus **G5**
8 Schönlaterngasse **H5**
9 Stephansdom **F5**
10 Universitätskirche **H5**

Restaurants ▼

1 Figlmüller **G5**
2 Griechenbeisl **G4**
3 Konstantin Filippou **H4**
4 Motto am Fluss **H3**
5 Pizza Bizi **F5**
6 Plachuttas Gasthaus
   zur Oper **E8**
7 Walter Bauer **G5**
8 Weibels Wirtshaus **G5**

Quick Bites ▼

1 Café Frauenhuber **F6**
2 Café Schwarzenberg.... **F8**
3 Haas & Haas
   Teahouse **F5**
4 Kleines Café **G6**
5 Zanoni & Zanoni **F4**

Hotels ▼

1 Grand Hotel Wien **F8**
2 Hotel Bristol **E8**
3 Hotel Imperial **F9**
4 König von Ungarn **G5**
5 Palais Coburg **G7**
6 The Ring Hotel **E8**
7 The Ritz-Carlton,
   Vienna **G8**
8 Ruby Lissi **H4**

KEY

① *Exploring Sights*
① *Restaurants*
① *Quick Bites*
① *Hotels*

folks can watch movies outside during the annual film festival. ⊠ *Rathausplatz 1, 1st District* ☎ *01/52550* Ⓜ *Trams 1, 2, or D/Rathaus.*

Römermuseum

MUSEUM | The Hoher Markt harbors one wholly unexpected attraction: underground ruins of a Roman military camp dating from the 2nd and 3rd centuries. You'll see fragments of buildings, pieces of pottery, children's toys, and statues, idols, and ornaments. Kids can learn about everyday life with interactive games. ⊠ *Hoher Markt 3, 1st District* ☎ *01/535–5606* ⊕ *www.wienmuseum. at* 🎟 *€7* ⊙ *Closed Mon.* Ⓜ *U1 or U4/ Schwedenplatz.*

Ruprechtskirche (*St. Ruprecht's Church*)

RELIGIOUS SITE | North of the Kornhäusel Tower, this is the city's most venerable church, believed to have been founded in 740; the oldest part of the present structure (the lower half of the tower) dates from the 11th century. Set on the ancient ramparts overlooking the Danube Canal, it is serene and unpretentious. ⊠ *Ruprechtsplatz, 1st District* Ⓜ *U1 or U4/Schwedenplatz.*

Schönlaterngasse (*Street of the Beautiful Lantern*)

NEIGHBORHOOD | Once part of Vienna's medieval Latin Quarter, Schönlaterngasse is the main artery of a historic neighborhood that has blossomed in recent years, thanks in part to government *Kulturschillinge*—or renovation loans. Streets are lined with beautiful Baroque town houses (often with colorfully painted facades), now distinctive showcases for art galleries, boutiques, and coffeehouses. At No. 5 you'll find a covered passage that leads to the historic **Heiligenkreuzerhof** courtyard. The picturesque street is named for the ornate wrought-iron wall lantern at Schönlaterngasse 6. Note the Baroque courtyard at Schönlaterngasse 8—one of the city's prettiest.

The quarter's most famous house is the **Basiliskenhaus**. According to legend, on June 26, 1212, a foul-smelling basilisk (half rooster, half toad, with a glance that could kill) took up residence in the courtyard well, poisoning the water. An enterprising apprentice dealt with the problem by climbing down the well armed with a mirror; when the basilisk saw its own reflection, it turned to stone. The petrified creature can still be seen in a niche on the building's facade. Be sure to peek into the house's miniature courtyard for a trip back to medieval Vienna. ⊠ *1st District* Ⓜ *U3/Stubentor, U3/Stephansplatz, U4/Schwedenplatz.*

Schottenkirche (*Scots Church*)

RELIGIOUS SITE | From 1758 to 1761, Bernardo Bellotto did paintings of the Freyung looking north toward the Schottenkirche; the pictures, which hang in the Kunsthistorisches Museum, are remarkably similar to the view you see today. A church has stood on the site of the Schottenkirche since 1177, when the monastery was established by monks from Ireland—Scotia Minor, in Latin, hence the name "Scots Church." The present edifice dates from the mid-1600s, when it replaced its predecessor, which had collapsed because of weakened foundations. The interior, with its ornate ceiling and a surplus of cherubs and angels' faces, is in stark contrast to the plain exterior. The adjacent **Museum im Schottenstift** includes the celebrated late-Gothic high altar dating from about 1470. The winged altar is fascinating for its portrayal of the Holy Family in flight into Egypt—with the city of Vienna clearly identifiable in the background. ⊠ *Freyung 6, 1st District* ☎ *01/534–98–600* ⊕ *www.schottenstift.at* 🎟 *Church free, museum €8* ⊙ *Closed Sun. and Mon.* Ⓜ *U2/Schottentor.*

Schweizertor (*Swiss Gate*)

BUILDING | Dating from 1552 and decorated with some of the earliest classical motifs in the city, the Schweizertor leads from In der Burg through to the oldest section of the palace, a small courtyard known as the Schweizer Hof. The gateway is painted maroon, black, and gold, giving a fine Renaissance flourish to the building's facade. ⊠ *Hofburg, 1st District* Ⓜ *U3/Herrengasse.*

Secession Building

MUSEUM | If the Academy of Fine Arts represents the conservative attitude toward the arts in the late 1800s, then its antithesis can be found in the building immediately behind it to the southeast: the Secession Pavilion, one of Vienna's preeminent symbols of artistic rebellion. Rather than looking to the architecture of the past, like the revivalist Ringstrasse, it looked to a new antihistoricist future. In its heyday, it was a riveting trumpet-blast of a building and is today considered by many to be Europe's first example of full-blown 20th-century architecture.

The Secession began in 1897, when 20 dissatisfied Viennese artists, headed by Gustav Klimt, "seceded" from the Künstlerhausgenossenschaft, the conservative artists' society associated with the Academy of Fine Arts. The movement promoted the radically new kind of art known as Jugendstil, which found its inspiration in both the organic, fluid designs of Art Nouveau and the related but more geometric designs of the English Arts and Crafts movement. The Secession building, designed by the architect Joseph Olbrich and completed in 1898, was the movement's exhibition hall. The lower story, crowned by the entrance motto *Der Zeit Ihre Kunst, Der Kunst Ihre Freiheit* ("To Every Age Its Art, To Art Its Freedom"), is classic Jugendstil: the restrained but assured decoration (by Koloman Moser) complements the facade's pristine flat expanses of cream-color wall. Above the entrance motto sits the building's most famous feature, the gilded openwork dome that the Viennese were quick to christen "the golden cabbage" (Olbrich wanted it to be seen as a dome of laurel, a subtle classical reference meant to celebrate the

triumph of art). The plain white interior was also revolutionary; its most unusual feature was movable walls, allowing the galleries to be reshaped and redesigned for every show. One early show, in 1902, was a temporary exhibition devoted to art celebrating the genius of Beethoven; Klimt's *Beethoven Frieze* was painted for the occasion, and the fragments that survived can be admired in the basement. Guided tours are given daily 10 am to 1 pm. ⊠ *Friedrichstrasse 12, 1st District* ☎ *01/587–53–070* ⊕ *www.secession.at* 🎫 *€9.50* ⊙ *Closed Mon.* Ⓜ *U4/Karlsplatz.*

Silberkammer (*Royal Silver Collection*)

MUSEUM | Fascinating for its behind-the-scenes views of state banquets and other elegant affairs, there are more than forks and finger bowls here. Stunning decorative pieces vie with glittering silver and gold for your attention. Highlights include Emperor Franz Josef's vermeil banqueting service, the jardinière given to Empress Elisabeth by Queen Victoria, and gifts from Marie Antoinette to her brother Josef II. The fully set tables give you a view of court life. ⊠ *Hofburg, Michaelertrakt, 1st District* ☎ *01/533–7570* 🎫 *€15, includes admission to Kaiserappartements, €36 with Sisi Museum* Ⓜ *U3/Herrengasse.*

Spanische Reitschule (*Spanish Riding School*)

ARTS VENUE | On the grounds of the Imperial Palace is the world-famous Spanish Riding School, a favorite for centuries, and no wonder: who can resist the sight of the white Lipizzaner horses going through their masterful paces? For the last 300 years they have been perfecting their haute école riding demonstrations to the sound of Baroque music in a ballroom that seems to be a crystal-chandeliered stable. The interior of the riding school, the 1735 work of Fischer von Erlach the Younger, makes it Europe's most elegant sports arena. From August to June, evening performances are held mostly on weekends, and morning exercises with music are held mostly on weekdays. Booking months ahead is a good idea. ✉ *Michaelerplatz 1, 1st District* ☎ *01/533–9031* ⊕ *www.srs.at* ✎ *From €53; morning exercises from €19; guided tour €19* ⊙ *Closed late Jul. and Aug.* Ⓜ *U3/Herrengasse.*

★ **Stephansdom** (*St. Stephen's Cathedral*)
RELIGIOUS SITE | Vienna's soaring centerpiece, this beloved 12th-century cathedral enshrines the heart of the city. Originally the structure was to have had matching 445-foot-high spires, but funds ran out, and the lack of symmetry makes the cathedral instantly identifiable from its profile. Though heavily damaged in World War II, it's difficult now to tell what was original and which parts of the walls and vaults were reconstructed. It's a stylistic jumble ranging from 13th-century Romanesque to 15th-century Gothic. To explore the cathedral in detail, buy the English-language description sold in the Dom Shop. One particularly masterly work: the stone pulpit attached to the second freestanding pier left of the central nave, carved by Anton Pilgram between 1510 and 1550; most intriguing are its five sculpted figures. Many notable events occurred here, including Mozart's marriage in 1782 and his funeral in December 1791. Enjoy the bird's-eye views from the cathedral's beloved **Alter Steffl** (Old Stephen Tower), reached via 343 steps. ✉ *Stephansplatz, 1st District* ☎ *01/515–52–3054* ⊕ *www.stephanskirche.at* ✎ *Cathedral only free. || €6 all-inclusive guided tour tickets include the catacombs, North Tower, and South Tower.* Ⓜ *U1 or U3/Stephansplatz.*

Stock-im-Eisen
MEMORIAL | Set into the building on the west side of Kärntner Strasse is one of the city's odder relics, an ancient tree trunk studded with blacksmiths' nails. Researchers in the 1970s identified the trunk as a 600-year-old spruce. Since the Middle Ages, any apprentice metalworker who came to Vienna to learn his trade

---

Bird's-Eye View

A good introduction to Vienna is from a view high above it, and the city's preeminent panoramic lookout point is the observation platform of Vienna's mother cathedral, the Stephansdom. The young and agile will make it up the 343 steps of the south tower in 8 to 10 minutes; the rest will make it in closer to 20. There's also an elevator to the terrace of the north tower, which gives pretty much the same view. From atop, you can see that St. Stephen's is the veritable hub of the city's wheel.

---

hammered a nail into the trunk for good luck. During World War II, when there was talk of moving the relic to a museum in Munich, it mysteriously disappeared (and then reappeared perfectly preserved after the threat of removal had passed). ✉ *Stock-im-Eisen-Platz, Kärntner Strasse and Singerstrasse, 1st District* Ⓜ *U1 or U3/Stephansplatz.*

Third Man Portal
HOUSE | This doorway (up the incline) was made famous in 1949 by the classic film *The Third Man*. It was here that Orson Welles, as the malevolently knowing Harry Lime, stood hiding in the dark, only to have his smiling face illuminated by a sudden light from the upper-story windows of the house across the alley. To get to this apartment building from the nearby Schottenkirche, follow Teinfaltstrasse one block west to Schreyvogelgasse on the right. ✉ *Schreyvogelgasse 8, 1st District* Ⓜ *U2/Schottentor.*

Universität Wien (*University of Vienna*)
COLLEGE | The oldest university in the German-speaking world (founded in 1365), the main section of the university is a massive block in Italian Renaissance style designed by Heinrich Ferstel and

The Spanish Riding School is a traditional riding school for Lipizzaner horses that perform their haute école equestrian skills to audiences in the Hofburg Palace.

built between 1873 and 1884. Statues representing 38 important men of letters decorate the front of the building, while the rear, which encompasses the library (with nearly 2 million volumes), is adorned with sgraffito. ⊠ *Dr. Karl Lueger-Ring 1, 1st District* ☎ *01/4277–17676, 01/4277–176–01 guided tours* ⊕ *www. univie.ac.at* 🎫 *€5* Ⓜ *U2/Schottentor.*

Universitätskirche (*Jesuit Church*)
RELIGIOUS SITE | The church was built around 1630. Its flamboyant Baroque interior contains a fine trompe-l'oeil ceiling fresco by Andrea Pozzo, the master of visual trickery, who was imported from Rome in 1702 for the job. You might hear a Mozart or Haydn mass sung here in Latin on many Sundays. ⊠ *Dr.-Ignaz-Seipl-Platz, 1st District* ☎ *01/5125–2320* Ⓜ *U3 Stubentor/Dr.-Karl-Lueger-Platz.*

Volksgarten
CITY PARK | Just opposite the Hofburg is a green oasis with a rose garden, a shining white 19th-century Greek temple, and a rather wistful white-marble monument to Empress Elisabeth,

Franz Josef's Bavarian wife, who died of a dagger wound inflicted by an Italian anarchist in Geneva in 1898. If not overrun with latter-day hippies, these can offer spots to sit for a few minutes while contemplating Vienna's most ambitious piece of 19th-century city planning: the Ringstrasse. ⊠ *Burgring 1, 1st District* Ⓜ *Tram: 1, 2, or D/Rathausplatz, Burgtheater.*

Wien Museum Beethoven Pasqualatihaus
HOUSE | Beethoven lived in the Pasqualatihaus multiple times between 1804 and 1815, including while he was composing his only opera, *Fidelio*. He also composed his Seventh Symphony and Fourth Piano Concerto when this was his home. Today this small apartment houses a commemorative museum (in distressingly modern style). After navigating the narrow and twisting stairway, you might well ask how he maintained the jubilant spirit of the works he wrote there. Note particularly the prints that show what the window view out over the Mölker bastion was like when Beethoven lived here, and the

current view too—it's a fantastic fourth-floor look out onto the Ringstrasse. ✉ *8 Mölker Bastei, 1st District* ☎ *01/535–8905* 🌐 *www.wienmuseum.at* 🎟 *€5* 🕒 *Closed Mon.* [M] *U2/Schottentor.*

★ **Wiener Staatsoper** (*Vienna State Opera*)
ARTS VENUE | The Vienna Staatsoper vies with the cathedral for the honor of emotional heart of the city—it's a focus for Viennese life and one of the chief symbols of resurgence after World War II. The first of the Ringstrasse projects to be completed (in 1869), the opera house suffered disastrous bomb damage in the last days of World War II (only the outer walls, the front facade, and the main staircase survived). The original design was followed in the 1945–1955 reconstruction, though with a postwar look, and sight lines from some of the front boxes are poor. But this is one of the world's half-dozen greatest opera houses, and a performance here can be the highlight of a Vienna trip. If tickets are sold out, some performances are shown live on a huge screen outside the building. Tours of the Opera House are given regularly, but starting times vary according to rehearsals. ✉ *Opernring 2, 1st District* ☎ *01/514–44–2606* 🌐 *www.staatsoper.at* 🎟 *From €10 for standing room tickets, €10 for guided tours* 🕒 *No performances Jul.–Aug.* [M] *U1, U2, or U4 Karlsplatz.*

🍴 Restaurants

DO & CO Albertina
$$ | **INTERNATIONAL** | When you're ready to collapse after taking in all the art at the fabulous Albertina, take a break at the museum's on-site eatery where you will find a variety of options including sushi, Mediterranean, and Italian. In summer you can sit outside on one of the city's nicest terraces and enjoy the view of the Burggarten. **Known for:** lovely terrace with a view of the Burggarten; bar seating for snacks and other light fare; sushi and gazpacho. [$] *Average main: €22* ✉ *Albertina Museum, Albertinaplatz 1, 1st District* ☎ *01/532–9669* 🌐 *www.doco.com/restaurants* [M] *U1, U2, or U4/Karlsplatz/Opera.*

Esterházykeller
$ | **WINE BAR** | The origins here go back to 1683, when this spot opened as one of the city's official *Stadtheuriger* (wine taverns), to provide Turk-fighting soldiers with wine before going off to battle. Below the Esterházy palace, the atmosphere is like that of a cozy cave, with the maze of rooms offering some of the best wines of any cellar in town, plus a typical Viennese menu noontime and evenings. **Known for:** history as one of the city's official wine taverns; great wine list (duh); meat-heavy food menu. [$] *Average main: €14* ✉ *Haarhof 1, 1st District* ☎ *01/533–3482* 🌐 *www.esterhazykeller.at* [M] *U1 or U4/Stephansplatz.*

Figlmüller
$$ | **AUSTRIAN** | This Wiener schnitzel institution might be touristy, but it's known for breaded veal and pork cutlets so large they overflow the plate and still attracts locals, too. The cutlet is hammered—you can hear the mallets pounding from a block away—so that the schnitzel winds up wafer-thin. **Known for:** huge schnitzel; delicious potato salad; second location at Bäckerstrasse 6. [$] *Average main: €19* ✉ *Wollzeile 5, 1st District* ☎ *01/512–6177* 🌐 *www.figlmueller.at* [M] *U1 or U3/Stephansplatz.*

Gösser Bierklinik
$ | **AUSTRIAN** | Dating back four centuries, this engaging old-world house sits in the heart of Old Vienna. It is one of the country's top addresses for beer connoisseurs and serves brews, both draft and bottled, *Dunkeles* (dark) and *Helles* (light), from the Gösser brewery in Styria. **Known for:** covered courtyard; authentically Austrian beer and cheese; sandwiches and schnitzel. [$] *Average main: €17* ✉ *Steindlgasse 4, 1st District* ☎ *01/533–7598* 🌐 *www.goesser-bierklinik.at* 🕒 *Closed Sun. No lunch weekdays July and Aug.* [M] *U3/Herrengasse.*

Griechenbeisl

$$ | AUSTRIAN | Neatly tucked away in a quiet and quaint area of the Old City, this ancient inn goes back half a millennium (Mozart, Beethoven, and Schubert all dined here). Yes, it's touristy, yet the food, including all the classic hearty dishes like goulash soup, Wiener schnitzel, and *Apfelstrudel,* is as good as that in many other beisl. **Known for:** old-world charm; classic Austrian dishes; famous patrons. $ *Average main: €22* ✉ *Fleischmarkt 11, 1st District* ☎ *01/533–1977* ⊕ *www.griechenbeisl.at* Ⓜ *U1 or U4/Schwedenplatz.*

★ Konstantin Filippou

$$$$ | INTERNATIONAL | In a stunningly short time, Filippou has made a remarkable impression on the Vienna dining elite, evident from its Michelin star and its Gault Millau Chef of the Year award. A seat at the prized kitchen table allows a view into the kitchen to watch the chef preparing the meal, including the famous escargot seasoned with horseradish and watercress. **Known for:** frequently changing, six-course tasting menu with wine pairing; outdoor garden dining in spring and summer; one of the top restaurants in Vienna (and most expensive). $ *Average main: €145* ✉ *Dominikanerbastei 17, 1st District* ☎ *01/51–22–229* ⊕ *www.konstantinfilippou.com* ⊘ *Closed weekends and last 3 wks of Aug.*

Melker Stiftskeller

$ | WINE BAR | Down and down you go, into one of the friendliest cellars in town, where *Stelze* (roast pork) is a popular feature, along with outstanding regional wines—Grüner Veltliner among them—by the glass or, rather, mug. This was originally the storehouse for wines from the Melk Abbey in the Danube Valley and dates from 1438, but was rebuilt in the 18th century. **Known for:** fantastic wine cellar; several centuries of history; roast pork and other Austrian classics. $ *Average main: €17* ✉ *Schottengasse 3, 1st District* ☎ *01/533–5530* ⊕ *www.melkerstiftskeller.at* ⊘ *Closed Sun. and Mon. No lunch* Ⓜ *U2/Schottentor.*

Motto am Fluss

$$$ | CONTEMPORARY | Even though night owls flock to the bar at Motto am Fluss until the wee hours, this sleek eatery serves an inspired selection of dishes when the sun is up, too, like tuna steak with creamy avocado sauce. The building overlooks the Danube and resembles an ocean liner, with a retro 1950s interior of checkerboard floors below and gigantic, globe-mirrored lamps above. **Known for:** sprawling dining room with great river views; 1950s retro decor; creative breakfast fare. $ *Average main: €17* ✉ *Franz-Josefs Kai, 1st District* ☎ *01/25255* ⊕ *www. mottoamfluss.at.*

Pizza Bizi

$ | FAST FOOD | Most people are drawn in by the thick aroma of buttered garlic wafting down the street; though for some, the attraction is watching the bakers toss the pizza pies into the air before popping them into the oven. Pizza Bizi is arguably one of the best slices of New York–style pizza you'll find anywhere in Europe. **Known for:** amazing pizza and pasta buffet; standing-room only seating; cash-only policy. $ *Average main: €4* ✉ *Rotenturmstrasse 4, 1st District* ☎ *01/513–3705* ⊕ *www. pizzabizi.at.*

Plachuttas Gasthaus zur Oper

$$ | AUSTRIAN | In case its name doesn't give it away, the proximity to the opera house should be a clue that among the dinner guests will be many of the city's regular operagoers, sitting for a meal before the show. Located on a side street near Kärntnerstrasse, this restaurant focuses on traditional Austrian dishes. **Known for:** beef from small Austrian farms; top-notch comfort foods; the "best schnitzel in Vienna". $ *Average main: €20* ✉ *Walfischgasse 5–7, 1st District* ☎ *01/512–2251* ⊕ *www. plachutta-oper.at.*

★ Restaurant Edvard

$$$$ | INTERNATIONAL | This gourmet establishment at the Palais Hansen Kempinski Hotel earned a Michelin star within months after opening. Now chef Norman Etzold has taken over the kitchen, continuing to prepare masterpieces for Vienna diners. **Known for:** three-course dinners served family-style and prepared tableside by the chef; daily afternoon teas; plenty of local patrons. $ Average main: €55 ⊠ Schottenring 24, 1st District ☎ 01/2361000 ⊕ www.kempinski.com ⊘ Closed Sun. and Mon.

★ Restaurant Grüne Bar

$$$$ | AUSTRIAN | The classic Austrian dessert, the Sachertorte, resulted from a family saga that began with Franz Sacher, Prince von Metternich's pastry chef, and ended with Franz's son and his wife, Anna, opening the 19th-century hotel. Today, the Restaurant Grüne Bar continues the tradition of creating some of Vienna's finest cuisine. **Known for:** famous Sachertorte chocolate cake; traditional Austrian fare with some more inventive dishes; lots of Vienna history. $ Average main: €42 ⊠ Hotel Sacher, Philharmonikerstrasse 4, 1st District ☎ 01/514–56840 ⊕ www.sacher.com ⊘ Closed Mon. and Aug. Ⓜ U1, U2, or U4/Karlsplatz/Opera.

Restaurant Hansen

$$ | MEDITERRANEAN | This fashionable establishment is in the basement of the 19th-century Vienna Stock Exchange and shares an enormous space with the flower shop Lederleitner. The chef creates a new menu of Mediterranean specialties each week. **Known for:** weekly changing menu; excellent Sunday brunch; superb contemporary art. $ Average main: €22 ⊠ Wipplingerstrasse 34, 1st District ☎ 01/532–0542 ⊕ www.hansen.co.at/en/restaurant ⊘ Closed Sun. No dinner Sat. Ⓜ U2/Schottenring.

Veggiezz

$ | VEGETARIAN | Vienna's favorite vegan restaurant has three locations in the city. The menu is varied, with wraps, burgers (veggie, of course), tofu dishes, and delicious quinoa concoctions. **Known for:** great veggie burgers; modern yet cozy decor; good value for price. $ Average main: €12 ⊠ Opernring 6, 1st District ☎ 1/890–0032 ⊕ www.veggiezz.at Ⓜ U1/U2 Karlsplatz.

Vestibül

$$$ | AUSTRIAN | Attached to the Burgtheater, this was once the carriage vestibule of the emperor's court theater. Today, the dining room is full of splendor and a menu that changes frequently, but diners can expect the best from one of Austria's most celebrated chefs. **Known for:** frequently changing menu; welcoming and friendly chef; Hummerkrautfleisch, a cabbage and lobster dish. $ Average main: €28 ⊠ Universitätsring 2, 1st District ☎ 01/532–49–99–10 ⊕ www.vestibuel.at ⊘ Closed Sun. and 3 wks in Aug. No lunch Sat. Ⓜ Tram: 1 or 2.

Walter Bauer

$$$$ | AUSTRIAN | Hidden away in one of the quietest quarters of historic Vienna, this charming and unpretentious Michelin-starred restaurant serves the very best in traditional cuisine. Even the everyman Leberkäse—an artery-blocking loaf of pork, bacon, corned beef, and onions—is turned into a delectable delight (and served with a dash of mustard). **Known for:** Austrian cuisine with the highest-quality ingredients; revolving door of Austria's top chefs; excellent wine list. $ Average main: €62 ⊠ Sonnenfelsgasse 17, 1st District ☎ 01/512–9871 ⊘ No lunch Mon. Closed weekends and mid-July–mid-Aug. Ⓜ U1 or U3/Stephansplatz.

Weibels Wirtshaus

$$ | **AUSTRIAN** | Down an old cobbled lane between Singerstrasse and Schuler-strasse and a stone's throw from the cathedral, Weibels Wirtshaus is one of the coziest places to have a lazy lunch or a quiet dinner. The dinner menu changes with the season; in summer try the cold cucumber soup with cilantro shrimp, and strawberry-rhubarb mousse for dessert. **Known for:** seasonally changing menu; delightful garden terrace; intimate and romantic seating upstairs. $ *Average main: €22* ⊠ *Kumpfgasse 2, 1st District* ☎ *01/512–3986* ⊕ *www.weibel.at* Ⓜ *U1 or U3/Stephansplatz.*

Wrenkh Restaurant and Cooking Salon

$ | **INTERNATIONAL** | Vienna's vegetarian pioneer extraordinaire Christian Wrenkh prefers teaching cooking classes to standing in the kitchen several times a week, but his two sons run the res-taurant show: roughly two-thirds of the menu is vegetarian, with delightful dishes like wild-rice risotto with mush-rooms, Greek fried rice with vegetables, or tofu, tomato, and basil tarts. The minimalist-style bistro, with mid-century modern decor that looks a tad like a modish hotel, offers affordable lunches and dinners. **Known for:** best vegetarian menu in Vienna; culinary classes taught by master chef; reasonable prices. $ *Average main: €16* ⊠ *Bauernmarkt 10, 1st District* ☎ *01/533–1526* ⊕ *www.wrenkh-wien.at* ☉ *Closed Sun.* Ⓜ *U1 or U3/Stephansplatz.*

Würstelstand am Hohen Markt

$ | **FAST FOOD** | Hot on the trail of the "Best Sausage" designation, the legend-ary Würstelstand am Hohen Markt serves the best *Bürenwurst* and American-style hot dogs. As with most of the Würs-telstands, or "Imbiss" kiosks, there is a surprising amount of food on offer. **Known for:** local favorites like Käserkrain-er (cheese-filled sausages) and Bosna (bratwurst with onions); wine, beer, and champagne available; late-night hours.

$ *Average main: €3* ⊠ *Hoher Markt, corner of Marc-Aurel-Strasse, 1st District* ⊟ *No credit cards.*

★ Zum Schwarzen Kameel

$$$$ | **AUSTRIAN** | Back when Beethoven dined at the Black Camel, it was already a foodie landmark. Since then, it has been renovated (but only in 1901) and more recently split into a Delikatessen and a restaurant. **Known for:** house specialty Beinschinken; deli sandwich-es from family recipe; elegant dining room. $ *Average main: €35* ⊠ *Bogn-ergasse 5, 1st District* ☎ *01/533–8125* ⊕ *www.kameel.at* ☉ *Closed Sun.* Ⓜ *U3/Herrengasse.*

☕ Coffee and Quick Bites

Café Bellaria

$ | **AUSTRIAN** | Located steps from the Volkstheater and close to the Kunsthis-torisches Museum and the Muse-umsQuartier, the Bellaria is a legendary resting spot between sights and beloved by locals for its live piano playing, great desserts, and relaxed café cuisine. **Known for:** one of Vienna's historic cafes; terrific desserts; warm and familial atmosphere. $ *Average main: €7* ⊠ *Bellariastrasse 6, 1st District* ☎ *1/523–5320* ⊕ *www.cafebellaria.at* Ⓜ *U2/U3 Volkstheater.*

★ Café Central

$ | **CAFÉ** | Made famous by its illustrious guests, the Café Central is one of the most famous cafés in all of Vienna. The soaring ceiling and gigantic columns are hallmarks of the landmark, which was home to Viennese literati as well as world game changers at the turn of the last century, including Leon Trotsky, who mapped out the Russian Revolution here beneath portraits of the Imperial family. **Known for:** Leon Trotsky hangout; stand-ard café fare and desserts; crowds of tourists. $ *Average main: €15* ⊠ *Herren-gasse 14, at Strauchgasse, 1st District* ☎ *01/533–3764–24* ⊕ *www.cafecentral.wien* Ⓜ *U3/Herrengasse.*

The Café Sacher is Vienna's most popular café and the perfect place to sample Vienna's most famous dessert, Sachertorte.

Café Frauenhuber

$ | **CAFÉ** | You can retreat to Café Frauen-huber, billed as Vienna's oldest café, to find some peace and quiet away from the busy shoppers on Kärntnerstrasse. Breakfast is a go-for-broke affair, and might include a pot of tea (or coffee), a glass of prosecco, fresh-squeezed orange juice, toast, and fresh salmon with a dash of horseradish. **Known for:** extravagant breakfast buffet; local hangout with few tourists; traditional velvet-seat decor. $ *Average main: €15* ⊠ *Himmelp-fortgasse 6, 1st District* ☏ *01/512–5323* ⊕ *www.cafe-frauenhuber.at* Ⓜ *U1 or U3/Stephansplatz.*

Café Hawelka

$ | **CAFÉ** | Practically a shrine—indeed, almost a museum—the Hawelka was the hangout of most of Vienna's modern artists, and the café has acquired an admirable art collection over the years. The Hawelka is most famous for its *Buchteln,* a baked bun with a sweet filling, served fresh from the oven. **Known for:** Buchteln, a baked sweet bun with a sweet filling; famous former guests ; impressive art collection. $ *Average main: €10* ⊠ *Dorotheergasse 6, 1st District* ☏ *01/512–8230* ⊕ *www.hawelka. at* Ⓜ *U1 or U3/Stephansplatz.*

★ Café Landtmann

$ | **CAFÉ** | A favorite of politicians and theater stars (the Burg is next door, the Rathaus across the street) since 1873, this was Sigmund Freud's favorite café (he lived within walking distance). If you want a great meal at almost any time of day, including options of several schnitzels, or just a slice of decadent cake, there are few places that can beat this one. **Known for:** house specialty "Franz Landtmann," mix of espresso, brandy, and whipped cream; lots of history and famous guests; glass-enclosed veranda. $ *Average main: €23* ⊠ *Dr.-Karl-Lueger-Ring 4, 1st District* ☏ *01/24–100–100* ⊕ *www.landtmann.at* Ⓜ *U2/Schottenring.*

Café Mozart

$$ | **CAFÉ** | The café, named after the monument to Mozart (now in the Burggarten) that once stood outside, is overrun with sightseers, but the waiters manage to remain calm even when customers run them ragged. Crystal chandeliers, a brass-and-oak interior, comfortable seating, and delicious food—the Tafelspitz is excellent—add to its popularity. **Known for:** Tafelspitz that locals love; fabulous decor; role in the classic movie The Third Man. $ *Average main: €18* ✉ *Albertinaplatz 2, 1st District* ☎ *01/24–100–200* ⊕ *www.cafe-mozart.at* Ⓜ *U1, U2, or U4/Karlsplatz/Opera.*

★ Café Sacher

$ | **CAFÉ** | Arguably the most famous café in Vienna, it is the home of the legendary Sachertorte, a dense chocolate torte with fresh aprioct jam in the center. This legend began as a *Delikatessen* opened by Sacher, court confectioner to Prince von Metternich, the most powerful prime minister in early-19th-century Europe. **Known for:** alleged origin of the famous Sachertorte cake; tasty savory options; live piano music daily. $ *Average main: €12* ✉ *Hotel Sacher, Philharmonikerstrasse 4, 1st District* ☎ *01/514560* ⊕ *www.sacher.com* Ⓜ *U1, U2, or U4/Karlsplatz/Opera.*

Café Schwarzenberg

$ | **CAFÉ** | Located near the Hotel Imperial, this is an ideal spot for a coffee and cake or a meal after a performance at the Musikverein or Konzerthaus, both just a couple of minutes away. Open until midnight, it has a good choice of food and pastries. **Known for:** large outdoor terrace; live piano music Wednesday, Friday, and weekends; late-night hours. $ *Average main: €16* ✉ *Kärntnerring 17, 1st District* ☎ *01/512–8998* ⊕ *www.cafe-schwarzenberg.at/en* Ⓜ *U2/Schottentor.*

★ Demel

$ | **BAKERY** | The display cases are filled to the brim at the world-renowned Demel, a 200-year-old pastry shop and chocolatier, famous for sweetmeats. Chocolate lovers will want to try the Viennese Sachertorte (two layers of dense chocolate cake, with apricot jam sandwiched between and chocolate icing on top) and compare it with its competition at Café Sacher. **Known for:** famous Sachertorte; crowds of tourists; elegant decor. $ *Average main: €10* ✉ *Kohlmarkt 14, 1st District* ☎ *01/535–1717* ⊕ *www.demel.at.*

★ Haas & Haas Teahouse

$ | **INTERNATIONAL** | Situated in the courtyard of the Stephansplatz, with a direct view of stunning St. Stephen's Cathedral, this teahouse is a rare find in a city steeped in the tradition of coffeehouses. It is a cozy tea parlor, indeed, with a selection of more than 200 brews and a particularly splendid afternoon tea menu. **Known for:** English-style afternoon tea served daily; extensive menu of international dishes; small spot by the cathedral. $ *Average main: €17* ✉ *Stephansplatz 4, 1st District* ☎ *01/5129770* ⊕ *www.haas-haas.at* Ⓜ *U1 or U3 Stephansplatz.*

Kleines Cafe

$ | **AUSTRIAN** | This landmark café is on one of the most charming squares in Vienna. The "Little Cafe" is open daily for coffee, cocktails, and light snacks, and few places are more delightful to sit and relax on a warm afternoon or evening. $ *Average main: €5* ✉ *Franziskanerplatz 3, 1st District.*

Oberlaa

$ | **BAKERY** | Popular with the locals and a great value, you'll find irresistible confections such as the Oberlaa Kurbad cake, truffle cake, and chocolate-mousse cake here. The lemon torte is filled with a light, fruity lemon cream and a thin layer of almond paste. **Known for:** lots of tasty desserts and cakes; gift-wrapped candy options; gluten- and lactose-free treats. $ *Average main: €8* ✉ *Neuer Markt 16, 1st District* ☎ *01/513–2936* ⊕ *www.oberlaa-wien.at.*

Veganista

$ | **INTERNATIONAL** | Vienna's most popular vegan ice cream maker has 11 locations scattered across Vienna's districts, but the one in the first district is closest to Vienna's major sights (there is a weather-permitting kiosk at the MuseumsQuartier, too). They're known for traditional flavors as well as nods to local and seasonal tastes like poppy seed and damson plums. **Known for:** seasonal flavors; "Inbetwiener" ice cream sandwich cookie; popular chain across Vienna. [$] *Average main: €7* ✉ *Tuchlauben 12, 1st District* 🌐 *www.veganista.at* [M] *U1/U3 Stephansplatz.*

Zanoni & Zanoni

$ | **ITALIAN** | Between Rotenturmstrasse and Bäckerstrasse, this place dishes up 25 or more flavors of smooth, Italian-style gelato, including mango, caramel, and chocolate chip, and has frozen yogurt and vegan ice cream, too. **Known for:** variety of flavors; good coffee; busy in the evenings. [$] *Average main: €5* ✉ *Am Lugeck 7, 1st District* ☎ *01/512–7979* 🌐 *www.zanoni.wien.*

Hotels

Ambassador

$$$ | **HOTEL** | Franz Lehár, Marlene Dietrich, the Infanta Isabel of Spain, and Mick Jagger are just a few of the celebrities who have stayed at this old dowager (from 1866). **Pros:** good value for location; convenient to shopping and dining; apartments available. **Cons:** very busy neighborhood; rooms feel a tad dated ; elevator doesn't reach all floors. [$] *Rooms from: €230* ✉ *Kärntner Strasse 22, 1st District* ☎ *01/961–610* 🌐 *www.ambassador.at* 🛏 *89 rooms* 🍴 *No meals.*

Benediktushaus

$$ | **B&B/INN** | You can stay in this guesthouse of a monastery, in the heart of Vienna, without following the dictum *ora et labora* (pray and work), though you will get to see how the monks live by the credo. **Pros:** superb location; serene vibes and setting; excellent breakfast spread. **Cons:** reception hours limited; church bells start ringing early; no TV and limited Wi-Fi. [$] *Rooms from: €140* ✉ *Freyung 6a, 1st District* ☎ *01/534–989–00* 🌐 *www.benediktushaus.at* 🛏 *21 rooms* 🍴 *Free breakfast.*

Do & Co Hotel

$$$$ | **HOTEL** | Inside the glass-and-stone Haas House, which reflects St. Stephen's Cathedral in its facade, you'll discover this unique boutique hotel. **Pros:** elegant ambience; most lavish breakfast in town; well-stocked minibar. **Cons:** glass walls in bathroom might bother more modest guests; hotel is in a pedestrian-only zone so can be a hassle with a car; staff sometimes isn't the most friendly. [$] *Rooms from:* ✉ *Stephansplatz 12, 1st District* ☎ *01/241–880* 🌐 *www.docohotel.com* 🛏 *43 rooms* 🍴 *No meals.*

Grand Hotel Wien

$$$ | **HOTEL** | With one of the great locations on the Ringstrasse, just across from the Musikverein and a minute on foot from the Staatsoper, the Grand oozes old-world splendor. **Pros:** three superb restaurants; good shopping next door; larger-than-average rooms. **Cons:** desk staff can seem haughty; check-in can be slow; some rooms could use freshening up. [$] *Rooms from: €220* ✉ *Kärntner Ring 9, 1st District* ☎ *01/515–800* 🌐 *www.grandhotelwien.com* 🛏 *205 rooms* 🍴 *No meals.*

★ The Guesthouse

$$$$ | **HOTEL** | Smack behind the Albertina and the Staatsoper, this authentically Austrian boutique hotel is an absolutely delightful addition to the Vienna lodging scene, with fabulous views of the heart of the Innere Stadt. **Pros:** modern design by Sir Terence Conran; mini fridge stocked with full-size bottles of wine included in rate; great restaurant and bakery onsite. **Cons:** standard rooms are a tad small; no real lobby; breakfast is popular here with non-guests, too, so it can

be hard to get a table. $ *Rooms from: €280* ✉ *Fuehrichgasse 10-a, 1st District* ☎ *01/512–1320* ⊕ *www.theguesthouse.at* ↩ *39 rooms* |○| *No meals.*

Hotel Am Stephansplatz

$$$ | HOTEL | You aren't likely to find a better location than this serene hotel, which sits directly across from the front entrance of St. Stephen's Cathedral. **Pros:** top location; great breakfast-bar views; excellent staff. **Cons:** busy location; noisy area at night; not very local. $ *Rooms from: €240* ✉ *Stephansplatz 9, 1st District* ☎ *01/534–050* ⊕ *www.hotelamstephansplatz.at* ↩ *56 rooms* |○| *Free breakfast.*

Hotel Bristol

$$$$ | HOTEL | For those wanting an Old Austria feel with modern conveniences, look no further than the Bristol. **Pros:** across the street from the Opera House; old school elegance ; historic charm. **Cons:** location is very busy and can be noisy ; some rooms could use an upgrade; period style may not be to everyone's tastes. $ *Rooms from: €320* ✉ *Kärntner Ring 1, 1st District* ☎ *01/515–160* ⊕ *www.bristolvienna.com* ↩ *150 rooms* |○| *No meals.*

Hotel Imperial

$$$$ | HOTEL | One of the landmarks of the Ringstrasse, this hotel has exemplified the grandeur of imperial Vienna ever since it was built. **Pros:** discreet, unpretentious staff; excellent restaurant and café; palatial. **Cons:** some rooms are on the small side; bathrooms can be tiny; restaurant and bar staff sometimes seem untrained. $ *Rooms from: €430* ✉ *Kärntner Ring 16, 1st District* ☎ *01/501–100* ⊕ *www.luxurycollection.com/imperial* ↩ *128 rooms* |○| *No meals.*

★ Hotel Sacher Wien

$$$$ | HOTEL | FAMILY | One of Europe's legends, originally founded by Franz Sacher, chef to Prince Metternich—for whom the famous chocolate cake was invented—this hotel dates from 1876 but has delightfully retained its old-world atmosphere-mit-Schlag while also providing luxurious, modern-day comfort. **Pros:** retains its hisotrical ambience , decadent breakfast buffet; family-run and service-oriented –ratio of staff to guests is more than two to one. **Cons:** you'll need reservations for the bar and dining as it is popular; located on a very busy street; popular dining options mean public areas are not always restful. $ *Rooms from: €560* ✉ *Philharmonikerstrasse 4, 1st District* ☎ *01/514–560* ⊕ *www.sacher.com* ↩ *149 rooms* |○| *No meals.*

★ Hotel Topazz Lamee

$$$ | HOTEL | Recently merged into one hotel, the Topazz and Lamee hotels offer spectacular architecture, central locations, a focus on sustainability and innovation, and supreme style and comfort. **Pros:** a designer's dream; roof terrace with cathedral views; oval window seats in rooms with oval windows. **Cons:** some rooms on the snug side; street can be noisy at night; no restaurant on-site. $ *Rooms from: €295* ✉ *Lichtensteg 2 & 3, 1st District* ☎ *01/532–2250* ⊕ *www.hoteltopazzlamee.com* ↩ *64 rooms* |○| *No meals.*

König von Ungarn

$$$ | HOTEL | In a 16th-century house in the shadow of St. Stephen's Cathedral, this dormered hotel began catering to court nobility in 1746 and today lets you choose between "classicism" and "designer" rooms. **Pros:** central yet peaceful; historic property and rooms have individual character; elegant restaurant set directly below the apartment where Mozart once lived. **Cons:** some rooms are less lavish and a tad old-fashioned; tour buses pass regularly; some rooms may feel cramped. $ *Rooms from: €245* ✉ *Schulerstrasse 10, 1st District* ☎ *01/515–840* ⊕ *www.kvu.at* ↩ *44 rooms* |○| *Free breakfast.*

Le Méridien Vienna

$$$ | **HOTEL** | The supercool "art and tech" lobby here, adorned with Mies van der Rohe–style sofas and ottomans and nouvelle fluorescent-light panels, is a fine introduction to a stylish and pampering stay in the heart of the city. **Pros:** next door to the museums; complimentary minibar; spacious bathrooms with modern showers. **Cons:** lacks "Vienna" character; housekeeping can be erratic; the popular bar can be disruptive. [$] *Rooms from: €230* ✉ *Robert-Stolz-Platz 1, 1st District* ☎ *01/588–900* 🌐 *www.lemeridienvienna.com* 🛏 *294 rooms* 🍴 *No meals.*

Palais Coburg

$$$$ | **HOTEL** | In this 19th-century regal residence, the lobby is sleek white stone and plate glass, embodying the hotel's philosophy of "preserving the past—shaping the future." Suites are in modern or imperial style, and many of them are spectacular, two-story showpieces, the best done in gilded-yellow Biedermeier or Empire style. **Pros:** luxurious atmosphere; Michelin-starred restaurant; luxurious wine cellar. **Cons:** breakfast menu is limited; fitness facilities are not up to par; not in city center. [$] *Rooms from: €780* ✉ *Coburgbastei 4, 1st District* ☎ *01/518–180* 🌐 *www.palais-coburg.com* 🛏 *33 rooms* 🍴 *No meals.*

★ Palais Hansen Kempinski Vienna

$$$$ | **HOTEL** | This Renaissance Revival–style structure, built in 1873 as an exhibition hall, was transformed 140 years later into a luxe hotel, which pays homage to the grand beginnings while also incorporating modern-day amenities. **Pros:** extensive spa; historic site; central location. **Cons:** posh prices; breakfast can lack variety; some staff can seem dismissive. [$] *Rooms from: €370* ✉ *Schottenring 24, 1st District* ☎ *01/236–1000* 🌐 *www.kempinski.com/en/vienna/palais-hansen* 🛏 *152 rooms* 🍴 *Free breakfast.*

Park Hyatt Vienna

$$$$ | **HOTEL** | Much care was taken to preserve the integrity and historical significance of the elegant building that houses one of Vienna's newer luxury hotels. **Pros:** fuses historic character with contemporary design; remarkable location; extravagant breakfasts. **Cons:** staff can be unfriendly; concierge advice hit-or-miss; room issues may not be resolved quickly. [$] *Rooms from: €520* ✉ *Am Hof 2, 1st District* ☎ *01/227–401–234* 🌐 *www.vienna.park.hyatt.com* 🛏 *184 rooms* 🍴 *No meals.*

Pension Nossek

$$$ | **HOTEL** | A family-run establishment on the upper floors of a 19th-century apartment building, the Nossek lies at the heart of Vienna's pedestrian and shopping area. **Pros:** central location; family oriented; Mozart once lived here. **Cons:** a little dated in appearance; entrance can be hard to find; street is noisy with the windows open. [$] *Rooms from: €180* ✉ *Graben 17, 1st District* ☎ *01/533–704–111* 🌐 *www.pension-nossek.at* 🛏 *31 rooms* 🍴 *Free breakfast.*

★ Radisson Blu Style Hotel

$$ | **HOTEL** | Behind the hotel's Art Nouveau facade, London interior designer Maria Vafiadis has paid tribute to Viennese Art Deco, and the result is überstylish yet comfortable. **Pros:** design lovers will love the look; central location; quiet area of old city. **Cons:** limited reception desks can make check in slow; not all room rates include breakfast; staff can sometimes seem arrogant. [$] *Rooms from: €175* ✉ *Herrengasse 12, 1st District* ☎ *01/227–803–214* 🌐 *www.radissonblu.com/stylehotel-vienna* 🛏 *78 rooms* 🍴 *No meals.*

The Ring Hotel

$$$ | **HOTEL** | Following the trend toward smaller boutique properties, this luxury lodging takes its place alongside some of Vienna's opulent grand hotels. **Pros:** good blend of character and modern comfort; most rooms are well sized;

state-of-the-art gym and spa with stunning views. **Cons:** breakfast isn't the best value; rooms feel a bit dated; trams frequently thunder around the block. [$] *Rooms from: €260* ✉ *Kärntner Ring 8, 1st District* ☎ *01/221–22* 🌐 *www.thering-hotel.com* 🛏 *68 rooms* 🍴 *No meals.*

The Ritz-Carlton, Vienna

$$$$ | **HOTEL** | From a Ringstrasse Palace to a Ritz-Carlton, all the fineries you'd expect from the brand are here, including ceiling frescoes and open fireplaces in the poshest of its suites. **Pros:** rooftop terrace is a choice spot to watch the sun set over the city; professional staff; good location. **Cons:** amenities at the club lounge here may not be as good as other Ritz-Carlton's; building's layout sometimes requires random stair climbing; some rooms look a little worn. [$] *Rooms from: €440* ✉ *Schubertring 5–7, 1st District* ☎ *01/311–88, 01/311–88111* 🌐 *www.ritzcarlton.com/en/hotels/europe/vienna* 🛏 *245 rooms* 🍴 *No meals.*

Ruby Lissi

$ | **HOTEL** | Thanks to the rather stark decor, you may feel like you're going to the office, but all visions of work will be forgotten when you enter the wide-open breakfast-lounge-bar space; there's no formal reception area, just a self-check-in spot. **Pros:** great location with good restaurants and nightlife nearby; interesting design mix of retro and modern; music lovers can rent a guitar and jam on their own in-room Marshall box. **Cons:** the unembellished white rooms can seem cold; no reception; basic rooms are on the small side. [$] *Rooms from: €138* ✉ *Fleischmarkt 19, 1st District* ☎ *01/205–551–80* 🌐 *www.ruby-hotels.com* 🛏 *107 rooms* 🍴 *No meals.*

Nightlife

BARS

ignacio vinos e ibéricos

BARS/PUBS | This classy but casual Spanish wine bar pours exceptional Iberian wines and serves small and large tapas to nibble on, too. It's also a fully-stocked wine shop in case you want to grab a bottle for your hotel room. Service is friendly and welcoming and in warmer weather they have a few tables outside. It's the perfect place for a casual bite and a glass or two to wind down after a day of sightseeing. Reservations are recommended (it's a tiny space with few seats). ✉ *Salztorgasse 7, 1st District* ☎ *01/922–0851* 🌐 *ignacio.at* ⏲ *Closed Sun.*

Motto am Fluss

BARS/PUBS | In a nod to its location, this hip place resembles a sleek ocean liner gliding down the Danube Canal (the location is also the mooring station for the *Twin City Liner,* which regularly cruises between Vienna and Bratislava). The bar is all glass and chrome, lending it an ultramodern feel. Silver spheres dangle from the ceiling like drops of mercury. The inside is stylish but most locals flock to the outdoor terrace to enjoy the water views and al fresco vibe. ✉ *Schwedenplatz 2, 1st District* ☎ *01/25–225–11* 🌐 *www.mottoamfluss.at.*

Volksgarten Club

BARS/PUBS | Back in 1870, Viennese used to come to the Volksgarten to waltz, drink champagne, and enjoy the night air in a candlelit garden. Today it's a nightclub where glammed-up locals flock to go clubbing, mostly to house and party music. ✉ *Burgring 1, 1st District* ☎ *01/532–4241* 🌐 *www.volksgarten.at* [M] *U2/3 MuseumsQuartier.*

Vienna in Film: *The Third Man*

Nothing has done more to create the myth of postwar Vienna than Carol Reed's classic 1949 film *The Third Man*. The bombed-out ruins of this proud, imperial city created an indelible image of devastation and corruption in the war's aftermath. Vienna was then divided into four sectors, each commanded by one of the victorious armies—American, Russian, French, and British. But their attempts at rigid control could not prevent a thriving black market.

Reed's film version of the Graham Greene thriller features Vienna as a leading player, from the top of its Ferris wheel to the depth of its lowest sewers—"which run right into the Blue Danube." It was the first British film to be shot entirely on location. The film is screened several times a week at the Burg Kino.

JAZZ CLUBS

In the last few decades, Austria has produced some great jazz talents. World-renowned saxophonist Wolfgang Puschnig, for example, holds a professorship at Vienna's Music University. He and his colleagues have inspired young musicians who can be found performing in the city's many jazz clubs.

Jazzland

MUSIC CLUBS | In a cellar under St. Ruprecht's church, this is the granddaddy of Vienna's jazz clubs and is the oldest jazz venue in Austria. Thanks to the pioneering work of the club's founder, Axel Melhardt, Austrian jazz musicians have grooved with the best American stars. The club also serves excellent, inexpensive, and authentic cuisine. ✉ *Franz-Josefs-Kai 29, 1st District* ☎ *01/533–2575* ⊕ *www.jazzland.at.*

Porgy & Bess

MUSIC CLUBS | Porgy & Bess is one of the top jazz clubs of Europe and is a fixed point on the international jazz scene. ✉ *Riemergasse 11, 1st District* ☎ *01/512–8811* ⊕ *www.porgy.at.*

🎭 Performing Arts

FILM

Artis International

FILM | The Artis cinema has six screens showing the latest blockbusters (all in English) several times a day. ✉ *Shulter-gasse 5, 1st District* ☎ *01/535–6570.*

Burg Kino

FILM | Carol Reed's Vienna-based classic *The Third Man,* with Orson Welles and Joseph Cotton, is screened two or three times a week in English. Hollywood's latest releases are usually shown here in the original English version. ✉ *Opernring 19, 1st District* ☎ *01/587–8406* ⊕ *www.burgkino.at.*

Filmmuseum

FILM | Located in the Albertina, the Filmmuseum has one of the most ambitious and sophisticated schedules around, with a heavy focus on English-language films. It's stylish Filmbar serves drinks and snacks spills out onto the street. It's open until well past midnight and often hosts lectures and retrospectives, but note that it is closed in July. ✉ *Augustinerstrasse 1, 1st District* ☎ *01/533–7054* ⊕ *www.filmmuseum.at.*

MUSIC
Hofburg Palace Concert Halls

MUSIC | Much of the Imperial Palace is used today for orchestral concerts. The Festsaal, the largest hall of the Hofburg and originally conceived as a throne room, hosts frequent Strauss and Mozart concerts. If dripping opulence is a must, the Zeremoniensaal, considered the most magnificent hall of the palace, is an unparalleled venue for experiencing Vienna's classical soul. ✉ *Hofburg Palace, Heldenplatz, 1st District* ☎ *01/587–2552* ⊕ *www.hofburgorchester.at.*

Konzerthaus

MUSIC | The Konzerthaus, home to three performance halls. The Grosser Konzerthaussaal, Mozartsaal, and Schubertsaal are all esteemed venues for a range of musical genres, including classical, cabaret, pop, and jazz. The lineup has included greats like Mnozil Brass, Dianne Reeves, Goran Bregović, and the Herbert Pixner Projekt. ✉ *Lothringerstrasse 20, 1st District* ☎ *01/242–002* ⊕ *www. konzerthaus.at.*

★ Musikverein

MUSIC | The city's most important concert halls are in the 1869 Gesellschaft der Musikfreunde, better known as the Musikverein. This magnificent theater holds six performance spaces, but the one that everyone knows is the venue for the annual New Year's Day Concert—the Goldene Saal. Possibly the world's most beautiful music hall, it was designed by the Danish 19th-century architect Theophil Hansen, a passionate admirer of ancient Greece who festooned it with an army of gilded caryatids. Surprisingly, the smaller Brahms Saal is even more sumptuous—a veritable Greek temple with more caryatids and lots of gilding and green malachite. What Hansen would have made of the four subsidiary halls added in 2004 and set below the main

theater will forever remain a mystery, but the avant-garde Gläserne, Hölzerne, Metallene, and Steinerne Säle (Glass, Wooden, Metal, and Stone Halls) make fitting showcases for contemporary music. In addition to being the main venue for the Wiener Philharmoniker and the Wiener Symphoniker, the Musikverein hosts many of the world's finest orchestras. ✉ *Bösendorferstrasse 12A, 1st District* ☎ *01/505–8190* ⊕ *www.musikverein.at.*

★ Sala Terrena

MUSIC | The most enchanting place to hear Mozart in Vienna (or anywhere, for that matter) is the exquisite 18th-century Sala Terrena, where Mozart himself played. In this intimate room (it seats a maximum of 80 people), a chamber group in historic costumes offers concerts in a jewel box overrun with Rococo frescoes in the Venetian style. Said to be the oldest concert hall in Vienna, the Sala Terrena is part of the German Monastery, where, in 1781, Mozart lived and worked for his despised employer, Archbishop Colloredo of Salzburg. ✉ *Singerstrasse 7, 1st District* ☎ *01/911–9077* ⊕ *mozarthaus.at/en/sala-terrena.*

Wiener Kursalon

MUSIC | If the Mozart symphonies and the whirling waltzes of Strauss are your thing, catch a Mozart and Strauss concert at the Wiener Kursalon, a majestic palace-like structure built in the Italian Renaissance Revival style in 1865 and set in Vienna's sylvan Stadtpark. Here, in gold-and-white salons, the Salonorchester Alt Wien performs concerts of the works of "Waltz King" Johann Strauss and famous works by Wolfgang Amadeus Mozart. You'll hear waltzes, polkas, and operetta melodies. ✉ *Johannesgasse 33, 1st District* ☎ *01/512–5790* ⊕ *www. kursalonwien.at.*

OPERA
Kammeroper

OPERA | Lesser-known and alternative operas and operettas are performed at the Kammeroper, the smallest and most intimate of Vienna's opera houses, to sold-out crowds under the artistic direction of Sebastian F. Schwarz. ⊠ *Fleischmarkt 24, 1st District* ☎ *01/588–30–1010* ⊕ *www.theater-wien.at.*

Vienna State Opera House (Staatsoper)
(*State Opera House*)

OPERA | One of the world's great opera houses, the Staatsoper has been the scene of countless musical triumphs and a center of unending controversy over how it should be run and by whom. A performance takes place virtually every night from September to June, drawing on the vast repertoire of the house, with an emphasis on Mozart, Verdi, and Wagner. Guided tours are given year-round. ⊠ *Opernring 2, 1st District* ☎ *01/514–440* ⊕ *www.wiener-staatsoper.at.*

THEATER
Burgtheater

THEATER | The Austrian National Theater is among the leading German-language theaters of the world. The Burgtheater's repertoire frequently mixes German classics with more modern and controversial pieces. The Burg also emphasizes works by Austrian playwrights, incluing Elfriede Jelinek, who won the 2004 Nobel Prize for Literature. The Burg's smaller house, the Akademietheater, draws on much the same group of actors for classical and modern plays, but performances are in a more relaxing setting. ⊠ *Dr.-Karl-Lueger-Ring 2, 1st District* ☎ *01/514–444–4140* ⊕ *www.burgtheater.at.*

Kammerspiele der Josefstadt

THEATER | This well-respected theater offers a season of modern dramas and comedies. ⊠ *Rotenturmstrasse 20, 1st District* ☎ *01/42–700–359* ⊕ *www.josefstadt.org.*

Ronacher Theater

THEATER | Extensively restored in recent years, the Ronacher presents the latest musical smash hits from Broadway in a magnificent, traditional space with ornate details, a painted ceiling and a two-ton chandelier. ⊠ *Seilerstätte 9, 1st District* ☎ *01/58885* ⊕ *www.musicalvienna.at.*

Shopping

ANTIQUES
★ Dorotheum

ANTIQUES/COLLECTIBLES | The Dorotheum was the first imperial auction house, established in 1707 by Emperor Josef I as a pawnshop. Occupying the former site of the Dorothy Convent (hence the name), it has built up a grand reputation over the years. If you're looking for something truly special—an 18th-century oil portrait or a real fur, a Rococo mirror or a fine silk fan, a china figurine or sterling-silver spoon, an old map of the Austrian Empire or even a stuffed parrot—the best place to try and find it is Dorotheum, Vienna's fabled auction house. Have you ever wanted to see how the Austrian aristocracy once lived, how their sumptuous homes were once furnished? Well, don't bother with a museum—you can inspect their antique furnishings, displayed as if in use, for free, and without the eagle eyes of sales personnel following your every move.

The neo-Baroque building was completed in 1901 and deserves a walk-through (you can enter from Spiegelgasse and exit on Dorotheergasse) just to have a look, even if you only admire the gorgeous stuccoed walls and palatial interiors, or peek into the glass-roofed patio stocked with early-20th-century glass, furniture, and art. With more than 600 auctions a year, this has become one of the busiest auction houses in Europe. There are auctions held frequently throughout the week, though not Saturday, and it's closed entirely Sunday. And if you don't fancy bidding for something, there are sale areas on the ground and second floors where loads of stuff can simply be bought off the floor. ⊠ *Dorotheergasse 17, 1st District* ☏ *01/515–600* ⊕ *www.dorotheum.com/en.html.*

Gallery Dr. Sternat

ANTIQUES/COLLECTIBLES | Just around the corner from the Opera House, this is one of the more traditional art galleries in the city. Austrian paintings, Viennese bronzes, Thonet furniture, and beautiful Biedermeier pieces crowd the small space. ⊠ *Lobkowitzplatz 1, 1st District* ☏ *01/512–2063* ⊕ *www.sternat.com.*

Kulcsar Antiques

ANTIQUES/COLLECTIBLES | This is your best bet for some of the finer collectibles in the city. Peter Kulcsar's special focus is on silverware, watercolors, and objets d'art. ⊠ *Spiegelgasse 19, 1st District* ☏ *01/512–7267* ⊕ *www.kulcsar.at.*

BOOKS

Buchhandlung Morawa

BOOKS/STATIONERY | This could be the best-stocked bookstore in Vienna, with titles on everything under the sun. Thankfully, help is always at hand if you can't find that specific one you're looking for. The magazine and newspaper section is particularly impressive. ⊠ *Wollzeile 11, 1st District* ☏ *01/51–37–51–34–50* ⊕ *www.morawa-buch.at.*

Freytag & Berndt

BOOKS/STATIONERY | If you're planning a hiking holiday in Austria or beyond, stock up on the necessary maps at Freytag & Berndt, which holds the best and most extensive selection of maps and travel books in Vienna. ⊠ *Wallnerstrasse 3, 1st District* ☏ *01/533–8685* ⊕ *www.freytag-berndt.com.*

Frick

BOOKS/STATIONERY | Four floors of books, including an English-language section, can be found at the largest Frick location in the city. Art history and guidebooks on Vienna and Austria are here, but you can also find small gift items like calendars and cards. The staff is helpful, and bargains can often be found in the trays by the door. ⊠ *Graben 27, 1st District* ☏ *01/533–9914* ⊕ *www.buchhandlung-frick.at.*

Wolfrum

BOOKS/STATIONERY | Art-book lovers will adore Wolfrum. If you have money to burn, you can also spring for a Schiele print or special art edition to take home. ⊠ *Augustinerstrasse 10, 1st District* ☏ *01/512–5398* ⊕ *www.wolfrum.at.*

CERAMICS, GLASS, AND PORCELAIN

Albin Denk

CERAMICS/GLASSWARE | If you want to enter an old-fashioned interior that has changed little from the time when Empress Sisi shopped here, Albin Denk is the place. The shop is filled with glass cases holding everything from armies of kitsch porcelain figurines as well as modern glassware and ceramics. ⊠ *Graben 13, 1st District* ☏ *01/512–4439* ⊕ *www.albindenk.at.*

Augarten

CERAMICS/GLASSWARE | The best china in town can be found at this flagship store, designed by Philipp Bruni, which has a sleek, modern design that shines a contemporary light on the traditional side of historic porcelain products. ⊠ *Spiegelgasse 3, 1st District* ☏ *01/512–1494* ⊕ *www.augarten.com.*

Berger

CERAMICS/GLASSWARE | Crafting made-to-order, handmade ceramics for his customers for 40 years, Herr Berger has now been joined in the business by his daughter Lisa. Here you might find a hand-crafted ceramic stove made to measure for your Alpine chalet, or a decorative wall plate blooming with a hand-painted flowering gentian. ⊠ *Weihburggasse 17, 1st District* ☏ *01/512–1434.*

Lobmeyr

CERAMICS/GLASSWARE | Nearly 200 years old, this shop is world renowned for its exquisite glassware. One of its collections is housed in the Museum of Modern Art (MoMA) in New York and its chandeliers have graced opera houses (including New York's Metropolitan Opera) and private homes for centuries. This is one of the only stores left in Vienna that retains its interior of imperial glory, yet allows the cutting edge of design to enter its realm. (See the breathtakingly beautiful black Rococo mirrors by Austrian designer Florian Ladstätter.) Even if you're not buying, head upstairs to the glass museum. ✉ *Kärntner Strasse 26, 1st District* ☎ *01/512–5088* ⊕ *www.lobmeyr.at.*

Swarovski

JEWELRY/ACCESSORIES | Ireland has its Waterford, France its Baccarat, and Austria has Swarovski, purveyors of some of the finest cut crystal in the world. You'll find your typical collector items and gifts here, but also high-style fashion accessories (Paris couturiers now festoon their gowns with Swarovski crystals the way they used to with ostrich feathers), crystal figurines, and home accessories. This flagship store is a cave of coruscating crystals that gleam and glitter. Breathtakingly beautiful window displays change monthly. ✉ *Kärntner Strasse 24, 1st District* ☎ *01/324–0000* ⊕ *www.swarovski.com.*

CHRISTKINDLMÄRKTE

Altwiener Christkindlmarkt

OUTDOOR/FLEA/GREEN MARKETS | This festive seasonal market is held on one of Vienna's cozier squares. ✉ *Freyung, 1st District.*

Rathausplatz Christkindlmärkte

OUTDOOR/FLEA/GREEN MARKETS | The biggest holiday market is the one on Rathausplatz, in front of the Gothic fantasy that is Vienna's city hall. An ice rink is set up around it and remains for ice-skaters to

Christkindlmärkte

Vienna keeps the Christmas flame burning perhaps more brightly than any other metropolis in the world. Here, during the holiday season, no fewer than nine major *Christkindlmärkte* (Christmas Markets) proffer their wares, with stands selling enough wood-carved Austrian toys, crèche figures, and Tannenbaum ornaments to tickle anybody's mistletoes. Many of the markets have food vendors selling *Glühwein* (mulled wine) and *Kartoffelpuffer* (potato patties).

enjoy into the New Year. ✉ *Rathausplatz 1, 1st District.*

CLOTHING

Anukoo

CLOTHING | Fair-trade fashion is the philosophy behind Anukoo. The designs here are fresh, and only organic material is used in the relaxed dresses, T-shirts, trousers, and more. ✉ *Lichtensteg 1, 1st District* ☎ *01/5352886* ⊕ *www.anukoo.com* Ⓜ *U1/U3/Stephansplatz.*

Callisti

CLOTHING | Chic and avant-garde, the designs here have a definite biker's edginess with a fair amount of leather on many items. The womenswear brand is all made by Austrian designer Martina Mueller Callisti. ✉ *Weihburggasse 20, 1st District* ☎ *676/301–301–0* ⊕ *www.callisti.at.*

Grandits

CLOTHING | This men's shop has a great selection of both business and casual wear from a variety of labels, including Armani, Boss, Ralph Lauren, and Versace. ✉ *Rotenturmstrasse 10, 1st District* ☎ *01/512–6389* ⊕ *www.grandits.at.*

Lena Hoschek

CLOTHING | One of the shooting stars of Austria's fashion industry, Lena Hoschek finds inspiration in traditional styles. She uses floral fabrics and traditional Austrian costume dresses (dirndls) to create petticoat dresses, blouses, and outfits worn by pop stars and celebrities. Singer Katy Perry is just one of many who love her figure-hugging fashions. ⊠ *Goldschmiedgasse 7A, 1st District* ☎ *01/50–30–92–00* ⊕ *www.lenahoschek.com.*

Loden-Plankl

CLOTHING | The Austrians take special pride in their traditional clothing (called trachten) and think naught of the kitschy von Trapp clan when doing so. Lederhosen and dirndls are worn at festivals and special occasions, and men's and women's *trachtenjacken* are worn in daily attire. Perhaps the best place to purchase traditional clothing is at Loden-Plankl, which stocks hand-embroidered jackets and lederhosen for kids. The building, opposite the Hofburg, is a centuries-old treasure. ⊠ *Michaelerplatz 6, 1st District* ☎ *01/533–8032* ⊕ *www.loden-plankl.at.*

Mühlbauer Headwear

CLOTHING | This fourth-generation, family-run brand has been making hats in Austria since 1903 and today its headwear has gained fame from the patronage of customers from around the world, including celebrities like Madonna and Yoko Ono. The high-quality designs are timeless and each piece contains their iconic cursive letter 'M'- shaped hat pin. The selection is broad enough to include elegant designs as well as hats for everyday wear. ⊠ *Seilergasse 10, 1st District* ☎ *01/512–2241* ⊕ *www.muehlbauer.at.*

Peek & Cloppenburg

CLOTHING | British star architect Sir David Chipperfield designed the six-story P & C store. With the longest facade on the Kärntner Strasse, huge windows, and almost a complete lack of ornamentation, it can't be missed. Find the best-known upmarket fashion labels, as well as inexpensive off-the-rack garb. ⊠ *Kärntner Strasse 29, 1st District* ☎ *0800/20–28–04* ⊕ *www.peek-cloppenburg.at.*

Schella Kann

CLOTHING | Fashionistas make a beeline for the flagship store of this Austrian women's clothing designer and national treasure. Extravagant and trendy, these are clothes you never want to take off. ⊠ *Spiegelgasse 15, 1st District* ☎ *01/997–2755* ⊕ *www.schellakann.com.*

Sir Anthony

CLOTHING | For a classic suit-and-tie look, this is the place to shop. But Sir Anthony may also surprise those interested in nontraditional clothing. A second location is nearby at the Ringstrassen-Gallerien. ⊠ *Kärntner Strasse 21–23, 1st District* ☎ *01/512–6835* ⊕ *www.sir-anthony.com.*

Sisi

CLOTHING | Traditional Austrian attire goes gorgeously modern at this boutique from Sissy Schranz. A charming take on the nostalgic styles donned in the days of beloved Empress Sisi, these creations are elegant yet versatile. A range of clothing from Austria's best designers are showcased here, as well as accessories, jewelry, and hats. ⊠ *Annagasse 11, 1st District* ☎ *01/513–0518* ⊕ *www.sisi-vienna.at.*

Steffl

DEPARTMENT STORES | One of Vienna's most prominent department stores, Steffl stocks just about everything. It's moderately upscale without being overly expensive. Celebrate your shopping finds with a drink in the top-floor Sky Bar, which boasts views of the Giant Ferris Wheel and St. Stephen's Cathedral. ⊠ *Kärntner Strasse 19, 1st District* ☎ *01/93–05–66–10* ⊕ *www.steffl-vienna.at.*

Sturm am Parkring

CLOTHING | Come here for dapper suits for well-dressed men. They also have a decent selection of coats. ⊠ *Parkring*

Coffeehouse 101

The coffeehouse culture is as much a part of the Austrian soul as Mozart is. There are more than 1,600 coffeehouses in Vienna, and its café culture has spread throughout Europe, even all the way to western Ukraine. The *Wiener Kaffeehäuser*—the cafés known for centuries as "Vienna's parlors," might be facing competition from places like Starbucks in recent years, but nothing will ever diminish the place coffeehouses hold with Austrians. Newspapers were started and run from them; revolutions started within them. Nothing else can replace the traditonal coffeehouse experience: their sumptuous, red-velvet-padded booths; the marbletop tables; the rickety yet indestructible Thonet bentwood chairs; the coffee served on small silver platters, and, with it, a shot-sized glass of water; the waiters, dressed in Sunday-best outfits; the pastries, cakes, strudels, and rich tortes; the newspapers, magazines, and journals; and a sense that here time stands still. Set aside a morning or an afternoon, and settle down in the one you've chosen. Read awhile, catch up on your letter writing, or plan tomorrow's itinerary: there's no need to worry about overstaying your welcome, even over a single small cup of coffee.

In Austria coffee is never merely coffee. It comes in countless forms and under many names. Ask a waiter for *ein Kaffee* and you'll get a vacant stare. If you want a black coffee, you must ask for a *kleiner* or *grosser Schwarzer* (small or large black coffee, small being the size of a demitasse cup). If you want it strong, add the word *gekürzt* (shortened); if you want it weaker, *verlängert* (stretched). If you want your coffee with cream, ask for a *Brauner* (again *gross* or *klein*); say *Kaffee Creme* if you wish to add the cream yourself (or *Kaffee mit Milch extra, bitte,* if you want to add milk, not cream). Others opt for a *Melange*, a mild roast with steamed milk (which you can even get *mit Haut,* with skin, or *Verkehrter,* with more milk than coffee). The usual after-dinner drink is espresso. Most delightful are the coffee-and-whipped-cream concoctions, universally cherished as *Kaffee mit Schlag.* A customer who wants more whipped cream than coffee asks for a *Doppelschlag.* Hot black coffee in a glass with one knob of whipped cream is an *Einspänner* (literally, "one-horse coach"—as coachmen needed one hand free to hold the reins). Or you can go to town on a *Mazagran*, black coffee with ice and a tot of rum, or *Eiskaffee*, cold coffee with ice cream and whipped cream. Or you can simply order *eine Portion Kaffee* and have an honest pot of coffee and jug of hot milk. Most coffeehouses offer hot food until about an hour before closing time.

2, 1st District ☎ 01/706–4600 ⊕ www.sturm-parkring.at.

Tostmann Trachten

CLOTHING | Fancy having your very own tailor-made Austrian dirndl or lederhosen? Tostmann Trachten will create a bespoke one just for you, or you can browse the ready-made selection. There is also a nice selection of men's sweaters. ⊠ *Schottengasse 3A, 1st District* ☎ *01/533–5331* ⊕ *www.tostmann.at.*

FLEA MARKETS

Am Hof

OUTDOOR/FLEA/GREEN MARKETS | On Friday and Saturday from March to early November, a small outdoor market with arts, crafts, and collectibles takes place on Am Hof. It's open 10 am to 6 pm. ⊠ *Am Hof, 1st District.*

FOOD AND CANDY

Gerstner K. u. K. Hofzuckerbäcker

FOOD/CANDY | At Gerstner K. u. K. Hofzuckerbäcker, which is spread out over three floors, you can pick up a true taste of Vienna to bring home. The famed "Sisi" cake (a layer cake with chocolate, buttercream, and whipped cream) as well as handmade cakes, truffles, and pralines are ready for purchase from this traditional confectioner for the Imperial and Royal Court. On the second floor is a café where you can enjoy a coffee and cake with a view of the State Opera. The third floor holds a restaurant. The opulent old-world-Vienna decor is as decadent as the fancy cakes. ⊠ *Kärntner Strasse 51, 1st District* ☎ *01/526–1361* ⊕ *www.gerstner-konditorei.at.*

GALLERIES

Bel Etage

ANTIQUES/COLLECTIBLES | This gallery specializes in Viennese Jugendstil with furniture and accessories, but also has an impressive selection of paintings by Austrian artists and small collections of watches and silverware. There's a second location at Dorotheergasse 12, a 10-minute walk away. ⊠ *Mahlerstrasse 5, 1st District* ☎ *01/512–2379* ⊕ *www.eletage.com.*

Lukas Feichtner Gallery

ART GALLERIES—ARTS | Opposite Vienna's House of Music, Lucas Feichtner's two-story gallery is abundant with natural light, which helps showcase the array of bold works ranging from photography to collage. National and international artists, such as Petar Mirkovic and Styliano Schico, are represented here. ⊠ *Seilerstätte 19, 1st District* ☎ *0676/338–7145* ⊕ *www.feichtnergallery.com.*

GIFTS AND SOUVENIRS

Alt-Österreich

ANTIQUES/COLLECTIBLES | Are you looking for a vintage postcard, a hand-carved walking stick, a classic record, or even an old photograph of the Opera House from before the war? Head to Alt-Österreich—its name translates as "Old Austria"—and you'll find that this treasure trove has just about everything dealing with that time-burnished subject. ⊠ *Himmelpfortgasse 7, 1st District* ☎ *01/512–1296.*

HAMTIL & SÖHNE

GIFTS/SOUVENIRS | For a taste of Vienna HAMTIL & SÖHNE has an upscale selection of design items including glass and porcelain from Lobmeyr and Augarten as well as fun items like a cookie cutter shaped like the Prater Ferris wheel. They have a second store (closed Sun.) at Wollzeile 9, a 10 minute walk away. ⊠ *Herrengasse 2, 1st District* ☎ *01/535–0565* ⊕ *www.hamtil.at.*

★ Herzilein Papeterrie

BOOKS/STATIONERY | This gorgeous paper shop is a joy to wander around. There is a lovely selection of paper products, but also cards, wrapping paper, small gifts, and leather goods. There's a second location (a 10 minute walk away) at Am Hof 5. ⊠ *Wollzeile 18, 1st District* ☎ *67–64/20–54–52* ⊕ *www.herzilein-papeterie.at.*

Österreichische Werkstätten

GIFTS/SOUVENIRS | An Austria's cooperative for arts and crafts stocks Austrian handicrafts of the finest quality. It has everything from brass or pewter candlesticks to linen tablecloths to embroidered brooches and scarves. ⊠ *Kärntner Strasse 6, 1st District* ☎ *01/512–2418* ⊕ *www.oew.at.*

Petit Point Kovacec

GIFTS/SOUVENIRS | For that Alt Wien flourish, choose a needlepoint handbag, pill box, or brooch from one of the oldest shops in the city center—family-run for nearly a hundred years. ⊠ *Kärntner Strasse 16, 1st District* ☎ *01/512–4886* ⊕ *www.petitpoint.eu.*

JEWELRY

A. E. Köchert

JEWELRY/ACCESSORIES | One of Vienna's original purveyors to the Imperial Court, A. E. Köchert has been Vienna's jeweler of choice for nearly two centuries. In the 19th century, Emperor Franz Josef commissioned 27 diamond-studded stars for the Empress Elizabeth's legendary auburn hair. A new European trend was born, and today "Sisi's stars" are again fashionable after Köchert started reissuing them. Plus, if you're ever in need of a crown, Köchert will craft one for you. ⊠ *Neuer Markt 15, 1st District* ☎ *01/512–5828* ⊕ *www.koechert.com.*

Bucherer

JEWELRY/ACCESSORIES | For one of the best selections of watches head to Bucherer's, a famous Swiss watch store, where the gold- and diamond-jewelry selections are also top-notch. ⊠ *Kärntner Strasse 2, 1st District* ☎ *01/512–6730* ⊕ *www.bucherer.com.*

Ernst A. Haban

JEWELRY/ACCESSORIES | This small shop might be hard to find (look for the Tissot sign), but once you do, you'll find a large watch selection. Reingold also specializes in jewelry design, especially pearls and diamonds. ⊠ *Kärntner Strasse 16, 1st District* ☎ *01/512–7103* ⊕ *www. habanwatches.com* ☉ *Closed Sun.*

Juwelier Heldwein

JEWELRY/ACCESSORIES | This established Vienna jeweler has been creating a range of jewelry, watches, silverware, and gifts since 1902. Now run by the fourth generation of the Heldwein family, the shop sells not only its own designs, but those from the likes of Carrera y Carrera, Georg Jensen, and more. ⊠ *Graben 13, 1st District* ☎ *01/512–5781* ⊕ *www.heldwein.at.*

Pomellato Boutique

JEWELRY/ACCESSORIES | In Vienna's prestigious "Golden Quarter," this Italian fine jewelry store offers a unique collection of precious stones and silver. ⊠ *Tuchlaubenhof 7A, 1st District* ☎ *1/905–2324* ⊕ *www.pomellato.com.*

Susanne Kitz

JEWELRY/ACCESSORIES | Austrian designer Susanne Kitz designs both exclusive leather bags and unique jewelry pieces. Her central Vienna shop features items that are at once bold and elegant. ⊠ *Weihburggasse 7, 1st District* ☎ *01/512–8648* ⊕ *www.susannekitz.com.*

MUSIC

Arcardia

MUSIC STORES | In case you bump into Placido Domingo or Anna Netrebko, you can buy a picture here so you can have it autographed. Arcadia, in the Opera House, stocks a grand selection of the latest releases (CDs) from the operatic world, quite a few classic rarities, plus some opera and classical music-related books ⊠ *Staatsoper, Opernring 2, 1st District* ☎ *01/513–9568.*

EMI

MUSIC STORES | Helpful sales assistants are at the ready if you're looking for any special titles at EMI—one of the big mainstays for classical music. The selections run the gamut from ethno to pop and they sell both CDs and vinyl. ⊠ *Kärntner Strasse 30, 1st District* ☎ *01/512–3675* ⊕ *www.emistore.at.*

PERFUMES

J.B. Filz Perfumery

PERFUME/COSMETICS | The perfumery to the Imperial Court, J.B. Filz has been creating beautiful scents since 1809. Bring back memories of Vienna with its Wiener Lieblingsduft, or try the Eau de Lavande, a scent made with three different kinds of lavender and suitable for both men and women, or Café de Vienne, a delicate blend of coffee and vanilla. ⊠ *Graben 13, 1st District* ☎ *01/512–1745* ⊕ *www. parfumerie-filz.at.*

Chapter 4

LEOPOLDSTADT AND ALSERGRUND

DISTRICTS 2 AND 9

4

Updated by
Caroline Sieg

 Sights
★★★★☆

 Restaurants
★★★☆☆

 Hotels
★★☆☆☆

 Shopping
★★★☆☆

 Nightlife
★★★☆☆

NEIGHBORHOOD SNAPSHOT

TOP EXPERIENCES

■ **Giant Ferris wheel:** Take in the city views while riding the Giant Ferris Wheel at the vintage Prater Amusement Park

■ **Sigmund Freud Museum:** Visit the birthplace of psychoanalysis and ring the bell on the door of the world-famous professor, just like his patients did over a hundred years ago.

■ **Stroll along the Praterstrasse:** Wander along the boulevard of Praterstrasse from the city center to the Prater and you'll find plenty of cafes and restaurants along the way.

■ **The Karameliter District:** Explore the area around the Karamelitermarkt to find the city's hippest cafes, restaurants, and cozy wine bars.

■ **Augarten Porzellanmanufaktur:** Learn about the history of this 300-year-old porcelain factory and see porcelain artists at work.

■ **Cafe Landtmann:** Enjoy a specialty coffee at this historic coffeehouse, Freud's local coffeeshop.

GETTING HERE

The main transport stations to Leopoldstadt are the U2 to Taborstrassse or Praterstern, or the U1 to Netsroyplatz or Praterstern. For Alsergrund, hop on the U2 to Schottentor or the U4 to Rosslauergelände or Friendsbrücke.

PLANNING YOUR TIME

Both Leopoldstadt and Alsergrund are quiet during the weekend but tend to be livelier on Friday evenings, and during the day and evening on Saturday and Sunday. Like most of the city, Sunday evenings are particularly quiet. If you are interested in Jewish history, allow time for a walking tour of the area.

QUICK BITES

■ **o.m.k. deli.** Upmarket Asian takeout joint offering ramen to sushi to bowls, plus coffee, wine, and beer. ⊠ *Praterstrasse 16, Leopoldstadt* ⊕ *www.o-m-k.com* Ⓜ *U1/ Nestroyplatz.*

■ **Weinschenke am Karmelitermarkt.** One of Vienna's most popular burger joints offers veggie and meat options at this market location (cash only). ⊠ *Karmelitermarkt Stand 10–12, Leopoldstadt* ⊕ *www.weinschenke-wien.com/standorte* Ⓜ *U2/ Taborstrasse.*

■ **Der Wiener Deewan.** Pay what you like for vegetarian Pakistani comfort food (think curries, dahl, and rice) at this casual little gem. ⊠ *Liechtensteinstrasse 10, Alsergrund* ⊕ *deewan.at* Ⓜ *U2/ Schottentor.*

Walk across the Danube Canal on Schwedenbrücke or Marienbrücke and you'll reach the vibrant 2nd District, Leopoldstadt, one of Vienna's trendiest neighborhoods, filled with quality coffee shops, the hip Karmelitermarkt, and a clutch of quirky restaurants.

It's also home to the Prater, the former royal hunting grounds, and Vienna's iconic *Riesenrad* (Ferris wheel), and MuTh, the concert hall and permanent home of the world-famous Vienna Boys' Choir, as well as Vienna's oldest Baroque park, the Augarten, which is anchored by a 300-year-old porcelain factory. Neighboring Alsergrund, District 9, was once Sigmund Freud's neighborhood, and today is a mostly residential neighborhood with a University District, lots of restaurants, boutiques, and lovely early-20th-century apartment buildings.

The beauty of Leopoldstadt is that it connects Vienna's vibrant present with its complicated past. It was named Leopoldstadt—Leopold's city—in the late 1670s after Leopold I, the archduke of Austria expelled a flourishing Jewish community from the area due to growing anti-semitism in the city. The non-Jewish population thanked Leopold by naming the district after him. However, this expulsion did not prevent a new settlement of Jews in the city, and only a few decades later, this part of the city once again became the focus of Jewish settlers and a hub of Jewish life in Vienna. By the late 1800s and early 1900s, Leopoldstadt was known as the Jewish Quarter or *Mazzes Insel* (Matzoh Island), until this population was again targeted during the Kristallnacht pogroms of

November 1938 after the annexation of Austria by Nazi Germany and then wiped out by the Holocaust.

In 1938, about 200,000 Jews lived in Vienna, most of them within the 2nd and 9th Districts. With the invasion of the Nazis, the Jews were suddenly deprived of all their rights, their jobs, and their homes. About two thirds of Austrian Jews were able to emigrate before the borders closed. Those who could not— some 60,000 Jewish men, women, and children—were deported to concentration camps and murdered.

As you wander Leopoldstadt today, you have to mostly imagine the vanished world of Vienna's Jewish quarter pre-World War II, as the area was heavily bombed during the war. But you will find subtle, poignant memorials to commemorate the Jews who once lived here. Hundreds of brass *stolpersteine*, or stumbling blocks, set into the pavement in front of residences from which people were deported mark a "Path of Remembrance" through Leopoldstadt. Plaques also commemorate the Austrians who helped and hid Jews. A project of artist Lukas Maria Kaufmann and the Jewish Museum Vienna positioned deconstructed Jewish Stars made of light tubes to mark the parts of the city where synagogues or houses of prayer once stood. There are 25 in all, six in the 2nd District.

In recent years, many Eastern European Jews have moved to this part of Vienna and revived the tradition of Jewish culture in the 2nd District. You'll see individuals and families in full Orthodox dress as you explore, and find quality Kosher restaurants, grocery stores, and cafes scattered throughout the district. You'll also find Austrian, Georgian, Japanese, and Italian eateries that have popped up here in the past few years. Karmelitermarkt itself has become a haven for high-end coffee shops and innovative kitchens.

Leopoldstadt

Leopoldstadt, or the 2nd District, is best known for Vienna's famous giant ferris wheel and Prater park but you won't want to miss the Augarten park, anchored by a procelain factory and home to the Vienna Boy's Choir. Walk through its quiet, leafy backstreets and you'll find the *real* Vienna—friendly and filled with locals.

Sights

Augarten
NATIONAL/STATE PARK | **FAMILY** | An elegant oasis of sculpted trees and elaborate formal gardens, Augarten Park dates to the beginning of the 17th century when this area was used as a small hunting area and lodge. In 1705, formal gardens were established by designer Jean Trehet, and the *Lustschloss* (a kind of pleasure palace or retreat for entertainment) was rebuilt after being destroyed by Ottoman troops. Today, the palace is the headquarters of the *Augarten Porzellanmanufaktur* (Augarten porcelain factory), one of Europe's oldest porcelain factories. In 1775, the Augarten was opened to the public by Emperor Joseph II and the inscription *"Allen Menschen gewidmeter Erlustigungs-Ort von Ihrem Schaetzer"* ("A place of amusement dedicated to all people by their Cherisher")

can still be read at the main gate to the Augarten from Obere Augartenstrasse. Gravel paths crisscross the park's 128 acres under the shade of leafy chestnuts, lime, ash, and maple trees. There's also a sprawling playground, a lovely cafe in the park's center, and two *Flaktürme* (Flak Towers), built by the Nazis to defend Vienna against air-raids during WWII. At the southern tip of Augarten is MuTH (Musik and Theatre), the 400-seat concert hall and home to the Vienna Boys Choir. Next door is a summer outdoor theater. ✉ *Obere Augartenstrasse 1, 2nd District/Leopoldstadt* Ⓜ *U2/Taborstrasse.*

★ **Augarten Porzellanmanufaktur** (*Augarten Porcelain Manufactory*)
MUSEUM | Founded in 1718, Europe's second-oldest porcelain factory is located in a former pleasure palace in Augarten Park, and is indeed a pleasure palace for lovers of hand-made and painted porcelain. This company is renowned for its high-quality porcelain, delicate patterns, and constant innovation in its design and production. Augarten porcelain is still produced and painted by the hands of employees in the manufactory, just as it has been for almost 300 years. One wing of the factory houses a museum, designed around the 18th century bottle kiln that reaches to the roof top of the first level. Guided tours of the factory (Monday to Thursday at 10:15 am and 11:30 am) take visitors behind the scenes to see creators at work and to explain the different phases of the process as well as the history and evolution of the art. Your wonder, appreciation, and awe at the final creations and the fact that it takes a porcelain artist three months to create will be put to good use in the gift shop. Visitors looking for a more immersive experience can book a two-day seminar on the creation and painting of porcelain. ✉ *Augarten Park, Obere Augartenstrasse 1, 2nd District/Leopoldstadt* ☎ *01/211–24200* ⊕ *www.augarten.com* 💲 *€14 tour.*

Monumental concrete Flak Towers are a remnant of WWII when they were used as platforms for anti-aircraft guns. Today they serve as a reminder of darker times and a home to thousands of pigeons.

Johann Strauss Wohnung (*Johann Strauss Residence*)

HOUSE | The most popular composer of all, waltz king Johann Strauss the Younger, composed the "Blue Danube Waltz"—Austria's unofficial national anthem—at this house in 1867. Standing in the huge salon of this belle-epoque building, you can well imagine what a sumptuous affair a Strauss soirée would have been. Artifacts include Strauss's Amati violin. ✉ *Praterstrasse 54, 2nd District/Leopoldstadt* ☎ *01/214–0121* ⊕ *www.wienmuseum.at/en/locations/johann-strauss-wohnung* 🎫 *€5* ⊙ *Closed Mon.* Ⓜ *U4/Nestroyplatz.*

★ **Karmelitermarkt**

MARKET | The market and lively surrounding area is one of Vienna's coolest food and drink hotspots and its sunny picturesque square is a favorite option for breakfasting and people-watching over coffee. The market itself has more than 80 vendors and has existed since 1671, making it one of Vienna's oldest—and yet it never gets old. There's a farmer's market on Saturday and new spots serving international and Viennese cuisine are popping up all the time. Quieter and more spacious than the buzzing 6th and 7th districts, this area is a great alternative to the busier central areas. Allow ample time to wander the surrounding streets and linger in cafes and boutiques. ✉ *Karmelitermarkt, 2nd District/Leopoldstadt* Ⓜ *U2 Taborstrasse.*

Kriminalmuseum (*Criminal Museum*)

HOUSE | The vast and macabre museum is entirely devoted to Viennese murders of the most gruesome kind. The most grisly displays are, appropriately situated in the cellar. Murderers and their victims are depicted in photos and newspaper clippings, and many of the actual instruments used in the killings are displayed, axes seeming to be the most popular. It also traces the penal system of the Middle Ages through displays of historial documents as well as objects used to execute and torture people. The museum is housed in the "soap-boiler house," one of the oldest and most spectacular

Leopoldstadt and Alsergrund

Sights ▼

1 Augarten..........................**E2**
2 Augarten
Porzellanmanufaktur **E3**
3 Johann Strauss Wohnung........**G5**
4 Karmelitermarkt....................**E4**
5 Kriminalmuseum...................**E4**
6 Prater **I5**
7 Schubert Geburtshaus............**A2**
8 Sigmund Freud Museum..........**B4**
9 Votivkirche.........................**B5**

Restaurants ▼

1 Café Ansari.........................**F5**
2 Das Loft.............................**F6**
3 Ramasuri............................**F5**
4 Restaurant Kim.....................**A3**
5 Schöne Perle.......................**E4**
6 Skopik & Lohn......................**E4**

Quick Bites ▼

1 Balthasar **G5**
2 Café Landtmann **B6**
3 Schweizerhaus **J5**

Hotels ▼

1 Hollmann Beletage.................**E6**
2 Meininger Hotel Vienna
Downtown Franz...................**D3**
3 Meininger Hotel Vienna
Downtown Sissi....................**E4**
4 The Rooms..........................**J3**
5 SO/ Vienna..........................**F5**

buildings in Leopoldstadt and is across the Danube Canal from Schwedenplatz, about a 15-minute walk from the core of the Innere Stadt (or the Inner City/City Center). ✉ *Grosse Sperlgasse 24, 2nd District/Leopoldstadt* ☎ *01/664–300–5677* 🌐 *www.kriminalmuseum.at* 🎟 *€8* 🕑 *Closed Mon.–Wed.* [M] *U2/Taborstrasse.*

★ Prater

AMUSEMENT PARK/WATER PARK | In 1766, to the dismay of the aristocracy, Emperor Josef II decreed that the vast expanse of imperial parklands known as the Prater would henceforth be open to the public. East of the inner city between the Danube Canal and the Danube proper, the Prater is a public park to this day, notable for its long promenade (the Hauptallee, more than 4½ km [3 miles] in length); the traditional amusement-park rides; a planetarium; and a small but interesting museum devoted to the Prater's long history. If you look carefully, you can discover a handful of children's rides dating from the '20s and '30s that survived the fire that consumed most of the Volksprater in 1945.

At the amusement park there are 250 rides, many of which will make thrill-ride enthusiasts happy, and on hot days, there is a water park to splash around in. For little ones, there is an interactive ride featuring polar bears and penguins. Madame Tussauds is also on-site if you want a photo with famous Austrian native sons and daughters (Arnold Schwarzenegger comes to mind). The best-known attraction is the 200-foot Ferris wheel that figured so prominently in the 1949 film *The Third Man.* It was one of three built in Europe at the end of the 19th century (the others were in England and France, but have long since been dismantled); the wheel was badly damaged during World War II, but restored shortly thereafter. Its progress is slow and stately (a revolution takes 10 minutes), and the views from its cars are magnificent, particularly toward dusk. ✉ *Riesenradplatz, 2nd District/Leopoldstadt* 🎟 *Park free, Ferris wheel €12* [M] *U1/Praterstern.*

🍴 Restaurants

Café Ansari

$ | **MEDITERRANEAN** | Run by a Georgian couple with Lebanese roots, this stylish and airy restaurant is part modern Viennese coffehouse, part Mediterranean escape. The light-filled interior features a beautifully tiled bar area with Lebanese tile, ornate lamps, and vases filled with fresh flowers, while the shady terrace is a perfect spot to slowly enjoy specialties like *khinkali* (meat-filled dumplings) and *khachapuri* (cheese-filled bread), along with Georgian wines, and specialty teas and coffees. **Known for:** authentic Mediterranean and Georgian fare; Georgian breakfast; lovely terrace on a quiet street. [$] *Average main: €15* ✉ *Praterstrasse 15, 2nd District/Leopoldstadt* ☎ *01/276–5102* 🌐 *cafeansari.at.*

★ Das Loft

$$$$ | **INTERNATIONAL** | Dine at Vienna's poshest restaurant while taking in the stunning, 360-degree panoramic vistas of the city's skyline from the 18th floor of the Sofitel Stephansdom. The gourmet meals, often made with seasonal, locally-sourced fare, are just as fabulous as the view. **Known for:** top-notch cuisine from Austria's premier chefs; gorgeous views especially at sunset; dress code after 6 pm. [$] *Average main: €100* ✉ *Praterstrasse 1, 2nd District/Leopoldstadt* ☎ *1/906168110* 🌐 *www.dasloftwien.at.*

Ramasuri

$ | **AUSTRIAN** | With tables set outside amidst flowering plants and trees, in the middle of cobbled Nestroyplatz, it is no wonder this is one of Vienna's favorite breakfast and brunch spots. the menu is huge with plenty of vegetarian options, but if you're here for a leisurely breakfast or brunch, go with the eponymous

Ramasuri sandwich, with Madame Crousto bread (from one of Vienna's best bakeries, Öfferl), wildflower cheese scrambled eggs, candied bacon, chard, and sundried tomatoes. Drinks, coffees, and service are excellent, so this is a perfect stop at any time of day. **Known for:** Ramasuri sandwich; greenery-filled terrace; tasty vegetarian options. [$] *Average main: €12* ✉ *Praterstrasse 19, 2nd District/Leopoldstadt* ☎ *676/466–8060* 🌐 *ramasuri.at.*

Schöne Perle

$ | **AUSTRIAN** | **FAMILY** | This "beautiful pearl" is one of the most popular dining spots for locals in Leopoldstadt. It offers traditional Austrian comfort food, including Tafelspitz—boiled beef, the favored dish of Emperor Franz Josef—and Wiener schnitzel, but its real palate pleasers are the wide selection of vegetarian dishes on the menu. **Known for:** Austrian comfort food; cash-only policy; crowds at dinner, so make a reservation. [$] *Average main: €16* ✉ *Grosse Pfarrgasse 2, 2nd District/Leopoldstadt* ☎ *664–2433–593* 🌐 *www.schoene-perle.at* 💳 *No credit cards.*

Skopik & Lohn

$$ | **AUSTRIAN** | Many restaurants have set up shop in former stalls on the market square in the artsy neighborhood that has sprung up around Karmelitermarkt, just across the Donaukanal, including Skopik & Lohn. The menu features international fare, such as roast chicken with figs and chestnuts, and linguine with fresh chanterelle mushrooms (which only grow two months out of the year). **Known for:** wide selection of international fare; artist Otto Zitko's massive doodling spree on the ceiling; hip neighborhood hangout. [$] *Average main: €20* ✉ *Leopoldsgasse 17, 2nd District/Leopoldstadt* ☎ *01/219–8977* 🌐 *www.skopikundlohn.at* 🕒 *Closed Sun. and Mon.* [M] *U2/Taborstrasse.*

Coffee and Quick Bites

★ Balthasar

$ | **CAFÉ** | One of Vienna's most popular third-wave coffeehouses brews and lives up to its hype and long lines with exceptional coffee, stylish decor, delicious baked goods and sandwiches, and a sustainable focus. It's also just a cool place to hang with all the cool people. **Known for:** trendy spot; pleasant and large outdoor seating area; exceptional third-wave coffee. [$] *Average main: €5* ✉ *Praterstrasse 38, 2nd District/Leopoldstadt* ☎ *01/946–9536* 🌐 *balthasar.at* 🕒 *Closed Sun.* 💳 *No credit cards* [M] *U1/Nestroyplatz.*

Schweizerhaus

$ | **AUSTRIAN** | When you're at the Prater, try to eat at Schweizerhaus, which has been serving frothy mugs of beer, roast chicken, and *Stelze* (a huge hunk of crispy roast pork on the bone) for more than 100 years. The informal setting, with wood-plank tables indoors or in the garden in summer, adds to the fun. **Known for:** huge beer garden is always crowded; pork knuckle; pretzels and beer. [$] *Average main:* ✉ *Strasse des 1. Mai 116, 2nd District/Leopoldstadt* ☎ *01/728–0152* 🕒 *Closed Nov.–Feb.* [M] *U1/Nestroyplatz.*

Hotels

Meininger Hotel Vienna Downtown Franz

$ | **HOTEL** | **FAMILY** | Brother hotel to its sister "Sissi"—six blocks away—this member of the Meininger budget hotel chain offers the same hip style and out-for-fun clientele, but has room rates that are slightly higher (these can be bargained lower, depending on daily availability). **Pros:** rare underground parking on-site; options for family or group travel; easy to make new friends. **Cons:** not a very quiet or peaceful atmosphere; with no air-conditioning, rooms can be very hot in summer; can feel like a college dorm. $ Rooms from: €100 ⊠ Rembrandtstrasse 21, 2nd District/ Leopoldstadt ☎ 01/720–882–065 ⊕ www. meininger-hotels.com/en/hotels/vienna/ downtown-franz ⇆ 131 rooms ⦿ No meals.

Meininger Hotel Vienna Downtown Sissi

$ | HOTEL | FAMILY | Part of the popular Meininger chain of budget hotels, this was the first of three to open in Vienna, all offering hip design, plugged-in clientele, and some of the best deals in town. **Pros:** kitchen available to guests; decent breakfast bar; sociable atmosphere. **Cons:** only one elevator; 15-minute walk to city center; no air-conditioning. $ Rooms from: €110 ⊠ Schiffamtsgasse 15, 2nd District/Leopoldstadt ☎ 01/720–882–066 ⊕ www.meininger-hotels.com/en/hotels/ vienna/downtown-sissi/ ⇆ 102 rooms ⦿ No meals.

The Rooms

$ | B&B/INN | With no two rooms alike, this tranquil, tiny guesthouse north of the Danube—it's in the 22nd District, beyond the 2nd District on the U1 metro line—exudes an exotic aura, and the charming, friendly, and ever-so-helpful owners are ready to assist when needed. **Pros:** excellent breakfast; friendly vibe; beautiful hospitality. **Cons:** outside center; accomodations differ greatly in size; no real public spaces. $ Rooms from: €115 ⊠ Schlenthergasse 17, 22nd District/ Donaustadt ☎ 01/664–431–6830 ⊕ www. therooms.at ⇆ 4 rooms ⦿ Free breakfast Ⓜ U1/Kagran.

★ SO/Vienna

$$$$ | HOTEL | Minimalist luxury can be a contradiction, but the SO/Vienna, a Sofitel hotel, it's pulled off with supreme elegance, and here, on the border of the 2nd District, it's paired with outstanding city skyline views. **Pros:** outstanding views; incredible restaurant; amazing spa. **Cons:** monochromatic palate can feel cold to some; deep bathtubs can

be difficult to maneuver; some rooms could use freshening up. $ Rooms from: €320 ⊠ Praterstrasse 1, 2nd District/Leopoldstadt ☎ 01/906–160 ⊕ www.sofitel. com/Vienna ⇆ 180 rooms ⦿ No meals Ⓜ U4 or U1/Schwedenplatz.

Nightlife

DANCE CLUBS
Fluc

DANCE CLUBS | One of the leaders and originals of nightlife in Vienna's 2nd District, the Fluc attracts world-famous DJs, who praise the small venue as one of the best in Europe. It is on the site of a converted passageway, so its thick, soundproof walls mean DJs can max out the volume. ⊠ Praterstern 5, 2nd District/ Leopoldstadt ☎ 01/218–28–24 ⊕ www. fluc.at.

Performing Arts

MUSIC
★ MuTh

MUSIC | A play on the words music and theater, MuTh is the concert hall and permanent home of the world-famous Vienna Boys' Choir (Wiener Sängerknaben). Since it opened in 2012, the 400-seat theater has become the official music center inside the Augarten, the oldest Baroque garden in Vienna. Here the legendary Vienna Boys' Choir performs music that ranges from classical to world music to pop. The vast stage has some of the finest acoustics in Vienna and is equipped with an orchestra pit, specially designed seating, and distinctive acoustic panels. The building itself combines a unique mix of Baroque and modern architecture and includes a café, shop, and seminar room where musical education and other performances take place. ⊠ Am Augartenspitz 1, 2nd District/Leopoldstadt ⊕ www.muth.at.

★ **Wiener Sängerknaben** (*Vienna Boys' Choir*)

MUSIC | The beloved Vienna Boys' Choir, known here as the Wiener Sängerknaben, isn't just a set of living dolls out of a Walt Disney film (like the 1962 movie *Almost Angels*); its pedigree is royal, and its professionalism such that the choir regularly appears with the best orchestras in the world. The troupe was founded by Emperor Maximilian I in 1498, but with the demise of the Hapsburg Empire in 1918, it became its own entity and began giving public performances in the 1920s to keep afloat.

From mid-September to late June, the apple-cheeked lads sing mass at 9:15 Sunday mornings in the Hofburgkapelle. Written requests for seats should be made at least six weeks in advance. Tickets are also sold at ticket agencies and at the box office (open Friday 11–1 and 3–5). Expect to pay a top price of €38 for a seat near the nave, and note that only the 10 side-balcony seats allow a view of the choir. On Sunday at 8:45 am, any unclaimed tickets are sold at the entrance. If you miss hearing the choir at a Sunday mass, you may be able to catch it in a more popular program in the Musikverein. ✉ *Hofmusikkapelle, Hofburg-Schweizerhof, 1st District* ☎ *01/216–3942* ⊕ *www.wsk.at.*

Shopping

CLOTHING
Bocca Lupo

CLOTHING | This luxury boutique features vintage fashion by well-known designers. See if you can track down a classic Hermès scarf, Louis Vuitton purse, or a fabulous, new-to-you cocktail dress. ✉ *Praterstrasse 14, 2nd District/Leopoldstadt* ☎ *01/904–3776* ⊕ *www.boccalupo.at.*

Song

CLOTHING | This former fur factory in Vienna's 2nd District has been transformed into a fashion temple. The stylish interior design is by architect Gregor Eichinger. A lover of the avant-garde styles, Song combines the finest luxury labels with its own fashion designs, plus contemporary styles from young, up-and-coming designers. Shop for fashion, bags, shoes, and furniture here. The website is regularly updated with a variety of events. ✉ *Praterstrasse 11–13, 2nd District/Leopoldstadt* ☎ *01/532–2858* ⊕ *www.song.at.*

FOOD
Kaas am Markt

FOOD/CANDY | Local cheeses, meats, and breads, fresh farm produce, and handmade specialty items look and taste delicious here. Stop by for an excellent breakfast, a snack, an afternoon tipple with a plate of cheese or the weekday three-course lunch (for the latter, get here on the early side to nab a table). ✉ *Karmelitermarkt 33–36, 2nd District/Leopoldstadt* ☎ *69/91–81–40–60–1* ⊕ *www.karmeliter.at* ⊘ *Closed Sun.*

GIFTS
Supersense

GIFTS/SOUVENIRS | Proudly announcing itself as a store with the "World's Most Analog Products," here you can record yourself on vinyl, buy Polaroid cameras, film, and accessories, and find letterpress prints (made on an operational letterpress on-site), or kits. You can also find books, handcrafted glassware, and ceramic coffee cups to go, or just browse the unique goods over a coffee. ✉ *Praterstrasse 70, 2nd District/Leopoldstadt* ☎ *01/969–0832* ⊕ *the.supersense.com* ⊘ *Closed Sun.*

Activities

Dianabad

SWIMMING | A great pool for children, complete with waterslides and a pirate-shaped swimming pool. ☎ *1/219–8181–10* ⊕ *www.dianabad.at.*

Alsergrund

The 9th District, Alsergrund, is located just north of the central district, Innere Stadt, and across the Danube from Leopoldstadt. It's long broad streets lined with elegant late-19th-century buildings are home to the University of Vienna and a large community of artists and students, and the lively music scene, nightlife, and beer gardens that accompany one of Europe's largest universities. But it's the district's notable former residents, including Franz Schubert (born here), Ludwig van Beethoven (died here in his apartment at Schwarzspanierstrasse 15), and Sigmund Freud (lived and worked here), that attract most visitors. Freud's home, the site of the Vienna Sigmund Freud Museum, is one of Vienna's top attractions.

Sights

Schubert Geburtshaus (*Schubert's Birthplace*)

HOUSE | Unlike most of Vienna's composers, Schubert was a native of Vienna. The modest but charming two-story house was not as idyllic then as it is today. When Schubert was born, it was home to 16 families who were crammed into as many studio apartments within the house. Many of the composer's personal items are displayed here, including his spectacles, which he allegedly didn't remove to sleep, as he was so anxious to begin composing as soon as he woke up. ⊠ *Nussdorferstrasse 54, 9th District/* *Alsergrund* ☎ *01/317–3601* ⊕ *www.wienmuseum.at* 🎫 *€5* ⊙ *Closed Mon.* Ⓜ *Streetcar 37 or 38 to Canisiusgasse.*

★ **Sigmund Freud Museum** (*Freud Haus*)

HOUSE | Not far from the historic Hofburg district, the marvels and pains of the 20th century come into focus here at the the former practice and private quarters of the father of psychoanalysis. The museum outlines Sigmund Freud's work and peronal life, as well as his impact on the world of psychology via memorabilia, private letters, biographical details, photos, films, and a library, It's housed in the apartment where Freud and his wife lived from 1891–1938 and raised their six children. The waiting-room furniture is original but the consulting room and study furniture (including the famous couch) can be seen only in photographs. The collection of telegrams (photocopies of the originals) from the State Department is chilling; they chronicle frantic efforts to help the Freud family escape Austria after the Nazi Anschluss in 1938. ⊠ *Berggasse 19, Apt. 6, 9th District/Alsergrund* ☎ *01/319–1596* ⊕ *www.freud-museum.at* 🎫 *€14* Ⓜ *U2/Schottentor.*

Votivkirche (*Votive Church*)

RELIGIOUS SITE | When Emperor Franz Josef was a young man, he was strolling along the Mölker Bastei, one of the few remaining portions of the old city wall, when he was taken unawares and stabbed in the neck by a Hungarian revolutionary. He survived, and in gratitude his family ordered that a church be built exactly on the spot he was looking at when he was struck down. The neo-Gothic church was built of gray limestone with two openwork turrets and was finally completed in 1879, after 23 years of construction. ⊠ *Rooseveltplatz, 9th District/Alsergrund* ☎ *01/406–1192* ⊕ *www.votivkirche.at* ⊙ *Closed Mon.* Ⓜ *U2/Schottentor.*

The neo-Gothic Votivkirche was built as a votive to thank God for saving Emperor Franz Josef from an attempted assassination.

🍴 Restaurants

Restaurant Kim

$$$$ | **ASIAN FUSION** | Since establishing herself as Austria's most inventive Asian chef, Korean-born Sohyi Kim continues to impress with her celebrated Asian-fusion cuisine. Every night, she dreams up "lite surprise" lunches for her guests, and 10-course "full surprise" dinners; yes, that means diners have no idea what exactly they are going to get. **Known for:** surprise full-course dinners and lunches featuring Asian-fusion dishes; reservations recommended; small, intimate space. 💲 *Average main: €70* ✉ *Währinger Strasse 46, 9th District/Alsergrund* ☎ *0664/4258866* ⊕ *www.kim.wien* 🕙 *Closed Sun.–Tues.* Ⓜ *U6 Währinger Strasse-Volksoper.*

☕ Coffee and Quick Bites

★ Café Landtmann

$ | **CAFÉ** | Opened in 1873, this legendary coffeehouse boasts an elegant interior and a guest list that includes regulars like Freud, Mahler, Kalman, Marlene Dietrich, and Paul McCartney. Its proximity to the Burgtheater, Rathaus, and Parliament makes it a local for today's celebrities and politicians, too. **Known for:** old world charm; specialty coffees like the Wiener Melange (similar to a cappuccino); traditional pastries. 💲 *Average main: €13* ✉ *Universitätsring 4, 9th District/Alsergrund* ☎ *01/241–00120* ⊕ *www.landtmann. at/en* Ⓜ *U2 Schottentor.*

Hotels

Hollmann Beletage

$$$ | HOTEL | Tucked away in the center of town just a short walk from the cathedral, this intimate boutique hotel has a quiet but convenient location. **Pros:** in the heart of the city; modern rooms; great breakfast. **Cons:** hotel entrance is hard to find; no restaurant; no views. $ *Rooms from: €175* ✉ *Köllnerhofgasse 6, 1st District* ☎ *01/961–1960* ⊕ *www.hollmann-beletage.at* ⊅ *26 rooms* ⦿ *Free breakfast.*

Performing Arts

FILM

Votiv Kino

FILM | This artsy theater features more alternative film options, with most movies shown in their original language with German subtitles. There are also special children's performances on the weekends. The cinema also has a lovely cafe offering wine, beer and light snacks. ✉ *Währingerstrasse 12, 9th District/ Alsergrund* ☎ *01/317–3571* ⊕ *www. votivkino.at.*

OPERA

Volksoper

OPERA | Opera, operetta, and ballet are performed at the Volksoper, just on the outer edge of the Innere Stadt at Währinger Strasse and Währinger Gürtel. Prices here are significantly lower than at the Staatsoper, and performances can be every bit as rewarding. This theater has a packed calendar, with offerings ranging from the grandest opera, such as Mozart's *Don Giovanni*, to an array of Viennese operettas, including Johann Strauss's *Die Fledermaus*, to Broadway musicals. Most operas and musicals are sung in German. The opera house is at the third stop on streetcar Nos. 41, 42, or 43, which run from Schottentor, U2, on the Ring. ✉ *Währinger Strasse 78, 9th District/Alsergrund* ☎ *01/513–1513* ⊕ *www.volksoper.at* Ⓜ *U6/Währinger Strasse–Volksoper.*

Chapter 5

LANDSTRASSE AND WIEDEN

DISTRICTS 3 AND 4

Updated by
Caroline Sieg

👁 **Sights**
★★★★☆

🍴 **Restaurants**
★★★★★

🛏 **Hotels**
★★★☆☆

🛍 **Shopping**
★★★☆☆

🍸 **Nightlife**
★☆☆☆☆

NEIGHBORHOOD SNAPSHOT

TOP EXPERIENCES

- **The Kiss:** Air kiss Gustav Klimt's famous work at the Upper Belvedere museum.

- **Austrian Bubbly:** Press pause and join the locals for a glass of Austrian sparkling wine at tiny, convivial Sekt Comptoir.

- **Karlskirche:** Gape at Vienna's greatest Baroque structure, the impressive Karlskirche.

- **Hundertwasserhaus:** Contemplate the tapestry of color at the public-housing complex designed by Friedensreich Hundertwasser.

- **Steirereck im Stadtpark:** Splurge on a tasting menu at this two-Michelin-star hotspot housed in a former dairy in the middle of a city park.

GETTING HERE

Vienna's 3rd district is one of the best connected areas of the city. Not only is the U3 one of the most useful metro lines in town, but the train station/mall Wien Mitte (literally meaning Vienna's center) also connects it with the U4 and a bunch of Schnellbahn lines (city trains) that will take you to either end of the city within 20 minutes. For Wieden take the U1, U2, U4 to Karlsplatz.

PLANNING YOUR TIME

To explore the Belvedere's upper and lower palaces and the palace gardens you will need at least three hours. If you plan to explore the Permanent or the Temporary art exhibitions at leisure, you may need more time. Belvedere Palace is busiest from 11 am to 2 pm, with long lines to enter the attraction. Both Landstrasse and Wieden are quiet during the week and get livelier on the weekends so plan your visit accordingly.

QUICK BITES

- **Soulkitchen.** Soups, bowls, and plates with a focus on Vietnamese and Persian fare (many of them vegan). ⊠ *Hintere Zollamtsstraße 2, Landstrasse* ⊕ *www.soulkitchenvienna. at* Ⓜ *U3/U4 Landstrasse.*

- **Hiddenkitchen Park.** Great salads, soups, and small plates in an airy space. ⊠ *Invalidenstrasse 17–19, Landstrasse* ⊕ *www. hiddenkitchen.at* Ⓜ *U3/U4 Landstrasse.*

- **Bánh Mì Vienna.** One of the city's favorite: Vietnamese Bánh Mì sandwiches and salads. ⊠ *Faulmanngasse 1, Wieden* ⊕ *banh-mi4. eatbu.com* Ⓜ *U1/U2/U4 Karlsplatz.*

VIEWFINDER

- Most people focus on the two palaces and the gardens between them at Belvedere Palace. But go around to the front of Upper Belvedere Palace (the opposite side to the museum entrance). Then walk out beyond the small lake and look back for the best photo of the palace and best backdrop in Vienna.

Well-to-do Landstrasse, Vienna's 3rd District, and its next-door neighbor Wieden, the 4th District, are home to some of the city's most significant sights, from the palace-turned-art-gallery the Belvedere, where you will find the largest collection of Gustav Klimt's paintings in the world, to the quirky and iconic Hundertwasserhaus, and the Baroque masterpiece, the Karlskirche.

The 3rd District is also home to the city's diplomatic quarter with several embassies housed in former palaces, but for all its imperial elegance and architectural interest, Landstrasse is calm and peaceful, with a genuine neighborhood feel and lots of small shops and cafes with real character. Wieden has a little more edge and cool nightlife options.

Next to Stephansplatz, Karlsplatz is one of the inner city's busiest hubs. It sprawls along the Ringstrasse to encompass the magnificent Baroque Karlskirche and an exquisite Jugendstil pavilion designed by Otto Wagner, the architect of the partly elevated tram system to the outer boroughs (now part of the U4 and U6 subway lines). From Karlsplatz, you can travel eastward on the Ringstrasse to visit the stunning Museum for Applied Arts and the romantic Stadtpark with its gilded statue of Johann Strauss, or head in the other direction to Prince Eugene's Belvedere Palace, a treasure trove of art spanning the centuries.

The focal landmark of Weiden is the elaborate Baroque church of Karlskirche.

Built in the 18th century, Karlskirche is an elegant, domed cathedral. There is a 32.5-meter long platform from which visitors can enjoy views of the exquisite frescos. Karlskirche is set within Karlsplatz and Resselpark park and garden.

👁 Sights

★ Belvedere Palace

CASTLE/PALACE | One of the most splendid pieces of Baroque architecture anywhere, the Belvedere Palace—actually two imposing palaces separated by a 17th-century French-style garden parterre—is one of the masterpieces of architect Lucas von Hildebrandt. Built outside the city fortifications between 1714 and 1722, the complex originally served as the summer palace of Prince Eugene of Savoy. Much later it became the home of Archduke Franz Ferdinand, whose assassination in 1914 precipitated World War I. Though the lower palace is impressive in its own right, it is the much larger upper palace, used for state receptions, banquets, and balls, that is acknowledged as Hildebrandt's

The gardens of the Belvedere Palace are among the the best baroque gardens in Austria, if not Europe, so allow time on your visit to simply wander the grounds of the complex.

masterpiece. The upper palace displays a wealth of architectural invention in its facade, avoiding the main design problems common to palaces: monotony on the one hand and pomposity on the other.

Hildebrandt's decorative manner here approaches the Rococo, that final style of the Baroque era when traditional classical motifs all but disappeared in a whirlwind of seductive asymmetric fancy. The main interiors of the palace go even further: columns are transformed into muscle-bound giants, pilasters grow torsos, capitals sprout great piles of symbolic imperial paraphernalia, and the ceilings are aswirl with ornately molded stucco. The result is the finest Rococo interior in the city.

Both the upper and lower palaces of the Belvedere are museums devoted to Austrian painting. The Belvedere's main attraction is the collection of 19th- and 20th-century Austrian paintings, centering on the work of Vienna's three preeminent early-20th-century artists:

Gustav Klimt, Egon Schiele, and Oskar Kokoschka. Klimt was the oldest, and by the time he helped found the Secession movement he had forged an idiosyncratic painting style that combined realistic and decorative elements in a way that was revolutionary. *The Kiss*—his greatest painting—is here on display. Schiele and Kokoschka went even further, rejecting the decorative appeal of Klimt's glittering abstract designs and producing works that ignored conventional ideas of beauty.

An ambitious 2016 European Union initiative brought 3-D technology to the Belvedere. The project, entitled AMBAVis (Access to Museums for Blind and Visually-Impaired Persons), transformed Klimt's *The Kiss* into a remarkable and unprecedented interactive experience. Finger-tracking technology allows viewers to scan the relief, prompting audio to play. ⊠ *Prinz-Eugen-Strasse 27, 3rd District/ Landstrasse* ☎ *01/795–57–134* ⊕ *www. belvedere.at* 🖾 *From €9* Ⓜ *U1, U2, or U4/ Karlsplatz; then Tram D or Tram 71.*

Belvedere 21

MUSEUM | The Belvedere's museum of contemporary art is housed in the structure originally built for the 1958 World Expo, the design of which won architect Karl Schwanzer the Grand Prix d'Architecture that year. The structure was modified and reopened in 2011 as a space to showcase the best of Austrian modern art of the past 70 years ⊠ *Arsenalstrasse 1, 3rd District/Landstrasse* ⊕ *www. belvedere.at* ☏ *€9* ⊘ *Closed Mon. and Tues.* Ⓜ *U1/ Südtirolerplatz; Tram D, 18 or O (station Quartier Belvedere).*

Fälschermuseum (*Museum of Art Fakes*)

MUSEUM | This museum is a must-see for those who like a bit of cunning cloak and dagger—an utterly unique collection that includes a myriad of magnificent forgeries in both arts and letters, and offers captivating backstories on how the faked pieces came to be. On display are fakes of Chagall and Rembrandt, as well as the infamous "Hitler Diaries" that were front-page news in the 1980s. ⊠ *Löwengasse 28, 3rd District/Landstrasse* ⊕ *www. faelschermuseum.com* ☏ *€6* ⊘ *Closed Mon.* Ⓜ *Tram 1 to Hetzgasse.*

Hundertwasserhaus

HOUSE | To see one of Vienna's most architecturally intriguing buildings, travel eastward from Schwedenplatz or Julius-Raab-Platz along Radetzkystrasse. Here you'll find the Hundertwasserhaus, a 52-apartment public-housing complex designed by the late Austrian avant-garde artist Friedensreich Hundertwasser, arguably Austria's most significant postmodernist artist. The complex looks like a colorful patchwork of gingerbread houses strung precariously together, and was highly criticized when it opened in 1985. Time heals all wounds, even imaginary assaults to the senses, and now the structure is a beloved thread of the Viennese architectural tapestry. It is across the street from the city's beloved Kunsthaus Wien, which also sprang from Hundertwasser's imagination.

⊠ *Löwengasse and Kegelgasse, 3rd District/Landstrasse* Ⓜ *U1 or U4/Schwedenplatz, then Tram N to Hetzgasse.*

★ Karlskirche

RELIGIOUS SITE | Dominating the Karlsplatz is one of Vienna's greatest buildings, the Karlskirche, dedicated to St. Charles Borromeo. This giant Baroque church is framed by enormous freestanding columns, mates to Rome's famous Trajan's Column. These columns may be out of keeping with the building as a whole, but were conceived with at least two functions in mind: one was to portray scenes from the life of the patron saint, carved in imitation of Trajan's triumphs, and thus help to emphasize the imperial nature of the building; and the other was to symbolize the Pillars of Hercules, suggesting the right of the Hapsburgs to their Spanish dominions, which the emperor had been forced to renounce. The end result is an architectural tour de force.

The Karlskirche was built in the early 18th century on what was then the bank of the River Wien. The church had its beginnings in a disaster. In 1713 Vienna was hit by a brutal outbreak of plague, and Emperor Charles VI made a vow: if the plague abated, he would build a church dedicated to his namesake, St. Charles Borromeo, the 16th-century Italian bishop who was famous for his ministrations to Milanese plague victims. In 1715 construction began, using an ambitious design by Johann Bernhard Fischer von Erlach that combined architectural elements from ancient Greece (the columned entrance porch), ancient Rome (the Trajanesque columns), contemporary Rome (the Baroque dome), and contemporary Vienna (the Baroque towers at either end). When it was finished, the church received decidedly mixed press. History, too, delivered a negative verdict: the Karlskirche spawned no imitations, and it went on to become one of European architecture's curiosities. Still, when seen lighted at night, the building is magical in its setting.

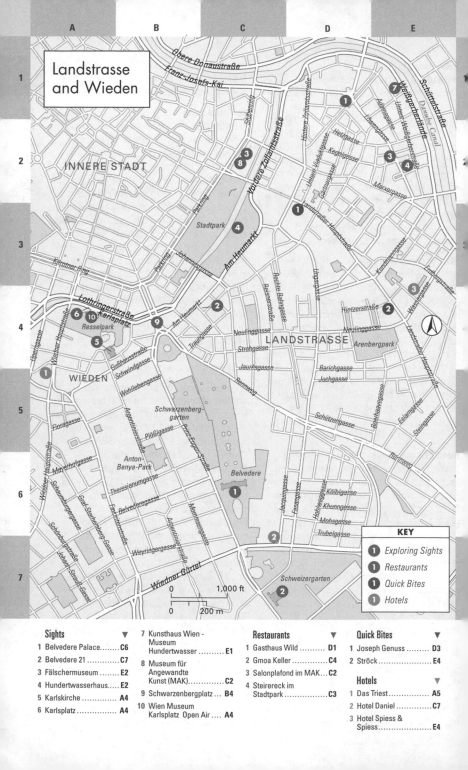

Landstrasse and Wieden

KEY
1 Exploring Sights
1 Restaurants
1 Quick Bites
1 Hotels

0   1,000 ft
0   200 m

The main interior of the church utilizes only the area under the dome and is conventional despite the unorthodox facade. The space and architectural detailing are typical High Baroque; the fine vault frescoes, by J. M. Rottmayr, depict St. Charles Borromeo imploring the Holy Trinity to end the plague. If you are not afraid of heights take the panorama elevator up into the sphere of the dome and climb the top steps to enjoy an unrivaled view to the heart of the city. ⊠ *Karlsplatz, 4th District/Wieden* ☏ *01/504–6187* ⊕ *www. karlskirche.at* ☞ *€8* Ⓜ *U1, U2, or U4 Karlsplatz.*

Karlsplatz

PLAZA | As with the Naschmarkt, Karlsplatz was formed when the River Wien was covered over at the turn of the 20th century. At the time, architect Otto Wagner expressed his frustration with the result—too large a space for a formal square and too small a space for an informal park—and the awkwardness is felt to this day. The buildings surrounding the Karlsplatz, however, are quite sure of themselves; the area is dominated by the classic Karlskirche, made less dramatic by the unfortunate reflecting pool with its Henry Moore sculpture, wholly out of place, in front. On the south side of the Resselpark, that part of Karlsplatz named for the inventor of the screw propeller for ships, stands the Technical University (1816–1818). In a house that occupied the space closest to the church, Italian composer Antonio Vivaldi died in 1741; a plaque marks the spot. On the north side, across the heavily traveled roadway, are the Künstlerhaus (built in 1881 and still in use as an exhibition hall) and the Musikverein. The latter, finished in 1869, is now home to the Vienna Philharmonic. The downstairs lobby and the two halls upstairs have been restored and glow with fresh gilding. The main hall has what may be the world's finest acoustics.

Some of Wagner's finest Secessionist work can be seen two blocks east on the northern edge of Karlsplatz. In 1893 Wagner was appointed architectural supervisor of the new Vienna City Railway, and the matched pair of small pavilions he designed, the Otto Wagner Stadtbahn Pavilions, at No. 1 Karlsplatz, in 1898 are among the city's most ingratiating buildings. Their structural framework is frankly exposed (in keeping with Wagner's belief in architectural honesty), but they are also lovingly decorated (in keeping with the Viennese fondness for architectural finery). The result is Jugendstil at its very best, melding plain and fancy with grace and insouciance. ⊠ *4th District/Wieden* Ⓜ *U1, U2, or U4/Karlsplatz.*

Kunsthaus Wien - Museum Hundertwasser

MUSEUM | This art museum mounts outstanding international exhibits in addition to showings of the vibrant works by avant-garde artist Friedensreich Hundertwasser. He designed this building, along with the nearby apartment building called Hundertwasserhaus. The building itself is pure Hundertwasser, a crayon box of colors, irregular floors, windows with trees growing out of them, and sudden architectural surprises, all of which make a wholly appropriate setting for modern art. ⊠ *Untere Weissgerberstrasse 13, 3rd District/Landstrasse* ☏ *01/712–0491–0* ⊕ *www.kunsthauswien.com* ☞ *€11 museum; €12 museum and current exhibit* Ⓜ *U1 or U4/Schwedenplatz, then Tram N or O to Radetzkyplatz.*

Museum für Angewandte Kunst (MAK)

(*Museum of Applied Arts*)
MUSEUM | This fascinating museum contains a large collection of Austrian furniture, porcelain, art objects, and priceless Oriental carpets. The Jugendstil display devoted to Josef Hoffmann and his Secessionist followers at the Wiener Werkstätte is particularly well done. The newest permanent collection

is based on Asian design, showcasing Japanese woodcuts, lacquer work, color stencil plates, and Chinese porcelain. The MAK also showcases changing exhibitions of contemporary works, and the museum shop sells furniture and other objects (including great bar accessories) designed by young local artists. ✉ *Stubenring 5, 1st District* ☎ *01/711–36–0* 🌐 *www.mak.at* 🎫 *€14* 🕒 *Closed Mon.* [M] *U3/Stubentor.*

Schwarzenbergplatz

PLAZA | The center of this square is marked by an oversize equestrian sculpture of Prince Schwarzenberg—he was a 19th-century field marshal for the imperial forces. See if you can guess which building is the newest—it's the one on the northeast corner (No. 3) at Lothringerstrasse, an exacting reproduction of a building destroyed by war damage in 1945 and dating only from the 1980s. The military monument occupying the south end of the square behind the fountain is the **Russian War Memorial,** set up at the end of World War II by the Soviets; the Viennese, remembering the Soviet occupation, call its unknown soldier the "unknown plunderer." South of the memorial is the stately **Schwarzenberg Palace,** designed as a summer residence by Johann Lukas von Hildebrandt in 1697 and completed by Fischer von Erlach, father and son. ✉ *3rd District/Landstrasse* [M] *Tram: Schwarzenbergplatz.*

Wien Museum Karlsplatz Open Air (*Museum of Viennese History*)

MUSEUM | Housed in an incongruously modern building at the east end of the Karlsplatz, this museum, which possesses Viennese historical artifacts and treasures (everything from 16th-century armor to paintings by Schiele and Klimt to the preserved facade of Otto Wagner's *Die Zeit* offices) is closed for renovation until roughly 2024. During renovations, the museum exterior will host rotating (and free!) open air exhibits surrounding the building. ✉ *Karlsplatz, 4th District/Wieden* ☎ *01/505–8747–0* 🌐 *www.wien-museum.at* [M] *U1, U2, or U4 Karlsplatz.*

🍴 Restaurants

Gasthaus Wild

$ | **AUSTRIAN** | The best place for a bite of traditional food near the Kunsthaus Wien and the Hundertwasser House is Gasthaus Wild. Formerly a wine tavern, it's now a down-to-earth beisl (the equivalent of a pub, also called a *gasthaus*), where the menu changes regularly but almost always features local dishes. **Known for:** wild game when in season; great wine list; extensive dessert menu. [$] *Average main: €17* ✉ *Radetzkyplatz 1, 3rd District/Landstrasse* ☎ *01/920–9477* 🌐 *www.gasthaus-wild.at* [M] *Tram: O/Radetzkyplatz.*

Gmoa Keller

$ | **AUSTRIAN** | One of the friendliest places in Vienna, this wood-panelled wonderful old cellar—just across the street from the Konzert Haus—offers some of the heartiest home cooking in town. Come here to enjoy dishes that hail from Carinthia, one of the best being the *Kas'nudeln* (potatoes and spinach pasta filled with cheese and onion), best served with green leaf salad. **Known for:** dishes from the Carinthia region of the country; cozy and gregarious atmosphere. [$] *Average main: €14* ✉ *Am Heumarkt 25, 3rd District/Landstrasse* ☎ *01/712–5310* 🌐 *www.gmoakeller.at* 🕒 *Closed Sun.* [M] *U4/Stadtpark.*

Salonplafond im MAK

$$$ | **AUSTRIAN** | Set within the Museum of Applied Arts (MAK), this warm and stylish restaurant offers fresh, locally grown fare under high, coffered ceilings and with furnishings and flatware to feed appetites for design. Everything is

either made on-site or commissioned from independent local enterprises. **Known for:** fresh and locally grown cuisine; large terrace overlooking green space; fresh and modern design. [$] *Average main: €28* ✉ *Museum of Applied Arts, Stubenring 5, 1st District* ☎ *01/226–0046* 🌐 *www.salonplafond.wien* [M] *U3/Stubentor.*

★ Steirereck im Stadtpark
$$$$ | **AUSTRIAN** | Considered one of the world's 50 best restaurants and holding two Michelin stars, this eatery is definitely the most raved-about place in Austria. Winning dishes include delicate wild boar's head with "purple haze" carrots, turbot in an avocado crust, or char in beeswax, yellow turnips, and cream. **Known for:** buzzy dishes using herbs from on-site rooftop garden; the more casual Meierei on the lower floor; selection of more than 120 cheeses. [$] *Average main: €70* ✉ *Stadtpark, Am Heumarkt 2A, 3rd District/Landstrasse* ☎ *01/713–3168* 🌐 *steirereck.at* 🕓 *Closed weekends* [M] *U4/Stadtpark.*

Coffee and Quick Bites

Joseph Genuss
$ | **BAKERY** | Each morning, the bread here is baked fresh—kneaded by hand—using what the owners call an ancient recipe that uses only organic ingredients. All of the breads are whole grain, and include varieties such as honey lavender, sourdough walnut, and sourdough pumpkinseed. **Known for:** amazing flavors of bread including honey lavender and sourdough walnut; delicious breakfast menu; bright and airy. [$] *Average main: €6* ✉ *Landstrasser Hauptstrasse 4, 3rd District/Landstrasse* ☎ *1710–2881* 🌐 *www.joseph.co.at.*

Ströck
$ | **AUSTRIAN** | Long known as a reliable haunt for breads and strudels, Ströck has multiple locations throughout the city. Open for evening and weekend meals, the eateries serve only organic, locally grown goods. **Known for:** popular with locals; good value for money; wide variety of bakery options. [$] *Average main: €5* ✉ *Landstrasser Hauptstrasse 82, 3rd District/Landstrasse* ☎ *01/204–39–99–93–057* 🌐 *www.stroeck.at.*

Hotels

Das Triest
$$$ | **HOTEL** | Transformed by Sir Terence Conran into an ultrasleek ocean liner, this design hotel was once a postal-coach station on the route between Vienna and the Italian port city of Trieste; the original cross vaulting remains in the lounges and in some suites. **Pros:** lovely courtyard garden; lively bar; decent breakfast included. **Cons:** some rooms on the small side; street-facing rooms may be noisy due to trams; street not very attractive. [$] *Rooms from: €210* ✉ *Wiedner Hauptstrasse 12, 4th District/Wieden* ☎ *01/589–180* 🌐 *www.dastriest.at* 🛏 *72 rooms* 🍴 *Free breakfast.*

Hotel Daniel
$$$ | **HOTEL** | For a decidedly unchainlike hotel experience, try the urban Daniel, which is decked out in industrial decor and puts the shower right in the room (the toilet has a separate space.) The hotel is good for those who like a casual vibe and minimalistic look. **Pros:** excellent access to the Belvedere; popular restaurant serving all day; Airstream trailer for rent. **Cons:** no closet: just a bench for your luggage; a 10-minute walk to sights; attracts a party crowd which can be loud. [$] *Rooms from: €180* ✉ *Landstrasser Gürtel 5, 3rd District/Landstrasse* ☎ *01/901–310* 🌐 *www.hoteldaniel.com* 🛏 *116 rooms* 🍴 *Free breakfast.*

Vienna's Trendiest Neighborhood

Paris has the Latin Quarter, London has Notting Hill, and the bohemian district in Vienna is the **Freihaus** sector in the 4th District (Wieden), one of Vienna's trendiest neighborhoods.

In the 17th century, Freihaus provided free housing to the city's poor, hence the name "Freihaus," which means Free House. The complex was destroyed in the Turkish siege of 1683, then rebuilt on a much larger scale, becoming arguably the largest housing project in Europe at the time. It was a city within a city, including shops and the old Theater auf der Wieden, in which Mozart's *The Magic Flute* premiered. A slow decline followed, spanning Franz Josef's reign from the mid-19th century to the early 20th century, with some of the area razed before World War I and finished off during World War II.

But in the late 1990s a group of savvy local merchants revitalized the area, opening funky art galleries, antiques shops, espresso bars, trendy restaurants, and boutiques. Freihaus is small, stretching from Karlsplatz to Kettenbrückengasse, which encompasses part of the Naschmarkt, the city's largest open-air market. Two of the best streets are Operngasse and Schleifmühlgasse.

★ Hotel Spiess & Spiess

$$ | B&B/INN | Considered by many to be the best B&B in Vienna, this small, family-run inn offers comfortable, spacious, and exquisitely furnished rooms. **Pros:** suites great for families; spacious rooms; on-site sauna. **Cons:** not in the city center; residential neighborhood lacks the flair of downtown; flight of stairs to climb to reception. $ *Rooms from:* ⊠ *Hainburgerstrasse 19, 3rd District/Landstrasse* ☎ *01/714–8505* ⊕ *www.spiess-vienna.at* 🛏 *22 rooms* ⭤ *Free breakfast.*

Nightlife

BARS

Café Malipop

CAFES—NIGHTLIFE | While most visitors come to Vienna for its elegant and grand coffeehouses, you should not miss an opportunity for a coffee or beer at a less prim and polished local institution like Café Malipop. This quirky, no frills spot has been open since 1979 and it is as much revered for its divebar warmth and abundance of character as for its excellent vinyl collection and strict owner, Frau Margit, who has a set of rules (i.e., no kissing) which must be followed by patrons. ⊠ *Ungargasse 10, 3rd District/Landstrasse* ☎ *01/713–3441.*

Johnnys

BARS/PUBS | Near the Naschmarkt, Johnny's is the classic, every-city-has-one good old Irish bar. Good beer, inexpensive meals, quiz nights, and live music make this pub a popular hangout. Note that it's cash only, and often filled with smokers. ⊠ *Schleifmühlgasse 11, 4th District/Wieden* ☎ *01/587–1921* ⊕ *www.johnnys-pub.at* Ⓜ *U4/Kettenbrückengasse.*

★ Sekt Comptoir

BARS/PUBS | This tiny sparkling wine bar exclusively pours bubbly from it's own Szigeti vineyard in Burgenland, a wine-focused region. It's a few steps away from the popular Naschmarkt. The vibe is jovial and friendly and bartenders are walking-talking encyclopedias of sparkling wine. ⊠ *Schleifmühlgasse 19, 4th District/Wieden* ☎ *06/644–325388* ⊕ *www.sektcomptoir.at* Ⓜ *U4/ Kettenbrückengasse.*

DANCE CLUBS
Club Schikaneder
MUSIC CLUBS | In the middle of the Frei-haus Quarter, the Schikaneder serves as both an independent, experimental movie theater and a very popular bar filled with the city's artists. It screens a few films daily (in original languages with German subtitles), hosts art exhibits, and offers first-class DJ lineups regularly. ⊠ *Marga-retenstrasse 22–24, 4th District/Wieden* ☎ *01/585–2867* ⊕ *www.schikaneder.at* Ⓜ *U1, U2, or U4/Karlsplatz.*

★ Club U
DANCE CLUBS | "U" stands for under-ground, and fittingly, Club U is located below one of the two Jugendstil pavilions that Otto Wagner built when designing Vienna's subway. One of the best dance halls for alternative music in the city, it has outdoor seating, live music, a great atmosphere, and excellent DJs. ⊠ *Karl-splatz, Künstlerhauspassage, 4th District/ Wieden* ☎ *01/505–9904* ⊕ *www.club-u.at* Ⓜ *U1, U2, or U4/Karlsplatz.*

Performing Arts

OPERA
★ Letztes Erfreuliches Operntheater
OPERA | What would *La Traviata* be like with two soloists and a piano? Or how about a *Tosca* where you can join in the chorus? Stefan Fleischhacker's Letztes Erfreuliches Operntheater (otherwise known as the Last Enjoyable Opera Theat-er, or L.E.O. for short) offers marvelously funny and entertaining performances of grand operas that are appropriate for audi-ences of all ages (and much shorter than their originals). For a small donation, bread

and wine are also available. ⊠ *Ungargasse 18, 3rd District/Landstrasse* ☎ *01/712–1427* ⊕ *www.theaterleo.at.*

Shopping

BOOKS
Babette's
BOOKS/STATIONERY | More than 2,000 cookbooks from every corner of the world are piled on every conceivable space in Bernadette Wörndl's shop. Exotic aromas linger in the air; Wörndl is skilled at creating superb dish-es, which she serves herself at the counter. Spices are also for sale, and cooking classes are held regularly (call to arrange an English class). ⊠ *Schleif-mühlgasse 17, at Mühlgasse, 4th Dis-trict/Wieden* ☎ *01/585–5165* ⊕ *www. babettes.at.*

CHRISTKINDLMÄRKTE
Karlsplatz Christkindlmärkte
OUTDOOR/FLEA/GREEN MARKETS | The Christ-mas market at Karlsplatz has some of the more refined stands in town, selling top-quality homemade wares. ⊠ *Karl-splatz, 4th District/Wieden.*

CLOTHING
Collins Hüte
CLOTHING | This is one of the Vienna's most historic and best sources for such accessories as scarves, gloves, and especially hats, from modern creations to traditional Austrian felt and feather hats. ⊠ *Opernpassage, 1st District* ☎ *01/587–1305* ⊕ *www.collins-hats.at.*

Flo Vintage
CLOTHING | For preworn fashions, enter this vintage world extraordinaire. Here you'll find pieces from 1880 through 1980, which might include that pearl-embroidered Charleston dress you always wanted, or a fabulous antique kimono. Besides bags, shoes,

and jewelry, there are also hats and even sheer silk stockings. ⊠ *Schleif-mühlgasse 15A, 4th District/Wieden* ☎ *01/586–0773* ⊕ *www.flovintage.com*.

Pregenzer

CLOTHING | The timeless fashions, shoes, and accessories here are either created by or selected by Jutta Pregenzer. Brands include those from Austrian, German, and Italian designers. ⊠ *Schleifmühl-gasse 4, 4th District/Wieden* ☎ *01/586–5758* ⊕ *www.pregenzer.com*.

GALLERIES

Gallery Georg Kargl

ART GALLERIES—ARTS | The Schleifmühl-gasse has recently emerged as one of Vienna's most renowned gallery districts. Among the top contemporary galleries here is this one, located inside a former print shop. ⊠ *Schleifmühlgasse 5, 4th District/Wieden* ☎ *01/585–4199* ⊕ *georg-kargl.com*.

GIFTS AND SOUVENIRS

★ gabarage upcycling design

GIFTS/SOUVENIRS | Old skis become coat stands, bowling pins turn into vases, traffic signs are transformed into lamps, and garbage bins find new lives as chairs here at the fabulously offbeat Gabarage. ⊠ *Schleifmühlgasse 6, 4th District/Wieden* ☎ *01/585–7632* ⊕ *www.gabarage.at*.

Chapter 6

NEUBAU, MARIAHILF, AND JOSEFSTADT

DISTRICTS 6, 7, AND 8

Updated by
Caroline Sieg

 Sights   Restaurants   Hotels   Shopping   Nightlife
★★★★★   ★★★★★   ★★★★★   ★★★★★   ★★★★★

NEIGHBORHOOD SNAPSHOT

TOP EXPERIENCES

■ **MuseumsQuartier:** Museum-hop, shop, linger at cafes, have lunch, have drinks, then museum-hop some more in the "MQ," Vienna's largest museum complex.

■ **Otto Wagner Houses:** The most popular residential buildings designed by Austria's favorite architect Otto Wagner can be found close to each other at Linke Wienzeile, next to Naschmarkt.

■ **Spittelberg Quarter:** Get lost in the cobbled, pedestrianized streets and alleys of one of Vienna's trendiest areas, home to the Spittelberg Christkindlmärkte.

■ **Coffee with Locals:** Indulge in a coffee and cake at Cafe Sperl, a casual but traditional Viennese coffeehouse beloved by locals.

■ **Cake by Oma:** The cozy and crowded Vollpension cafe hires grandmothers (and a few grandfathers) to bake and serve cakes and bridge communications with baked goods.

■ **Ammutsøn Craft Beer Dive:** Sample brews from Austrian and European craft breweries at this friendly spot tucked into a cobbled alley.

GETTING HERE

Neubau and Mariahif are best reached on the U4 via Pilgrimgasse, the U3 to Neubausegasse or Zieglergasse or the U2 to MuseumsQuartier. Josefstadt is easy to get to via the U6 to Josefstädterstrasse or the U2 to Rathaus.

PLANNING YOUR TIME

The area is busy with shoppers from Monday to Saturday, but this is also the best time to cruise the many boutiques. The MuseumsQuartier area is liveliest on the weekends. Sundays are great if you want to wander around without the shopping crowds, while Neubau is loud and lively on weekend evenings.

QUICK BITES

■ **Drechsler.** Lively and friendly hangout with international nibbles next to the Naschmarkt. ✉ *Linke Wienzeile 22, Mariahilf* ⊕ *www.drechsler-wien.at* Ⓜ *U4/Kettenbrückengasse.*

■ **Ulrich.** Serving coffee and cake plus cheese plates, soups, salads, flatbreads, and small plates, the convivial atmosphere and friendly vibes are always a treat. ✉ *Sankt-Ulrichs-Platz 1, Neubau* ⊕ *ulrichwien.at* Ⓜ *U2/3/Volkstheater.*

■ **Bao Bar.** Classic baos, kimchi fries, and rice bowls are top notch—and spicy if you request it—at the spot that attracts both students and busy shoppers. ✉ *Zollergasse 2, Neubau* ⊕ *www.baobar.at* Ⓜ *U3/Zieglergasse.*

PAUSE HERE

Stock up on cheese-stuffed peppers, pfefferoni, falafel, appel strudel, fermented grape juice, coffees, and myriad snack samples from Naschmarkt's delicious stalls and then take your feast out of the market to a bench in Alfred-Grünwald-Park, just across the street.

Just beyond the city center, Vienna's 7th District, Neubau, is often referred to as Vienna's coolest and most bohemian neighborhood. The streets are filled with indie boutiques, galleries, vintage shops, and cool cafes and populated with the accompanying trendy creatives and students.

Vienna's most cutting-edge art complex lies just beyond the two sandstone giants of the Kunsthistorisches Museum (filled with centuries of art) and Naturhistorisches Museum (focusing on natural history) set on the Heldenplatz, the huge square in front of the Hofburg. The MuseumsQuartier is made up of several galleries showing art ranging from Expressionist to modern art to avant-garde. There's even a breathtaking museum for children. Hipsters flock to the cafés and restaurants in and around the former 18th-century riding stables.

When you exit MuseumsQuartier, walk up Burggasse to Spittelberggasse, where you will find the Spittelberg Quarter and its Baroque and Biedermeier buildings. Emperor Josef II supposedly frequented the neighborhood's "houses of pleasure." A plaque at the Witwe Bolte restaurant on Gutenberggasse reminds strollers that his majesty was thrown out of one establishment during a clandestine visit.

Sitting between Wieden and Neubau and backing onto the MuseumsQuartier, Mariahilf, the 6th District, is a little more residential than its neighbor, but still quietly trendy. Densely populated with a diverse population, this neighborhood is full of cultural activities, bookstore-cafés

and mellow, low-lit bars where you can linger into the early morning hours. Most visitors linger on Mariahilferstrasse, Vienna's main shopping street packed with all the High Street brands. Head to Gumpendorfstrasse to uncover the indie side of this district.

Located near Vienna City Hall, Vienna's 8th District, Josefstadt, is the smallest of Vienna's 23 districts and was named after the Holy Roman Emperor Joseph I. What it lacks in size, it makes up for in elegance as one of Vienna's most architecturally impressive districts. Here, you'll find a quiet residential vibe close to all the city-center action.

 Sights

Architekturzentrum Wien (*Vienna Architecture Center*)
MUSEUM | Besides the permanent show of Austrian architecture in the 20th and 21st centuries, an Encyclopaedia of Architects featuring more than 1000 master builders, urban planners, and theorists who did work in Vienna from 1770 to 1945 and an impressive image archive of photographs tracing Austrian architecture from 1980 to 2005, the center holds major exhibitions presenting the breadth of architecture history

Hundreds of masterworks of Austrian modern art collected by the passionate art lover Dr. Rudolf Leopold are shown in the Leopold Museum near the Imperial Palace.

and visions of what is to come. ⊠ *MuseumsQuartier, Museumsplatz 1, 7th District/Neubau* ☎ *01/522–3115* ⊕ *www.azw.at* ⊠ *€9* Ⓜ *U2/MuseumsQuartier; U2 or U3/Volkstheater.*

Dritte Mann Museum (*Third Man Museum*)

MUSEUM | Close to the Naschmarkt, this shrine for film-noir aficionados offers an extensive private collection of memorabilia dedicated to the classic film, *The Third Man,* directed by Carol Reed and shot entirely on location in Vienna. Authentic exhibits include cinema programs, autographed cards, movie and sound recordings, and first editions of Graham Greene's novel, which was the basis of the screenplay. Also here is the original zither used by Anton Karas to record the film's music, which started a zither boom in the '50s. In the reading corner, you can browse through historic newspaper articles about the film. Note that the museum is only open on Saturday, from 2 to 6. ⊠ *Pressgasse 25, 4th District/Wieden* ☎ *01/586–4872* ⊕ *www.3mpc.*

net ⊠ *€9.50* ⊙ *Closed Sun.–Fri.* Ⓜ *U4/Kettenbrückengasse.*

Haydnhaus (*Joseph Haydn House*)

MUSIC | Joseph Haydn spent the last twelve years of his life at this house and so it is fitting that the permanent exhibition at his final residence-turned-museum focuses on the last years of the composer's life. The museum is small but offers insight into the Vienna of Haydn's last days as well as an opportunity to stand where one of the world's greatest composers stood and imagine him at work in this very space. You'll see his fortepiano and his clavichord (which was later owned by Brahms), as well as medals, certificates, and gifts Haydn had received and displayed with pride. The small garden has been recreated according to historical models, so you can sit here and imagine the great master admiring his fruit trees as he created melodies. Haydn bought the house—which was then considered to be in the suburbs—and added another floor, where his valet stayed. He moved in at the age of 65 in 1797 and lived here until his death on May 31, 1809. He was the most famous composer in all of Europe in the final years of his life and displays on the ground floor of the house show portraits and comments from his many famous visitors. These last years were also one of the most creatively productive periods of his life; Haydn created the two oratorios "The Creation" (1796–1798) and "The Seasons" (1799–1801) while living here. There's a first-edition score of the latter on display. ✉ *Haydngasse 19, 6th District/ Mariahilf* 🕾 *01/596–1307* ⊕ *www.wien-museum.at/en/locations/haydnhaus* 🚇 *€5* Ⓜ *U4/Pilgramgasse or U3/Zieglergasse.*

Hofmobiliendepot (*Imperial Furniture Depot*)

MUSEUM | In the days of the Hapsburg Empire, palaces remained practically empty if the ruling family was not in residence. Cavalcades laden with enough furniture to fill a palace would set out in anticipation of a change of scene, while another caravan accompanied the royal party, carrying everything from traveling thrones to velvet-lined portable toilets. Much of this furniture is on display here, allowing a glimpse into everyday court life. The upper floors contain re-created rooms from the Biedermeier to the Jugendstil periods, and document the tradition of furniture making in Vienna. Explanations are in German and English. ✉ *Mariahilferstrasse 88, entrance on Andreasgasse, 7th District/Neubau* 🕾 *01/524–3357* ⊕ *www.hofmobiliende-pot.at* 🚇 *€10.50* 🕓 *Closed Mon.* Ⓜ *U3 Zieglergasse/follow signs to Otto-Bauer-Gasse/exit Andreasgasse.*

Kunsthalle Wien (*Vienna Art Gallery*)

MUSEUM | The gigantic rooms here are used for temporary exhibitions of avant-garde art, including photography, video, film, and new-media projects. The museum prides itself on finding artists who break down the borders between art genres and explore the connection between art and social change. ✉ *MuseumsQuartier, Museumsplatz 1, 7th District/Neubau* 🕾 *01/521–8933* ⊕ *www.kunsthallewien.at* 🚇 *€8* Ⓜ *U2 MuseumsQuartier; U2 or U3/ Volkstheater.*

Leopold Museum

MUSEUM | Filled with pieces amassed by Rudolf and Elizabeth Leopold, the Leopold contains one of the world's greatest collections of Austrian painter Egon Schiele, as well as impressive works by Gustav Klimt and Oskar Kokoschka. Other artists worth noting are Josef Dobrowsky, Anton Faistauer, and Richard Gerstl. Center stage is held by Schiele (1890–1918), who died young, along with his wife and young baby, in the Spanish flu pandemic of 1918. His colorful, appealing landscapes are here, but all eyes are invariably drawn to the artist's tortured depictions of nude mistresses, orgiastic self-portraits, and provocatively sexual couples, all elbows and organs. ✉ *MuseumsQuartier, Museumsplatz 1, 7th District/Neubau* 🕾 *01/525–700* ⊕ *www.leopoldmuseum. org* 🚇 *€14* 🕓 *Closed Mon. and Tues. Sept.–May* Ⓜ *U2 MuseumsQuartier; U2 or U3/Volkstheater.*

mumok (*Museum Moderner Kunst Stiftung Ludwig*)

MUSEUM | In a sleek edifice constructed of dark stone, the Museum moderner Kunst Stiftung Ludwig Wien (mumok) houses the national collection of 20th-century art. Spread over eight floors, the collection is largely a bequest of Peter Ludwig, a billionaire industrialist who collected top-notch modern art. The top works here are of the American pop-art school, but all the trends of the last century, from Nouveau Réalisme to Viennese Actionism, vie for your attention. Names include René Magritte, Max Ernst, Andy Warhol, Jackson Pollock, Cy Twombly, and Nam June Paik, to name a few. ✉ *MuseumsQuartier, Museumsplatz 1, 7th District/Neubau* 🕾 *01/525–000* ⊕ *www.mumok.at* 🚇 *€13* Ⓜ *U2/Muse-umsQuartier; U2 or U3/Volkstheater.*

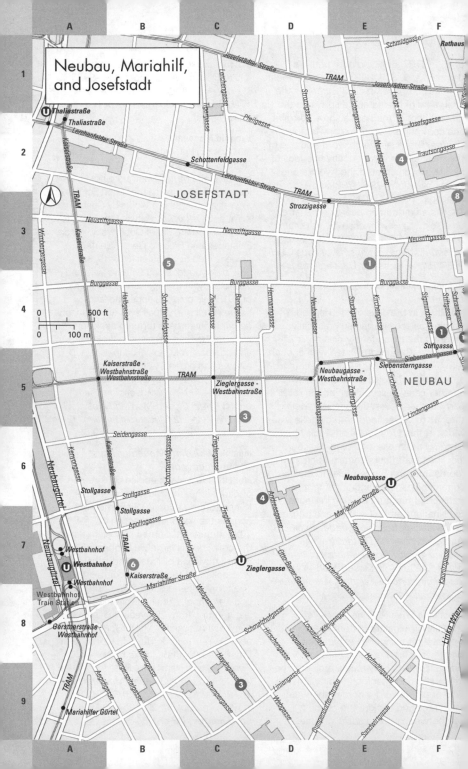

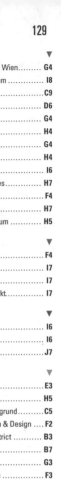

Sights ▼

Restaurants ▼

Quick Bites ▼

Hotels ▼

★ **MuseumsQuartier** (*Museum Quarter*)
MUSEUM | **FAMILY** | The MQ—as many call it—is a sprawling collection of galleries housed in what was once the Imperial Court Stables, the 260-year-old Baroque complex designed by Fischer von Erlach. Where once 900 cavalry horses were housed, now thousands of masterworks of the 20th and 21st centuries are exhibited, all in a complex that is architecturally an expert and subtle blending of historic and cutting-edge. The Architekturzentrum, Kunsthalle, Leopold Museum, mumok, and ZOOM Kinder Museum are all part of the MuseumsQuartier, and the Quartier21 showcases up-and-coming artists and musicians in the huge Fischer von Erlach Wing. Modern-art lovers will find it easy to spend at least an entire day here, and with several cafés, a lovely inner courtyard perfect for lounging and people-watching, restaurants, gift shops, and bookstores, you won't even need to venture anywhere else. ✉ *Museumsplatz 1, 7th District/Neubau* ☎ *01/523–5881* ⊕ *www.mqw.at* 🎫 *€13 to €34* Ⓜ *U2/MuseumsQuartier; U2 or U3/Volkstheater.*

Naschmarkt
MARKET | The area between Linke and Rechte Wienzeile is home to the Naschmarkt, Vienna's largest and most famous outdoor produce market. It's certainly one of Europe's great open-air markets, where packed rows of polished and stacked fruits and vegetables compete for visual appeal against stacks fragrant spices, redolent of Asia or the Middle East. Come for the atmosphere and the exotic prices, but note that the prices for meats, fruits, vegetables and cheeses here tend to be higher than other places in the city. Wine stores and gourmet food shops round out the offerings. In winter, many stalls shorten their hours. On Saturday, a lively flea market takes place at the tail end of the market. Be sure you get the correct change and watch the scales when your goods are weighed. ✉ *Between Linke and Rechte Wienzeile, 4th District/Wieden* ⊕ *www. wienernaschmarkt.eu* Ⓜ *U1, U2, or U4/Karlsplatz (follow signs to Secession).*

Otto Wagner Houses
HOUSE | The apartment houses that line the Wienzeile are an attractive, if rather ordinary, lot, but two stand out: **Linke Wienzeile 38 and 40**—the latter better known as the "Majolica House"—designed (1898–1899) by the grand old man of Viennese fin-de-siècle architecture, Otto Wagner. A good example of what Wagner was rebelling against can be seen next door, at **Linke Wienzeile 42**, where decorative enthusiasm has blossomed into Baroque-revival hysteria. Wagner banished classical decoration and introduced a new architectural simplicity, with flat exterior walls and plain, regular window treatments meant to reflect the orderly layout of the apartments behind them. There the simplicity ended. For exterior decoration, he turned to his younger Secessionist cohorts Joseph Olbrich and Koloman Moser, who designed the ornate Jugendstil patterns of red-majolica-tile roses (No. 40) and gold stucco medallions (No. 38) that gloriously brighten the facades of the adjacent house—so much so that their Baroque-period neighbor is ignored. The houses are privately owned. ✉ *Linke Wienzeile, 6th District/Mariahilf* Ⓜ *U1, U2, or U4/Karlsplatz.*

Spittelberg Quarter
HISTORIC SITE | The Spittelberg is like a slice of Old Vienna, a perfectly preserved little enclave that allows you to experience the 18th century by strolling along cobblestone pedestrian streets lined with pretty Baroque town houses. The quarter—one block northwest of Maria-Theresien-Platz off the Burggasse—offers a fair visual idea of the Vienna that existed outside the city walls a century ago. Most buildings have been replaced, but the engaging 18th-century survivors at Burggasse 11 and 13 are adorned with religious and secular decorative

The Neue City

Early one day in 1911, Emperor Franz Josef started out on a morning drive from the Hofburg, when he was stunned to come upon the defiantly plain Looshaus, constructed just opposite the Michaelerplatz entrance to the imperial palace. Never again, it was said, did the royal carriage use the route, so offensive was this modernist building to His Imperial Highness. One can only imagine the emperor's reaction to the Haas-Haus, built in 1985 on Stephansplatz. Here, across from the Gothic cathedral of St. Stephen's, famed architect Hans Hollein designed a complex whose elegant curved surfaces and reflecting glass interact beautifully with its environment. The architecture proved an intelligent alternative to the demands of historicism on the one hand and aggressive modernism on the other.

This balancing act has always been a particular challenge in Vienna. For a few critics, the Gaudiesque eccentricities of the late Friedensreich Hundertwasser did the trick (besides the Kunsthaus museum he is also responsible for the multicolor, golden-globe-top central heating tower that has become almost as much a part of the skyline as St. Stephen's spire). But for all their charm, they have now been overshadowed by the Viennese modernism of today. By far the most exciting urban undertaking has to be the Spittelau Viaducts, just across from the Hundertwasser power plant. This revitalization plan for the Wiener Gürtel, perhaps Vienna's busiest thoroughfare, includes public-housing apartments, offices, and artists'

studios that interact with the arched bays of the viaduct, a landmarked structure built by Otto Wagner. Responsible for the staggering three-part complex, partly perched on stilts, is star architect Zaha Hadid. A pedestrian and bicycle bridge connects the whole project to the University of Business, the North Railway Station, and the Danube Canal.

A discreet example of Vienna's new architecture is the vast Museums-Quartier. Hidden behind the Baroque facade of the former imperial stables, the design by Laurids and Manfred Ortner uses its enclosed space to set up a counterpoint between Fischer von Erlach's riding school and the imposing new structures built to house the Leopold Museum and the Modern Art Museum. From the first, old and new collide: to enter the complex's Halle E + G, you pass below the Emperor's Loge, whose double-headed imperial eagles now form a striking contrast to a silver-hue steel double staircase. Other important projects—notably the underground Jewish history museum on Judenplatz (look for a stark cube memorial by English sculptor Rachel Whiteread); the Gasometer complex, a planned community recycled from the immense brick drums of 19th-century gasworks; the ellipse-shape Uniqa Tower on the Danube Canal designed by Heinz Neumann, and the ecologically responsible Donau City—are among the architectural highlights on tours now organized by the Architecture Center (AZW) of the Museums-Quartier; its maps and brochures can be used for self-guided tours.

sculpture, the latter with a niche statue of St. Joseph, the former with cherubic work-and-play bas-reliefs. Around holidays, particularly Easter and Christmas, the Spittelberg quarter, known for arts and handicrafts, hosts seasonal markets offering unique and interesting wares. Promenaders will also find art galleries and lots of restaurants. ✉ *Off Burggasse, 7th District/Neubau* [M] *U2 or U3/ Volkstheater.*

TBA21 (*Thyssen-Bornemisza Art Contemporary*)
ARTS VENUE | While her father, Baron H. H. Thyssen-Bornemisza, amassed one of the greatest collections of Old Master paintings, Francesca von Habsburg has chosen to spearhead Austria's avant-garde scene at her TBA21, short for Thyssen-Bornemisza Art Contemporary. New media installations, puppet rock operas, and exhibits by hot new international artists keep people talking. ✉ *Köstlergasse 1, 6th District/Mariahilf* ☎ *01/513–98560* 🌐 *tba21.org.*

ZOOM Kindermuseum (*ZOOM Children's Museum*)
MUSEUM | **FAMILY** | Kids of all ages enjoy this outstanding museum, where they can experience the fine line between the real and virtual worlds, making screenplays come to life by becoming directors, sound technicians, authors, and actors. For the little ones there's an "ocean" where kids and parents enter a play area inhabited by magical underwater creatures. The museum operates like little workshops, with the staff very hands-on and available to the children. You must book your tickets for a specific admission time, so reserve via the website before you go. ✉ *MuseumsQuartier, Museumsplatz 1, 7th District/Neubau* ☎ *01/524–7908* 🌐 *www.kindermuseum.at* 🎫 *€16–18 for family ticket* 🕓 *Closed Mon.* [M] *U2/MuseumsQuartier; U2 or U3/ Volkstheater.*

Noshing at Naschmarkt 🍴

There are so many enticing snack stands in the Naschmarkt that it's hard to choose. A host of Turkish stands offer juicy *döner* sandwiches—thinly sliced, pressed lamb, turkey, or veal with onions and a yogurt sauce in a freshly baked roll. A number of Asian noodle and sushi stalls offer quick meals, and many snack bars offer Viennese dishes. At the Karlsplatz end of the Naschmarkt is the Nordsee glass-enclosed seafood hut.

🍴 Restaurants

Amerlingbeisl
$ | **AUSTRIAN** | If you're lucky, you can snag a table in the idyllic garden of this low-key pub, hidden away inside a delightful Biedermeyer cobbled courtyard. The staff is young, hip, and carefee, and will gladly serve you breakfast until 3pm—both traditional Viennese-style plus vegan and vegetarian options. **Known for:** hip and young crowds; large breakfast buffet on Sunday; weekly cocktail specials. [$] *Average main: €13* ✉ *Stiftgasse 8, 7th District/Neubau* ☎ *1/526–1660.*

Do-An
$ | **INTERNATIONAL** | This bustling restaurant in a stall along the Naschmarkt is a prime place to stop for a bite and watch the crowds go by. The menu is as diverse as the customers, and includes various Turkish mainstays, such as tzatziki and falafel, and a variety of international choices. **Known for:** mostly Turkish cuisine, including falafel and tzatziki; fun market atmosphere; breakfast until 4pm. [$] *Average main: €11* ✉ *Naschmarkt Stand 412–415, 6th District/Mariahilf* ☎ *01/585–8253* 🌐 *www.doan.at.*

Vienna's best-known market, Naschmarkt, has around 120 market stands and restaurants for a colorful culinary offering.

Drechsler

$ | **AUSTRIAN** | This lively cafe-restaurant, conveniently located next to the Naschmarkt, is best known for its breakfast (served until 4 pm every day) and for its classic coffee house feel with contemporary decor (one wall is decorated with ripped posters.) Lunch options like baked sweet potato, homemade sage gnocchi, and Styrian baked chicken (a classic dish from Styria, a region in Austria known for its wine and food) hold their own to brunch favorites like avocado toast with poached eggs and salmon and blueberry pancakes. It's a popular stop for a late-afternoon cocktail or late-night coffee. **Known for:** excellent breakfasts; open late; popular with a cool crowd. [$] *Average main: €12* ✉ *Linke Wienzeile 22, 6th District/Mariahilf* ☎ *01/581-2044* 🌐 *www.drechsler-wien.at.*

★ Neni am Naschmarkt

$ | **ISRAELI** | Smack in the middle of of the Naschmarkt, Neni is a perennially-popular spot run by an Israeli-Austrian family, serving up Israeli-Middle-Eastern specialties from tabouli to lamb, plus a few fusion dishes (think bok choy and salmon with sesame tahini). They've beeen so successful that they now have locations in other cities across Europe and a few cookbooks, but this is the original location. **Known for:** great Naschmarkt location; small plates alongside full meals; local hotspot. [$] *Average main: €12* ✉ *Naschmarkt , Stand 510, 6th District/Mariahilf* ☎ *01/585–2020* 🌐 *www.neni.at* [M] *U4/Pilgrimgasse.*

Coffee and Quick Bites

★ Cafe Sperl

$ | **CAFÉ** | Coffee in Vienna is designed to be savored and enjoyed, and one of the most splendid places in Vienna to do just that is at the Sperl. Featured in Hollywood films *A Dangerous Method* and *Before Sunrise,* the venerable café—commandeered way back when as the café for artists—is more than just a fantastically pretty face. **Known for:** the go-to café for artists; live music on Sunday; great people-watching at the window tables. [$] *Average main: €12*

✉ *Gumpendorferstrasse 11, 6th District/ Mariahilf* ☎ *01/586–4158* 🌐 *www.cafesperl.at* ⏲ *Closed Sun. in July and Aug.*

Phil

$ | **AUSTRIAN** | Cozy yet vast, this place near the Naschmarkt bucks the trend of the grand, old-school Vienna coffeehouses and offers itself up as a café, shop, and salon all in one. Inside you'll find shelves with a constant rotation of books, DVDs, and vinyl records, all for sale. **Known for:** unique take on the Vienna coffeehouse; everything from books to furniturefor sale; evening lectures and films. [$] *Average main: €7* ✉ *Gumpendorferstrasse 10, Vienna* ☎ *1/581–0489* 🌐 *www.phil.info.*

★ Vollpension

$ | **CAFÉ** | *Oma* is the word for Grandma in German, and if you ever wished you had one of your own to make you homemade *kuchen* (cake) or simple, hearty Austrian meals, make a beeline for Vollpension. This delightful cafe-restaurant employs Austrian grandmas (and a few grandpas) who make their favorite cake recipes for you to enjoy. **Known for:** authentic grandmas baking cakes and chatting; delicious cakes and coffee; very popular cafe. [$] *Average main: €10* ✉ *Schleifmühlgasse 16, 4th District/Wieden* ☎ *01/585–0464* 🌐 *www.vollpension.wien* [M] *Karlsplatz.*

Hotels

Altstadt

$$$ | **HOTEL** | When contemporary-arts patron Otto E. Wiesenthal hired premier Italian architect Matteo Thun to revamp this lodging, the results were exquisitely decorated, sensuous chambers oozing atmosphere from the Vienna era of Freud and Klimt. **Pros:** breakfast included in room rate; amazing private art collection; excellent staff. **Cons:** small reception area; outside the city center; building is not exclusive to the hotel. [$] *Rooms from: €179* ✉ *Kirchengasse 41, 7th District/ Neubau* ☎ *01/522–6666* 🌐 *www.altstadt.at* 🛏 *45 rooms* 🍴 *Free breakfast.*

Das Tyrol

$$$$ | **HOTEL** | On a bustling Mariahilferstrasse corner, this small, luxurious hotel is a good choice for those who want to be next door to the MuseumsQuartier and near some fun shopping, too. **Pros:** plentiful breakfast; good location for shoppers; lots to see for art lovers. **Cons:** rooms differ greatly in size; busy street not so attractive; no restaurant. [$] *Rooms from: €310* ✉ *Mariahilferstrasse 15, 6th District/Mariahilf* ☎ *01/587–5415* 🌐 *www.das-tyrol.at* 🛏 *30 rooms* 🍴 *Free breakfast.*

Hotel am Brillantengrund

$ | **HOTEL** | The eclectic hotel—picture a 1950s theme in a 19th-century building—is a popular hangout for local creatives who mingle seamlessly with guests, making it difficult to distinguish between who's staying and those who come for breakfast or a drink. **Pros:** excellent Filipino restaurant on-site; rates include great breakfast; characterful and charming design. **Cons:** no air-conditioning; minimal toiletries; small bathrooms. [$] *Rooms from: €110* ✉ *Bandgasse 4, 7th District/Neubau* ☎ *01/523–3662* 🌐 *www.brillantengrund.com* 🛏 *35 rooms* 🍴 *Free breakfast.*

Hotel Rathaus Wein & Design

$$$ | **HOTEL** | Rooms at this wine-themed boutique hotel are named after Austria's top winemakers, with a bottle of their latest vintage on display (sorry, it's not included in the room price). **Pros:** top-notch staff with extensive wine knowledge; local wine excursions available; excellent buffet breakfast. **Cons:** no restaurant; no in-room coffee machine but you can call for complimentary coffee service; economy rooms are a tad cramped. [$] *Rooms from: €179* ✉ *Langegasse 13, 8th District/Josefstadt* ☎ *01/400–1122* 🌐 *www.hotel-rathaus-wien.at* 🛏 *39 rooms* 🍴 *Free breakfast.*

Max Brown 7th District

$$ | **HOTEL** | A hip hotel in hip Neubau, the Max Brown offers bright, spacious rooms decorated with plants, record players, and a mix of midcentury and modern furnishings and art. **Pros:** quirky, cool design; excellent breakfast; Award-winning Seven North restaurant on-site. **Cons:** common areas can get busy; some noise carries into rooms; no minibar. [$] *Rooms from: €127* ✉ *Schottenfeldgasse 74, 7th District/Neubau* ☎ *01/376–1070* 🌐 *maxbrownhotels.com/7th-district-vienna* 🛏 *144 rooms* 🍴 *No meals* [M] *U6/Burggasse-Stadthalle.*

Ruby Marie

$ | **HOTEL** | Located just off the lively Mariahilferstrasse, the Ruby Marie is one of three Ruby hotel properties in Vienna. **Pros:** a variety of public spaces; funky vibe; good shopping location. **Cons:** neighborhood isn't relaxing; staff might be too laid-back for some; no separate shower space. [$] *Rooms from: €90* ✉ *Kaiserstrasse 2–4, 7th District/Neubau* ☎ *01/205–639–700* 🌐 *www.ruby-hotels.com* 🛏 *186 rooms* 🍴 *Free breakfast.*

Sans Souci Hotel

$$$$ | **HOTEL** | "Sans souci" means "without worry" and you truly do shed all worries and traveler weariness as you step through the doors of this elegant boutique hotel in the MuseumsQuartier. **Pros:** nice summer terrace; great location near Mariahilferstrasse's trendy shops and within the MuseumsQuartier; great spa, bar, and restaurant. **Cons:** beige-and-wood color schemes are a bit bland; minimum six nights for apartments; rooms on the lower floors may have tram noise. [$] *Rooms from: €280* ✉ *Burggasse 2, 7th District/Neubau* ☎ *01/522–2520* 🌐 *www.sanssouci-wien.com* 🛏 *63 rooms* 🍴 *Free breakfast.*

★ 25hours Hotel Wien

$$$ | **HOTEL** | A circus theme predominates at this bohemian addition to the city's lodging scene, each room containing exceptionally illustrated wallpaper of old-time big-top themes by German artist Olaf Hajek and quirky vintage furnishings. **Pros:** surprising and fun design and atmosphere; trendy rooftop bar with city views; nice bikes with curated bike routes of the city for guests. **Cons:** rooftop bar gets overcrowded; may not appeal to those looking for a more conservative stay; standard rooms can feel cramped. [$] *Rooms from: €210* ✉ *Lerchenfelder Strasse 1–3, 7th District/Neubau* ☎ *01/521–510* 🌐 *www.25hours-hotels.com/hotels/wien/museumsquartier* 🛏 *217 rooms* 🍴 *No meals.*

Nightlife

BARS

★ Ammutsøn Craft Beer Dive

BREWPUBS/BEER GARDENS | The excellent craft beer bar serves up rotating beers on tap from a variety of microbreweries. There's usually at least one Austrian brew on tap alongside a United Nations of beers, and despite their name, the brick and wood-filled space has a vibe that's more rustic and cozy than divey. Staff are incredibly knowledgable and always happy to give you a taste before committing to a full mug. ✉ *Barnabitengasse 10, 6th District/Mariahilf* 🌐 *www.ammutson.com* [M] *U3/Neubaugasse.*

Café Carina

BARS/PUBS | In a cavernous subway station, Café Carina is dazzling in its dinginess. It's offbeat, artistic, and action packed—you get the sense that anything can happen here, from an air-guitar competition to an evening of 1980s hits. On weekends expect it to be packed. ✉ *Josefstädterstrasse 84 at Stadtbahnbogen, 8th District/Josefstadt* ☎ *01/4064322* 🌐 *www.cafe-carina.at* [M] *U6/Josefstädterstrasse.*

DANCE CLUBS
Café Leopold
CAFES—NIGHTLIFE | In the MuseumsQuartier, this café-bar is hidden inside the large, white cube that is the Leopold Museum. Tables are scattered outside on the plaza at night, and in summer the restaurant vibe morphs into a bar and trendy hangout in the evenings. ⊠ *Leopold Museum, Museumsplatz 1, 7th District/Neubau* ☎ *01/522–2391* ⊕ *www.cafeleopold.wien* Ⓜ *U2 or U3/MuseumsQuartier.*

🎭 Performing Arts

DANCE
Tanzquartier Wien (*DanceQuarter Vienna*)
DANCE | Austria's foremost center for contemporary dance performances is Tanzquartier Wien. The season runs from September to June, and is followed by the so-called Factory Season, when the center concentrates solely on the projects presented in its dance studios. ⊠ *Museumsplatz 1, 7th District/Neubau* ☎ *01/581–3591* ⊕ *www.tqw.at.*

FILM
English Cinema Haydn
FILM | One of the city's original movie theaters, this family-run place shows blockbuster movies (some in 3-D) on four screens. ⊠ *Mariahilferstrasse 57, 6th District/Mariahilf* ☎ *01/587–2262* ⊕ *www. haydnkino.at.*

OPERA
Theater an der Wien
OPERA | This beautiful Rococo-style historic theater located in Mariahilf is more than 200 years old. It was used and abused for decades as a contemporary musical venue, but now the building—which is closely linked to Beethoven, who lived here—has renewed its role as an opera house, attracting an international crowd. It's open year-round, and hosts a premiere nearly every month. The selection of works performed here is tremendous, including Janáček, Prokofiev, Britten, Handel, Monteverdi, Rossini, and Bach. ⊠ *Linke Wienzeile 6, 6th District/Mariahilf* ☎ *01/58885, 01/588–301010* ⊕ *www.theater-wien.at.*

Theater in der Josefstadt
THEATER | The Theater in der Josefstadt, the oldest theater still in operation, stages classical and modern works year-round in a space once run by the great producer and teacher Max Reinhardt. The theater had, of late, been seeming to gather layers of dust, but happily director Herbert Föttinger has restored its reputation for more avant-garde and daring productions. ⊠ *Josefstädterstrasse 26, 8th District/Josefstadt* ☎ *01/42–700–300* ⊕ *www. josefstadt.org.*

Vienna's English Theater
THEATER | For English-language theater—mainly classic comedies and dramas—head for this cozy and charming venue. The season runs early September to early July. ⊠ *Josefsgasse 12, 8th District/Josefstadt* ☎ *01/402–1260* ⊕ *www.englishtheatre.at.*

THEATER
Raimund Theater
THEATER | Originally built as a theater for the people, the Raimund staged popular folk plays in its early days. It then moved on to opera for a spell before becoming a leading venue for long-running musicals. Here, lovers of the genre can enjoy such hits as *Hair* and *Mamma Mia!* ⊠ *Wallgasse 18, 6th District/Mariahilf* ☎ *01/58885, 01/588–301010* ⊕ *www. musicalvienna.at.*

👜 Shopping

BOOKS AND STATIONERY
Sous-Bois
BOOKS/STATIONERY | Lovely cards, notepads, planners, pens, and even art books can be found in this crafty 7th District shop. Items are carefully chosen from a global selection of artists and designs. ⊠ *Neustiftgasse 33, 7th District/Neubau* ☎ *699/13–06–68–78* ⊕ *www.sous-bois.at.*

CHRISTKINDLMÄRKTE
Spittelberg Christkindlmarkt
OUTDOOR/FLEA/GREEN MARKETS | The city's most fashionable love this artsy market, held in Spittelberg's enchanting Biedermeier quarter. ✉ *Burggasse and Siebensterngasse, 7th District/Neubau.*

CLOTHING
Arnold's
CLOTHING | This appealing boutique stocks a wide range of sought-after international brands and labels for urban fashionistas, like Wood Wood, Scarti Lab, and Edwin. A large selection of menswear and shoes include Arnold's own signature T-shirts. ✉ *Siebensterngasse 52, 7th District/Neubau* ☎ *01/923–1316* ⊕ *www.arnolds.at.*

Art Point
CLOTHING | Russian designer Lena Kvadrat treats Viennese hipsters to cutting-edge fashion, unveiling two collections each year. ✉ *Neubaugasse 35, 7th District/Neubau* ☎ *01/522–0425* ⊕ *www.artpoint.eu.*

Bisovsky
CLOTHING | Haute couture and prêt-à-porter are by appointment only in Susanne Bisovsky's Neubau district studio. Email or phone ahead for an appointment. ✉ *Seidengasse 13/6, 7th District/Neubau* ☎ *699/11–17–67–55* ⊕ *www.bisovsky.com.*

EbenBERG
CLOTHING | Billing itself as an ethical concept store, EbenBERG combines the designs of Laura Ebenberg with a carefully crafted lineup of other sleek designers who share her vision of using organic and fair-trade materials. ✉ *Neubaugasse 4, 7th District/Neubau* ☎ *699/15–28–72–26.*

Ferrari Zöchling
CLOTHING | For those with a love of creative prints, Romana Zöchling's label Ferrari Zöchling designs very eye-catching clothing. Sometimes bold, sometimes mellow, but always artistic, Romana takes inspiration from the art and photography that she often uses in her prints. ✉ *Kirchengasse 27, 7th District/Neubau* ☎ *66/41–21–11–27* ⊕ *www.ferrarizoechling.com* ⊙ *Closed Mon. and Tues.*

Lila
CLOTHING | Informal women's fashion from designer Lisi Lang is found at this store. Her label offers lovely pieces that will go perfectly in many wardrobes. ✉ *Kirchengasse 7, 7th District/Neubau* ⊕ *www.lila.cx.*

Maronski
CLOTHING | Austrian fashion label Maronski's designs for women are well cut in beautiful colors and very mix-and-matchable. Organic cotton and bamboo material is used for a fresh and comfortable feel. ✉ *Neubaugasse 7, 7th District/Neubau* ☎ *699/11–34–74–54* ⊕ *www.maronski.at.*

Nachbarin
CLOTHING | European avant-garde fashion can be found here, where select labels include Veronique Leroy, Amber & Louise, and Elena Ghisellini. ✉ *Gumpendorfer Strasse 17, 6th District/Mariahilf* ☎ *01/587–2169* ⊕ *www.nachbarin.co.at.*

Nfive
CLOTHING | Neutral, unadorned walls are as minimalistic as the fashion on sale here at Nfive. Helmut Lang, Isabel Marant, Tiger of Sweden, Filippa K, Vanessa Bruno, and many more labels (both men and women's) are on offer. ✉ *Neubaugasse 5, 7th District/Neubau* ☎ *01/523–8313* ⊕ *www.nfive.at.*

Ulliko
CLOTHING | Ullrike Kogelmüller, known as Ulliko, creates two lines every year of pure yet modern designs and has them manufactured locally. Her aesthetic is geometrical shapes of red, black, and white with an occasional appearance of grey. ✉ *Kirchengasse 7, 7th District/Neubau* ☎ *699/12–84–39–22* ⊕ *www.ulliko.com.*

Wabisabi

CLOTHING | Local designer Stefanie Wippel creates breezy, easy-to-wear pieces that flatter any figure. ✉ *Lindengasse 20, 7th District/Neubau* ☎ *644/54–51–280* ⊕ *www.alle-tragen-wabi-sabi.at.*

DEPARTMENT STORES

Grüne Erde

HOUSEHOLD ITEMS/FURNITURE | Beautiful scents greet you upon entering Grüne Erde, a shop specializing in organic household goods, ecologically sound furniture and tableware, natural cosmetics, and "fashion with responsibility." The name literally translates to "green earth," and products are created using natural materials and with sustainability in mind. ✉ *Mariahilferstrasse 11, 6th District/Mariahilf* ☎ *01/520–3410* ⊕ *www.grueneerde. com.*

FLEA MARKETS

Flohmarkt am Naschmarkt

OUTDOOR/FLEA/GREEN MARKETS | In back of the Naschmarkt, stretching along the Linke Wienzeile from the Kettenbrück-engasse U4 subway station, you'll find the city's most celebrated flea market. It offers a staggering collection of items, ranging from serious antiques to plain junk. It's held every Saturday, rain or shine, from 6:30 am to around 2 pm. ✉ *6th District/Mariahilf.*

GIFTS AND SOUVENIRS

★ Das Goldene Wiener Herz

GIFTS/SOUVENIRS | Das Goldene Wiener Herz produces some truly unique items. It's best known for mugs and glasses decorated with real gold. The store's name translates to the "golden Viennese heart," and classic Viennese traditions from Art Nouveau artwork to the famous wine *heurigers* are reflected in the motifs throughout the shop. ✉ *Kirchberggasse 17, 7th District/Neubau* ☎ *68/03–23–26–66* ⊕ *www.dgwh.at.*

HOUSEHOLD ITEMS AND FURNITURE

Die Werkbank

HOUSEHOLD ITEMS/FURNITURE | This small shop has a bold concept: absolutely everything at Die Werkbank is completely handcrafted. From contemporary furniture to jewelry and ceramics, something truly memorable will be discovered by any shopper who stops by to browse. ✉ *Breite Gasse 1, 7th District/Neubau* ☎ *65/05–24–81–36* ⊕ *www.werkbank.cc.*

SHOES AND LEATHER GOODS

Freitag Bags

SHOES/LUGGAGE/LEATHER GOODS | This is the Vienna location of the Swiss brand Freitag, known for its selection of one-of-a-kind bags, backpacks, purses, and other accessories made from old truck tarpaulins. ✉ *Neubaugasse 26, 7th District/Neubau* ☎ *01/523–3136* ⊕ *www.freitag.ch.*

Ina Kent

SHOES/LUGGAGE/LEATHER GOODS | The Ina Kent brand, whose creations are all handmade in Vienna, says they are "exploring the ambivalence between aesthetics and functionality" and that they sell "bags with potential." That pretty much nails their stylish, leather handbags, since most have adjustable straps so you can switch up the bag to various options like a backpack, a tote, or just adjust it to yield a shorter or longer strap. Wallets and other accessories are also on offer, often with adjustable elements, too. ✉ *Siebensterngasse 50, 7th District/Neubau* ☎ *699/1477–7477* ⊕ *inakent.com* Ⓜ *U3/Neibaugasse.*

SHOPPING MALLS

BahnhofCity Wien West

SHOPPING CENTERS/MALLS | Located in the Westbahnhof train station at one end of the busy Mariahilferstrasse shopping zone, BahnhofCity has about 80 shops selling clothing, electronics, shoes, sporting goods, and more. There's also a food court, plus a small grocery store that's open Sunday. ✉ *Mariahilferstrasse, 6th District/Mariahilf* ⊕ *www.bahnhofcitywienwest.at.*

Chapter 7

GREATER VIENNA

DISTRICTS 10, 11, 13, 14, 15, 16, 19, 20, 21, 22

Updated by
Caroline Sieg

 Sights
★★★★★

 Restaurants
★★☆☆☆

 Hotels
★☆☆☆☆

 Shopping
★★☆☆☆

 Nightlife
★☆☆☆☆

NEIGHBORHOOD SNAPSHOT

TOP EXPERIENCES

- **Schloss Schönbrunn:** Marvel at this rococo palace/primary summer home of the Hapsburgs.

- **Schönbrunn Gardens:** Explore the orangery, the partially forested Schlosspark, and the graceful baroque gardens of the Great Parterre, and get lost in the Irrgarten maze.

- **Kirche Am Steinhof:** While the glowing copper dome of this church can be seen from miles away, Otto Wagner's architectural masterpiece should be visited up close.

- **Tiergarten Schönbrunn:** The world's oldest continuously operating zoo has a canopy trail through the Vienna Woods treetops where you will find yourself at eye level with numerous bird species and enjoying palace views.

- **Wagenburg/Imperial Carriage Museum:** Wow at the Imperial Carriage, historic sports cars, and children's gala carriages as part of the fleet of more than 600 vehicles used by the Viennese court on show at this museum.

- **Heurige (Wine Taverns):** Visit a local heurige where you can drink Vienna-grown wine in a cozy space, or among the vines at the winery itself.

PLANNING YOUR TIME

Schloss Schönbrunn is best visited on weekday mornings to avoid the crowds. In general, weekends in Greater Vienna tend to be busier than weekdays, but this is also the most lively time to explore this area. Plan on touring the palace in the morning and reserve the afternoon for exploring the gardens on the palace grounds.

Some heuriger are only open on weekends, and sometimes on Fridays, so aim to visit on a weekend afternoon or early evening. You don't need a tour to experience the heuriger, just show up, order some wine, and enjoy the lively atmosphere.

QUICK BITES

- **Magdas Kantine.** Modern, airy cantine with tasty soups, salads, and snacks that employs workers with limited job opportunities. ⊠ *Absberggasse 27, 10th District/Favoriten* ⊕ *www.magdas-kantine.at.*

- **Gota Coffee Experts.** One of Vienna's favorite third-wave coffee roasters serves paninis, meat and cheese-filled croissants, chia puddings, and cakes (including gluten-free options) alongside its expertly-made caffeine concoctions. ⊠ *Mariahilferstrasse 192, 15th District/Rudolfsheim-Fünfhaus* ⊕ *www.gota.coffee* Ⓜ *U4/Schönbrunn.*

- **Cafe Dommayer.** Owned by Austria's Cafe Oberlaa empire, this traditional cafe (Strauss used to hang out here) serves omelettes, sandwiches, and cakes. ⊠ *Auhofstrasse 2, 13th, Hietzing* ⊕ *www.oberlaa-wien.at* Ⓜ *U4/Schönbrunn.*

GETTING HERE

Greater Vienna is well-connected to the center via public transport. Schloss Schönbrunn is best reached by taking the U4 subway to the Schönbrunn stop. Most heuriger within the city limits are located in Grinzing, which can be reached by taking tram 38 until the end station, Grinzing.

Forming a concentric second circle around the 2nd through 9th Districts, Vienna's suburbs—Districts 10 to 23— are largely residential, home to families, beautiful parks, and thriving multicultural neighborhoods. Only a few hold attractions of interest to visitors, but venturing outside the city center offers a glimpse into the *real* Vienna, where locals outnumber visitors.

The 11th District, Simmering, contains one of Vienna's architectural wonders, Gasometer, a former gasworks that has been remodeled into a housing and shopping complex. The 13th District, Hietzing, was once home to aristocrats and royalty and is still one of Vienna's most affluent neighborhoods. Here, you'll find the highlight of Greater Vienna and indeed, the highlight of Imperial Austria, the fabulous palace and gardens of Schloss Schönbrunn, a must-see on any Vienna itinerary.

The Schloss Schönbrunn (Schönbrunn Palace) complex embodies Imperial elegance, interrupted only by tourist traffic, and flows unbroken throughout the grounds. Here, you step back three centuries into the heart of a powerful and growing empire and follow it through to defeat and demise in 1918. Around the main palace you'll find much to see and do (and fewer crowds), including a fountain with a little maiden carrying a water jar, after whom the complex is named, and outbuildings that served as entertainment centers when the court moved to Schönbrunn in summer, with a zoo, theater, fake Roman ruins, greenhouses, and walkways.

Beyond Hietzing are a few local-filled neighborhoods worth exploring if you have the time. The 14th District, Penzing, is one of Vienna's hidden gems, with excellent restaurants and cafes. This outer edges of this long, stretched district are edged by the Vienna Woods. The 19th District, Döbling, is Vienna's poshest neighborhood and also bears the nickname "the Noble District" because of all the embassies on its chestnut-tree-lined streets. The 19th also incorporates several other neighborhoods within its borders, in particular the wine villages of Grinzing, Sievering, Nussdorf, and Neustift am Walde. Vienna's *heuriger* (wine taverns), one of which used to be Beethoven's local, are a popular excursion from Vienna with a smattering of nibbles and the cacophany of locals enjoying their home-grown tipples. The 22nd District, Donaustadt, now called Donau City, is a modern business and shopping complex that has grown around the United Nations center. This district also has several fantastic stretches for

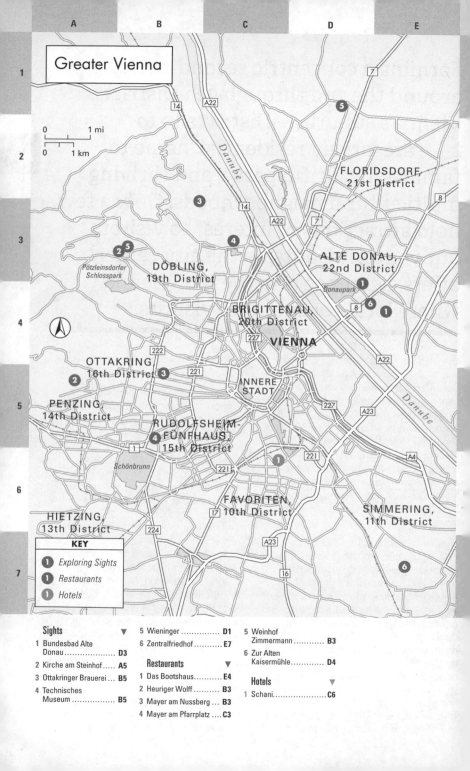

Greater Vienna

0 — 1 mi
0 — 1 km

FLORIDSDORF, 21st District

DÖBLING, 19th District

Pötzleinsdorfer Schlosspark

ALTE DONAU, 22nd District

Donaupark

BRIGITTENAU, 20th District

VIENNA

OTTAKRING 16th District

INNERE STADT

PENZING 14th District

RUDOLFSHEIM-FÜNFHAUS 15th District

Schönbrunn

FAVORITEN, 10th District

SIMMERING, 11th District

HIETZING, 13th District

KEY

- 1 *Exploring Sights*
- 1 *Restaurants*
- 1 *Hotels*

Sights ▼

1 Bundesbad Alte Donau **D3**

2 Kirche am Steinhof **A5**

3 Ottakringer Brauerei ... **B5**

4 Technisches Museum **B5**

5 Wieninger **D1**

6 Zentralfriedhof **E7**

Restaurants ▼

1 Das Bootshaus **E4**

2 Heuriger Wolff **B3**

3 Mayer am Nussberg ... **B3**

4 Mayer am Pfarrplatz **C3**

5 Weinhof Zimmermann **B3**

6 Zur Alten Kaisermühle **D4**

Hotels ▼

1 Schani **C6**

sunbathing along Alte Donau (Old Danube), with waterside cafes nearby.

It may be helpful to know the neighborhood names of other residential districts: the 10th/Favoriten; 12th/Meidling; 15th/Funfhaus; 16th/Ottakring; 17th/Hernals; 18th/Währing; 20th/Brigittenau; 21st/Floridsdorf; and 23rd which includes Liesing and the edge of the Vienna Woods.

Favoriten, 10th District

Favoriten is one of Vienna's largest districts. In the area closest to the city center, you'll see a mix of grand residential buildings peppered with previous factories in what used to be a largely industrial area. Come here for the Brotfabrik, one of the city's best modern performance spaces housed in a former bread factory.

Hotels

Schani

$ | **HOTEL** | The German word *Schani* means "friendly servant," and everything about this relaxed hotel exudes friendliness: from the inviting lounging spaces, including a back patio surrounded by trees, the lively coworking space in the lobby, and the friendly staff. **Pros:** there's a tram stop outside the front door; SMART hotel with mobile check-in, room selection, and mobile keys; coworking space in lobby. **Cons:** rooms are quite compact; no restaurant; the shower and sink are separated from the room by a curtain. [$] *Rooms from: €110* ✉ *Karl-Popper-Strasse 22, 10th District/Favoriten* ☎ *01/955–0715* 🌐 *www.hotelschani.com* 🛏 *134 rooms* 🍴 *No meals.*

Performing Arts

Brotfabrik (*Bread Factory*)

ART GALLERIES—ARTS | A former bread factory once slated for demolition is now the site of Vienna's most celebrated contemporary art venue. Ateliers, galleries, showrooms, and studios for artists-in-residence are set up inside, making it akin to an urban artists' colony. It showcases some of the country's premier artists, as well as many up-and-comers. ✉ *Absberggasse 27, 10th District/Favoriten* ☎ *01/982–3939* 🌐 *www.brotfabrik.wien.*

Simmering, 11th District

Simmering is a mainly residential area worth venturing to for a visit to the Central cemetery, where many of the great composers are buried.

Sights

Zentralfriedhof (*Central Cemetery*)

CEMETERY | Austrians take seriously the pomp of a funeral, brass bands and all, and nowhere is that more evident than the Central Cemetery. A streetcar from Schwarzenbergplatz takes you to the front gates of the cemetery that contains the graves of most of Vienna's great composers: Ludwig van Beethoven, Franz Schubert, Johannes Brahms, the Johann Strausses (father and son), and Arnold Schönberg, among others. Find your way around with the help of an audio guide, which can be rented for a small fee. For a hefty fee, Fiakers are on standby for a carriage ride around the beautiful grounds. The monument to Wolfgang Amadeus Mozart is a memorial only; the approximate location of his unmarked grave can be seen at the now deconsecrated St. Marx-Friedhof at Leberstrasse 6–8. ✉ *Simmeringer Hauptstrasse, 11th District/Simmering* [M] *Tram: 71 to St. Marxer Friedhof, or on to Zentralfriedhof Haupttor/2.*

While the views of the palace from the Gloriette are stunning, be sure to take in the view of the Gloriette from the park and gardens below.

Hietzing, 13th District

The 13th district of Vienna, Hietzing, is popular with tourists as it is the location of both the city zoo and the Schönbrunn Palace and gardens.

Sights

Gloriette

BUILDING | At the crest of the hill, topping off the Schönbrunn Gardens, sits a Baroque masterstroke: Johann Ferdinand von Hohenberg's Gloriette, now restored to its original splendor. Perfectly scaled, the Gloriette—a palatial pavilion that once offered royal guests a place to rest and relax on their tours of the palace grounds and that now houses a welcome café—holds the vast garden composition together and at the same time crowns the ensemble with a brilliant architectural tiara. This was a favorite spot of Maria Theresa's, though in later years she grew so obese—not surprising, given that she bore 16 children in 20 years—it took six men to carry her in her palanquin to the summit. ■ TIP→ **From the rooftop viewing platform you can enjoy an impressive panoramic view of Vienna and the Vienna Woods.** ✉ *Schönbrunn Palace, Schönbrunner Schlossstrasse, 13th District/ Hietzing* ⊕ *www.schoenbrunn.at* 🎟 *viewing platform €4.50 or free with Vienna Pass* Ⓜ *U4/Schönbrunn.*

Otto Wagner Hofpavillon

BUILDING | The restored imperial subway station known as the Hofpavillon is just outside the palace grounds (at the northwest corner, a few yards east of the Hietzing subway station). Designed by Otto Wagner in conjunction with Joseph Olbrich and Leopold Bauer, the Hofpavillon was built in 1899 for the exclusive use of Emperor Franz Josef and his entourage. Exclusive it was: the emperor used the station only once. The exterior, with its proud architectural crown, is Wagner at his best, and the lustrous interior is one of the finest examples of Jugendstil decoration in the city. ⊠ *Schönbrunner Schlossstrasse, 13th District/Hietzing* ☎ *01/877–1571* ✉ *€5* Ⓜ *U4/Hietzing.*

Palmenhaus

GARDEN | On the grounds of Schönbrunn Palace is this huge greenhouse filled with exotic trees and plants. ⊠ *Schönbrunn Palace, Schönbrunner Schlossstrasse, 13th District/Hietzing* ☎ *01/877–5087* ⊕ *www.schoenbrunn.at* ✉ *€7* Ⓜ *U4/ Schönbrunn.*

★ **Schönbrunn Gardens** (*Palace Park*)

CASTLE/PALACE | The palace grounds entice with a bevy of splendid divertissements, including a grand zoo (the Tiergarten) and a carriage museum (the Wagenburg). Climb to the Gloriette for a panoramic view out over the city as well as of the palace complex. If you're exploring on your own, seek out the intriguing Roman ruin. The marble *schöner Brunnen* ("beautiful fountain") gave its name to the palace complex. Then head over the other side of the gardens to the playground and the newly grown maze. ⊠ *Schönbrunner Schlossstrasse, 13th District/Hietzing* ⊕ *www.schoenbrunn.at* Ⓜ *U4/Schönbrunn.*

★ **Schönbrunn Palace**

CASTLE/PALACE | Originally designed by Johann Bernhard Fischer von Erlach in 1696 and altered considerably for Maria Theresa 40 years later, the huge Hapsburg summer residence lies just a few subway stops west of Karlsplatz on the U4. The breathtaking view that unfolds once you go past the main courtyard is one of the supreme achievements of Baroque planning: the sculpted marble fountain; the carefully planted screen of trees behind; the sudden, almost vertical rise of the grass-covered hill beyond, with the **Gloriette** a fitting crown. Within the palace, the state salons are equally as splendid. Forty of the 1,441 rooms are open to the public, and two are of special note: the Hall of Mirrors, where the six-year-old Mozart performed for Empress Maria Theresa in 1762, and the Grand

Gallery, where the Congress of Vienna (1815) danced at night after carving up Napoléon's collapsed empire during the day. ⊠ *Schönbrunner Schlossstrasse, 13th District/Hietzing* ☎ *01/811–13–239* ⊕ *www.schoenbrunn.at* ✉ *€18 for Imperial Tour (Franz Josef's rooms); €22 Grand Tour (includes Maria Theresa's rooms)* Ⓜ *U4/Schönbrunn.*

Tiergarten Schönbrunn (*Schönbrunn Zoo*)

ZOO | FAMILY | Part of the imperial summer residence of Schönbrunn, a UNESCO World Heritage Site, the world's oldest zoo has retained its original Baroque design, but new settings have been created for both the animals and the public so that entertainment is combined with conservation and education. Founded in 1752, Schönbrunn Zoo is the oldest continuously operating zoo in the world and also one of the most popular— it has been voted Europe's best zoo five times. The more than 700 animal species housed here include koalas, lions, pandas, hippos, orangutans, and Siberian Tigers. There's also a fantastic canopy trail with a suspension bridge through the forest for up-close views of birds and open-air terrariums. ⊠ *Schönbrunner Schlosspark, Schönbrunner Schlossstrasse, 13th District/Hietzing* ☎ *01/877–92–940* ⊕ *www.zoovienna.at* ✉ *€22* Ⓜ *U4/Schönbrunn.*

Tiroler House

HOUSE | This Tyrolean-style building to the west of the Gloriette was a favorite retreat of Empress Elisabeth; it now includes a restaurant. ⊠ *Schönbrunner Schlosspark, Schönbrunner Schlossstrasse, 13th District/Hietzing* Ⓜ *U4/Schönbrunn.*

Wagenburg (*Imperial Carriage Museum*)

MUSEUM | Most of the carriages on display here are still roadworthy, and in fact Schönbrunn dusted off the black royal funeral carriage for the burial ceremony of Empress Zita in 1989. There are also a number of sleighs in the collection, including one upholstered in leopard skin.

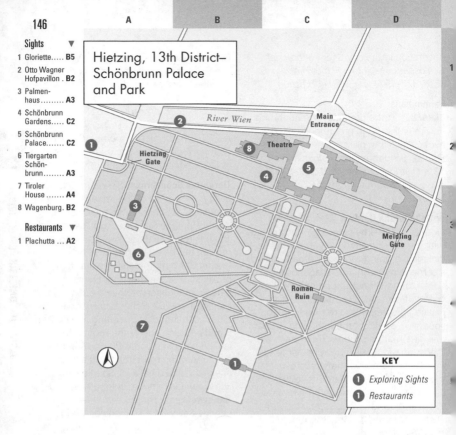

Hietzing, 13th District–
Schönbrunn Palace
and Park

River Wien

Main Entrance

Hietzing Gate

Theatre

Meidling Gate

Roman Ruin

KEY

❶ *Exploring Sights*

❶ *Restaurants*

Today a special Sisi trail leads through the museum; on show are some of her famous gowns, carriages, personal objects, and paintings, highlighting the empress's life from marriage to her tragic death. ⊠ *Schönbrunner Schlosspark, Schönbrunner Schlossstrasse, 13th District/Hietzing* ☏ *01/877–3244* ⊕ *www. kaiserliche-wagenburg.at/* ⊠ *€10* Ⓜ *U4/ Schönbrunn.*

🍴 Restaurants

Come for the palace, gardens, and zoo but don't plan to stay for dinner. If you need a quick coffee (and maybe cake) pause after all that sightseeing, Café Gloriette in the palace park of Schönbrunn Gardens is a great bet.

Plachutta

$$$ | **AUSTRIAN** | This traditional, white-tablecloth spot is known for it's Tafelspitz, a boiled-beef dish popular in both Austria and Germany and great on a chilly winter day. If that's not your thing, they also do a few hearty seafood plates, but this is a meat-focused classic local insitution. **Known for:** traditional Austrian dishes and old-school vibe; outdoor seating; close to Schönbrunn. Ⓢ *Average main: €28* ⊠ *Auhofstrasse 1, 13th District/Hietzing* ☏ *1/877–70–870* ⊕ *www.plachutta-hietzing.at* Ⓜ *U4/Schonbrunn.*

Wine in Vienna

For a memorable experience, sit at the edge of a vineyard in the outskirts of the city with a tankard of young white wine and listen to the *Schrammel* quartet playing sentimental Viennese songs. The wine taverns in this region sprang up in 1784 when Josef II decreed that owners of vineyards could establish their own private wine taverns, with the provision that the vintners rotate their opening times among them; soon the Viennese discovered it was cheaper to go out to the wine than to bring it inside the city walls, where taxes were levied.

These taverns in the wine-growing districts vary from the simple front room of a vintner's house to ornate settings. Named after the "new" wine, the true *Heurige* is open for only a few weeks a year to allow vintners to sell a certain quantity of their production, tax-free, when consumed on their own premises. The choice is usually between a "new" and an "old" wine, but you can also ask for a milder or sharper wine according to your taste. Most *Heurigen* are happy to let you sample the wines before you order. You can also order a *Gespritzter*, half wine and half soda water. If you visit in the fall, be sure to order a glass of *Sturm*, a cloudy drink halfway between grape juice and wine, with a delicious yeasty fizz. Don't be fooled by its sweetness; it goes right to your head.

Tourist traps still abound in Grinzing, where for years busloads descended on the picturesque wine village on Vienna's outskirts to drink new wine, but there are also worthy Heurigen destinations in Stammersdorf, Sievering, Nussdorf, or Neustift. And these days you can usually find fine dinners to accompany the excellent wine.

7

Greater Vienna HIETZING, 13TH DISTRICT

🛏 Hotels

While there are hotels in this area, we don't really recommend staying in Hietzing. It's a suburban area with very few noteworthy dining options and no nightlife to speak of, and far enough from the city center that, with the exception of Schönbrunn, it's a bit of a trek to visit most of the the main sights.

 Performing Arts

MUSIC
Schlosstheater Schönbrunn
MUSIC | For nearly 80 years, the theater has been associated with the University of Music and Performing Arts. Here visitors can watch student performances of both opera and dramatic arts. ⊠ *Schönbrunner Schloss, Schönbrunner Schlossstrasse 47, 13th District/Hietzing* ☎ *0664–1111–600* ⊕ *www.mdw.ac.at/ gesangundmusiktheater.*

THEATER
Marionettentheater Schloss Schönbrunn
PUPPET SHOWS | FAMILY | Historical recordings of Mozart's *Magic Flute* and other favorites are on the program at this magnificent puppet theater in Schönbrunn Palace. These outstanding performances fill a whole evening, with programs designed for adults as well as for children. ⊠ *Schönbrunn Palace, Schönbrunner Schlossstrasse 47, 13th District/Hietzing* ☎ *01/817–3247* ⊕ *www. marionettentheater.at.*

Shopping

CHRISTKINDLMÄRKTE

Schönbrunn Christkindlmarkt

OUTDOOR/FLEA/GREEN MARKETS | All the glitter and gilt of the season frames the market held at the Hapsburgs' Schönbrunn. The Schönbrunn market offers the one of the best selection of works by Austrian and Viennese designers of all the city's Christmas markets. ⊠ *Schönbrunn Palace, Schönbrunner Schlossstrasse, 13th District/Hietzing.*

Penzing, 14th District

Penzing and the west side of Vienna feel like the undiscovered secret of the city. Public transport connections are excellent so you can easily make your way around.

 Sights

Kirche Am Steinhof (*The Church of St. Leopold*)

RELIGIOUS SITE | Otto Wagner's most exalted piece of Jugendstil architecture, the first church of the Modernism period in Europe, lies in the suburbs: the church on the grounds of the old Vienna City Psychiatric Hospital. Wagner's design here unites functional details (rounded edges on the pews to prevent injury to the patients, how would the building be cleaned, and how many people have an unobstructed view of the high altar) with a soaring, airy dome and stained glass by Koloman Moser. ⊠ *Baumgartner Höhe 1, 14th District/Penzing* ☎ *01/91060* ⏰ *€12* Ⓜ *U4/Unter-St.-Veit; then Bus 47A to Psychiatrisches Krankenhaus. U2/Volkstheater; then Bus 48A.*

Technisches Museum

MUSEUM | About a 10-minute walk from Schönbrunn Palace is the Technical Museum , which traces the evolution of industrial development over the past two centuries. On four floors you'll find actual locomotives from the 19th century, a Tin Lizzie, airplanes from the early days of flying, as well as examples of factory life, how electric lighting took the place of gas lamps, and how mountain highway tunnels are constructed. ⊠ *Mariahilferstrasse 212, 14th District/Penzing* ☎ *01/899–98–0* ⊕ *www.tmw.at* ⏰ *€14* Ⓜ *U3 or U6/Westbahnhof, then Tram 52 or 58/Penzingerstrasse.*

 Activities

Trail Center Hohe Wand Weise

HIKING/WALKING | A full-service hiking and climbing center located in Vienna's 14th District. ⊕ *www.hohewandwiese.com/de/trailcenter.*

Rudolfsheim Fünfhaus, 15th District

While not home to any major "sights," this multicultural district has markets at Johnstrasse, eclectic cafes, restaurants, and many brunch spots dotted around Märzstrasse and the top of Mariahilfer strasse, and you'll find great local Turkish bakeries and Balkan supermarkets. It's well connected with tramlines and the U3.

Ottakring, 16th District

Home to the famous Ottakring brewery, Vienna's last remaining brewery within the city limits, this district has a bohemian charm. It's home to Brunnenmarkt which is the less touristy equivalent of Naschmarkt. Yppenplatz square is a glorious spot to linger over brunch and people watch (Frida's, Caffee am Yppenplatz, and Wirr am Brunnenmarkt are all good options.) The Ottakringer Brauerei (brewery) hosts a number of cool food festivals, pop up markets, and festivals throughout the year so it's worth checking ahead to see if there's anything happening while you're in town.

Sights

★ **Ottakringer Brauerei** (*Ottakringer Brewery*)
WINERY/DISTILLERY | Founded in 1837, and located in the historic workers' district of the same name and featuring an in-house well from which the water for the entire production is still sourced, the independent Ottakring Brewery is a traditional brewery with roots. It also has a creative, modern outlook, beer tastings, tours, workshops, festivals, and a craft beer sub-brand (BrauWerk) offering IPAs, Porters, and Vienna Pale Ales with fun names and flavors, which add up to a thoroughly cool old brand and a must-do beer experience. Register in advance online for guided tours (Monday to Friday 9 to 5:30). ■ **TIP→ Guided tours meet at the Ottakringer Shop, Ottakringer Strasse 95.** ✉ *Ottakringer Platz 1, Vienna* ☎ *664/618–2129* 🌐 *www.ottakringerbrauerei.at/en* 🎫 *€9 tour (incl. tasting).*

Dobling, 19th District

Away from the bustle of the city, and backing onto Vienna's vineyards and the Kahlenberg hill, the 19th District is a stunning district filled with charming cottages and villas and the best *heuriger* (wine taverns). Be sure to check opening hours before you visit as some heurige can be booked for events or just closed without much notice. Many smaller heurige are only open on specific weekends or days during the season from May to November. Allow time to wander around from tavern to tavern and to get comfortable in a perfect little courtyard.

The 38 tram drops you in the heart of Grinzing, or the 60 to Rodaun that will end up in ten minute walking distance to some smaller local heuriger. You can also avail of the super cute Vienna Heurigen Express—a hop-on hop-off shuttle that starts at the bottom of Kahlenberg and runs on Saturday to get you between the heurigers dotted along the hillside.

Restaurants

Heuriger Wolff
$ | **AUSTRIAN** | **FAMILY** | In the heart of the vine village of Neustift am Walde, this inn dating from 1609 sticks to tradition. The selection of white wine includes Grüner Veltliner, Riesling, and Chardonnay, and reds of Blauburger and Zweigelt. **Known for:** historical wine tavern; traditional Viennese dishes; great value lunch specials. [$] *Average main: €13* ✉ *Rathstrasse 44–46, 19th District/Döbling* ☎ *01/440–2335* 🌐 *www.wienerheuriger.at* [M] *U4/U6/Spittelau; Bus: 35A/Neustift am Walde.*

★ **Mayer am Nussberg**
$ | **AUSTRIAN** | **FAMILY** | Situated smack in the Mayer winery vines with sweeping views of Vienna, this rustic outdoor spot is a great place to enjoy local wines while relaxing among the rows of grapes that produced your tipple. It's a convivial atmosphere and family-friendly, with picnic tables, a few highly-coveted reclining lounge chairs and play areas for kids. **Known for:** vineyard setting; good food and wine; popular with locals. [$] *Average main: €15* ✉ *Kahlenberger Str. 213, 19th District/Döbling* ☎ *01/370–1287* 🌐 *www.mayeramnussberg.at/en* 🕒 *Closed Mon.–Thurs. Closed in inclement weather.*

Mayer am Pfarrplatz
$$ | **AUSTRIAN** | **FAMILY** | Heiligenstadt is home to this *heurige* in one of Beethoven's former abodes; he composed his 6th Symphony, as well as parts of his 9th Symphony ("Ode to Joy") while staying in this part of town. The à la carte offerings and buffet are plentiful, and include traditional Viennese dishes like Tafelspitz (boiled beef with horseradish). **Known for:** generous buffet of regional Austrian classics; Beethoven history; excellent Riesling house wines. [$] *Average main: €19* ✉ *Pfarrplatz 2, 19th District/Döbling* ☎ *01/370–7373* 🌐 *www.pfarrplatz.at* 🕒 *No lunch weekdays* [M] *Tram: D/Nussdorf from the Ring.*

★ Weinhof Zimmermann

$ | AUSTRIAN | A winding walk up a tree-lined lane brings you to the garden of one of the city's most well-known heuriger. Here you will find one of the finest, most peaceful views around along with specialty wine like the Grüner Veltliner. **Known for:** buffet of traditional dishes, including schnitzel and strudels; excellent Austrian wines in a cozy space; great views of both the countryside and city. $ *Average main: €15* ✉ *Mitterwurzergasse 20, 19th District/Döbling* ☎ *01/440–1207* ⊕ *www.weinhof-zimmermann.at* ⊘ *Closed Mon. and Nov.–mid-Mar.* Ⓜ *U2/Schottentor; Tram: 38/Grinzing.*

 Activities

Kahlenberg Forest Rope Park

CLIMBING/MOUNTAINEERING | FAMILY | Vienna's most popular local mountain, Kahlenberg, has one of the biggest ropes courses in Austria. There are 17 courses with several degrees of difficulty and aside from the fun and adrenaline rush, these courses offer lovely views of the Vienna Woods. Visit after dark on Friday or Saturday to experience the woods lit up with lanterns (until 11 pm). ✉ *Josefsdorf 47, 19th District/Döbling* ☎ *1/3200476* ⊕ *www.waldseilpark.at* Ⓜ *Bus: 38A/Elisabethwiese.*

The 20th, 21st, and 22nd Districts

Situated in the northeast and eastern sides of Vienna on the edge of the Danube, the 20th, 21st, and 22nd Districts make up Floridsdorf (which includes Stammersdorf), the Alte Donau, and Donaustadt. Huge swaths of this area are of no interest to visitors, but there are a few areas worth exploring. Stammersdorf is home to several heuriger (the best of the lot is Wieninger), the Alte Donau area—a closed-off channel of the Danube that now forms a recreational lake—has several excellent spots to swim, sunbathe, and eat in summer, and Donaustadt also offers some excellent waterside eating and drinking haunts.

 Sights

Bundesbad Alte Donau

POOL | FAMILY | Once a military swimming school designed to harden soldiers, this 100-year-old public outdoor bath, situated on the Old Danube is today a local hotspot in summer for soft exercise and relaxation. Facilities include changing rooms, bathrooms, showers, and lockers, and there are lots of shady areas for picnics and lounging. Bundesbad is especially popular with families with its expansive play area, small in-water slides, and kids programs in summer, but the rafts, table tennis, on-site cafe-restaurant, and boules mean you'll find students and elderly locals, too. ■**TIP**➔ **You can't rent towels here so bring your own.** ✉ *Arbeiterstrandbadstrasse 93, 22nd District/Donaustadt* ☎ *01/263–3667* ⊕ *www.burghauptmannschaft.at* 🎟 *€5* ⊘ *Closed in bad weather* Ⓜ *U1/Alte Donau.*

★ Wieninger

WINERY/DISTILLERY | The driving force behind the WienWein group, pioneer Fritz Wieninger is a masterful vintner. He exports to the United States and elsewhere, but luckily there are some bottles left to be savored in this pleasant, tree-shaded inner courtyard and tavern. The food is not typical heuriger fare; instead, expect more contemporary choices, like roasted scampi burgers with mango-avocado dip. It's across the Danube in Stammersdorf, one of Vienna's oldest heurige regions. ✉ *Stammersdorferstrasse 78, 21st District/Floridsdorf* ☎ *01/290–1012* ⊕ *heuriger-wieninger.at* ⊘ *Closed late Dec.–mid-May. Lunch only Sat. and Sun.* Ⓜ *U2, U4/Schottenring; Tram: 31/Stammersdorf.*

🍴 Restaurants

★ Das Bootshaus

$ | **SEAFOOD** | In summer the alfresco tables—most peppered on a wide, floating dock on top of the water—offers a sublime, Mediterranean-summer vibe. In winter, the indoor space centers around a fireplace in a space reminiscent of a traditional British rowing club: Chesterfield leather benches and plump sofas, copper and oak under a high, white ceiling where English crystal chandeliers and two rowing boats hang. **Known for:** homage to rowing; idyllic setting with city views; great seafood. [$] *Average main: €14* ✉ *An der unteren Alten Donau 61, 22nd District/Donaustadt* ☎ *01/24100–811* 🌐 *www.dasbootshaus.at* [M] *Tram 25 Arminenstrasse.*

Zur Alten Kaisermühle

$ | **AUSTRIAN** | This vast waterside patio alongside the shimmering Danube is where you want to be on a long summer's evening in Vienna, having drinks, enjoying good food, and watching boats bob at the dock. It's also pretty popular in fall and winter, when you can cozy up with a mulled wine in the charming indoor section featuring wood-beams and exposed brick.The menu includes Viennese and traditional Austrian cuisine with seasonal specialties, as well as steak, seafood, and Mediterranean delicacies. **Known for:** regional specialties; greenery-filled patio by the water; popular beer garden. [$] *Average main:* ✉ *Fischerstrand 6, 20th District/Alte Donau* ☎ *01/263–3529* 🌐 *www.kaisermuehle.at* 🕒 *Closed Mon. and Tues. late Sept.–early Apr.* [M] *U1/Alte Donau.*

DAY TRIPS FROM VIENNA

8

Updated by
Joseph Reaney

 Sights
★★★★★

 Restaurants
★★★☆☆

 Hotels
★★★★☆

 Shopping
★★☆☆☆

 Nightlife
★★☆☆☆

WELCOME TO DAY TRIPS FROM VIENNA

TOP REASONS TO GO

★ **Abbey with a view:** The magnificent Benedictine Baroque splendor of Melk Abbey leaves you breathless.

★ **Step into Slovakia:** Easily reached by boat, bus or train, Bratislava offers a towering Renaissance castle, a historic Old Town, and a buzzy café and pub culture.

★ **Lakeside cycling:** Pedal across the plains surrounding Neusiedl, one of Central Europe's largest lakes, stopping to explore scenic hamlets.

★ **Bold architecture:** Internationally renowned for its daring architecture, Linz—capital of Upper Austria—has taken a leading role in contemporary art, style, and design.

★ **Verdant vistas:** Travel in tranquility by boat or bike through the Wachau Valley. Perhaps the Danube's most picturesque stretch lies between the towns of Krems and Melk.

★ **Hop into Hungary:** Head just across the border to the fairytale Hungarian city of Sopron, famed for its cobbled medieval Inner Town.

1 **Carnuntum and Hainburg an der Donau.** Discover the remains of Carnuntum and follow in the footsteps of composer Joseph Haydn.

2 **Marchegg.** This tiny Weinviertel town close to the border with Slovakia is a great base for exploring Schlosshof.

3 **Bratislava.** Famed for its medieval Old Town overlooked by a grand Renaissance castle, Slovakia's capital is just a short trip downriver (by catamaran) from Vienna.

4 **Neusiedl am See.** Situated at the northern tip of the vast Neusiedl Lake, this resort town is a great base for exploring the area by bike, boat, or car.

5 **Eisenstadt.** It may be the largest settlement in the Neusiedl region, but Eisenstadt remains a small and eminently strollable city, overlooked by the pretty Schloss Esterházy.

6 **Rust.** Come for the charming historic center, the chimney-dwelling birdlife, and the delicious *beerenauslese* dessert wine.

7 **Sopron.** Located just across the border, Sopron offers a beautiful and proudly Hungarian city that mixes Celtic, Roman, German, Slavic, and Magyar influences.

8 **Baden.** Taking a trip to the spa town of Baden bei Wien means following the Vienna Woods' southern trail past ancient monasteries, fertile plains, and bucolic vineyards.

9 **Klosterneuburg and Korneuburg.** These two villages, which sit across the Danube from one another, are home to an impressive Augustinian abbey and a particularly photogenic castle.

10 **Krems.** Marking the start of the Wachau section of the Danube, Krems is itself a pretty riverside city with a lovely cobbled Old Town.

11 **Dürnstein.** Amid stiff competition, Dürnstein is perhaps the prettiest town on the Danube, with the ruins of its medieval hilltop castle jutting out over verdant vineyards.

12 **Melk.** The gigantic Benedictine abbey in Melk is one of Austria's most photographed buildings. Take a snap from the riverside then climb the cobbled streets for a peek inside.

13 **Linz.** Austria's third-largest city basks in amazing cutting-edge design. You can experience exciting insights into the latest technology at one of its incredible museums.

The area along the Danube and around Vienna is drenched in history. Composers like Johann Strauss were inspired by the woodlands and river, and Joseph Haydn and Anton Bruckner both lived in the region and left their traces. A trip here unfolds like a treasured picture book, with Roman ruins, medieval castles, and Baroque monasteries perching precariously above the river. This is where the Nibelungs—later immortalized by Wagner—caroused operatically, and where Richard the Lionheart was locked in a dungeon and held for (a substantial) ransom for nearly two years.

Passenger boats can take you along the Danube on pleasure cruises that stop at quaint villages. Aside from the Danube, water sports are on offer in the Neusiedl Lake area, where the Viennese go to escape the city. Biking both in the lake area and along the Danube is becoming increasingly popular, and the nearby town of Baden, a favorite haunt of Beethoven, offers superb postpedaling spa relaxation.

In the towns and hamlets throughout the region, time seems to be on pause. Colorful 17th- and 18th-century buildings now serve as hotels and inns, with old-fashioned charm and well-made traditional food that invites you to sit outdoors and savor the countryside. No one is in a hurry here. But not everything is old-fashioned. A little exploring, especially in the vineyards around Neusiedl Lake, will turn up eateries pushing the envelope with modern cuisine, matched with top-notch local wines. Time suddenly leaps forward in Linz, which has more and more modern buildings punctuating the skyline along with its churches and castles, helping the city to become a unique melange of past and future.

MAJOR REGIONS

Weinviertel and Bratislava. Austria's Weinviertel (Wine District) has been largely neglected by the "experts," and its deliciously fresh wines reward those who enjoy partaking of the grape without the all-too-frequent fuss and nonsense that goes with it. Situated to the north and east of Vienna, this is a lovely region to tour by car for a day. You could even put aside two or three days to truly savor the region's wines (which are generally on the medium-dry or dry side, like the popular Blaufränkisch reds) and attractions like the Roman town of Carnuntum and the Baroque castle near Marchegg. Further east lies Bratislava, the Slovakian capital renowned for its medieval Old Town and exciting nightlife.

Neusiedl Lake, Sopron, and Baden. To the southeast of Vienna, Neusiedl Lake occupies a strange world. One of the largest lakes in Europe, it is a bizarre body of warm, brackish water, fed by underground springs and encircled by a thick belt of tall reeds. The habitat of more than 250 species of birds, it is also a magnet for anglers, boaters, and windsurfers. Relax on the beach in Neusiedl am See, or head down the western shore to Eisenstadt for some historical sightseeing. Nearby Rust prides itself on its wine-making tradition. Further south, just across the Austria–Hungary border, Sopron offers daytrippers an entirely different culture, language, and perspective. And northwest of here (southwest of Vienna) lies the famous spa city of Baden, seperated from the capital only by the Vienna Woods.

West Along the Danube. The Romans used to say, "Whoever controls the Danube controls all of Europe." That may no longer be true, but the scenery is still something to behold. There are riverside highlights to be found near Vienna, particularly the hilltop fortifications in Klosterneuburg and Korneuburg, but the loveliest stretch of the Danube's Austrian course runs through the narrow defiles of the Wachau; from the art gallery-laden town of Krems to the spectacular abbey-topped Melk. Further west still lies culture-crammed Linz, Austria's third-largest city. Visiting today, it's hard to believe that for years after the Second World War, the River Enns near Linz marked the border between the western (U.S., British, and French) and eastern (Russian) occupation zones.

Planning

When To Go

Most of the regions around Vienna and along the Danube are best seen in the temperate months between mid-March and mid-November; not much is offered for winter sports and a number of hotels as well as sights close in the winter. The glorious riverside landscape takes on a fairy-tale quality when apricot and apple trees burst into blossom late April to mid-June. Others might prefer the early to mid-autumn days, when the vineyards on the terraced hills turn reddish-blue and a bracing chill settles on the Danube. From mid-September until the beginning of October, the Bruckner Festival in Linz joins forces with Ars Electronica, combining the classic with the contemporary. No matter the season, crowds jam the celebrated abbey at Melk; you're best off going first thing in the morning before the tour buses arrive, or at midday, when the throngs have receded.

Getting Here

To get to the area between Linz and Weinviertel you can fly into the airport in Vienna or take a EuroCity train to Vienna or Linz. Once here, driving is the most convenient and scenic way to explore the region, especially if you're visiting the smaller towns and villages. If you don't want to drive, opt for the train—rather than a bus—for the main routes and longer distances. Local trains that stop at every station take a long time to get anywhere, but if you have time to spare, train rides can be fun and there are great views of the countryside from the broad windows.

AIR

The northern part of eastern Austria is served by Flughafen Wien (Vienna International Airport) at Schwechat, 19 kilometers (12 miles) southeast of the city center.

Linz Airport (also know as Blue Danube Airport Linz) is a good alternative if you want to start your journey in calmer surroundings. Located just 20 minutes from the city center by car or train, the airport is serviced regularly by Lufthansa, Austrian Airlines, and several low-cost airlines.

BOAT

You can take a day trip by boat from Vienna or Krems and explore one of the stops, such as Dürnstein or Melk. Boats run from mid-April to late October. One of the most popular boat companies to ply the Danube is Brandner Schifffahrt. Along this stretch of the river, bridges are few and far between, so old-fashioned tow ferries (attached to cables stretched across the river) allow a speedy crossing for people, cars, and bikes for a small fee.

Consider traveling from Vienna to Bratislava by Twin City Liner catamaran. It's fun, comfortable, and fast too, with the whole journey taking just 75 minutes. Sit on the upper deck for the best views.

BOAT INFORMATION Brandner Schifffahrt. ✉ *Welterbeplatz 1, Krems* ☎ *07433/259021* ⊕ *www.brandner.at.* **Twin City Liner.** ✉ *Schiffstation Wien City, Franz-Josefs-Kai 2, Vienna* ☎ *01/904–88–80* ⊕ *www.twincityliner.com/en.*

BUS

While most of the region is sufficiently covered by trains, some destinations are quicker and easier to reach by bus. For example, to get to Rust on Neusiedl Lake, take the regular Bus 200 from Vienna Central Station. Alternatively, you can pick up Bus 285 or 286 from Neusiedl am See or Eisenstadt.

Most services are run by the Austrian railroad system and the Austrian postal service, but some connections to smaller towns are operated by Blaguss Reisen. Between all three, you can get almost anywhere in the region by bus, assuming you have the time.

BUS INFORMATION Blaguss Reisen. ☎ *050/6550* ⊕ *www.blaguss.at.*

CAR

The Weinviertel to the north is accessed by major highways but not by autobahns, while taking Route 9 east will get you to Carnuntum and Hainburg an der Donau. Turn north here onto Route 49 for Marchegg, or continue east to Bratislava.

To get to Neusiedl am See, take the scenic Route 10, or for Eisenstadt, take the A3 south. From the latter, turn east onto Route 52 for Rust, or continue south on Routes 16 and 84 for Sopron in Hungary.

Baden can be reached by taking the E59 autobahn south in the direction of Graz and turning west onto Route 210 for the last few kilometers.

For the Danube, the main routes along the north bank are the A22, S5, and A3, while the south bank is a choice between the A1 and a collection of lesser roads. Car rental is easiest in Vienna or Linz.

TRAIN

The train system is excellent, and reliable trains run frequently from Vienna's Schnellbahn stations to most of the destinations around Vienna.

Heading east, there are hourly trains running from Wien-Mitte (Landstrasser Bahnhof) to Petronell-Carnuntum (50 minutes), with the same trains continuing on to Hainburg (one hour). A fast train runs from Vienna Central Station to Bratislava (one hour), via Marchegg.

Trains depart from Vienna Central Station frequently for the 40-minute ride to Neusiedl am See. The same train continues on to Eisenstadt, taking another 30 minutes. The fast train from Vienna Central Station to Sopron takes one hour 15 minutes. Trains also leave the same station regularly for Baden (30 minutes).

Regional rail tracks run parallel to the north and south banks of the Danube, and while trains reach all the larger towns and cities in the region, they miss the smaller towns of the Wachau Valley along the Danube's south bank. You can combine rail and boat transportation along this route, taking the train upstream and crisscrossing your way back on the river.

TRAIN INFORMATION ÖBB. ☎ *05/1717* ⊕ *www.oebb.at.*

Hotels

Although there are some luxury hotels in Linz and a few castle-hotels along the Danube, in general accommodations in the countryside are no frills. That said, the region has become much more heavily traveled than it was a generation ago, and many lodgings have been upgraded and restyled to attract the growing number of guests. Establishments are generally family-run, and there is usually somebody on staff who speaks English. You'll probably have to carry your own bags, and sometimes climb stairs in older buildings. Booking ahead is a good idea, as most places have relatively few rooms, particularly rooms with private baths. The standard country pillows and bed coverings are down-filled, so if you're allergic to feathers, ask for other blankets. Accommodations in private homes are cheaper still, and these bargains are usually identified by signs reading *"zimmer frei"* (room available) or *"frustück-spension"* (bed-and-breakfast).

Some hotels offer half-board, with dinner in addition to buffet breakfast. The half-board rate is usually an extra €15–€30 per person. Occasionally, quoted room rates for hotels already include half-board accommodations, though a discounted rate is generally offered if you prefer not to take the evening meal; inquire when booking. Rooms rates include taxes and service, and usually breakfast—although this is likely little more than bread or rolls with slices of ham and cheese. In summer, nights are generally cool, but days can get uncomfortably hot. Most older hotels don't have air-conditioning, and rooms can get stuffy; whenever possible, see the rooms before checking in.

Accommodations in the bigger cities of Bratislava and Sopron are rather more varied, with options ranging from cheap and cheerful hostels to luxe, five-star hotels. *Hotel reviews have been shortened. For full information, visit Fodors.com.*

Restaurants

With only a few exceptions, food in this region is on the simple side. The basics are available in abundance: roast meats, customary schnitzel variations, game (in season), fresh vegtables, and standard desserts such as *Palatschinken* (crepes filled with jam or nuts, topped with chocolate sauce) and *Apfelstrüdel*. However, imaginative cooking is beginning to spread, and most places have fresh fish and other lighter fare. You'll find at least one vegetarian course on most menus.

Around Neusiedl Lake, the local Pannonian cooking, strongly influenced by neighboring Hungary, showcases such spicy dishes as *gulyas* (goulash) flavored with paprika. You'll also find fresh fish, goose, game, and an abundance of fresh local vegetables. Along the Danube, restaurants make the most of the river views. Simple *Gasthäuser* are everywhere, but better dining is more often found in country inns. Restaurants, whether sophisticated and stylish or plain and homey, are often rated as much by their wine as by their cuisine. As bigger cities, food and drink options across the borders in Bratislava and Sopron are significantly more varied.

Dining in the Austrian countryside is a casual affair. Meal times are usually from noon to 2 pm for lunch and from 6 to 10 for dinner. It's rare to find a restaurant that serves all afternoon, so plan ahead. It's a good idea to reserve a table, especially for Sunday lunch, which is a popular time for families to get together. As in Vienna, tipping is usually rounded to the nearest euro. When in doubt, tip 5%. *Restaurants reviews have been shortened. For full information, visit Fodors.com.*

What it Costs in Euros

	$	$$	$$$	$$$$
RESTAURANTS				
	under €12	€12–€17	€18–€22	over €22
HOTELS				
	under €100	€100–€135	€136–€175	over €175

Tours

One-day tours to Bratislava usually include a boat ride one direction. For the Vienna Woods and Baden, short half-day tours give only a quick taste of the region; if you have more time, investigate further.

Tours from Vienna also take you to Melk and back by bus and boat. These tours usually run about eight hours, with a stop at Dürnstein. Bus tours operate year-round except as noted, but the boat runs only mid-April to late October. For details, check with your hotel or with Vienna Sightseeing Tours.

Vienna Sightseeing

GUIDED TOURS | In addition to its city tours, this company offers a number of whole and half-day trips to nearby attractions. You can visit Bratislava, traveling there by bus and returning by catamaran; head to the Danube Valley, including a guided tour of Melk Abbey; or explore the pretty Vienna Woods, with a walking tour in Baden. Tours run year-round, though some transport options are seasonal. ⊠ *Opernring 3-5/Top 17-24, Vienna* ☎ *01/712–46–83* ⊕ *www.viennasightseeing.at* 🎫 *€44.*

Visitor Information

For information on Lower Austria, call the Niederösterreich Tourismus in Vienna. Local tourist offices in the Vienna Woods, including those in Baden, are generally open weekdays. The Weinviertel region also has several tourist centers, while there are regional tourist information offices for Neusiedl Lake in Eisenstadt (Burgenland Tourismus) and Neusiedl am See (Neusiedler See Tourismus). There are helpful local *Fremdenverkehrsämter* (tourist offices), listed in the individual towns.

If you plan on seeing many museums, galleries, and castles in Lower Austria— which includes Vienna, Baden, Melk, Krems, and the Weinviertel—consider getting the Niederösterreich-Card (Lower Austria Card), which allows free entry to more than 300 sites and offers a host of discounts on concerts, rail travel, and accommodations. It costs €63 for the whole year (spring to spring), and is available at tourist information offices, Raiffeisen banks, tobacco shops, and online at ⊕ *www.niederoesterreich-card.at.*

CONTACTS Burgenland Tourismus. ⊠ *Johann Permayer-Strasse 13, Eisenstadt* ☎ *02682/633840* ⊕ *www.burgenland. info.* **Neusiedler See Tourismus.** ⊠ *Obere Hauptstrasse 24, Neusiedl am See* ☎ *02167/8600* ⊕ *www.neusiedler- see.com.* **Niederösterreich Tourismus.** ☎ *02742/9000–9000* ⊕ *www.niederoes- terreich.at.* **Upper Austria.** ⊠ *Freistaed- ter Strasse 119, Linz* ☎ *0732/221022* ⊕ *www.upperaustria.com.*

Carnuntum and Hainburg an der Donau

42 km (26 miles) southeast of Vienna.

Until a few years ago, the village of Car- nuntum was a yawning backwater on the Austrian plain and, along with its slightly larger neighbor, Hainburg, was the last stop before the Iron Curtain. But the fall of the wall turned the main road into a major throughway connecting East to West. The development of the Carnun- tum archaeological complex and the rise of the Donau-Auen National Park (the last remaining intact wetlands in Central Europe) turned this once-forgotten region into a significant destination for travelers.

GETTING HERE AND AROUND

From Vienna, take the A4 east directly to Petronell-Carnuntum. By train, take the S7, a local service that departs from Wien-Mitte/Landstrasse or Wien-Nord/ Praterstern; from here, buses run to Hainburg via Bad Deutsch-Altenburg. The tiny village of Rohrau, Joseph Haydn's birthplace, is five kilometers (three miles) south of Petronell on Route 211. There is a bus service, but it takes a very long and circuitous route; better to take a taxi or even walk it.

 Sights

★ **Carnuntum**

ARCHAEOLOGICAL SITE | FAMILY | The remains of the important Roman legion- ary fortress and civil town of Carnuntum, which once numbered 55,000 inhabit- ants, extend about five kilometers (three miles) along the Danube from the tiny vil- lage of Petronell to the next town of Bad Deutsch-Altenburg. The recent discovery here of an ancient school of gladiators delighted archaeologists and significantly raised Carnuntum's stature, and rightfully so. Visitors can tour the grounds, which include two amphitheaters (the first one seating 8,000) and the foundations of former residences, reconstructed baths, and trading centers—some with mosaic floors. The ruins are quite spread out, with the impressive remains of a Roman arch, the **Heidentor** (Pagans' Gate), a 15-minute pleasant walk from the main excavations in Petronell. You can experience what Roman life was like circa AD 380 in the elegantly furnished Villa Urbana. Many of the excavated finds are housed at the Museum Carnuntinum at Bad Deutsch-Altenburg. The star of the collection is a carving of Mithras killing a bull. Guided tours in English are available in July and August at noon; otherwise they are in German only. ⊠ *Haupt- strasse 1A, Petronell* ☎ *02163/33770* ⊕ *www.carnuntum.at* 🎫 *€12* ☉ *Closed mid-Nov.–mid-Mar.*

Haydn's Birthplace (*Haydn-Geburtshaus Rohrau*)

HOUSE | Just a five-minute drive south of Petronell, the tiny village of Rohrau was the birthplace of Joseph Haydn—and the quaint, reed-thatched cottage where the composer, son of the local blacksmith, was born in 1732 is now a small muse- um. You'll see a pianoforte he is sup- posed to have played, as well as letters and other memorabilia. The furnishings are homey, if a bit spartan. After Haydn had gained worldwide renown, he is said to have returned to his native Rohrau

Situated near the border between Vienna and the Bratislava, the ancient Roman city of Carnuntum was once even larger than Vienna.

and knelt to kiss the steps of his humble home. Concerts are occasionally held on the grounds. ⊠ *Obere Hauptstrasse 25, Rohrau* ☎ *02164/2268* ⊕ *www.haydnge-burtshaus.at* ✉ *€5* ⊘ *Closed Mon. and Nov.–mid-Feb.*

Schloss Rohrau

CASTLE/PALACE | Also in Rohrau, this palace is where Haydn's mother worked as a cook for Count Harrach. It also has one of the best private art collections in Austria, with an emphasis on 17th- and 18th-century Spanish and Italian painting; weekend tours are available Easter through October. The upper level has been renovated and turned into private apartments; there is now also a good restaurant on the grounds serving Austrian fare. Be mindful of the peacocks that wander the grounds, and sometimes beyond. ⊠ *Schloss Rohrau 1, Rohrau* ☎ *02164/225316* ⊕ *www.schloss-rohrau. at* ✉ *€12* ⊘ *Closed Nov.–Easter.*

Schlossberg Castle Ruins (*Burgruine Heimenburg*)

ARCHAEOLOGICAL SITE | Situated in the heart of Hainburg, these castle ruins (easily approached on foot) are equally appealing for the castle's long and illustrious history and the lovely views from the top. During the 11th century, Hainburg was a fortified town on the far eastern front of the Holy Roman Empire, and in 1252, Przemsyl Ottaker, the king of Bohemia, married Duchess Margarethe of Austria here, a union designed to considerably expand his kingdom. The castle had been built shortly before that with part of the ransom received from the capture of King Richard the Lionheart in Dürnstein. The Schloss was attacked many times, most severely by the 1683 Turkish invasion, which also took the lives of 8,000 residents, nearly the entire community. Each summer the town hosts "Burgspiele Hainburg," where open-air plays (often Shakespeare) are performed in German on the castle grounds. ⊠ *Schlossbergstrasse, Hainburg an der Donau* ☎ *02165/67365* ✉ *Free.*

Wienertor

BUILDING | The imposing "Vienna Gate" still represents the entrance to the medieval town of Hainburg on the Danube, and buses, tractors, and a steady stream of cars still squeeze through its passage daily. The town is encircled by remarkably well-preserved 13th-century walls with 12 gates and towers, including the Wienertor, which is the largest extant medieval gate in Europe. In 1683, the Turks devastated the town, leaving only a handful of survivors, including composer Josef Haydn's grandfather (who, as a small boy, scrambled up a chimney and hid from the marauders). Climb up inside the Wienertor, now a museum, and see an impressive supply of weaponry left behind by the invaders—clearly in a hurry to get to Vienna—as well as a stockpile from other ancient wars. A view out the narrow window offers a charming look down at the winding main street and the church steeple. While you can always stop by and view the exterior of the tower, inside access is only available Sunday and holidays. ✉ *Hainburgerstrasse 1, Hainburg an der Donau* ☎ *06642/261630* 🌐 *www.wienertor.at* 🎟 *€4* 🕘 *Closed Mon.–Sat. and Nov.–Apr.*

Hotels

Hotel Altes Kloster

$$ | **HOTEL** | Adjacent to the historic Kulturfabrik (once the Imperial Royal Tobacco Factory) and just around the corner from where little Joseph Haydn used to have his music lessons, this 17th-century monastery retains all its historic serenity in the sleepy, romantic town of Hainburg. **Pros:** live piano music in the restaurant-café; quiet and peaceful setting; five-minute walk to town center. **Cons:** carpeting in rooms may aggravate allergies; not all staff speak English; no air-conditioning. [$] *Rooms from: €105* ✉ *Fabriksplatz 1a, Hainburg an der Donau* ☎ *02165/64020* 🌐 *www.altes-kloster.com* 🛏 *52 rooms* 🍴 *Free breakfast.*

Marchegg

52 km (32 miles) northeast of Vienna.

This tiny corner of the lower Weinviertel is known as the Marchfeld, for the fields stretching east to the March River that form the border with Slovakia. Known as the granary of Austria, the region is home to an elegant Baroque castle that, while totally renovated, has lost none of its gracious charm over the centuries.

GETTING HERE AND AROUND

From Vienna, take the A4 highway east to Bad Deutsch-Altenburg, then turn onto the B49, which goes directly north to Marchegg. Trains go from Vienna Central Station to Marchegg several times daily. To get from here to Schlosshof, jump on the free shuttle bus starting at Marchegg train station; it runs mid-March through mid-November and there are timetables on the Schlosshof website.

Sights

★ Schlosshof

CASTLE/PALACE | **FAMILY** | A true Baroque gem, this castle is shining even more brilliantly since the completion of extensive restorations. The product of that master designer and architect Johann Lukas von Hildebrandt, who in 1732 reconstructed the square castle into an elegant U-shape building, the Schloss opens up on the eastern side to a marvelous Baroque formal garden that gives way toward the river. The famed landscape painter Bernardo Bellotto, noted for his Canaletto-like vistas of scenic landmarks, captured the view before the reconstruction. His three paintings were used as a guide for restoring the gardens to their Baroque appearance.

The castle was once owned by Empress Maria Theresa, mother of Marie Antoinette. You can visit the suite the empress used during her royal visits, faithfully re-created down to the tiniest details, as well as the two-story chapel in which she prayed.

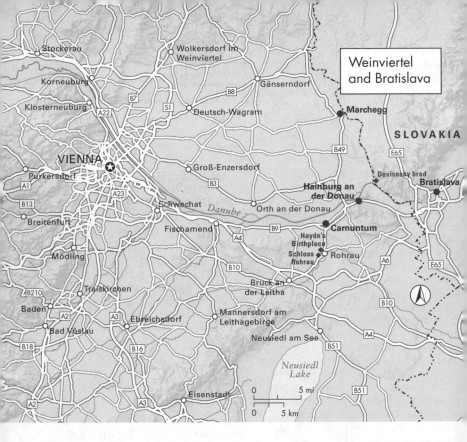

In 2016, the Schlosshof added some highly popular adventure paths to the interactive visitor experience. Children can play the roles of stable boys and maidens, performing various chores and encountering blacksmiths, falconers, or bakers along the path. You might stumble upon a large estate farm that is home to horses, goats, donkeys, and several other animals. The complex also includes a restaurant and pâtisserie, both with indoor and outdoor seating. Guided tours and audio tours of the castle and garden are available in English, but it's also possible to wander around the buildings and grounds on your own. The castle is about eight kilometers (five miles) south of Marchegg. Be sure to enjoy the panaromic view (you can even see across the border into Slovakia and it's capital Bratislava from here). If you come in winter, you can enjoy the charming Adventmarkt set up on the sprawling grounds. ⊠ *Schlosshof 1, Schlosshof* ☏ *02285/20000* ⊕ *www.schlosshof.at* 🎟 *€18.*

Bratislava, Slovakia

66 km (42 miles) east of Vienna.

Slovakia may be one of the world's youngest nations, but the country—and its capital Bratislava—has a long and illustrious history. Settled since the Neolithic era, Bratislava and the area around has spent much of this time as a component of a larger state, from the Roman Empire to the Kingdom of Hungary, the Hapsburg Monarchy to Czechoslovakia. In 1993, Slovakia became an independent state, and since then Bratislava has blossomed into a thriving, modern European capital—while still retaining its charming historic center.

The city's most visible attraction is its enormous white Renaissance castle, perched on a rocky hill overlooking the Danube. But head down to ground level and you'll find there are plenty of other charms to this city, from the extensive Old Town that combines medieval and Gothic architecture to the thriving restaurant and nightlife culture that seriously rivals Vienna. Most of the top attractions are free (or very cheap) to experience, but if you want to dig a little deeper, it's worth picking up a **Bratislava Card**. This will give you entry into 16 museums and galleries in the city and around, including the Museum of Viticulture and Devín Castle, as well as a one-hour guided tour of the Old Town and free public transportation. The card is valid for 24, 48, and 72 hours, at €20, €25, and €28 respectively. Pick it up at the tourist information or on the Visit Bratislava website.

GETTING HERE AND AROUND

Bratislava has a small international airport served by budget airlines including Ryanair and Wizzair; a 40-minute bus brings you in the city center. For long-haul destinations and national carriers, fly to and from Vienna.

To reach Bratislava from the Austrian capital, you can come by car (about one hour east on Route 9) or with a fast train (via Marchegg, also one hour). Alternatively, take to the water with the Twin City catamaran (75 minutes).

Once you're in town, ditch the car: the Old Town is almost completely pedestrianized, and small enough to walk around, while regular buses and trams will take you to destinations further afield.

AIRPORT INFORMATION Bratislava Airport. (*Letisko M. R. Štefánika*) ✉ *Ivanská cesta, Bratislava* ☎ *02/330–333–53* ⊕ *www.bts.aero.*

RESTAURANTS AND HOTELS

Bratislava has a small but excellent selection of quality boutique hotels, as well as several fine restaurants and casual

Weinstrasse Cycling

A great way to see Carnuntum and the towns along the Danube is by bicycle. Bike routes are well marked, extensive, and in excellent condition. Many shops in Vienna rent bikes, and some hotels have bikes available to their guests. For the most part, you can take a bike free of charge on the local and regional trains, which makes it easy to explore a larger area. And you'll be in good company: weekend cycle tours along the Danube are popular with the Viennese and the neighboring Slovaks.

dining options. Despite using the same currency, you will usually get more bang for your euro in Bratislava than in Vienna.

What it Costs in Euros			
$	$$	$$$	$$$$
RESTAURANTS			
under €10	€11–€15	€16–€20	over €20
HOTELS			
under €80	€81–€105	€106–€135	over €135

VISITOR INFORMATION

CONTACTS Visit Bratislava. ✉ *Klobučnícka 2, Bratislava* ☎ *02/544–194–10* ⊕ *www.visitbratislava.com.*

Sights

★ **Bratislavský hrad** (*Bratislava Castle*) **CASTLE/PALACE** | With roots dating back more than a millennium—it was first mentioned in 907 for its role in a battle between Bavarians and Hungarians—Bratislava Castle was significantly rebuilt in the Renaissance style in the mid-16th century. It's this enormous, rectangular form with four stocky towers that you can see today (though it incorporates architectural features from throughout its history, and the dazzling white paint job is distinctly 20th century). Walk up the (steep) castle hill and pass through one of the four entrance gates (probably **Viedenská brána** or **Leopoldova brána**) for incredible views of the town and the Danube below. The grounds are free to enter, so you can soak up the vistas as long as you like; make sure you visit the beautiful **Baroková záhrada** (Baroque Garden) while you're at it. You only need to pay if you want to head inside, either for the **SNM-Historical Museum**, which is a little sparse but does include access to the **Crown Tower** via a narrow passageway, or any of the regularly-changing temporary exhibits. ⊠ *Zámocká 2, Bratislava* ☎ *02/204–831–10* ⊕ *www. bratislava-hrad.sk.*

Devínsky hrad (*Devín Castle*)
CASTLE/PALACE | Located on the confluence of the Morava and Danube rivers that form the border between Slovakia and Austria, just 10½ kilometers (6½ miles) west of Bratislava, lies this extraordinary ruined castle. Built on the top of a high crag, the enormous Devín Castle is one of the oldest in the region, first mentioned in written sources in 864. You can learn about the history of castle and the village (all the way back to Neolithic times) in a fascinating exhibition within the castle walls. Enjoy the sweeping views from the top of the ruined Upper Castle, and take a snap of the famous **Maiden's Tower**, a tiny watchtower precariously balanced on a lone rock that has spawned countless legends of imprisoned women leaping to their deaths. In summer, there are kid-friendly medieval-themed events held in and around the castle. To reach Devín, take Bus 29 from Bratislava (30 minutes) or drive west out of the city on Devínska cesta. ⊠ *Muránská 1050/10, Bratislava* ☎ *02/657–301–05* ⊕ *www.muzeum.bratislava.sk* 🖻 *€5* 🕙 *Closed Mon.*

Grasalkovičov palác (*Grassalkovich Palace*)
GOVERNMENT BUILDING | This grand Rococo-style summer residence was built in 1780 for Count Anton Grassalkovich, advisor to Empress Maria Theresa (who was crowned in Bratislava in 1761). Today, it's the official residence of the President of the Slovak Republic so it isn't possible to see inside, but come at 1 pm any day of the week to witness the ceremonial Changing of the Guard. You can also head around the back of the palace to explore the lovely Prezidentská záhrada (Presidental Garden), a public park that's an oasis of manicured lawns, sculpted hedges, and gorgeous flower displays. It also has a number of avant garde sculptures, including the playful *Fountain of Youth* by Slovak sculptor Tibor Bártfay. ⊠ *Hodžovo námestie 2978/1, Bratislava* ☎ *02/578–881–55* ⊕ *www. prezident.sk.*

Hlavné Námestie
PLAZA | Bratislava's main square is the beating heart of the city, home to some of its most interesting history, architecture, and artworks. The centerpiece of the square is **Maximiliánova fontána** (Maximilian's Fountain), erected in 1572 as a public water supply. The knight on top is said to bow once a year, on New Year's Eve, though only for those pure of heart and born in Bratislava. The square is ringed by a number of beautiful Gothic and Baroque buildings, many of which are now embassies. The most notable of these is the **Stará radnica** (Old Town Hall), which is actually a mishmash of different houses built at various stages from the 14th century onwards; look for the cannonball embedded in the town hall's tower. Opposite, on the corner outside Café Mayer, is the **Schöne Náci** (Nice Nazi) statue, depicting a famous local eccentric who cheerfully wandered the streets in top hat and tails. As well as the permanent fixtures, the square also hosts regular markets, concerts, and political events. ⊠ *Bratislava.*

Bratislava, with its compact old town, charming city streets, and outdoor café culture, is a wonderful day trip from Vienna.

Hviezdoslavovo námestie (*Hviezdoslav Square*)

PLAZA | This charming, tree-shaded promenade is named for renowned Slovak poet Pavol Országh Hviezdoslav and lined with some of the city's grandest buildings—now mainly embassies, hotels, and restaurants. The "square" starts with a **statue of Hviezdoslav** and ends at **Morový stĺp**, a beautiful Baroque trinity column. Just east of Hviezdoslav Square is the old **Slovenské národné divadlo** (Slovak National Theatre) building, while just around the corner crowds gather to see the popular **Čumil** (Rubberneck) sculpture; a cheeky bronze chap peeping out from under a manhole cover. ⊠ *Bratislava.*

Kostol svätej Alžbety (*Blue Church*)

RELIGIOUS SITE | Bratislava's most striking Secession (Art Nouveau) style building, the Church of St. Elizabeth is noted for its powder blue exterior, which extends all the way up to its 120-foot round tower. The unusual color scheme continues throughout the early-20th-century building, from the blue ceramic roof tiles, mosaics, and maiolica (tin-glazed pottery) decorations outside, to the baby blue pews and arches inside. The church once functioned as the chapel of the school opposite, which is evident in the two buildings' similar design elements (though the school has a rather more traditional color scheme). ⊠ *Bezručova 2, Bratislava* ⊕ *www.modrykostol.fara.sk.*

Michalská brána (*Michael's Gate*)

MUSEUM | The last gate standing from Bratislava's original 13th century city walls, Michael's Gate was rebuilt in the Baroque style in 1758; that's when the onion dome was added. Look up to the top of the tower to see the dome, as well as a statue of the archangel Michael slaying a dragon; or look down to see a bronze plate showing the distances to different world capitals. Also of note is the remarkably skinny house on the northwest side of the gate, now a fast food joint. For a small fee, you can climb the tower for views over the city; your ticket also includes entry to the small Museum of Arms within the gate, as well as the nearby Pharmacy Museum, a fascinating exhibition on 16th century medicine. ⊠ *Michalská ulica 22, Bratislava* ☎ *02/544–330–44* ⊕ *www. muzeum.bratislava.sk* 🎫 *€4.50 (tower and museum)* ⊙ *Closed Mon. (tower and museum).*

Primaciálny palác (*Primate's Palace*)
CASTLE/PALACE | This gorgeous Neoclassical building, constructed between 1778 to 1781 for the Archbishop József Batthyány—"primate" is a title given to a bishop; nothing to do with monkeys—played a vital role in European history in 1805. That's when the palace's Hall of Mirrors was used to sign the fourth Peace of Pressburg, which effectively brought an end to the Holy Roman Empire. Today, you can visit the beautiful hall, elegantly furnished with period pieces, as well as the picture gallery with portraits of Hungarian rulers. Somewhat surprisingly, the palace also contains a rare collection of exquisite English tapestries from the time of King James I (1566–1625). ⊠ *Primaciálne námestie 2, Bratislava* ☎ *02/593–563–94* ⊕ *www.visitbratislava.com/places/primatial-palace* ⊙ *Closed Mon.*

Slovak National Collection of Wines
WINERY/DISTILLERY | Attached to the Museum of Viticulture—which traces the long history of winemaking in the Bratislava and Lower Carpathians region—is this beautiful 16th century wine cellar offering regular tastings. The national collection is made up of Slovakia's "Top 100 Wines," which are chosen from more than 600 entries each year; you can find everything from Tokajs to ice wines. Choose to sample two, four, or eight of the collection's wines and a professional sommelier will guide you through the experience. Alternatively, opt for the self-guided, all-you-can-drink "72 wines in 100 minutes" tasting. All tastings are available for individuals or groups, but it's best to call ahead to ensure an English-speaking guide. ⊠ *Radničná 577/1, Bratislava* ☎ *918–664–992* ⊕ *www.salonvin.sk* ⊙ *Closed Sun.–Mon.*

★ **St Martin's Cathedral** (*Katedrála svätého Martina*)
RELIGIOUS SITE | The enormous golden crown and cushion on top of this beautiful Gothic cathedral reveals that this was once a coronation church. In fact, it was *the* coronation church for Hungarian (and later Austrian) monarchs for more than 250 years; 19 different royals were crowned here between 1563 and 1830, including Empress Maria Theresa. The church was also one of the city's lines of defense, which explains the chunky walls, the arrow-slit windows, and the exceptionally tall (lookout) tower. Luckily, the interior is more delicate and decorative, with dramatic rib vaults, colorful stained glass windows, and a grand altar showing St. Martin in a traditional Hungarian hussar dress. Next to the cathedral lie the remains of the **Neologická Synagóga** (Neological Synagogue), demolished by the Communist government in the 1970s, and overlooked by the glorious facade of the **Lekáreň u Salvátora** (Pharmacy Salvator). ⊠ *Rudnayovo námestie 1, Bratislava* ☎ *02/544–313–59* ⊕ *www.dom.fara.sk.*

🍴 Restaurants

★ **Albrecht**
$$$$ | FRENCH | One of the city's most elegant fine dining experiences, Restaurant Albrecht near Bratislava Castle serves sumptuous, strictly seasonal French cuisine using the highest quality locally-sourced ingredients; menus often lists individual farms and producers. Head chef Jaroslav Žídek is known for his elaborate, multi-course tasting menus, but you can also order the dishes à la carte: opt for the tuna ceviche to start, the lamb back with sheep-cheese ravioli for main, and the plum dumplings to finish. **Known for:** multi-course tasting menus; great value lunch menu; five minutes by taxi from the Old Town. $ *Average main: €30* ⊠ *Mudroňova 4237/82, Bratislava* ☎ *902–333–888* ⊕ *www.hotelalbrecht.sk/restauracia* ⊙ *Closed Sun.*

Roxor

$$ | **BURGER** | Melt-in-the-mouth eco-farm beef, crunchy double-cooked fries, and crisp craft beers are the order of the day at this excellent burger joint. There are half a dozen burger options to choose from, including veggie mushroom and vegan patty ones; all are cooked medium as standard and served with tasty sides like rosemary or garlic fries, kimchi, and coleslaw. **Known for:** Bratislava's best burgers; homemade pineapple-curry mayo; a little way out of the Old Town. $ *Average main: €15* ✉ *Šancová 19, Bratislava* ☎ *02/210–205–00* ⊕ *www. roxorburger.sk.*

Zylinder

$$$ | **AUSTRIAN** | With dishes based on traditional Austro-Hungarian recipes, this well-located café and restaurant makes a pleasant stop for lunch or dinner. Expect everything from traditional Austrian schnitzel and *tafelspitz* (boiled beef served with minced apples) to Hungarian beef goulash and *somlói galuska* (sponge trifle), as well as Slovakian specialties like *halušky* (small potato dumplings with sheep cheese, sautéed bacon, and sour cream). **Known for:** tasty beef broth with noodles; great location on Hviezdoslav Square; big portions and good value for area. $ *Average main: €16* ✉ *Hviezdoslavovo námestie 19, Bratislava* ☎ *903–123–134* ⊕ *www.zylinder.sk.*

☕ Coffee and Quick Bites

★ Konditorei Kormuth

$$ | **CAFÉ** | It may look unassuming from the street, but step inside and it becomes immediately apparent why this is considered one of Europe's most beautiful cafes. The walls and ceilings throughout the interior are plastered in majestic Renaissance-style frescoes, while seemingly every nook and cranny of the old building is filled with antiques, some dating back to the 16th century. **Known for:** stunningly decorative interior; delicious cakes and pastries; entrance fee. $ *Average main: €10* ✉ *Sedlárska 363, Bratislava* ☎ *02/544–325–37* ⊕ *www.konditoreikormuth.sk* ⊙ *Closed Mon.–Tue.*

Koun

$ | **FAST FOOD** | In recent years, Bratislava has been taken over by ice cream stores, and today it's hard to find an Old Town street without a high-quality gelato option. But if you have to choose only one scoop while you're in town, opt for Koun (pronounced "cone"). **Known for:** incredible lemon cake ice cream; sunny decor and even sunnier staff; half-hidden on a side street off Hviezdoslav Square. $ *Average main: €5* ✉ *Paulínyho 1, Bratislava* ☎ *948–687–795* ⊕ *www.koun.sk* ⊙ *Closed Mon.*

Hotels

Loft Hotel

$$ | **HOTEL** | Standing out from the Old Town crowd with its industrial-style decor incorporating exposed brick walls, distressed wooden floors, shabby leather sofas, and retro advertising prints, Loft offers a different kind of hotel experience. **Pros:** sixth floor rooms have gorgeous garden views; free snacks and wine for guests; popular Fabrika brewpub downstairs. **Cons:** industrial decor isn't to all tastes; underground parking is €20 a day; wood floors can be noisy. $ *Rooms from: €85* ✉ *Štefánikova 864/4, Bratislava* ☎ *901–902–680* ⊕ *www.lofthotel.sk* ⇥ *111 rooms* ⊙| *No meals.*

★ Marrol's Boutique Hotel

$$$ | **HOTEL** | A romantic boutique gem in the heart of the Old Town, Marrol's is set within a 19th century burgher's house and oozes period charm, with its opulent chandeliers, deep leather armchairs, and charming wood paneling. **Pros:** free minibar full of drinks; lovely plant-covered Summer Terrace; underground parking available. **Cons:** breakfast is nothing special; service isn't always with a smile; noise in corridors carries. $ *Rooms* *from: €110 ✉ Tobrucká 6953/4, Bratislava ☎ 02/577–846–00 🌐 www.hotelmarrols.sk 🛏 54 rooms 🍴 Free breakfast.*

Roset Hotel

$$$ | **HOTEL** | Built in 1903 in the Secession (Art Nouveau) style, this sophisticated hotel, which is conveniently located by the Old Town, offers 27 spacious and elegant suites, a spa with fitness center, sauna, and jacuzzi, and the time-honored Tulip Café. **Pros:** beautiful turn-of-the-century building; in-suite massages available; incorporates famous old literary café. **Cons:** breakfast is underwhelming; mattresses are a little hard; some rooms need sprucing up. [$] *Rooms from: €115 ✉ Štúrova Ulica 10, Bratislava ☎ 917–373–209 🌐 www.rosethotel.sk 🛏 27 rooms 🍴 Free breakfast.*

🍸 Nightlife

Grand Cru Wine Gallery

WINE BARS—NIGHTLIFE | This popular Old Town bar is the perfect place to sample some high-quality Slovakian wines. Amiable owner Martin Pagáč is always on hand to talk you through individual vintages and answer questions. ✉ *Zámočnícka 404/8, Bratislava ☎ 908–656–259 🌐 www.facebook.com/GrandCruWineGallery.*

KC Dunaj

DANCE CLUBS | Set within a Communist-era shopping mall but now reclaimed by a younger, hipper crowd, this lively bar and club venue hosts regular live concerts, club nights, theater events, and more. ✉ *Nedbalova 435/3, Bratislava ☎ 904–330–049 🌐 www.kcdunaj.sk.*

★ Kláštorný pivovar

BREWPUBS/BEER GARDENS | For a great tasting, great value beer, you won't beat the homebrew at this popular brewpub—it's just €3.70 for a whole liter of Monastic Beer served straight from the tap. Enjoy it with tasty Slovak pub food like grilled sausages, baked pork knuckle, and *halušky* (potato dumplings with sheep's cheese) ✉ *Námestie SNP 469/8, Bratislava ☎ 907–976–284 🌐 www.klastornypivovar.sk.*

UFO

BARS/PUBS | Situated at the top of the observation tower on the UFO bridge, this swanky bar offers the chance to enjoy delicious cocktails, spirits, and wines while overlooking the Danube and the city below. There's also a well-regarded restaurant here, but beware: the sky-high setting also means sky-high prices. ✉ *Most SNP 1, Bratislava ☎ 02/625–203–00 🌐 www.u-f-o.sk.*

🎫 Performing Arts

Slovenské národné divadlo (*Slovak National Theater*)

THEATER | Whether at the grand, 18th-century, Neo-Renaissance building in the heart of the Old Town, or at the shiny, art-filled, 21st century building downriver, the Slovak National Theater knows how to put on a show. The regular, high-quality operas, ballets, and drama performances are typically around €20 a ticket. ✉ *New Slovak National Theater, Pribinova 17, Bratislava ☎ 02/204–722–89 🌐 www.snd.sk.*

👜 Shopping

BEER

100 Pív

LOCAL SPECIALTIES | A small bottle shop on the edge of the Old Town, 100 Pív has hundreds of beers available to buy, with a big focus on local craft breweries. There are always some beers on tap, so you can try before you buy. ✉ *Medená 111/33, Bratislava ☎ 948–405–409 🌐 www.100piv.sk.*

FASHION

NOX Vintage

CLOTHING | A favorite with lovers of vintage and retro fashion, this Old Town store has rack upon rack of clothes, bags, and shoes, as well as few items of furniture and homeware. ✉ *Ventúrska 3,*

Bratislava ☎ 905–861–879 ⊕ www.face-book.com/NOXvintage ⊗ Closed Sun.

GIFTS AND SOUVENIRS
Slávica
GIFTS/SOUVENIRS | You'll find everything from clothing and jewelry to art prints and ceramics from local producers at this hip design store near Laurence's Gate. ⊠ *Laurinská 19, Bratislava ☎ 917–968–736 ⊕ www.slavicadesign.sk.*

Neusiedl am See

50 km (31 miles) southeast of Vienna.

At the north end of the lake for which it is named is a pleasant resort town with good facilities. Direct hourly commuter trains from Vienna have made it very popular, so you won't be alone here. To reach the lake, where you can rent small boats, swim, or just relax on the beach, follow the main street for three blocks east of the Hauptplatz and turn right on Seestrasse. In the town itself, visit the ruins of the 13th-century hill fortress, Ruine Tabor, and the 15th-century parish church near the town hall.

GETTING HERE AND AROUND
Trains leave from Vienna Central Station frequently every day and take 40 minutes. By car, take the A4 motorway southeast; you'll switch to the A50 then the B51 just north of Neusiedl am See (follow the signs).

VISITOR INFORMATION
CONTACTS Tourism Neusiedl am See. ⊠ *Untere Hauptstrasse 7 ☎ 02167/2229 ⊕ www.neusiedlamsee.at.*

 Hotels

Hotel Wende
$$$$ | HOTEL | This sprawling three-story hotel complex is close to the lake and has more than standard amenities, whether you want to get a relaxing massage or to rent bicycles and set off

Bicycling Around Neusiedl

The plains around Neusiedl Lake, upon which sit tiny, undisturbed hamlets amid unspoiled scenery, are perfect for leisurely bicycling. Practically every village has a bike-rental shop (*Fahrradverleih* or *Radverleih*), but on weekends demand is so great that it's a good idea to reserve in advance. A bike route encircles the lake, which means it passes through Hungary (you can shorten the route by taking the ferry between Illmitz beach and Mörbisch). Bike route maps are available at tourist offices.

on the path that begins at its doorstep. **Pros:** friendly and knowledgeable staff; spacious lobby; very good location. **Cons:** little charm; outdated televisions; no air conditioning. Ⓢ *Rooms from: €189* ⊠ *Seestrasse 40 ☎ 02167/8111 ⊕ www.hotel-wende.at ⊗ Closed at start of Feb.* ⤳ *104 rooms* ⓘ⦿❘ *Free breakfast.*

Eisenstadt

58 km (336 miles) south of Vienna.

Burgenland's provincial capital, Eisenstadt, is a really small town. Nevertheless, it has an illustrious history and enough sights to keep you busy for a half day, if not quite a full one. Although the town has existed since at least the 12th century, it only rose to significance in the 17th century when it became the seat of the Esterházys, a princely Hungarian family that traces its roots to Attila the Hun. The original Esterházy made his fortune by marrying a succession of wealthy landowning widows. Esterházy's support was largely responsible for the Habsburg reign in Hungary under the Dual

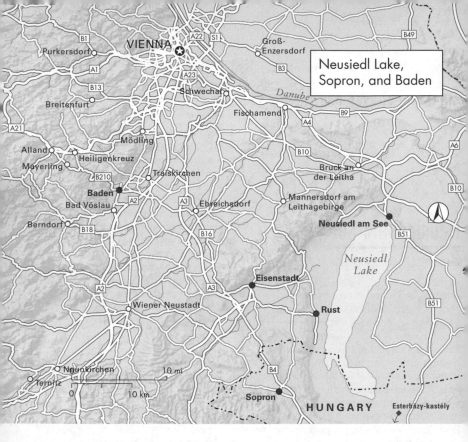

Neusiedl Lake, Sopron, and Baden

Monarchy. At one time the family controlled a far-flung agro-industrial empire, and it still owns vast forest resources. The composer Joseph Haydn lived in Eisenstadt for some 30 years while in the service of the Esterházy family. When Hungary ceded Burgenland to Austria after World War I, its major city, Sopron, elected to remain a part of Hungary, so in 1925 tiny Eisenstadt was made the capital of the new Austrian province.

Eisenstadt's main draw is the former palace, Schloss Esterházy, and the tourist office can tell you about its other attractions, including the Museum of Austrian Culture, the Diocesan Museum, the Fire Fighters Museum, Haydn's little garden house, and an assortment of churches.

GETTING HERE AND AROUND

Eisenstadt is connected to Vienna and Neusiedl am See by direct train and to Rust and other places throughout Burgenland by bus. By car from Vienna, take the A3 south to the edge of town.

VISITOR INFORMATION

CONTACTS Eisenstadt Tourismustour.
✉ Hauptstrasse 21 ☎ 02682/67390
⊕ www.eisenstadt-tourismus.at.

 Sights

Haydn-Haus

HOUSE | The composer Joseph Haydn lived in the simple house on a street that now bears his name from 1766 until 1778. Now a house museum—the house itself, and especially its flower-filled courtyard with the small back rooms, is quite delightful— it contains several first editions of his music and other memorabilia. A guided costumed tour involves tales about love and music in the real Haydn's life. ✉ *Joseph-Haydn-Gasse 21* ☎ *02682/719–6000* 🌐 *www.haydnhaus.at* 🎫 *€5* 🕑 *Closed mid-Nov.–Mar. and Mon. Apr.–Aug.*

Österreichisches Jüdisches Museum (*Austrian Jewish Museum*)
MUSEUM | From 1671 until 1938, the streets Wertheimergasse and Unterbergstrasse formed the boundaries of the Jewish ghetto. During that time Eisenstadt had a considerable Jewish population; today the Österreichisches Jüdisches Museum recalls the experience of Austrian Jews throughout history. A fascinating private synagogue in the complex survived the 1938 terror and is incorporated into the museum. ✉ *Unterbergstrasse 6* ☎ *02682/65145* 🌐 *www.ojm.at* 🎫 *€5* 🕑 *Closed Nov.–Apr. and Mon.*

★ **Schloss Esterházy** (*Esterházy Palace*)
CASTLE/PALACE | The former palace of the ruling princes reigns over the town. Built in the Baroque style between 1663 and 1672 on the foundations of a medieval castle and later modified, it is still owned by the Esterházy family, who lease it to the provincial government for use mostly as offices. The Esterházy family rooms are worth viewing, and the lavishly decorated Haydn Room, an impressive concert hall where the composer conducted his own works from 1761 until 1790, is still used for presentations of Haydn's works, with musicians often dressed in period garb. The hall is one of several rooms on a guided tour (in English on request if there are at least 10 people) that lasts about 30 minutes. The cellar has the largest wine museum in Austria with 700 objects including a massive wine barrel and historical grape press. A tour of the princess's apartment includes objects relating to three royal women. The park behind the palace is pleasant for a stroll or a picnic, and in late August it's a venue for the Burgenland wine week—Eisenstadt hosts the "Festival of 1,000 Wines"—when there's a two-hour wine tour and tasting at the palace. ✉ *Esterhazyplatz 1* ☎ *02682/719–63004* 🌐 *www.esterhazy.at/schloss-esterhazy* 🎫 *€12; €28 for all exhibitions and wine museum* 🕑 *Closed weekdays in mid-Nov.–Mar.*

Haydn Fully at Rest

Composer Joseph Haydn's body was returned to Eisenstadt for burial at the request of Prince Esterházy in 1821. The head, however, had been stolen by phrenologists and eventually became the property of the Gesellschaft der Musikfreunde, a Viennese musical society. A new marble tomb was built for Haydn in 1932 at Eisenstadt's Bergkirche, but the head was not returned until 1954. In the meantime a substitute head had been placed with the remains. Both skulls are now in the marble tomb.

🍴 Restaurants

★ **Taubenkobel**
$$$$ | **ECLECTIC** | Consistently ranked as one of the top restaurants in Austria, the "Dovecote" is a rambling, elegantly restored 19th-century farmhouse located halfway between Eisenstadt and Rust in the village of Schützen. The seasonally changing seven-course menu has featured dishes such as saddle of lamb with mangold blossoms and asparagus in saffron sauce. **Known for:** fresh herbs taken from nearby meadows; menu that changes seasonally; packages that include wine pairings and hotel stays. [$] *Average main: €138* ✉ *Hauptstrasse 27, Schützen am Gebirge* ☎ *02684/2297* 🌐 *www.taubenkobel.com* 🕑 *Closed Mon.–Tue., and mid-Nov.–Feb.*

🛏 Hotels

Hotel Ohr
$$$$ | **HOTEL** | Personal service is the hallmark of this family-run hotel and restaurant close to the town center, with a selection of comfortable "four-star" rooms attractively furnished in natural woods and whites with pastel accents, along with some slightly older (and smaller) "three-star" rooms. **Pros:** spacious rooms; excellent food in cozy restaurant; bicycles available to rent. **Cons:** no real lobby; a/c in only some rooms; only 10 of the 39 rooms are "four star". [$] *Rooms from: €170* ✉ *Rusterstrasse 51* ☎ *02682/62460* 🌐 *www.hotel-ohr.at* 🔑 *39 rooms* 🍴 *Free breakfast.*

Rust

71 km (44 miles) southeast of Vienna.

Picturesque Rust, a UNESCO World Cultural Heritage site, is easily the most popular village on the lake for the colorful pastel facades of its houses and for lake sports. Tourists flock here in summer to see storks nesting atop the Renaissance and Baroque houses in the well-preserved historic center.

GETTING HERE AND AROUND

By car from Vienna, take the A4 south then, just after Eisenstadt, take the B52 east about 14½ kilometers (nine miles). Bus service is also available directly from Vienna and from Neusiedl am See (via Eisenstadt).

VISITOR INFORMATION

CONTACTS Tourismusverband Freistadt Rust. ✉ *Conradplatz 1* ☎ *02685/5020* 🌐 *www.freistadt-rust.at.*

👁 Sights

Fischerkirche (*Fisherman's Church*)
RELIGIOUS SITE | The restored Gothic Fischerkirche is off the west end of the Rathausplatz. Built between the 12th and 16th centuries, it is surrounded by a defensive wall and is noted for its 15th-century frescoes and an organ from 1705. The church sometimes has classical concerts. Tours are available but must be arranged in advance. ✉ *Rathausplatz 16* ☎ *02685/502* 🎫 *€2, €4 with tour.*

Kremayrhaus Stadtmuseum
MUSEUM | Three decades ago, local arts patron Rudolf Kremayr bestowed to Rust one of the most stunning buildings on the town's main square. Today, it is the town's museum, with the lavishly decorated interior home to some of Rust's most important historical archives. The chimney room, an outbuilding off the courtyard, is where local exhibitions and small concerts are held. ✉ *Conradplatz 2* ☎ *0676/8416–0623.*

Seebad Rust
BEACH—SIGHT | A causeway leads through nearly a mile of reeds to the Seebad beach and boat landing, where you can take a sightseeing boat either as a round-trip or to another point on the lake. You can also rent a boat, swim, or enjoy a waterside drink or snack at an outdoor table. ✉ *Ruster Bucht 2* 🌐 *www.seebadrust.at.*

Weingut Feiler-Artinger
WINERY/DISTILLERY | Like many family-run wineries in Rust (most in Austria are family businesses), this one in the heart of town produces white and red sweet wine from the vineyards around Rust. Many are for sale, including a selection of organic wines. ✉ *Hauptstrasse 3* ☎ *02685/237* 🌐 *www.feiler-artinger.at* 🕒 *Closed Sun.*

🍴 Restaurants

For a small town, Rust has a great dining scene that makes the most of the delicious freshwater fish found in Neusiedl Lake. If you're visiting during summer, look out for *steckerl*, a delicious, locally-caught fish that's grilled barbecue-style with spices.

Buschenschank Schandl

$$ | AUSTRIAN | The Schandl family of Rust is one of the best-known wine growers of the Neusiedl Lake area; their devotees come for wine tastings and stay for dinner..The simple but satisfying buffet offers a selection of sausages, salads, cheeses, and pickles, as well as a few hot dishes, to complement the wine. **Known for:** generous buffet with sausages and salads; large courtyard for outdoor summer dining; family wine for sale at adjacent shop. $ *Average main: €15* ✉ *Hauptstrasse 20* ☎ *02685/20484* ⊕ *www.buschenschankschandl.at* ⊘ *No lunch weekdays. Closed Tue.–Wed. in Mar.–Jun. and Oct.–Nov.*

Rusterhof

$$ | AUSTRIAN | A lovingly renovated burgher's house—the town's oldest—at the top of the main square houses an excellent and imaginative restaurant. The menu depends on what's fresh, and might include grilled fish or Wiener schnitzel made with organic veal. **Known for:** terrace view over main street; fresh and organic menu; four lovely apartments also available. $ *Average main: €17* ✉ *Rathausplatz 18* ☎ *02685/60793* ⊕ *www.rusterhof.com* ⊘ *Closed Mon.*

 Hotels

Hotel Sifkovits

$$ | HOTEL | FAMILY | This charming hotel run by the Hallwirth family has lovely and tastefully redecorated rooms in a prime location, close to the lake and a block away from Rust's bustling center. **Pros:** spacious and welcoming lobby; quiet rooms; large park behind the hotel. **Cons:** rooms facing the street can be noisy; room decor not for everyone; gets booked up early. $ *Rooms from: €125* ✉ *Am Seekanal 8* ☎ *02685/20460* ⊕ *www.sifkovits.at* ⊘ *Closed Dec.–Mar.* ⇨ *27 rooms* ❤️ *Free breakfast.*

🎭 Performing Arts

★ **Oper im Steinbruch** (*Opera in St. Margarethen Quarry*)

OPERA | Three kilometers (two miles) west of Rust, outside the tiny village of St. Margarethen, is Römersteinbruch, a delightful rock quarry used for outdoor opera performances for six weeks during July and August. It's one of the three largest outdoor opera venues in Europe, seating 7,000 nightly. The opera changes annually—previous operas have included Puccini's *Turandot* and Bizet's *Carmen*, with a Passion play running every fifth year—and performances also include a dazzling fireworks display. Ticket prices range from around €40 up to nearly €150. It's a good idea to bring a seat cushion, if possible, to soften the metal chairs. Bus trips from Vienna and back to see performances can be arranged through several tour agencies. You can buy tickets online or at the ticket office in Eisenstadt. ✉ *Römersteinbruch 1* ☎ *02682/65065* ⊕ *www.operimsteinbruch.at.*

Sopron, Hungary

80 km (50 miles) south of Vienna.

Lying just across the Hungarian border, close to the southern shore of Neusiedler Lake, Sopron is one of Central Europe's most picturesque cities, packing a frankly incredible array of historic monuments into a very small area.

Sopron is often called Hungary's most faithful town, as its residents voted to remain part of Hungary (rather than join Austria) in 1921 after World War I. Today's city of 60,000 was a small Celtic settlement more than 2,300 years ago. During Roman times, as Scarabantia, it stood on the main European north–south trade route, the Amber Road, and also happened to be near the junction with the east–west route used by Byzantine merchants. In AD 896 the Magyars conquered the Carpathian basin and later named the city Suprun, after a medieval Hungarian warrior; after the Hapsburgs took over the territory during the Turkish wars of the 16th and 17th centuries, they renamed it Ödenburg. The city suffered greatly during World War II, until it was "liberated" by the Soviet Red Army in April 1945. Decades of Communist rule followed, until protests on the nearby Austria-Hungary border in 1989 helped to instigate the fall of the Berlin Wall.

Despite the centuries of upheaval, Sopron's historic core has survived and been painstakingly restored; the city even won a 1975 Europe Prize Gold Medal for Protection of Monuments. Today, the horseshoe-shaped Belváros (Inner Town), a wondrous mix of Gothic, Baroque, and Renaissance architecture protected by city walls (one set built by Romans, the other by medieval Magyars), attracts visitors from far and wide. Most come on a day-trip from Vienna, or as a stopover between the Austrian and Hungarian capitals.

GETTING HERE AND AROUND

The easiest way to get to Sopron is by train, with regular services leaving from Vienna's Central Station. The journey takes around 1¼ hours. You can also reach Sopron by train from Eisenstadt (30 minutes, via Wulkaprodersdorf). Driving from Vienna is easy and takes around an hour: head south on the A3 and B16, which becomes Route 84 once you cross the border.

Sopron is a small city, so it's easy to navigate on foot. Most of the city sights are in Belváros, but even those outside are still within walking distance. To get to attractions outside the city, like Eszterházy Palace and Széchenyi Mansion, you can take a bus or drive.

RESTAURANTS AND HOTELS

The selection of quality hotels in Sopron is modest, but always improving. Dining tends to be casual, and many restaurants have outdoor seating terraces during warmer months, usually from May through September. Both hotels and restaurants are, as a general rule, cheaper in Sopron than in Vienna and around. Prices are quoted in the local currency, Hungarian forints (HUF), though euros are widely accepted. Typically, it's in the region of 350 HUF to €1, but always check the current exchange rate before you travel.

What it Costs in Hungarian Florint			
$	$$	$$$	$$$$
RESTAURANTS			
under 2,500 HUF	2,500–5,000 HUF	5,001–7,500 HUF	over 7,500 HUF
HOTELS			
under 25,000 HUF	25,000–37,500 HUF	37,501–50,000 HUF	over 50,000 HUF

VISITOR INFORMATION

CONTACTS Tourinform. ⊠ *Szent György utca 2, Sopron* ☎ *99/951–975* ⊕ *www. turizmus.sopron.hu.*

Sights

Esterházy-kastély (*Esterházy Palace*)
CASTLE/PALACE | A 30-minute drive east of Sopron in the town of Fertőd, and near the southern shore of Neusiedl Lake, this magnificent yellow baroque and rococo palace is often referred to as the Hungarian Versailles. Built between 1720 and 1760 as a residence for the Hungarian noble family, it was badly damaged in World War II but has since been painstakingly restored. Step through the intricate wrought-iron gate entrance to discover the palace's 126 lavishly decorated rooms, including the Banqueting Hall with its ceiling fresco of Apollo in his chariot, the beautiful library with almost 22,000 volumes, and the enormous Sala Terrena with its heated marble floor. There's also a three-story-high concert hall, where classical concerts are held

throughout the summer as part of the International Haydn Festival; Joseph Haydn was the court conductor to the Eszterházy family here for 30 years. Before you leave, take a walk around the ornamental French-style gardens. ⚠ **Not to be confused with Schloss Esterházy in Eisenstadt, also a 30-minute drive but north, not east. This was the family's main residence; see the Eisenstadt section for more.** ✉ *Joseph Haydn utca 2, Fertod* ☎ *99/537–640* 🎫 *2,500 HUF.*

Fő tér (Main Square)

PLAZA | The city's attractive main square is dominated by the early Gothic Soproni Nagyboldogasszony templom(Blessed Mary Benedictine Church), better known as the Goat Church for reasons both fantastical—it's said the church was financed with treasure found by a billy goat—and practical—goats feature on the coat of arms of the *actual* church financiers. It's a real mishmash of styles, with a Gothic choir, a rococo main altar, and a Baroque red-marble pulpit, along with recently-discovered medieval tombs. Outside stands the 18th-century Szentháromság-szobor (Holy Trinity Column), Hungary's finest plague memorial and among the first anywhere to feature a twisted column.

Facing the square are three very different but equally fascinating museums. Fabricus Ház (Fabricius House) is a beautiful Baroque mansion with an exhibits on ancient city history: highlights include the remains of a Roman bathhouse and the 1,200-year-old Cunpald Goblet. The Storno Ház (Storno House) is Sopron's finest Renaissance-era building with a collection of furniture, porcelain, sculptures, and paintings belonging to the Stornos, a rags-to-riches dynasty of chimney sweeps-turned-art restorers. types. And the Fehér Angyal Patikamúzeum (Angel Pharmacy Museum) is a real-life 17th century apothecary that now houses a collection of period pharmaceutical tools, books, potions, and lotions. ✉ *Sopron.*

Mária-oszlop (Mary's Column)

PUBLIC ART | With its finely sculpted biblical reliefs, the column is a superb specimen of Baroque design. It was erected in 1745 to mark the former site of the medieval Church of Our Lady, which was destroyed by Sopron citizens in 1632 because they feared the Turks would use its steeple as a strategic firing tower. ✉ *Várkerület 62, Sopron.*

Ó-zsinagóga (Old Synagogue)

RELIGIOUS SITE | This medieval synagogue is now a religious museum complete with stunning stained-glass windows, a stone mikvah (a ritual bath for women), and old Torahs on display. Built around 1300, the synagogue endured several incarnations over the centuries, including a stint as a hospital (in the 1400s) and a residential building (in the 1700s); the existing facade dates from 1734. The synagogue was once at the heart of the city's Jewish ghetto, and a plaque honors the 1,640 Jews of Sopron—85% of the city's total population—who were murdered by the Nazis. ✉ *Új utca 22, Sopron* ☎ *99/311–327* 🎫 *800 HUF* ⊘ *Closed Mon. and Oct.–Mar.*

Széchenyi kastély (Széchenyi Mansion)

HOUSE | This pretty manor house, situated 13 kilometers (eight miles) southeast of Sopron, is the family seat of the Széchenyi family. Mostly completed in the neoclassical style but heavily rebuilt after World War II, the property is now home to the Széchenyi Museum, which tells the family's story through reconstructed rooms and period furnishings. The star of the show is Count István Széchenyi, known as the "Greatest Hungarian" for his achievements as a politician, writer, reformer, and generous patron: his money helped establish the Hungarian Academy of Sciences and build the Chain Bridge in Budapest. You'll find an immodest number of István portraits throughout the property, as well as interactive exhibits on some of his projects. ■**TIP→ Information within each**

Just over the border in Hungary, Sopron is especially charming in winter when you'll find festive Christmas decorations and markets.

room is scarce for non-Hungarian speakers, so be sure to pick up an English-language brochure on your way in. ⊠ *Kiscenki utca 7, Sopron* ☎ *30/4471–1248* ⊕ *www.szeche-nyiorokseg.hu* ✉ *1,400 HUF* ☉ *Closed Mon.*

Szent György utca (*St. George Street*)
NEIGHBORHOOD | This beautiful Inner Town street runs south from Fő tér to Orsolya tér, where there's an interesting fountain showing Jesus using his crucifix to pierce a snake with an apple. As you walk down the street, you will come across an eclectic mix of architecture co-existing in a surprisingly harmonious fashion. The **Erdody Vár** (Erdody Palace) at No. 16 is Sopron's richest rococo building. Two doors down, at No. 12, stands the **Eggen-berg Ház** (Eggenberg House), where the widow of Prince Johann Eggenberg held Protestant services during the harshest days of the Counter-Reformation and beyond. Today, it's home to the **Macskakő Múzeum**, an interactive children's muse-um about the everyday lives of people liv-ing in ancient times. But the street takes its name from **Szent György templom** (St. George's Church), a 14th-century Catholic church so sensitively "Baroqued" some 300 years later that its interior is still as soft as whipped cream. ⊠ *Sopron.*

★ **Tuztorony** (*Fire Tower*)
BUILDING | This symbol of Sopron's endurance—and entranceway to the Inner Town—is 200 feet high, with foundations dating to the days of the Árpád dynasty (9th–13th centuries) and perhaps back to the Romans. The tower is remarkable for its uniquely harmoni-ous blend of architectural styles: it has a Romanesque base rising to a circular balcony of Renaissance loggias topped by an octagonal clock tower that is itself capped by a brass Baroque onion dome and belfry. The upper portions were rebuilt after most of the earlier Fire Tower was, ironically, destroyed by the Great Fire of 1676, started by students roasting chestnuts in a high wind (today a dou-ble-headed eagle weathervane helps to predict wind direction; it's said that if the eagles face north and south it's going

to rain). On the inside of the gate, you'll find a depiction of "Hungaria" receiving the loyalty of Sopron's kneeling citizens. Climb the 200-step spiral staircase to the top of the tower for lovely views of the town and surrounding countryside. It's from here that tower watchmen warned of approaching enemies and tolled the alarm for fire or the death of a prominent citizen. And occasionally, musicians would serenade the townsfolk from here. ✉ *Fő tér 5* ☎ *99/311–327* 🌐 *www.tuztorony.sopron.hu* 🎟 *1,400 HUF.*

Várfalsétány (*Bailey Promenade*)
ARCHAEOLOGICAL SITE | Starting near the Fire Tower and following the route of Sopron's medieval town walls, the Bailey Promenade makes for a lovely stroll. The oldest part of city walls were built in the 14th century but some sights along the way are even older: look out for ancient gate foundations, remnants of the Roman town of Scarbantian. Some sections of the promenade close overnight. ✉ *Sopron.*

🍴 Restaurants

Corvinus
$ | **HUNGARIAN** | Set on the ground floor of the historic Storno House on Sopron's delightful cobblestone main square, Corvinus combines a café, pub, pizzeria, and restaurant all in one. Among the traditional Hungarian specialties are a meaty soup with a baked-on pastry cap, and roast venison goulash with porcini mushrooms. **Known for:** in beautiful 500-year-old building; cheese-heavy vegan options; good value for central location. [$] *Average main: 2000 HUF* ✉ *Fő tér 8, Sopron* ☎ *99/505–035* 🌐 *www.corvinusetterem.hu.*

El Gusto
$$ | **INTERNATIONAL** | This attractive and popular café-bistro is a great stop for breakfast, brunch, lunch, and dinner or just a takeaway coffee and ice cream. Enjoy an international menu of soups, salads, pizzas, paninis, and burgers (along with a few local specialties) in the simple Scandi-style interior, or else sit outside on the pleasant street terrace. **Known for:** simple but warm decor; burgers and pizza; excellent coffee and cakes. [$] *Average main: 3,250 HUF* ✉ *Várkerület 79, Sopron* ☎ *70/3723–961* 🌐 *www.elgusto.hu.*

★ Erhardt
$$$ | **HUNGARIAN** | On a quiet side street a block from Várkerület, away from the main tourst drag, this excellent restaurant serves delicious, inventive dishes in a choice of beautiful settings: take your pick from the wood-beamed rooms upstairs, the beautiful 18th century brick-vaulted wine cellar below, or the leafy garden terrace outside. The menu features high quality, overwhelmingly meaty and fishy Hungarian fare, like roasted duck breast and paprika catfish (though vegetarian options like delicious barley-stuffed peppers do exist). **Known for:** curd-cheese dumplings with fruit; choice of beautiful settings; combined dinner and wine tasting for 11,600 HUF. [$] *Average main: 5500 HUF* ✉ *Balfi út 10, Sopron* ☎ *99/506–711* 🌐 *www.erhardts.hu.*

Jégverem Fogadó
$$ | **HUNGARIAN** | A short walk from the Inner Town, this charming restaurant is a perennial favorite for its cozy, rustic interior of wooden-beamed ceilings, cast iron light fittings, and checkered tablecloths, as well as for its "guzzle guts" menu of homemade Hungarian specialities, often with an inventive twist. In warm weather, you can also sit outside in the lovely, leafy courtyard. **Known for:** gigantic portions; poppy seed bread and butter pudding; bargain lunch menus. [$] *Average main: 3,000 HUF* ✉ *Jégverem utca 1, Sopron* ☎ *99/510–113* 🌐 *www.jegverem.hu.*

Hopsz

$$ | CAFÉ | Offering something a little different, this cool café and grill is a real bright spot in a rather drab part of town. Sit in the achingly-hip interior—all funky artworks, bold patterns, and bright prints—to enjoy a menu of delicious international dishes, or sit out on the plant pot–covered terrace in summer. **Known for:** cool interior with eclectic artworks; great food early 'til late; a 10-minute walk from the center. $ Average main: 2,800 HUF ⊠ Gyár utca 1-3, Sopron ☎ 99/333–355 ⊕ www.hopszsopron.hu.

 Hotels

Hotel Wollner

$$ | HOTEL | Tucked inside the city center, this quiet and charming 18th century peach-colored hotel has been restored to its original splendor, with comfortable rooms boasting arched ceilings, comfy beds, and spacious bathrooms. **Pros:** a property with oodles of history; convenient Inner Town location; the garden incorporates medieval town wall. **Cons:** traditional furnishings not to all tastes; no elevator or A/C; no parking facilities. $ Rooms from: 34,000 HUF ⊠ Templom utca 20, Sopron ☎ 99/524–400 ⊕ www.wollner.hu ➾ 18 rooms ⦿ Free breakfast.

Pannonia Hotel

$$ | HOTEL | This elegant, antique-filled hotel has a long and illustrious past, starting in the 17th century as the Golden Hind, when it welcomed stagecoaches traveling between Vienna and Budapest. **Pros:** convenient central location; big rooftop terraces with views; rooftop basketball court. **Cons:** some stains on carpets; no tea and coffee in rooms; breakfast isn't included. $ Rooms from: 26,000 HUF ⊠ Várkerület 75, Sopron ☎ 99/312–180 ⊕ www.pannoniahotel. com ➾ 79 rooms ⦿ No meals.

★ Sopronbánfalvi Kolostor Hotel

(*Pauline-Carmelite Monastery of Sopronbánfalva*)

$$$ | HOTEL | If you're looking for a memorable stay in Sopron, look no further than this extraordinary 12th-century monastery-turned-hotel. **Pros:** this is a truly one-of-a-kind stay; an audio guide introduces the property; Refektórium restaurant is one of Sopron's finest. **Cons:** some rooms have single beds; hotel services are limited; a 40-minute walk (or 10-minute taxi) from the center. $ Rooms from: 46,000 HUF ⊠ Kolostorhegy utca 2, Sopron ☎ 99/505–895 ⊕ www.banfalvakolostor. hu ➾ 20 rooms ⦿ All-inclusive.

 Nightlife

Cézár Pince

WINE BARS—NIGHTLIFE | Come for the wine, stay for the decor: this beautiful 17th-century wine cellar sits beneath a gorgeous Gothic building that once played host to the Diet of Hungary (the medieval kingdom's parliament). Today, you can sample a good selection of local vintages, along with a wide choice of meat and cheese platters. ⊠ Hátsókapu utca 2, Sopron ☎ 99/311–337 ⊕ www. cezarpince.hu.

🎭 Performing Arts

★ Fertőrákosi Barlangszínház (*Fertőrákos Cave Theater*)

CONCERTS | For a unique entertainment experience, it's hard to beat this cave theater, carved out of a limestone quarry eight kilometers (five miles) northeast of Sopron. The 760-seat theater has amazing natural acoustics, which make for memorable classical music performances, pop and rock concerts, and musical theater productions. Arrive an hour early to enjoy the walking trail around the quarry, with lovely lookout points over the southern shore of Lake Neusiedl and a fun paleontological exhibition. ⊠ Fő utca 1, Sopron ☎ 99/530–404 ⊕ www.fertorakosikofejto.hu.

🛍 Shopping

ART
Septem
ART GALLERIES | Stylised SEP7EM, this cozy little art gallery and shop showcases works by contemporary Sopron artists, as well as prints of classic Hungarian artworks. All are available to buy. ⊠ *Kolostor utca 7, Sopron* ⊕ *www.septem.hu* ⊗ *Closed Sun. and Mon.*

CERAMICS
Esterházy Márkabolt
CERAMICS/GLASSWARE | This small shop is devoted to the renowned Herend hand-painted porcelain (the company first gained international acclaim when England's Queen Victoria ordered a dinner set for Windsor Castle in 1851). ⊠ *Várkerület 98, Sopron* ☎ *99/508–712* ⊕ *www.herend.com* ⊗ *Closed Sun.*

Zsolnay Porcelán Márkabolt
CERAMICS/GLASSWARE | If you can't make it to the less expensive factory outlet in Pécs, you can purchase exquisite Zsolnay porcelain here. A tiny room lined with glass cabinets displays the delicate wares. ⊠ *Előkapu 11, Sopron* ☎ *99/505–252* ⊕ *www.zsolnay.hu.*

COSMETICS
L'Apotheca Kozmetika
PERFUME/COSMETICS | This cute little boutique sells organic cosmetics—including face creams, shower gels, and body lotions—crafted to recipes by local pharmacist Tömea Glöckner. ⊠ *Színház utca 4, Sopron* ☎ *20/298–7494* ⊕ *www.lapotheca.com* ⊗ *Closed Sun.*

WINE
Natura Vinotéka
WINE/SPIRITS | Situated on Várkerület, the main shopping street that partly circles the outside of the Old Town, this is a good place to look for fine Sopron wines, whether the peppery red kékfrankos or the spicy white zöld veltelini. ⊠ *Várkerület 24, Sopron* ☎ *30/986–6488* ⊕ *www.sopronivinoteka.hu* ⊗ *Closed Sun.* Ⓜ *9400.*

Baden

38 km (24 miles) southwest of Vienna.

The Weinstrasse brings you to the serenely elegant spa town of Baden. Since antiquity, Baden's sulfuric thermal baths have attracted both the ailing and the fashionable from all over the world. When the Romans came across the springs, they dubbed the town Aquae; the Babenbergs revived it in the 10th century; and with the visit of the Russian czar Peter the Great in 1698, Baden's golden age began. Austria's Emperor Franz II spent 31 successive summers here. Later in the century, Emperor Franz Josef was a regular visitor, his presence inspiring many of the regal trappings the city still displays. It was in Baden that Mozart composed his "Ave Verum"; where Beethoven spent 15 summers and wrote large sections of his Ninth Symphony and *Missa Solemnis*; where Franz Grillparzer wrote his historical dramas; and where Josef Lanner, both Johann Strausses (father and son), Carl Michael Ziehrer, and Karl Millöcker composed and directed many of their waltzes, marches, and operettas.

GETTING HERE AND AROUND
A streetcar was built in the 19th century for the sole purpose of ferrying the rich Viennese from their summer homes in Baden to the opera in Vienna—the last stop is directly in front of the opera house. Today, the modern streetcar still winds its way through Vienna's suburbs on its 50-minute journey to Baden, though things only start to get scenic about 25 minutes before Baden, when the car passes through the wine villages. A faster option is to take the train. It's about a half hour from Westbahnhof, and most trains are double-deckers (so you can sit up top and have a great view of the countryside).

VISITOR INFORMATION

CONTACTS Baden. ✉ *Brusattiplatz 3* ☎ *02252/86800–600* 🌐 *www.tourismus.baden.at.*

Sights

Arnulf Rainer Museum

MUSEUM | A former 19th-century bathhouse—one which Emperor Franz Josef frequented on his visits to Baden—was converted in 2009 to a museum highlighting Austria's internationally renowned abstract artist Arnulf Rainer. Exhibits also include other contemporary greats, including Damien Hirst. Rainer's work has been displayed in the Museum of Modern Art in New York and other noteworthy museums. ✉ *Josefsplatz 5* ☎ *02252/209–196* 🌐 *www.arnulf-rainer-museum.at* 🎫 *€6.*

Beethoven Haus

HOUSE | Known locally and affectionately as Beethoven's *Haus der Neunten,*or Ninth House, since he composed his Ninth Symphony while living at this address, the house was fully restored after workers discovered artwork within that dated back to the time Beethoven lived there. The art, which hung on the walls of Beethoven's summer apartment, has been fully restored as well. ✉ *Rathausgasse 10* ☎ *02252/86800–630* 🌐 *www.beethovenhaus-baden.at* 🎫 *€6* 🕒 *Closed Mon.*

Casino Baden

CASINO—SIGHT | The ornate Casino Baden—with a bar, restaurant, and gambling rooms—still includes traces of its original 19th-century touches, but has been enlarged and, in the process, overlaid with glitz rivaling that of Las Vegas. Evening attire is expected, and jackets are available on loan at the coat check. Casual dress is only acceptable in the Jackpot Casino. ✉ *Kaiser Franz-Ring 1* ☎ *02252/44496* 🌐 *www.casinos.at/en/baden.*

Kurpark Baden

CITY PARK | One of the biggest draws to Baden, outside of the spa, is the vast, lovely, sloping Kurpark almost smack in the middle of town. It was created back in 1792 for Austria's beloved Empress Maria Theresa. But as her highness only occasionally made her way to this Vienna outpost, the locals were free to enjoy it themselves, and they've been doing so ever since. In summer the park is in full flush: concerts are held each weekend afternoon under the hundred-year-old music pavilion, and operettas are performed at the arena (it's fitted with a glass dome, which comes out when it rains.) ✉ *Kaiser Franz-Ring* 🌐 *www.tourismus.baden.at/historischer-kurpark.*

Puppen- und Spielzeugmuseum (*Doll and Toy Museum*)

MUSEUM | Children of all ages will enjoy this enchanting museum, which has four rooms with dolls dating from the late 1700s to the 1950s, alongside other exhibits. ✉ *Erzherzog Rainer-Ring 23* ☎ *02252/86800–578* 🌐 *www.puppenmuseum-baden.at* 🎫 *€4* 🕒 *Closed Mon.*

Restaurants

Rudolfshof

$$ | **AUSTRIAN** | Enjoy a walk through the Kurpark, where you'll find this 19th-century hunting lodge. The fine restaurant serves traditional dishes from the region, including Wiener and chicken schnitzel, pork fillet, and venison stew. **Known for:** traditional and hearty Austrian fare; excellent local wine; beautiful views from the terrace. [$] *Average main: €16* ✉ *Gaminger Berg 5* ☎ *02252/209–2030* 🌐 *www.rudolfshof.at* 🕒 *Closed Mon.–Tues.*

Hotels

Krainerhütte

$$ | HOTEL | Located about seven kilometers (four miles) outside Baden in a beautiful wooden area is this beautiful, typical Alpine house with sleek, modern rooms (think lots of balconies and natural wood). **Pros:** beautiful location; great for hiking or outdoor seminars; nice restaurant with vegan options. **Cons:** often gets booked up; some noise from nearby highway; restaurant doesn't serve after 9 pm. $ *Rooms from: €125* ✉ *Helenental 41* ☎ *02252/44511* ⊕ *www.krainerhuette. at* ⬏ *73 rooms* ❍ *Free breakfast.*

Schloss Weikersdorf

$$ | HOTEL | Set within beautiful grounds, this restored Imperial castle is minutes from the town center, on the edge of a vast public park. **Pros:** helpful staff; beautiful surroundings; sometimes offers special last-minute rates. **Cons:** rooms vary greatly in size; can feel crowded; a/c only in the Residenz wing. $ *Rooms from: €105* ✉ *Schlossgasse 9–11* ☎ *02252/48301* ⊕ *www.hotelschlossweikersdorf.at* ⬏ *164 rooms* ❍ *Free breakfast.*

Klosterneuburg and Korneuburg

12 km (7½ miles) northwest of Vienna.

The quiet, moderate-size town of Klosterneuburg, on the south/west (Vienna) side of the Danube, feels much farther from the big city than just a few miles. In antiquity the area was a Roman fort, and its modern habitation began in the 11th century. Just south of Klosterneuburg lies the charming little vintners' village of Kahlenbergerdorf, an excellent spot to stop and sample the local wines.

To the north of here, just across the river on the north/east (Krems) bank, lies Korneuburg. The town is best known for its spectacular castle, which lies a short walk from the center, but also has a few other interesting sights that make it worth a stop, including a beautiful neo-Gothic town hall (1864), which dominates the central square and incorporates a 15th-century tower.

GETTING HERE AND AROUND

Commuter trains from Vienna's Franz-Josefs-Bahnhof and buses from the Heiligenstadt station leave frequently for the short trip to Klosterneuburg. By car from Vienna, follow the riverside Route B14 north.

For Korneuburg, commuter trains go frequently from Vienna's Praterstern and Central stations. Get off at Korneuburg Bahnhof for the town center and Leobendorf-Burg Kreuzenstein for the castle. By car, take the A22 to Exit 16, and then follow Route B3.

There is a regular taxi ferry service between the two towns running April through September. The journey takes five or 10 minutes (depending on direction) and it's a 25-minute walk at either end to reach the town centers.

VISITOR INFORMATION

CONTACTS Tourismus Klosterneuburg.
✉ *Freizeitzentrum Happyland, In der Au 2–4* ☎ *02243/32038* ⊕ *www.klosterneuburg.net/en.*

 Sights

★ Burg Kreuzenstein

CASTLE/PALACE | Seemingly lifted from the pages of a German fairy tale, Burg Kreuzenstein bristles with storybook turrets and towers. Sitting atop a hillside three kilometers (two miles) beyond Korneuburg, "Castle Cross-stone" is, in fact, a 19th-century architectural fantasy built to conjure up "the last of the knights"—Emperor Maximilian I himself. Occupying the site of a previously destroyed fort, the enormous structure was built by Count Nepomuk Wilczek between 1879 and 1908. Using old elements and Gothic and Romanesque bits and pieces, the castle was carefully laid out according to the rules of yore, complete with a towering Burgtor, "kennel" corridor (where attackers would have been cornered), Gothic arcades, and tracery parapet walls. Discover the Burghof courtyard, with its half-timbered facade and Baltic loggia, a festival and banquet hall, a library, a stained-glass chapel, vassal kitchens, and the Narwalzahn, a room devoted to hunting trophies (if you've ever wanted to see a "unicorn horn," here's your chance). Guided tours are available on the hour.

A group of falconers keeps peregrine falcons and other birds of prey near the castle grounds, and there are regular shows April through October. ■TIP➜ **The quickest and most pleasant way to reach the castle is to take the suburban train (S-Bahn) to Leobendorf, followed by a 45-minute uphill walk. Only cash payment is accepted, and there is no ATM at the castle.** ⊠ *Leobendorf bei Korneuburg* ☎ *0664/163–2700* ⊕ *www.kreuzenstein. com* ⊠ *€12*.

★ **Stift Klosterneuburg**
RELIGIOUS SITE | The great Augustinian abbey Stift Klosterneuburg dominates the town. The structure has undergone many changes since the abbey was established in 1114, most recently in 1892, when Friedrich Schmidt, architect of Vienna's City Hall, added neo-Gothic embellishments to its two identifying towers. Inside the abbey church, treasures include the carved-wood choir loft and oratory, the large 17th-century organ, beautifully enameled 1181 Verdun Altar in the Leopold Chapel, stained-glass windows from the 14th and 15th centuries, and a Romanesque candelabra from the 12th century. In an adjacent outbuilding there's a huge wine cask over which people slide; the exercise, called *Fasslrutsch'n,* takes place during the Leopoldiweinkost, the wine tasting around St. Leopold's Day on November 15. The

Stiftskeller, with its atmospheric underground rooms, serves standard Austrian fare and wine bearing the Klosterneuburg label. There are several different tours available covering religious artifacts, imperial rooms and treasures, wine making, and the garden. ■TIP➜ **Guided tours are in German, but audio guides with English and other languages are available.** ⊠ *Stiftsplatz 1* ☎ *02243/411–0* ⊕ *www. stift-klosterneuburg.at* ⊠ *€9 (additional €2–€5 for tours).*

Krems

80 km (50 miles) northwest of Vienna.

Krems marks the beginning (when traveling upstream) of the Wachau section of the Danube. The town is closely tied to Austrian history; here the ruling Babenbergs set up a dukedom in 1120, and the earliest Austrian coin was struck in 1130. In the Middle Ages, Krems looked after the iron trade, while neighboring Stein traded in salt and wine.

Set at the center of a thriving wine-producing area, charming Krems is perhaps most famed for the cobbled streets of its pedestrianized Altstadt (Old Town), which is virtually unchanged since the 18th century. Highlights here include the Steinertor city gate, the Renaissance-style Rathaus and, up a steep hill, the 13th century Piarist Church, one of the oldest in Lower Austria.

According to Austrian law, any town that houses a jail must receive massive funding for the arts—and Krems fits the bill. Consequently, the town is brimming with culture, most notably with its Kunstmiele, or Arts Mile (⊕ *www.kunstmeile. at*). Starting at the Dominikanerkirche in the town center, it heads west for 1.6 kilometers (one mile) to the Minoritenkirche. All the big-ticket galleries, like the Karikaturmuseum, Landesgalerie Niederösterreich, and Kunsthalle Krems, are at the western end of the trail.

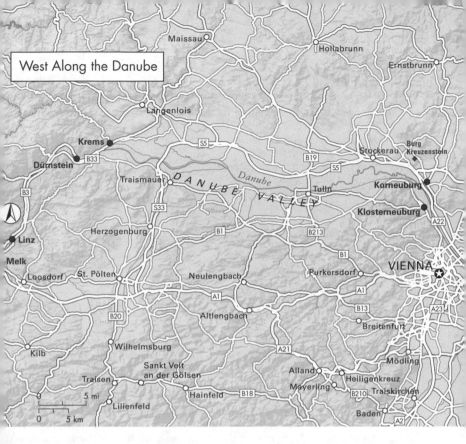

West Along the Danube

GETTING HERE AND AROUND
By car from Vienna, take the A22 to the Knoten Floridsorf exit, then following the S5 to Krems. Direct trains from Vienna's Franz-Josefs-Bahnhof to Krems take a little over an hour, while trains from Vienna's Westbahnhof require a change in St. Pölten.

VISITOR INFORMATION
CONTACTS Krems Tourismusinformation.
✉ Museumkrems, Körnermarkt 14
☎ 02732/82676 ⊕ www.krems.info.

 Sights

Steinertor
BUILDING | The sole survivor of the original four 15th century city gates—the rest of them were razed in the late 1800s, along with the city wall—Steiner Tor remains one of the most recognizable symbols

of Krems. A plaque on one side reveals its three major stages of development—construction in 1480 (on the orders of Holy Roman Emperor Friedrich III), a Baroque refurb in 1754 (under the reign of Maria Theresa), and a significant renovation in the 1950s—while the other side has coats of arms and other decorative adornments. Look out also for the memorial to a catastrophic ice flood in January 1573. ✉ Obere Landstrasse.

Karikaturmuseum (Caricature Museum)
MUSEUM | In 2016, Austrians grieved the death of Manfred Deix, whose world-famous works are housed here ("Deixfiguren" became so popular that the word was added to the German dictionary). More than 250 works from the 20th century to the present can also be viewed here, including a large collection of English-language political satire and

Wachau Wines

The epitome of Austrian viticulture is found in the Wachau, those few precious kilometers of terraced vineyards along the north bank of the Danube River. There are few nicer ways to spend an afternoon than to travel to the fabled wineries of the valley and sample the golden nectar coaxed from the vines. It's usually possible to stop in and meet the winemaker, who will be happy to pour you a taste from the latest vintage and share some of the secrets of the trade.

Straddling both sides of the Danube is the Kremstal, centering on the medieval town of Krems. This wine-growing region is home to some of the finest white wines in Europe. The elegant, long-lived Rieslings are world-renowned, but the special glory of Austria is the Grüner Veltliner, an indigenous grape that can produce anything from simple *Heurigen* thirst-quenchers to wines of a nobility that rival the best of Burgundy.

Other popular grapes here include the intensely fragrant Traminer and the Grauburgunder (more familiar as Pinot Gris). There are even some full-bodied reds, like Cabernet Sauvignon and Pinot Noir. To sample some of these wines, you may be tempted to make an excursion to one of the nearby wineries like Salomon, Malat, or Zöhrer. Toni Zöhrer runs vineyard tours—his wines have been among the most successful in recent challenges.

A little farther upriver, near Dürnstein, there are even more wineries to discover, including F.X. Pichler, Knoll, and Jamek. For more information on Wachau wineries, visit ⊕ *www.vinea-wachau.at.*

caricature. ⊠ *Steiner Landstrasse 3a* ☎ *02732/908010* ⊕ *www.karikaturmuseum.at* ▨ *€10.*

Kunsthalle Krems

MUSEUM | An old tobacco factory is now a showcase for quirky and contemporary art by both known and unknown artists from the 19th to 21st centuries. Notable examples include Martha Jungwirth and Gregor Schmoll. Tickets include entry to the Dominikanerkirche in the Old Town, which often holds Kunsthalle exhibitions focusing on current artists from around the world. ⊠ *Steiner Landstrasse 5* ☎ *02732/908010* ⊕ *www.kunsthalle.at* ▨ *€10* ۝ *Closed Mon.*

★ Landesgalerie Niederösterreich (*State Gallery of Lower Austria*)

MUSEUM | When it opened in 2019, the Landesgalerie instantly became the most eye-catching building in Krems. Well, its gracefully swooping, tent-like, zinc-tiled and glass-dotted roof isn't exactly easy to ignore. Step inside and things get even more interesting, with its 3,000 square meters of exhibition space dedicated to visual artworks from the last two centuries. Visitors can enjoy prints, paintings, photographs, sculptures, and installations from renowned Lower Austrian artists including Leo Navratil and Christa Hauer-Fruhmann. The on-site Restaurant Poldi Fitzka is well worth a visit too. ⊠ *Steiner Landstrasse 1* ☎ *02732/908010* ⊕ *www.lgnoe.at/en* ▨ *€10* ۝ *Closed Mon.*

🍴 Restaurants

Gasthaus Jell

$$$ | **AUSTRIAN** | In the heart of the medieval Altstadt is this storybook stone cottage run by Ulli Amon-Jell (pronounced "Yell"), who serves the tried-and-true recipes of her grandmother and great-grandmother, with a bit of her own

modern flair added to the mix. Snails *au gratin* in garlic herb butter, roast kidneys with bacon and onion, and gazpacho with buttery parmesan dumplings are popular items on the menu. **Known for:** enormous portions; delicious marillenknödel; preserves and other jarred delicacies for sale. [$] *Average main: €18* ✉ *Hoher Markt 8* ☎ *02732/82345* 🌐 *www.amon-jell.at* 🕒 *Closed Mon. No dinner weekends.*

Kaiser von Österreich

$$$$ | **AUSTRIAN** | At this landmark in Krems's Old Town district, you'll find excellent regional cuisine along with an outstanding wine selection (some of these vintages come from the backyard). Owner-chef Haidinger learned his skills at Bacher, across the Danube in Mautern, so look for fresh river fish on the ever-changing set menus, along with locally-hunted wild boar and venison. **Known for:** fresh and locally sourced produce; selection of gluten-free foods; need to make reservations at least a day ahead. [$] *Average main: €43* ✉ *Körnermarkt 9* ☎ *0800/400–171–052* 🌐 *www.kaiser-von-oesterreich.at* 🕒 *Closed Sun. and Mon. No lunch.*

Wellen.Spiel

$$ | **AUSTRIAN** | This riverside bar-restaurant, overlooking the landing station from which the Danube to Melk cruises depart, makes a lovely spot for breakfast, lunch, or dinner. Local specialties like freshly-caught fish and *flammkuchen* (a pizza-like pie slathered in crème fraîche, onions, and bacon bits) sit alongside no-fuss favorites like burritos, burgers, and steaks. **Known for:** lovely riverside setting; tasty steckerl fish served with grilled vegetables; unpasteurized beers. [$] *Average main: €18* ✉ *Welterbeplatz 1* ☎ *02732/75055* 🌐 *www.wellenspiel.at.*

🛏 Hotels

Alte Post

$ | **B&B/INN** | The oldest inn in Krems, which for almost 140 years was a mail-route post house, is centered on an adorable Renaissance-style courtyard topped with a flower-bedecked arcaded balcony and storybook mansard roof. **Pros:** cool historical vibe; excellent restaurant with large portions; ideal Old Town location. **Cons:** old-fashioned; most rooms have shared shower and toilet facilities; restaurant can get very busy. [$] *Rooms from: €95* ✉ *Obere Landstrasse 32* ☎ *02732/822760* 🌐 *www.altepost-krems.at* 🕒 *Closed Dec.–Mar.* 🛏 *23 rooms* 🍴 *Free breakfast.*

Arte Hotel Krems

$$$ | **HOTEL** | Located a little out of the center but very convenient for a host of art galleries including the Kunsthalle Krems, the Landesgalerie Niederösterreich, and the Karikaturmuseum, this hip, youthful hotel offers spacious, comfortable rooms with funky and colorful design elements. **Pros:** near the Arts Mile and cruise terminal; lovely views of surrounding vineyards; breakfast includes homemade bircher muesli. **Cons:** 20-minute walk from center; style over function in places (like desks without plug sockets); no tea or coffee in rooms. [$] *Rooms from: €155* ✉ *Dr.-Karl-Dorrek-Strasse 23* ☎ *02732/71123* 🌐 *www.arte-krems.at* 🛏 *91 rooms* 🍴 *Free breakfast.*

LOISIUM Wine and Spa Hotel

$$$$ | **HOTEL** | The town of Langenlois, about 10 kilometers (six miles) north of Krems, is home to one of the region's most luxurious accommodation options; a luxury hotel and wellness spa set within a sleek, ultramodern complex. **Pros:** lovely setting among vineyards; fun wine tour and tasting; extensive spa facilities. **Cons:** air conditioning is unreliable; modern design not to everyone's taste;

Danube River Cruises

A cruise up the Danube to the Wachau Valley is a tonic in any season. A parade of storybook-worthy sights—fairy-tale castles-in-air, medieval villages, and Baroque abbeys crowned with "candle-snuffer" cupolas—unfolds before your eyes. Remember that it takes longer to travel north: the trip upstream to Krems, Dürnstein, and Melk will be longer than the return back to Vienna, which is why many travelers opt to return to the city by train, not boat. Keep your fingers crossed: rumor has it that on some summer days the river takes on an authentic shade of Johann Strauss blue.

Brandner Schifffahrt Leapfrog ahead by train from Vienna and start your cruise in Krems. A short walk takes you to the Schiffstation Krems piers, where river cruises run by Brandner Schifffahrt from April through October depart at 10:05 am for a ride to glorious Melk Abbey, via Dürnstein. It's €26.50 one way, or €31.50 return. Other options include special day and evening cruises with oompah band concerts, wine cruises, and the like. There is an occasional "crime cruise" (in German) with a murder mystery to be solved. ✉ *Welterbeplatz 1, Krems* ☎ *07433/259021* 🌐 *www.brandner.at* 🎫 *€26.50 one way.*

DDSG Blue Danube Schifffahrt If you want to start your Danube sightseeing cruise in Vienna, DDSG is the company to go with. Boats depart from the company's piers at Handelskai 265 (by the Reichsbrücke bridge). There are thematic and brunch cruises as well, and you can also get trips from Krems to Melk. The ticket office is at the Vienna piers (take the U-Bahn line U1 to Vorgartenstrasse). Wannabe captains can also steer the ship for 15 minutes, while the real captain observes. ✉ *Handelskai 265, Vienna* ☎ *01/58880* 🌐 *www.ddsg-blue-danube.at* 🎫 *€59 round-trip.*

minimum two-night stay on summer weekends. [$] *Rooms from: €305* ✉ *Loisium-Allee 2, Langenlois* ☎ *02734/77100* 🌐 *www.loisium.com* 🛏 *82 rooms* 🍴 *Free breakfast.*

Dürnstein

85 km (53 miles) northwest of Vienna.

If a beauty contest were held among the towns along the Wachau Danube, chances are Dürnstein would be the winner—as you'll see when you arrive along with droves of tourists. The town is small, so leave the car or ship and walk the narrow streets. The main street, Hauptstrasse, is lined with picturesque 16th-century residences.

If you want to enjoy Dürnstein fully, without the crowds of day-trippers, stay overnight. Particularly during the summer solstice, when hundreds of boats bearing torches and candles sail down the river at twilight to honor the longest day of the year—a breathtaking sight best enjoyed from the town and hotel terraces over the Danube. In October or November the grapes from the surrounding hills are harvested by volunteers from villages throughout the valley—locals garnish their front doors with straw wreaths if they can offer tastes of the new wine, as members of the local wine cooperative, the Winzergenossenschaft Wachau.

GETTING HERE AND AROUND

Dürnstein is eight kilometers (five miles) west of Krems on Route B3. Buses go from Krems/Donau Bahnhof at least once an hour in the daytime. It is also a stop on the Krems to Melk cruise route.

VISITOR INFORMATION

CONTACTS Fremdenverkehrsverein Dürnstein-Loiben . ✉ *Dürnstein 32* ☎ *02711/200* 🌐 *www.duernstein.at.*

Sights

★ Richard the Lionheart Castle (*Ruine Dürnstein*)

CASTLE/PALACE | It may involve a steep, 30-minute climb up to 500 feet above the town, but the ruins of this famous castle—and its spectacular views up and down the Danube—make it well worth the effort. The name (in English at least) comes from the fact the castle once held Richard the Lionheart of England, who was captured by Leopold V on his way back home from the Crusades. It's said that Leopold had been insulted by Richard while they were in the Holy Land, so when the English nobleman was shipwrecked and had to head back home through Austria dressed (clearly not very convincingly) as a peasant, Leopold pounced. Richard was subsequently imprisoned in the tower of the castle for four months (1192–1193), before Leopold turned his prisoner over to the emperor, Henry VI. Henry held him for months longer until ransom was paid by Richard's mother, Eleanor of Aquitaine. ✉ *Dürnstein.*

Stiftskirche

RELIGIOUS SITE | Set among terraced vineyards, the town is landmarked by its gloriously Baroque Stiftskirche, dating from the early 1700s, which sits on a cliff overlooking the river. This cloister church's combination of luminous blue facade and stylish Baroque tower is considered the most beautiful of its kind in Austria. ✉ *Dürnstein 1* 🌐 *www.stift-duernstein.at.*

Restaurants

Loibnerhof

$$$$ | **AUSTRIAN** | It's hard to imagine a more idyllic setting for a memorable meal than this lovely restaurant in Unterloiben, a five-minute drive southeast of Dürnstein—especially if the weather is nice and tables are set out in the fragrant apple orchard. One of the oldest restaurants in the area, its kitchen offers inventive variations on regional themes, like Wachau fish soup, crispy roast duck, and foie gras parfait. **Known for:** unique Butterschnitzel (panfried veal with pork); outdoor dining at apple orchard; historic atmosphere. [$] *Average main: €30* ✉ *Unterloiben 7* ☎ *02732/82890* 🌐 *www.loibnerhof.at* 🕒 *Closed Mon.–Tue. and Jan.*

Hotels

★ Gasthaus Prankl

$$ | **HOTEL** | **FAMILY** | Located about a third of the way between Durnstein and Melk in the charming town of Spitz, the Gasthaus Prankl is a Danube gem, located in an old shipmaster's house dating back to 1680. **Pros:** romantic ambience; divine Danube views; huge rooms. **Cons:** only one room is wheelchair accessible; restaurant closes at 8:30 pm; Spitz is short on attractions. [$] *Rooms from: €130* ✉ *Hinterhaus 16, Spitz* ☎ *02713/2323* 🌐 *www.gasthaus-prankl.at* 🔑 *8 rooms* 🍴 *Free breakfast.*

Richard Löwenherz

$$$$ | **B&B/INN** | Built up around the former church of a vast 700-year-old convent, this noted inn overlooks the Danube. **Pros:** überromantic; outstanding restaurant serves regional specialties; heated swimming pool in garden. **Cons:** rooms can get hot in summer; no elevator; bathrooms are bland. [$] *Rooms from: €214* ✉ *Dürnstein 8* ☎ *02711/222* 🌐 *www.richardloewenherz.at* 🕒 *Closed Nov.–mid-Apr.* 🔑 *37 rooms* 🍴 *Free breakfast.*

Sänger Blondel

$$ | **B&B/INN** | Nearly under the shadow of the Baroque spire of Dürnstein's parish church, this popular hotel-restaurant welcomes you with a lovely, sunny-yellow, flower-bedecked facade. **Pros:** great value for money; beautiful garden; helpful staff can suggest excursions. **Cons:** no elevator; outdated room style; rooms could be bigger. [$] *Rooms from: €129* ✉ *Dürnstein 64* ☎ *02711/253* 🌐 *www.saengerblondel.at* 🕒 *Closed Nov.–mid-Mar.* 🛏 *16 rooms* 🍴 *Free breakfast.*

★ Schloss Dürnstein

$$$$ | **HOTEL** | One of the most famous hotels in Austria, this 17th-century early-Baroque castle on a rocky terrace with exquisite views over the Danube was once the preserve of the princes of Starhemberg. **Pros:** an elegant and historic property; great indoor and outdoor pools; exquisite views from the terrace. **Cons:** no air-conditioning; very expensive for the area; some bathrooms are small. [$] *Rooms from: €25976* ✉ *Dürnstein 2* ☎ *02711/212* 🌐 *www.schloss.at* 🛏 *47 rooms* 🍴 *Free breakfast.*

Melk

86 km (54 miles) west of Vienna.

One of the most impressive sights in all of Austria, the abbey of Melk is best approached in mid- to late afternoon, when the setting sun ignites the abbey's ornate Baroque yellow facade. As you head eastward paralleling the Danube, the abbey, shining on its promontory above the river, comes into view. It easily overshadows the town, but remember that the riverside village of Melk itself is worth exploring. A self-guided tour (in English, from the tourist office) will point you toward the highlights and the best spots from which to photograph the abbey.

GETTING HERE AND AROUND

To reach Melk from Vienna, drive on the A1 west or take one of the regular trains from Westbahnhof. From Krems, drive south on the B3, take a bus from Krems/Donau Bahnhof or, best of all, take to the water on a boat cruise (three hours).

VISITOR INFORMATION

CONTACTS Wachau Info-Center Melk. ✉ *Kremser Strasse 5* ☎ *02752/51160.*

Sights

★ Stift Melk (*Melk Abbey*)

RELIGIOUS SITE | Part palace, part monastery, part opera set, this masterpiece of Baroque architecture looms high above the Danube thanks to its upward-reaching twin towers, its grand 208-foot-high dome, and, of course, its site high up on a rocky outcrop. The Benedictine abbey has a history that extends back to its establishment in 1089, but the glorious building you see today is architect Jakob Prandtauer's reconstruction, completed in 1736, in which some earlier elements are incorporated.

A tour of the building includes the main public rooms: a magnificent library, with more than 100,000 books, nearly 2,000 manuscripts, and a superb ceiling fresco by the master Paul Troger; the Marmorsaal, whose windows on both sides enhance the ceiling frescoes and give them a curved effect; and the glorious *Stiftskirche* (abbey church) of Saints Peter and Paul, an exquisite example of the Baroque style. Look out for some quirky features along the way, like a "reusable coffin" that subtly opens at the bottom, and the hidden door in the library. There are guided tours in English every day at 3 pm. Be sure to leave time for exploring the gardens, a lovely mix of manicured lawns and wild woodland with amazing river views. ✉ *Abt-Berthold-Dietmayr-Strasse 1* ☎ *02752/5550* 🌐 *www.stiftmelk.at* 🎫 *€12.50 (€14.50 with tour).*

Hotels

Hotel zur Post

$$$ | HOTEL | Situated right in the center of town, this typical village hotel combines the traditional friendliness of family management with spacious, comfortable, and pleasantly furnished rooms. **Pros:** close to the abbey; friendly and accommodating; in-house sauna. **Cons:** parking area behind the hotel is small; noise from the abbey's bells can be intrusive; rooms with a/c cost extra. [$] *Rooms from: €148* ✉ *Linzer Strasse 1* ☎ *02752/52345* 🌐 *www.post-melk.at* 🕓 *Closed Jan.* 🛏 *30 rooms* 🍴 *Free breakfast.*

Linz

185 km (115 miles) west of Vienna, 132 km (82 miles) northeast of Salzburg.

The capital of Upper Austria—set where the Traun River flows into the Danube—is a fascinating mix of the old and new. On the one hand, Austria's third-largest city has been casting a spell for centuries, thanks to the beautiful old houses on the vast medieval square, its Baroque cathedral with twin towers (and a fine organ over which composer Anton Bruckner once presided), and its unique historic railroad track that leads to the top of the Pöstlingberg. But on the other hand, it's also one of Austria's most modern, cosmopolitan, and cultural cities, with groundbreaking theaters and concert halls, hi-tech museums and galleries, and a dedication to creating a bike-friendly, traffic-free city center. Every September, Linz hosts the internationally renowned Ars Electronica Festival, designed to promote artists, scientists, and the latest technical gadgets. It's just one of many reasons Linz was named a UNESCO City of Media Arts in 2014.

If you plan to see a lot while you're in the city, consider purchasing the **Linz Card**, available online or at the tourist office. Valid for public transportation and free entry into some museums, including the Ars Electronica Center and the Schlossmuseum, the card also provides discounts on entry to the zoo, botanical gardens, St. Florian's Abbey, and other venues. The card comes in three versions: one day (€16), two day (€27, including a round-trip on the Pöstlingbergbahn), and three day (€35, including the Pöstlingbergbahn and a €5 restaurant voucher).

GETTING HERE AND AROUND

Linz Airport is served by Austrian Airlines, Lufthansa, and Ryanair. Regular flights connect with Vienna, Frankfurt, London Stansted, and more. The Linz airport is in Hörsching, about 12 kilometers (7½ miles) southwest of the city. Buses run between the airport and the main train station according to flight schedules. High speed trains connect to cities across Austria, as well as international destinations like Munich in Germany and Prague in the Czech Republic.

The city center is easy to manage on foot. The heart of the city—the Altstadt (Old Town)—has been turned into a pedestrian zone; either leave your car at your hotel or use the huge parking garage under the main square in the center of town. Distances are not great, and you can take in the highlights of the city in half a day; though longer is better.

Easy-to-use trams take visitors to sites of interest not directly in the city center. If in doubt, grab a cab; there are many taxi stands in Linz. From Linz, you can also take the delightful LILO (Lizner Lokalbahn) interurban line, which makes the run up to Eferding.

AIRPORT INFORMATION LILO (Linzer Lokalbahn). ☎ *0732/771670* 🌐 *www.linzer-lokalbahn.at.* **Linz Airport.** (*Blue Danube Airport Linz*) ✉ *Flughafenstrasse 1* ☎ *07221/6000* 🌐 *www.linz-airport.com.* **ÖBB.** ☎ *05/1717* 🌐 *www.oebb.at.*

The white marble Holy Trinity column in Linz's Main Square was erected in gratitude for catastrophes the city had survived and as protection again fire, war, and plague.

VISITOR INFORMATION

CONTACTS Linz Tourism. ✉ *Altes Rathaus, Hauptplatz 1* ☎ *0732/7070–2009* ⊕ *www. linztourismus.at.*

 Sights

Alter Dom (*Old Cathedral*)
RELIGIOUS SITE | Hidden away off the Graben, a narrow side street off the Taubenmarkt above the Hauptplatz, is this Baroque gem (1669–1678). The most striking feature of the Old Church, or Ignatiuskirche as it's also known, is its single nave with side altars. Anton Bruckner was the organist here from 1856 to 1868. ✉ *Domgasse 3* ⊕ *www. dioezese-linz.at.*

Altes Rathaus (*Old Town Hall*)
GOVERNMENT BUILDING | At the lower end of the main square, the original 1513 building was mostly destroyed by fire and replaced in 1658–1659. Its octagonal corner turret and lunar clock, and some vaulted rooms, remain, and you can detect traces of the original Renaissance

structure on the Rathausgasse facade. The present exterior dates from 1824. The approach from Rathausgasse 5, opposite the Kepler Haus, leads through a fine, arcaded courtyard. On the facade here you'll spot portraits of Emperor Friedrich III, the mayors Hoffmandl and Prunner, the astronomer Johannes Kepler, and the composer Anton Bruckner. The building houses a museum dedicated to the history of Linz and a rather odd museum of dentistry. ✉ *Hauptplatz 1.*

★ **Ars Electronica Center**
MUSEUM | **FAMILY** | Just across the Nibelungen Bridge from the Hauptplatz, this highly acclaimed "Museum of the Future," opened in 2009, pays tribute to the confluence of art, technology, and society. Permanent features at the museum include the 3-D cinema room, which allows you to fly over Renaissance cathedrals or explore ancient civilizations, as well as exhibits on the latest developments in robotics and the origins of the universe—all with English explanations. As well as its permanent exhibits, the

center also hosts annual festivals, with a different theme each year. Allow at least half a day to experience all the cybersites here. When you need a break, visit the Cubus Café Restaurant Bar on the third floor for refreshments and a spectacular view overlooking the Danube and Lentos Kunstmuseum opposite. ✉ *Ars-Electronica-Strasse 1* ☎ *0732/72720* ⊕ *www.ars.electronica.art* 🖅 *€11.50* ⊙ *Closed Sun. and Mon.*

Dreifaltigkeitssäule (*Trinity Column*)

MEMORIAL | One of the symbols of Linz is the 65-foot Baroque column in the center of the Hauptplatz. Made in 1723 from white Salzburg marble, the memorial offers thanks from an earthly trinity—the provincial estates, city council, and local citizenry—for deliverance from the threats of war (1704), fire (1712), and plague (1713). On Saturdays, from March through October, there's a popular flea market centered around the column, while on Tuesdays and Fridays there is a farmers' market. ✉ *Hauptplatz.*

Landhaus

GOVERNMENT BUILDING | A magnificent renaissance building erected in the 16th century, the Landhaus is today the seat of the Upper Austrian provincial government. Look inside to see the arcaded courtyard with the Planet Fountain (honoring Johannes Kepler, the astronomer who taught here when it was the city's college) and the Hall of Stone on the first floor, above the barrel-vaulted hall on the ground floor. This hall, the Steinerner Saal, was probably the setting for a noted concert given by the Mozart children in October 1762, from which Count Pálffy hurried back to Vienna to spread the word about the musical prodigies. Adjoining the building is the **Minoritenkirche,** or Church of the Minor Friars. Once part of the monastery, the present building dates from 1758 and has a delightful Rococo interior with side-altar paintings by Kremser Schmidt and a main altar by Bartolomeo Altomonte. ✉ *Landhausplatz 1.*

Lentos Kunstmuseum

MUSEUM | Taking its name from the ancient Celtic settlement that was the origin of the city of Linz, this contemporary art gallery hugs the banks of the Danube on the Altstadt side of the river. Designed by Zurich architects Weber and Hofer, the building alone is worth a visit: its long, low-slung "shoe-box" gray-glass structure picks up the reflection of the water and, at night, it's brightly lit in shimmering blue or red. Inside, the collection contains an impressive number of paintings by Austrian Secession maestros Klimt, Schiele, and Kokoschka, along with works by other artists, including sculptures by Alfred Hrdlicka and one of the famous silkscreen portraits of Marilyn Monroe by Andy Warhol. All in all, the museum has about 1,500 artworks, more than 10,000 sketches, and nearly 1,000 photographs. The gallery's excellent café-bar-restaurant has an outdoor terrace with beautiful views of the river. ✉ *Ernst-Koref-Promenade 1* ☎ *0732/7070–3600* ⊕ *www.lentos.at* 🖅 *€8* ⊙ *Closed Mon.*

Mural Harbor

PUBLIC ART | Just a 30-minute walk from the Old Town but a whole world away, Linz's old industrial Hafenviertel (Harbor Quarter) is now home to one of Europe's largest open-air graffiti galleries. Almost every inch of the area's old warehouses, containers, and other industrial facades have been taken over by colorful and evocative works by international street artists like Aryz, Lors, Nychos, and Roa, as well as local Austrian talent. There are about 300 artworks altogether, and you can see them all on a two-hour guided tour (€20), although this is currently only available in German. Alternatively, just stroll up and down Industriezeile yourself—many of the most impressive artworks are visible from the street. ✉ *Mural Harbor Gallery, Industriezeile 40* ☎ *0664/6575–142* ⊕ *www.muralharbor.at.*

Neuer Dom (New Cathedral)

RELIGIOUS SITE | In 1862, the bishop of Linz engaged one of the architects of Cologne cathedral to develop a design for a grand cathedral in the French neo-Gothic style to accommodate 20,000 worshipers, at that time one-third of the population of Linz. According to legend, the tower was not to be higher than that of St. Stephen's in Vienna. The result was the massive 400-foot tower, shorter than St. Stephen's by a scant 6½ feet. Nevertheless, the "New Cathedral"—also known as the Mariendom or Maria-Empfängnis-Dom—was, and remains, the largest cathedral in the country. It contains gorgeous stained-glass windows depicting scenes from Linz's long history, and you can also climb the tower for lovely views over the city. There are also regular organ recitals held here; check the schedule online. ⊠ Herrenstrasse 26 ☎ 0732/946100 ⊕ www.mariendom.at.

Nordico

MUSEUM | At the corner of Dametzstrasse and Bethlehemstrasse you'll find the city museum. The building dates from 1610, while its extensive collection of art, photography, and archaeology follows local history from pre-Roman times to the mid-1880s. ⊠ Dametzstrasse 23 ☎ 0732/7070–1912 ⊕ www.nordico.at ⊠ €6.50 ⊗ Closed Mon.

★ Pöstlingberg

VIEWPOINT | FAMILY | When you want to escape the hustle and bustle of Linz, just hop on the electric railway Pöstlingbergbahn for a scenic ride up to the famous mountain belvedere, the Pöstlingberg. The narrow-gauge marvel has been making the journey since 1898, and today the line extends to Hauptplatz. Europe's steepest non-cog mountain railway gains 750 feet in elevation in a journey of roughly four kilometers (2½ miles) in just 20 minutes, with neither pulleys nor cables to prevent it from slipping. Halfway up is the Linz Zoological Garden and a children's petting zoo, but it's at the top where you'll enjoy the best views, with the city and the wide sweep of the Danube filling the foreground and the snowcapped Alps on the horizon. Also here is the Church of the Seven Sorrows of the Virgin (Sieben Schmerzen Mariens), an immense and opulent twin-towered Baroque pilgrimage church (1748) visible for miles around. Kids will enjoy the Grottenbahn, or Dragon Express, where they're whisked through a world of dwarves, forest creatures, and other fairy-tale folk, while adults can drink in the views—along with a glass of chilled white wine—from the terrace of the Pöstlingberg Schlössl restaurant. ⊠ Pöstlingbergbahn Bergstation, Am Pöstlingberg 9 ☎ 0732/3400–7506 ⊕ www.linzag.at/poestlingberg ⊠ €4 one way, €6.70 round-trip.

Schlossmuseum (Castle Museum)

CASTLE/PALACE | The massive four-story Linz Schloss (Linz Castle) was rebuilt as a palace by Friedrich III around 1477, literally on top of a castle that dated from 799. Today, its south wing is a modern, glass and steel building that contains one of the best provincial museums in the country. The Schlossmuseum's permanent exhibition traces the development of art, culture, science, and technology in Upper Austria from prehistory, through the Romans, to the Middle Ages, while temporary exhibitions do a deep-dive on particular aspects of local history. Look out for Beethoven's Hammerklavier among the historical musical instruments. Outside, check out the **Friedrichstor** (the Frederick Gate), with the A.E.I.O.U. monogram—some believe it stands for the Latin sentence meaning "All Earth pays tribute to Austria"—then stop for a drink or a bite in the **Schloss Café**, with its lovely shaded terrace affording lordly views of the Danube and the opposite bank. ■ TIP→ **Getting up to the castle requires a short uphill walk. Avoid the steep and unshaded steps off Römerstrasse and opt for the gentler walk up Hofgasse instead.** ⊠ Schlossberg 1 ☎ 0732/772–052–300 ⊕ www.ooelkg.at ⊠ €6.50 ⊗ Closed Mon.

Stadtpfarrkirche

RELIGIOUS SITE | This city parish church dates from 1286 and was rebuilt in Baroque style in 1648. The tomb in the right wall of the chancel contains Frederick III's heart and entrails (the corpse is in Vienna's St. Stephen's Cathedral). The ceiling frescoes are by Altomonte, and the figure of Johann Nepomuk (a local saint) in the chancel is by Georg Raphael Donner, with grand decoration supplied by the master designer Hildebrandt. ✉ *Pfarrplatz 20* ☎ *0732/776120* ⊕ *www.dioezese-linz.at/pfarre/4208.*

★ Stift St. Florian (*St. Florian Abbey*)

RELIGIOUS SITE | Located 14 kilometers (8½ miles) southeast of Linz, this palatial Augustinian abbey—one of the most spectacular Baroque showpieces in Austria—was built in 1686 to honor the spot on the River Enns where St. Florian was drowned by pagans in 304. Landmarked by three gigantic "candle-snuffer" cupolas, it's centered on a mammoth **Marmorsaal** (Marble Hall), covered with frescoes honoring Prince Eugene of Savoy's defeat of the Turks, and a sumptuous **library** filled with 140,000 volumes. Guided tours of the abbey also take in the magnificent, three-story **figural gateway**, covered with symbolic statues; the **Kaiserzimmer,** a suite of 13 opulent salons with the "terrifying bed" of Prince Eugene (it's adorned with wood-carved figures of captives); and the over-the-top **abbey church,** home to an enormous organ once played by composer Anton Bruckner. You'll also see one of the great masterworks of the Austrian Baroque, Jakob Prandtauer's **Eagle Fountain Courtyard,** with its richly sculpted figures. If you find one day isn't enough to see it all, there are also rooms where you can spend the night in the abbey grounds (from €104 per night, including breakfast). Getting to the abbey is easy: there are regular buses from Linz's Volksgarten. ✉ *Stiftstrasse 1, St. Florian* ☎ *07224/89020* ⊕ *www.stift-st-florian.at* ☝ *Tour €10.50 (€14 incl. Imperial Apartments).*

 Restaurants

★ Herberstein

$$$$ | **EUROPEAN** | Tucked away inside the historic Kremsmünsterhaus, this elegant restaurant rocks a mod-retro look with cozy tables, muted lighting, and attractive stonework. The cuisine is Austrian with a touch of Asia, as evidenced by the selection of wok dishes and an excellent sushi bar. **Known for:** delicious corn cream soup; courtyard seating; sushi making classes available. $ *Average main: €25* ✉ *Altstadt 10* ☎ *0732/786161* ⊕ *www.herberstein-linz.at* ◷ *Closed Sun. No lunch.*

Muto

$$$$ | **FUSION** | There's a reason why the two-man creative team at this innovative Old Town restaurant chose the name "Muto." Meaning "transform" in Latin, it reflects their food philosophy; taking quality regional and seasonal ingredients and transforming them into delicious dishes with unusual and surprising flavor and texture combinations. The two seven-course menus (one for meat-eaters at €75 and one for vegetarians at €65) are always changing—just one more way in which this restaurant constantly surprises. **Known for:** innovative and playful dishes; cozy and casual interior; unlike anywhere else in Linz. $ *Average main: €75* ✉ *Altstadt 7* ☎ *0732/770377* ⊕ *www.mutolinz.at* ◷ *Closed Sun.–Tue. No lunch.*

Promenadenhof

$$$ | **AUSTRIAN** | The atmosphere here is that of a spacious, contemporary Gasthaus, with a fabulous roofed garden filled with flowers. The varied menu of regional cuisine is reasonably priced and has a touch of the Mediterranean, with plenty of vegetarian options available. **Known for:** delicious Linzertorte; excellent service; wine from the cellar available by the glass. $ *Average main: €20* ✉ *Promenade 39* ☎ *0732/777661* ⊕ *www.promenadenhof.at* ◷ *Closed Sun.*

★ Verdi

$$$$ | **AUSTRIAN** | It may be some way out of town, but the exquisite food, intimate atmosphere, and gorgeous views at this fine dining restaurant make it worth a special trip. Passionate owner-chef Erich Lukas crafts clever, seasonal set menus that combine Austrian and Mediterannean influences to great effect. **Known for:** seasonal menus using local ingredients; terrace seating in summer; gets booked up very quickly. $ *Average main: €35* ✉ *Pachmayrstrasse 137* ☎ *0732/733005* ⊘ *Closed Sun.–Mon. No lunch.*

Coffee and Quick Bites

Café Traxlmayr

$ | **CAFÉ** | One of Austria's grand old coffeehouses, this is the only one of its kind in Upper Austria. It's the perfect place to savor a cup of coffee, read the newspapers, and enjoy a light meal. **Known for:** grand coffeehouse atmosphere; delicious homemade cakes; outside terrace in summer. $ *Average main: €6* ✉ *Promenade 16* ☎ *0732/773353* ⊕ *www.cafe-traxlmayr.at.*

🛏 Hotels

★ Arte Hotel Linz

$$ | **HOTEL** | Around the corner from Ars Electronica Center and just across the river from the Old Town, this avant-garde boutique hotel offers stylish and spacious bedrooms with quirky light fixtures and tailor-made artworks by local creatives. **Pros:** bright and cheerful decor; peaceful location away from the crowds; has a (small) gym and sauna. **Cons:** breakfast buffet not included and a bit sparse; decor feels a bit cheap in places; artworks divide opinion. $ *Rooms from: €110* ✉ *Fiedlerstrasse 6* ☎ *0732/733733* ⊕ *www.arte-linz.at* ⇆ *73 rooms* ⦿ *No meals.*

Schwarzer Bär

$$$ | **HOTEL** | The birthplace of the renowned Mozart tenor Richard Tauber (1891–1948), the "Black Bear" is a traditional house filled with memorabilia on a side street in the center of the Old Town, a block from the pedestrian zone. **Pros:** great Old Town location; on-site underground parking; good bistro and rooftop bar. **Cons:** variance in room size; street noise can be heard from some rooms; friendly service not guaranteed. $ *Rooms from: €140* ✉ *Herrenstrasse 11* ☎ *0732/772477* ⊕ *www.linz-hotel.at* ⇆ *50 rooms* ⦿ *Free breakfast.*

Wolfinger

$$$ | **HOTEL** | Set within a 500-year-old former nunnery, the centrally located Wolfinger has been a hostelry since the late 1700s, and that gives the interior some real charm. **Pros:** great location for museums and restaurants; charming rooms; very helpful and friendly staff. **Cons:** old fittings in some rooms; a few rooms share bathrooms; no a/c. $ *Rooms from: €149* ✉ *Hauptplatz 19* ☎ *0732/7732–910* ⊕ *www.hotelwolfinger.at* ⇆ *50 rooms* ⦿ *Free breakfast.*

Nightlife

Linz is far livelier than even most Austrians realize. The city's most happening neighborhood, known as the Bermuda Triangle, has dozens of hip bars and lounges centered around three narrow Old Town streets—Klosterstrasse, Altstadt, and Hofgasse—while the OÖ Kulturquartier off Landstrasse has recently become another popular late-night hangout spot.

★ Boiler Room

BARS/PUBS | The city's coolest cocktail bar can be found within this long and atmospheric vaulted cellar just off the Hauptplatz. Expert mixologists serve an array of unique, crafty cocktails, incorporating everything from port wine to peanut butter. ✉ *Domgasse 5* ☎ *0676/944–2019* ⊕ *www.boiler-room.at.*

Casino Linz

CASINOS | Located in the Hotel Schiller-park, the casino has roulette, blackjack, poker, and slot machines (and a formal dress code). The less formal Jackpot Casino does not require a jacket and tie. Note that a passport is required for entry. The Jackpot Café, located on the ground floor, is open until late. ✉ *Rainerstrasse 2–4* ☎ *0732/654487* ⊕ *www.casinos.at/linz.*

Easy Bar

BARS/PUBS | This cocktail bar has been a mainstay of the Linz bar scene for about three decades and is still going strong. ✉ *Baumbachstrasse 14* ☎ *732/770090* ⊕ *www.cocktailbareasy.at.*

Josef

BARS/PUBS | This hopping establishment has its own home-brewed beer on tap, light snacks, and hearty regional dishes, and is open every day (except Sundays) from 11 am until 1 am.. ✉ *Landstrasse 49* ☎ *0732/773165* ⊕ *www.josef.eu.*

Paul's

BARS/PUBS | Virtually in the shadow of the New Cathedral, this hip stone-and-glass bar serves a great selection of Austrian wines and beers, including their own (superb) pale ale. They're open from early 'til late and do good food (including mean burgers) all day long—come at lunch for the bargain set menu (€11 for three courses). ✉ *Herrenstrasse 36* ☎ *0732/783338* ⊕ *www.pauls-linz.at.*

Performing Arts

Brucknerhaus

CONCERTS | A vast array of concerts and recitals are presented in the noted Brucknerhaus, the modern hall on the south bank of the Danube. Every September it's home to the International Bruckner Festival. The venue also hosts some events for Ars Electronica, a festival that explores art, science, and society. ✉ *Untere Donaulände 7* ☎ *0732/775230* ⊕ *www.brucknerhaus.at.*

★ Landestheater Linz

ARTS CENTERS | Designed by British architect Terry Pawson and considered Europe's most state-of-the-art opera house, the Landestheater—also known as the Musiktheater am Volksgarten—is now the stage for hit musicals and orchestra and choir performances, along with hosting a youth theater. The Main Hall seats 1,200 with several smaller halls seating up to 270 each. The remarkable Sound Foyer was created in cooperation with Ars Electronica Future Lab. Visitors to the theater, whether they see a show or not, are welcome to stop in and experience the technological wonder of the so-called sound path. ✉ *Am Volksgarten 1* ⊕ *www.landestheater-linz.at.*

Posthof

ARTS CENTERS | Located at the docks near the Mural Harbor Gallery, the Posthof has been one of the largest venues for contemporary arts not only in Austria, but in all of Europe, for more than 30 years. It's a multidisciplinary arts center, offering live music (of all genres, from reggae to techno), cabaret, dance, theater, literature, and more. Some 220 events are hosted each year throughout the September through June season. ✉ *Posthofstrasse 43* ☎ *0732/781800* ⊕ *www.posthof.at.*

Shopping

Linz is a good place to shop; prices are generally lower than those in resorts and the larger cities, and selections are varied. The major shops are found in the main square and the adjoining side streets, in the old quarter to the west of the main square, in the pedestrian zone of the Landstrasse and its side streets, and in the Hauptstrasse of Urfahr, over the Nibelungen Bridge across the Danube. A helpful list of boutique shops can be found on the Linz Labyrinth website (⊕ *www.linzlabyrinth.at*).

GIFTS AND SOUVENIRS
O. Ö. Heimatwerk
GIFTS/SOUVENIRS | This is a good option if you're looking for local handmade goods and good-quality souvenirs. You'll find silver, pewter, ceramics, fabrics, and some clothing. In the summer, be on the lookout for good discounts. ⊠ *Landstrasse 31* ☎ *0732/773377* ⊕ *www.ooe-heimatwerk. at* ⊘ *Closed Sun.*

HANDICRAFTS
'S Fachl
GIFTS/SOUVENIRS | This quirky little Hauptplatz store, part of a small chain operating throughout Austria, Germany, and Switzerland, gives over its shelves (well, its stacked fruit crates) to a variety of small local producers. The handicrafts for sale are forever changing, but there's always something worth popping in for, whether its clothes, jewelry, beauty products, stationery, or craft beer. ⊠ *Hauptplatz 24* ☎ *0676/4203–016* ⊕ *www.fachl. at* ⊘ *Closed Sun.*

JEWELRY
Atelier Almesberger
JEWELRY/ACCESSORIES | Also known as Donau Stein Design (Danube Stone Design), this shop creates little works of wearable art from stones found along the river's shore. ⊠ *Hofgasse 7* ☎ *0670/6079–858* ⊕ *www.donausteindesign.com* ⊘ *Closed Sun.*

⚡ Activities

BICYCLING
Cyclists appreciate the relatively level terrain around Linz, and within the city there are 200 kilometers (125 miles) of marked cycle routes. Cycling at slow speeds is also allowed in the city's pedestrian zones. The international Donauradweg, or Danube Cycling Path, runs from Germany through Linz and to the Black Sea. Get bike maps from the tourist office.

Donau Touristik
BICYCLING | Rent bikes here, or book a guided cycling tour along the Danube River. Bikes rented in Linz can be returned at several points along the Danube Cycling Path. ⊠ *Lederergasse 4–12* ☎ *0732/2080* ⊕ *www.donaureisen.at.*

SALZBURG

Updated by
Joseph Reaney

● Sights	🍴 Restaurants	🛏 Hotels	🛍 Shopping	🍸 Nightlife
★★★★☆	★★★★☆	★★★★☆	★★★☆☆	★★★★★

WELCOME TO SALZBURG

TOP REASONS TO GO

★ **Fortress Hohensalzburg:** Ascend to the fortress on the peak and find the soul-stirring combination of gorgeous architecture in a stunning natural location.

★ **Baroque churches:** See the magnificent 16th- and 17th-century churches built not only to honor God but also to document the importance of the ruling prince-archbishops during the 17th century.

★ **Concerts, operas, and more:** Feel the spirit of 1,300 years of musical history as you listen to the music of Wolfgang Amadeus Mozart, arguably the greatest Western composer who ever lived, in the Marble Hall of Mirabell Palace.

★ **Steingasse:** After exploring the Altstadt, cross the River Salzach to take in the completely different atmosphere of the narrow, 16th-century Steingasse.

★ **Schloss Hellbrunn:** A Renaissance-inspired pleasure palace with trick fountains, a lush green lawn, and the gazebo that witnessed so much wooing in *The Sound of Music*.

Salzburg lies on both banks of the Salzach River, at the point where it's pinched between two mountains; the Kapuzinerberg on one side and the Mönchsberg on the other. In broader view are many other beautiful Alpine peaks.

1 The Altstadt. Salzburg is the only city in the world with 1,300 years of continuous music history, which you can experience in the Altstadt's many concert halls, churches, restaurants, bars, and even outdoors in city squares—particularly during the Salzburger Festspiele.

2 Around Fortress Hohensalzburg. The showstopping medieval fortress is an attraction on its own, but it also offers sweeping Salzburg views. To the west of the fortress, near Salzburg Airport, is the popular plane, helicopter and Formula One racing car museum Hangar-7.

3 The Neustadt. Across the river from the Altstadt and spreading north and east, the Neustadt is a place to simultaneously enjoy outstanding old and new architecture and some lovely green spaces, from Mirabellgarten to Friedhof St. Sebastian.

4 Day Trips from Salzburg. It's not only the gorgeous Schloss Hellbrunn that's within easy reach of Salzburg; other nearby highlights include the world's oldest salt mine and the chapel where the Christmas carol "Silent Night" was first sung.

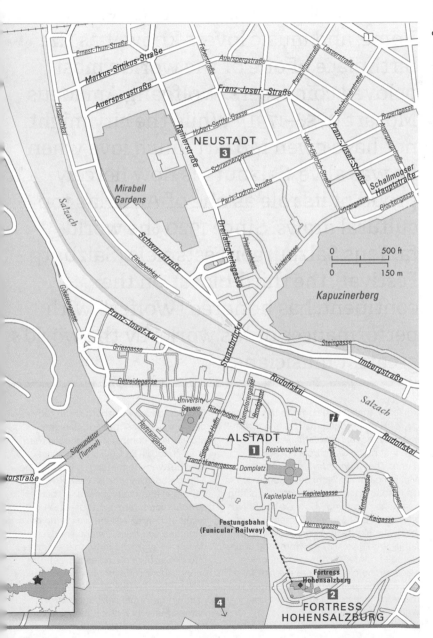

Art lovers call it the Golden City of High Baroque; historians refer to it as the Florence of the North or the German Rome; and music lovers know it as the birthplace of one of the world's most beloved composers, Wolfgang Amadeus Mozart (1756–1791). While the city might not have given Mozart much love when he was alive, Salzburg is now fiercely proud of its role as one of Austria's top cultural draws. Since 1920 the world-famous Salzburger Festspiele (Salzburg Festival), the third-oldest on the continent, has honored "Wolferl" with performances of his works by the world's greatest musicians.

Ironically, many who come to this golden city of High Baroque may first hear the instantly recognizable strains from the film that made Salzburg a household name: *The Sound of Music*. From the Mirabellgarten to Nonnberg Convent, it's hard to go anywhere without hearing someone humming "How Do You Solve a Problem Like Maria?" Filmed here in 1964, the film focuses on the von Trapp family who, like Mozart, were little appreciated at home; Austria was the only place on the planet where the film failed. Perhaps the locals at that time struggled to sympathize with a prominent family who fled the country.

Getting to know Salzburg is not too difficult, because most of its sights are within a comparatively small area. The Altstadt (Old City) is a compact area between the jutting outcrop of the Mönchsberg and the Salzach River. The cathedral and interconnecting squares surrounding it form what used to be the religious center, around which the major churches and the old archbishops' residence are arranged (note that entrance into all Salzburg churches is free). The Mönchsberg cliffs emerge unexpectedly behind the Old City, crowned to the east by the Hohensalzburg Fortress. Across the river is the Steingasse, a narrow medieval street once home to laborers, craftsmen, and traders serving the salt-mining industry, and just north of here lies the Neustadt (New City). Here, you'll find some of Salzburg's most popular attractions, including the Mozart Residence, the Mirabell Palace (and its manicured gardens), and the Marionettentheater, as well as some of its most luxurious heritage hotels.

It's best to begin by exploring the architectural and cultural riches of the Altstadt, then go on to the fortress. Afterward, cross the river to see the Neustadt. Ideally, you need two days to do it all. An alternative, if you enjoy exploring churches and castles, is to go directly up to the fortress, either on foot or by returning through the cemetery to the funicular railway.

Planning

When to Go

The high season in Salzburg is summer, particular during the Salzburger Festspiele (July and August). A visit in late spring or early autumn offers comfortable temperatures but thinner crowds. For winter sports enthusiasts, or those who like to wrap up for brisk walks, winter is also a good option—though it can get very busy around Christmas and New Year.

Salzburg has a milder climate than much of Austria. Summer visitors will be warm with temperatures around 75 to 85°F, while winter visitors can expect to shiver at around 15 to 25°F. Whenever you come, bring an umbrella as rain is always a possibility.

Festivals

Salzburger Festspiele

FESTIVALS | The biggest event on the Salzburg social calendar—as it has been since it was first organized by composer Richard Strauss, producer Max Reinhardt, and playwright Hugo von Hofmannsthal in 1920—is the world-famous Salzburg Festival, usually held late July through late August. The most star-studded events feature top opera stars and conductors and are very expensive, with keen audience members pulling out all the stops—think summer furs, Dior dresses, and white ties. However, other performances can be more relaxed and more reasonably priced, and events outside the main festival halls, the **Grosses Festspielhaus** (Great Festival Hall) and the **Haus für Mozart** (House for Mozart), located on the grand promenade of Hofstallgasse, are even cheaper. This street is especially dazzling at night, thanks to the floodlighted Fortress Hohensalzburg. There are also concerts and operas at other theaters in the city, including the Summer Riding School (Felsenreitschule), Kollegienkirche, and the Mozarteum. ■ TIP→ **Order your tickets early, as major performances sell out several months in advance.** ⊠ *Hofstallgasse 1* ☎ *0662/8045–500* ⊕ *www.salzburger-festspiele.at.*

Getting Here and Around

AIR

Salzburg Airport, four kilometers (2½ miles) west of the city center, is Austria's second-largest international airport. There are direct flights from London and other European cities to Salzburg, but not from the United States. For transcontinental travel, you can fly to Munich and take the 90-minute train ride to Salzburg, or you can take a transfer bus run by SMS. Taxis are the easiest way to get downtown from the Salzburg airport; the ride costs around €15 and takes about 20 minutes. O-Bus 10, which makes a stop by the airport every 15 minutes, runs down to Salzburg's Altstadt (about 20 minutes), while the equally regular O-Bus 2 drops off at the train station (about 25 minutes).

AIRPORT CONTACTS Munich International Airport (MUC). (*Flughafen München*) ⊠ *Nordallee 25, Munich* ☎ *089/975–00* ⊕ *www.munich-airport.de.* **Salzburg Airport (SZG).** ⊠ *Innsbrucker Bundesstrasse 95* ☎ *0662/85800* ⊕ *www.salzburg-airport.com.* **SMS.** (*Salzburger Mietwagenservice*) ⊠ *Wasserfeldstrasse 24A* ☎ *0622/81610* ⊕ *www.smsflughafentransfer.at.*

BUS

A tourist map (available from tourist offices in Mozartplatz and the train station) shows all bus routes and stops; there's also a color-coded map of the public transport network, so you should have no problem getting around. Virtually all buses and trolleybuses (O-Bus) run via Mirabellplatz and/or Hanuschplatz. Single bus tickets bought from the driver cost €2.90.

CONTACTS Salzburger Verkehrsverbund. (*Main ticket office*) ⊠ *Schallmooser Hauptstrasse 10* ☎ *0662/632900* ⊕ *www.salzburg-verkehr.at.*

CAR

If driving, the fastest and simplest routes into Salzburg are the autobahns. From Vienna, take the A1 west to Salzburg for the full 300 kilometers (186 miles). From Munich in Germany, take the A8 southeast for 145 kilometers (90 miles). From Villach near the Italy and Slovenia borders, take the A10 north for 198 kilometers (118 miles). The only advantage to having a car in Salzburg itself is that you can get out of the city for short excursions. The city center, on both sides of the river, is a pedestrian zone, and the rest of the city, with its narrow one-way streets, is a driver's nightmare.

TAXIS 81-11. ☎ *0662/8111* ⊕ *www.taxi.at.*

TRAIN

You can get to Salzburg by rail from most European cities. Salzburg Hauptbahnhof is north of the Neustadt, a 20-minute walk from the city center. The bus station and the suburban railroad station are at the square in front of the train station. A taxi to the center of town should take about 10 minutes and cost €10.

TRAIN INFORMATION ÖBB. ☎ *05/1717* ⊕ *www.oebb.at.* **Salzburg Hauptbahnhof.** ⊠ *Südtirolerplatz 1* ☎ *0435/1717* ⊕ *www.oebb.at.*

Hotels

It's difficult for a Salzburg hotel not to have a good location—you can find a room with a stunning view over the Kapuzinerberg or Gaisberg or one that simply overlooks a lovely Altstadt street—but it's possible. Salzburg is not a tiny town, and location is important. It's best to be near the historic city center; it's about a mile from the railway station to historic Zentrum (center), right around the main bridge of the Staatsbrücke. The Altstadt has a wide assortment of hotels and pensions, but there are few bargains. Also note that many hotels in this area have to be accessed on foot, as cars are not permitted on many streets. If you have a car, you may opt for a hotel or converted castle on the outskirts of the city. Many hostelries are charmingly decorated in *Bauernstil*, the rustic look of Old Austria; the ultimate in peasant-luxe is found at the world-famous Hotel Goldener Hirsch.

If you're looking for something really cheap (less than €60 for a double), clean, and comfortable, stay in a private home, though the good ones are all a little way from downtown.

The tourist information office can assist with booking B&Bs, farmhouses, and religious institutions, as well as hotels and apartments.

If you're planning to come at festival time (July and August), you must book as early as possible; try to reserve at least two months in advance. Prices soar over the already high levels—so much so that during the high season a hotel may edge into the next-higher price category.

Room rates include taxes and service charges. Many hotels include a breakfast in the room rate—check when booking—but the more expensive hostelries often do not. A property that provides breakfast and dinner daily is known as *halbpension,* and one that serves three meals a day is *vollpension.* If you don't have a reservation, go to one of the tourist information offices, either in the center (on Mozartplatz) or at the railway station. *Hotel reviews have been shortened. For full information, visit Fodors.com.*

Restaurants

Salzburg has some of the best—and most expensive—restaurants in Austria, so if you happen to walk into one of the Altstadt posh establishments without a reservation, you may get a sneer worthy of Captain von Trapp. Happily, the city is plentifully supplied with pleasant eateries, offering not only good, solid Austrian food (not for anyone on a diet), but also exceptional Italian dishes and *neue Küche* (nouvelle cuisine) delights. There are certain dining experiences that are quintessentially Salzburgian, including restaurants perched on the town's peaks that offer "food with a view" or rustic inns that offer "Alpine evenings" with entertainment. Some of the most distinctive places in town are the fabled hotel restaurants, such as those of the Goldener Hirsch or Restaurant S'Nockerl, the cellar of the Hotel Elefant.

For fast food, Salzburgers love their broiled-sausages street stands. Some say the most delicious fare is found at the Balkan Grill at Getreidegasse 33 (its recipe for spicy Bosna sausage has always been a secret). ■TIP➜ **For a quick lunch on weekdays, visit the market in front of the Kollegienkirche—a lot of stands offer a large variety of boiled sausages for any taste, ranging from mild to spiced.**

In the more expensive restaurants the set menus give you an opportunity to sample the chef's best; in less expensive ones they help keep costs down. Note, however, that some restaurants limit the hours during which the set menu is available. Many restaurants are open all day; otherwise, lunch is served from approximately 11 am to 2 pm and dinner from 6 to 10 pm. In more expensive restaurants it's always best to make a reservation. At festival time most restaurants are open seven days a week, and have generally more flexible late dining hours. *Restaurant reviews have been shortened. For full information, visit Fodors.com.*

What it Costs in Euros			
$	$$	$$$	$$$$
RESTAURANTS			
under €12	€12–€17	€18–€22	over €22
HOTELS			
under €120	€120–€170	€171–€270	over €270

Nightlife

Music in Salzburg is not just Mozart's greatest hits; the city's nightlife is actually much livelier than it is reputed to be. The "in" areas include the "Bermuda Triangle" (Steingasse and Imbergstrasse) and Kaigasse, while young people tend to populate the bars and discos around Gstättengasse and Rudolfskai. Salzburg loves beer, and has some of the most picturesque beer gardens in Austria. The Augustinerbräu is a legendary Munich-style beer hall.

Performing Arts

Before you arrive in Salzburg, do some advance research to determine the city's music schedule for the time you will be there, and make reservations; if you'll be attending the summer Salzburg Festival, this is a must. After you arrive in the city, any office of the Salzburg Tourist Office and most hotel concierge desks can provide you with schedules for all the arts performances held year-round in Salzburg, and you can find listings in the daily newspaper, *Salzburger Nachrichten*.

The Advent season transforms this picture-perfect city into an even more magical wonderland. Music fills the streets of the Old City during the Christmas markets. Warm up with a cup of *Glühwein* (mulled wine) from one of the numerous wooden stands and find the nearest festively attired brass ensemble for a lovely free concert.

To experience a true local tradition, get tickets to one of several Adventsingen performances. Folk singers, choral ensembles, children's choirs, traditional instrument ensembles, and actors weave music and theater into the Advent season. The stories and songs are typically in local dialect, which can be difficult for even High German speakers to understand, but the atmosphere and experience are worth it.

The spiritual surroundings of the St. Andrew's Church on Mirabellplatz offer the perfect atmosphere for the performances by Salzburger Advent (⊕ *www. salzburgeradvent.at*). Salzburg Advent Singing (⊕ *www.salzburgeradventsingen. at*) in the Great Festival Hall is the largest event of the season.

TICKETS Salzburg Ticket Service. ✉ *Mozartplatz 5* ☎ *0662/840310* ⊕ *www. salzburgticket.com*. **Salzburg Ticket Shop.** ✉ *Getreidegasse 5* ☎ *0662/825–858–16* ⊕ *www.salzburg-ticketshop.at*.

Shopping

For a small city, Salzburg has a wide spectrum of stores. The specialties are traditional clothing, like lederhosen and loden coats, jewelry, glassware, handicrafts, confectionary, dolls in native costume, Christmas decorations, sports equipment, and silk flowers. A *Gewürzsträussl* is a bundle of whole spices bunched and arranged to look like a bouquet of flowers; you can usually find some in the markets on Universitätsplatz. This old tradition goes back to the time when only a few rooms could be heated, and people and their farm animals would often cohabitate on the coldest days. You can imagine how lovely the aromas must have been—so this spicy room freshener was invented.

At Christmas there is a special **Advent market** on the Domplatz and the Residenzplatz, offering regional decorations, from the week before the first Advent Sunday until December 26, daily 9 am–8 pm. Stores are generally open weekdays 10 am–6 pm, and many on Saturday 10 am–5 pm. Some supermarkets stay open until 7:30 pm on Thursday or Friday. Only shops in the railway station, the airport, and near the general hospital are open on Sunday.

Tours

The Altstadt, composed of several interconnecting squares and narrow streets, is best seen on foot. Salzburg's official licensed guides offer a one-hour walking tour (€10) through the area every day at 12:15, and a more in-depth art and architecture 1½-hour tour (€15) Monday through Saturday at 2 pm, which start in front of the Information Center at Mozartplatz 5. A Salzburg Card reduces the fee.

Several local companies conduct 1½- to two-hour city tours. The tours are by minibus, since large buses can't enter the Old

City, and briefly cover the major sights, including Mozart's birthplace, the festival halls, major squares, churches, and the palaces at Hellbrunn and Leopoldskron. Bob's Special Tours is well-known to American visitors—the company offers a discount to Fodor's readers who book directly with it, show their Fodor's book, and pay cash. Salzburg Panorama Tours and Salzburg Sightseeing Tours offer similar tours.

To reach spots buses can't, ride along with one of Fräulein Maria's daily 3½-hour bicycle tours (€35).

Bob's Special Tours

SPECIAL-INTEREST | Bob's small vans allow access to the narrow streets of Salzburg that lumbering buses can't maneuver. Explore the city, nearby mountain regions, or *The Sound of Music* filming highlights on daily and seasonal tours. Experienced multilingual guides are available and there's a 10% discount for Fodor's readers (just show your guidebook and pay in cash). ⊠ *Rudolfskai 38* ☎ *0662/849511* ⊕ *www.bobstours.com* ☜ *From €55.*

Fräulein Maria's Bicycle Tour

BICYCLE TOURS | FAMILY | Ride through the streets of Salzburg singing the soundtrack favorites and learn a surprising amount of the city's history with fellow movie and musical fans on these *The Sound of Music*–themed small group bicycle tours. Guides share the von Trapp family cheer rain or shine with riders of all ages and abilities—inclement weather gear, tandem bikes, children's bikes, trailers, and baby seats are offered at no additional cost. ⊠ *Mirabellplatz 4* ☎ *0650/3426–297* ⊕ *www.mariasbicycletours.com* ☜ *Sound of Music Tour €30.*

Salzburg Panorama Tours

GUIDED TOURS | One of the most reliable, respected tour companies in the area offers a variety of themes and ways to become acquainted with Salzburg and the surrounding areas, either by bus,

on foot, or in a luxurious private car. The "Original *Sound of Music* Tour" hits the movie location highlights and includes much about the city itself. The "Walking City Tour" is the perfect introduction to Salzburg's architectural history, churches and cathedrals, and Mozart. Bus pick-up is available at several local hotels. ⊠ *Schrannengasse 2* ☎ *0662/8832–110* ⊕ *www.panoramatours.com* ☜ *From €21.*

Salzburg Sightseeing Tours

BUS TOURS | One of the oldest tour companies in the city, Salzburg Sightseeing Tours offers prepackaged programs—including the best of the city, *The Sound of Music* locations, and nearby Alpine highlights—or custom tours. The yellow hop-on, hop-off buses stop at the most famous Salzburg landmarks, with informative recorded audio guides between stops. The complete circuit (without getting off) takes an hour. All tickets include free access to all local Salzburg buses, as well as the Gaisberg bus (No. 151). ⊠ *Mirabellplatz 2* ☎ *0662/881616* ⊕ *www.salzburg-sightseeingtours.at* ☜ *From €21.*

Visitor Information

VISITOR INFORMATION Tourist Info Train Station. ⊠ *Salzburg Hauptbahnhof, Südtirolerplatz 1* ☎ *0662/88987–340* ⊕ *www.salzburg.info/en.* Tourist Info Mozartplatz. ⊠ *Mozartplatz 5* ☎ *0662/88987–330* ⊕ *www.salzburg.info/en.*

The Altstadt

Intent on becoming a patron of the arts, the prince-archbishop Wolf-Dietrich lavished much of his wealth on rebuilding Salzburg into a beautiful and Baroque city in the late 16th and early 17th centuries. In turn, his grand townscape came to inspire the young Joannes Chrysostomus Wolfgangus Theophilus Mozart. In fact, by growing up in the center of the city and composing already at five years of age, Mozart set lovely Salzburg itself to music. He was perhaps the most purely Austrian of all composers, a singer of the smiling Salzburgian countryside and of the city's Baroque architecture. So even if you're not lucky enough to snag a ticket to a performance of *The Marriage of Figaro* or *Don Giovanni* in the Haus für Mozart, you can still appreciate what inspired his melodies just by strolling through these streets.

Ever since the 1984 Best Film Oscar-winner *Amadeus,* the composer has been the 18th-century equivalent to a rock star. Born in Salzburg on January 27, 1756, he crammed a prodigious number of compositions into the 35 short years of his life, many of which he spent in Salzburg (he moved to Vienna in 1781). Indeed, the Altstadt revels in a bevy of important sights, ranging from his birthplace on the Getreidegasse to the abbey of St. Peter's, where the composer's *Great Mass in C Minor* was first performed.

◉ Sights

Alter Markt (*Old Market*)
MARKET | Right in the heart of the Old City is the Alter Markt, the old marketplace and former center of secular life in the city. The square is lined with 17th-century, middle-class houses, colorfully hued in shades of pink, pale blue, and yellow ocher. Look in at the old royal pharmacy, the **Hofapotheke,** whose ornate black-and-gold Rococo interior was built in 1760. Inside, the curious apothecarial smell can be traced to the shelves of Latin-labeled pots and jars. The pharmacy is still operating today and you can even have your blood pressure taken—but preferably not after drinking a *Doppelter Einspänner* (black coffee with whipped cream, served in a glass) in the famous Café Tomaselli just opposite. In warm weather, the café's terrace provides a wonderful spot for watching the world go by as you sip a *Melange* (another coffee specialty,

served with frothy milk), as does the chestnut tree-shaded Tomaselli garden at the top of the square.

Next to the coffeehouse you'll find the smallest house in Salzburg; note the slanting roof decorated with a dragon gargoyle. In the center of the square is the marble St. Florian's Fountain, dedicated in 1734 to the patron saint of firefighters. ⊠ *Salzburg.*

★ Dom zu Salzburg (*Salzburg Cathedral*)
RELIGIOUS SITE | Set within the beautiful Domplatz with the Virgin's Column in its center, this gorgeous cathedral is considered to be the first early-Italian Baroque building north of the Alps. There has been a cathedral on this spot since the 8th century, but the present structure dates from the 17th century. Its facade is of marble, its towers reach 250 feet into the air, and it holds 10,000 people. The church's simple sepia-and-white interior is a peaceful counterpoint to the usual Baroque splendor. Mozart was christened here (at the 14th-century font) and later served as the cathedral's organist, writing some of his compositions, such as the *Coronation Mass,* specifically for the cathedral. It was a good fit, as this is the only house of worship in the world with five independent fixed organs. Today, they are sometimes played together during special church-music concerts. ■TIP→ On Sunday and all Catholic holidays, mass is held at 10 am— the most glorious time to experience the cathedral's full splendor. ⊠ *Domplatz 1a* ☎ *0662/804–779–50* ⊕ *www.salzburger-dom.at/home.*

★ DomQuartier
MUSEUM | For the first time since the early 1800s, you can look down on the original heart of Salzburg as once only the powerful archbishops could, as you walk the top-floor corridors surrounding the Domplatz that connect the Residenz (palace), Dom (cathedral), and St. Peter's Abbey. In the Residenz, see the magnificent **State Rooms,** including the Kaisersaal

Salzburg's basilica in the heart of the historic center has been hit by no less than ten fires and has been entirely rebuilt three times over the centuries.

(Imperial Hall) and the Rittersaal (Knight's Hall). Of particular note are the frescoes by Johann Michael Rottmayr and Martino Altomonte depicting the history of Alexander the Great. Upstairs on the third floor is the **Residenzgalerie**, a princely art collection specializing in 17th-century Dutch and Flemish art and 19th-century paintings of Salzburg. On the State Rooms floor, Mozart's opera *La Finta Semplice* premiered in 1769 in the Guard Room. Also included is the fascinating **Dommuseum**, with cathedral art from the 8th to 18th centuries, as well as the **Museum St. Peter** with valuable art treasures from the monastery's collections. You'll also enjoy a beautiful balcony view of the cathedral interior, as well as expansive vistas of the city. The interior walkways make it particularly appealing on one of Salzburg's frequent rainy days. ✉ *Residenzplatz 1/Domplatz 1a* ☎ *0662/804–221–09* ⊕ *www.domquartier.at* 🎫 *€13* ◷ *Closed Tue.*

Franziskanerkirche (*Franciscan Church*)
RELIGIOUS SITE | The graceful, tall spire of the Franciscan Church stands out from all other towers in Salzburg; the church itself encompasses the greatest diversity of architectural styles. There was a church on this spot as early as the 8th century, but it was destroyed by fire. The Romanesque nave of its replacement is still visible, as are other Romanesque features, such as a stone lion set into the steps leading to the pulpit. In the 15th century the choir was built in Gothic style, then crowned in the 18th century by an ornate red-marble-and-gilt altar designed by Austria's most famous Baroque architect, Johann Bernhard Fischer von Erlach. Mass—frequently featuring one of Mozart's compositions—is celebrated here on Sunday at 9 am. ✉ *Franziskanergasse 5* ☎ *0662/843629.*

The Altstadt

NEUSTADT

Mirabell Gardens

Salzach

Auerspergstraße

Elisabethkai

Rainerstraße

Schwarzstraße

Elisabethkai

Gstättengasse

Franz-Josef-Kai

Griesgasse

Hagenauerplatz

Getreidegasse

University Square

Hofseilgasse

Reichenhaller Straße

Sigmundstor (Tunnnel)

Franziskanerga

Sigmundsto...

Neutorstraße

Johann-Wolf-Straße

Steinbruchstraße

KEY

1 *Exploring Sights*

1 *Restaurants*

1 *Quick Bites*

1 *Hotels*

Glockenspiel

LOCAL INTEREST | This famous carillon bell tower is perched on top of the **Neue Residenz** (New Residence), Prince-Archbishop Wolf-Dietrich's government palace. The carillon is a later addition, brought from today's Belgium in 1695 and finally put in working order in 1704. The 35 bells play classical tunes (usually by Mozart or Haydn) with charm and ingenuity at 7 am, 11 am, and 6 pm. On Sunday at 11:45 am, musicians perform in the "Trumpeter Tower" at Hohensalzburg Fortress, and their Baroque fanfares can be heard across the Old City. Details about the music selections are listed on a notice board across the square on the corner of the Residenz building. ⊠ *Mozartplatz 1* ☎ *0662/620–808–700* ⊕ *www. salzburgmuseum.at.*

Kollegienkirche (*Collegiate Church*)
RELIGIOUS SITE | Completed by Fischer von Erlach in 1707, this church, sometimes called the Universitätskirche, is one of the purest examples of Baroque architecture in Austria. Unencumbered by Rococo decorations, the modified Greek cross plan has a majestic dignity worthy of Palladio. ⊠ *Universitätsplatz* ☎ *0662/841327* ⊕ *www.kollegienkirche. at/en.*

Mönchsbergaufzug (*Mönchsberg Elevator*)
TRANSPORTATION SITE (AIRPORT/BUS/FERRY/TRAIN) | Just around the corner from the Pferdeschwemme horse fountain, at Anton-Neumayr Platz, you'll find the Mönchsberg elevator, which carries you up 60 meters through solid rock in less than 30 seconds. At the top, you'll find not only to the **Museum der Moderne** but also some lovely wooded paths that are great for walking and gasping—there are spectacular vistas of Salzburg. In summer, the elevator is a marvelous (and quick) way to escape the tiny, crowded streets of the Old City. ⊠ *Gstättengasse 13* ⊠ *Round-trip €3.90, one way €2.60.*

Mozart Monument (*Mozart Square*)
PUBLIC ART | In the center of Mozartplatz, on a marble plinth, stands this impressive bronze statue of Wolfgang Amadeus Mozart. Sculpted by Ludwig Schwanthaler and unveiled in 1842 in the presence of the composer's two surviving sons (how's that for pressure?), it was the first sign of public recognition Mozart received from his hometown since his death in Vienna in 1791. The statue, the first for a non-noble person in Austria, is very much a 19th-century stylized view of the composer, draped in a mantle and holding a page of music and a copybook. ⊠ *Mozartplatz.*

★ **Mozarts Geburtshaus** (*Mozart's Birthplace*)
HOUSE | This homage to Salzburg's prodigal son offers fascinating insights into his life and works, with carefully curated relics of Mozart's youth, listening rooms, and models of famous productions of his operas. As an adult, the great composer preferred Vienna to Salzburg, complaining that audiences in his native city were no more responsive than tables and chairs. Still, home is home, and this was Mozart's—when not on one of his frequent trips abroad—until the age of 17. Mozart was born on the third (in American parlance, the fourth) floor of this tall house on January 27, 1756, and his family lived here in the front apartment, when they were not on tour, from 1747 to 1773. As the child prodigy composed many of his first compositions in these rooms, it is fitting and touching to find Mozart's tiny first violin on display. ⊠ *Getreidegasse 9* ☎ *0662/844313* ⊕ *www. mozarteum.at* ⊠ *€12; combined ticket with Mozart-Wohnhaus €18.50.*

Museum der Moderne
MUSEUM | There are two branches of the Museum der Moderne in Salzburg: Mönchsberg and Rupertinum. The former enjoys one of Salzburg's most famous scenic spots, atop the sheer cliff face of the Mönchsberg. Clad in minimalist white

Music lovers flock to Mozart's birthplace which features his letters, memorabilia, furnishings, family portraits, and even locks of the composer's hair.

marble, the modern art museum has three exhibition levels, with graphics and paintings by Austrian and international artists like Oskar Kokoschka and Erwin Wurm, and a focus on large-scale installations and sculptural works. In the Altstadt below, the Rupertinum offers changing exhibitions of modern graphic art and interactive special exhibits within a lovely early-Baroque-era building. Both branches have superb dining options, but the Mönchsberg restaurant edges it for the spectacular city views (come in the evening to see the city illuminated). ✉ *Museum der Moderne Mönchsberg, Mönchsberg 32* ☎ *0662/842220* ⊕ *www.museumdermoderne.at* ✉ *€12 for both museums* ⊘ *Closed Mon. except during Salzburg Festival.*

Petersfriedhof (*St. Peter's Cemetery*)
CEMETERY | Eerie but intimate, this is the oldest Christian graveyard in Austria, dating back to 1627. Enclosed on three sides by elegant wrought-iron grilles, Baroque arcades contain chapels belonging to Salzburg's old patrician families. The graveyard is far from mournful: the individual graves are tended with loving care, decorated with candles, fir branches, and flowers—especially pansies (because the name means "thoughts"). In Crypt XXXI is the grave of Santino Solari, architect of the cathedral; in XXXIX that of Sigmund Haffner, a patron for whom Mozart composed a symphony and named a serenade. The final communal Crypt LIV (by the so-called catacombs) contains the body of Mozart's sister Nannerl and the torso of Joseph Haydn's younger brother Michael (his head is in St. Peter's church). The cemetery is in the shadow of the Mönchsberg mount; note the early-Christian tombs carved in the rock face. ✉ *Sankt-Peter-Bezirk 1* ☎ *0662/844–576–0.*

Pferdeschwemme (*Horse Pond*)
FOUNTAIN | If Rome had fountains, so, too, would Wolf-Dietrich's Salzburg. The city is studded with them, and none is so odd as this monument to all things equine. You'll find it if you head to the western end of the Hofstallgasse on Herbert-von-Karajan-Platz, named after

Mozart: Marvel and Mystery

"Mozart is sunshine." So proclaimed Antonín Dvořák—and how better to sum up the prodigious genius of Wolfgang Amadeus Mozart (January 27, 1756 to December 5, 1791)? Listening to his Rococo orchestrations, his rose-strewn melodies, and his insouciant harmonies, many listeners seem to experience nothing short of giddiness. Scientists have found Mozart's music can cause the heart to pound, bring color to the cheeks, and provide the expansive feeling of being thrillingly alive. Yet, Mozart must have sensed how hard it is to recognize happiness, which is often something vaguely desired and not detected until gone. It is this melancholy undercurrent that makes Mozart modern—so modern that he is now the most popular classical composer, having banished Beethoven to second place. Shortly after *Amadeus* won the 1984 Oscar for best film—with its portrayal of Mozart as a giggling, foul-mouthed genius—*Don Giovanni* began to rack up more performances than *La Bohème.* The bewigged face graces countless "Mozartkugeln" chocolates, while Mostly Mozart festivals pay him homage across the pond. But a look behind the glare of the spotlights reveals that this blond, slightly built tuning fork of a fellow was a quicksilver enigma.

Already a skilled pianist at age three, the musical prodigy was dragged across Europe by his father, Leopold, to perform for empresses and kings. In a life that lasted a mere 35 years, he spent 10 of them on the road—a burden that contributed to making him the first truly European composer. Growing up in Salzburg, the *Wunderkind* became less of a *Wunder* (as well as less of a *Kind*) as time went by. Prince-Archbishop Hieronymus von Colloredo enjoyed dissing his resident composer by commanding him to produce "table music" with the same disdainful tone he commanded his chef's dinner orders. Being literally forced to sit with those cooks, Mozart finally rebelled. In March 1781 he married Constanze Weber and set out to conquer Vienna.

Hated by Mozart's father, Constanze is adored today, since we now know she was Mozart's greatest ally. She no doubt heartily enjoyed the fruits of his first operatic triumph, the naughty *Abduction from the Seraglio* (1782). His next opera, *The Marriage of Figaro* (1786), to no one's surprise, bombed. Always eager to thumb his nose at authority, Mozart had adapted a Beaumarchais play so inflammatory in its depiction of aristos as pawns of their own servants, it soon helped ignite the French Revolution. In revenge, wealthy Viennese society gave a cold shoulder to his magisterial *Don Giovanni* (1787). Mozart was relegated to composing, for a lowly vaudeville house, the now immortal *Magic Flute* (1790), and to ghosting a *Requiem* for a wealthy count. Sadly, his star only began to soar after a tragic, early death in 1791.

Salzburg's second-greatest musical son, the legendary conductor who was the music director of the Salzburg Festival for many decades. On the Mönchsberg side of the square is the Pferdeschwemme—a royal trough, constructed in 1695, where prize horses used to be cleaned and watered; as they underwent this ordeal they could delight in the frescoes of their pin-up fillies on the rear wall. The Baroque monument in the middle represents the antique legend of the taming of a horse, Bellerophon and his mount, Pegasus. ⊠ *Herbert-von-Karajan-Platz 11.*

Rathaus (*Town Hall*)
GOVERNMENT BUILDING | Where Sigmund-Haffner-Gasse meets the Getreidegasse you will find the Rathaus, an insignificant building in the Salzburg skyline—no doubt reflecting the historical weakness of the burghers vis-à-vis the Church, whose opulent monuments are evident throughout the city. On the other hand, this structure is a prime example of the Italian influence in Salzburg's architecture. Originally this was a family tower (and the only one still remaining here), but it was sold to the city in 1407. ⊠ *Rathausplatz and Kranzlmarkt.*

Residenz
CASTLE/PALACE | At the very heart of Baroque Salzburg, the Residenz overlooks the spacious Residenzplatz and its famous fountain. The palace in its present form was built between 1600 and 1619 as the home of Wolf-Dietrich, the most powerful of Salzburg's prince-archbishops. See inside with a visit to the **Dom-Quartier**. The palace courtyard has the lovely setting for Salzburg Festival opera productions since 1956—mostly the lesser-known treasures of Mozart. ⊠ *Residenzplatz 1.*

★ Salzburg Museum (*Neue Residenz*)
MUSEUM | Encompassing six different buildings, the Salzburg Museum's largest location is the 17th-century Neue Residenz (New Residence). This building

was Prince-Archbishop Wolf-Dietrich's "overflow" palace—he couldn't fit his entire archiepiscopal court into the main Residenz across the plaza—and as such, it features 10 state reception rooms that were among the first attempts at Renaissance-style design in the North. The permanent exhibition focuses on the city's artistic, cultural, and historical development. The Mirror Hall contains an archaeological collection including remains of the town's ancient Roman ruins. The Panorama Passage, lined with archaeological excavations from the Neue Residenz, leads to the Panorama Museum, home to the spectacular Sattler Panorama. One of the few remaining 360-degree paintings in the world, it shows the city of Salzburg in the early 19th century. The Art Hall hosts three major special exhibitions a year. ⊠ *Mozartplatz 1* ☎ *0662/620–808–0* ⊕ *www.salzburgmuseum.at* ☜ *€9 inc. Panorama Museum* ⊘ *Closed Mon.*

Spielzeugmuseum (*Toy Museum*)
MUSEUM | **FAMILY** | On a rainy day this is a delightful diversion for both young and old, with an interactive collection of dolls, teddy bears, model trains, and wooden sailing ships. Special Punch and Judy–style *Kasperltheater* puppet shows leave everyone laughing. Performances are held every Wednesday at 3 pm. ⊠ *Bürgerspitalgasse 2* ☎ *0662/620–808–300* ⊕ *www.spielzeugmuseum.at* ☜ *€5; theater performances €5.50* ⊘ *Closed Mon.*

Stiftkirche St. Peter (*St. Peter's Abbey*)
RELIGIOUS SITE | The most sumptuous church in Salzburg, St. Peter's is where Mozart's famed *Great Mass in C Minor* premiered in 1783, with his wife, Constanze, singing the lead soprano role. Wolfgang directed the orchestra and choir and also played the organ. During the Salzburger Festspiele, the work is performed here during a special church-music concert. The porch has beautiful Romanesque vaulted arches from the original structure built in the

12th century. The interior was decorated in the voluptuous late-Baroque style when additions were made in the 1770s. Note the side chapel by the entrance, with the unusual crèche portraying the Flight into Egypt and the Massacre of the Innocents. Behind the Rupert Altar is the "Felsengrab," a rock-face tomb where—according to a legend—St. Rupert himself was originally buried. To go from the sacred to the profane, head for the abbey's legendary St. Peter Stiftskeller restaurant, adjacent to the church. ✉ *Sankt-Peter-Bezirk 1* ☎ *0662/844576* 🌐 *www.erzabtei.at.*

Get Carded

Planning to see a lot? Consider purchasing the Salzburg Card, which gives you no-cost entry to all city museums and sights, free public transport, and discounts on concerts and cultural events. The cards are good for 24, 48, or 72 hours (at €29, €38, and €44 respectively) and even less November through April. Children under 15 pay half.

🍴 Restaurants

★ Balkan Grill

$ | **HOT DOG** | Known simply as "The Bosna Grill," this tiny sausage stand has become a cult destination for locals and international travelers. Find the long line of hungry people in the tiny passageway between the busy Getreidegasse and the Universitätsplatz to try this Bulgarian-inspired, Salzburg-born specialty: two thin, grilled bratwurst sausages in a toasted white bread bun, topped with chopped onions, fresh parsley, and a curry-based seasoning mixture that's been a secret since the owner, Zanko Todoroff, created it more than 50 years ago. **Known for:** phenomenal curry sausage; long lines; cash-only policy. [$] *Average main: €4* ✉ *Getreidegasse 33* ☎ *0662/661835* 🌐 *www.hanswalter.at/infos-zum-bosna-stand.html* 💳 *No credit cards.*

Bärenwirt

$$ | **AUSTRIAN** | Regionally sourced, top-quality ingredients elevate the traditional Austrian dishes in this inviting Wirtshaus, just north of the Old City. Since 1663, locals have shared mugs of beer from the neighboring Augustinerbräu brewery in these warmly lighted, wood-paneled rooms, adorned with traditional Salzburg-style heating ovens and cushioned benches. **Known for:** cozy atmopshere; delicious (mostly meat-heavy) dishes; homemade schnapps. [$] *Average main: €16* ✉ *Müllner Hauptstrasse 8* ☎ *0662/422404* 🌐 *www.baerenwirt-salzburg.at.*

Blaue Gans

$$$$ | **AUSTRIAN** | In a 500-year-old building with vaulted ceilings and windows looking out onto the bustling Getreidegasse, the restaurant of the Blaue Gans Hotel offers innovative, modern interpretations of traditional Austrian cooking. The fresh flavors are evident in dishes like the house-smoked *Lachsforelle* (salmon trout) and perfectly prepared beef carpaccio. **Known for:** great service; historic building; excellent Austrian and German wine list. [$] *Average main: €23* ✉ *Blaue Gans Hotel, Getreidegasse 41–43* ☎ *0662/842–491–54* 🌐 *www.blauegans.at* 🕒 *Closed Sun. except during festival.*

Glüxfall

$$ | **MODERN EUROPEAN** | A personalized, choose-your-own-breakfast-adventure menu (served until 1 pm) lets you savor several beautifully prepared, whimsically presented small dishes without encroaching on your date's plate. Mix and match two, four, or six sweet and savory choices: venison carpaccio with lingonberry chutney; heart-shape waffle with sour-cherry sauce; or nonalcoholic Bloody Mary shooter with a salmon canapé. **Known for:** well-crafted cocktails; creative brunch and breakfast dishes;

Shopping Streets

For centuries, Getreidegasse has been the main shopping street in the Old City center. Today you'll find elegant international fashion houses, traditional Austrian clothiers, and familiar international brands, all with intricate wrought-iron signs conforming with Salzburg's strict Altstadt conservation laws. There are also a number of arcades—mostly flower bedecked and opening into delightful little courtyards—that link Getreidegasse to the river and the Universitätsplatz. The southern end of Getreidegasse becomes Judengasse, once the heart of the city's medieval Jewish community, which is also packed with shops and galleries festooned with more of Salzburg's famous wrought-iron signs.

Wiener Philharmoniker-Gasse—named after the world-famous Vienna Philharmonic Orchestra, in recognition of the unique contribution it makes annually to the Salzburger Festspiele—blossoms with an open-air food market every Saturday morning, while there is also a fruit-and-vegetable market on Universitätsplatz every day except Sundays and holidays. Across the river, Linzergasse is less crowded and good for more practical items. There are also interesting antiques shops in the medieval buildings along Steingasse and on Goldgasse.

peaceful courtyard. $\boxed{\text{S}}$ *Average main: €14* ⊠ *Franz-Josef-Kai 11* ☎ *0662/265017* ⊕ *www.gluexfall.at* ⊘ *Closed Mon.–Tues. No dinner Sun.*

KOLLER+KOLLER am Waagplatz

$$$ | AUSTRIAN | With white-linen tablecloths, candles, flowers, and windows opening onto the street, this is one of Salzburg's most pleasant restaurants. Menu selections consist of local fish, mouthwatering steaks, traditional Austrian dishes, and game in season. **Known for:** Austrian classics; lovely outdoor seating in summer; notable business lunch. $\boxed{\text{S}}$ *Average main: €22* ⊠ *Waagplatz 2* ☎ *0662/842156* ⊕ *www.kollerkoller.com.*

Pan e Vin

$$$$ | ITALIAN | This cozy Old City restaurant offers some lovely Italian and Mediterranean specialties on its extensive (and expensive) menu. Try the roasted veal chop with truffle ravioli. **Known for:** 600-year-old building; extensive Austrian wine list; surprisingly expensive. $\boxed{\text{S}}$ *Average main: €35* ⊠ *Gstättengasse 1* ☎ *0662/844666* ⊕ *www.panevin.at* ⊘ *Closed Sun.*

St. Peter Stiftskeller

$$$$ | AUSTRIAN | Legends swirl about this famous Altstadt beer cellar: locals claim that Mephistopheles met Faust here, others say Charlemagne dined here, and some believe Columbus enjoyed a glass of its famous Salzburg Stiegl beer just before he set sail for America in 1492. But there is no debating the fact that this place—first mentioned in a document dating from 803—is Austria's oldest restaurant. **Known for:** the country's oldest restaurant; historical dining spaces; sophisticated Austrian classics. $\boxed{\text{S}}$ *Average main: €26* ⊠ *St. Peter Bezirk 1/4* ☎ *0662/841–268–0* ⊕ *www.stpeter.at.*

Triangel

$$$ | AUSTRIAN | See and be seen among the Salzburg Festival glitterati in Triangel's large outdoor seating area, or cozy up in the intimate dining room of this organic-farming-focused Austrian restaurant. The endless pounding coming from the kitchen tells you that the Wiener schnitzel is a popular choice, but if you have to pick one dish, make it

Oma's Schweinsbraten; owner Franzi's grandmother's roast pork belly recipe. **Known for:** crowd of Salzburg Festival artists; organic ingredients; old-school roast pork belly recipe. $ *Average main: €18* ✉ *Wiener Philharmoniker Gasse 7* ☎ *0662/842229* 🌐 *www.triangel-salzburg.co.at* 🕓 *Closed Sun.–Mon.*

Zum Eulenspiegel

$$ | **AUSTRIAN** | This spot allures with rustic wooden furniture, old folio volumes, antique weapons, and open fireplaces. Tables gleaming with white linen are set in wonderful nooks and crannies reached by odd staircases and charming salons. **Known for:** ingredients sourced from bio-farm; rustic and charming ambience; central location near Mozart's birthplace. $ *Average main: €16* ✉ *Hagenauerplatz 2* ☎ *0662/843180–0* 🌐 *www.zum-eulenspiegel.at.*

Zum Wilden Mann

$$ | **AUSTRIAN** | Here you'll find a true time-tinged feel of an old Salzburg *Gasthaus,* right down to a huge ceramic stove next to wooden chairs that welcomed generations of locals as they tucked into enormous plates of *Bauernschmaus* (Farmer's Feast): roast pork, ham, sausage, sauerkraut, and a massive dumpling. Pair it with a frothy-headed mug of the hometown "liquid bread"—Stiegl beer—from the oldest private brewery in Austria. **Known for:** huge meat-filled plates; traditional local vibe; beer from Austria's oldest private brewery. $ *Average main: €14* ✉ *Getreidegasse 20* ☎ *0662/841787* 🌐 *www.wildermann.co.at* 💳 *No credit cards* 🕓 *Closed Sun.*

Coffee and Quick Bites

★ Café Tomaselli

$ | **AUSTRIAN** | This inn opened its doors in 1705 as an example of that newfangled thing, a Wiener Kaffeehaus (Vienna coffeehouse), and was an immediate hit. Enjoying its 11 types of coffee was none other than Mozart's beloved, Constanze, who often dropped in, as her house was just next door. **Known for:** historic Vienna coffeehouse; delicious Erdbeerschüsserl (cream cake with strawberries); gorgeous upstairs terrace. $ *Average main: €10* ✉ *Alter Markt 9* ☎ *0662/844–488–0* 🌐 *www.tomaselli.at* 💳 *No credit cards.*

Espresso Fabrizi

$ | **AUSTRIAN** | Named after the former Italian owner of this historic house (note the beautiful small archway passage), this is a top spot for tasting Marzemino, the red wine Don Giovanni drinks in Mozart's opera. But there are plenty of other goodies here: some of the best Italian coffees in the city; outstanding Austrian *Apfel oder Topfenstrudel* (apple or cheese pie); and one of the the best Salzburger *Nockerl*. **Known for:** great menu of wine and prosecco; traditional Austrian desserts; fantastic Italian coffee. $ *Average main: €9* ✉ *Getreidegasse 21* ☎ *0662/845914* 🌐 *www.espresso-fabrizi.com* 💳 *No credit cards* 🕓 *No dinner.*

220GRAD

$$ | **EUROPEAN** | Whether you're craving a stellar late breakfast (served until 2 pm) or you're on the hunt for a carefully crafted espresso, you'll want to put this lively café on your daytime itinerary. The husband-and-wife team infuses care and quality into each step, from farm to cup, which takes them around the world to meet growers. **Known for:** great breakfasts and brunches; seasonal specialties; amazing coffee roasted by the owners. $ *Average main: €14* ✉ *Chiemseegasse 5* ☎ *0662/881–665–50* 🌐 *www.220grad.com* 🕓 *Closed Sun. and Mon. No dinner.*

Hotels

Arthotel Blaue Gans

$$$$ | **HOTEL** | The sleek, contemporary style of the Blue Goose boutique art hotel counters the building's centuries-old pedigree and offers guests a stellar location at the top of the main shopping street and steps away from the

Grosses Festspielhaus. **Pros:** wonderful art throughout; near the city's major sights; close to shopping. **Cons:** on a noisy street; can be hard to get a reservation; front-desk staff can seem scattered. $ Rooms from: €300 ⊠ Getreidegasse 41–43 ☎ 0662/842491 ⊕ www.blaue-gans.at ⇆ 35 rooms ⊙ No meals.

★ **Goldener Hirsch**

$$$$ | **HOTEL** | Celebrities from Picasso to Pavarotti have favored the Golden Stag for its legendary gemütlichkeit and away-from-it-all feel. **Pros:** unbeatable location but never noisy; clever blend of the modern and historic; restaurant has Salzburg's best steaks. **Cons:** there are better breakfasts in the Old City; low ceilings can be a hazard; easy to get lost in the maze of corridors. $ Rooms from: €585 ⊠ Getreidegasse 37 ☎ 0662/80840 ⊕ www.goldenerhirsch.com ⇆ 70 rooms ⊙ No meals.

Hotel am Dom

$$ | **HOTEL** | Tucked away on a tiny street near Residenzplatz, this small boutique hotel in a 14th-century building offers stylish, comfortable rooms, some with oak-beam ceilings. **Pros:** rustic atmosphere; well-kept rooms; air-conditioning throughout. **Cons:** few amenities; no on-site parking; elevator doesn't reach the top-floor rooms. $ Rooms from: €160 ⊠ Goldgasse 17 ☎ 0662/842765 ⊕ www.hotelamdom.at ⇆ 14 rooms ⊙ No meals.

Hotel Elefant

$$$$ | **HOTEL** | With its cozy rooms, fantastic central location, and excellent on-site restaurant and bar, Hotel Elefant is an old Salzburg favourite. **Pros:** lots of history; quiet yet centrally located street; unusual welcome from elephant sculpture in lobby. **Cons:** some rooms are cramped; difficult to access with a car; room temperature can vary widely. $ Rooms from: €275 ⊠ Sigmund-Haffner-Gasse 4 ☎ 0662/843397 ⊕ www.hotelelefant.at ⇆ 31 rooms ⊙ Free breakfast.

Hotel Neutor

$$ | **HOTEL** | A two-minute walk from the Old City, next to the historic tunnel that plows through the Mönchsberg, and directly in front of a stop on several bus lines, this basic hotel has location and transportation covered. **Pros:** excellent location; easy access to public transportation; parking available. **Cons:** on a busy street; very dated interior; staff could use some hospitality training. $ Rooms from: €165 ⊠ Neutorstrasse 8 ☎ 0662/844–1540 ⊕ www.neutor.com ⇆ 90 rooms ⊙ No meals.

Hotel Wolf

$$ | **B&B/INN** | The embodiment of Austrian gemütlichkeit, just off Mozartplatz, the small, family-owned, in-the-center-of-everything Hotel Wolf offers spotlessly clean and cozy rooms in a rustic building from the year 1429. **Pros:** plenty of atmosphere; in a historic house; lovely breakfast. **Cons:** parking is a problem; no air-conditioning or fans; staff can sometimes be unhelpful. $ Rooms from: €150 ⊠ Kaigasse 7 ☎ 0662/843–453–0 ⊕ www.hotelwolf.at ⇆ 16 rooms ⊙ Free breakfast.

Radisson Blu Hotel Altstadt

$$$$ | **HOTEL** | This venerable 1372 building, one of the city's oldest inns, is an impressive riverside landmark with its buff pink facade and iron lanterns. **Pros:** central location; expansive river views; generous breakfast buffet. **Cons:** can be difficult to find parking but valet service available; chain-hotel feel; can be noisy. $ Rooms from: €300 ⊠ Rudolfskai 28 ☎ 0662/848–571–0 ⊕ www.radissonhotels.com ⇆ 62 rooms ⊙ No meals.

Schloss Mönchstein

$$$$ | **HOTEL** | With gorgeous gardens and hiking trails, it's little wonder the 19th-century naturalist Alexander von Humboldt called this retreat outside the city center a "small piece of paradise." Catherine of Russia and the Duchess of Liechtenstein are among the notables who have stayed in the gable-roofed, tower-studded mansion, with its lovely

Evening Music Abounds

Salzburg is most renowned for the Salzburger Festspiele, centred around the Altstadt, but much of the city's special charm can be best discovered and enjoyed off-season and in other parts of the city. Riches include chamber concerts held in Mirabell Palace and the Fortress, as well as bountiful sacred music choices at the cathedral or any of the other churches offering impressive backdrops. Salzburg concerts by the Mozarteum Orchestra and the Camerata are now just as popular as the Vienna Philharmonic's program in the Musikverein in Vienna. In the Neustadt, the Landestheater season runs from September to June, and don't miss the chance to be enchanted and amazed by the skill and artistry of the Marionettentheater.

rooms that combine clever design and modern luxuries with heritage features and timeless elegance. **Pros:** luxurious rooms; lovely panoramic views; extensive and exclusive spa. **Cons:** outside of city center; need a car to get around; a/c is a bit noisy. $ *Rooms from: €450* ⊠ *Mönchsberg Park 26* ☎ *0662/848–555–0* ⊕ *www.monchstein.at/en* ⊘ *Closed Feb.* ⥱ *24 rooms* ⦿ *Free breakfast.*

 Nightlife

BARS AND PUBS
★ Augustinerbräu
BREWPUBS/BEER GARDENS | One of the largest beer cellars in Europe and the only one of its kind in Austria, the celebrated Augustinerbräu is at the north end of the Mönchsberg, a short walk from the Old City. Pick up a stone jug of strong, frothy, 10-week aged Märzen beer, made using the same recipe since 1621 and served directly from wooden kegs. With communal, dark-wood tables and beautifully restored chandeliers, the halls overflow with cheerful locals, and outside, where massive chestnut trees shade the sprawling garden, you'll find a complete cross section of Salzburg society. If you're feeling hungry, shops in the huge monastery complex sell a vast array of salads, breads, and pastries, as well as sausages and spit-roasted chicken. Advent and Lent offer special beers, because the Catholic church decreed that "drinking does not interrupt fasting." You can tour the brewery by appointment on weekday afternoons (€16.90 per person); call or register online. ⊠ *Lindhofstrasse 7* ☎ *0662/431246* ⊕ *www.augustinerbier.at.*

Sternbräu
BARS/PUBS | The Sternbräu is a mammoth Bierkeller with eight rambling halls festooned with tile stoves, paintings, and wood beams. The chestnut-tree beer garden or the courtyard are divine on hot summer nights. Many travelers head here for the **Sound of Salzburg Show** (⊕ *www.soundofsalzburg.info*), a popular evening event presented May through October, which includes unforgettable songs from *The Sound of Music*, traditional Salzburg folk songs, and a medley of Austrian operettas. The show costs €39 including a drink, but you can combine with a Sternbräu meal for €59. ⊠ *Griesegasse 23* ☎ *0662/842140* ⊕ *www.sternbrau.com.*

🎭 Performing Arts

MUSIC

There is no shortage of concerts in this most musical of cities. Customarily, the Salzburg Festival hosts the Vienna Philharmonic, and the Staatskapelle Dresden is in residence during the Easter Festival, but other orchestras can be expected to take leading roles as well. The Kulturvereinigung fills the Festival Hall during the fall and winter with more top-notch concerts and operas. In addition, there is Mozart Week (late January), which offers many musical gems—in recent seasons Daniel Barenboim, Pierre Boulez, and Nikolaus Harnoncourt have conducted the Vienna Philharmonic, while Sir John Eliot Gardiner, Rene Jacobs, and Marc Minkowski led other world-renowned orchestras—as well as Salzburg Cultural Days (October), and the Dialogues Festival (December). The Palace Concerts and the Fortress Concerts are year-round solo and chamber music mainstays. Find experimental works in the black box theater at the ArgeKultur.

Salzburger Kulturvereinigung

MUSIC | World-class guest orchestras and Salzburg's own Mozarteum Orchestra appear in the Grosses Festspielhaus and the Great Hall of the Mozarteum during the fall and winter under the auspices of the Salzburg Cultural Association. If you visit over *Sylvester* (New Year's Eve), you can experience the Austrian tradition of the brass-and-wind-powered New Year's Concert. It also created Salzburg Cultural Days, filling the autumn off-season with top talent and exciting performances. ✉ *Waagplatz 1A* ☏ *0662/845346* ⊕ *www.kulturvereinigung.com.*

OPERA

Salzburger Festspiele

OPERA | Eyes from all corners of the world are on this city during the Salzburger Festspiele, which mounts a full calendar of magnificently produced operas every summer, and even more during the Whitsun Festival in May. These performances are held in three main venues along Hofstallgasse in the Old City: the **Grosses Festspielhaus** (Great Festival Hall), which opened in 1960 and seats more than 2,150; the **Haus für Mozart** (House for Mozart), with its massive lobby frescoes by Salzburg painter Anton Faistauer; and the **Felsenreitschule** (the Rocky Riding School), which was hewn out of the rock of the Mönchsberg during the 17th century and offers a setting that is itself as dramatic as anything presented on stage. There are also performances at the **Landestheater** (State Theater) across the river and at numerous other smaller venues, where lieder recitals and chamber works dominate. ✉ *Hofstallgasse 1* ☏ *0662/804 5500* ⊕ *www.salzburgerfestspiele.at* ☏ *From €15.*

THEATER

Jedermann (Everyman)

THEATER | This morality play, by Hugo von Hofmannsthal, is famously performed annually (in German) in the front courtyard of the cathedral. A centerpiece of the Salzburger Festspiele, the play begins with a rousing medieval parade of performers through the streets of the Altstadt, spilling onto the stage for a colorful, intense, and moving presentation of the allegorical story of wealthy, selfish Jedermann's final journey before death. Few of the thousands packing the plaza are unmoved when, at the height of the banquet, church bells around the city ring out and the voice of Death is heard calling "Jedermann—Jedermann—Jed-er *mann*" from the Franziskanerkirche tower, followed by echoes of voices from other steeples and from atop the Fortress Hohensalzburg. ✉ *Domplatz.*

📖 Shopping

ANTIQUES

A.E. Köchert

JEWELRY/ACCESSORIES | As the Imperial Court Jeweler and Personal Jeweler to Emperor Franz Josef I, the Köchert goldsmiths have crafted such world-renowned treasures as the Austrian imperial crown and the diamond stars adorning Empress Sisi's hair in her famous portrait. Today's sixth-generation jeweler creates modern pieces using traditional techniques, replicas of the "Sisi Stars," and offers stunning antique jewelry in the firm's small Salzburg outpost. ✉ *Alter Markt 15* ☎ *0662/843398* ⊕ *www.koechert.com* ☾ *Closed Sun.*

Madero CollectorsRoom

ANTIQUES/COLLECTIBLES | It's worth a short trip around the southeast tip of the Mönchsberg into Nonntal to discover the impressive collection of mid-20th-century furniture, contemporary design pieces, and delicate porcelain and glassware; all celebrating the tradition of European craftsmanship and offered at a variety of price levels. ✉ *Nonntaler Hauptstrasse 10* ☎ *0662/844008* ⊕ *www.madero.at.*

CONFECTIONARY AND SCHNAPPS

Cafe Konditorei Fürst

FOOD/CANDY | If you're looking for the kind of *Mozartkugeln* (chocolate marzipan confections) you can't buy at home, try the store that claims to have invented them in 1890. It still produces the candy by hand, according to the original (and secret) family recipe. When here—or at the café's three other locations around town—you can also stock up on the *Bach Würfel* (coffee, nut, and chocolate truffle) and other delicacies ✉ *Brodgasse 13* ☎ *0662/843–759–0* ⊕ *www.original-mozartkugel.com.*

Schatz Konditorei

FOOD/CANDY | Salzburg locals have relied on this small family-owned bakery since 1877 to satisfy their cravings for *Cremeschnitte* (vanilla custard cream

Sweet Souvenirs

Mozartkugeln, candy balls of pistachio marzipan rolled in nougat cream and dipped in dark chocolate, which bear a miniportrait of Mozart on the wrapper, are omnipresent in Salzburg. Those handmade by Konditorei Fürst cost more but can be purchased individually. In summer, ask for a thermos bag to prevent melting. You can find mass-produced products like those from Mirabell or from the German competitor Reber almost everywhere. Discounts are easy to find in supermarkets or duty-free shops.

between puff-pastry layers), *Rigo-Jancsi* (Hungarian chocolate sponge cake, chocolate mousse, and chocolate glaze), *Himbeer-Obers-Souffle* (strawberry-cream souffle), apple strudel, and other mouthwatering selections from the 30 to 50 daily cakes and pastries. ✉ *Schatz Passageway, Getreidegasse 3* ☎ *0662/842792* ⊕ *www.schatz-konditorei.at* ☾ *Closed Sun.*

Sporer

WINE/SPIRITS | Leave room in your suitcase for a few bottles from the excellent selection of house brands and locally produced distilled Austrian schnapps, liqueurs, brandies, festive punch, spirits, and wines at this fourth-generation family-owned shop and tavern. Locals look forward to the Christmas markets so they can warm up from the inside with their annual fix of orange-flavored Sporer Punsch, which you can purchase year-round in the store. Chat with the friendly owners and regular customers at the small bar while you sample the wares. ✉ *Getreidegasse 39* ☎ *0662/845431* ⊕ *www.sporer.at* ☾ *Closed Sun.*

CRAFTS
Christmas in Salzburg
SPECIALTY STORES | Rooms of gorgeous Christmas-tree decorations, notably an abundance of hand-painted blown egg ornaments for all holidays, fill this charming year-round shop. ✉ *Judengasse 11* ☎ *0664/535–711–1* ⊕ *www.christmas-in-salzburg.at.*

Gehmacher
HOUSEHOLD ITEMS/FURNITURE | Find chic European traditional to modern-style home design and accessories at this centrally located furniture store. ✉ *Alter Markt 2* ☎ *0662/845506* ⊕ *www.gehmacher.at* ⊘ *Closed Sun.*

Glaskunst Kreis (*Handwerkskunst in Glas*)
CERAMICS/GLASSWARE | Explore the finely crafted, hand-etched, traditionally blown glass pieces in this specialty shop. ✉ *Sigmund-Haffner-Gasse 14* ☎ *0662/841323* ⊕ *www.glaskunstkreis.com* ⊘ *Closed Sun.*

Salzburger Heimatwerk
CERAMICS/GLASSWARE | Salzburg ladies choose fabrics for their custom made *Dirndln* from the store's floor-to-ceiling wall of colorful linen, silk, and cotton. They can also outfit their homes with locally produced ceramics, hand-stenciled linens, and regional cookbooks at good prices. ✉ *Residenzplatz 9* ☎ *0662/844110* ⊕ *www.salzburgerheimatwerk.at* ⊘ *Closed Sun.*

TRADITIONAL CLOTHING
Dschulnigg
CLOTHING | This is a favorite among elegant Salzburgers for *Trachten,* the traditional Austrian costume including lederhosen and dirndl (region-specific dresses with white blouse, printed skirts, and apron). You can also get high-quality field and hunting gear, and unique home decorations. ✉ *Griesgasse 8* ☎ *0662/842–376–0* ⊕ *www.jagd-dschulnigg.at* ⊘ *Closed Sun.*

Jahn-Markl
CLOTHING | Admire the traditional craftsmanship of the leather clothing and other goods here, some made to order. ✉ *Residenzplatz 3* ☎ *0662/842610* ⊕ *www.jahn-markl.at.*

Madl
CLOTHING | Flair and elegance distinguish the traditional Austrian designs here. ✉ *Getreidestrasse 13* ☎ *0662/845457* ⊕ *www.madlsalzburg.at.*

Around Fortress Hohensalzburg

According to a popular saying in Salzburg, "If you can see the fortress, it's just about to rain; if you can't see it, it's already raining." Fortunately, there are plenty of days when spectacular views can be had of Salzburg and the surrounding countryside from the top of this castle.

Sights

★ Fortress Hohensalzburg
CASTLE/PALACE | **FAMILY** | Founded in 1077, the Hohensalzburg is Salzburg's acropolis and the largest preserved medieval fortress in Central Europe. Brooding over the city from atop the Festungsberg, it was originally founded by Salzburg's Archbishop Gebhard. Over the centuries the archbishops gradually enlarged the castle, using it sometimes as a residence, then as a siege-proof haven against invaders and their own rebellious subjects. The grim exterior belies the lavish state rooms inside, such as the glittering **Golden Room**, the **Castle Museum** (dedicated to life in the fortress over the centuries), and the **Rainer's Museum,** with its collections honoring Salzburg's former home regiment. There's also a torture chamber not far from the exquisite late-Gothic **St. George's Chapel**, the **World of Strings** marionette theater,

Around Fortress Hohensalzburg

ALSTADT

University Square

Residenzplatz

Domplatz

Kapitelplatz

Kapitelgasse

Herrengasse

Festungsbahn (Funicular Railway)

Festungsgasse

Festungsgasse

Nonnberggasse

Rudolfskai

KEY

1 Exploring Sights

1 Restaurants

1 Hotels

FORTRESS HOHENSALZBURG

0   500 ft
0   150 m

and a deafening 200-pipe organ. To reach the fortress, walk up the zigzag path that begins just beyond the Stieglkeller on the Festungsgasse, or take the **Festungsbahn** (funicular railway; round-trip ticket includes museum admission) from behind St. Peter's Cemetery.
■ **TIP→ Climb up the 100 tiny steps to the Recturm, a grand outpost with a sweeping view of Salzburg and the mountains.** ✉ *Mönchsberg 34* ☎ *0662/842–430–11* ⊕ *www.salzburg-burgen.at* 🎫 *€9.90 funicular and castle; €15.70 inc. all museums.*

★ Hangar-7

MUSEUM | FAMILY | Red Bull founder Dietrich Mateschitz opens his fantasy toy chest for all to admire: vintage airplanes, helicopters, motorbikes, and Formula One racing cars gleam under the glass and steel of this modern multipurpose dome. The Flying Bulls, Red Bull's aerobatics experts, and their pristine fleet call this home when not circling the world on their frequent air-show tours. Watch daytime takeoffs and landings from under the shadow of a massive, silver World War II bomber at the Carpe Diem Lounge-Café or in the sunny Outdoor Lounge. The Mayday Bar is an affordable way to experience the evening atmosphere if you can't get a table at the popular Ikarus restaurant. ✉ *Salzburg Airport, Wilhelm-Spazier-Strasse 7A* ☎ *0662/2197* ⊕ *www.hangar-7.com.*

Nonnberg Convent

RELIGIOUS SITE | Just below the south side of the Fortress Hohensalzburg— and best visited in tandem with it—the Stift Nonnberg was founded right after 700 AD by St. Rupert. His niece St. Erentrudis was the first abbess; in the archway a late-Gothic statue of Erentrudis welcomes visitors. The church is more famous these days as "Maria's convent"—both the one in *The Sound of Music* and that of the real Maria on which the movie was based. She returned to marry her Captain von Trapp here in the Gothic church (as it turns out, no filming was done here—"Nonnberg" was re-created in the film studios of Salzburg-Parsch). Each May evening at 7 pm the nuns sing a 15-minute service called Maiandacht in the old Gregorian chant. Their beautiful voices can be heard also at the 11 pm mass on December 24. Parts of the private quarters for the nuns, which include some lovely, intricate wood carvings, can be seen by prior arrangement. ■ **TIP→ To see the frescoes located below the Nuns' Gallery as well as the altar in St. John's Chapel, ask at the convent entrance for the key.** ✉ *Nonnberggasse 2* ☎ *0662/841607* 🌐 *www.benediktinerinnen.de.*

🍴 Restaurants

★ Ikarus

$$$$ | **MODERN EUROPEAN** | This extraordinary Michelin-starred restaurant, set with the ultramodern Hangar-7 and overlooking its gleaming vehicle collection, offers a unique and exciting dining concept: a different renowned chef every month. The guest chefs come from all over the world and serve a mind-boggling array of cuisines—the only guarantees are that the ingredients will be fresh, the set menus (usually at least six courses) will be of exceptional quality, and the check at the end will make your eyes water. **Known for:** unique setting and concept; extensive wine list and expert pairing; incredibly expensive. [$] *Average main: €250* ✉ *Hangar-7, Wilhelm-Spazier-Strasse 7A* ☎ *0662/21970* 🌐 *www.hangar-7.com* 🕒 *No lunch Mon.–Thu.*

🛏 Hotels

★ Schloss Leopoldskron

$$$ | **HOTEL** | Expansive grounds surround this historic palace immortalized in *The Sound of Music,* located less than a kilometer (⅔ mile) southwest of Fortress Hohensalzburg, which was originally built in the 18th century for Archbishop Leopold von Firmian. **Pros:** idyllic lakeside setting; smart and reasonably priced rooms; free bicycles available from reception. **Cons:** the closest bus stop is a 12-minute walk; no on-site restaurant; too far from the action for some. [$] *Rooms from: €186* ✉ *Leopoldskronstrasse 56–58* ☎ *0662/839–830* 🌐 *www.schloss-leopoldskron.com* 🛏 *55 rooms* 🍽 *Free breakfast.*

🍸 Nightlife

Stieglkeller

BREWPUBS/BEER GARDENS | Sample the selections of this hometown-pride brew under the shade of chestnut trees as you watch the sun set over the rooftops and steeples of the Old City. The noted local architect Ceconi devised this sprawling place around 1901. The Keller is partly inside the Mönchsberg hill, right under the Festung Hochsalzburg, so its cellars guarantee the quality and right temperature of the drinks. It's a great place to stop for lunch, an afternoon snack, or an evening *Prost* with friends. Just beware: climbing up the relatively steep incline is easier than stumbling down after a few *Grosses* (large beers). ✉ *Festungsgasse 10* ☎ *0662/842681* 🌐 *www.stieglkeller.at* 🕒 *Closed Feb.*

🎟 Performing Arts

MUSIC

Salzburger Festungskonzerte

MUSIC | The concerts performed by the Salzburg Mozart Ensemble and the Mozart Chamber Orchestra are presented in the grand Golden Hall at Festung Hohensalzburg and often include

The name Hohensalzburg translates into "High Salzburg Fortress" which is fitting considering the castle's location atop Festungsberg directly overlooks Salzburg's old town quarter.

works by Mozart. A special candle-light-dinner-and-concert ticket is offered. ✉ *Festung Hohensalzburg, Mönchsberg 34* ☎ *0662/825858* ⊕ *www.salzburghighlights.at* 🎫 *€36–€44.*

The Neustadt

Across the River Salzach from the Old City is the Neustadt (New City) area of historic Salzburg, where you'll find Mirabell Palace and Gardens, the Landestheater, and the Mozart Residence, among other highlights. If you want to see the most delightful Mozart landmark in this section of town, the Zauberflötenhäuschen—the mouthful used to describe the little summerhouse where he finished composing *The Magic Flute*—can be viewed when concerts are scheduled in the adjacent Mozarteum. Overlooking the Neustadt to the south is the tree-shrouded hill Kapuzinerberg, flanked by the medieval Steingasse and topped by the Kapuzinerkloster (Capuchin Monastery).

Sights

Dreifaltigkeitskirche (*Holy Trinity Church*)
RELIGIOUS SITE | The Makartplatz—named after Hans Makart, the most famous Austrian painter of the mid-19th century—is dominated at the top (east) end by Fischer von Erlach's first architectural work in Salzburg, built 1694–1702. It was modeled on a church by Borromini in Rome and prefigures von Erlach's Karlskirche in Vienna. Dominated by a lofty, oval-shape dome—which showcases a painting by Johann Michael Rottmayr—this church was the result of the archbishop's concern that Salzburg's Neustadt was developing in an overly haphazard manner. The church interior is small but perfectly proportioned, surmounted by its dome, whose trompe-l'oeil fresco seems to open up the church to the sky above. ✉ *Dreifaltigkeitsgasse 13* ☎ *0662/877495.*

The Sound of Music Sights in Salzburg

After Mozart, Salzburg's biggest cultural draw is the Hollywood extravaganza *The Sound of Music*, which was filmed here in 1964. A popular tourist exercise is to make the town's acquaintance by visiting some of the sights featured in, or connected to, the much-loved movie, so here's our pick of musical must-sees:

Mirabellgarten

The undoubted star of "Do Re Mi," the Mirabellgarten features heavily throughout the second half of the song, when Maria and the von Trapp childen dance their way through the grounds. You can follow their footsteps by marching around the Pegasus Fountain, waltzing under the Greek fencing statues, and hopping up and down the North Terrace steps.

Residenzplatz

It features in the movie for a mere 20 seconds, but the Baroque horse fountain in the Residenzplatz gets a starring turn during the song "I Have Confidence," when Maria displays her determination by splashing the water. Incidentally, as she wanders away from the fountain, you can see the looming Fortress Hohensalzburg in the background.

Schloss Hellbrunn

Although the palace itself doesn't feature in the movie—it was Schloss Leopoldskron (now a hotel) that stood in for the von Trapp family home—it has one of the movie's most famous sets. Take a stroll in Schloss Hellbrunn's gardens and you'll soon come across the pavilion from the iconic song "Sixteen Going on Seventeen."

Nonnberg Abbey

The convent seen in the film may have been a Hollywood set, but it was heavily inspired by the beautiful abbey where the real-life Maria was a novitiate. A few features, like the abbey gates, are sure to look familiar to fans of the film. A five-minute walk from here takes you to Petersfriedhof, where the von Trapps hide towards the end of the movie.

Villa Trapp

Now a popular hotel in the southern suburb of Aigen, the Villa Trapp was—as the name suggests—once the home of the real von Trapp family. This beautiful white-and-yellow mansion is a lovely place to stay during a visit to Salzburg, with house and garden tours explaining more about the real-life events that inspired the hit musical.

Friedhof St. Sebastian (*St. Sebastian's Cemetery*)

CEMETERY | This final resting place for many members of the Mozart family, in the shadows of St. Sebastian's Church, offers a peaceful respite from the store-lined Linzergasse. Prince-Archbishop Wolf-Dietrich commissioned the cemetery in 1600 to replace the old cathedral graveyard, which he planned to demolish. It was built in the style of an Italian *campo santo* (sacred field), with arcades on four sides, and in the center of the square he had the Gabriel Chapel, an unusual, brightly tiled Mannerist mausoleum, built for himself; he was interred here in 1617. Several famous people are buried in this cemetery, including the medical doctor and philosopher Theophrastus Paracelsus, who settled in Salzburg in the early 16th century (his grave is by the church door). Around the chapel is the grave of Mozart's widow, Constanze, alongside her second husband, Georg

The origins of the famous Salzburg Christmas market go all the way back to the late 15th century.

Nikolaus Nissen, and possibly her aunt Genoveva Weber (by the central path leading to the mausoleum). According to the latest research, Mozart's father, Leopold, came to rest in the unmarked community grave here, too. If the gate is closed, enter through the back entrance around the corner in the courtyard. ⊠ *Linzergasse 41.*

Kapuzinerberg (*Capuchin Hill*)
MOUNTAIN—SIGHT | To the south of the New City, and directly opposite the Mönchsberg on the other side of the river, Kapuzinerberg hill is crowned by several interesting sights. By ascending a stone staircase near Steingasse 9, you can start your climb up the peak. At the top of the first flight of steps is a tiny chapel, **St. Johann am Imberg,** built in 1681. Farther on are a signpost and gate to the **Hettwer Bastion,** part of the old city walls and one of Salzburg's most spectacular viewpoints. At the summit is the gold-beige **Kapuzinerkloster** (Capuchin Monastery), originally a fortification built to protect the one bridge crossing the river. It

is still an active monastery so cannot be visited, except for the church. The road down—note the Stations of the Cross along the path—is called Stefan Zweig Weg, after the great Austrian writer and critic who rented the **Paschingerschlössl** house by the monastery until 1934, when he fled Austria. Continue along to the northeast end of the Kapuzinerberg road for a well-earned meal with a stunning 180-degree view from the garden of the **Franziskischlössl.** There are also luxurious suites here if you want to stay overnight (⊕ www.franziskischloessl.at). ⊠ *Salzburg.*

★ **Marionettentheater** (*Marionette Theater*)
ARTS VENUE | FAMILY | The Salzburger Marionettentheater is both the world's greatest marionette theater and a surprisingly sublime theatrical experience. Many critics have noted that viewers quickly forget the strings controlling the puppets, which assume lifelike dimensions and provide a very real dramatic experience. The Marionettentheater is

identified above all with Mozart's operas, which seem particularly suited to the skilled puppetry. Their repertoire extends to Rossini (*The Barber of Seville*) and Strauss (*The Bat*), among others, as well as numerous fairy tales. *The Sound of Music* has also been performed here since 2007. For children, the theater recommends its one-hour afternoon performances, usually shortened version of their headline shows. All productions are accompanied by historic recordings and are subtitled in several languages. The theater itself is a Rococo concoction. The company is famous for its world tours but is usually in Salzburg during the summer and around major holidays. ✉ *Schwarzstrasse 24* ☎ *0662/872406* ⊕ *www.marionetten.at* 🎟 *€20–€40*.

★ **Mirabellgarten** (*Mirabell Gardens*)

GARDEN | FAMILY | Enter the gardens from the Rainerstrasse and head for the Rosenhügel (Rosebush Hill). That way, you'll arrive at the top of the steps where Julie Andrews and her seven charges showed off their singing ability in *The Sound of Music*. This is also an ideal vantage point to admire the formal gardens and one of the best views of Salzburg, which shows how harmoniously architects of the Baroque period laid out the city. The center of the gardens—one of Europe's most beautiful parks, partly designed by Fischer von Erlach as the grand frame for the Mirabell Palace—is dominated by four large groups of statues representing the elements water, fire, air, and earth. The most famous section is the **Zwerglgarten** (Dwarfs' Garden), with its 12 statues of "Danubian" dwarves sculpted in marble. The **Heckentheater** (Hedge Theater) is an enchanting natural stage setting that dates from 1700. ✉ *Mirabellplatz 3*.

★ **Mozart-Wohnhaus** (*Mozart Residence*)

HOUSE | FAMILY | The Mozart family moved from its cramped quarters in Getreidegasse to this house on the Hannibal Platz, as it was then known, in 1773. Wolfgang Amadeus Mozart lived here until 1780, his sister Nannerl stayed here until she married in 1784, and their father Leopold lived here until his death in 1787. The house is accordingly referred to as the Mozart Residence, signifying that it was not only Wolfgang who lived here. During the first Allied bomb attack on Salzburg in October 1944, the house was partially destroyed, but was reconstructed in 1996. Mozart composed the "Salzburg Symphonies" here, as well as all five violin concertos, church music, and some sonatas, and parts of his early operatic masterpieces, including *Idomeneo*. Take the informative audio tour for an introduction to the museum's interesting collection of musical instruments—like his own pianoforte in the Dance Master Hall—as well as books from Leopold Mozart's library, family letters, and portraits. Before you leave, take a peek inside the Mozart Audio Visual Collection, an archive of thousands of Mozart recordings as well as films and video productions, all of which can be listened to or viewed on request. ✉ *Makartplatz 8* ☎ *0662/874–227–40* ⊕ *www.mozarteum.at* 🎟 *€12; combined ticket with Mozarts Geburtshaus €18.50*.

Mozarteum

MUSIC | Organizer of the important Mozart Week held every January and the forward-looking Dialogue Festival held during the first week of December, the Mozarteum is the center for scholarly research and continued support of Mozart's life and works. The libraries, containing rare editions and significant publications, are open to the public. Thousands flock here for its packed calendar of concerts. ✉ *Schwarzstrasse 26* ☎ *0662/889400* ⊕ *www.mozarteum.at*.

Schloss Mirabell (*Mirabell Palace*)

CASTLE/PALACE | The "Taj Mahal of Salzburg," Schloss Mirabell was built in 1606 by the wealthy and powerful Prince-Archbishop Wolf-Dietrich for his mistress, Salomé Alt, and their 15 children. Such was the palace's beauty that it was taken over by succeeding prince-archbishops,

Sights ▼

1 Dreifaltigkeitskirche **E7**
2 Friedhof St. Sebastian **G6**
3 Kapuzinerberg **J7**
4 Marionettentheater **D7**
5 Mirabellgarten **D5**
6 Mozarteum **E6**
7 Mozart-Wohnhaus **E7**
8 Schloss Mirabell **D5**
9 Steingasse **H8**

Restaurants ▼

1 DaxLueg **J2**
2 Die Weisse **I4**
3 Pfefferschiff **J2**
4 Zum Fidelen Affen **F7**

Quick Bites ▼

1 Café Bazar **E8**
2 Café Sacher **E8**

Hotels ▼

1 Gersberg Alm **J2**
2 Goldenes Theater **I5**
3 Hotel Amadeus **G6**
4 Hotel Auersperg **H4**
5 Hotel Bristol **E7**
6 Hotel Sacher Salzburg **E7**
7 Hotel Stein **F8**
8 Motel One Salzburg Mirabell **B1**
9 NH Salzburg **H5**
10 Sheraton Grand Salzburg **C4**
11 Stadtkrug **F7**
12 Star Inn Zentrum **C9**
13 Villa Trapp **J9**
14 Wolf-Dietrich **G5**

including Franz Anton von Harrach, who brought in Lukas von Hildebrandt to give the place a Baroque face-lift in 1727. A disastrous fire hit in 1818, but happily, three of the most spectacular set pieces of the palace—the Chapel, the Marble Hall, and the Angel Staircase—survived. The Marble Hall is now used for civil wedding ceremonies and is regarded as the most beautiful registry office in the world. The young Mozart and his sister gave concerts here. The magnificent marble Angel Staircase is romantically draped with white marble putti. ■ TIP→ Try to catch a candlelight chamber music concert during your visit. ⊠ *Mirabellplatz 4* ☎ *0662/80720.*

Steingasse

NEIGHBORHOOD | Stretching south from the Neustadt and walled in on one side by the bare cliffs of the Kapuzinerberg, this narrow medieval street was originally the ancient Roman entrance into the city from the south. The houses stood along the riverfront before the Salzach was regulated. Nowadays it's a fascinating mixture of shops and nightclubs, but with its tall houses the street still manages to convey an idea of how life used to be in the Middle Ages. The **Inneres Steintor** marks the entrance to the oldest section of the street; here on summer afternoons the light can be particularly striking. House No. 23 on the right still has deep, slanted peep-windows for guarding the gate. House No. 31 is the birthplace of Josef Mohr, the poet of "Silent Night, Holy Night" fame (not No. 9, as is incorrectly noted on the wall). ⊠ *Salzburg.*

🍴 Restaurants

DaxLueg

$$ | **AUSTRIAN** | If you really want to enjoy food with a view, drive three kilometers (two miles) north along the B1 Linzer Bundesstrasse to Mayrwies and turn right up through the woods. Here you can take in a view of Salzburg from the mountainside perch of this former

Cycling in Salzburg

Find bike and e-bike rental points along the Salzach, and visit local bookstores for maps of the extensive network of cycle paths. Check out the interactive map at ⊕ *www.radlkarte.info* to plan your trip. The **Hellbrunner Allee** from Freisaal to Hellbrunn Palace is an enjoyable run, taking you past Frohnburg Palace and a number of elegant mansions on either side of the tree-lined avenue. The more adventurous can go farther afield, taking the **Salzach cycle path** north to the village of Oberndorf, or south to Golling and Hallein.

Rupertialm (St. Rupert's Pasture), a famous scenic lookout even in Mozart's time. **Known for:** stunning panoramic views; Alpine chalet charm; seasonal dishes and garnishes. $ *Average main: €15* ⊠ *Daxluegstrasse 5, Hallwang bei Salzburg* ☎ *0662/665800* ⊕ *www.daxlueg.at* ☉ *Closed Mon.–Tues.*

Die Weisse

$$ | **AUSTRIAN** | This *Weissbierbrauerei* combines the original charm of one of Salzburg's most historic breweries and adds a high-ceilinged, wood-paneled modern bar to satisfy the many locals who consider it to be the ultimate private retreat (so much so that from Wednesday through Saturday it's best to make a reservation). The beer garden really hits the spot on a hot summer day, but all year long you can savor traditional Bavarian style *Weisswurst* (veal sausages with sweet mustard) as well as the usual array of tempting Salzburg delights. **Known for:** original beers brewed on-site; local neighborhood vibe; Bavarian-style sausages. $ *Average main: €17* ⊠ *Rupertgasse 10* ☎ *0662/872246* ⊕ *www.dieweisse.at* ☉ *Closed Sun.*

★ Pfefferschiff

$$$$ | ECLECTIC | The Pepper Ship is one of the most acclaimed restaurants in Salzburg, despite being five kilometers (three miles) northeast of the Neustadt. It's in a pretty, renovated rectory (dated 1640) and adjacent to a pink-and-cream chapel. **Known for:** beautifully composed seasonal set menus; impressive Austrian wine list; country-chic atmosphere. Ⓢ *Average main: €29 ⊠ Söllheim 3 ☎ 0662/661242 ⊕ www.pfefferschiff.at ☉ Closed Sun.–Mon.*

Zum Fidelen Affen

$$ | AUSTRIAN | The name means "At the Faithful Ape," which explains the monkey motifs in this popular Gasthaus dominated by a round, copper-plated bar and stone pillars under a vaulted ceiling. Besides the beer on tap, the kitchen offers tasty Austrian dishes, such as *Schlutzkrapfen,* handmade cheese ravioli with a light topping of chopped fresh tomatoes, or a big salad with juicy *Backhendl* (breaded, fried chicken). **Known for:** large portions of traditional Austrian dishes; fun party vibe; big crowds. Ⓢ *Average main: €17 ⊠ Priesterhausgasse 8 ☎ 0662/877361 ⊕ www.fideleraffe.at ☉ Closed Sun. No lunch Sat.*

☕ Coffee and Quick Bites

Café Bazar

$ | CAFÉ | Sip a *Melange* (frothy milk coffee) under the shade of the leafy trees at this people-watching coffeehouse institution on the Salzach River. Salads, soups, and toasted ham-and-cheese sandwiches served with ketchup satisfy savory cravings; homemade Topfen- and Apfelstrudel beckon from the glass case of house-made tortes. **Known for:** homemade cakes; sumptuous traditional coffeehouse atmosphere; beautiful river views from the terrace. Ⓢ *Average main: €8 ⊠ Schwarzstrasse 3 ☎ 0662/874278 ⊕ www.cafe-bazar.at.*

Café Sacher

$$ | AUSTRIAN | Red-velvet banquettes, sparkling chandeliers, and lots of gilt mark this famous gathering place, a favorite of well-heeled Salzburgers and an outpost of the celebrated Vienna landmark. It's a perfect choice for a leisurely afternoon pastry. **Known for:** elegant Salzburg decor; famous homemade Sachertorte; top-rate coffee. Ⓢ *Average main: €12 ⊠ Hotel Sacher Salzburg, Schwarzstrasse 5–7 ☎ 0662/889–772– 384 ⊕ www.sacher.com.*

Hotels

Gersberg Alm

$$ | HOTEL | FAMILY | A picture-perfect Alpine chalet on the lofty perch of the Gersberg, high above Salzburg, this hotel is less than 15 minutes by car from the Neustadt. **Pros:** beautiful hilltop location; pleasant rooms; great restaurant. **Cons:** outside the city; car is required; balconies are shared. Ⓢ *Rooms from: €139 ⊠ Gersberg 37 ☎ 0662/641257 ⊕ www.gersbergalm.at ⬯ 40 rooms* ⅋ *Free breakfast.*

Goldenes Theater

$ | HOTEL | Close enough to the top of the Linzergasse shopping district and the theaters in the Neustadt but far enough to offer a respite from the summer crowds, this simple hotel is a decent value choice. **Pros:** close to Linzergasse shops; quiet terrace; free street parking at weekends. **Cons:** on a busy street; some rooms are quite dated; garage parking extra. Ⓢ *Rooms from: €115 ⊠ Schallmooser Hauptstrasse 13 ☎ 0662/881681 ⊕ www.gt-hotel-salzburg.com ⬯ 58 rooms* ⅋ *Free breakfast.*

Hotel Amadeus

$$ | HOTEL | Renovated in 2017, the guest rooms in this 500-year-old house are individually decorated, featuring wooden floors and antique armoires among understated modern accents. **Pros:** charming and airy decor; historic house; free tea and coffee all day. **Cons:**

church bell next door sounds every 15 minutes 6 am through 11 pm; breakfast a little sparse; reception desk not open 24 hours. [$] *Rooms from: €151* ✉ *Linzergasse 43* ☎ *0662/871401* 🌐 *www.hotelamadeus.at* 🛏 *20 rooms* 🍴 *Free breakfast.*

★ Hotel Auersperg

$$$ | HOTEL | FAMILY | A lush, green oasis is tucked between the two buildings that comprise the Auersperg: the hotel, built in 1892 by the noted Italian architect Ceconi, and its neighboring villa. **Pros:** family-friendly; great breakfast; hidden urban oasis. **Cons:** on a busy intersection; not in the city center; "villa" building not as convenient. [$] *Rooms from: €205* ✉ *Auerspergstrasse 61* ☎ *0662/889440* 🌐 *www.auersperg.at* 🛏 *55 rooms* 🍴 *Free breakfast.*

Hotel Bristol

$$$$ | HOTEL | There is little wonder that this pale-yellow palace, just across the river from the Altstadt and with stunning historic detail and fine artwork, has attracted an impressive roster of royal and celebrity guests. **Pros:** some fantastic views; charming accommodations; elegant restaurant. **Cons:** some decor is a little dated; lower-floor rear rooms lack views; non-suite rooms can be cramped. [$] *Rooms from: €400* ✉ *Makartplatz 4* ☎ *0662/873557* 🌐 *www.bristol-salzburg.at* 🕓 *Closed Feb. and Mar.* 🛏 *60 rooms* 🍴 *Free breakfast.*

★ Hotel Sacher Salzburg

$$$$ | HOTEL | FAMILY | Wonderfully located right on the Salzach River, this mammoth heritage hotel has attracted guests from the Beatles and the Rolling Stones to Hillary and Chelsea Clinton, but the owners, the Gürtler family, will ensure that even if you don't have a Vuitton steamer trunk you'll feel welcome. **Pros:** wonderful Altstadt views; good riverside location; plenty of top-notch dining options. **Cons:** gets overcrowded during festival time; very expensive (and without breakfast); service can be slow. [$] *Rooms from: €420* ✉ *Schwarzstrasse 5–7* ☎ *0662/889770* 🌐 *www.sacher.com/en/salzburg* 🛏 *109 rooms* 🍴 *No meals.*

Hotel Stein

$$$ | HOTEL | Standing tall over the Staatsbrücke and looking across at the Old City, Hotel Stein provides a high-end, design-forward, adults-only accommodation option at the very heart of Salzburg. **Pros:** convenient Neustadt location; stunning features from Venetian glassblower Barovier & Toso; terrace restaurant with amazing view. **Cons:** decor won't be to everyone's tastes; little original architecture left; service isn't always great. [$] *Rooms from: €205* ✉ *Giselakai 3* ☎ *0662/874–346–0* 🌐 *www.hotelstein.at* 🛏 *56 rooms* 🍴 *No meals.*

Motel One Salzburg Mirabell

$ | HOTEL | This budget friendly, thoroughly modern, and recently redesigned riverside hotel is a 10-minute walk north of the Mirabellgarten, but it's very convenient for the main train station. **Pros:** lovely riverfront location; close to both city and train station; free drink in bar on arrival. **Cons:** a bit of a walk from everywhere; no tea or coffee in rooms; small bathrooms. [$] *Rooms from: €97* ✉ *Elisabethkai 58–60* ☎ *0662/885200* 🌐 *www.motel-one.com* 🛏 *119 rooms* 🍴 *No meals.*

NH Salzburg

$$$ | HOTEL | Part of a Spanish hotel chain, this pretty building is in a nice location, around the corner from Linzergasse (the shopping street leading to the Salzach River) and five minutes away from the beautiful Mirabellgarten. **Pros:** in a historic setting; tasty breakfast; underground parking on-site. **Cons:** noisy common areas; popular with groups so can get crowded; rooms could be freshened up. [$] *Rooms from: €190* ✉ *Franz-Josef-Strasse 26* ☎ *0662/882–041–0* 🌐 *www.nh-hotels.com* 🛏 *140 rooms* 🍴 *Free breakfast.*

Sheraton Grand Salzburg

$$$ | HOTEL | With the lovely Mirabellgarten virtually at its back door, this modern hotel tastefully blends in with the belle-epoque buildings that surround it. **Pros:** spacious rooms; good on-site meal options; fantastic park-facing location. **Cons:** often filled with conferences; chain-hotel feel; breakfast not included as standard. $ *Rooms from: €250* ✉ *Auerspergstrasse 4* ☎ *0662/889990* ⊕ *www.marriott.com/ hotels/travel/szgsi-sheraton-grand-salzburg* ⇨ *166 rooms* ⦿ *No meals.*

Stadtkrug

$$$ | HOTEL | Snuggled under the monument-studded Kapuzinerberg and a two-minute walk from the bridge leading to the center of the Altstadt, the Stadtkrug (dated 1353) hits an idyllic, romantic, and quiet vibe, thanks to its mountainside setting. **Pros:** great Neustadt location; lots of charm; helpful staff. **Cons:** parking off-site; four levels mean stairs to climb; no air-conditioning. $ *Rooms from: €200* ✉ *Linzergasse 20* ☎ *0662/873545* ⊕ *www.stadtkrug.at* ⇨ *40 rooms* ⦿ *Free breakfast.*

Star Inn Zentrum

$$ | HOTEL | Behind the Mönchsberg, this no-frills hotel stands close to the center of the historic section, and if you want to fit in a quiet morning stroll through the area, this is a decently priced option. **Pros:** excellent location; close to public transportation; friendly staff. **Cons:** front rooms on a busy street; spartan, outdated rooms; the standard rooms are small. $ *Rooms from: €160* ✉ *Hildmannplatz 5* ☎ *0662/846–846* ⊕ *www.starinnhotels. com* ⇨ *86 rooms* ⦿ *No meals.*

★ Villa Trapp

$$ | HOTEL | Stay at the home of the real von Trapp family in the southern suburb of Aigen, 3½ kilometers (2¼ miles) south of the Neustadt, where each of the comfortable rooms is individually decorated. **Pros:** quiet out-of-town location; a dream for fans of The Sound of Music; gorgeous views. **Cons:** far outside the city center;

no 24-hour reception; no air-conditioning. $ *Rooms from: €170* ✉ *Traunstrasse 34* ☎ *0662/630860* ⊕ *www.villa-trapp.com* ⇨ *14 rooms* ⦿ *No meals.*

Wolf-Dietrich

$$$ | HOTEL | This small, family-owned hotel is an inviting choice, with some of the guest rooms including attractive sitting areas; rooms in the back look out over the looming Gaisberg and the cemetery of St. Sebastian. **Pros:** elegantly decorated rooms; simple but well-appointed spa; great location. **Cons:** nearby church bells ring constantly; rooms vary wildly; not all rooms have air-conditioning. $ *Rooms from: €199* ✉ *Wolf-Dietrich-Strasse 7* ☎ *0662/871275* ⊕ *www.salzburg-hotel.at* ⇨ *29 rooms* ⦿ *Free breakfast.*

ⓨ Nightlife

Fridrich

WINE BARS—NIGHTLIFE | This cozy little bar on the narrow Steingasse serves well-crafted drinks, an extensive selection of Austrian wines, antipasti, cold smoked locally caught fish, and small portions of savory Austrian favorites like *Faschierte Laibchen* (finely minced meatballs with bread and pickles) and *Krautfleckerl* (square pasta with caramelized onions, shredded white cabbage, sweet wine, and cumin). Eclectic music runs the gamut from Tarantino soundtracks to Italian music to jazz. ✉ *Steingasse 15* ☎ *0676/375–642–1.*

Gablerbräu

BARS/PUBS | Many like to stop here for a cold beer, but you should ponder the historic vibes, too. In this old inn Richard Mayr—a star of Vienna's State Opera House—was born. He later became one of the organizers of the music festival. After studying the parlor of Mayr's parents—a dark, wood-carved, neo-Gothic interior from the end of the 19th century—head for a table and order yourself a drink or a bite to eat. ✉ *Linzergasse 9* ☎ *0662/88965* ⊕ *www.gablerbrau.at.*

Schloss Hellbrun was the summer playhouse of the archbishop of Salzburg, built to entertain, delight, and soak with its trick fountains hidden throughout the gardens.

Performing Arts

MUSIC

★ Mozarteum

MUSIC | Two institutions share the address in this building finished just before World War I—the International Foundation Mozarteum, set up in 1870, and the University of Music and Performing Arts, founded in 1880. The former organizes the annual Mozart Week festival in January. Many important concerts are offered from October to June in its two recital halls, the Grosser Saal (Great Hall) and the Wiener Saal (Vienna Hall). Behind the Mozarteum is the famous **Zauberflöten-häuschen**—the little summerhouse where Mozart composed parts of *The Magic Flute,* with the "encouragement" of his frantic librettist Emanuel Schikaneder; he locked the composer inside to force him to finish. ⊠ *Schwarzstrasse 26* ☎ *0662/88940* ⊕ *www.mozarteum.at* ⊙ *Closed Sat.–Sun.*

★ Schlosskonzerte Mirabell

CONCERTS | Classical soloists and chamber ensembles perform in more than 230 concerts each year in the legendary Marmorsaal (Marble Hall) at **Mirabell Palace,** where Mozart performed. Concerts begin at 8 pm and last 1½ hours. ⊠ *Mirabell Palace, Mirabellplatz 4* ☎ *0662/828695* ⊕ *www.salzburg-palace-concerts.com* 🎫 *From €34.*

OPERA

Salzburger Landestheater (*Salzburg State Theater*)

DANCE | This neo-Baroque gem has nearly 1,000 seats and presents roughly 25 productions a year, including opera, theater, and ballet. Mozart is always in the repertoire, and it is continuing to expand into daring new works. The Mozarteum Orchester Salzburg is its regular orchestra, and the theater has its own opera, theater, and dance ensembles. You can purchase tickets from the theater's box office. For those unable to catch a show or who want to see behind the scenes, guided tours (€5) take place every second Saturday at 2 pm. ⊠ *Schwarzstrasse 22* ☎ *0662/871–5120* ⊕ *www.salzburger-landestheater.at.*

★ Salzburger Marionettentheater

OPERA | FAMILY | This delightful, acclaimed cultural institution has string-puppet shows devoted to opera, with a particularly renowned production of *Così fan tutte* to its credit. The Marionettentheater not only performs operas by Mozart, but also goodies by Rossini, the younger Strauss, Offenbach, Humperdinck, Mendelssohn (who wrote the music for the troupe's delightful show devoted to William Shakespeare's *A Midsummer Night's Dream*), and a fairy-tale version of *The Sound of Music,* all accompanied by historic recordings. Performances are staged during the first week of January, during Mozart Week (late January), from May through October, and in December. ⊠ *Schwarzstrasse 24* ☎ *0662/872406* ⊕ *www.marionetten.at* ☒ *From €18.*

THEATER
ARGEkultur

CONCERTS | The heart of Salzburg's contemporary art and culture scene beats at this modern, multipurpose performance venue. Its two performance spaces host envelope-pushing experimental music concerts, modern dance and theater performances, Austrian cabaret evenings, and poetry slams. The Open Mind Festival in November is the big annual event, featuring productions created especially for the festival. ⊠ *Ulrike-Gschwandtner-Strasse 5* ☎ *0662/848784* ⊕ *www.argekultur.at.*

🛍 Shopping

TRADITIONAL CLOTHING
Lanz

CLOTHING | A good selection of loden coats and *dirndln* in the signature "Lanz cut" can be found at this famous Salzburg Trachten maker, known for leading the modern revival of traditional Austrian clothing. ⊠ *Schwarzstrasse 4* ☎ *0662/874272* ⊕ *www.lanztrachten.at* ⊗ *Closed Sun.*

Day Trips from Salzburg

Travel just a short way out of Salzburg and you'll find a whole host of other attractions, from skyscraping mountain peaks to subterranean salt mines, and from grand old palaces to music-filled chapels. All these sights lie within a 30-minute drive of the city and are also easily accessible by bus, train, or bicycle.

Sights

Gaisberg and Untersberg

MOUNTAIN—SIGHT | Salzburg's "house mountains" are so called because of their proximity to the city, with Gaisberg lying to the east and Untersberg to the south.

To reach Gaisberg, you can take the Albus No. 151 bus from Mirabellplatz right up to the summit of the mountain, where you'll be rewarded with a spectacular panoramic view of the Alps and the Alpine foreland. The bus leaves four times a day weekdays and six times a day weekends and takes about a half hour.

The Untersberg is the mountain Captain von Trapp and Maria climbed as they escaped the Nazis in *The Sound of Music.* In the film they were supposedly fleeing to Switzerland; in reality, the climb up the Untersberg would have brought them almost to the doorstep of Hitler's retreat at the Eagle's Nest above Berchtesgaden in Germany. A cable car from St. Leonhard, about 13 km (eight miles) and a 30-minute bus ride south of Salzburg, takes you 6,020 feet up to the top of the Untersberg for a breathtaking view. In winter you can ski down (you arrive in the village of Fürstenbrunn and taxis or buses take you back to St. Leonhard); in summer there are a number of hiking routes from the summit. ⊠ *Gaisberg Gaisbergspitze Bus Stop, Gaisberg 32* ☒ *€7.20 return bus.*

★ **Hallein Salt Mine** (*Salzwelten Hallein*)
MINE | The second-largest town of the region, 15 kilometers (10 miles) south of Salzburg, Hallein was once famed for its caves of "white gold"—or salt. "Hall" is the old Celtic word for salt, and this treasure was mined in the neighboring Dürrnberg mountain, which you can now visit in the form of Hallein Salt Mine. It's the oldest salt mine in the world and probably also the most fun: you get to explore the subterranean world by foot, boat, and even slide. You can get to Hallein by regular bus, by car, or by bicycle alongside the River Salzach, then it's a lovely, 40-minute walk (or seven-minute taxi) up to the mine. ⊠ *Ramsaustrasse 3, Hallein-Taxach* ⊕ *www.salzwelten.at/de/hallein* ⊡ *€23* ⊙ *Closed Sept.–Mar.*

Keltenmuseum (*Museum of the Celts*)
MUSEUM | FAMILY | It's not all about salt: the town of Hallein is also home to one of the largest Celtic art and history museums in Europe. Here, you can discover Ice Age burial grounds and settlements, as well as more modern history in the form of some 70 oil paintings that show the working conditions of the area's salt mines (okay, so it's mostly about salt). ⊠ *Pflegerplatz 5, Hallein-Taxach* ☎ *06245/80783* ⊕ *www.keltenmuseum.at* ⊡ *€7.50.*

★ **Schloss Hellbrunn** (*Hellbrunn Palace*)
CASTLE/PALACE | FAMILY | Just six kilometers (four miles) south of Salzburg, Schloss Hellbrunn was the prince-archbishops' pleasure palace, built early in the 17th century. Nowhere else can you experience so completely the realm of fantasy that the grand Salzburg archbishops indulged in. The castle has some fascinating rooms, including an octagonal music room and a banquet hall with a trompe-l'oeil ceiling. Look out for the homemade "unicorn." Hellbrunn Park became famous far and wide because of its **Wasserspiele**, or trick fountains. In the formal gardens, an outstanding mechanical theater includes exotic and humorous fountains spurting water from strange places at unexpected times. The **Monatsschlösschen**, the old hunting lodge, contains an excellent folklore museum. The **Steintheater** (Stone Theater) is an old quarry made into the earliest open-air opera stage north of the Alps. The former palace deer park has become a **zoo**. On the estate grounds is the little gazebo from *The Sound of Music* ("I am 16, going on 17")—though the doors are locked. To reach Schloss Hellbrunn from Salzburg Altstadt, take bus 25.
■**TIP→ Consider going one stop further on the bus to the zoo; there's a lovely walk from here through the park into the palace gardens.** ⊠ *Fürstenweg 37, Hellbrunn* ☎ *0662/8203–720* ⊕ *www.hellbrunn.at* ⊡ *€13.50* ⊙ *Closed Nov.–Mar.*

Stille Nacht Kapelle
TOWN | The little village of Oberndorf, 18 kilometers (11 miles) north of Salzburg, has just one claim to fame: it was here on Christmas Eve, 1818, that the world-famous Christmas carol "Silent Night" was sung for the first time. It was composed by the organist and schoolteacher Franz Gruber to a lyric by the local priest, Josef Mohr. The church was demolished and replaced in 1937 by this tiny commemorative chapel containing a copy of the original composition (the original is in the Salzburg Museum), stained-glass windows depicting Gruber and Mohr, and a Nativity scene. Behind the chapel, the Heimatmuseum documents the history of the carol. You can get to Oberndorf by the local train (opposite the main train station), by car along the B156 Lamprechtshausener Bundesstrasse, or by bicycle along the River Salzach.
■**TIP→ Every December 24 at 5 pm, a traditional performance of the carol—two male voices plus guitar and choir—in front of the chapel is the introduction to Christmas.** ⊠ *Salzburg* ⊕ *www.stillenacht-kapelle.at.*

Chapter 10

EASTERN ALPS

Updated by
Caroline Sieg

 Sights
★★★★★

 Restaurants
★★★☆☆

 Hotels
★★★☆☆

 Shopping
★★☆☆☆

 Nightlife
★☆☆☆☆

WELCOME TO EASTERN ALPS

TOP REASONS TO GO

★ **Grossglockner Highway:** The towering peaks along this panoramic alpine road make it one of Austria's most spectacular mountain passes.

★ **Photogenic Heiligenblut:** This jewel of a photo-op town has a slender church steeple and gorgeous mountain backdrop.

★ **The lake at Velden:** The lakeshore of this upscale town is lined with hotels and the fabulous villas of Austria's rich and famous.

★ **Bad Kleinkirchheim:** The province of Carinthia's best-known and most fashionable ski resort is home to the greatest downhill racer of all time, Franz Klammer. Join him—or follow in his tracks—on the slopes.

★ **Eisriesenwelt:** This wonder of nature (the name translates to "the giant ice world") is one of the biggest ice caves in the world—don't miss this unforgettable experience.

★ **The Bad Gastein cure:** This is, perhaps, the most famous of all Alpine thermal mountain spas.

Austria's Eastern Alps straddle four provinces: Carinthia, East Tyrol, Salzburgerland, and Styria. Imposing mountain ranges ripple through the region, isolating Alpine villages whose picture-postcard perfection has remained unspoiled through the centuries. The mountainous terrain makes some backtracking necessary if you're interested in visiting the entire area, but driving through the spectacular scenery is part of the appeal of touring the region.

1 Zell am See. Situated about halfway between Salzburg and Innsbruck and at the foot of a famous Alpine viewpoint (whose summit is reached by aerial ropeway), this picturesque lakeside town is a popular winter and summer resort.

2 Grossglockner High Alpine Road. This spectacular alpine pass wiggles through the heart of Hohe Tauern National Park toward the highest peak in Austria, the Grossglockner, offering incredible views along the way.

3 Heiligenblut. One of the most picturesque spots on the Grossglockner Road, this Alpine village lures skiers, hikers, and photographers.

4 Bad Gastein. This charming spa town offers a stunning high Alpine landscape, world-class skiing, and mineral-rich waters.

5 Filzmoos. A little Alpine village facing the Gosaukamm mountains, this hidden gem is equally enchanting in summer as in winter.

6 Werfen. A picture-perfect base for exploring the nearby ice caverns, castles, and has one of Austria's top restaurants.

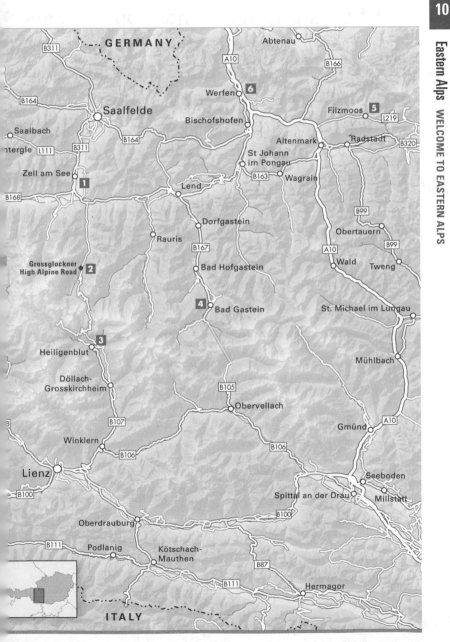

The entire Eastern Alps region is a feast of dramatic countryside, with breathtaking scenery and mountainous terrain that offers great winter sports opportunities. Here, majestic peaks, many well over 9,750 feet, soar above glaciers that give way to sweeping Alpine meadows ablaze with flowers in spring and summer. Long, broad valleys (many names have the suffix -au, meaning "water-meadow") are basins of rivers that cross the region between mountain ranges, sometimes meandering, sometimes plunging.

The land is full of ice caves and salt mines, deep gorges and hot springs. Tourism thrives through the towns and villages, with resorts such as Heiligenblut, in the shadow of the Grossglockner, Austria's highest mountain, a major draw for hikers and climbers and the namesake for the adjacent Grossglockner High Alpine Road, Austria's most famous and stunning mountain pass road Wherever you go, you'll find a range of good lodging, solid local food, and friendly folk. Western Carinthia and Salzburg province are dotted with quaint villages that have charming churches, lovely mountain scenery, and access to plenty of outdoor action⬚from hiking and fishing in summer to skiing in winter.

MAJOR REGIONS

Across the Grossglockner Pass. This is the excursion over one of the longest and most spectacular highways through the Alps, the Grossglockner High Alpine Road/Highway, which is a true engineering marvel. To explore this region from Salzburg, head south on the A10 highway and take Route 311 to enter the valley to **Zell am See**. Go south over the **Grossglockner Highway** to **Heiligenblut**. (The trip can be done by car or bus.) If the Grossglockner road is closed due to weather conditions, you must drive west of Zell am See to Mittersill toward Lienz via the 5-km (3-mile) Felbertauern toll tunnel (€11 one way) under the Tauern mountains. Exiting the tunnel, continue on Route 107 to Heiligenblut.

Salzburgerland. Glaciers, hot springs, luxurious hotels, and tranquil lakes are the enticing combinations this Austrian region serves up superlatively. Gold and silver mined from the mountains were the source of many local fortunes; today glittering gold jewelry finds many buyers in the shops of **Bad Gastein's** Kaiser Wilhelm Promenade. To set off on this trip, head south from Salzburg on the A10 and take the Bischofshofen exit toward St. Johann im Pongau, which gets you to Route 311 and, 17 km (11 miles) later, the Route 167 junction. From Zell am See, head east on Route 311 to pass Bruck, continue through Taxenbach to Lend, and turn south at the intersection of Route 167.

The SalzburgerLand Card includes admission to thermal baths (including Bad Gastein) and museums, trains and cable-car rides, a 24-hour Salzburg-City card, and more—190 attractions in all. It's definitely worth the money if you plan to do more than a couple of activities in the area. A six-day card costs €66; a 12-day card costs €81. Cards can be purchased from May till October 26. ⊕ *www.salzburgerlandcard.com.*

Planning

When to Go

Snowy conditions can make driving a white-knuckle experience, but winter also brings extensive, superb skiing throughout the region—and it's somewhat cheaper here than at the better-known resorts in Tyrol. In summer the craggy mountain peaks and lush meadows provide challenge and joy to hikers, trail runners, and mountain-bike enthusiasts, while spelunkers head into the bowels of the behemoths. Placid lakes and meandering mountain streams attract anglers for some of the best fishing to be found in the country.

Getting Here and Around

Driving is the best and most efficient way to explore this area; the roads are good and you can stop to picnic or just to marvel at the scenery. There is a cost to driving these roads, though, as tunnels, passes, and panoramic roads often have tolls. Bus and train travel is also a relatively hassle-free option.

AIR

The busiest airport in the Eastern Alps region is the Mozart airport in Salzburg, larger and with more connections than the one in Carinthia at Klagenfurt. Both have frequent connections to other Austrian cities and points in Europe, but neither has scheduled overseas direct flights, except to the United Kingdom.

BUS

As is typical throughout Austria, where trains don't go the buses do, though some side routes are less frequently covered. Coordinating your schedule with that of the buses is not as difficult as it sounds. Austrian travel offices are helpful in this regard, or bus information is available in Klagenfurt and Salzburg. The Postbus network is extensive throughout Austria, with services remaining reliable even through adverse weather, including heavy snow. You can take Postbus 650/651 from the Zell am See train station up and over the mountains to the Grossglockner glacier at Kaiser-Franz-Josefs-Höhe, a 2½-hour trip. The bus runs twice a day from late June to the end of September. There's also a connecting bus from the glacier to Heiligenblut twice a day, so you can start the route from there, too.

BUS INFORMATION Postbus. ☎ *43/051717* ⊕ *www.postbus.at.*

CAR

If you're coming from northern Italy, you can get to the Eastern Alps from Villach on the E55/A13 in Italy, which becomes the A2 and then the A10; from Klagenfurt, farther east in Carinthia, taking the

A2 autobahn is quickest. The fastest route from Salzburg is the A10 autobahn, but you'll have to take two tunnels into account at a total cost of €12.50 (Tauern- and Katschbergtunnel). In summer on certain weekends (especially during Germany's official holidays), the A10 southbound can become one very long parking lot, with hour-long waits before the tunnels. Taking the normal road over the passes, although long, is a very attractive option, but you won't be the only person who thought of it. A good alternative to the busy Tauern Highway is the Tauern Motorail link, connecting Bad Gastein with Carinthia (Mallnitz) through an 8-km (5-mile) tunnel. It's a 20-minute ride and cars are transported from one side to the other by train while passengers ride in a proper carriage. One way costs €17. Prices are per car, including all passengers. If coming from abroad, don't forget to buy the autobahn vignette (sticker) for Austria; unless you get an annual pass, your options are as follows: €9.40 for 10 days or €27.40 for two months.

Be aware that the Grossglockner High Alpine Highway is closed from the first heavy snow (mid-November or possibly earlier) to mid-May or early June. Though many of the other high mountain roads are kept open in winter, driving them is nevertheless tricky and you may even need tire chains.

TRAIN

Salzburg is the main hub for visiting the Eastern Alps, with frequent rail service from Vienna. Bad Gastein is also connected to Vienna, but with fewer direct trains; to get to Zell am See you must change trains in Salzburg. Most of the towns in the Eastern Alps are reachable by train, but the Grossglockner is reachable in a practical sense only by road.

If your onward travel plans from the Eastern Alps point you in the direction of Vienna, or you plan to travel to Carinthia after flying into Vienna, keep in mind the route via the **Semmering Railway.** It is now a section of rail travel that is part of the Austrian network, but the 41 km (25 miles) that is still called the Semmering is probably the most spectacular regular-gauge train journey you will ever take— and it has been in constant use for more than 160 years. Built between 1848 and 1854, it traverses high mountain terrain between Gloggnitz, southwest of Vienna, to Murzzuschlag over the Semmering Pass. It's commonly referred to as the world's first true mountain railway and is a marvel of civil engineering. It features 14 tunnels, 16 viaducts (some of them two stories), and more than 100 curved stone bridges and 11 small iron ones. It's possible to incorporate traveling this wonder on your way to or from Vienna and Klagenfurt, Heiligenblut, or Zell am See. Get information about tickets and timetable from ÖBB (Austrian Railways).

TRAIN INFORMATION Österreichisches Bundesbahn/Austrian Railways. ☎ *05/1717* ⊕ *www.oebb.at/en.*

Hotels

This part of Austria can be relatively inexpensive (for the lowest rates, try to avoid weekends, when city-folk arrive for a weekend escape), except for the top resort towns of Bad Gastein and Zell am See. Even there, budget accommodations are available outside the center of town or in pensions. Note that room rates include taxes and service and almost always breakfast (except in the most expensive hotels) and one other meal, which is usually dinner. *Halbpension* (half-board), as this plan is called, is de rigueur in most lodgings. However, most will offer a breakfast-buffet-only rate if requested. Most hotels provide in-room phones and TVs. A few of the smaller hotels still take no credit cards. In the prominent resorts summer prices are often as much as 50% lower than during ski season. *Hotel reviews have been shortened. For full information, visit Fodors.com.*

Restaurants

Although this region contains fine restaurants—in fact, two of the country's top dozen dining establishments are here—most of the traditional dining options in the small towns of the Eastern Alps will take place in *Gasthöfe* or *Gasthäuser*—chalet-style country hotels and inns with flower-decked balconies and overhanging eaves. You'll also find a small but growing range of more contemporary options, from trendy eateries serving moderns twists on local fare and/or international food (some in boutique hotels) to Third wave coffee shops that serve small bites alongside excellent coffee sourced from from top-quality independent roasters. Note that many inns and other smaller establishements are often closed in the off-season, particularly November and possibly April or May. *Restaurant reviews have been shortened. For full information, visit Fodors.com.*

What it Costs in Euros

	$	$$	$$$	$$$$
RESTAURANTS				
	under €16	€16–€20	€21–€30	over €30
HOTELS				
	under €130	€130–€155	€156–€210	over €210

Visitor Information

For information about Carinthia, contact Kärntner Tourismus. The central tourist board for East Tyrol is Osttirol Information. For information about Salzburg Province, contact Salzburger Land Tourismus. The main tourist bureau for Styria is Steiermark Information.

Many individual towns have their own *Fremdenverkehrsamt* (tourist office); these are listed under the specific towns.

CONTACTS Visit Carinthia. ✉ *Völkermarkter Ring 21–23, Klagenfurt* ☎ *0463/3000* ⊕ *www.visitcarinthia.at.* **Osttirol Information.** ✉ *Mühlgasse 11, Innsbruck* ☎ *050/212–212* ⊕ *www.osttirol.com.* **Salzburgerland Tourismus.** ✉ *Wiener Bundesstrasse 23, Postfach 1, Hallwang bei Salzburg* ☎ *0662/6688–44* ⊕ *www.salzburgerland.com.* **Steiermark Information.** ✉ *St. Peter-Hauptstrasse 243, Graz* ☎ *0316/4003–0* ⊕ *www.steiermark.com/en.*

Zell am See

108 km (67 miles) southwest of Salzburg.

This lovely lakeside town got its name from the monks' cells of a monastery founded here in about 790. It has excellent skiing and is busy throughout the winter. But it is now also one of Austria's most popular summer destinations, with an idyllic setting that's hard to beat, and the town can get very crowded in the peak season of July and August. If you want to stay in the town center, booking well ahead of time is strongly advised.

Zell am See is one of Europe's top vacation destinations for Middle Eastern tourists. In 2014, the town faced controversy after the city authorities issued a booklet offering "cultural advice" to visitors—it pointed out that Austrian shopkeepers don't expect customers to haggle over prices, and that eating on the floor in hotel rooms is very much a no-no. Visitors were advised not to wear burqas and to "adopt the Austrian mentality." Press, media, and some local businesses criticized the booklet, saying it unfairly stigmatized Arab visitors, and the tourist office swiftly withdrew the booklet within a few months. When Austria imposed a ban on full face coverings in 2017, local establishments worried it would negatively affect tourism from this region, but in fact, it lead to criticism by police after it mainly resulted in the issuing of warnings against people wearing ski gear and costumes. In general many local officials turn a blind eye to veiled visitors.

GETTING HERE AND AROUND

Enter the Pongau valley from the A10 highway from Salzburg by taking Exit 47 Pongau/Bischofshofen to merge onto Route B311, Bruckner Bundesstrasse.

VISITOR INFORMATION

CONTACTS Zell am See. ⊠ *Brucker Bundesstrasse 1A* ☎ *06542/770* ⊕ *www. zellamsee-kaprun.com.*

Sights

Pinzgauer Railroad

TRANSPORTATION SITE (AIRPORT/BUS/FERRY/ TRAIN) | This romantic narrow-gauge train winds its way under steam power on a two-hour trip through the Pinzgau, following the Salzach River valley westward 54 km (34 miles) to Krimml. Nearby are the famous Krimml waterfalls, with a 1,300-foot drop, which you can see from an observation platform or explore close at hand if you don't mind a steep hike. Be sure to take a raincoat and sneakers. A one-day ticket is included with a SalzburgerLand Card. ☎ *06542/40600* ⊕ *www. pinzgauer-lokalbahn.info* 🚂 *Zell am See to Krimml €11, round-trip €18.60.*

Schloss Rosenberg

BUILDING | In the town center, visit the very handsome 16th-century Schloss Rosenberg, which now houses the Rathaus (town hall). ⊠ *Brucker Bundestrasse 2.*

Schmittenhöhe

MOUNTAIN—SIGHT | A cable car will take you virtually from the center of Zell am See up to the Schmittenhöhe, at 6,453 feet, for a far-reaching panorama that takes in the peaks of the Glockner and Tauern granite ranges to the south and west and the very different limestone ranges to the north. You can have lunch at the Berghotel at the top. Four

other cable-car trips are available up this mountain, part of the ski-lift system in the winter, but open in the summer for walkers and mountain bikers. ⊕ *www. schmitten.at/en.*

St. Hippolyt Pfarrkirche (*Parish Church*) **RELIGIOUS SITE** | Unusually fine statues of St. George and St. Florian can be found on the west wall of the splendid Romanesque St. Hippolyt Pfarrkirche, built in 1217. The tower was added about two centuries later, and the church itself was beautifully renovated in 1975. ⊠ *Stadtplatz.*

Thumersbach

TOWN | Several locations offer up stunning vistas of the town and its environs. On ground level, take a boat ride to the village of Thumersbach, on the opposite shore, for a wonderful reflected view of Zell am See.

Vogtturm

BUILDING | This more than 1000-year old tower, built in the 11th century and the oldest building in the town, houses a local history museum with details about local folklore, old costumes, and artifacts, as well as rotating exhibits featuring works and objects by local design companies or artists. It's open Wed.–Sun. from 2 to 6 pm—but opens earlier (around 11 am) if it's a rainy day! ⊠ *Stadtplatz* ☎ *0664/586–2706* ⊕ *www. vogtturm.at* ⊗ *Closed Mon.–Tues.*

Votter's Vehicle Museum

MUSEUM | Beautiful (and not so beautiful) cars and motorcycles from the 1950s, 1960s, and 1970s are on display here, including the remarkable one-person Messerschmitt Bubble Car and other, dare we say more appealing, automobiles. With around 200 exhibits, this is a great place to visit for a few hours on a rainy/bad-weather day. ⊠ *Schlossstrasse 32, Kaprun* ☎ *0699/1717–1342* ⊕ *www. oldtimer-museum.at* 🎟 *€9.90.*

Take the legendary cable car from Zell am See to the summit of Schmittenhöhe for stunning views of the town and lake below.

🍴 Restaurants

Kraftwerk Restaurant & Winebar

$$ | AUSTRIAN | Housed in a converted 1934 powerstation with exposed brick walls and beams, this stylish two-story restaurant serves creative regional Austrian fare along with an excellent wine list. It's modern but rustic, industrial but welcoming, and authentic regional cuisine but creatively presented. **Known for:** excellent wine list; unique space; inventive Austrian mountain cuisine. ⓈAverage main: €16 ✉ Schmittenstrsse 12a ☎ 06643/888016 ⊕ www.kraft-werk-restaurant.at ⊗ Closed Sun.

Restaurant Zum Hirschen

$$$ | AUSTRIAN | In the hotel of the same name, the restaurant is in a charming, typically Austrian stube—all wood paneled and cozy—and serves regional specialties and international cuisine. Its popularity extends to locals and visitors

alike, which makes for a good atmosphere. **Known for:** traditional wood-paneled ambience, both elegant and cozy; popularity with locals and visitors alike; excellent-value set lunch. ⓈAverage main: €29 ✉ Dreifaltigkeitsstrasse 1 ☎ 06542/774–0 ⊕ www.hotel-zum-hir-schen.at ⊗ Closed Oct. and Nov.

Steinerwirt1493

$$$ | AUSTRIAN | As the name suggests, the Steinerwirt dates back almost as far as Columbus's Atlantic voyage. It is family run, and its newest generation of owners and staff have brought modernity to the cuisine while maintaining the original Alpine flair. **Known for:** amazing history of more than 500 years; high-end interpretation of Austrian favorites; combination of tradition and modern flair. ⓈAverage main: €23 ✉ Dreifaltigkeitsgasse 2 ☎ 06542/72502 ⊕ www.steinerwirt.com ⊗ Closed early Nov.–1st wk in Dec. and last 2 wks of May.

Coffee and Quick Bites

Bella Bean

$ | **CAFÉ** | Opened in 2020, this specialty Third-wave coffee shop and roastery brews excellent cups of java and serves small bites like yogurt, fuit, and pastries in a cool, contemporary setting. **Known for:** inhouse roastery; expert staff; small bites. [$] *Average main: €5* ✉ *Schlossplatz 2a* ☎ *06642/352193* 🌐 *www.bellabean.at* 🕒 *Closed Sun.*

Hotels

Grand Hotel Zell am See

$$$$ | **HOTEL** | **FAMILY** | In the style of the great turn-of-the-twentieth-century resort hotels, this palatial lake house is the best located address in Zell am See, with direct beach access and wonderful lake views. **Pros:** great location; big standard rooms; kids' club for ages 3–10 and other child-friendly services. **Cons:** some rooms face noisy railroad; rooms with a view are more expensive; no air-conditioning, which is common with most Austrian hotels as the mountain climate is normally mild. [$] *Rooms from: €270* ✉ *Esplanade 4–6* ☎ *06542/788* 🌐 *www.grandhotel-zellamsee.at* 🛏 *132 rooms* 🍴 *Free breakfast.*

★ Salzburgerhof

$$$$ | **HOTEL** | The well-located five-star hotel, styled like an oversized chalet with modern annexes on either side, stands out with its lovely courtyard garden, a natural swimming pool, and the best spa in the area. **Pros:** the region's best place to stay; rooms have balconies with views; big standard rooms. **Cons:** rooms at rear of building are near railroad tracks; standard rooms do not face garden; some rooms are looking a little tired and could use an update. [$] *Rooms from: €400* ✉ *Auerspergstrasse 11* ☎ *06542/7650* 🌐 *www.salzburgerhof.at* 🕒 *Closed Nov.* 🛏 *70 rooms* 🍴 *Free breakfast.*

Schloss Prielau

$$$$ | **B&B/INN** | Attentive hosts Anette and Andreas Mayer take extra special care of their guests in this fairy-tale castle, with its turreted towers and striped shutters. **Pros:** eye-popping architecture; very personal feeling; private lake beach is only five minutes' walk. **Cons:** 20-minute walk to town; no elevator; no air-conditioning (a lack that is common in most Austrian mountain hotels). [$] *Rooms from: €290* ✉ *Hofmannsthalstrasse 12* ☎ *06542/729–110* 🌐 *www.schloss-prielau.at* 🕒 *Closed Nov.* 🛏 *9 rooms* 🍴 *Free breakfast.*

Steinerwirt1493

$$$ | **HOTEL** | Redesigned by Austrian architects in a minimalistic and modern style that distances itself from the local Alpine kitsch, this centrally located boutique hotel has a lot to offer. **Pros:** has its own art gallery; in the center of Zell am See; known for great cuisine. **Cons:** no swimming pool (there is an outdoor Jacuzzi); some noise from the nearby railroad station; some rooms are quite small. [$] *Rooms from: €195* ✉ *Dreifaltigkeitsgasse 2* ☎ *06542/72502* 🌐 *www.steinerwirt.com* 🕒 *Closed early Nov.–1st wk in Dec. and last 2 wks of May* 🛏 *28 rooms* 🍴 *Free breakfast.*

Nightlife

The emphasis in Zell is more on drinking than on dancing, but the scene does change periodically.

Crazy Daisy

BARS/PUBS | This restaurant-café and dance pub is in the center of town. It has legendary status among skiers and boarders, serves hot mulled wine in the winter along with heaters and blankets, and has a great summertime scene on the terrace. There's also regular live music. ✉ *Salzmannstrasse 8* ☎ *06542/725260* 🌐 *crazy-daisy.at.*

⚡ Activities

BICYCLING

The area around Zell am See is ideal for bicycling. From April to October, bike tours run from south of Zell am See up to St. Johann and Salzburg via the Tauern cycle route.

Adventure Service

BICYCLING | Mountain-bike tours, Segway tours, and other outdoor activities including rafting, canyoning, climbing, and paragliding are available. They also rent e-bikes. ✉ Steinergasse 5–7 ☎ 06542/73525 ⊕ www.adventureservice.at.

Sport Achleitner

BICYCLING | If you left your two wheels at home, you can rent some here for €12 per day for a city bike, €25 for a mountain bike, or €32 for an e-bike. Renting by the week is more economical. In the winter the bikes give way to ski and board rentals. ✉ Postplatz 2 ☎ 06542/73581 ⊕ www.sport-achleitner.at.

FISHING

The lake's tranquil waters offer fine fishing, and many hotels in the area have packages for avid anglers.

SKIING

Zell am See-Kaprun

SKIING/SNOWBOARDING | There's good skiing on the slopes immediately above the town. Most of the runs are intermediate, but there are good areas for beginners, too, and experts will find some steepish, sweeping runs on which to have fun if not be truly tested. Towering over Zell am See, the Schmittenhöhe has tree-lined runs that will feel familiar to Colorado and New England skiers. Kitzsteinhorn mountain, which rises to 10,499 feet above Kaprun, has year-round glacier skiing and was the first glacier ski area in Austria. Together these mountains offer 57 lifts, with 130 km (80 miles) of prepared slopes. In addition, there are more than 200 km

(124 miles) of cross-country trails and eight ski schools. ☎ 06542/770 tourist office ⊕ www.zellamsee-kaprun.com.

WATER SPORTS

Boating—from paddleboating to sailing—and swimming are excellent on the uncrowded Zeller See.

Edis Wasserskischule

WATER SPORTS | Powerboats are restricted on many Austrian lakes, but there is this waterskiing school at Thumersbach. ✉ Strandbad, Lindenallee, Thumersbach ☎ 0664/2068506 ⊕ www.ediswasserski.com ⊘ Closed Oct.–early May.

Grossglockner High Alpine Road

46 km (29 miles) from Bruck to Heiligenblut.

One of the best-known roads in the Alps, the Hochalpenstrasse—rising to more than 8,000 feet and containing 36 hairpin bends, with spectacular views the whole way—leads you deep into the Hohe Tauern National Park. The highway is generally open from early May to early November, but only during daylight hours. There's a toll of €37 for regular or hybrid cars or €27 for 100% electric cars.

GETTING HERE AND AROUND

From Zell am See head south toward Bruck an der Grossglocknerstrasse, and continue on the B107. After the toll station in Ferleiten on the north side of the Grossglockner peak, the highway begins its many hairpin turns and continues to Heiligenblut.

VISITOR INFORMATION

CONTACTS **Grossglockner Hochalpenstrasse/ Grossglockner High Alpine Road.** ✉ Rainerstrasse 2, Salzburg ☎ 0662/873673–0 ⊕ www.grossglockner.at.

The spectacular Grossglockner High Alpine Road is one of Austria's top attractions and the highest point of the country.

Sights

Grossglockner Hochalpenstrasse (*Grossglockner High Alpine Highway*)
SCENIC DRIVE | This is the excursion over the longest and most spectacular highway through the Alps. The road was completed in 1935, after five years of labor by 3,200 workers. From Heiligenblut the climb begins up the Carinthian side of the Grossglockner Mountain. The peak itself—at 12,461 feet the highest point in Austria—is to the west. The Grossglocknerstrasse twists and turns as it struggles to the 8,370-foot Hochtor, the highest point on the through road and the border between Carinthia and Salzburg Province.

A side trip on the Edelweiss-Strasse leads to the scenic vantage point at the **Edelweissspitze.** It's an unbelievable view out over East Tyrol, Carinthia, and Salzburg, including 19 glaciers and 37 peaks rising above the 9,600-foot mark. The rare white edelweiss—the von

Trapps sang its praises in *The Sound of Music*—grows here. Though the species is protected, don't worry about the plants you get as souvenirs; they are cultivated for this purpose. ■**TIP**➔ **It is strictly forbidden to pick a wild edelweiss (or several other plant species), should you happen to come across one.**

You can get somewhat closer to Grossglockner peak than the main road takes you by following the highly scenic but steep Gletscherstrasse westward up to the Gletscherbahn on the Franz-Josef-Plateau, where you'll be rewarded with absolutely breathtaking views of the Grossglockner peak and surrounding Alps, of the vast glacier in the valley below, and, on a clear day, even into Italy. ☎ *0662/873673 road information* ⊕ *www.grossglockner.at* ✉ *€37 regular or hybrid vehicle or €27 100% electric cars for a one-day pass, €59 per vehicle (all types) for 3-week pass* ⊙ *Closed in Winter, roughly Nov.–April.*

Hohe Tauern National Park

NATIONAL/STATE PARK | This is one of the most varied and unspoiled landscapes on the planet—high Alpine meadows, deep evergreen woods, endless spiraling rock cliffs, and glacial ice fields—and at 1,786 square km (690 square miles) it's the largest national park of central Europe. It touches on three provinces (Salzburg, Carinthia, and Tyrol) and includes the Grossglockner mountain group. The Grossglockner Hochalpenstrasse passes through the park. The hardier traveler may want to spend a few days hiking and lodging at any one of several refuges, where you may occasionally be treated to very rustic, homemade victuals (cheeses and hams). ⊕ *www.hohetauern.at.*

Heiligenblut

54 km (34 miles) south of Zell am See.

One of the most photographed places in the country, Heiligenblut remains one of Austria's most picturesque Alpine villages. With the majestic Grossglockner—Austria's highest mountain—for a backdrop, the town cradles the pilgrimage church of St. Vincent. Nowhere else does a steeple seem to find such affirmation amid soaring peaks. Some say the best time to experience this little slice of Alpine nirvana is after a leisurely dinner at one of the many Gasthöfe, gazing out at the starry firmament over the Hohe Tauern range. Others relish standing around an early-morning fire used by hikers setting out to conquer the mighty foothills of the Grossglockner peaks. It's the famed mountain-climbing school and climbing and skiing possibilities (there are 40 peaks higher than 10,000 feet here) that draw flocks of all-out active types.

GETTING HERE AND AROUND

You can get to Heiligenblut from Zell am See via the Grossglockner pass or via Lienz. In winter, Heiligenblut is a ski resort of some repute; buses also run from the village to other nearby ski areas.

VISITOR INFORMATION
CONTACTS Heiligenblut. ⊠ *Hof 4* ☎ *04824/2001* ⊕ *www.heiligenblut.at.*

Sights

Alten Pocher
HISTORIC SITE | A replica 16th-century gold mining village, Alten Pocher is more than 5,906 feet above sea level. Miners prospected in the Hohe Tauern for gold from the 14th to the end of the 19th century, and it was considered one of the most important gold-mining regions of its day. Today, visitors can rent rubber boots and a panning bowl to try their luck in the Fleissbach. Many caves were created through grueling labor by thousands of miners over this period, under the most arduous conditions (of course, the owners of the mines themselves lived comfortable and rich lives). ⊠ *Heiligenblut* ⊠ *Gold panning €9, open-air mining museum free; €4 with guide* ⊙ *Closed mid-Sept.–mid-July.*

Church of St. Vincent
RELIGIOUS SITE | According to local legend, St. Briccius, after obtaining a vial of the blood of Jesus, was buried by an avalanche, but when his body was recovered the tiny vial was miraculously found hidden within one of the saint's open wounds. The town gets its name, Heiligenblut (Holy Blood), from this story. Today the relic is housed in the Sakramenthäuschen, the chapel of this small but beautiful Gothic church. Completed in 1490 after more than a century of construction under the toughest conditions, the church is marked by its soaring belfry tower. Sublimely, the sharply pointed spire finds an impressive echo in the

conical peak of the Grossglockner. St. Vincent's contains a beautifully carved late-Gothic double altar nearly 36 feet high, and the Coronation of Mary is depicted in the altar wings, richly carved by Wolfgang Hasslinger in 1520. The region's most important altarpiece, it imparts a feeling of quiet power in this spare, high church. The church also has a noble crypt and graveyard, the latter sheltering graves of those lost in climbing the surrounding mountains. ⊠ *Heiligenblut* ☎ *04824/2700.*

Hotels

Chalet-Hotel Senger

$$$ | B&B/INN | A peaceful location and great views make this farmhouse chalet a great choice. **Pros:** romantic; beautiful mountain views; cozy alpine-chic. **Cons:** 10-minute walk to town; very comfortable but doesn't claim to be luxurious; closed part of spring and part of late fall. Ⓢ *Rooms from: €185* ⊠ *Hof 23* ☎ *04824/2215* ⊕ *www.romantic.at* ⊙ *Closed 1 wk after Easter–June and Oct.–mid-Dec.* ↳ *19 rooms* ⍥ *Free breakfast.*

Hotel Lärchenhof

$$$$ | HOTEL | FAMILY | This charming hotel is a true *panoramagasthof*—a guesthouse with spectacular views. **Pros:** a good spa; wonderful country hotel atmosphere; very quiet location. **Cons:** some double rooms are on the small side; uphill walk back from the village; so lovely you won't want to leave. Ⓢ *Rooms from: €220* ⊠ *Hof 70* ☎ *04824/2262* ⊕ *www.hotellaerchenhof.at/en* ↳ *23 rooms* ⍥ *Free breakfast.*

Hunguest Hotel Heiligenblut

$$$$ | HOTEL | FAMILY | This family-friendly hotel, a short distance from the town center, runs its own kindergarten on weekdays where you can leave the kids while you hit the slopes. **Pros:** perfect for families; lots of activities; mountain views. **Cons:** not the quietest location in town;

sauna is small; views from the rooms vary. Ⓢ *Rooms from: €222* ⊠ *Winkl 46* ☎ *04824/4111* ⊕ *www.hotel-heiligenblut.at/* ⊙ *Closed Easter–May and Oct.–mid-Dec.* ↳ *112 rooms* ⍥ *Free breakfast.*

Nationalpark Lodge Grossglockner

$$$$ | HOTEL | FAMILY | This wooden chalet in the center of the village offers old-fashioned charm and modern amenities. **Pros:** very friendly staff; restaurant focuses on organic local produce; lots of children's activities. **Cons:** some rooms on the small side; bells from neighboring church can be loud; rooms at the front can suffer from road noise. Ⓢ *Rooms from: €215* ⊠ *Hof 6* ☎ *04824/2244* ⊕ *www.nationalparklodge.at/en/* ⊙ *Closed May–mid-June, Oct., and Nov.* ↳ *50 rooms* ⍥ *Free breakfast.*

Activities

HIKING AND MOUNTAIN CLIMBING

This is a hiker's El Dorado during summertime, with more than 240 km (150 miles) of marked pathways and trails in all directions. There are relatively easy hikes to the Naturlehrweg Gössnitzfall-Kachlmoor (1½ hours), Wirtsbauer-Alm (two hours), and the Jungfernsprung (one hour), which ends atop a 500-foot cliff above the Mölltal.

Guided Tours

HIKING/WALKING | Enjoyable group or private guided tours are run by the national park service. These could include walks conducted by a national-park ranger to the foot of the Grossglockner, to see sure-footed ibex in their natural habitat jumping about on seemingly sheer rock walls; a hike to the Pasterze Glacier, the largest in Austria; or a hike to the Mollschlucht gorge, much of it a via ferrata route—not for the fainthearted. ☎ *04824/2700–20 national park programs office* ⊕ *www.hohetauern.at, www.heiligenblut.at* ⍥ *From €12 for short group tour; from €200 per person for private one- to three-day tours.*

Heiligenblut Climbing Park
CLIMBING/MOUNTAINEERING | The park has a high-ropes course, climbing wall, zip line, children's playground, and restaurant. The via ferrata has two routes of varying levels of difficulty, which take you along spectacular waterfalls and cliffs. The high-ropes course is at the Gasthof Sonnblick, where the Brandstatter family can give information and make bookings. ✉ *Hof 21* ☎ *04824/21310* 🌐 *www.sonnblick-heiligenblut.at* 🎫 *€20.*

Bad Gastein

54 km (34 miles) southeast of Zell am See.

Though it traces its roots all the way back to the 15th century, this resort, one of Europe's leading spas, gained renown only in the 19th century, when VIPs from emperors to impecunious philosophers flocked to the area to "take the cure." Today Bad Gastein retains much of its allure. The stunning setting—a mountain torrent, the Gasteiner Ache, rushes through the town—adds to the attraction. Much of the town has a solid though timeworn elegance, and some of the aging buildings are in need of a spruce-up. But the old buildings still dominate the townscape, giving it a wonderful feeling of substance and history. The baths themselves, however, are state-of-the-art, as evidenced by the massive **Felsentherme Gastein** and the nearby **Thermalkurhaus.**

A special tradition in Bad Gastein is the old pagan *Perchtenlaufen* processions in January. People wear huge and intimidating masks and make lots of noise to chase the winter away, bringing good blessings for the new year. However, it can be an excuse for excessive drinking by some costume-wearing youths, who often, sadly, cross the line to unruliness.

GETTING HERE AND AROUND

Bad Gastein is serviced by many rail lines, with many expresses running from Salzburg and Klagenfurt. You can also reach the town by bus from Salzburg.

VISITOR INFORMATION

CONTACTS Bad Gastein Tourist Office. ✉ *Kaiser-Franz-Josef-Strasse 27* ☎ *06432/3393–114* 🌐 *www.gastein.com.*

🍴 Restaurants

Betty's Bar
$ | **INTERNATIONAL** | This casual, light-filled little bar-café a few steps from the center of town is the perfect spot to pick up coffee and baguettes or to linger for hours over champagne and cocktails. There's a cozy interior and welcoming outdoor tables, and a great wine, beer, and cocktail list. **Known for:** lively spot; great wine and cocktails; Flammkuchen (thin, cripsy flatbreads). [$] *Average main: €10* ✉ *Kaiser-Franz-Josef-Strasse 17* ☎ *0650/6272627* 🌐 *www.hellobettysbar.com.*

The Blonde Beans
$ | **CAFÉ** | This tiny, Swedish-run Third-wave coffee shop brews beans from a premium Swedish coffee roaster and serves homemade *Kanelbullar* (Swedish cinnamon buns), as well as vanilla and cardamom variations, plus house-crafted bagels and gourmet sandwiches. It's a great place to grab a sandwich to take on your hike. **Known for:** quality coffee; homemade cinammon buns and bagels; take-out food. [$] *Average main: €5* ✉ *Bahnhofplatz 4* ☎ *0660/1385366* 🌐 *www.theblondebeans.com* 🕒 *Closed Sun. and Thurs. Closed early Oct.–late Nov. and late April–early June.*

Jägerhäusl
$$ | **AUSTRIAN** | With green wood paneling and a red timber ceiling, the restaurant is both historic and traditional but exceptionally stylish. It's also right in the old town center, and has a garden and cozy wooden parlors. **Known for:** warm, family

Did You Know?

Picturesquely set in a high valley of the Hohe Tauern mountain range, Bad Gastein is known for the Gastein Waterfall and a variety of Belle Époque hotel buildings.

atmosphere; traditional Austrian dishes; good pizzas. $ *Average main: €17* ✉ *Kaiser-Franz-Josef-Str. 9* ☎ *06434/20254* ☉ *Closed Nov.*

★ Mondi Bellevue Alm

$$$ | AUSTRIAN | Idyllically set on the east side of the Stubnerkogel, directly on the ski slope, this Alpine hut is one of the oldest in Europe, remarkably well preserved, with wooden interiors and a huge open fire. Wooden parlors and a big terrace, with a spectacular view over Bad Gastein, invite visitors in for a substantial meal, followed by a couple of drinks after a hike or long skiing day. **Known for:** tempting and substantial Austrian delicacies and desserts; fabulous views; cozy atmosphere. $ *Average main: €21* ✉ *Bellevue-Alm-Weg 6* ☎ *06434/3881–26* ⊕ *www.bellevuealm.at* ▭ *No credit cards* ☉ *Closed Nov.–early Dec.*

 ## Hotels

Alpenblick

$$ | HOTEL | Perched high above the town, the Alpenblick has a sweeping view of the valley, and is an ideal base for skiers, hikers, and anyone who wants a quiet stay away from the town center. **Pros:** fabulous lofty location with great views; laid-back vibe; family ownership provides a warm welcome. **Cons:** 15-minute walk to town and a bit steep on your way back; poor Wi-Fi service; some rooms are outdated. $ *Rooms from: €135* ✉ *Kötschachtalerstrasse 17* ☎ *06434/20620* ⊕ *www.alpenblick-gastein.at* ☉ *Closed Nov.–mid-Dec.* ⇨ *40 rooms* ⦿ *Free breakfast.*

★ Haus Hirt Alpine Spa Hotel

$$$ | HOTEL | FAMILY | This stylish Alpine lodge, on a hillside about a half mile from the town center, has good amenities for families, spectacular views, and a style that cleverly combines Alpine traditional with contemporary-chic. **Pros:** glorious position with fabulous views; organic breakfast buffet; free transportation. **Cons:** spa and pool are small and can get packed during winter; a 20-minute walk to town; repeat customers mean early reservations are needed. $ *Rooms from: €260* ✉ *Kaiserhofstrasse 14* ☎ *06434/2797–48* ⊕ *www.haus-hirt.com* ☉ *Closed Nov.* ⇨ *32 rooms, 9 suites* ⦿ *All-inclusive.*

Hotel Miramonte

$$$$ | HOTEL | A somewhat retro-style hotel, with original '50s and '60s elements, is a chic retreat that caters well to the sophisticated traveler, from mostly spacious bedrooms with balconies to high-quality meals. **Pros:** large terrace, yoga at the waterfall, and firepit encourage connection with outdoors; direct access to thermal water spring from the mountains; panorama rooms have balconies with views of mountains and valley. **Cons:** no swimming pool; limited parking; 15-minute walk to center of Bad Gastein. $ *Rooms from: €320* ✉ *Reitlpromenade 3* ☎ *06434/2577* ⊕ *www.hotelmiramonte.com* ☉ *Closed Nov.* ⇨ *36 rooms* ⦿ *Free breakfast.*

Regina Hotel

$$$$ | HOTEL | This family-run, chic boutique hotel offers designer rooms a mere 5 minute walk from the town center. **Pros:** stylish rooms, most with balconies; elegant restaurant and bar ; panoramic views. **Cons:** the restaurant-bar can be noisy late in the evening; the buzzy vibe might not appeal to those seeking mountain solitude; the cheapest rooms have no balconies or views and feel cramped. $ *Rooms from: €280* ✉ *K. H. Waggerl Strasse 5* ☎ *0643/421610* ⊕ *dasregina.com* ☉ *Closed early Oct.–early Dec. and late-April–late June* ⇨ *32* ⦿ *Free breakfast.*

Activities

Bad Gastein will keep guests entertained with all sorts of events from snowboarding competitions to llama trekking (popular with families). You will not be bored.

HIKING

Stubnerkogel Cable Car

HIKING/WALKING | Take the Stubnerkogel gondola lift 2¼ km (1½ miles) above sea level, where spectacular views over the Gastein Valley will take your breath away. A suspension bridge will make you go weak in the knees, and the modern Panorama platform guarantees a view of the Grossglockner. In summer, many hikes are possible from here, while in winter the cable car is used to access the ski slopes. One round-trip is included with the SalzburgerLand Card. ☎ *06434/232–2415* 🖂 *€27.50 round-trip.*

SKIING

Although not as well-known to outsiders as other resorts, the Gastein Valley is very popular with Austrians. There are a number of ski areas here, with a free shuttle bus running between them. The main access to the Bad Gastein area is by the Stubnerkogelbahn gondola, and it's possible to link with the Bad Hofgastein sector at Angertal. Sportgastein, quite exposed and with a remote feel, and Graukogel, with some protected wooded runs, are both above Bad Gastein and are not linked with any of the other sectors. Graukogel is delightful and all too often ignored by visitors—it's a great place for family skiing, with super views and a good mountain restaurant. Farther down the valley is the Dorfgastein area, which links with Grossarl on the far side of the Kreuzkogel. All in all, the valley has good and varied skiing for all levels, including a wealth of intermediate runs, but there are also a few challenges to be found. There are 43 ski lifts, and all the sectors have decent rental shops. You can get information on skiing conditions in all the areas from the tourist office.

Filzmoos

74 km (46 miles) northeast of Bad Gastein.

One of the most romantic villages in Austria, Filzmoos is still something of a well-kept secret. Though skiing in the nearby Dachstein mountains is excellent, the relatively inexpensive winter resort (which is part of the Salzburger Sportwelt ski area) has yet to be fully discovered by foreign tourists. During the summer months meandering mountain streams and myriad lakes attract anglers eager for trout, while hikers come to challenge the craggy peaks.

Filzmoos calls itself a "balloon village," not only for the International Hot Air Balloon Week every January, but because hot-air-balloon trips are a popular attraction for visitors and a great way to see the spectacular region.

GETTING HERE AND AROUND

Head south on the A10 highway and take Exit 60-Eben onto Filzmooserstrasse-L219.

VISITOR INFORMATION

CONTACTS Filzmoos. 🖂 *Filzmoos 50* ☎ *06453/8235* ⊕ *www.filzmoos.at.*

Sights

Salzburger Dolomitenstrasse (*Salzburg Dolomites Highway*)

SCENIC DRIVE | From Filzmoos, rejoin Route 99/E14 again at Eben im Pongau. Here you can take the A10 autobahn north to Salzburg if you're in a hurry. But if you have time for more majestic scenery and an interesting detour, continue about 4 km (2½ miles) on Route 99/E14, and turn north on Route 166, the Salzburger Dolomitenstrasse, for a 43-km (27-mile) swing around the Tennen mountains. ■**TIP→ Be careful, though, to catch the left turn onto Route 162 at Lindenthal; it will be marked to Golling. Head for Abtenau**

With spectacular ice formations and frozen waterfalls, Eisriesenwelt is the largest—and arguably the most beautiful—ice cave in the world.

Restaurants

★ Hubertus

$$$$ | **AUSTRIAN** | Every last detail, from romantic furnishings to the doting service, is done to perfection here, making this restaurant the best in the area. Chef Johanna Maier's way with trout is exquisite, but don't overlook the game, roast poultry, or veal sweetbreads. **Known for:** wonderful, tempting presentation of dishes; use of local produce; elegant surroundings. $ *Average main: €32* ⊠ *Am Dorfplatz 1* ☎ *06453/8204* ⊕ *www. johannamaier.at* ☉ *Closed mid-Apr.–mid-May and mid-Oct.–mid-Dec. No lunch.*

🛏 Hotels

Alpenkrone

$ | **HOTEL** | **FAMILY** | From the balconies of this hotel above the town center you'll have a great view of the surrounding mountains. **Pros:** great value; friendly staff; wonderful location. **Cons:** steep climb from town; not in the center of the action; hotel not very lively after dinnertime. $ *Rooms from: €140* ⊠ *Filzmoos 133* ☎ *06453/8280–0* ⊕ *www.alpenkrone. com* ☉ *Closed Easter–mid-May and mid-Oct.–mid-Dec.* ⇨ *57 rooms* ⏋ *No meals.*

Werfen

30 km (19 miles) west of Filzmoos.

The small size of Werfen, adorned with 16th-century buildings and a lovely Baroque church, belies its importance, for it's the base for exploring three extraordinary attractions: the largest and most fabulous ice caverns in the world; one of Austria's most spectacular castles; and a four-star culinary delight, Obauer. These riches place Werfen on a par with many larger and more highly touted Austrian cities. That said, this is a lovely spot to visit but it's best to stay in Filzmoos and explore Werfen on a day trip.

GETTING HERE AND AROUND

Werfen is close to the A10 highway; take Exit 43 and follow the signs to the town. Many trains from Salzburg stop here.

VISITOR INFORMATION

CONTACTS Werfen. ⊠ *Markt 24* ☎ *06468/5388* ⊕ *www.werfen.at.*

Sights

Burg Hohenwerfen

CASTLE/PALACE | From miles away you can see Burg Hohenwerfen, one of Europe's most formidable fortresses (it was never taken in battle), which dates from 1077. Though fires and renovations have altered its appearance, it maintains historic grandeur. Hewn from the rock on which it stands, the castle was called a "plume of heraldry radiant against the sky" by Maximilian I. It has black-timber-beamed state rooms, an enormous frescoed Knights' Hall, and a torture chamber. Eagles and falcons swoop above, adding to the medieval feel. The fortress has been used as a prison and police training center, but now it harbors Austria's first museum of falconry where the birds are rigorously trained. ■**TIP→ Shows with music, falconry, and performers in period costume are held at least twice a month; call ahead or check website for dates and times and save money by buying tickets online.** ⊠ *Burgstrasse* ☎ *06468/7603* ⊕ *www.salzburg-burgen. at* 🖾 *€16.50 including tour and birds-of-prey performance and funicular or €13 (online price); €12.50 without funicular.* ☉ *Closed Mon.*

Eisriesenwelt (*Ice Caves*)

CAVE | The "World of the Ice Giants" houses the largest known complex of ice caves, domes, galleries, and halls in Europe. It extends for some 42 km (26 miles) and contains a fantastic collection of frozen waterfalls and natural formations. Drive to the rest house, about halfway up the hill, and be prepared for some seriously scenic vistas. Then walk 15 minutes to the cable car, which takes you to a point about 15 minutes on foot from the cave, where you can take a 1¼-hour guided tour. The entire adventure takes about half a day. And remember, no matter how warm it is outside, it's below freezing inside, so bundle up, and wear appropriate shoes. You must be in reasonable shape, as there are 700 steps, but there's a restaurant with a terrace and a view where you can recover after the tour. You can also take a bus to the cable car from the Werfen train station. Buses run at 8:18 am, 10:18 am, 12:18 pm, and 2:18 pm. There are also transfers about every 25 minutes from the bus departure point at Gries, which is about a five-minute walk from the rail station. ⊠ *Eishohenstrasse 30* ☎ *06468/5248* ⊕ *www.eisriesenwelt.at/ en* 🖾 *€28, including cable car.*

Restaurants

★ Obauer

$$$$ | CONTEMPORARY | Among Austria's top dining spots, Obauer is presided over by the brothers Karl and Rudolf, who share chef-de-cuisine responsibilities. Thanks to their flair, this has become a culinary shrine, especially for Salzburgers and Germans. **Known for:** alfresco dining in the summer months in its charming garden; modern alpine cuisine; a fabulous collection of wines from the extensive cellar. Ⓢ *Average main: €35* ⊠ *Markt 46* ☎ *06468/52120* ⊕ *www.obauer.com.*

Chapter 11

SALZKAMMERGUT

Updated by
Jacy Meyer

 Sights
★★★★☆

 Restaurants
★★★★★

 Hotels
★★★★★

 Shopping
★★★★☆

 Nightlife
★★★☆☆

WELCOME TO SALZKAMMERGUT

TOP REASONS TO GO

★ **Fairy-tale landscape:** With spectacular alpine panoramas, dramatic alpine and subalpine lakes, and charming picture-postcard villages, this region is appropriately renowned for its scenery.

★ **Bad Ischl:** This town, where the rich and famous have long come for the healing waters, was Emperor Franz Josef's summer retreat in the 19th century.

★ **Cradle of culture:** Vienna and Salzburg may get all the credit, but the composers who made those cities cultural capitals also came to this part of Austria to hear the music in the air.

★ **Sports abound:** You'll find swimming, sailing, surfing, hiking, biking, climbing, and horseback riding in summer, and skiing, cross-country skiing, snow-shoeing, tobogganing, sleigh rides and more in winter.

★ **Thrills and chills:** Stand on a glass viewing platform at 5fingers with 400 meter drops to the stunning valleys below and then hike into the spectacular Dachstein ice caves.

To the west of Bad Ischl are the best known of all the Salzkammergut's 76 lakes—the Wolfgangsee and the Mondsee (*See* is German for "lake"). Not far to the south-east of these lakes lies one of Austria's loveliest spots, Gosau am Dachstein. Here the Gosau lakes are backdropped by a spectacular sight that acts as a landmark for many leagues: the Dachstein peak. Another scenic wonder is the storybook village of Hallstatt, huddled between mountain and lake.

Whether you start out from Salzburg or set up a base in Bad Ischl—the heart of the Lake District—it's best to take in the beauties of the Salzkammergut in perhaps two separate courses: first around the Fuschlsee, Mondsee, the Wolfgangsee, and Bad Ischl; then south-west to Gosau am Dachstein and back to the Hallstätter See.

1 St. Wolfgang. This charming market town is on the steep banks of the Wolfgangsee. Ferries, including an 1873 paddle steamer, cruise the lake, which is ringed by mountains.

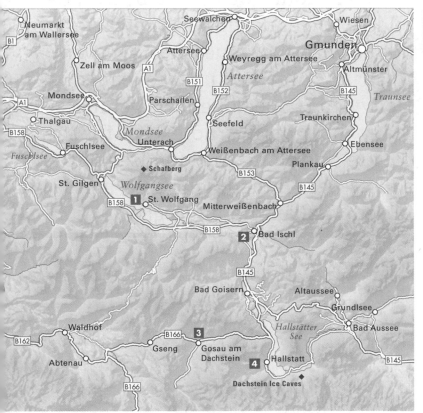

2 Bad Ischl. A spa town with a riverside location has a famous pastry shop and lots of reminders of its most famous visitor, Emperor Franz Joseph. His villa is one of the area's top attractions and the thermal spas are still a draw for Austrians and visitors from around the world.

3 Gosau am Dachstein. One of the most beautiful places in Austria, this cozy alpine village offers the most beautiful valley landscapes, complete with magical lakes, glacier views, hiking trails, and all manner of alpine winter activities. You may want to stay a while to really commit this special beauty to memory.

4 Hallstatt. This village on Lake Hallstatt's western shore is the stuff of Austrian fairytales with its colorful Alpine houses, cobblestone streets, a funicular, and one of the world's oldest salt mines. There are no bad views of this idyllic mountain town but you will have to share it with crowds of tourists (unless you visit in the off season or plan to stay a few days.)

Remember the exquisite opening scenes of *The Sound of Music*? Castles reflected in water, mountains veiled by a scattering of downy clouds, flower-strewn valleys dotted with cool blue lakes: a view of Austria as dreamed up by a team of Hollywood's special-effects geniuses—so many thought. But, no, except for the bicycle ride along the Mondsee, those scenes were filmed right here, in Austria's fabled Salzkammergut region.

The Lake District of Upper Austria, centered on the region called the Salzkammergut (literally, "salt estates"), offers stunning sights: soaring mountains and needlelike peaks; a glittering necklace of turquoise lakes; forested valleys populated by the *Rehe* (roe deer) immortalized by Felix Salten in *Bambi*—this is Austria at its most lush and verdant. Some of these lakes, like the Hallstätter See, remain quite unspoiled, partly because the mountains act as a buffer from busier, more accessible sections of the country. Another—historic—reason relates to the presence of the salt mines, which date back to the Celtic era; with salt so common and cheap nowadays, many forget it was once a luxury item mined under strict government monopoly, and the Salzkammergut was closed to the casually curious for centuries, opening up only after Emperor Franz Josef made Bad Ischl—one of the area's leading spa towns (even then, studded with *salt*water swimming pools)—his official summer residence in 1854.

A favorite passion for Austrians is *das Wandern*, or hiking. The Lake District has many miles of marked trails, including the BergeSeen Trail, which stretches 350 km (217 miles) and connects 35 of the region's lakes. The trail can be explored in stages, most of which end in one of the Salzkammergut's lovely towns. Cycling, popular among locals and visitors, offers an athletic way to see miles of landscape at a doable pace. Within this pastoral perfection you can stay in age-old *Schloss*-hotels or modern villas, dine in fine restaurants, and shop for the linens, ceramics, woodcarvings, and painted glass of the region.

MAJOR REGIONS

St. Wolfgang and Bad Ischl. Between its romantic lakes surrounded by Alpine peaks, this region is perfect for both water sports in summer and skiing in winter. The charming Bad Ischl's old-fashioned buildings document the town's importance in the days of the Hapsburgs.

The mountains forming Austria's backbone may be less majestic than other Alps at this point, but they are also considerably less stern; glittering blue lakes and villages nestle safely in valleys without being constantly under the threatening eye of an avalanche from the huge peaks. Here you'll find what travelers come to the Lake District for: elegant restaurants, Baroque churches, meadows with green space and privacy, lakeside cabanas, and forests that could tell a tale or two.

Gosau and Hallstatt. The sight from atop the Dachstein mountain range gives the impression of being on top of the world. The picturesque towns in this region are full of Austrian folklore and tradition, and have inspired many composers, painters, and poets.

It's hard to imagine anything prettier than this region of the Salzkammergut, which takes you into the very heart of the Lake District. The great highlight is Gosau am Dachstein—a beauty spot that even the least impressionable find hard to forget. But there are other notable sights, including Hallstatt and the Dachstein Ice Caves.

Planning

When to Go

Year-round, vacationers flock to the Lake District, but late fall is not the best time to visit the region. It could be rainy and cold, and many sights are closed or operate on a restricted schedule. By far the best months are July and September. August sees the countryside overrun with families on school holidays and music lovers from the nearby Salzburg Music Festival (even so, who can resist a visit to Bad Ischl on August 18, when Emperor Franz Josef's birthday is still celebrated). Others like to visit Hallstatt for its annual procession across the lake,

held on Corpus Christi day (weather permitting, around the last weekend in May, or the Sunday after)—a Catholic, and therefore, national holiday all over Austria. December finds several small picturesque markets in the villages around the Wolfgangsee and traditional *Adventsingen* concerts in churches throughout the region.

Getting Here and Around

AIR

By air, the Lake District is closer to Salzburg than to Linz. The Salzburg airport is about 53 km (33 miles) from Bad Ischl, heart of the Salzkammergut; the Linz airport (Hörsching) is about 75 km (47 miles).

BUS

BUS INFORMATION ÖBB/Postbus.
☎ *05/1717* ⊕ *www.postbus.at.*

CAR

Driving is by far the easiest and most convenient way to reach the Lake District; traffic is excessive only on weekends (although it can be slow on some narrow lakeside stretches). From Salzburg you can take Route 158 east to Fuschl, St. Gilgen, and Bad Ischl or the A1 autobahn to Mondsee. Coming from Vienna or Linz, the A1 passes through the northern part of the Salzkammergut; get off at the Steyrermühl exit or the Regau exit and head south on Route 144/145 to Gmunden, Bad Ischl, and Bad Goisern. But keep in mind that gasoline is expensive in Austria.

TRAIN

The geography of the area means that rail lines run mainly north–south. Where the trains don't go, buses do, so if you allow enough time you can cover virtually all the area by public transportation. The main bus routes through the region are Bad Ischl to Gosau, Hallstatt, Salzburg, and St. Wolfgang; Mondsee to St. Gilgen and Salzburg; St. Gilgen to Mondsee; Salzburg to Bad Ischl, Mondsee, St. Gilgen, and Strobl.

TRAIN INFORMATION ÖBB—Österreichisches Bundesbahn. ☎ *05/1717* ⊕ *www. oebb.at.*

Hotels

In the grand old days, the aristocratic families of the region would welcome paying guests at their charming castles. Today most of those castles have been, if you will, degentrified: they are now schools or very fine hotels. But you needn't stay in a castle to enjoy the Salzkammergut—there are also luxurious lakeside resorts, small country inns, even guesthouses without private baths. Although our hotel reviews cover the best in every category, note that nearly every village, however small, also has a *Gasthaus* or village inn; the ubiquitous *Hotel-*or *Gasthof zur Post* is usually a solid choice. Many hotels offer half-board, with dinner in addition to buffet breakfast included in the price (although the most expensive hotels will often charge extra for breakfast). The half-board room rate is usually an extra €20–€35 per person. Occasionally, quoted room rates for hotels already include half-board accommodations, though a "discounted" rate is usually offered if you prefer not to take the evening meal. Inquire when booking. *Hotel reviews have been shortened. For more information, visit Fodors.com.*

Restaurants

Culinary shrines are to be found around Mondsee. However, in many of the towns of the Salzkammergut, you'll find country inns with dining rooms but few independent restaurants, other than the occasional simple *Gasthäuser.*

Fresh, local lake fish is on nearly every menu in the area, so take advantage of the bounty. The lakes and streams are home to several types of fish, notably trout, carp, and perch. They are prepared in numerous ways, from plain breaded

(*gebacken*), to smoked and served with *Kren* (horseradish), to fried in butter (*gebraten*). Look for *Reinanke,* a mild whitefish straight from the Hallstättersee. Sometimes at country fairs and weekly markets you will find someone charcoaling fresh trout wrapped in aluminum foil with herbs and butter: it's worth every euro. *Knödel*—bread or potato dumplings sometimes filled with either meat or jam—are a tasty specialty. Desserts are doughy as well, though *Salzburger Nockerl,* a sabayon-based soufflé, consists mainly of sugar, beaten egg whites, and air. And finally, keep an eye out for seasonal specialties: spring is *Spargelzeit* (white asparagus time), in summer restaurants often serve chanterelle mushrooms (*Eierschwammerl*) with pasta, and in October it's time for delicious venison and game during the *Wildwochen* (game weeks). *Restaurant reviews have been shortened. For more information, visit Fodors.com.*

What it Costs in Euros			
$	$$	$$$	$$$$
RESTAURANTS			
under €12	€12–€17	€18–€22	over €22
HOTELS			
under €100	€100–€135	€136–€175	over €175

Tours

Daylong tours of the Salzkammergut, offered by Salzburg Sightseeing Tours and Salzburg Panorama Tours, whisk you all too quickly from Salzburg to St. Gilgen, St. Wolfgang, Fuschl, and Mondsee.

Salzburg Panorama Tours

GUIDED TOURS | Tours through the Salzkammergut depart from Salzburg and include a four-hour tour (departs daily at 2 pm, May–October) or an eight-hour combined tour that includes a visit to the salt mine (departs at 8:45 am, May–October). Private guided tours are also available. Bookings are best made online up to 24 hours prior to departure, but you can also go to the meeting place (Mirabellplatz) at least 15 minutes before the tour starts for last-minute tickets. ⊠ *Schrannengasse 2/2, Salzburg* ☎ *0662/883211* ⊕ *www. panoramatours.com* ✉ *From €50.*

Salzburg Sightseeing Tours

GUIDED TOURS | A four-hour tour of the Salz-kammergut (with stops in St. Gilgen and St. Wolfgang) leaves from Mirabellplatz in Salzburg daily at 1:45 pm, May–October. The price includes a boat trip on Lake Wolfgang. ⊠ *Mirabellplatz 2, Salzburg* ☎ *0662/881616* ⊕ *www.salzburg-sightseeingtours.at* ✉ *Salzkammergut tour €50.*

Visitor Information

Most towns in the Salzkammergut have their own *Tourismusverband* (tourist office), which is listed in the specific towns. The main tourist offices for the provinces and regions are Salzkammergut and Upper Austria. Upper Austria and the Salzkammergut comprise the backbone of the Dachstein range.

VISITOR INFORMATION **Salzkammergut Tourist Information Office.** ⊠ *Salinenplatz 1, Bad Ischl* ☎ *06132/26909* ⊕ *www. salzkammergut.at.* **Upper Austria Tourist Information Center.** ⊠ *Freistädterstrasse 119, Linz* ☎ *0732/221022* ⊕ *www.ober-oesterreich.at.*

St. Wolfgang

19 km (12 miles) southeast of St. Gilgen, 50 km (31 miles) southeast of Salzburg.

The town has everything: swimming and hiking in summer, cross-country skiing in winter, and natural feasts for the eye at every turn. Here you'll find yourself in the Austria of operetta fame. Indeed, St. Wolfgang became known

around the world thanks to the inn called the **Weisses Rössl,** which was built right next to the landing stage in 1878. It featured prominently in a late-19th-century play that achieved fame as an operetta by Ralph Benatzky in 1930. Ironically, the two original playwrights, Gustav Kadelburg and Oskar Blumenthal, had another, now destroyed, Weisses Rössl (along the road from Bad Ischl to Hallstatt) in mind. In the years following World War II, the composers Samuel Barber and Gian Carlo Menotti spent summer vacations here, too.

GETTING HERE AND AROUND

A lovely way to enter the picture-book town of St. Wolfgang is to leave your car at Strobl, at the southern end of the Wolfgangsee, and take one of the steamers that ply the waters of the lake. Strobl itself is a delightful village, but not as fashionable as St. Wolfgang; if you prefer a quiet vacation base, this may be its attraction for you. Between St. Wolfgang and Strobl, the Wolfgangsee retains its old name of "Abersee." The earliest paddleboat on the lake is still in service, a genuine 1873 steamer called the *Kaiser Franz Josef.* Service is regular from May to mid-October, and on the Advent weekends. The view of the town against the dramatic mountain backdrop is one you'll see again and again on posters and postcards. If you decide to drive all the way to town, be prepared for a crowd. Unless your hotel offers parking, you'll have to park on the fringes of town and walk a short distance, as the center is a pedestrian-only zone.

VISITOR INFORMATION
CONTACTS **Wolfgangsee.** ⊠ *Au 140* ☎ *06138/8003* ⊕ *wolfgangsee.salzkammergut.at.*

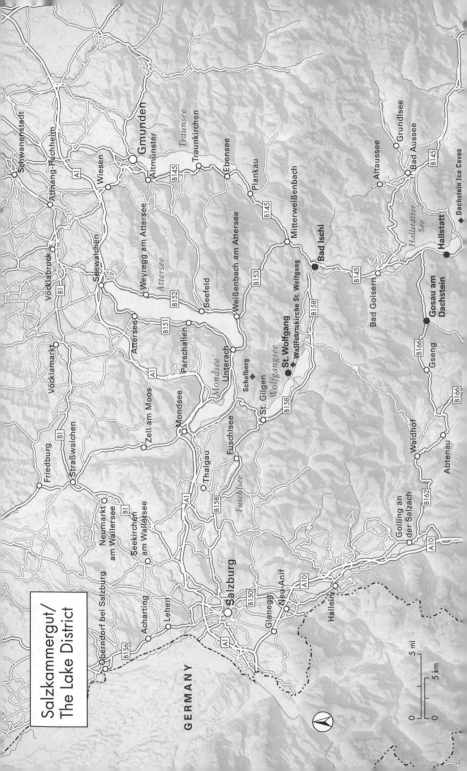

Salzkammergut/ The Lake District

GERMANY

Oberndorf bei Salzburg
B156
Acharting
Lehen
Friedburg
B1
Straßwalchen
Neumarkt am Wallersee
Seekirchen am Wallersee
B1
Zell am Moos
Mondsee
Mondsee
Thalgau
B158
Fuschlsee
Fuschlsee
St. Gilgen
Unterach
Schafberg ◆
Wolfgangsee
St. Wolfgang
Wallfahrtskirche St. Wolfgang ◆
Parschallen
B151
Attersee
Attersee
B152
Seefeld
Weißenbach am Attersee
Weyregg am Attersee
B153
Seewalchen
Schörfling
Wiesen
Vöcklamarkt
Vöcklabruck
B1
Attnang-Puchheim
A1
Schwanenstadt

Salzburg
B150
Glanegg
Neu-Anif
A10
Hallein
Golling an der Salzach
A10
Abtenau
B162
Waldhof
B166
Gseng
B166
Gosau am Dachstein
Bad Goisern
B145
Bad Ischl
B158
Mitterweißenbach
Plankau
Ebensee
Traunkirchen
Traunsee
Gmunden
Altmünster
B145
A1

Bad Aussee
Grundlsee
Altaussee
B145
Hallstatt
Hallstätter See
◆ Dachstein Ice Caves

5 mi
5 km
N

Steam Train to Schafberg

From May to mid-October, the SchafbergBahn cog railway trip from St. Wolfgang to the 5,800-foot peak of the Schafberg offers a great chance to survey the surrounding countryside from what is acclaimed as the "belvedere of the Salzkammergut lakes." The mountain is also a hiker's paradise—take advantage of one-way train tickets for a less strenuous afternoon. Pause for refreshments at one of two inns on the peak. On a clear day you can almost see forever, or at least as far as the Lattengebirge mountain range west of Salzburg. Crowds waiting for trains are likely, so start out early to get a seat by a window for the best view; call the ticket office to reserve a spot at your preferred departure time. ☎ 06138 /22320 ⊕ www. schafbergbahn.at

◉ Sights

Wallfahrtskirche St. Wolfgang (*Pilgrimage Church*)

RELIGIOUS SITE | You shouldn't miss seeing Michael Pacher's great altarpiece in the 15th-century Wallfahrtskirche, one of the finest examples of late-Gothic woodcarving to be found anywhere. This 36-foot masterpiece took 10 years (1471–81) to complete. The paintings and carvings on this winged altar were used as an *Armenbibel* (a Bible for the poor)—illustrations for those who couldn't read or write. You're in luck if you're at the church on a sunny day, when sunlight off the nearby lake dances on the ceiling in brilliant reflections through the stained-glass windows. Visit the Wolfgangsee Tourist Office website for a list of frequent concerts in the sanctuary and *Pfarramt* (rectory). ⊠ *Markt.*

🍽 Restaurants

Zum Weissen Hirschen

$$$ | **AUSTRIAN** | This roomy and friendly Austrian restaurant is wood-paneled and bright but if the weather allows, sit outside on their shady lakeside terrace to soak in the excellent views. Highlights from the menu include the *Hausruck* beef tartare, local fish soup, and for dessert, the delightful *Kaiserschmarrn* (a lightly sweetened pancake). **Known for:** local specialties; lakeside terrace; Kaiserschmarrn (a lightly sweetened pancake). $ *Average main: €21* ⊠ *Markt 73* ☎ *6138/2238* ⊕ *www.weisserhirsch.at.*

🛏 Hotels

Cortisen am See

$$$ | **B&B/INN** | A large chalet-style structure with a glowing yellow facade, "At the Court" has become one of St. Wolfgang's most stylish and comfortable hotels. **Pros:** in the center of the village; has a sauna and spa; unique atmosphere. **Cons:** front rooms face busy street; not family-friendly; no air-conditioning. $ *Rooms from: €150* ⊠ *Pilger Strasse 15* ☎ *06138/2376* ⊕ *www.cortisen.at* ⇱ *32 rooms* ⦿ *Free breakfast.*

Gasthof Zimmerbräu

$ | **B&B/INN** | This pleasant, rustic, and central Gasthof began four centuries ago as a brewery and opened its doors to guests in 1895, and though it's not directly on the lake, it does maintain its own bathing cabana on the shore. **Pros:** all rooms have balconies; wonderful staff; excellent breakfast. **Cons:** not on the lake; noisy until evening; Wi-Fi can be spotty. $ *Rooms from: €90* ⊠ *Markt 89* ☎ *06138/2204* ⊕ *www.zimmerbraeu.com* ⊗ *Closed Jan.– Mar.* ⇱ *27 rooms* ⦿ *Free breakfast.*

Landhaus zu Appesbach
$$$$ | **HOTEL** | Secluded, quiet, and offering excellent service, this old ivy-covered manor hotel is tucked away from the hubbub of the village and offers sailboats and rowboats to enjoy the direct lake access. **Pros:** peaceful atmosphere; quiet location; excellent service. **Cons:** need a car to get around; some rooms are more modern than others; 20-minute walk to the town center. [$] *Rooms from: €210* ✉ *Au 18* ☎ *06138/2209* 🌐 *www.appesbach.com* 🕒 *Closed Nov. and Jan.–Easter* 🛏 *20 rooms* 🍴 *Free breakfast.*

Weisses Rössl
$$$$ | **HOTEL** | Family-owned since the 1800s, the "White Horse" guest rooms and apartments, in nine connected houses, are full of the country charm, flowered fabrics, and quaint furniture brought to the big screen in the movie version of the idyllic Austrian operetta of the same name. **Pros:** notable restaurant; excellent location; wonderful spa and pools. **Cons:** very touristy; noisy location; some rooms are dated. [$] *Rooms from: €235* ✉ *Markt 74* ☎ *06138/2306* 🌐 *www.weissesroessl.at* 🕒 *Closed early Mar.–early Apr.* 🛏 *91 rooms* 🍴 *Free breakfast.*

Performing Arts

Free brass-band concerts are held on the Marktplatz in St. Wolfgang every Saturday evening at 8:30 in May, and on both Wednesday and Saturday at 8:30 pm from June to September. Folk events are usually well publicized with posters (if you're lucky, Benatzky's operetta *Im Weissen Rössl* might be on the schedule). The Wallfahrtskirche also hosts regular concerts, putting its two wonderful organs on proud display. Not far from St. Wolfgang, the town of Strobl holds a Day of Popular Music and Tradition in early July—"popular" meaning brass band, and "tradition" being *Tracht,* the local costume. Check with the regional tourist office for details. Advent is the region's largest event with traditional Christmas markets, nativity scenes, and plenty of special concerts.

Bad Ischl

56 km (35 miles) southeast of Salzburg, 16 km (10 miles) southeast of St. Wolfgang.

Many travelers used to think of Bad Ischl primarily as the town where Zauner's pastry shop is located, to which connoisseurs drove miles for the sake of a cup of coffee and a slice of *Guglhupf,* a lemon sponge cake studded with raisins and nuts. Pastry continues to be the best-known drawing card of a community that symbolizes, more than any other place except Vienna itself, the Old Austria of resplendent uniforms, balls, waltzes, and operettas.

Although the center is built up, the town is charmingly laid out on a peninsula between the Rivers Traun and Ischl. Bad Ischl was the place where Emperor Franz Josef chose to establish his summer court, and it was here that he met and fell in love with his future empress, the troubled Sisi, though his mother had intended him for Sisi's elder sister. Today you can enjoy the same sort of pastries *mit Schlag* (whipped cream) that the emperor loved. Afterward, you can hasten off to the town's modern spa, one of the best known in Austria.

You'll want to stroll along the shaded **Esplanade,** where the pampered and privileged of the 19th century loved to take their constitutionals, usually after a quick stop at the **Trinkhalle,** a spa pavilion in high 19th-century Austrian style, still in the middle of town on Ferdinand-Auböck-Platz.

GETTING HERE AND AROUND

Bad Ischl is accessed easily via various routes. From St. Wolfgang, backtrack south to Strobl and head eastward on Route 158. To get to the town directly from Salzburg, take the A1 to Mondsee, then Routes 151 and 158 along the Wolfgangsee and the Mondsee. There are many buses that depart hourly from Salzburg's main train station; you can also travel by train via the junction of Attnang-Puchheim or Stainach-Irdning (several transfers are required)—a longer journey than the bus ride, which is usually 90 minutes. There are also many regular bus and train connections between Gmunden and Bad Ischl.

VISITOR INFORMATION

CONTACTS Bad Ischl. ✉ *Auböckplatz 5* ☎ *06132/27757* ⊕ *badischl.salzkammergut.at.*

Sights

Kaiservilla

HOUSE | In Bad Ischl the quickest way to travel back in time to the gilded 1880s is to head for the mammoth Kaiservilla, the imperial-yellow (signifying wealth and power) residence, which looks rather like a miniature Schönbrunn: its ground plan forms an "E" to honor the empress Elisabeth. Archduke Markus Salvator von Habsburg-Lothringen, great-grandson of Franz Josef, still lives here, but you can tour parts of the building to see the ornate reception rooms and the surprisingly modest residential quarters (through which sometimes even the archduke guides visitors with what can only be described as a very courtly kind of humor). It was at this villa that the emperor signed the declaration of war against Serbia, which officially marked the start of World War I. The villa is filled with Hapsburg and family mementos, none more moving than the cushion, on display in the chapel, on which the head of Empress Elisabeth rested after she was stabbed by an Italian assassin in 1898. ✉ *Kaiserpark* ☎ *06132/23241* ⊕ *www.kaiservilla.at* 💰 *€15.40; grounds only €5.20* ⊗ *Closed Nov., Thurs.–Tues. in Jan.–Mar., and weekdays in Dec.*

Museum der Stadt Bad Ischl

MUSEUM | Fascinating is the only word to describe this museum, which occupies the circa 1880 Hotel Austria—the favored summer address for Archduke Franz Karl and his wife Sophie (from 1834 on). More momentously, the young Franz Josef got engaged to his beloved Elisabeth here in 1853. After taking in the gardens (with their Brahms monument), explore the various exhibits, which deal with the region's salt, royal, and folk histories. Note the display of national folk costumes, which the emperor wore while hunting. From December until the beginning of February, the museum shows off its famous *Kalss Krippe,* an enormous mechanical Christmas crèche. Dating from 1838, it has about 300 figures. The townsfolk of Ischl, in fact, are famous for their Christmas "cribs," and you can see many of them in tours of private houses opened for visits on select dates in January. ✉ *Esplanade 10* ☎ *06132/25476* ⊕ *www.stadtmuseum.at* 💰 *€5.50; special exhibits, €3.10; combined ticket to the museum and Lehár Villa, €9.50* ⊗ *Closed Mon., Tues., Nov., and Mon.–Thurs. in Jan.–Mar.*

Photo Museum (Marmorschlössl Bad Ischl)

MUSEUM | Don't overlook the small but elegant "marble palace" built near the Kaiservilla for Empress Elisabeth, who used it as a teahouse; this now houses a photography museum. The permanent collection offers an interesting overview of the history of analog photography, with a nice tribute to the empress. The marriage between Franz Josef and Elisabeth was not an especially happy one; a number of houses bearing women's names in Bad Ischl are said to have been quietly given by the emperor to his various lady friends (Villa Schratt was given to Katharina Schratt, the emperor's nearly official mistress). You'll first need to purchase a ticket to the museum or park to visit. ✉ *Kaiserpark* ☎ *06132/24422* ⊕ *www.ooelkg.at* 🖼 *Museum and Kaiserpark €7.20* ⊘ *Closed Nov.–Apr.*

Stadtpfarrkirche St. Nikolaus

RELIGIOUS SITE | In the center of town, St. Nikolaus Parish Church graces Ferdinand-Auböck-Platz. It dates back to the Middle Ages, but was enlarged to its present size during Maria Theresa's time in the 1750s. The decoration inside is in the typically gloomy style of Franz Josef's era (note the emperor's family portrayed to the left above the high altar). Anton Bruckner used to play on the old church organ. ✉ *Kirchengasse 2.*

Villa Lehár

HOUSE | A steady stream of composers followed the aristocracy and the court to Bad Ischl. Anton Bruckner, Johannes Brahms (who composed his famous *Lullaby* here as well as many of his late works), Johann Strauss the Younger, Carl Michael Ziehrer, Oscar Straus, and Anton Webern all spent summers here, but it was the Hungarian-born Franz Lehár, composer of *The Merry Widow,* who left the most lasting musical impression, the Lehár Festival. Named in his honor, it is Bad Ischl's summer operetta festival, which always includes at least one Lehár work. With the royalties he received from his operettas, he was able to settle into the sumptuous Villa Lehár, where he lived from 1912 until his death in 1948. Now a museum, it contains a number of the composer's fin-de-siècle period salons, which can be viewed only on guided tours. ✉ *Lehárkai 8* ☎ *06132/26992* ⊕ *www.stadtmuseum.at/ hg_leharvilla.php* 🖼 *€5.80; combined ticket to Villa and Bad Ischl Museum €9.50* ⊘ *Closed Mon., Tues., and Oct.–Apr.*

 Restaurants

★ Café Zauner

$ | **CAFÉ** | If you haven't been to Zauner, you've missed a true highlight of Bad Ischl. The desserts—particularly the house creation, *Zaunerstollen,* a chocolate-covered confection of sugar, hazelnuts, and nougat—have made this one of Austria's best-known pastry shops. **Known for:** fabulous cakes; gorgeous space; royal history. 🟤 *Average main: €6* ✉ *Pfarrgasse 7* ☎ *06132/23310–20* ⊕ *www.zauner.at.*

Grand-Café & Restaurant Zauner

$$$ | **AUSTRIAN** | If you enjoyed a cake at the acclaimed Café Zauner, you may want to visit their second location for something heartier. The Zauner restaurant specializes in Austrian classics and wine, including beef and dumplings and Styrian chicken salad. **Known for:** riverside seating; friendly service; special Würstel. 🟤 *Average main: €18* ✉ *Hasnerallee 2* ☎ *6132/23722* ⊕ *www.zauner.at.*

🛏 Hotels

Goldener Ochs

$ | **HOTEL** | The "Golden Ox" is in a superb location in the town center, with the sparkling River Traun a few steps away. **Pros:** great value; close to the major sights; lovely private wellness spa. **Cons:** traffic noise in front rooms; no a/c; need to book ahead for popular times. 🟤 *Rooms from: €81* ✉ *Grazerstrasse 4* ☎ *06132/23529* ⊕ *www.goldenerochs.at* ⮌ *62 rooms* ⦿ *All meals.*

Performing Arts

The main musical events of the year in the Salzkammergut are the July and August operetta festivals held in Bad Ischl.

Landscape as Muse

For nearly two centuries the Salzkammergut Lake District has been a wellspring of inspiration to great artists and composers. Richard Strauss, Gustav Klimt, and Franz Lehár are just a few of the greats who ventured here to holiday and, as souvenirs of their trips, left behind immortal symphonies and paintings.

It was in the 19th century that the region was discovered. French philosopher Jean Jacques Rousseau's "back to nature" theories and the Romantic movement of the 19th century made tourism fashionable. And the Salzkammergut was opened for the first time to visitors (previously, the "salt-mine" region was a private preserve of the Hapsburgs).

Following the example of Emperor Franz Josef and other royals, painters and poets soon began flocking to this region to enjoy the "simple life." The region's spas also attracted aristos by the boatload. Archduke Rudolf—brother of the emperor and pupil of Beethoven (for whom the composer wrote his *Missa solemnis*)—was the first Hapsburg to enjoy the cure in Bad Ischl. The sensitive souls of the composers of the Romantic era were highly attracted by the beauty of the landscape. Little wonder that listeners can hear its reflection in the music written here: listen to the scherzo movement of Gustav Mahler's Third Symphony and you'll know where its cuckoo theme and wistful post horn come from. Then when the Salzburg Music Festival hit its stride in the 1930s, many of the great artists involved—Hugo von Hofmannsthal and Richard Strauss among them—liked to escape to summerhouses in the hills after performing in town. Today, you can follow in Johannes Brahms's footsteps and walk over a meadow on a sunny day or through a silent forest, or climb a mountain to renew mind and spirit.

Kongress- und Theaterhaus

MUSIC | A number of events grace the imperial interiors of the Kongress- und Theaterhaus each season. Musical performances are held throughout the year, including Advent concerts. The biggest draw is the summer Lehár Festival. Operetta and classic musical theater lovers flock to Bad Ischl during July and August for favorite standards like *The Merry Widow* and *My Fair Lady.* Tickets are sold online, at local tourist offices, and on-site. Pre-sales for the upcoming season begin in October. ✉ *Kurhausstrasse 8* ☎ *06132/23420* ⊕ *www.leharfestival.at* 🎫 *Tickets from €26–€83.*

Gosau am Dachstein

67 km (42 miles) southeast of Salzburg, 10 km (6 miles) northwest of the Hallstättersee.

Lovers of scenic beauty should not leave the Hallstatt region without taking in Gosau am Dachstein, considered the most beautiful spot in Austria by 19th-century travelers but often unaccountably overlooked today.

Instead of driving around the area, it's worthwhile to take a serious walk (about 2½ hours, depending on your speed), departing from the tourist information office not far from the crossroads known as the Gosaumühle. Passing by churches, the road follows the valley over the meadows. From Gosauschmied Café on, it's a romantic way through the forest to the first Gosau lake, the Vorderer Gosausee (Front Gosau Lake), which is the crown jewel, some 8 km (5 miles) to the south of the village itself. Beyond a sparkling, almost fjordlike basin of water rises the amazing Dachstein massif, majestically reflected in the lake's mirrorlike surface. Aside from a restaurant and a gamekeeper's hut, the lake is undefiled by man-made structures. At the right hour—well before 2:30 pm, when due to the steepness of the mountain slopes, the sun is already withdrawing—the view is superb. Then you may choose to endure the stiff walk to the other two lakes set behind the first and not as spectacularly located (in fact, the third is used by an electric power station and therefore not always full of water, yet it remains the closest place from which to view the glittering Dachstein glacier). Hiking to the latter two lakes will take about two hours. You can also take a cable car up to the Gablonzer Hütte on the Zwieselalm (you might consider skiing on the Gosau glacier); or tackle the three-hour hike up to the summit of the Grosser Donnerkogel.

At day's end, head back for Gosau village, settle in at one of the many Gasthöfe (reserve ahead) overhung with wild gooseberry and rosebushes (or stay at one of Gosau's charming *Privatzimmer* accommodations). Cap the day off with a dinner of fried *Schwarzrenterl*, a delicious regional lake fish. To get to Gosau, travel north or south on Route 145, turning off at the junction with Route 166, and travel 36 km (20 miles) east through the ravine of the Gosaubach River.

GETTING HERE AND AROUND

This lovely spot is 10 km (6 miles) west of the Hallstätter See, just before the Gschütt Pass: you travel either by bus (eight daily from Bad Ischl to Gosau) or car. The village makes a good lunch stop, and, with its many Gasthöfe and pensions, could be a base for your excursions.

VISITOR INFORMATION

CONTACTS Gosau am Dachstein. ✉ *Gosauseestrasse 5* ☎ *5/95095* 🌐 *dachstein.salzkammergut.at.*

🍴 Restaurants

Kirchenwirt

$$$ | AUSTRIAN | Adjacent to Gosau's pretty parish church, this inn is evidence of the venerable tradition of placing town restaurants next to houses of worship (on Sunday farmers would attend the service then head for the nearest table and discuss the past week's events). Today, the restaurant is a popular place, with local specialties and lovely views from the terrace. **Known for:** large portions of regional cusine; beautiful mountain views; friendly hosts. [$] *Average main: €21* ✉ *Wirtsweg 18* ☎ *06136/8196* 🌐 *www.kirchenwirt-peham.at.*

🛏 Hotels

Hotel Koller

$$$$ | HOTEL | One of the most charming hotels in Gosau, the peaked gables and weather vanes of this 1850s-era villa give a fairy-tale aura when seen from its pretty park. **Pros:** cheerful interiors; pretty views; friendly staff. **Cons:** no elevator; rooms vary in size; bathrooms are a little outdated. [$] *Rooms from: €200* ✉ *Pass-Gschütt-Strasse 353* ☎ *06136/8841* 🌐 *www.hotel-koller.com* 🕒 *Closed Nov. and 1 month around Easter (dates vary)* 🛏 *22 rooms* 🍽 *Free breakfast.*

Hallstatt

89 km (55 miles) southeast of Salzburg, 19 km (12 miles) south of Bad Ischl.

As if rising from Swan Lake itself, the town of Hallstatt is the subject of thousands of travel posters. "The world's prettiest lakeside village" perches precariously on what seems the smallest of toeholds, one that nevertheless prevents

Take a guided tour of the Dachstein Ice Cave and learn how its frozen waterfalls and magnificent ice formations were created as you head deeper into the icy landscape.

it from tumbling into the dark waters of the Hallstättersee. Down from the steep mountainside above it comes the Mühlbach waterfall, a sight that can keep you riveted for hours. Today, the town is a magnet for tourists, and accordingly a bit too modernized, especially considering that Hallstatt is believed to be the oldest community in Austria. More than 1,000 graves of prehistoric men have been found here, and it has been such an important source of relics of the Celtic period that this age is known as the Hallstatt epoch.

GETTING HERE AND AROUND

Arriving in Hallstatt is a scenic spectacle if you come by train, with the entire village arrayed on the other side of the lake; from the train station, a boat, the *Stefanie,* takes you across the Hallstättersee to the town, leaving every hour. You can take the train from Bad Ischl or via the Stainach-Irdning junction. To get to Hallstatt from Bad Ischl by car, head south on Route 145 to Bad Goisern (which also has curative mineral springs,

but never achieved the cachet of Bad Ischl). Just south of town, watch for signs for the turnoff to the Hallstättersee. Since the lake is squeezed in between two sharply rising mountain ranges, the road parallels the shore, with spectacular views. From Bad Ischl, you can also take a half-hour bus ride to Hallstatt.

VISITOR INFORMATION
CONTACTS Hallstatt. ⊠ *Seestrasse 99* ☎ *5/95095–30* ⊕ *www.hallstatt.net.*

 Sights

Archaeological Excavation
ARCHAEOLOGICAL SITE | A unexpected peek into the Celtic past is offered at the DachsteinSport Janu shop. A decade ago, its intention to put a new heating system in the cellar unexpectedly turned into a historical excavation when workmen found the remains of a Celtic dwelling, now on view to visitors. ⊠ *Seestrasse 50* ☎ *06134/8298* ⊕ *www. dachsteinsport.at/ausgrabungen/ueber- blick.php* ⊠ *Free* ☉ *Closed Sun.*

Hallstatt's 16th-century Alpine houses and alleyways are home to charming cafes and shops.

★ Dachstein Ice Caves

CAVE | This is one of the most impressive sights of the eastern Alps—vast ice caverns, many of which are hundreds of years old and aglitter with ice stalactites and stalagmites, illuminated by an eerie light. The most famous sights are the **Rieseneishöhle** (Giant Ice Cave) and the **Mammuthöhle** (Mammoth Cave), but there are other caves and assorted frozen waterfalls in the area. The cave entrance is at about 6,500 feet, accessed via cable car and a hike (or you can hike all the way), but still well below the 9,750-foot Dachstein peak farther south. If you visit in August, you can enjoy the Friday Ice Sounds concert series under the Parsifal Dome of the Dachstein cave. Tickets for these special shows include a cave tour and buffet dinner at the Erlebnisrestaurant Schönbergalm. ■ **TIP→ Be sure to wear warm, weatherproof clothing and good shoes; inside the caves it is very cold, and outside the slopes can be swept by chilling winds. Start before 2 pm to see both caves.** ✉ *34 Winkl* ✥ *From Hallstatt, take the scenic road around the bottom of the lake to Obertraun; then follow the signs to the cable car (Dachsteinseilbahn). From the cable-car landing, a 15-minute hike up takes you to the entrance (follow signs "Dachsteineishöhle")* ☎ *05/0140* ⊕ *www.dachstein-salzkammergut.com/ en/* ✉ *Giant Ice and Mammoth Cave €37.50 each; combined ticket €44.00; cable car €33 round-trip; Ice Sounds concert €75* ⊘ *Closed Nov.–Apr.*

5fingers

VIEWPOINT | **FAMILY** | This unique, hand-shaped observation platform features 5 "fingers" stretching out 400 meters above the spectacular views of Lake Hallstatt, Hallstatt, and the Inner Salzkammergut below. One of the platforms is made entirely from glass (not for the fain hearted) and another enables visitors to gain their own personal view of the Hallstatt World Heritage site through a large picture frame. The walk to 5fingers can be easily completed in about 20 minutes from the Dachstein Krippenstein cable car. ✉ *Obertraun* ⊕ *dachstein.salzkammergut.at* ✉ *Free* Ⓜ *Dachstein Krippenstein cable car.*

Michaelerkirche (*St. Michael's*)
RELIGIOUS SITE | The Hallstatt market square, now a pedestrian area, is bordered by colorful 16th-century houses and this 16th-century Gothic church, which is picturesquely situated near the lake. Within, you'll find a beautiful winged altar, which opens to reveal nine 15th-century paintings. The *Karner* (charnel house) beside the church is a rather morbid but regularly visited spot. Because there was little space to bury the dead over the centuries in Hallstatt, the custom developed of digging up the bodies after 12 or 15 years, piling the bones in the sun, and painting the skulls. Ivy and oak-leaf wreaths were used for the men, alpine flowers for the women, and names, dates, and often the cause of death were inscribed. The myriad bones and skulls are now on view in the charnel house, also known as the "*Beinhaus*" (bone house), which has a stunning setting overlooking the lake. Each year at the end of May the summer season kicks off with the Fronleichnahm (Corpus Christi) procession, which concludes with hundreds of boats out on the lake. ✉ *Kirchenweg 40.*

Museum Hallstatt
MUSEUM | **FAMILY** | Go back 7,000 years and discover the orgins of Hallstatt and its salt mines at this museum. The exhibits include holographic representations, video animations, and a 3-D journey through time. ✉ *Seestrasse 56* ☎ *06134/8280* 🌐 *www.museum-hallstatt.at* 🎫 *€10* 🕑 *Closed Mon. and Tues. in Nov.–Mar.*

Salzwelten
MINE | Salt has been mined in this area for at least 4,500 years, and the Hallstatt mines of the Salzberg Mountain are the oldest in the world. These "show mines" are in the Salzbergtal valley, accessed either by paths from the village cemetery or, much more conveniently, via a funicular railway that leaves from the southern end of the village. From the railway a 10-minute walk takes you to a small-scale miner's train (tall people, beware), which heads deep into the mountain. Inside, you can famously slide down the wooden chutes once used by the miners all the way down to an artificial subterranean lake, once used to dissolve the rock salt. At the entrance to the mines you'll find an Iron Age cemetery and a restaurant. ■ **TIP→ Buy a "Salzerlebnis" (Salt Adventure) combination ticket from the ÖBB (Austrian Railway) that offers an all-inclusive value fare for travel to and from Hallstatt as well as the salt mine tour.** ✉ *Salzbergstrasse 21* ☎ *06132/200–2400* 🌐 *www.salzwelten.at* 🎫 *Funicular €10 one way, €18 round-trip; mine and tour €24; combination ticket for cable car and salt mines €34* 🕑 *Closed Jan.* ☞ *No children under 4 yrs.*

Schifffahrt Boat Trips
TRANSPORTATION SITE (AIRPORT/BUS/FERRY/TRAIN) | The same company that ferries train passengers across the lake to Hallstatt also runs three other vessels offering summer boat tours around the lake via Obertraun to the south (50 minutes) or Obersee to the north (80 minutes). You can also link boat trips with hiking along the shore between pick-up points. ✉ *Am Hof 126* ☎ *06134/8228* 🌐 *www.hallstattschifffahrt.at* 🎫 *South lake trip: €8 one way, €12 round-trip; North lake trip: €8–€9 one way, €15 round-trip; full-day unlimited-ride pass, €22; bikes, €5* 🕑 *No south trip early Oct.–May; no north trip early Oct.–mid-July.*

🍴 Restaurants

Bräugasthof
$$$$ | **AUSTRIAN** | In a city famed for tourist crowds, most restaurants are hit or miss, but the Bräugasthof, with its delicious fish dishes and gorgeous lake views, is definitely a hit. Flavors from Austria, Slovakia, and Hungary infuse the regional menu. **Known for:** terrace on the lake; fresh trout; delicious soups. [$] *Average main: €25* ✉ *Seestrasse 120* ☎ *06134/20673* 🌐 *www.brauhaus-lobisser.com* 💳 *No credit cards.*

Hotels

Bräugasthof

$$ | **B&B/INN** | With an idyllic lakeside perch, this former 16th-century brewery (*bräugasthof*) offers distinctive charm. **Pros:** cozy rooms; lakefront setting; fabulous views from balcony rooms. **Cons:** noisy during the day; room furnishings are a bit old; historical building so it's a little creaky. $ *Rooms from: €135* ✉ *Seestrasse 120* ☎ *06134/8221* ⊕ *www.brauhaus-lobisser.com* ➽ *8 rooms* ⊙ *Free breakfast.*

Grüner Baum

$$$$ | **HOTEL** | Glowing with a daffodil-yellow facade, sitting directly on the shore of the lake, and at the foot of a picture-perfect square, this traditional inn is one of Hallstatt's most memorable accommodations. **Pros:** great location on the lake; pretty views; lovely sauna. **Cons:** breakfast can be chaotic; parking is outside town; popular with groups. $ *Rooms from: €220* ✉ *Marktplatz 104* ☎ *06134/8263-0* ⊕ *www.gruenerbaum.cc* ➽ *20 rooms* ⊙ *Free breakfast.*

Activities

ADVENTURE SPORTS
Outdoor Leadership

CANOEING/ROWING/SKULLING | If you're ready for a true Alpine adventure, just name your fear factor—from family-friendly to daredevil—and Heli and Anja Putz's company has you covered, with a full team of skilled outdoor guides ready to take you kayaking, canyoning, climbing, rafting, paragliding, or skiing throughout the Salzkammergut. These experts know the mountains and caves like they're walking through their own backyards, and they personally created many of the half- and full-day routes that they offer. All necessary equipment is meticulously maintained and available for rent. Call or email 3–4 days in advance to arrange your tour. ✉ *Steinach 4, Bad Goisern* ☎ *6135/6058* ⊕ *www.outdoor-leadership.com.*

BOATING
Sport Zopf

BOATING | This company organizes two-hour rafting tours on the Hallstättersee, traveling from Steeg to Lauffen. No prior experience is required, and Zopf supplies all the equipment. Trips take place on Wednesday and Saturday afternoons from May to September, and must be prebooked by telephone. Private trips can be arranged for groups of six or more. ✉ *Obere Marktstrasse 6, Bad Goisern* ☎ *0664/360670* ⊕ *www.zopf.co.at* ☞ *€50.*

HIKING

There are many great hiking paths around Hallstatt; contact the local tourist office for information about the path along the Echerntal to Waldbachstrub past pleasant waterfalls, or the climb to the Tiergartenhütte, continuing on to the Wiesberghaus and, two hours beyond, the Simony-Hütte, spectacularly poised at the foot of the Dachstein glacier. From here, mountain climbers begin the ascent of the Hoher Dachstein, the tallest peak of the Dachstein massif.

Chapter 12

CARINTHIA AND GRAZ

12

Updated by
Jacy Meyer

 Sights
★★★★☆

 Restaurants
★★★★☆

 Hotels
★★★☆☆

 Shopping
★☆☆☆☆

 Nightlife
★★☆☆☆

WELCOME TO CARINTHIA AND GRAZ

TOP REASONS TO GO

★ **The Wörthersee:** In spring, pleasure-seekers check into mansions-turned-hotels, boat on the crystalline lake, and party until the wee hours.

★ **Burg Hochosterwitz:** Walt Disney drew the inspiration for Snow White from this magnificent castle on top of a mountain.

★ **Gurk Cathedral:** Supported by 100 marble pillars, the most splendid of all the region's Romanesque churches features the original chair of St. Hemma.

★ **Graz:** A UNESCO City of Design, this fresh, young, creative city offers an all-year-round cultural program with events for all tastes.

★ **Museum in a Palace:** Actually, there are four museums—plus the gorgeous Prunkräume (state rooms) in Graz's Schloss Eggenberg, itself a museum piece that sheds light on Austria's past.

★ **Rogner Bad Blumau:** This natural-spring-water resort, a two-hour train ride northeast of Graz, was designed by artist Friedensreich Hundertwasser.

Carinthia is protected in the northwest by the vast Hohe Tauern range and the impossibly high and mighty Grossglockner. Along its northern borders are the bulky Nockberge National Park and the massive crests of the Noric mountain range, and to the east are the grassy meadows on the slopes of the Saualpe and Koralpe. Completing the circle in the south and bordering Slovenia and Italy are the steep, craggy Karawanken Mountains and Carnic Alps. Lying serenely in the valleys between these rocky mountains are the long, meandering Drau and Gail rivers and more than 100 lakes, including the best known and largest, the Wörthersee, as well as the Ossiacher See and Faaker See.

1 Klagenfurt. This laidback little city is ideally located on Lake Wörthersee, one of Europe's largest and warmest Alpine lakes which becomes one of Austria's largest skating rinks in winter. Klagenfurt is a perfect base for exploring the Carinthian outdoors.

2 Hochosterwitz. An impressive castle (considered one of Austria's most impressive medieval castles) and a massive hike; Hochosterwitz wows in more ways than one.

3 Gurk. A pilgrimage destination, Gurk's cathedral is a Romanesque dream set in beautiful surroundings.

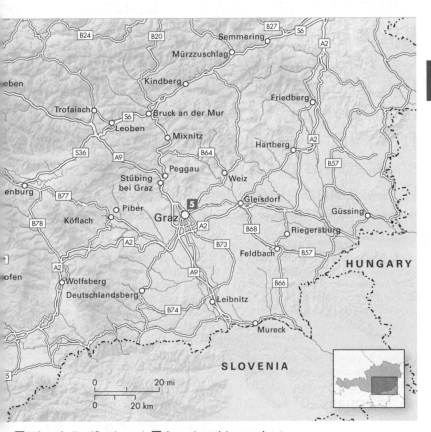

4 Friesach. Fortifications consisting of a town wall and water-filled moat, castle buildings, churches, monasteries and many small monuments of art make Friesach one of Carinthia's most atmospheric towns.

5 Graz. Austria's second-largest city by population often plays second-best to Vienna and Salzburg, but Austrian's know this historic city is a vibrant destination that doesn't need to brag about its two distinct titles: UNESCO World Heritage site and UNESCO City of Design.

While lesser-known than the mountainous terrain of Tyrol or the culture-rich cities of Vienna and Salzburg, the southern provinces of Carinthia and Styria with its capital Graz—located directly above Italy and Slovenia and 2½ hours by train from Vienna—beckon visitors with spectacular mountain ranges, abundant forests, and glass-clear lakes.

Art lovers gravitate to such architectural landmarks as the Romanesque Gurk Cathedral, a host of Baroque town halls, and the medieval fantasy of the 9th-century castle Hochosterwitz. The provinces' summer season is custom tailored for bicycling, fishing, hiking, and water sports.

The area has a rich history and a distinguished musical past, and the sophistication and beauty of Graz may surprise you.

MAJOR REGIONS

Carinthia. On the eastern end of Wörthersee, the region's biggest lake, the Carinthian capital Klagenfurt prides itself on its charming city center and mellow lifestyle. The unspoiled Gurktal region attracts both hikers and art lovers. Blessed with verdant forests and Romanesque architecture, the northeastern corner of Carinthia enchants visitors with its pristine landscape.

Heading north from Klagenfurt you enter genuine, rural, Austrian countryside.

Small villages, farms, wide pastures, and forests unfold while driving over smooth hills. Burg Hochosterwitz, perched on a steep hill, can be seen from far away. A popular place of pilgrimage is Gurk Cathedral, a Romanesque basilica from the 12th century and an important building full of European religious art. Friesach, a medieval town, and one of the oldest in Carinthia, is another highlight on this route.

Graz. Austria's second-largest city headlines as one of Europe's best preserved Renaissance town centers, dating to an era when Graz, not Vienna, was the capital. Italian architects, in fact, came to Graz to gain design experience and shaped the city with their exquisite building skills. Located in the Grazer basin and crossed by the Mur River, Graz has now turned into a lively meeting point for art and culture. The surrounding countryside boasts vineyards, thermal spas, and mountains.

Planning

When to Go

Because of the bulwark of mountains that protect it from the cold winds of the north, the Carinthian and Styrian climate is milder than that of the rest of Austria, and it also boasts more sunshine. Consequently, the lakes maintain an average summer temperature of between 75°F and 82°F.

To see the province in its best festive dress of blue and emerald lakes framed by wooded hills and rocky peaks, and also do some swimming, come between mid-May and early October. Early spring, when the colors are purest and the crowds not yet in evidence, and fall, are perhaps the best times for quiet sightseeing. Christmas in Graz and Klagenfurt is a visual spectacle, with whole sections of the cities turned into a Christmas market. Winter in the area is an enigma: the Semmering Mountains mark the eastern tail end of the Alps—north of the divide can be overcast and dreary while the area to the south basks in sunshine.

Getting Here and Around

AIR

Klagenfurt airport (KLU), just northeast of Klagenfurt, is served by Austrian Airlines and Eurowings. Several flights daily connect the provincial capital with Vienna and Köln/Bonn, Germany. In summer, charter flights will take you from here to several popular Mediterranean tourist destinations.

The northern part of eastern Austria is served by Vienna's international airport at Schwechat, 19 km (12 miles) southeast of the city center.

Graz has its own international airport at Feldkirchen, just south of the city, with flights to and from many major European cities, like Amsterdam, Zurich, and Berlin. Austrian Airlines and Lufthansa are the most ubiquitous carriers there.

AIRPORT INFORMATION Graz Airport. (*GRZ*) ☎ *0316/2902172* ⊕ *www. flughafen-graz.at.*

CAR

If you are driving, the most direct route from Vienna is via the Semmering mountain pass through Styria to Graz and on to Klagenfurt. Or take the heavily traveled A2 from Vienna to Graz and farther south. From Salzburg, the A10 autobahn tunnels beneath the Tauern range and the Katschberghöhe to make a dramatic entry into Carinthia, although the parallel Route 99, which runs "over the top," is the more scenic route. A pretty alternative here that leads you straight into the Nock Mountains or Gurk Valley is to leave the A10 at St. Michael after the Tauern Tunnel, head toward Tamsweg, and then take Route 97 through the Mur Valley; at Predlitz the pass road begins its climb over the steep Turracherhöhe into the Nock Mountains. The fork to Flattnitz, the most scenic way into the Gurk Valley, is at Stadl. Several mountain roads cross over from Italy, but the most traveled is Route 83 from Tarvisio.

TRAIN

As in all of Austria, post-office or railway (*Bundesbahn*) buses go virtually everywhere, but you'll have to allow plenty of time and coordinate schedules carefully so as not to get stranded in some remote location.

The main rail line south from Vienna parallels Route 83, entering Carinthia north of Friesach and continuing on to Klagenfurt and Villach. From Salzburg, a line runs south, tunneling under the Tauern mountains and then tracing the Möll and Drau river valleys to Villach. The main international north–south route connecting Vienna and northeastern Italy runs through Graz and is traversed by EuroCity trains from Munich and Salzburg.

Services on the main routes are fast and frequent. Trains depart hourly from Vienna Hauptbanhof (Central Station) to Graz for a 2½-hour ride, and from Salzburg five times a day for a four-hour ride.

TRAIN INFORMATION ÖBB—National Train Information. ☎ 05/1717 ⊕ www. oebb.at.

Festivals

Lovers of classical music will enjoy Carinthischer Sommer, a festival in July and August with a heavy emphasis on sacred and chamber music. The Musikforum Viktring near Klagenfurt brings together world-renowned classical, electronic, and jazz artists. Through the summer and early fall, villages big and small celebrate their patron saints. These festivals are called Kirtag and feature music, dance, horseback-riding competitions, and lots of wine and beer. The Styriarte Festival in Graz, from June to July, has classical music on the program. The Styrian Autumn Festival, a celebration of contemporary art in October, or the Spring Festival, an electronic-music event, are just two examples of the many events taking place in Graz throughout the year.

Hotels

Accommodations range from luxurious lakeside resorts to small inns, and even include guesthouses without private baths. Accommodations in private homes are cheaper still. These bargains are usually identified by signs reading "Zimmer frei" (room available) or "Frühstückspension" (bed-and-breakfast). Summers are never too hot, and it cools off delightfully at night, which means that most hotels are not equipped with air-conditioning. Some hotels offer half-board, which includes dinner in addition to buffet breakfast (although most $$$$ hotels will charge extra for breakfast). The half-board room rate is usually an extra €15–€30 per person.

Occasionally, quoted room rates for hotels already include half-board accommodations, though a "discounted" rate is usually available if you prefer not to take the evening meal. Inquire when booking. *Hotel reviews have been shortened. For full information, visit Fodors.com.*

Restaurants

Through much of Carinthia you'll discover that, other than simple *Gasthäuser* (wine taverns), most dining spots are not independent establishments but belong to country inns. Carinthia's peasant tradition is reflected in its culinary specialties, such as *Kärntner Käsnudeln* (giant ravioli stuffed with a ricotta-like local cheese and a whisper of mint), *Sterz* (polenta served either sweet or salty), and *Hauswürste* (smoked or air-cured hams and sausages, available at butcher shops).

Styria, bordering on Slovenia, has a hearty cuisine with Slavic overtones; a typical dish is *Steirisches Brathuhn* (roast chicken turned on a spit). The intensely nutty *Kürbiskernöl* (pumpkinseed oil) is used in many soup and pasta dishes, as well as in salad dressings, or to top off vanilla ice cream.

Carinthia is full of lakes and rivers that abound with carp, pike, perch, eel, bream, crawfish (in a rather short season), and, best of all, a large variety of trout. The most popular way of serving Austrian brook trout and rainbow trout is *blau* (blue), the whole fish simmered in a court bouillon and served with drawn butter. Or try it *Müllerin*—sautéed in butter until a crisp brown. In summer, try *kalte Räucherforelle* (cold smoked trout) with lemon or horseradish as a delicate hors d'oeuvre. *Restaurant reviews have been shortened. For full information, visit Fodors.com.*

What it Costs in Euros

	$	$$	$$$	$$$$
RESTAURANTS				
	under €12	€12–€17	€18–€22	over €22
HOTELS				
	under €100	€100–€135	€136–€175	over €175

Tours

The official tourist office for the province is Kärnten Werbung in Velden. The Kärnten Card costs €42, works between April and October, and includes access to more than 100 museums, attractions, lifts, and other sites of interest in the province. It can be purchased in many hotels, and some offer the card to their guests for free for the duration of their stay.

Visitor Information

CONTACTS Kärnten Werbung. ✉ Völkermarkter Ring 21-23, Klagenfurt ☎ 463/3000 ⊕ www.visitcarinthia.at.

Klagenfurt

329 km (192 miles) southwest of Vienna, 209 km (130 miles) southeast of Salzburg.

Klagenfurt became the provincial capital in 1518, so most of the delightful sites here date from the 16th century or later. However, a group of attention-getting Carinthian architects has also breathed new life into old buildings. The town is an excellent base for excursions to the rest of Carinthia. In the city center you can't miss the *Lindwurm,* Klagenfurt's emblematic dragon with a curled tail, which adorns the fountain on Neuer Platz (New Square). Legend has it that the town was founded on this spot, where the beast was destroyed by resident peasants back in days of yore (but the notion of Klagenfurt's dragon became more intriguing when the fossilized cranium of a prehistoric rhinoceros was found nearby).

GETTING HERE AND AROUND

If you come from Italy, Klagenfurt can be reached via the southern highway, A2, which continues all the way to Graz and Vienna. Coming from Salzburg take the A10, via Villach. It's well connected by railway from Salzburg and Vienna. Several buses serve the route daily from Graz. A system of public buses connects Klagenfurt and its surroundings. Centrally located Heiligengeistplatz is the major bus hub. Bus tickets can be purchased from the driver (€1.50/€2.30). Take bus No. 10 or No. 20 to explore the Wörthersee (towards Strandbad). Klagenfurt itself is compact and easy to explore on foot. Bicycles can be rented through a shared bicycle scheme called Nextbike; a rental station at the tourism office is open April–October.

VISITOR INFORMATION

CONTACTS Klagenfurt. ⊠ *Neuer Platz 5* ☏ *0463/287–463–0* ⊕ *www.visitklagenfurt.at.*

Sights

Alter Platz

PLAZA | The old town square of Klagenfurt, or Alter Platz, is still the center of the city. Brightly colored buildings dating from the 12th century frame this pedestrian meeting area. A Trinity Column representing God, Jesus Christ, and the Holy Spirit, dating from 1680, now stands in the Alter Platz. These columns

were built all over Europe as a thanks to God from the people for having survived the plague that killed nearly 25 million Europeans during the Middle Ages. The brightly colored yellow building is the old town hall. ⊠ *Alter Platz.*

Domkirche (*Cathedral*)

RELIGIOUS SITE | South of Neuer Platz (take Karfreitstrasse) is the Domkirche, completed as a Protestant church in 1581, given over to the Jesuits and reconsecrated in 1604, and finally declared a cathedral in 1787. The 18th-century side-altar painting of St. Ignatius by Paul Troger, the great Viennese Rococo painter and teacher, is a fine example of the qualities of transparency and light he introduced to painting. ⊠ *Domplatz.*

Landhaus (*District Government Headquarters*)

GOVERNMENT BUILDING | One of the most notable sights of the city is the Landhaus, with its towers and court with arcaded stairways. It was completed in 1590, and at the time formed a corner of the city wall. The only interior on view is the dramatic **Grosser Wappensaal** (Great Hall of Heraldry), which contains 665 coats of arms of Carinthia's landed gentry. On the ceiling is a stirring rendition of the Fürstenstein investiture ceremony portrayed by Fromiller, the most important Carinthian painter of the Baroque period. The Gasthaus im Landhaushof, on the ground floor, is well worth a stop for lunch. ⊠ *Landhaushof 1* ☏ *463/57757–215* ⊕ *www.landesmuseum.ktn.gv.at* 🎟 *€4* ⏱ *Closed Sun. in May–Oct., closed Sun.–Mon. in Nov.–Apr.*

Minimundus

AMUSEMENT PARK/WATER PARK | **FAMILY** | From Klagenfurt, bypass the autobahn and instead take Villacher Strasse (Route 83) to the Wörther Lake, Austria's great summer resort area. You'll pass by the entrancing Minimundus, literally "miniature world," with around 150 1:25 scale models. Structures include copies of the White House, the Taj Mahal, the Eiffel

Tower, and the Gur-Emir Mausoleum from Uzbekistan, all built when possible from the original materials. Net proceeds support needy children and families in Carinthia. ⊠ *Villacher Strasse 241* ☎ *0463/21194–0* ⊕ *www.minimundus.at* ⌚ *€15* ⊘ *Closed Nov.–mid-Dec.*

Museum Moderner Kunst Kärnten

MUSEUM | This museum displays works by modern and contemporary artists. It pays special attention to avant-garde artists with roots in Carinthia. Maria Lassnig, Arnulf Rainer, and Bruno Gironcoli, some of the heavyweights of post–World War II art, hail from the region. The museum also fosters the young art scene by showing works by emerging artists such as Hans Schabus and Heimo Zobernig. ⊠ *Burggasse 8* ☎ *050/53616252* ⊕ *www. mmkk.at* ⌚ *€5* ⊘ *Closed Mon.*

Reptilien Zoo

ZOO | FAMILY | Adjacent to Minimundus is the Reptilien Zoo, featuring crocodiles, cobras, rattlesnakes, and several kinds of hairy spiders, as well as colorful fish from the nearby Wörther Lake. ⊠ *Villacher Strasse 237* ☎ *0463/23425* ⌚ *€15* ⊘ *Closed Nov.*

Robert Musil Museum

MUSEUM | In the house where Robert Musil—author of the celebrated novel *The Man Without Qualities*—was born in 1880, the Robert Musil Museum displays documents and photographs belonging to him, as well as first editions of his work. Additional permanent exhibition space is given to lyricist Christine Lavant and author Ingeborg Bachmann. Musil's writing focused on the cultural disintegration and spiritual crisis of his day. He fled Nazi-occupied Austria in 1938 and died penniless in Switzerland in 1942. Note the portraits of all three of the museum's subjects, spray painted by French street artist Jef Aérosol, that decorate the building's exterior. ⊠ *Bahnhofstrasse 50* ☎ *0463/501–429* ⊕ *www.musilmuseum. at* ⌚ *€2.50* ⊘ *Closed weekends.*

St. Egyd (*Stadthauptpfarre St. Egid*)

RELIGIOUS SITE | North of Neuer Platz (go along Kramergasse for two blocks, then angle left to the Pfarrplatz) is the parish church of St. Egyd, with its eye-catching totem-pole bronze carving by Austrian avant-garde artist Ernst Fuchs in the second chapel on the right. In the next chapel is the crypt of Julian Green (1900–1998), the noted French-born American novelist whose works include *The Closed Garden* and *The Other One.* He perceived the city as a sanctuary of peace in the world and decided he wanted to be buried here. ⊠ *Pfarrhofgasse 4/A* ⊕ *www.st-egid-klagenfurt.at.*

SIDETRIPS FROM KLAGENFURT

↗ Klopeinersee

With water temperatures averaging 28°C (82°F) from spring to fall, this lake is a popular spot for sunbathing. Surrounded by gentle mountains, it's a little over 1½ km long (1 mile long) and 1 km wide (½ mile wide), and motorboats are not allowed. To reach the Klopeinersee, take the west Völkermarkt/Tainach exit from the A2 autobahn and follow signs to the lake. It's about a 30-minute drive east of Klagenfurt. For information on lakeside hotels and pensions, as well as hiking and biking in the region, contact Klopeinersee Tourismus. ⊠ *Klopein* ⊕ *www. klopeinersee.at.*

↗ Pyramidenkogel

On the shore of the Wörthersee, a winding 5-km (3-mile) road ascends to the 2,790-foot observation tower, the Pyramidenkogel; take its elevator (or the climb 441 steps) up to its three platforms and you can see out over half of Carinthia. The quickest way down is via the slide (separate ticket required) which promises to have you at ground level within 18 seconds. ⊠ *Linden 62, Keutschach Am See* ☎ *04273/2443* ⊕ *www.pyramidenkogel.info* ⌚ *€14.*

🍴 Restaurants

Bar-Bistro 151
$$$ | **CONTEMPORARY** | Inventive dishes, excellent staff, and an inviting atmosphere sum up a visit to 151. Chef Markus Vidermann cooks up a small but fascinating menu of Austrian and international flavors, including vegan options and multiple-course tasting menus. **Known for:** top service; creative cocktails; beautiful atmosphere. [$] *Average main: €20* ✉ *Höhenweg 151* ☎ *676/615–1151* 🌐 *www.151.at* 🕘 *Closed Sun.*

Bierhaus zum Augustin
$ | **AUSTRIAN** | This rustic brewery is in one of the oldest buildings in Klagenfurt and attracts a mixed and lively clientele. The excellent beer produced here pairs perfectly with the local cuisine. **Known for:** great home-brewed beer menu; large portions of Austrian classics; awesome courtyard. [$] *Average main: €13* ✉ *Pfarrhofgasse 2* ☎ *0463/513–992* 🌐 *www.gut-essen-trinken.at/das-augustin/* 🕘 *Closed Sun.*

Bistro Ricardo
$$$ | **PORTUGUESE** | This welcoming Portuguese restaurant may be a welcome break for those looking for an adventurous, non-Austrian meal. Creative vegetarian dishes like the polenta and mushrooms make Ricardo's a nice non-schnitzel change. **Known for:** creative vegetarian dishes; tasting platters; creative use of Port. [$] *Average main: €28* ✉ *Tabakgasse 3* ☎ 🕘 *Closed Sun.*

Gasthaus Pumpe
$ | **AUSTRIAN** | When nothing but a hearty goulash will do, the Gasthaus Pumpe is the top Klagenfurt choice. Fresh Puntingammer beer on tap is just one of the highlights of this humble spot which is popular with locals looking to hang out with friends and enjoy a few beers and large plates of sausage, schnitzel, or other Austrian delights. **Known for:** excellent goulash; large plates are good for groups; lively atmosphere. [$] *Average main: €14* ✉ *Lidmannskygasse 2* ☎ *0463/571–96* 🕘 *Closed Sun.*

Maria Loretto
$$$ | **SEAFOOD** | Gorgeous is the word to describe this spot's perch, which offers a view over the Wörthersee and makes a fitting backdrop for some of the area's best seafood. This former villa offers several romantic dining rooms in champagne and red tones, or you can sit outdoors on the wraparound terrace overlooking the glistening water. **Known for:** lake views; beautiful terrace; amazing seafood like trout caviar. [$] *Average main: €22* ✉ *Lorettoweg 54* ☎ *0463/24465* 🌐 *www.restaurant-maria-loretto.at* 🕘 *Closed Tues. in Oct., Mon.–Tues. in Nov.*

Osteria Veneta
$$ | **ITALIAN** | One of the best places in the city for fresh fish and seafood, including polenta con schie and spaghetti alle vongole. Located on a neighborhood side street, the exterior is unassuming while the interiors are rustic Italian. **Known for:** seafood pasta dishes; fish selection; large terrace. [$] *Average main: €22* ✉ *Kardinalplatz 3* ☎ *0463/915710,* 🌐 *www.osteriaveneta.at* 🕘 *Closed Sun.*

🛏 Hotels

City Hotel zum Domplatz
$ | **HOTEL** | Just a few steps from the center's main square, this convenient little hotel is a good choice for leisure or business travelers on a budget. **Pros:** quiet courtyard; good breakfast; complimentary tea and apples. **Cons:** no elevator; no meals other than breakfast; parking is off-site. [$] *Rooms from: €94* ✉ *Karfreitstrasse 20* ☎ *0463/54320* 🌐 *www.cityhotel-klagenfurt.at* 🛏 *12 rooms* 🍴 *Free breakfast.*

Sandwirth
$$$ | **HOTEL** | Once *the* watering hole of Klagenfurt society, the Sandwirth now features streamlined furniture and innovative works of art that recast vintage landscape photographs in a new light,

while retaining the 19th-century yellow facade. **Pros:** business friendly; good café/restaurant; fitness area and sauna. **Cons:** lobby is used for conference coffee breaks at times; no parking; breakfast is not included. [$] *Rooms from: €140* ⊠ *Pernhartgasse 9* ☎ *0463/56209* ⊕ *www. sandwirth.at* ⇆ *100 rooms* ⦿| *No meals.*

Seepark Hotel

$$$ | HOTEL | Designed by a group of young Austrian architects, this hotel attracts business and leisure travelers alike, thanks to its position on the shores of the Wörthersee. **Pros:** five-minute walk to Wörthersee lake; modern design; lake views from third floor and higher. **Cons:** street-facing rooms are noisy; breakfast is expensive; out of town. [$] *Rooms from: €150* ⊠ *Universitätsstrasse 104* ☎ *0463/204–4990* ⊕ *www.seeparkhotel. at* ⇆ *142 rooms* ⦿| *No meals.*

Nightlife

For a true after-hours scene in Klagenfurt, head for the Pfarrplatz-Herrengasse area, where you'll find a number of intimate bars and cafés.

🎭 Performing Arts

Stadttheater Klagenfurt

OPERA | A large variety of operas, operettas, plays, and ballets are performed year-round at the Stadttheater in Klagenfurt, an inviting Art Nouveau building designed by the famous theater architects Helmer and Fellner of Vienna and completed in 1910. The box office is open Monday through Saturday 9–6. ⊠ *Theaterplatz 4* ☎ *0463/54064* ⊕ *www. stadttheater-klagenfurt.at.*

Hochosterwitz

20 km (12 miles) northwest of Klagenfurt.

Like the impenetrable fortress it is, Burg Hochosterwitz looms over the surrounding countryside. This medieval building sits at 564 feet high, and on a clear day you can see it from nearly 20 miles away. It's a roughly 20-minute drive from Klagenfurt.

GETTING HERE AND AROUND

From Klagenfurt, head northeast on St. Veiterstrasse and merge onto S37. The castle is well signposted and can be seen from far away.

Sights

★ Hochosterwitz

CASTLE/PALACE | FAMILY | The dramatic castle of Hochosterwitz crowns the top of a steep, isolated outcropping, looking as if it has just emerged from the pages of a fairy tale. It was in this castle that the forces of "Pocket-Mouthed Meg" (Margarethe Maultasch) were tricked by two slaughtered oxen dropped onto the heads of its soldiers. Those inside the fortress were starving, but the strategy succeeded, and, dispirited by such apparent proof of abundant supplies, the Tyrolese abandoned the siege. The most recent fortifications were added in the late 1500s against invading Turks; each of the 14 towered gates is a small fortress unto itself. Inside, there's an impressive collection of armor and weaponry plus a café-restaurant in the inner courtyard. There's a glass elevator (accommodating wheelchairs) from a point near the parking-lot ticket office. The hike up the rather steep path to Hochosterwitz adds to the drama. Your reward at the summit is spectacular vistas from every vantage point. There's a restaurant in the castle

12

Carinthia and Graz HOCHOSTERWITZ

and a food stand in the upper parking park. Get to the castle on the back road from Treibach or via Route 83/E7. ⊠ *Hochosterwitz 1, Launsdorf* ☎ *04213/2020* ⊕ *www.burg-hochosterwitz.com* ☎ *€15, elevator €9* ⊘ *Closed mid-Nov.–Mar.*

Gurk

47 km (29 miles) north of Klagenfurt.

Gurk is located in central Carinthia in the Gurk Valley, surrounded by high mountain meadows and magnificent forests. The actual center of the valley is characterized by the two mighty towers of the cathedral.

GETTING HERE AND AROUND
Take the Klagenfurter Schnellstrasse S37; at Pöckstein, turn left onto Gurktalstrasse B93.

Sights

Dom (*Cathedral*)
RELIGIOUS SITE | Gurk's claim to fame is its massive Romanesque Dom topped by two onion cupolas and considered the most famous religious landmark in Carinthia. It was founded in the 11th century by Hemma, Countess of Zeltschach, who after losing her two sons and husband decided to turn to religious works. She tied two oxen to a cart and let them walk until they stopped on their own. At that spot, she founded a cloister and gave all her belongings to the church to build a cathedral. Construction on the cathedral began in 1140 and ended in 1200, though Hemma wasn't canonized until 1938. Her tomb is in the crypt, whose ceiling, and hence the cathedral itself, is supported by 100 marble pillars. The Hemma-Stein, a small, green-slate chair from which she personally supervised construction, is also here, and alleged to bring fertility to barren women. In the church itself, the high altar is one of the most important examples of the early Baroque in Austria.

Note the *Pietà* by George Rafael Donner, who is sometimes called the Austrian Michelangelo. Be sure to visit the bishop's chapel, which features rare late-Romanesque and Gothic frescoes. At the end of August and in early September, a concert series is held in the cathedral. Tours may be restricted by church services, but run daily at 11 and 2:30. Advanced reservations are required. ⊠ *Domplatz 11* ☎ *04266/8236–12* ☎ *Tours: church, bishop's chapel, and crypt €9; church and crypt €5.50* ⊘ *Treasury closed Nov.–Apr.*

Friesach

22 km (13 miles) northeast of Gurk.

The oldest settlement in Carinthia, romantic Friesach is great for wandering. The town is peppered with red-roofed buildings encircled by an old stone wall. There is a well-preserved medieval town center and a Romanesque parish church, as well as Petersburg Castle, home to the Friesach City Museum, which features exhibits on the town's history and culture. Friesach has many medieval marvels; be sure to stop in at the tourist office for information on all of them.

GETTING HERE AND AROUND
Take the Klagenfurter Schnellstrasse S37 coming from the south.

VISITOR INFORMATION
CONTACTS Friesach Tourism. ⊠ *Fürstenhofplatz 1* ☎ *04268/221340* ⊕ *www.friesach-tourismus.at.*

Sights

★ Burgbau
BUILDING | FAMILY | How was a medieval castle built? The team at Burgbau are finding out, building a castle to exacting medieval standards: no electricity, no modern tools, and only natural materials. The aim is not only to build an "authentic" castle, but also to keep these heritage crafts alive. When complete,

the complex will include a residential tower, residential building with a chapel, castle courtyard, farm buildings, and a castle garden. The site can only be visited as part of a guided tour. You will you see stone workers, ironmongers, and carpenters at work and discover the how and why of medieval construction practices. In June, September and October, tours are at 11 am and 3 pm; in July and August, tours are at 11 am, 1:30 pm and 3 pm. ✉ *St. Veiterstrasse 30* ☎ *4366/5448856* 🌐 *www.burgbau.at* 🎟 *€11* 🕒 *Closed Nov.–Apr.*

Dominican Monastery

RELIGIOUS SITE | The Dominican Monastery of St. Nikolaus von Myra is named after St. Nikolaus, the man who eventually became pop culture's Saint Nick and Santa Claus. The monastery is near the town's moat, and was rebuilt in 1673, though the church nearby dates from 1217. Take a moment to notice the stone statue of the Virgin Mary inside the monastery, and the massive crucifix. ✉ *Stadtgrabengasse 5.*

Hauptplatz

PLAZA | It's easy to find the Hauptplatz (main square), with its old town hall and gleaming, multicolor, pastel facades. As you stroll you'll discover aspects of the medieval-era town: beautiful stone houses, the double wall, and the towers, gates, and water-filled moat. ✉ *Hauptplatz, off Kirchgasse or Herrengasse.*

Schloss Petersberg

CASTLE/PALACE | From a footpath at the upper end of the Hauptplatz, behind the Raiffeisenbank, take a steep 20-minute climb up 323 steps to the impressive remains of Schloss Petersberg. (An easier path to see the 12th- and 13th-century castle can be found next to Villa Bucher.) The **Stadtmuseum** (city museum) displays the history of the oldest city in Carinthia. Additionally, make a stop at the **Petersbergkirche,** a Romanesque church first built in 1130. ✉ *North of Hauptplatz off Kirchgasse* 🕒 *Museum closed Nov.–mid-Apr.*

Stadtpfarrkirche

RELIGIOUS SITE | The 12th-century Romanesque Stadtpfarrkirche (parish church) has some excellent stained glass in the choir. ✉ *Friesach.*

🍴 Restaurants

Villa Bucher

$$$ | **AUSTRIAN** | Pause your medieval wanderings to indulge in classic Carinthian dishes, homemade noodles, and of course a selection of fish dishes at the restaurant in Friesach's most popular hotel. Interiors are simple and classy, but the best spot is perched on the terrace with a view of the square. **Known for:** historic wine cellar; large terrace; traditional menu. [$] *Average main: €20* ✉ *Hauptplatz 11* ☎ *04268/25100* 🌐 *www.metnitztalerhof.at* 🕒 *Closed Wed., Sun. lunch only.*

🛏 Hotels

Villa Bucher

$$$ | **HOTEL** | This delightful hotel is decorated in modern country house style and boasts a prime location on the main medieval town square. **Pros:** some rooms have balconies overlooking the castle ruins; in the center of town; free parking. **Cons:** reception has limited opening hours; Wi-fi can be spotty; no A/C. [$] *Rooms from: €138* ✉ *Hauptplatz 11* ☎ *04268/25100* 🌐 *www.metnitztalerhof.at* 🛏 *24 rooms* 🍴 *Free breakfast.*

Graz

200 km (125 miles) southwest of Vienna, 285 km (178 miles) southeast of Salzburg.

Austria's second-largest city, Graz is graceful, welcoming, and far from the usual tourist routes. Instead of visitors, it's the large university population that keeps the sidewalk cafés, trendy bars, and chic restaurants humming in the vibrant Altstadt. The modern-art museum, the Kunsthaus, has a startling biomorphic blue shape that looms over rooftops like some alien spaceship. Along with this, the annual Styriarte summer music festival has become one of the most prestigious cultural draws in the country, and the city opera theater now attracts top companies like the Bolshoi. Graz is far from the cultural backwater it once was; in fact, it was appointed a UNESCO City of Design in 2011.

With its skyline dominated by the squat 16th-century clock tower, this stylish city has a gorgeous and well-preserved medieval center whose Italian Renaissance overlay gives it, in contrast to other Austrian cities, a Mediterranean feel. The name Graz derives from the Slavic *gradec,* meaning "small castle"; there was probably a fortress atop the Schlossberg hill as early as the 9th century. By the 12th century a town had developed at the foot of the hill, which in time became an imperial city of the ruling Hapsburgs. Graz's glory faded in the 17th century when the court moved to Vienna, but the city continued to prosper as the provincial capital of Styria, especially under the enlightened 19th-century rule of Archduke Johann.

In 1811, the archduke founded the Landesmuseum Joanneum, making it the oldest public museum in Austria. This museum complex, with 17 museums in Graz and Styria, has notable collections of art, archaeology, and armor, as well as fossils and folklife artifacts. A €15, 24-hour ticket allows you entry to all collections and exhibitions.

GETTING HERE AND AROUND

Streetcars and buses are an excellent way of traveling within the city. Single tickets (€2.50) can be bought from the driver or kiosks, and one-day and multiple-ride tickets are also available. All six streetcar routes converge at Jakominiplatz near the south end of the Old City. One fare may combine streetcars and buses as long as you take a direct route to your destination. Driving in the Graz city center is not advisable, because there are many narrow, one-way, and pedestrian streets and few places to park. In Graz, taxis can be ordered by phone.

If you're pressed for time, choose which part of the Old City you'd rather see: the lower section, with its churches, historical houses, and museums, or the upper town, with its winding wooded paths, famous clock tower, and the Schlossberg, the lookout point of the city. The best time to visit is between April and October, when the weather is at its most inviting.

CONTACTS Public Transport Graz.
✉ *Jakoministrasse 1, Graz* ☎ *0316/887– 4224* ⊕ *www.holding-graz.at/linien.html.* **Taxis.** ☎ *0316/878, 0316/889, 0316/2801.*

WALKING TOURS

Guided walking tours of Graz in English and German are conducted Mon.–Sat. at 2:30. Registration is required. The meeting point for these tours is Tourist Information at Herrengasse 16. The cost is €13.50.

VISITOR INFORMATION

CONTACTS Grazer Tourismus. ✉ *Herrengasse 16, Graz* ☎ *0316/8075–0* ⊕ *www. graztourismus.at.*

◉ Sights

Burg

CASTLE/PALACE | The scanty remains of this former imperial palace now house government offices. Most of this uninspired structure is from the 19th and 20th centuries, but two noteworthy vestiges of the original 15th-century stronghold remain: the **Burgtor** (palace gate), which opens into the sprawling **Stadtpark** (municipal park), and the unusual 49-step, 26-foot carved stone double-spiral **Gothic staircase** from 1494 to 1500, in the hexagonal tower at the far end of the first courtyard. While meandering around

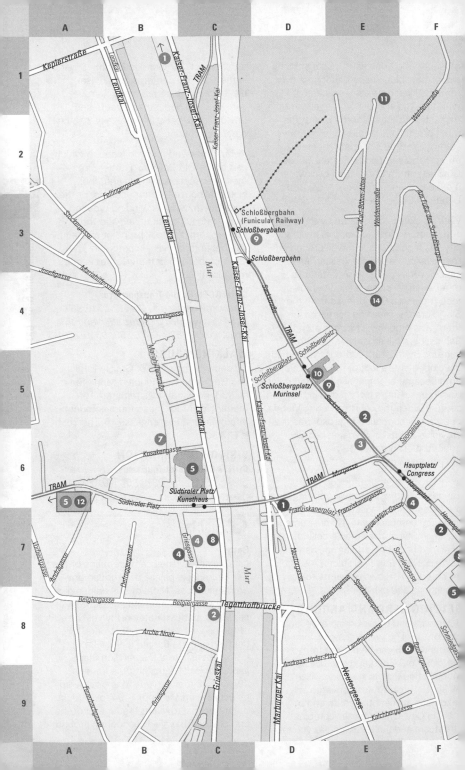

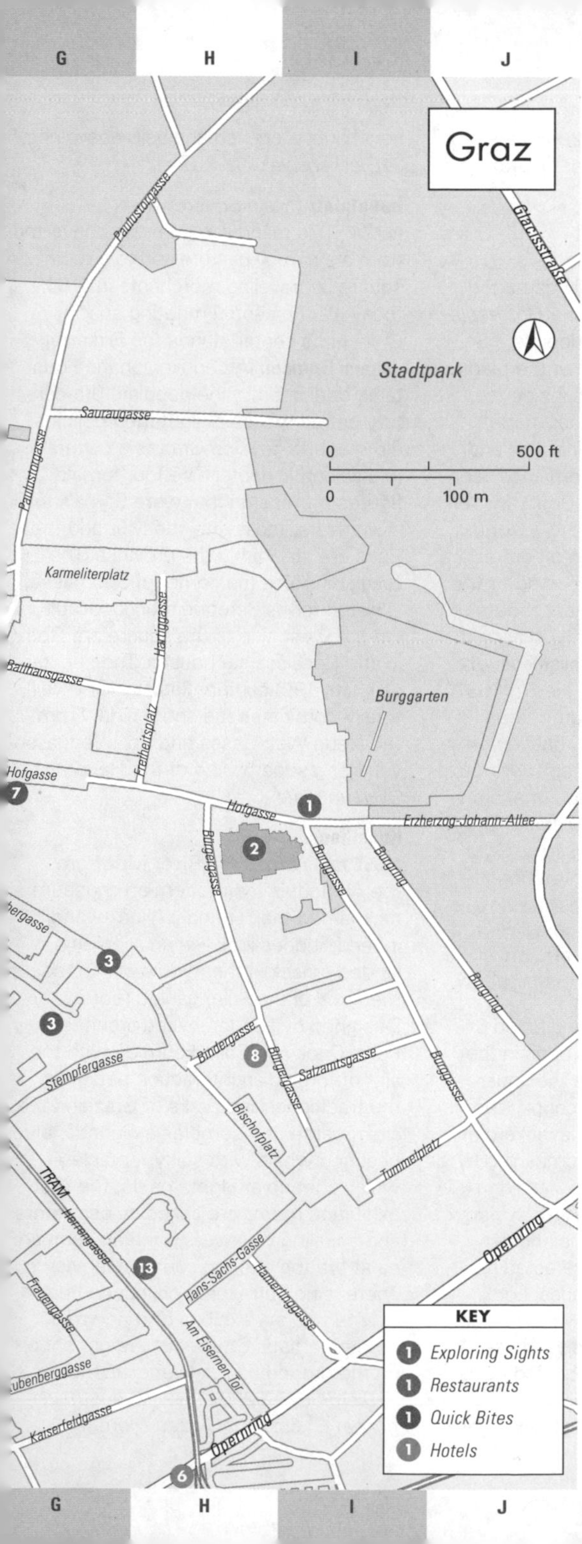

Graz

Stadtpark

Karmeliterplatz

Burggarten

KEY

1 *Exploring Sights*

1 *Restaurants*

1 *Quick Bites*

1 *Hotels*

take note of the *Spor,* a statue of a seed, which represents the center of Graz. ✉ *Hofgasse 15, Graz.*

Domkirche (*Graz Cathedral*)
RELIGIOUS SITE | On the cathedral's south exterior wall is a badly damaged 15th-century fresco called the *Gottesplagenbild,* which graphically depicts contemporary local torments: the plague, locusts, and the Turks. Step inside to see the outstanding high altar made of colored marble, the choir stalls, and Konrad Laib's *Crucifixion* from 1457 (considered one of the top late-Gothic panel paintings of German-speaking Europe). The 15th-century reliquaries on either side of the triumphal arch leading to the choir were originally the bridal chests of Paola Gonzaga, daughter of Ludovico II of Mantua. The Baroque **Mausoleum** of Emperor Ferdinand II, who died in 1637, adjoins the cathedral. Its sumptuous interior is partly a design by native son Fischer von Erlach, and his only work to be seen in Graz. Call ahead to make an appointment to visit the Friedrichskapelle and Konrad Laib. ✉ *Burggasse 3, Graz* ☎ *0316/8041890 for appointments* 🎫 *Mausoleum €6; Friedrichskapelle and Konrad Laib €3* ⊙ *Mausoleum closed Mon., Wed., and Thurs. in Jan.–Apr.*

Glockenspielplatz
PLAZA | Every day at 11 am and 3 and 6 pm two mullioned windows open in the mechanical clock high above the square, revealing a life-size wooden couple, the man adorned in lederhosen, a tankard of beer in his upraised fist, accompanied by a dirndl-clad Austrian maiden. An old folk tune plays and they dance on the window ledges before returning to their hidden perch. The musical box was erected in 1905 by the owner of the house. Look into the courtyard at No. 5, which has an impressive 17th-century open staircase. The house at No. 7 has an arcaded Renaissance courtyard. Have a typical Austrian meal right next door at **Glöckl Bräu,** where they brew their own beer. Every time a new barrel is opened, the bells above ring. ✉ *Glockenspielplatz 4, Graz.*

Hauptplatz (*Main Square*)
PLAZA | This triangular area was converted from a swampy pastureland to a town square by traveling merchants in 1164; today it's the central meeting spot of Graz. In its center stands the **Erzherzog Johann Brunnen** (Archduke Johann Fountain), dedicated to the popular 19th-century patron whose enlightened policies did much to develop Graz as a cultural and scientific center. The four female figures represent what were Styria's four main rivers; today only the Mur and the Enns are still within the province. The **Luegg House,** at the corner of Sporgasse, is noted for its Baroque stucco facade. On the west side of the square are Gothic and Renaissance houses. The spectacular, late-19th-century **Rathaus** (City Hall) totally dominates the south side. From the Neue-Welt-Gasse and Schmiedgasse you get a superb view of the Hauptplatz. ✉ *Hauptplatz, Graz.*

Kunsthaus
MUSEUM | Across the River Mur from the Altstadt is the modern-art museum nicknamed the "Friendly Alien"—and indeed, it does look like an alien ship landed smack in the middle of the town's medieval orange-tile, gabled roofs. Designed by London-based architects Peter Cook and Colin Fournier, with the aim of forging an interaction between the traditional landmarks of Graz and the avant-garde, it resembles a gigantic, blue, beached whale with spiky tentacles—which light up at night. Inside, the vast exhibition rooms are linked by escalators and spiraling walkways, with an open arena at the top offering spectacular views. There is no permanent collection here, only temporary exhibits of renowned modern artists. Check out the gift shop on the ground floor. ✉ *Lendkai 1, Graz* ☎ *0316/8017–9200* ⊕ *www.kunsthaus-graz.at* 🎫 *€9.50* ⊙ *Closed Mon.*

Landesmuseum Johanneum

MUSEUM | The oldest public museum in Austria is a vast complex located between Neutorgasse, Kalchberggasse, and Raubergasse. The Joanneum Quarter holds the natural history collections, the Neue Galerie Graz, and the Bruseum, dedicated to Styrian artist Günter Brus. The Natural History Museum showcases exhibitions from all of Joanneum Universal Museum's natural sciences departments, including botany, geology, paleontology, mineralogy, and zoology. The Neue Galerie's permanent collection features art from the 19th and 20th centuries. ⊠ *Joanneumsviertel, access Kalchberggasse, Graz* ☎ *0316/8017 9100* ⊕ *www.museum-joanneum.at* ⊠ *Natural History Museum or Neue Galerie Graz €9.50; 24-hour ticket valid for all museums of Landesmuseum €15* ⊗ *Closed Mon.*

Landeszeughaus

MUSEUM | **FAMILY** | With 32,000 items on display, the Styrian Armory is the largest preserved arsenal in the world, and one of the biggest attractions in Graz. Built between 1642 and 1644 on behalf of the Styrian nobility, the four-story armory still contains the 16th- and 17th-century weapons intended for use by Styrian mercenaries in fighting off the Turks. Empress Maria Theresa closed the armory in 1749, due to extended periods of peace; however, it remained intact to illustrate the history of the area. The collection includes more than 3,000 suits of armor (some of which are beautifully engraved), thousands of halberds, swords, firearms, cannons, and mortars—some hanging off the ceiling, others projecting off the walls, and still more sitting on the floor. The sheer quantity of displays can be daunting, so thankfully the most unusual items are highlighted, sometimes in striking displays. ⊠ *Herrengasse 16, Graz* ☎ *0316/8017–9810* ⊕ *www.museum-joanneum.at* ⊠ *€9.50, 24-hour ticket valid for all museums of Landesmuseum €15* ⊗ *Closed Mon. and Tues.*

Murinsel Island

Murinsel Island isn't actually an island but a floating platform, designed by modernist artist Vito Acconci in honor of the city's designation as the European Capital of Culture in 2003. You can access it below the Kunsthaus, where a pedestrian walkway leads from the Haupt-Brucke bridge to the steel structure in the shape of a seashell. Murinsel includes a trendy café, amphitheater, showroom featuring Styrian interior design, and a small gift shop with contemporary Austrian products. It lights up in pretty colors at night.

Landhaushof

GOVERNMENT BUILDING | The main wing of the Styrian provincial parliament house was built starting in 1557 by Italian Domenico dell'Allio in the Renaissance Lombard style. Through an archway off Herrengasse, visitors can glimpse a magnificently proportioned three-floor courtyard, surrounding a bronze fountain and copper gargoyles dating from the 16th century. The striking Styrian coat of arms, which depicts a white panther on a green background, is painted as a mural on a nearby wall. In the summer you may discover a small market with sausages, beer, and live music; at Advent, it hosts a Nativity scene made of ice. ⊠ *Herrengasse 16, Graz.*

Palais Herberstein (*History Museum*)
MUSEUM | This 17th-century former city residence of the ruling princes houses the **Cultural History Collection.** In addition to a Baroque interior, the permanent collection of 35,000 items features items related to the political history of Graz and Styria. Palais Herberstein has a special focus on the "status symbols" that defined the

time; and as visitors walk down a red carpet they question the equivalent in the world today. ⊠ *Sackstrasse 16, Graz* ☎ *0316/8017–9800* ⊕ *www.museum-joanneum.at* 🖃 *€9.50; 24-hour ticket valid for all museums of Landesmuseum €15* ⊘ *Closed Mon. and Tues.*

Palais Khuenburg (*Graz Museum*)
CASTLE/PALACE | This was the birthplace in 1863 of Archduke Franz Ferdinand, heir to the throne of the Austro-Hungarian Empire. His assassination at Sarajevo in 1914 led directly to the outbreak of World War I. The palace is now home to the Graz Museum, whose exhibits trace the history of Graz and includes an old-time pharmacy. ⊠ *Sackstrasse 18, Graz* ☎ *0316/872–7600* ⊕ *www.grazmuseum.at* 🖃 *€7.*

★ Schloss Eggenberg
CASTLE/PALACE | FAMILY | This 17th-century palace, a UNESCO World Heritage site on the eastern edge of the city and the largest Baroque palace in Styria, is surrounded by a large park full of peacocks. Enjoy a guided tour of the **Prunkräume** (state rooms); they are noted for their elaborate stucco decorations and frescoes, and contain one of the few depictions of Osaka before 1615. There's also an arcaded courtyard lined with antlers.

The many attractions here include a traditional art gallery, a collection of coins, and an archaeology museum. The Alte Galerie (old gallery) contains a world-famous collection of art from the Middle Ages through the Baroque period. Among its treasures are works by Pieter Brueghel the Younger, Hans and Lucas Cranach, the *Admont Madonna* wood carving from 1400, and a medieval altarpiece depicting the murder of Thomas à Becket. At the Archaeology Museum, the holdings include a remarkable collection of Styrian archaeological finds, including the small and rather strange Strettweg ritual chariot from the 7th century BC. Stop by the outdoor café for a break, or wander through the park to relax in between

visits to the many sights. ⊠ *Eggenberger Allee 90, Graz* ☎ *0316/8017–9532* ⊕ *www.museum-joanneum.at* 🖃 *State rooms and guided tour €15; Alte Galerie, Archaeology Museum, Coin Cabinet and Park €9.50; 24-hour ticket valid for all museums of Landesmuseum €15* ⊘ *State Rooms closed Nov.–Mar., other museums closed Mon. and Nov.–Mar. requires as part of a guided tour.*

★ Schloßberg (*Palace Mountain*)
MILITARY SITE | FAMILY | The view from the summit of Graz's midtown mountain takes in the city and much of central Styria. A zigzagging stone staircase, beginning at Schlossbergplatz, leads to the top. It's 260 steps, so you may prefer to use the Schlossbergbahn funicular railway (Kaiser-Franz-Josef-Kai 38; €2.50) or an elevator carved through the rock face (Schlossbergplatz; €1.80). The Schlossberg, a Romanesque castle with Gothic elements turned Renaissance fortress, constitutes only a portion of this site, and is one of the few places not conquered by Napoléon. A few steps east of the funicular station at the top is the Glockenturm (bell tower), an octagonal structure from 1588 containing Styria's largest bell, the 4-ton Liesl, in the upper belfry. Its 101 chimes resound three times daily, at 7 am, noon, and 7 pm. The Open-Air Theater, to the north, is built into the old casements of the castle and has a retractable roof. Both opera and theater performances are presented here in summer. There are ruins of the older structure, and many a modern café here, too. ⊠ *Am Schlossberg 1, Graz* ☎ *0316/887–405.*

Stadtpfarrkirche (*Church of the Holy Blood*)
RELIGIOUS SITE | You can easily see the city parish church spire from Graz's main street. The church itself was built early in the 16th century from a 15th-century chapel, and later received Baroque touches and·an 18th-century spire. Tintoretto's *Assumption of the Virgin* decorates the altar. Badly damaged in World War II, the stained-glass windows were replaced in

1953 by a Salzburg artist, Albert Birkle, who included portrayals of Hitler and Mussolini as malicious spectators at the scourging of Christ (left window behind the high altar, fourth panel from the bottom on the right). ⊠ *Herrengasse 23, Graz* ☎ *0316/829–684.*

Uhrturm (*Clock Tower*)

CLOCK | This landmark, dating back to the 16th century, is the symbol of Graz. The clock has four giant faces that might at first confuse you—until you realize that the *big* hands tell the hour and the *small* hands the minutes. The clock was designed with only hour hands—smaller minute hands were added later. Nearby, notice a statue of a watchdog—he is said to represent a dog who once saved the daughter of an emperor from being kidnapped by a slighted lover. ⊠ *Schlossberg 3, Graz.*

 Restaurants

Aiola Upstairs

$$$$ | INTERNATIONAL | A tiny bar, café, and restaurant, Aiola is located at the top of the Schlossberg mountain fortress. The restaurant serves traditional Austrian breakfasts with a selection of bread, cheese, and meat, and dinner entrées such as porcini mushroom risotto and the Aiola-style grill plate, which includes beef, lamb, and cheese. **Known for:** gorgeous views; unique architecture; nice wine list. $ *Average main: €27* ⊠ *Schlossberg 2, Graz* ☎ *0316/818797* ⊕ *upstairs.aiola.at.*

Altsteirische Schmankerlstub'n

$$ | AUSTRIAN | A good choice to experience authentic Styrian cooking, this old Graz institution is reminiscent of a cozy country cottage. Salads are a must here, prepared with the Styrian specialty, *Kürbiskernöl,* or pumpkinseed oil. **Known for:** cozy decor (and seating arrangements); local Styrian cuisine; great vegetarian menu. $ *Average main: €14* ⊠ *Sackstrasse 10, Graz* ☎ *0316/833211* ⊕ *www.schmankerlstube.at* ⊟ *No credit cards.*

★ Die Herzl Weinstube

$$ | AUSTRIAN | Located in Mehlplatz, one of the oldest squares of Graz, Die Herzl restaurant opened in 1934 and is known for both its tavernlike atmosphere and its traditional Austrian cuisine. Seasonal entrées are mixed with typical Austrian dishes such as *Gemischter Salat* (a mix of cucumber, potato, and sauerkraut on lettuce) or the *Gebackener* Camembert (fried Camembert cheese served with tart berry chutney). **Known for:** traditional Austrian cooking; great local wine list; affordable lunch specials. $ *Average main: €13* ⊠ *Prokopigasse 12/Mehlplatz, Graz* ☎ *0316/824–300* ⊕ *www.dieherzl.at.*

Gasthaus zur Alten Press

$ | AUSTRIAN | Warm wooden parlors, romantic corners, and authentic Austrian cuisine define this rustic spot. Products are mainly local and seasonal, in keeping with the restaurant's slow-food philosophy. **Known for:** rustic and busy atmosphere; local and seasonal products; pumpkin and pumpkinseed dishes. $ *Average main: €13* ⊠ *Griesgasse 8, Graz* ☎ *0316/719–770* ⊕ *www.zuraltenpress.at* ⊙ *Closed Sun. No dinner Sat.*

Landhauskeller

$$$$ | AUSTRIAN | The magnificent centuries-old Landhaus complex also includes this popular traditional restaurant. Styrian beef is the main event here, but there are lots of other tasty dishes to choose from. **Known for:** beautiful courtyard seating; popular cocktail menu; Styrian beef dishes. $ *Average main: €23* ⊠ *Schmiedgasse 9, Graz* ☎ *0316/830276* ⊕ *www.landhauskeller.at* ⊙ *Closed Sun.*

Mangolds

$ | VEGETARIAN | FAMILY | This popular vegetarian restaurant offers tasty dishes served cafeteria-style and sold by weight. You can choose between at least five main courses plus salads and desserts (including whole-grain cakes.) Mangolds also serves freshly squeezed juice, wine, and coffee—the *Eiskaffee*

The clockworks of Graz's Clock Tower, made by Michael Sylvester Funck in 1712, are still working but have been driven electronically since the middle of the 20th century.

mit Schlag (iced coffee with vanilla ice cream and whipped cream) is addictive. **Known for:** vegetarian buffet; fresh juices; reasonable prices. [$] *Average main: €8* ✉ *Griesgasse 11, Graz* ☎ *0316/718002* 🌐 *www.mangolds.com* 💳 *No credit cards* 🕒 *Closed Sun.*

Peppino im Hofkeller

$$$$ | **ITALIAN** | With its vaulted ceiling and dark, gleaming wainscoting, Peppino im Hofkeller offers the most innovative Italian cuisine in the city. The chef serves a classic Italian menu that includes homemade pasta dressed with seasonal specialties and wonderfully fresh seafood. **Known for:** excellent Italian cooking; Sardinian wine list; good fish selection. [$] *Average main: €25* ✉ *Hofgasse 8, Graz* ☎ *0316/697511* 🌐 *www.peppino-hofkeller.at* 🕒 *Closed Sun. and Mon.*

Salon Marie

$$$ | **INTERNATIONAL** | Salon Marie offers a stylish setting with its chandeliers, greenery, and floor-to-ceiling street art by Josef Wurm. The expansive menu by Chef Aleš Rascan truly includes something for everyone, be it Holstein schnitzel, BBQ chicken, or vegan homemade spring rolls and falafel. **Known for:** cordon bleu; good wine list; showpiece bar. [$] *Average main: €18* ✉ *Grieskai 4-8, Graz* ☎ *0316/706683* 🌐 *www.salonmarie.at.*

Coffee and Quick Bites

Cafe Schwalbennest

$ | **CAFÉ** | A tiny old house turned coffee shop in the center of the city, Cafe Schwalbennest serves traditional Austrian cakes such as homemade sweet poppy seed and cheese-curd tort. It's also a great breakfast spot with regionally sourced cheese and meat, and has a nice Austrian wine list for later in the day. **Known for:** great breakfasts; homemade cakes; small space that fills up quickly. [$] *Average main: €5* ✉ *Franziskanerplatz 1, Graz* ☎ *0316/818892* 🌐 *www.schwalben.at* 💳 *No credit cards* 🕒 *Closed Mon.*

Sacher

$$$ | AUSTRIAN | Joining the expanding enterprise of Sacher cafés in Austria's most prominent cities, Graz's Sacher is everything you would expect from a Sacher Café—lots of gilt, crimson upholstery, sparking chandeliers, and Viennese dessert, including the rich chocolate Sachertorte. If you're hungry for a meal, there are breakfast, lunch, and dinner specialties. **Known for:** famed Sachertorte dessert; popular wine bar; typical Austrian cafe. $ *Average main: €20* ⊠ *Herrengasse 6, Graz* ☎ *0316/80050* ⊕ *www.sacher.com* ⊘ *Closed Sun.*

Hotels

Augarten Art Hotel

$$$ | HOTEL | A glass-and-chrome structure in the middle of a residential neighborhood, the Augarten has more than 400 pieces of art, from the 1960s to works by present-day Austrians, spread through every room and common area. **Pros:** extensive art collection; 24-hour pool and fitness area; luxurious guest rooms. **Cons:** a bit cold feeling; not in the city center; no on-site restaurant. $ *Rooms from: €175* ⊠ *Schönaugasse 53, Graz* ☎ *0316/20800* ⊕ *www.augartenhotel.at* ⮌ *57 rooms* ⊚ *Free breakfast.*

Das Weitzer

$$ | HOTEL | A large property on the river, Das Weitzer offers a modern stay in the heart of Graz which you can see from the upper floor rooms and sauna. **Pros:** rooftop sauna; popular cafe; spacious rooms for the price. **Cons:** area can be noisy at night so you may need to close windows; breakfast is expensive; Wi-fi can be inconsistent. $ *Rooms from: €139* ⊠ *Grieskai 12-16, Graz* ☎ *0316/7030* ⊕ *www.hotelweitzer.com* ⮌ *204 rooms* ⊚ *No meals.*

★ Erzherzog Johann

$$$ | HOTEL | Travelers who prefer a traditionally elegant city hotel will be happy with this historic establishment in a 16th-century building. **Pros:** central location; historical rooms; excellent café. **Cons:** rooms facing main street can be a bit noisy; limited parking in front of hotel; the decor may not be to everyone's tastes. $ *Rooms from: €149* ⊠ *Sackstrasse 3–5, Graz* ☎ *0316/811616* ⊕ *www.erzherzog-johann.com* ⮌ *57 rooms* ⊚ *No meals.*

★ Grand Hotel Wiesler

$$ | HOTEL | Five guesthouses were converted into Hotel Wiesler in 1870 and the property has seen several lives; today, this historic property offers stylish, modern rooms in seven different categories and sizes. **Pros:** variety of rooms for every budget; notable inhouse restaurant, Salon Marie ; modern, arty feel with personal touches. **Cons:** the hip restaurant can be busy; rooms facing the side street can be a bit dark; some rooms have open shower in room. $ *Rooms from: €135* ⊠ *Grieskai 4–8, Graz* ☎ *0316/70660* ⊕ *www.hotelwiesler.com* ⮌ *102 rooms* ⊚ *No meals.*

Hotel Daniel

$$ | HOTEL | Located next door to the train station, Hotel Daniel's young, fresh concept makes it the go-to budget option in Graz. **Pros:** great design; good value; close to train station. **Cons:** 10-minute walk from the city center; the outside looks a little run-down; no kettles in smart rooms. $ *Rooms from: €110* ⊠ *Europaplatz 1, Graz* ☎ *0316/711–0800* ⊕ *www.hoteldaniel.com* ⮌ *108 rooms* ⊚ *No meals.*

Hotel Gollner

$$$ | HOTEL | A popular hotel since the mid-1800s and family-owned for four generations, the friendly Gollner is close to the Jakominiplatz and about a 10-minute walk from the Old City. **Pros:** family-owned property with personalized service; some rooms face the backyard; bar is open 24/7. **Cons:** breakfast not included; not in the center of town; the basic rooms are quite small. $ *Rooms from: €150* ⊠ *Schlögelgasse 14, Graz* ☎ *0316/822521* ⊕ *www.hotelgollner.at* ⮌ *55 rooms* ⊚ *No meals.*

Hotel Mariahilf
$$ | **HOTEL** | A comfortable hotel in the center of things, the Mariahilf is across the river from the Old City close to the Kunsthaus. **Pros:** quiet central location; delicious breakfast; good value. **Cons:** no restaurant; area is a bit noisy at night; rooms could use some renovating. [$] *Rooms from: €110* ✉ *Mariahilferstrasse 9, Graz* ☎ *0316/713163* 🌐 *www.hotelmariahilf.at* 🛏 *45 rooms* 🍴 *Free breakfast.*

★ Hotel zum Dom
$$$ | **HOTEL** | Occupying the 18th-century Palais Inzaghi, the Dom has whimsically decorated rooms and works to combine the old history of Graz with the new modern style. **Pros:** great location; luxury in a historic building; friendly staff. **Cons:** some baths on the small side; noise from the street on weekends; breakfast not included. [$] *Rooms from: €154* ✉ *Bürgergasse 14, Graz* ☎ *0316/824800* 🌐 *www.domhotel.co.at* 🛏 *29 rooms* 🍴 *No meals.*

Schlossberg Hotel
$$$ | **HOTEL** | Contemporary art meets antiquity and modern convenience at this town house tucked up against the foot of the Schlossberg, which was turned into a hotel in 1982. **Pros:** tastefully furnished rooms; rooftop pool with a view; great art collection. **Cons:** longer walk to city center; expensive breakfast ; some rooms don't have much natural light. [$] *Rooms from: €170* ✉ *Kaiser-Franz-Josef-Kai 30, Graz* ☎ *0316/80700* 🌐 *www.schlossberg-hotel.at* 🛏 *62 rooms* 🍴 *No meals.*

Nightlife

Graz's after-hours scene is centered on the area around Prokopigasse, Bürgergasse, Mehlplatz, and Glockenspielplatz. Here you'll find activity until the early-morning hours.

Casino Graz
CASINOS | At the corner of Landhausgasse and Schmiedgasse in the Old City, Casino Graz offers American roulette, blackjack, poker tables, and more than 100 slot machines. Entry is free, but you are required to buy chips for €30. You must bring a passport and be at least 18. Men are expected to wear a jacket and tie;you can rent a jacket if you don't have one. ✉ *Landhausgasse 10, Graz* ☎ *316/832578* 🌐 *www.casinos.at.*

Performing Arts

Graz, a major university town, has a lively, avant-garde theater scene known especially for its experimental productions. Its **Schauspielhaus,** built in 1825, is the leading playhouse, and there are smaller theaters scattered around town. It is also known for its opera, concerts, and jazz. Contact the tourist office for current offerings.

Opernhaus Graz
DANCE | A 19th-century opera house, the Opernhaus Graz, with its resplendent Rococo interior, is a showcase for young talent and experimental productions as well as more conventional works; it stages three to five performances a week during its late September to June season. Tickets are generally available until shortly before the performances; prices start at €11.50. Call for information or stop by the office. ✉ *Kaiser-Josef-Platz 10, Graz* ☎ *0316/8000* 🌐 *www.oper-graz.com.*

Springfestival Graz
FESTIVALS | This five-day festival during mid-June, the largest of its kind in the country, serves as a showcase for the Austrian and European electronic music and art scene. Concerts take place across Graz in venues ranging from clubs and beaches to empty plots of land. Tickets can be purchased online in advance or during festival week at the various spots where performances take place. ✉ *Graz* 🌐 *www.springfestival.at.*

Styrian Autumn Festival

FESTIVALS | The annual Steirischer Herbst, or Styrian Autumn Festival, a celebration of the avant-garde with the occasional shocking piece in experimental theater, music, opera, dance, jazz, film, video, and other performing arts, is held in Graz from the end of September to the middle of October. ✉ *Graz* ⊕ *www.steirischer-herbst.at.*

Styriarte

FESTIVALS | The Styriarte festival (late June to mid-July) gathers outstanding classical musicians from around the world. Performances take place throughout the city including the Helmut-List-Halle and Schloss Eggenberg. The ticket office is located in the center of the city. ✉ *Sackstrasse 17, Graz* ☎ *0316/825000* ⊕ *www.styriarte.com.*

 # Shopping

Graz is a smart, stylish city with great shopping. In the streets surrounding Hauptplatz and Herrengasse you'll find top designer boutiques and specialty shops. Be on the lookout for traditional skirts, trousers, jackets, and coats of gray and dark-green loden wool; dirndls; modern sportswear and ski equipment; handwoven garments; and objects of wrought iron. Take time to wander around the cobblestone streets of the Altstadt near the cathedral, where you'll come across several little specialty shops selling exotic coffees, wine, and cheese.

Käse-Nussbaumer

FOOD/CANDY | For a wide selection of wine and cheese, as well as hard-to-find Styrian cheese varieties, go to Käse-Nussbaumer, near the Hauptplatz. ✉ *Paradeisgasse 1, Graz* ⊕ *www.delikatessen-nussbaumer.at* ⊗ *Closed Mon.*

Moser

BOOKS/STATIONERY | This three-story bookstore is at the end of Graz's main street, Herrengasse, near Jakominiplatz. Moser bustles with people buying postcards, CDs, children's books in multiple languages, and quirky gifts (though not from local dealers). There is a large selection of English fiction and nonfiction on the ground floor, as well as cookbooks with Austrian cuisine written in English. There is a basic no-frills coffee shop on the top floor, where shoppers can have a snack and peruse books before purchasing them. ✉ *Am Eisernen Tor 1, Graz* ☎ *0316/83–01–10.*

★ Steirisches Heimatwerk

CERAMICS/GLASSWARE | The Heimatwerk shop is associated with the local folklore museum and stocks a good variety of regional crafts and luxuries. ✉ *Sporgasse 23, Graz* ⊕ *www.heimatwerk.steiermark.at/.*

INNSBRUCK, TYROL, AND VORARLBERG

Updated by
Joseph Reaney

Sights	Restaurants	Hotels	Shopping	Nightlife
★★★★★	★★★★☆	★★★☆☆	★★☆☆☆	★★★★☆

WELCOME TO INNSBRUCK, TYROL, AND VORARLBERG

TOP REASONS TO GO

★ **The Ötz Valley:** Outdoors enthusiasts love hiking through this region because of rich green pastures in summer and glittering expanses of white in winter.

★ **Highly rated skiing areas:** Known around the world for its extensive and fashionable ski villages, from Kitzbühel to St. Anton am Arlberg, Tyrol often attracts celebrities and global glitterati to its resorts to experience the high-altitude good life, along with dedicated skiers keen to take on its challenging slopes.

★ **Music in Bregenz:** With the sun setting over the Bodensee (Lake Constance) and the Vienna Philharmonic Orchestra striking up the overture of *Rigoletto* on the world's biggest floating stage, this is an unparalleled place to see an opera or a musical.

★ **Top hospitality in a top village:** The Post Lech is a bit like the Vorarlberg mountain village itself—full of charming understatement. You'll never want to leave.

1 Innsbruck. A picturesque and lively university city, Innsbruck is set against a backdrop of soaring mountain peaks and has twice been host of the Winter Olympic Games.

2 Hall in Tirol. This medieval Tyrolean town, ringed by Alpine peaks and known for its castle and mint dating back to the 13th century, is a popular half-day trip from Innsbruck.

3 Zell am Ziller. Once a center for gold-mining, this little village is now a center for outdoor adventures, from skiing and tobogganing in winter to rafting and zip-lining in summer.

4 Kitzbühel. One of Austria's hippest winter resorts, famed for its non-stop, 145-kilometer (90-mile) Ski Safari, "Kitz" is also home to several golf courses and a major tennis tournament.

5 Stubaital. Perhaps the most beautiful mountain valley in Tyrol (although there's plenty of competition), Stubaital's majestic glaciers attract skiers and hikers all year round.

6 Sölden. A winter sports hub with a reputation as a party town, Sölden has fresh snow from October to May and an extensive, high-speed ski lift network to make the most of it.

7 St. Anton am Arlberg. Another town with a big ski reputation, St. Anton is also an appealing summer destination with modern cable cars taking hikers and bikers up to over 9,000 feet.

8 Ischgl and Galtür. As well as a skier's dream, Ischgl is the cultural hub of the Poznaun Valley. A little farther along, Galtür is the region's premier mountain-climbing base.

Bodensee

Bregenz 12

Dornbirn
Schwarzenber
Bezau
Hohenems
Feldkirch
Damüls
Lech
Zürs
Brand
A12
Stuben
Schruns
St. An
am Arlb
11
Isc
Galtür
LIECHTENSTEIN

SWITZERLAND

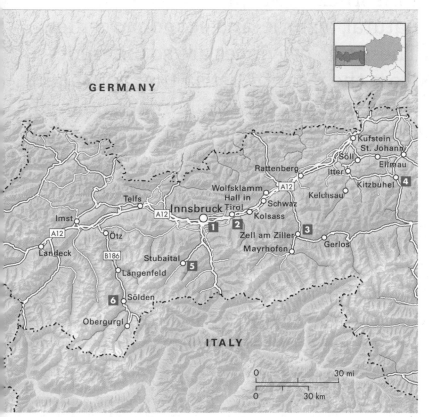

9 Zürs. Across the state border in Vorarlberg, out-of-the-way Zürs is one of Austria's top ski destinations, with lifts jutting out from the tiny village in almost every direction.

10 Lech. Six miles further up the valley, Lech is a picture-perfect ski resort with plush resorts and regular celebrity visitors (though good luck spotting them behind the ski masks).

11 Schruns-Tschagguns. Situated in the heart of the Montafon Valley, Schruns-Tschagguns offers top-class skiing at significantly lower rates than the nearby Arlberg resorts.

12 Bregenz. Vorarlberg's state capital and cultural hub, Bregenz is known for its beautiful Bodensee waterfront, its medieval Upper Town, and its on-the-lake opera festival.

The provinces of Tyrol and Vorarlberg make up the western tip of Austria with Innsbruck, the capital of Tyrol, as the natural, historic, and economic center. These two provinces are so different from the rest of Austria that you might think you've crossed a border, and in a way you have. The frontier between Tyrol and the province of Salzburgerland to the east is defined by mountains; four passes routed over them are what make access possible. To the west of Tyrol lies Vorarlberg—"before the Arlberg"—the mountain range straddling the border between the two provinces.

In winter you'll find unrivaled skiing and tobogganing. The famous Arlberg ski resorts are cult destinations for skiers from all over the world. In summer, Bregenz, the historic state capital of Vorarlberg, becomes the "Summer Capital of Austria" when the Bregenz Festival opens with a performance by the Viennese Symphonic Orchestra. Thousands flock to see operas and musicals by the likes of Giuseppe Verdi, Georges Bizet, and Wolfgang Amadeus Mozart, which take place on a huge floating stage with the Bodensee (Lake Constance) and the Swiss mountains as a backdrop.

Like most mountain peoples, Tyroleans are proud and independent—so much so that for many centuries the natives of one narrow valley fastness had little communication with their "foreign" neighbors in the next valley. Similarly, until a tunnel was cut through the Arlberg range, Vorarlberg was effectively cut off from the rest of the country in winter. The province has much in common with its neighbor, Switzerland. Both peoples are descended from the same ancient Germanic tribes that flourished in the 3rd century BC.

MAJOR REGIONS
Innsbruck. Innsbruck makes a good starting point for exploring western Austria. It's a city that preserves the charm of ancient times and has lots to offer: fascinating culture, stellar restaurants, and trendy nightclubs.

Tyrol. Radiating out from Innsbruck in all directions is Tyrol, a picture-perfect province of soaring mountain peaks and plunging green valleys. At the eastern end of the region is Kitzbühel, while at the western end is St. Anton; both are among Austria's most popular winter vacation destinations, and a joy to visit all year round. In between the two extremes lie charming villages, glossy ski resorts, medieval castles, and some of the world's most beautiful mountain scenery. To the south of Innsbruck lies two famous valleys: the Stubaital, a long Alpine glen lined with glaciers and accessible by narrow-gauge tram; and the Ötztal, home to the popular skiing and mountaineering hub of Sölden. To the west of Innsbruck lies the upper Inn Valley, a spectacular region of family-run farms perched on mountainsides and steep granite peaks flanking narrow valleys leading to some of Austria's finest ski areas. These include St. Anton am Arlberg, Ischgl, and Galtür. You'll need to car to experience it all. Most visitors take Route 171 west from Innsbruck along the banks of the Inn, rather than the autobahn, which hugs the cliffs along the way.

Vorarlberg. Austria's westernmost province is completely mountainous. It borders Germany to the north, Switzerland and Liechtenstein to the west, and Switzerland again to the south. Its nickname is Ländle, meaning "tiny province." The region is a haven for those who love the great outdoors. At its eastern end, right on the border with Tyrol, it is home to two of the country's most famous and exclusive ski resorts: Zürs and Lech. There's nowhere better in Austria for celebrity-spotting.

Farther west, things get even more secluded, as Schruns-Tschagguns in the Montafon valley offers acres of getaway space and privacy—it's no wonder that Ernest Hemingway came to Schruns to write *The Sun Also Rises*.

At Vorarlberg's northwestern edge lies the state capital of Bregenz. This eminently-strollable city is home to the world-famous annual opera festival Bregenzer Festspiele, where shows are performed on a floating platform on the Bodensee (Lake Constance).

Planning

When to Go

The physical geography of Tyrol and Vorarlberg makes them perfect for enjoying outdoor life year-round. Ski-crazy travelers descend on the resorts during the winter months; in summer, when the mountains are awash with wildflowers, campers' tents spring up like mushrooms in the valleys as hikers, bikers, climbers, and spelunkers take advantage of the soaring peaks. High season for summer activities is July through August, while the skiing season begins in many resorts in late November or early December and can go on until early May in the higher ski areas. If you're in Vorarlberg in summer, be sure to stop in Bregenz, when the city comes to life with the Bregenzer Festspiele (Bregenz Music Festival). Boat excursions to Switzerland and Germany are another must. You can even rent a boat and go out on the lake to do some fishing.

Getting Here and Around

AIR

All of Tyrol uses the Flughafen Innsbruck (Innsbruck Airport), three kilometers (two miles) west of the capital. It is served by a number of international airlines, including Austrian Airlines, British Airways, EasyJet, and Lufthansa. But for intercontinental flights, the main gateway airports for Tyrol and Vorarlberg are Munich in Germany and Zurich in Switzerland.

Zurich Airport is about 120 kilometers (75 miles) from Bregenz, with several direct Euro City express trains a day making the 1½-hour journey on the way to Munich. There are also trains, sometimes direct or with only one change, from Zurich Airport to many stations in Tyrol. Munich Airport is more convenient for the eastern part of Tyrol, with Kitzbühel less than two hours by car or train from the Bavarian capital.

AIRPORT INFORMATION Innsbruck Airport. (INN) ☎ 0512/22525 ⊕ www.innsbruck-airport.com.

AIRPORT TRANSFERS

From Innsbruck Airport, take the regular F Line bus into Innsbruck. It takes about 15 minutes to the train station, via the city center. Get your ticket (€2.30) from the machine by the bus stop, right outside the arrivals door, or from the bus driver. Taxis into Innsbruck should take no more than 10 minutes, and the fare is about €15.

From Zurich Airport to Bregenz, hop on one the regular express trains (1½ hours), or for Zürs and Lech there are winter bus transfers running several times a day Friday through Sunday. Book through the airline Swiss.

BUS

Bus lines operated by the railroads and post office connect all the towns and villages not served by train, using vehicles with snow chains when necessary in winter. Even so, some of the highest roads can become impassable for a few hours. And except in the most remote areas, buses are frequent enough that you can get around.

In Innsbruck the deluxe ski buses that depart from the Landestheater on Rennweg, across from the Hofburg, are the most convenient way to reach the six major ski areas outside the city. An Innsbruck Card (€66 for 72 hours) covers most routes on the transport system from the city and surrounding villages to the ski areas, as well as entrance fees to many sights, attractions, cable cars, and ski lifts. Many hotels even provide shuttle service to the ski bus stop.

BUS INFORMATION Postbus. ☎ 05/1717 ⊕ www.postbus.at.

CAR

Driving is the best way to see Tyrol and Vorarlberg, since it allows you to wander off the main routes at your leisure. The autobahns are fastest, but for scenery you're best off on the byways, as you can stop and admire the view. Be aware that roads can be treacherous in winter, and cars are not allowed on some mountain roads in the Arlberg without chains, which you can rent from many service stations. If you are renting a car in the winter, specify that you want winter tires—these will be sufficient to deal with fairly heavy snow on the road, although you will often be required to also carry snow chains. Roads with particularly attractive scenery are marked on highway maps with a parallel green line. To drive on Austria's autobahn, you will need a *vignette*, or sticker, available at almost all service stations. A 10-day sticker costs €9.40; for 60 days it's €27.40.

FERRY

From April to October, passenger ships of the Vorarlberg Lines fleet connect Bregenz with Lindau, Friedrichshafen, Meersburg, and Constance on the German side of the lake. Remember to bring your passport.

BOAT INFORMATION Vorarlberg Lines. ☎ 05574/42868 ⊕ www.vorarlberg-lines.at.

TRAIN

Direct trains from Munich serve Innsbruck. From here on, the line follows the Inn Valley to Landeck and St. Anton, where it plunges into an 11-kilometer (seven-mile) tunnel under the Arlberg range, emerging at Langen in Vorarlberg. It then continues to Bregenz, where you can change to the EuroCity Express to

Zurich (you can also change at Innsbruck for a more direct route to Zurich via Feldkirch) or go back to Munich. A line from Innsbruck to the south goes over the dramatic Brenner Pass (4,495 feet) into Italy.

Some of the most fascinating and memorable side trips can be made by rail. For example, two narrow-gauge lines steam out of Jenbach, one up to the Achensee, the other down to May-rhofen in the Zillertal. From Innsbruck, the narrow-gauge Stubaitalbahn—which starts off as a regular city tram and morphs into a train as it ascends into the mountains—runs south to Telfes and Fulpmes.

TRAIN INFORMATION ÖBB. ☎ *05/1717* ⊕ *www.oebb.at.*

Festivals

There is more here than just the Bregenz Festival. The annual Tyrolean calendar is packed with special events; a particularly charming festival is the Almabtrieb, when herds of cows come down from the high pastures in the fall, garlanded with flowers and surrounded by bands playing music. In winter, *fasching* is when young men parade through towns and villages wearing wooden masks as part of a ritual to scare away evil spirits, while the famous Hahnenkamm World Cup downhill ski race is held in Kitzbühel. There's also the Gauder Fest at Zell am Ziller, a traditional-costume festival, dur-ing the first weekend in May; the castle concerts and music and dance festivals in summer, primarily in Kufstein and Innsbruck; and the many village harvest festivals in the fall throughout Tyrol.

Hotels

In Innsbruck travelers do not seem to stay long, so there is a fast turnover and rooms are almost always available some-where. Some travelers opt to set up their base not in town but *overlooking* it, on the Hungerburg Plateau to the north perhaps, or in one of the nearby villages perched on the slopes to the south. In any case, the Innsbruck Tourist Office at ⊕ *www.innsbruck.info* offers an informa-tion and booking source for Innsbruck and the surrounding villages.

Book in advance if you're traveling in the region, especially Vorarlberg, in the winter high season and in July and August. Room rates include taxes and service and, almost always, a breakfast buffet. In the resort towns dinner will be included. *Halbpension* (half-board), which are plans that include breakfast and dinner, are usually the best deal. Hotel rates vary widely by season, the off-peak periods being March through May and September through November. Most hotels take credit cards. Note that at the most expensive hotels in the resort towns of Zürs/Lech, Kitzbühel, St. Anton, and Sölden, rooms can reach up to (and even beyond) €500 a night. If you're out for savings, it's a good idea to find lodgings in small towns nearby rather than in the bigger towns or in the resorts themselves; local tourist offices can help you get situ-ated, possibly even with accommodations in pensions (simple hotels) or *Bauernhöfe* (farmhouses). It's worth remembering that in Austria, cheap accommodations can still be of a very high standard, with large en suite rooms of sparkling cleanliness. Keep in mind that in hotel saunas and steam baths, nude people of both genders should be expected. Other patrons and man-agement will often take great exception to guests who enter a sauna wearing a swimsuit. Children under certain ages are usually not admitted. *Hotel reviews have been shortened. For full information, visit Fodors.com.*

Restaurants

The gastronomic scene of Austria's westernmost provinces is as varied as its landscape: first-rate gourmet restaurants, traditional inns, rustic local taverns, as well as international chains and ethnic cuisine are all part of the mix. In small towns throughout the region restaurants are often the dining rooms of country inns, and there are plenty of these. Austria used to have a reputation for substantial but stereotypical dishes of meat, dumplings, and sauerkraut, but things have changed considerably. Gourmet meals are available at many wonderful restaurants, often at much more reasonable prices than is typical of Europe's high-class dining scene. That said, in many villages you'll find inns catering largely to local farm workers, where the old favorites are still the order of the day—prepare to be filled rather than thrilled.

Most hotel restaurants will be closed in the off-season, usually November and April. In ski season breakfast is typically served early enough for you to hit the slopes in good time, and dinner is timed so that exhausted skiers can get an early night in preparation for the next day.

Restaurants range from grand-hotel dining salons to little *Wirtshäuser,* rustic restaurants where you can enjoy hearty local specialties such as *Tyroler Gröstl* (a skillet dish made of ham or pork, potatoes, and onions, with caraway seeds, paprika, and parsley), *Knödel* (dumpling) soup, or *Schweinsbraten* (roast pork with sauerkraut), while sitting on highly polished (and rather hard) wooden seats. Don't forget to enjoy some of the fine Innsbruck coffeehouses, famous for their scrumptious cakes and cappuccino. *Restaurant reviews have been shortened. For full information, visit Fodors.com.*

What it Costs in Euros

	$	$$	$$$	$$$$
RESTAURANTS				
	under €12	€12–€17	€18–€22	over €22
HOTELS				
	under €100	€100–€200	€201–€300	over €300

Visitor Information

The Innsbruck tourist office can be found on Burggraben in the heart of town. The headquarters for tourist information about Vorarlberg is in Bregenz. Other regional tourist offices (called either *Tourismusbüro, Verkehrsverein,* or *Fremdenverkehrsamt*) are found throughout the province using the contact information listed under particular towns. They are easily spotted—just look for the large "i" (for information) sign.

CONTACTS Austrian National Tourist Board. ☎ *00800/400–200–00* ⊕ *www.austria. info.* **Innsbruck Tourist Office.** ✉ *Burggraben 3, Innsbruck* ☎ *0512/59850* ⊕ *www.innsbruck.info.* **Tourist Information Vorarlberg.** ✉ *Poststrasse 11, Dornbirn* ☎ *05572/3770330* ⊕ *www.vorarlberg.at.*

Innsbruck

166 km (103 miles) southwest of Salzburg, 476 km (295 miles) southwest of Vienna.

The capital of Tyrol is one of the most beautiful towns of its size anywhere in the world, owing much of its charm and fame to its unique location. To the north, the steep, sheer sides of the Alps rise, literally from the edge of the city, like a shimmering blue-and-white wall—an impressive backdrop for the mellowed green domes and red roofs of the Baroque town tucked below. To the south, the peaks of the Tuxer

Mountain Sports

13

Hiking and Climbing

Tyrol has an abundance of more than 35,000 miles of well-maintained mountain paths that thread the countryside. Hiking is one of the best ways to experience the truly awesome Alpine scenery, whether you just want to take a leisurely stroll around one of the crystalline lakes mirroring the towering mountains or trek your way to the top of one of the mighty peaks. Mountain climbing is a highly organized activity in Tyrol, a province that contains some of the greatest challenges to devotees of the sport. The instructors at the Alpine School Innsbruck are the best people to contact if you want to make arrangements for a mountain-climbing holiday.

Skiing

Downhill was practically invented in **Tyrol**. Legendary skiing master Hannes Schneider took the Norwegian art of cross-country skiing and adapted it to downhill running. No matter where your trip takes you, world-class—and often gut-scrambling—skiing is available, from the glamour of Kitzbühel in the east to the imposing peaks of St. Anton am Arlberg in the west.

In the area east of Innsbruck, chic **Kitzbühel** is perhaps most famous for its "Ski Safari," a far-ranging system of ski lifts and trails, some floodlit at night, that allows you to ski for weeks without retracing your steps. **Alpbach** is one of the most popular resorts for families, with many not-too-challenging slopes and a reputation for being one of the most beautiful villages in Austria, full of heavily timbered traditional chalets surrounded by thickly wooded runs. The area around is collectively known as the **Ski Welt** (Ski World), where the villages of **Soll, Ellmau, Scheffau, Itter, Going, Brixen im Thale, Westendorf, Hopfgarten,** and **Kelchsau** form Austria's largest linked skiing area. It's dotted with cozy, welcoming mountain huts, many of which are family-friendly.

Innsbruck itself is at the center of a group of resorts easily reached by bus from the city. The best time to ski Innsbruck's slopes is January through March.

Southwest of the city, in the heart of Tyrol, is the Ötz Valley. From the Ötztal station you can go by bus to **Sölden,** a resort at 4,500 feet that has become almost as well-known for its party scene as for its superb skiing. The up-and-comers of Austrian ski resorts are **Ischgl** and **Galtür** in the Paznaun Valley bordering Switzerland. Here, good snow and a long ski season are assured on high-altitude slopes with a top station at 9,422 feet.

Close to the Arlberg Pass is **St. Anton,** which proudly claims to have one of the finest ski schools in the world. Although it has some nice piste skiing suitable for intermediates, St. Anton is known for being a challenge in the form of long, tough, and steep mogul runs and spectacular off-piste. It was in the Arlberg in the 1920s that Hannes Schneider started the school that was to become the model for all others. A short bus ride to the top of the pass brings you to **St. Christoph,** at 5,800 feet. If you care to mingle with royalty and celebrities on the lifts, the upscale ski villages of **Zürs** and **Lech,** on the Vorarlberg side of the pass, are the places for you.

Ski Areas

GERMANY

Bregenz
Hard
A14
Dornbirn
Schetteregg
Bezau
Damuls
Au-Schoppernau
L200
Warth-Schrocken
L193
Lech
L198
Bludenz
Zurs
L194
Bludenz
S16
St. Cristoph
Stüben
Tschagguns
Schruns
St. Anton
L188
Galtür
B188
Ischgl
Serfaus
B180
B171
Landeck
Landeck
B198
Imst
Imst
A12
L16
B186
Sölden
Hochgurgl
Vent
Obergurgl

Vils
Reutte
Reutte
B179
Lermoos
Ehrwald
Ehrwald
B189
Telfs
A12
Zirl
Vols
L13
Oetz

B177
Seefeld
Innsbruck
Watt
Hall in Tir
Telfes
Fulpmes
Fulpmes
B183
Stubaital
Neustift
Steinach am Brenner
A13
Matrei
am Brenner
Hintertux

B1
Achenkirch
Pertisau
Schwaz

SWITZERLAND

ITALY

and Stubai ranges undulate in the hazy purple distance.

Squeezed by the mountains and sharing the valley with the Inn River (Innsbruck means "bridge over the Inn"), the city is compact and very easy to explore on foot. Reminders of three historic figures abound: the local hero Andreas Hofer, whose band of patriots challenged Napoléon in 1809; Emperor Maximilian I (1459–1519); and Empress Maria Theresa (1717–80), the latter two responsible for much of the city's architecture. Maximilian ruled the Holy Roman Empire from Innsbruck, and Maria Theresa, who was particularly fond of the city, spent a substantial amount of time here.

GETTING HERE AND AROUND

Innsbruck Airport is only minutes from Innsbruck city center and is linked by frequent bus service.

Direct trains serve Innsbruck from Munich, Vienna, Rome, and Zurich, and all arrive at the train station, Innsbruck Hauptbahnhof, at SüdTyroler Platz. The station is outfitted with restaurants, cafes, a supermarket, and even a post office.

Innsbruck is connected by bus to other parts of Tyrol, and the bus terminal is beside the train station. In Innsbruck, most bus and streetcar routes begin or end at Maria-Theresien-Strasse, nearby Boznerplatz, or the main train station. One-way tickets cost €2.60 on the bus or streetcar, and you can transfer to another line with the same ticket as long as you continue in more or less the same direction in a single journey. You can get tickets from machines, or, at a slightly increased cost, from the driver.

If you're driving, remember that the Altstadt (Old City) is a pedestrian zone. Private cars are not allowed on many streets, and parking requires vouchers that you buy from blue coin-operated dispensers found around parking areas. Fees are usually around €1 per half hour.

In Innsbruck taxis are not much faster than walking, particularly along the one-way streets and in the Old City. Basic fare is €6.20 for the first 1.3 kilometer (0.8 mile) and €1.90 per km after that, so that most rides within the city limits will amount to between €8 and €12. Innsbruck Taxi 4 You is a good option if you want to call a cab. There are set fares for longer journeys (to a ski resort from the train station or airport, for example), but if you're prepared to haggle, these are negotiable, particularly on a quiet day when plenty of cabs are waiting in line. Let the driver know that you are aware of the alternatives available, such as train or bus.

Horse-drawn cabs, still a feature of Innsbruck life, can be hired at the stand in front of the Landestheater. Set the price before you head off; a half-hour ride will cost around €30.

Innsbruck's main tourist office is open daily except Sundays, 9 am through 6 pm. Tyrol's provincial tourist bureau, the Tyrol Werbung, is also in Innsbruck. The Österreichischer Alpenverein is the place to go for information on Alpine huts and mountaineering advice. It's open weekdays 9 am to 4:30 pm, with a break for lunch; it's mornings only on Fridays.

BUS INFORMATION Postbus. ☏ *05/1717* ⊕ *www.postbus.at.*

TAXI INFORMATION City Taxis. ☏ *0800/201148* ⊕ *www.taxi-292915.at.* **Innsbruck Taxi 4 You.** ☏ *0664/926–5557* ⊕ *www.innsbruck-taxi4you.com.*

TRAIN INFORMATION Innsbruck Hauptbahnhof. ✉ *Südtiroler Platz.* **ÖBB.** ☏ *05/1717* ⊕ *www.oebb.at.*

VISITOR INFORMATION
CONTACTS Innsbruck Tourist Office. ✉ *Burggraben 3* ☏ *0512/59850* ⊕ *www.innsbruck.info.* **Österreichischer Alpenverein.** ✉ *Olympiastrasse 37* ☏ *0512/595470* ⊕ *www.alpenverein.at.*

The Goldenes Dachl, the symbol of the city of Innsbruck, is tiled with 2,657 fire-gilded copper shingles.

Tirol Werbung. ☒ *Maria-Theresien-Strasse 55* ☎ *0512/72720* ⊕ *www.tirol.at.*

TOURS

The red **Sightseer** bus, a service of the Innsbruck Tourist Office, is the best way to see the sights of Innsbruck without walking. It features a recorded commentary in several languages, including English. There are two routes, both beginning from Maria-Theresien-Strasse in the Old City, but you can catch the bus from any of the nine marked stops, and jump off and on the bus whenever you like. The ride is free with your Innsbruck Card, or buy your ticket (€18) from the driver or at the tourist office.

 # Sights

Annasäule

MEMORIAL | St. Anne's Column, erected in 1706, commemorates the withdrawal of Bavarian forces in the war of the Spanish Succession on St. Anne's Day (July 26) in 1703. Along with the Triumphal Arch, it is one of the two most important sights on Maria-Theresien-Strasse. From here there is a classic view of Innsbruck's Altstadt (Old City), with the glorious Nordkette mountain range in the background. ☒ *Maria-Theresien-Strasse 18.*

Bergisel Ski Jump

RESTAURANT—SIGHT | This ski-jumping stadium towers over Innsbruck with a gloriously modern, concrete-and-glass observation deck and restaurant designed by world-celebrated architect Zaha Hadid. It opened in 2003, replacing the old stadium that no longer complied with modern requirements for ski jumping and crowd safety. There's a café at the base area, and if you're lucky you can have a beer while watching ski jumpers practice, even during the summer when they heavily water the slope (so they can still ski despite the lack of snow). ☒ *Bergiselweg 3* ☎ *0512/589259* ⊕ *www.bergisel.info* ☜ *€10* ⊙ *Closed Tue. Nov.–May.*

Club Innsbruck Card

Pick up a free Club Innsbruck card at your hotel for no-charge use of ski buses and reduced-charge ski-lift passes. For big savings, buy the all-inclusive **Innsbruck Card**, which gives you free admission to all museums, mountain cable cars, the Alpenzoo, and Schloss Ambras, plus free bus and tram transportation, including bus service to nearby **Hall in Tirol**. The card includes unlimited ride-hopping onboard the big red **Sightseer** bus, which whisks you in air-conditioned comfort to all of the major sights, and even provides recorded commentary in English and five other languages. Cards are good for 24, 48, and 72 hours at €49, €55, and €66 respectively, with a 50% discount for children ages 6 to 15, and are available at the tourist office, on cable cars, and in larger museums.

Domkirche zu St. Jakob

RELIGIOUS SITE | Innsbruck's cathedral was built between 1717 and 1724 on the site of a 12th-century Romanesque church. Regarded as possibly the most important Baroque building in Tyrol, its main attraction is the painting of the Madonna by Lucas Cranach the Elder, dating from about 1530 and displayed above the high altar. The tomb of Archduke Maximilian III, Master of the Teutonic Knights, dating from 1620, can be seen in the north aisle. ⊠ *Domplatz 6* ☎ *0512/583902* ⊕ *www.dibk.at* ✉ *Free.*

Ferdinandeum (*Tyrolean State Museum Ferdinandeum*)

MUSEUM | This state museum with a striking Florentine Renaissance Revival–style facade houses Austria's largest collection of Gothic art and 19th- and 20th-century paintings, including works by Rembrandt, Brueghel, and Klimt. There are also musical instruments and medieval armor, along with special exhibitions. Here you'll find the original coats of arms from the Goldenes Dachl balcony. Chamber music concerts are offered throughout the year. ⊠ *Museumstrasse 15* ☎ *0512/59489–109* ⊕ *www.tiroler-landesmuseen.at* ✉ *€12 combined ticket with Hofkirche, Volkskunstmuseum, and Zeughaus* ⊙ *Closed Mon.*

★ Goldenes Dachl (*Golden Roof*)

HOUSE | Any walking tour of Innsbruck should start at the Goldenes Dachl, which made famous the late-Gothic mansion whose balcony it covers. In fact, the roof is capped with 2,600 gilded copper tiles, and its refurbishment is said to have taken nearly 31 pounds of gold. The 15th-century house was owned by Maximilian I, who added a balcony in 1501 as a sort of "royal box" for watching street performances in the square below. The structure was altered and expanded at the beginning of the 18th century, and now only the loggia and the alcove are identifiable as original. The magnificent coats of arms representing Austria, Hungary, Burgundy, Milan, the Holy Roman Empire, Styria, Tyrol, and royal Germany are copies; you can see the originals in the Ferdinandeum. The Golden Roof building houses the **Goldenes Dachl Museum** with memorabilia and paintings from the life of Emperor Maximilian I. ⊠ *Herzog-Friedrich-Strasse 15* ☎ *0512/5360–1441* ✉ *€4.80 (Goldenes Dachl Museum)* ⊙ *Closed Mon.*

Grassmayr Bell Foundry

FACTORY | A visit to this 400-year-old bell foundry includes a tour of the foundry and a fascinating little museum, which will give you an idea of how bells are cast and tuned. There's also a sound chamber where you can try your hand at bell ringing. Guided tours in English can be arranged. ⊠ *Leopoldstrasse 53* ☎ *0512/59416* ⊕ *www.grassmayr.at* ✉ *€9* ⊙ *Closed Sun. year-round and Sat. Oct.–May.*

Hofburg (*Imperial Palace*)

CASTLE/PALACE | One of Innsbruck's most historic attractions is the Hofburg, or Imperial Palace, which Maximilian I and Archduke Sigmund the Rich commissioned to be built in late-Gothic style in the 15th century. Center stage is the **Giant's Hall**—designated a marvel of the 18th century as soon as it was topped off with its magnificent trompe-l'oeil ceiling painted by Franz Anton Maulpertsch in 1775. The Rococo decoration and the portraits of Hapsburg ancestors in the ornate, white-and-gold great reception hall were added in the 18th century by the Empress Maria Theresa. Look for the portrait of "Primal" (Primrose)—to use the childhood nickname of the empress's daughter, Marie Antoinette. Skip the 3D show at the end. ⊠ *Rennweg 1* ☎ *0512/587186* ⊕ *www.hofburg-innsbruck.at* ✉ *€9.50.*

Hofkirche (*Court Church*)

RELIGIOUS SITE | Close by the Hofburg, the Court Church was built as a mausoleum for Maximilian I (although he is actually buried in Wiener Neustadt, south of Vienna). The emperor's ornate black-marble tomb is surrounded by 24 marble reliefs depicting his accomplishments, as well as 28 larger-than-life-size bronze statues of his ancestors (real and imagined), including the legendary King Arthur of England. Freedom fighter Andreas Hofer is also buried here. Don't miss the 16th-century **Silver Chapel,** up the stairs opposite the entrance, with its elaborate altar and silver Madonna. The chapel was built in 1578 to be the tomb of Archduke Ferdinand II and his wife, Philippine Welser, the daughter of a rich and powerful merchant family. ■TIP➔ **Visit**

the chapel for picture taking in the morning; the blinding afternoon sun comes in directly behind the altar. ⊠ *Universitätsstrasse 2* ☎ *0512/59489–514* ✉ *€8; €12 combined ticket with Volkskunstmuseum, Ferdinandeum, and Zeughaus.*

Museum im Zeughaus

MUSEUM | The late-Gothic secular building that now houses the Zeughaus Museum was once the arsenal of Maximilian I. Today, displays include cartography, mineralogy, music, hunting weapons, coins, aspects of Tyrol's culture, and the province's wars of independence. ⊠ *Zeughausgasse 1* ☎ *0512/59489–11* ⊕ *www.tiroler-landesmuseen.at* ✉ *€12 combined ticket with Hofkirche, Volkskunstmuseum, and Ferdinandeum* ⊙ *Closed Mon.*

★ Nordkettenbahnen (*Nordkette Cable Car*)

VIEWPOINT | FAMILY | The Nordkette is Innsbruck's most famous mountain and it's possible to reach it directly from the city center. Hop on the funicular—the main station is just around the corner from the Hofburg—and in just eight minutes you'll be at the Hungerburg station, 2,822 feet above sea level. But that's just the start: from here, two more cable cars lead high into the mountains to the "Top Of Innsbruck," a viewing platform at 7,546 feet with staggering panoramic views of Innsbruck and the surrounding peaks. Along with the spectacular views, you can also enjoy a range of hiking and biking trails for every ability along the way, as well as restaurants, shops, cafes, and play parks for kids. There's also the **Alpenzoo**, which is home to an unusual collection of Alpine birds and animals, including many endangered species. Entry costs €17, including the Nordkettenbahnen up to the Hungerburg station. ⊠ *Nordkette Cable Car Station, Rennweg 3* ☎ *0512/293344* ⊕ *www.nordkette.com* ✉ *Funicular round-trip €9.90; cable-car round-trip €38.*

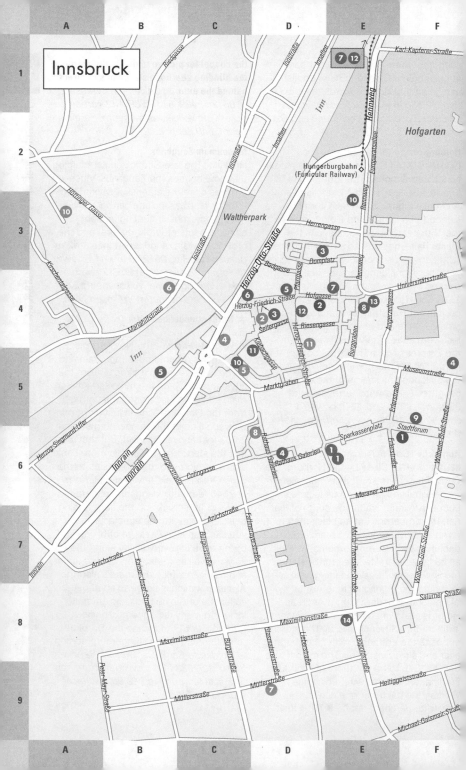

Sights ▼

1 Annasäule **E6**
2 Bergisel Ski Jump **H9**
3 Domkirche zu
  St. Jakob **D3**
4 Ferdinandeum............ **F5**
5 Goldenes Dachl......... **D4**
6 Grassmayr Bell
  Foundry **H9**
7 Hofburg **E4**
8 Hofkirche **E4**
9 Museum im Zeughaus ...**I4**
10 Nordkettenbahnen **E3**
11 Schloss Ambras **H9**
12 Stadtturm **D4**
13 Tiroler
  Volkskunstmuseum...... **E4**
14 Triumphpforte **E8**

Restaurants ▼

1 Das Schindler............ **E6**
2 Europastüberl **G6**
3 Goldener Adler.......... **D4**
4 Lichtblick **D6**
5 Markthalle................ **B5**
6 Ottoburg **C4**
7 Restaurant Seegrube ... **E1**
8 Schwarzer Adler......... **G3**
9 Sitzwohl................... **F5**
10 Thai-Li.................... **C5**
11 Weisses Rössl **D5**
12 Wirtshaus Schoneck.... **E1**

Quick Bites ▼

1 Cafe Central **F6**
2 Kröll **D4**

Hotels ▼

1 Adlers **H5**
2 Gasthof Goldener
  Adler **D4**
3 Grand Hotel Europa **G6**
4 Hotel Innsbruck.......... **C4**
5 Hotel Maximilian......... **C5**
6 Mondschein............. **B4**
7 Nala Individuell Hotel .. **D9**
8 The Penz................. **D6**
9 Schwarzer Adler........ **G3**
10 Tautermann.............. **A3**
11 Weisses Kreuz **D4**

Schloss Ambras
CASTLE/PALACE | This Renaissance castle, just outside Innsbruck but easily reached by regular or **Sightseer** bus, is now home to one of the oldest museums in the world. It all began when Archduke Ferdinand II was begrudgingly allowed to marry the commoner Philippine Welser, but only if the couple lived outside the city. He therefore had an existing 10th-century castle virtually rebuilt from scratch, and it was completed in 1556. He made sure the new castle, Schloss Ambras, had every luxury, including a sunken bath, acres of gardens, and statement rooms like the exquisite Spanish Hall, home to 27 full-length portraits of Tyrol rulers.

The initial 16th-century castle collections, started by avid collector Ferdinand, have been expanded over the years, and now contain a fascinating mix of natural, scientific, and artistic curios. In particular, look out for a suit of armor belonging to the court's giant Bartlmä Bont, and a series of portraits of "Hairy Man" Pedro Gonzalez and his children. ✉ *Schlossstrasse 20* ☎ *01525/24–4802* 🌐 *www.schlossambras-innsbruck.at* 🎫 *Apr.–Oct., €12; Dec.–Mar., €8* 🕒 *Closed Nov.*

Stadtturm
BUILDING | Innsbruck's looming City Tower was built in about 1460. It has a steep climb of 133 steps to the top, where the bulbous cupola was added in the 16th century, and from it there are magnificent views of the city and surrounding mountains. The 31-meter-high platform is a particularly good vantage point from which to view **Helbling House** on the corner across the square, right by Goldenes Dachl. This Gothic town house originally dates from the 15th century, though the colorful pink-and-white facade with its late-Baroque stuccos was added around 1730. ✉ *Herzog-Friedrich-Strasse 21* ☎ *0512/5871–13* 🎫 *€4.*

Tiroler Volkskunstmuseum (*Tyrolean Folk Art Museum*)
MUSEUM | In the same complex as the Hofkirche (with the same entrance), this museum is regarded as the most important collection of folk art in the Alpine region. Its wood-paneled parlors house furniture, including entire room settings from old farmhouses and inns, decorated in styles from Gothic to Rococo. In particular, look out for the traditional Tyrolean tiled stoves. Other exhibits include costumes, farm implements, cow bells, carnival masks, and musical instruments. ✉ *Universitätsstrasse 2* ☎ *0512/59489–514* 🌐 *www.tiroler-landesmuseen.at* 🎫 *€12 combined ticket with Hofkirche, Ferdinandeum, and Zeughaus.*

Triumphpforte
BUILDING | One of the icons of Innsbruck, the Roman-style Triumphal Arch was built in 1765 to commemorate both the marriage of emperor-to-be Leopold II (then Duke of Tuscany) to Spanish princess Maria Luisa, and the sudden death of Emperor Franz I, husband of Empress Maria Theresa. The south side clearly represents celebration, while the north side shows mourning motifs. ✉ *Leopoldstrasse 2.*

🍴 Restaurants

★ Das Schindler
$$$$ | **INTERNATIONAL** | One of Innsbruck's go-to gourmet experiences—its 14 Gault Millau points are a fine endorsement—this restaurant in the heart of the old town is known for its obsession with using local ingredients as much as possible, with absolutely no artificial additives. Details of suppliers, farms, and even local hunting grounds for the game on the menu are available for perusal. The interior is modern and the atmosphere is trendy. **Known for:** elegant decor; a true farm-to-table menu; very local ingredients. [$] *Average main: €28* ✉ *Maria-Theresien-Strasse 31* ☎ *0512/566969* 🌐 *www.dasschindler.at* 🕒 *Closed Sun.*

Europastüberl

$$ | **AUSTRIAN** | Here at the Grand Hotel Europa's acclaimed dining room you'll find creative cuisine that still draws on traditional recipes. Europastüberl achieves the difficult feat of combining coziness with elegance, with carved wood alcoves— the typical Tyrolean Stüberl—harboring intimate tables dressed with white linens and flickering candles. For more than 20 years, the signature dish here has been the Dover sole sautéed in butter. Other seasonal regional specialties include local game or house-made pastas like *tafelspitz*, an Austrian specialty of boiled beef and creamed spinach with fresh horseradish. The four- to seven-course prix-fixe menus are good options for those who can't settle on ordering just one thing, and the wine list includes a great selection of Austrian wines. **Known for:** the epitome of cozy Austrian elegance; excellent local wine menu; signature Dover sole sautéed in butter. $ *Average main: €22* ⊠ *Grand Hotel Europa, Südtirolerplatz 2* ☎ *0512/5931* ⊕ *www.grandhoteleuropa.at.*

Goldener Adler

$$ | **AUSTRIAN** | This restaurant is as popular with locals as it is with visitors. The kitchen takes a modern approach to traditional dishes, with pork medallions topped with ham and Gorgonzola, and veal steaks ladled with a creamy herb sauce that's as steeped in flavor as the restaurant is steeped in history. The traditional dining rooms on the arcaded ground floor and the summer-only terrace are popular places to eat, the former both romantic and private, and the latter good for people-watching. Start with a glass of *Sekt* (an Austrian sparkling wine) flavored with a dash of cassis—a kir royale—as you peruse the menu. The restaurant is also the breakfast room of the Goldener Adler hotel. **Known for:** Innsbruck's oldest restaurant (opened in 1390); alfresco dining in the summer; hearty portions of classical Austrian dishes. *Average main: €20* ⊠ *Herzog-Friedrich-strasse 6* ☎ *0512/571111* ⊕ *restaurant.goldeneradler.com.*

★ Lichtblick

$$$$ | **ECLECTIC** | This little restaurant's location on the seventh floor of the chic Rathausgalerie is as lofty as its reputation. The entire restaurant is encased in glass, providing you with sensational views of the Old City, and thanks to the creative menu, it has gained the reputation of one of Innbruck's best hidden gems. The kitchen offers captivating dishes made from fresh local ingredients. The menu changes often and the desserts are especially good. **Known for:** impressive location with wonderful views; imaginative and constantly changing menu; fantastic desserts. $ *Average main: €23* ⊠ *Rathaus Gallery, Maria-Theresienstrasse 18* ☎ *0512/566550* ⊕ *www.restaurant-lichtblick.at* ☉ *Closed Sun.*

Markthalle

$ | **AUSTRIAN** | This tidy indoor market offers plenty of farm-fresh produce, including a variety of cheeses, just-picked berries, and a wide choice of mushrooms. You'll also find pastas and other homemade delicacies, with its central location making it a good stop for an inexpensive lunch. It's basically a take-out place, but there are a few stand-up tables available to eat on. Go to the bakery for your choice of breads, and then browse the stalls to find your ideal fillings. There are usually more food stalls in the Marktplatz outside too. **Known for:** relaxed and bustling atmosphere; one of the city's best take-out lunch spots; amazing homemade breads. $ *Average main: €5* ⊠ *Herzog-Siegmund-Ufer 1-3, Marktplatz* ☎ *0512/4004–404* ⊕ *www.markthalle-innsbruck.at* ▤ *No credit cards* ☉ *Closed Sun.*

Ottoburg

$$$ | **AUSTRIAN** | This family-run restaurant offers excellent food, from burgers to Austrian specialties, and an extraordinary location in an ancient landmark. It was originally built in 1180, as a city watchtower, and retains much of its historical charm. Several of the

bay-window alcoves in the shuttered house have great views of the main square, while others overlook the river. Try the *Tafelspitz*, an Austrian specialty of boiled beef served with vegetables and horseradish, or the *Pfandl*, a fillet of pork and a steak served in an old-fashioned pan. On a sunny day, come early to get a table outside. **Known for:** truly historic atmosphere; delicious classic Austrian dishes; lovely outdoor seating. $ *Average main: €18* ⊠ *Herzog-Friedrich-Strasse 1* ☎ *0512/584338* ⊕ *www.ottoburg.at.*

Restaurant Seegrube

$$ | **AUSTRIAN** | **FAMILY** | Simply put, this restaurant in the Seegrube cableway station is one of the best dinners with a view in the country. At 6,500 feet high, the view of the city lights twinkling below makes a wonderful background for a romantic dinner. The food itself is mostly Tyrolean specialties including *gröstl*, a bacon, onion, and potato fry-up topped with a fried egg. During the week, a hearty breakfast including smoked salmon, sausages, and cheese feeds hungry hikers. During July and August, there is also a jazz brunch every Sunday, starting at 11 am. **Known for:** sublime views; delicious Tyrolean specialties; requires reservations in advance. $ *Average main: €16* ⊠ *Seegrube 1* ☎ *0512/303065* ⊕ *www.seegrube.at.*

Schwarzer Adler

$$$ | **AUSTRIAN** | This intimate, romantic restaurant on the ground floor of the Hotel Schwarzer Adler has leaded-glass windows and rustic embellishments offering the perfect backdrop for a memorable meal (in summer, this includes dining on the rooftop terrace). The innovative chefs present a new menu every couple of months based on regional seasonal specialties. The year-round classics, such as garlic soup with croutons or three kinds of local dumplings served with sauerkraut, are delicious choices. The paintings on display are constantly changing, acting as exhibitions for local artists,

with many works for sale. **Known for:** charming and intimate interiors; dining room doubles as an art gallery; gorgeous outdoor dining. $ *Average main: €22* ⊠ *Kaiserjägerstrasse 2* ☎ *0512/587109* ⊕ *www.schwarzeradler-innsbruck.com.*

★ Sitzwohl

$$$ | **MEDITERRANEAN** | Stylishly modern, with a functional yet intimate atmosphere, Sitzwohl has built up a solid reputation for superb cuisine, with an emphasis on Mediterranean and Tyrolean dishes. Chanterelle mushroom stew with dumplings or black gnocchi with wild salmon and fennel are favorites here. Lunchtime service is quick and efficient for business diners, but the evenings are more relaxed. In addition, chutneys, jams, and soups are available from the attached deli. **Known for:** attentive and quick service; some of the best food in the city; great produce from deli next door. $ *Average main: €20* ⊠ *Stadtforum Gilmstrasse* ☎ *0512/562888* ⊕ *www.restaurantsitzwohl.at* ⊗ *Closed Sun.*

Thai-Li

$$ | **THAI** | This Thai kitchen has quietly fashioned a reputation as one of the best and most popular dining spots in the Old Town. Thai-Li is short on elbow room, but long on excellent food presented with elegance and efficiency. Come for lunch when you can sit outside at the tables on the cobbled pavement. In the evening, start with skewers of grilled chicken and pork, fried prawns, and vegetables with a range of dipping sauces. For a main course, try one of the curry dishes, such as duck simmered in cooconutty red curry. Beverages include a good selection of teas, coffees, and fruit juices. Not to be confused with Thai-Li-Ba across town. **Known for:** very affordable menu; possibly the best Thai food in Tyrol; classic curry dishes. $ *Average main: €15* ⊠ *Marktgraben 3* ☎ *0512/562813* ⊕ *www.thaili.at* ⊗ *Closed Mon.*

Weisses Rössl

$$ | AUSTRIAN | This is Innsbruck's oldest restaurant, and the hunting pedigree of the area is reflected by the array of antlers adorning the walls in the authentically rustic dining rooms. Be aware that this is not a vegetarian's natural habitat, but meat lovers will enjoy the solid local standards, such as *Tiroler Gröstl*, a tasty hash, and Wiener schnitzel (veal, or pork if you prefer, cutlet), both of which taste even better on the outside terrace in summer. Ask about the specials that don't appear on the menu, such as wild game or freshly picked mushrooms. Because the place hosts regular local gatherings it can get quite lively; for a quieter experience, request a table in one of the smaller stubes. **Known for:** historic and atmospheric; classic Austrian meat-heavy staples; lively atmosphere. $ *Average main: €16* ⊠ *Kiebachgasse 8* ☎ *0512/583057* ⊕ *www.roessl.at* ⊘ *Closed Sun.*

★ Wirtshaus Schoneck

$$$$ | AUSTRIAN | With fine views of the city, an atmospheric bar, and veranda and garden for summer dining, this is one of Innsbruck's most exquisite restaurants. Housed in a former imperial hunting lodge across the River Inn from the city center, it has been earning fine-dining accolades since 1899, thanks to a menu that features Austrian staples with a sophisticated twist. The two-course business lunch is a great way to experience the menu at a reasonable price, with options like Viennese goulash with fried egg or bouillabaisse with garlic bread. The evening menus are always a surprise, with dishes decided by the chef that same day. **Known for:** excellent-value business lunches; impressive and historic setting; an ever-changing menu with Austrian classics. $ *Average main: €26* ⊠ *Weiherburggasse 6* ☎ *0512/272728* ⊕ *www.wirtshaus-schoeneck.com* ⊘ *Closed Sun.–Tues.*

☕ Coffee and Quick Bites

Cafe Central

$ | AUSTRIAN | Dark wooden paneling, crystal chandeliers, and the smell of coffee make this Viennese-style café a meeting point for intellectuals, artists, and students. International newspapers and magazines are available, as is a variety of cakes, pastries, and breakfast dishes. You can have breakfast any time of day, or choose something from the daily menu. A typical small dish to sample is *Kasnocken* (cheese dumplings with brown butter); more substantial choices might include traditional boiled beef. Enjoy your cappuccino with live piano accompaniment every Sunday from October to April. In summer, there is also terrace seating. **Known for:** film-noir atmosphere; breakfast available all day; live piano music and terrace seating in the summer. $ *Average main: €15* ⊠ *Hotel Central, Gilmstrasse 5* ☎ *0512/5920* ⊕ *www.hotel-cafe-central.at/en.*

Kröll

$ | CONTEMPORARY | The small bakery and café, a few steps from the Goldenes Dachl, offers homemade strudel (sweet or savory fillings wrapped in a fine pastry) and Italian coffee specialties. The café opens at 6 am every day of the year, until 11 pm in the summer and 9 pm in the winter. **Known for:** savory and sweet strudels; popular (and busy) spot; excellent coffee menu. $ *Average main: €8* ⊠ *Hofgasse 6* ☎ *0512/574347* ⊕ *www. strudel-cafe.at* ⊟ *No credit cards.*

Hotels

★ Adlers

$$ | HOTEL | One of Innsbruck's newer hotels, Adlers eclipses all with its panoramic vistas, and every room in the striking, supermodern building has floor-to-ceiling windows. **Pros:** best view in the city; handy for train station; spacious rooms. **Cons:** no on-site parking (€15-a-day parking nearby); windows don't open; a little way from the prettiest part of town. [$] *Rooms from: €124* ✉ *Bruneckerstasse 1* ☎ *0512/563100* ⊕ *www.adlers-inns-bruck.com* ⇄ *75 rooms* ◯| *No meals.*

★ Gasthof Goldener Adler

$$ | HOTEL | Perfectly located in the heart of the Old Innsbruck's pedestrian area, this is said to be one of Europe's oldest hotels, and since 1390 it has welcomed nearly every king, emperor, duke, or poet who passed through Innsbruck. **Pros:** perfect location; atmosphere of living history; exceptional breakfast buffet. **Cons:** beware the small steps in room doorways; no on-site parking; portrait-heavy trad decor is not for everyone. [$] *Rooms from: €160* ✉ *Herzog-Friedrich-Strasse 6* ☎ *0512/571111* ⊕ *www.goldeneradler. com* ⇄ *43 rooms* ◯| *Free breakfast.*

★ Grand Hotel Europa

$$ | HOTEL | Conveniently located opposite the train station, this top-notch hotel has provided lodging to the celebrated and wealthy in richly appointed, extremely comfortable rooms since it opened in 1869. **Pros:** spacious rooms; wonderful restaurant; opposite train station. **Cons:** on a busy square; a little way from the center; parking lot a walk away. [$] *Rooms from: €200* ✉ *Südtirol-erplatz 2* ☎ *0512/5931* ⊕ *www.grandho-teleuropainnsbruck.com* ⇄ *127 rooms* ◯| *Free breakfast.*

Hotel Innsbruck

$$ | HOTEL | With an ideal location in the heart of Innsbruck, there's an efficient and functional slant here rather than any wow factor—until you look out the window. **Pros:** lovely sauna area (including indoor pool); great location; family run. **Cons:** often has large groups; can be difficult to navigate; business feel rather than Tyrolean charm. [$] *Rooms from: €160* ✉ *Innrain 3* ☎ *0512/598680* ⊕ *www. hotelinnsbruck.com* ⇄ *109 rooms* ◯| *Free breakfast.*

★ Hotel Maximilian

$$ | HOTEL | FAMILY | The clean, modern lines within the vaulted interior of a historic building are immediately striking in this hotel, a couple of minutes from the center of the Old Town. **Pros:** great location; English-language TV channels; striking modern luxury. **Cons:** lack of Tyrolean character; no on-site parking; some rooms on the small side. [$] *Rooms from: €160* ✉ *Marktgraben 7–9* ☎ *0512/59967* ⊕ *www.hotel-maximilian.com* ⇄ *46 rooms* ◯| *Free breakfast.*

Mondschein

$$ | HOTEL | Among the city's oldest and pinkest houses, this warm and welcoming family-run hotel was built across the river from the Old Town in 1473. **Pros:** some rooms have "starry night sky" ceilings; has (expensive) on-site parking; convenient riverfront location. **Cons:** some rooms can be noisy; courtyard rooms are dark; some areas are looking tired. [$] *Rooms from: €115* ✉ *Mariahilfstrasse 6* ☎ *0512/227840* ⊕ *www.mondschein.at* ⇄ *34 rooms* ◯| *Free breakfast.*

Nala Individuell Hotel

$$ | HOTEL | Quirky, colorful, and unapologetically contemporary, Nala is a breath of fresh air in a city dominated by heritage hotels. **Pros:** quirky and colorful rooms; inviting terrace with mountain views; breakfast buffet includes strudel. **Cons:** check out is at 10:30 am; a short walk from the center; too primary colored for some. [$] *Rooms from: €189* ✉ *Müllerstrasse 15* ☎ *0512/584444* ⊕ *www.nala-hotel.at* ⇄ *57 rooms* ◯| *Free breakfast.*

The Penz

$$ | HOTEL | The ultramodern steel-and-glass architecture of this luxury hotel, designed by the renowned French architect Dominique Perrault, is a striking contrast to the Old Town and has a purposeful, business feel that will make traveling executives feel right at home. **Pros:** sleek design; great breakfast; popular rooftop bar. **Cons:** no spa or sauna; can feel a bit sterile for some; rooms above delivery entrance are noisy. $ *Rooms from: €130* ✉ *Adolf-Pichler-Platz 3* ☎ *0512/5756–570* ⊕ *www.the-penz.com* �''94 rooms ⊠ *Free breakfast.*

★ Schwarzer Adler
$$ | **HOTEL** | The vaulted cellars of this 500-year-old building were once stables for Emperor Maximilian's horses; now they host glittering events in atmospheric surroundings, and the hotel attracts those in search of a romantic experience. **Pros:** lovely spa; romantic ambience; every room is different. **Cons:** only one elevator; some rooms face busy street; smoking still tolerated in the bar. $ *Rooms from: €144* ✉ *Kaiserjägerstrasse 2* ☎ *0512/587109* ⊕ *www.schwarzeradler-innsbruck.com* ➭ *47 rooms* ⊠ *Free breakfast.*

Tautermann
$ | **HOTEL** | **FAMILY** | This solid red-shuttered house, a friendly family-run hotel, is within a five-minute walk of the city center, but is in a quiet area across the river. **Pros:** very quiet location outside the center; inexpensive rates; free parking. **Cons:** located up a steep hill; furnishings a little dated; no elevator. $ *Rooms from: €90* ✉ *Stamserfeld 5* ☎ *0512/281572* ⊕ *www.hotel-tautermann. at* ➭ *32 rooms* ⊠ *Free breakfast.*

Weisses Kreuz
$$ | **HOTEL** | **FAMILY** | Quirky, endearing, and in an unrivaled position over ancient stone arcades in the pedestrian heart of the Old Town, this hotel begs you to fall in love with it—and you might, as long as you put character and atmosphere above slick service and cutting-edge amenities. **Pros:** oozing with history and character; family-friendly and well located; breakfast served in original stube. **Cons:** parking is a short walk away; not all rooms are air-conditioned; touristy neighborhood can be noisy in evenings. $ *Rooms from: €105* ✉ *Herzog-Friedrich-Strasse 31* ☎ *0512/594790* ⊕ *www.weisseskreuz.at* ➭ *48 rooms* ⊠ *Free breakfast.*

Nightlife

Blue Chip
DANCE CLUBS | For dancing, this basement club on Landhaus Square is a leading hotspot and a magnet for students Wednesday through Saturday. DJs are highly rated, usually playing house music, hip-hop, and R&B. ✉ *Wilhelm-Greil-Strasse 17* ⊕ *www.chip-ibk.com.*

Casino Innsbruck
CASINOS | The jazzy casino next to the Marriott Hotel offers blackjack, baccarat, roulette, poker, and plenty of slot machines, as well as a bar. You must present your passport to enter the casino. Special meal-plus-gambling-chips packages are available in conjunction with the hotel. ✉ *Salurner Strasse 15* ☎ *0512/59350* ⊕ *www.casinos.at/en/innsbruck.*

Jimmy's Bar
BARS/PUBS | This upstairs bar is wildly popular and has built up a jazz-loving clientele. In the winter it's something of an après-ski hangout. You can expect lots of events here, from guest DJs to jam sessions and party nights. ✉ *Wilhelm-Greil-Strasse 17* ☎ *0699/172–215–55* ⊕ *www.jimmys.at.*

Krahvogel
BARS/PUBS | Known for its wide choice of beer—the drink of choice here rather than cocktails—Krahvogel is also something of a gastropub, with regional and international cuisine on offer. It's on one of Innsbruck's busiest shopping streets and attracts a good cross-section of customers, from tourists to local office workers and students. ✉ *Anichstrasse 12* ☎ *0512/580149* ⊕ *www.facebook.com/krahvogel.*

Performing Arts

It's said that Tyrol has more bandleaders than mayors. Folklore shows at the **Messehalle** and other spots around the city showcase authentic Tyrolean folk dancing, yodeling, and zither music. The tourist office and hotels have more details.

Festwochen der Alten Musik

FESTIVALS | Between mid-July and late August, the Festival of Early Music highlights music from the 14th to 18th centuries, performed by many of Europe's finest musicians in such dramatic settings as Innsbruck's beautiful Schloss Ambras and the Hofkirche. In summer there are frequent brass-band (*Musikkapelle*) concerts in the Old Town. During the Renaissance and in the Baroque era, Innsbruck was one of Europe's most important centers for music, and this is the oldest existing festival to celebrate such early music. ⊠ *Universitätsstrasse 1* ☎ *0512/5710–32* ⊕ *www.altemusik.at.*

Kongresshaus

CONCERTS | The original congress house was built by Archduke Leopold V in 1629 as the first freestanding opera house north of the Alps, and in the 19th century it was converted into the Dogana, or customs house. Destroyed during World War II, its remains were used to create this modern congress and events center in 1973. Concerts take place in the modern Saal Tirol. ⊠ *Rennweg 3* ☎ *0512/5936–1000* ⊕ *www.cmi.at/en.*

Tanzsommer Innsbruck

DANCE | The world's premiere dance companies have been visiting Innsbruck between the last week in June and mid-July for this international dance festival since 1992. The world-renowned Dance Theatre of Harlem and the Sao Paulo Dance Company, as well as Maracana, Brazil's Grupo Corpo, and Sankai Juku, all feature regularly. Visitors can join in dance workshops, too. Tickets are available through the tourist office or the festival office. ⊠ *Burggraben 3* ☎ *0512/577–677.*

Tiroler Landestheater

CONCERTS | Innsbruck's principal theater is said to be the world's oldest German-speaking theater. It was built in 1654 as the court opera house, but totally renovated in the classical style in 1846 and modernized and extended in the 1960s. Both operas and operettas are presented in the main hall, usually starting at 7:30 pm; plays and dance in the Kammerspiele start at 8 pm. Obtain tickets at the box office or at the city's main tourist office. ⊠ *Rennweg 2* ☎ *0512/520744* ⊕ *www.landestheater.at.*

Shopping

The best shops are along the arcaded Herzog-Friedrich-Strasse in the heart of the Altstadt; along its extension, Maria-Theresien-Strasse; and the adjoining streets Meraner Strasse and Anichstrasse. Innsbruck is the place to buy native Tyrolean clothing, particularly lederhosen (traditional brushed leather shorts and trousers) and loden (sturdy combed-wool jackets and vests). Look also for cut crystal and woodcarvings; locally handmade, delicate silver-filigree pins make fine gifts.

Boschi

GIFTS/SOUVENIRS | Reproductions of old pewterware, using the original molds when possible, are among the items you'll find here, along with locally produced, hand-decorated beer mugs with pewter lids. ⊠ *Kiebachgasse 8* ☎ *0512/589224* ⊕ *www.boschi.at* ⊗ *Closed Sun.*

Christmas Markets

CRAFTS | For sheer holiday delight, nothing tops the traditional Christmas markets, which features wooden and glass handicrafts, Christmas-tree decorations, candles, and Tyrolean toys and loden costumes. There are half a dozen different markets around Innsbruck and its environs, but the highlight is the one in the heart of the Old Town. Here, market stalls are set up around the giant, illuminated Christmas tree next to the Goldenes Dachl. The markets are open from mid-November until 6 January. ⊠ *Herzog-Friedrich-Strasse 15* ⊕ *www.christkindlmarkt. cc/en/markets/maria-theresien-strasse* ⊗ *Closed Jan.–mid-Nov.*

Culinarium

WINE/SPIRITS | This is *the* shop to buy Austrian wine, which has come on leaps and bounds in recent years, as well as wonderful schnapps and rum. You can try everything before you buy, and the talkative, friendly owner will be happy to advise. ⊠ *Pfarrgasse 1* 🕾 *0512/890589* ⊕ *www.facebook.com/ culinariuminnsbruck2020.*

Galerie Thomas Flora

ART GALLERIES | The droll graphics by Tyrolean artist Paul Flora on sale here provide much to smile at, and maybe you'll even find something to take home. ⊠ *Herzog-Friedrich-Strasse 5* 🕾 *0512/577402.*

Hubertus Moden Steinbock

CLOTHING | This is an outstanding source of dirndls, those attractive traditional costumes for women, with white blouses, dark skirts, and colorful aprons. It also has children's clothing. ⊠ *Sparkassenplatz 3* 🕾 *0512/585092* ⊕ *www. steinbock.at* ☺ *Closed Sun.*

Rathausgalerie

SHOPPING CENTERS/MALLS | Innsbruck's swish, central, glass-roofed indoor mall is home to luxury boutiques and world-famous brand names. Here you can shop, eat, and drink in style. ⊠ *Maria-Theresien-Strasse 18* 🕾 *0512/574861* ⊕ *www. rathausgalerien.at.*

Swarovski Crystal Worlds

CERAMICS/GLASSWARE | This dazzling Old Town gallery features a dazzling array of crystal products from the world-renowned maker, whose headquarters is in nearby Wattens, east of Innsbruck. ⊠ *Herzog-Friedrich-Strasse 39* 🕾 *05224/51080* ⊕ *www.swarovski.com/ innsbruck.*

Tiroler Heimatwerk

CLOTHING | Make this your first stop for high-quality souvenirs. The extremely attractive shop carries textiles and finished clothing, ceramics, carved wooden chests, and some furniture, but don't expect a bargain. You can also

have clothing made to order. ⊠ *Meraner Strasse 2* 🕾 *0512/582320* ⊕ *www.heimatwerk.co.at* ☺ *Closed Sun.*

Activities

GOLF
Golfclub Innsbruck-Igls

GOLF | It's the breathtaking views of surrounding mountains that make this a special golfing experience. About nine kilometers (5½ miles) outside Innsbruck, this club has two courses, an 18-hole championship course at Rinn and a nine-hole course at nearby Lans. Founded in 1935, the courses are among Austria's oldest, with concentric, partly hilly fairways on an ascending plateau. The golf club is open April through November. ⊠ *Oberdorf 11, Rinn* 🕾 *05223/78177* ⊕ *www.golfclub-innsbruck-igls.at* 🏌 *Rinn: €90 for 18 holes; Lans: €50 for 9 holes* 🏌 *Rinn: 18 holes, 6622 yards, par 71; Lans: 9 holes, 4662 yards, par 33.*

HIKING

Both easy paths and extreme slopes await hikers and climbers. From June to October holders of the Innsbruck Card can take free, daily, guided mountain hikes. The tourist office has a special hiking brochure.

HORSEBACK RIDING
Reitclub Innsbruck (*Campagnereitergesellschaft Tirol*)

HORSEBACK RIDING | Horseback riding can be arranged through Reitclub Innsbruck, which is based in the village of Igls just outside Innsbruck. ⊠ *Römerstrasse 50, Innsbruck-Igls* 🕾 *0664/516–5505* ⊕ *www. reitclub-innsbruck.com.*

ROCK CLIMBING
Alpine Auskunft

CLIMBING/MOUNTAINEERING | Whether you're an experienced climber or new learner, the man to contact for rock climbing in Tyrol is Mike Rutter at Alpine Auskunft. He has advice on everything from suitable climbing areas to guides

and courses. ⊠ *Meinhardstrasse 7–11*
☎ *0512/587828* ⊕ *www.alpine-auskunft.at.*

SKIING

Around Innsbruck you'll find everything
from the beginner slopes of the
Glungezer to the good intermediate
skiing of Axamer Lizum and Patscherkofel to the steep runs and off-piste
skiing of Seegrube. Your Innsbruck
Card includes transportation to the ski
areas and reduced prices on a number
of ski lifts. A variety of combination ski
passes are available that give access
to lifts at resorts around Innsbruck and
throughout Tyrol. For example, the Olym-
picWorld Ski Pass gives access to nine
mountains, with 300 kilometers (186
miles) of trails, including Nordketten-
bahn-Seegrube, Patscherkofel, Axamer
Lizum, Muttereralm, Kühtai, Rangger
Köpfl, Glungezer, Schlick 2000, and
Stubai Glacier. The tourist office can give
you more information and also sells all
necessary tickets.

Die Boerse

SKIING/SNOWBOARDING | You can book
all skiing needs, from equipment to lift
tickets at this store, tucked into an alley
just south of the Triumphpforte. You can
also hire instructors and book lessons
through the on-site Ski & Snowboard-
schule Innsbruck to meet you at your
hotel or one of the ski areas, or the
school can arrange transportation (at
extra cost). It can also arrange days out,
with instruction, at farther-flung resorts
such as St. Anton, Ischgl, or Solden.
One-on-one tuition starts at €140 for an
afternoon, with each additional person
€10. ⊠ *Leopoldstrasse 4* ☎ *660/21–
44–660* ⊕ *www.dieboerse.at, www.
skischule-innsbruck.com.*

SWIMMING

Around Innsbruck there are plenty of
lakes, but in town you have little choice
other than pools, indoors and out.

Freibad Tivoli

SWIMMING | Come here to swim under
the sun with a panoramic view of the
mountains. ⊠ *Purtschellerstrasse 1*
☎ *0512/502–7081* ⊕ *www.ikb.at/privat/
baeder/freibad-tivoli.*

Hallenbad Amraser Strasse

SWIMMING | If the weather goes south,
try this turn-of-the-20th-century indoor
swimming pool with an Art Nouveau
look. ⊠ *Amraser Strasse 3* ☎ *0676/836–
867–056* ⊕ *www.ikb.at/privat/baeder/
hallenbad-sauna-amraser-strasse.*

Hallenbad Höttinger Au

SWIMMING | This is a popular indoor
swimming facility, also boasting a
counterflow pool and sauna and
sunbeds. ⊠ *Fürstenweg 12* ☎ *0676/836–
867–076* ⊕ *www.ikb.at/privat/baeder/
hallenbad-sauna-hoettinger-au.*

Hall in Tirol

*9 km (7 miles) east of Innsbruck, 18 km
(5½ miles) northeast of the Stubaital
Valley.*

A few minutes by road east of Innsbruck
is what many say is the most beautiful
town in Tyrol—ancient Hall, wonderfully
preserved and with a historic center
actually larger than that of Innsbruck. The
town has a history of great prosperity—
salt mining in the Middle Ages made it
the most important commercial hub in
the region at the time (the High German
word *Hal* means salt mine). The town
received its municipal charter in 1286,
but even greater prestige was to come
nearly 200 years later when the provincial
mint was moved to the town.

GETTING HERE AND AROUND

From Innsbruck, take Highway A12 east.
There is frequent bus service between
Innsbruck and Hall on Route 4 (every 15
minutes), with a journey time of about
20 minutes. The Postbus system has
frequent services linking Hall with the

Eastern Tyrol

rest of Tyrol and beyond. Hall is also on the rail network.

VISITOR INFORMATION

CONTACTS Hall in Tirol. ⊠ *Unterer Stadtplatz 19, Hall in Tirol* ☎ *05223/45544* ⊕ *www.hall-wattens.at.*

 Sights

Burg Hasegg and Hall Mint

MUSEUM | Built to protect the salt mines and trade on the River Inn, Burg Hasegg was enlarged into a showpiece castle by Duke Siegmund and Emperor Maximilian I. Meanwhile, the first silver coin in Tyrol, the thaler—say it quickly and you'll realize it was the root of the modern word, dollar—emerged from the Münze (mint) in the center of Hall. In 1567, Ferdinand II moved the mint to Burg Hasegg, and thereafter the fortunes of the mint and the castle became intertwined. In the 18th century, 17 million Maria Theresa thaler were minted here and became a valued currency throughout the world. Today, you can visit the mint museum where you can even mint your own coin, as well as climb to the top of the Mint Tower for splendid views. ⊠ *Burg Hasegg 6, Hall in Tirol* ☎ *05223/5855–520* ⊕ *www.muenze-hall.at* 🎟 *€11 (inc. tower)* ⊘ *Closed Mon. all year; closed Sun. in Nov.–Mar., closed except groups mid-Jan.–mid-Mar.*

Damenstift (*Herz-Jesu-Basilika*)

RELIGIOUS SITE | Archduchess Magdelena, sister of Ferdinand II, founded the Damenstift Abbey, home of the silent order of Carmelite nuns, in 1567–69. While the abbey was abolished in 1783, the order survived, and today the remaining (mostly elderly) nuns can be found praying in the Collegiate Church (Herz-Jesu-Basilika) at the top of Eugenstrasse. A tiny plaque on the dramatic church facade—an example of the transition from the Renaissance to the Baroque style—confirms its links to the historic Damenstift. Sit quietly at the back of the church and witness the silent and extensive devotions of the nuns amidst the glorious interior of wood, marble, and gold. ⊠ *Jesuitenkirche , Eugenstrasse 14, Hall in Tirol* 🎟 *Free.*

Pfarrkirche St. Nikolaus

RELIGIOUS SITE | Hall in Tirol's most prominent building is this large, 13th-century Catholic church, boasting a dramatic interior of pinks, golds, and blacks with grand ceiling frescos. The undoubted highlight is the Waldaufkapelle, home to Florian Waldauf's rather gruesome collection of 45 skulls, said to be those of B-list saints. Waldauf, something of a fixer for Emperor Maximilian I at the beginning of the 16th century, began scouring Europe for relics to purchase, and eventually opened his prized collection to the public. Now, the skulls rest on individual embroidered cushions and are, rather oddly, topped with decorative headdresses. ⊠ *Pfarrplatz 1, Hall in Tirol* ☎ *05223/57914* ⊕ *www.pfarre-hall.at* 🎟 *Free.*

★ Wolfsklamm

TRAIL | If you're driving from Hall in Tirol to Zell am Ziller, this impressive gorge hike is the perfect stop along the way. Exhilarating and spectacular (but very safe), the climb starts in the village of Stans, follows walkways hewn from the mountainside and across bridges spanning the tumbling river and beside waterfalls—all protected by railings—and finally reaches the Benedictine monastery of St. Georgenberg. The whole thing takes about 90 minutes and features 354 steps. At the top, the monastery's sumptuously decorated Baroque church, precariously perched on a rocky peak, is worth a few minutes of your time. There is a decent restaurant, too, with a terrace dizzily located above a sheer drop of several hundred feet. ⊠ *Stans.*

Hotels

Garten Hotel Maria Theresia

$$ | **HOTEL** | Built in solid, substantial, flower-bedecked chalet style, this is a family hotel to the core, and the family that runs it is the epitome of true Tyrolean innkeeping and hospitality. **Pros:** very good value; family run and very friendly; excellent food. **Cons:** away from the prettiest district of Hall; bit of a walk to the town center; the bells of a nearby church may disturb some. [$] *Rooms from: €110* ✉ *Reimmichlstrasse 25, Heiligkreuz, Hall in Tirol* ☎ *05223/56313* 🌐 *www.gartenhotel.at* 🛏 *24 rooms* 🍴 *Free breakfast.*

Gasthof Badl

$$ | **HOTEL** | **FAMILY** | For a short stay, this gasthof can fit the bill at a budget price, offering a warm welcome and rooms that are sparkling clean, with all the comfort you need for an overnight stay. **Pros:** extremely friendly and family run; excellent value; great views on the river side. **Cons:** close to an autobahn so can be noisy; not in the center of town; friendly dogs roam the grounds. [$] *Rooms from: €110* ✉ *Haller Innbrücke 4, Ampass, Hall in Tirol* ☎ *05223/56784* 🌐 *www.badl.at* 🛏 *25 rooms* 🍴 *Free breakfast.*

Rettenberg Hotel

$ | **HOTEL** | Close to Hall in Tirol and very handy for Innsbruck, this comfortable hotel remains a place where you can feel part of a small community and actually meet locals in the bar. **Pros:** very reasonable prices; lots of local character; on-site spa with pool and bowling alley. **Cons:** rooms at the front can be noisy; smoking still allowed in the bar; main slopes are a drive or bus ride away. [$] *Rooms from: €59* ✉ *Mühlbach 6, Kolsass-Weer* ☎ *05224/68124* 🌐 *www.kolsass.at* 🛏 *45 rooms* 🍴 *Free breakfast.*

Zell am Ziller

60 km (38 miles) southeast of Innsbruck, 52 km (32 miles) southeast of Hall in Tirol.

Zell is the main town of the Zillertal, one of the many beautiful Alpine valleys of the Tyrol, and a real working community rather than just a resort town. It is notable for its traditional 500-year-old Gauder Fest, and has also developed into a center of summer activities. You can choose to stay in one of a dozen hotels or bed-and-breakfast pensions at surprisingly reasonable cost. Although Zell is considered the valley's main town, the bigger-name resort, especially for skiing, is Mayrhofen, a little farther up the valley and somewhat more expensive. In Zell, families enjoy the Fun-arena, which has water slides and a roller coaster for kids, while adults can try rafting or paragliding.

GETTING HERE AND AROUND

From Innsbruck, take Highway A12 or Route 171 to Wiesing; from here, the B169 will lead you to the Ziller Valley. Kids—and quite a few adults—will love the old steam engine of the Zillertalbahn pulling a few historical cars from Jenbach train station up the Zillertal to Zell, and then on to Mayrhofen, twice a day.

Sights

★ Gauder Fest

FESTIVAL | The more than 500-year-old Gauder Fest, held on the first weekend in May, is Austria's biggest folk festival. Thousands of visitors, many of them in traditional costume from Tyrol and other parts of Austria, pack the little market town of Zell am Ziller for the colorful skits, music, and singing—and great quantities of *Gauderbier,* a strong brew created for the occasion. You can hear some of the country's best singing by the valley residents and listen to expert harp and zither playing, for which the valley is famous. Tradition runs strong here, so even if you can't make it in May, there are other festival opportunities: witness the Perchtenlaufen, processions of colorfully masked well-wishers going the neighborhood rounds on January 5; or come for the annual Almabtrieb on the last September and first October days, when the cows (decorated with wreaths and bells) are herded back from the high Alpine pastures into the lower fields and barns. ✉ *Zell am Ziller* 🌐 *www.gauderfest.at.*

Krimml Waterfalls

BODY OF WATER | The tiered Krimml falls plunge down in three stages, with a total drop of 1,247 feet, making it the highest waterfall in Austria and one of Austria's most popular natural attractions. A path ascends through the woods beside the falls, with frequent viewing points. By car or bus, it's 35 minutes from Zell am Ziller over the Gerlos Pass. ✉ *Krimml* ☎ *06564/7212* 🌐 *www.wasserfaelle-krimml.at* 🎟 *€10 (includes water park); €4 to just walk the path beside the waterfall* 🕒 *Closed Nov.–mid-Apr.*

🍴 Restaurants

Hotel Gasthof Bräu

$$ | AUSTRIAN | FAMILY | The core of this frescoed building in the town center dates from the 16th century, but subsequent renovations have brought the five-story structure up to date. The three-room restaurant offers a menu with an emphasis on fish and game, and many ingredients come directly from the owner's own farm and fish ponds or from other local suppliers. Go for the trout, and make sure to taste the house beer from the on-site brewery, also the source of a special made-for-the-festival brew, Zillertel Gauderbier. The "Bräu" also has some nice rooms to stay the night; book early if you want to reserve a room during the Gauder Fest. **Known for:** beautifully decorated wood-paneled parlors; locally grown produce; beer from nearby family brewery. [$] *Average main: €17* ✉ *Dorfplatz 1* ☎ *05282/2313* 🌐 *www.hotel-braeu.at* 🕒 *Closed Apr. and mid-Oct.–mid-Dec.*

🏃 Activities

ZIP-LINING

Arena Skyliner

ZIP LINING | FAMILY | A development of the Flying Fox zip-line concept, the Skyliner has four lines where you can hurtle along at 50 kph (31 mph) and get a bird's-eye view of the area (on Line 3 you are more than 200 feet above the ground). The meeting point is at the top station of the Gerlosstein cable car. Minimum and maximum weight restrictions apply—40 kilos (88 pounds) and 120 kilos (265 pounds), respectively. ✉ *Dorfplatz 3a* ☎ *0664/44–19–283* 🌐 *www.zillertalarena.com/en/arena/sommer/arena-skyliner.html* 🎟 *€42.30.*

Kitzbühel

92 km (57 miles) east of Innsbruck, 78 km (49 miles) northeast of Zell am Ziller.

Kitzbühel is indisputably one of Austria's most fashionable winter resorts, although the town boasts a busy summer season as well. "Kitz" offers warm-season visitors a hefty program of hiking, cycling, golf, and lake swimming (at nearby Schwarzsee), along with outdoor concerts and plays. It also hosts the annual Austrian Open tennis tournament in July. In winter, many skiers are attracted by the famous Ski Safari—a carefully planned, clever combination of chairlifts, gondola lifts, draglifts, and runs that lets you ski for more than 145 km (91 miles) without having to walk a single foot. Kitzbühel is in perpetual motion and is busy December through mid-April, notably at the end of January for the famed **Hahnenkamm World Cup** downhill ski race. At any time during the season there's plenty to do, from sleigh rides to fancy-dress balls. And with parts of the town dating back to the 14th century, Kitzbühel is a scenic place to stay year-round. **■TIP→ In summer, visitors are offered free guest cards, which provide free access or substantially**

reduced fees for various activities, such as tennis, riding, and golf.

GETTING HERE AND AROUND

From Innsbruck, take the autobahn A12 or B171 west to the town of Wörgl, then the B170 to Kitzbühel. From here you can travel south on the B161/B108 to Matrei in Osttirol and to Lienz.

VISITOR INFORMATION

CONTACTS Kitzbühel Tourismus. ✉ *Hinterstadt 18* ☎ *05356/66660* 🌐 *www.kitzbuehel.com/en.*

Sights

Alpine Flower Garden Kitzbühel
GARDEN | Take the cable car up the Kitzbüheler Horn to this lovely garden at 6,500 feet. Amid glorious mountain scenery you will see hundreds of varieties of Alpine flowers in their native habitat, including varieties from other parts of the world. Guided tours are offered daily at 11 am from June to early September. ✉ *Kitzbühel* ☎ *05356/6951* 🌐 *www.kitzbuehel.com/en* 🎫 *Free; cable car: one way €22, round-trip €27.50.*

Church of St. Catherine (*Katharinenkirche*)
RELIGIOUS SITE | Built around 1350, this historic church houses a Gothic winged altar dating from 1515. Kitzbühel is also blessed with several other beautiful churches, including St. Andrew's (1435–1506) with its lavish Rococo chapel, and Christuskirche (1962) with its striking white bell tower. ✉ *Kitzbühel.*

Restaurants

★ Hallerwirt
$$ | AUSTRIAN | In the small village of Aurach about 5 km (3 miles) south of Kitzbühel, Hallerwirt is known for its great Austrian cuisine and charm. Old wooden floors and a ceramic stove in the parlor lend a period flair to this 400-year-old farmhouse. A colorful mix of people gathers here, and young and old enjoy the easygoing vibe. The congenial hosts, Monika and Jürgen Stelzhammer, take time to give everyone some good wine suggestions. The friendly staff serves specialties such as Jerusalem artichoke soup and fillet of lamb. **Known for:** warm welcome from the owners; charming surroundings; use of local produce. [$] *Average main: €18* ✉ *Oberaurach 4, Aurach bei Kitzbühel* ☎ *05356/64502* 🌐 *www.hallerwirt.at* 🕒 *Closed Mon.–Tue. and mid-Nov.–early Dec.*

Praxmair
$ | CAFÉ | Après-ski can't begin early enough for the casually chic crowds that pile into this famous café and pastry shop in the heart of Kitzbühel. For locals, the Praxmair is a meeting point for regular get-togethers, cabaret performances, and small events. The wood interior and a tiled stove give the place a special flair. **Known for:** bustling atmosphere; live après-ski music; tasty krapfen (jelly doughnuts). [$] *Average main: €10* ✉ *Vorderstadt 17* ☎ *05356/62646* 💳 *No credit cards* 🕒 *Closed Apr. and Nov.*

★ Tennerhof Gourmet
$$$$ | AUSTRIAN | Expect elegant dress and quiet conversations at this high-class restaurant, where Johannes Denk and his creative team have been awarded 17 Gault Millau points and previously held a Michelin star. Freshly picked herbs from the garden accompany almost every dish, from soup to sorbet, and imaginative dishes might include rainbow trout paired with a pig's trotter. Local game is a passion, and food and wine are presented by well-trained, white-gloved staff in one of the four cozy parlors that make up the *Kupferstube*. Menus range from four courses (€120) to seven courses (€185). **Known for:** cozy Tyrolean atmosphere; local produce from the on-site garden; great wine menu. [$] *Average main: €120* ✉ *Tennerhof Hotel, Griesenauweg 26* ☎ *05356/63181* 🌐 *www.tennerhof.com* 🕒 *Closed Mon.–Tue.; closed Apr.–May and Oct.–mid-Dec.*

Hotels

★ Rasmushof

$$$ | HOTEL | It's hard to imagine a better choice for a Kitzbühel stay than this superluxurious but relaxed former farmstead, with unrivaled year-round proximity to outdoor activities. **Pros:** fabulous location; breathtaking views; ski-in ski-out in winter. **Cons:** pretty pricey for the area; away from the town center; service in bar can be curt. 💲 *Rooms from: €255 ⊠ Hermann Reisch Weg 15 ☎ 05356/652520 ⊕ www.rasmushof.at 🛏 60 rooms ⦿ Free breakfast.*

★ Tennerhof

$$$$ | HOTEL | Adored by the rich and famous, from the Duke of Windsor to Kirk Douglas, this Alpine Shangri-la is at once rustic and glamorous, with gold chandeliers hung over country cupboards and silk-covered sofas next to shuttered windows. **Pros:** grand aristocratic flair; great breakfast; lovely garden. **Cons:** a little way from the town center and ski lifts; can be too fancy for some; very expensive. 💲 *Rooms from: €340 ⊠ Griesenauweg 26 ☎ 05356/63181 ⊕ www.tennerhof.com ⊙ Closed Apr.– May and Oct.–mid-Dec. 🛏 39 rooms ⦿ Free breakfast.*

★ Villa Licht

$$$ | B&B/INN | This adorable Hansel-and-Gretel chalet is home to eight self-catering apartments where hospitality and attention to detail are paramount. **Pros:** a short walk from town center; very quiet; lots of free parking. **Cons:** no restaurant (though plenty nearby); minimum five-night stays in high season; need to book well in advance. 💲 *Rooms from: €230 ⊠ Franz Reisch Strasse 8 ☎ 05356/62293 ⊕ www.villa-licht.at 🛏 8 apartments ⦿ Free breakfast.*

Nightlife

Fünferl

BARS/PUBS | Located in the center of town, this place is full of character and has many dedicated fans. It's good for late-evening cocktails and attracts a somewhat more mature and relaxed clientele who prefer conversation to partying. ⊠ *Franz-Reisch-Strasse 1 ⊕ www.club-takefive.com/fuen-ferl ⊙ Closed Sun.–Tues.*

Kitzbühel Casino

CASINOS | Few casinos can be located in such a charming and historic building as this, in the center of town. It offers baccarat, blackjack, roulette, and one-armed bandits. There's a restaurant and bar, and it's open late (usually until 3 am). A valid passport or driver's license is needed to enter. ⊠ *Hinterstadt 24 ☎ 05356/62300 ⊕ www.casinos.at/en/kitzbuehel.*

The Londoner

BARS/PUBS | Young people flock to this popular watering hole, one of the biggest-name bars in town. It gets packed by fans and racers alike on big ski-race days, and can be just too crammed to get in. ⊠ *Franz-Reisch-Strasse 4 ☎ 05356/71427 ⊕ www.thelondoner.at.*

Take Five

DANCE CLUBS | The dance-club crowd moves from place to place, but check out this hot spot in the center of Kitz. It has three bars and a spacious VIP area, and aims for a sophisticated atmosphere. ⊠ *Hinterstadt 22 ☎ 0664/308–1634 ⊕ www.club-takefive.com.*

🏃 Activities

GOLF

With four courses on its doorstep and a dozen more within an hour's drive, Kitzbühel may properly lay claim to being the golf center of the Alps. The Golf Alpin Card (⊕ *www.golf-alpin.at*) offers special deals, including five green fees for €360 or three for €225; it's available at several Kitzbühel hotels and golf clubs, or from the tourist office.

Golf Eichenheim

GOLF | Heady views of soaring Alpine peaks surrounding the course are mixed with leafy fringed fairways to give this 18-hole PGA-rated venue a unique appeal. The name, meaning "Oak Home," reflects the surroundings, and a round includes the opportunity to appreciate rare flora and fauna. If you work up an appetite, the clubhouse includes a gourmet restaurant. ⊠ *Eichenheim 8* ☎ *05356/66615–560* ⊕ *www.eichenheim. com* ✉ *Apr.–Jun. and Oct.–Nov. €80; Jul.–Sep. €99; 9 holes €40–€50* 🏌 *18 holes, 6662 yards, par 71.*

Golfclub Kitzbühel

GOLF | This pretty nine-hole course winds between ancient trees and water hazards with a fabulous backdrop of Alpine grandeur. The slightly hilly terrain is set around the Grand Spa Resort A-Rosa, and resort guests receive a discount. There are plenty of water hazards, with two of the greens located on islands. The course, built in 1955, is open from May to October and has a handicap limit of 36. ⊠ *Ried Caps 3* ☎ *05356/63007* ⊕ *www.golfclub-kitzbuehel.at* ✉ *€94 for 18 holes, €56 for 9 holes* 🏌 *9 holes, 5629 yards, par 70.*

Golf-Club Kitzbühel-Schwarzsee-Reith

GOLF | Amazing views to the Wilder Kaiser mountain range and the Kitzbuheler Horn peak nearby help to make this 18-hole course a treat for the senses. The par-72 course is varied, with wide fairways. A big surprise is sprung at the par-three 16th hole—called the Mousetrap—which is played over a small ravine. The course is open from May to October (in winter it's used by cross-country skiers), and holders of the Kitzbühel Guest Card get a 20% green fee discount. ⊠ *Golfweg-Schwarzsee 35* ☎ *05356/66660–70* ⊕ *www.kitzbuehel. com/golf-schwarzsee* ✉ *May–Jun. and Oct., €87 for 18 holes, €50 for 9 holes; Jul.–Sep., €95 for 18 holes, €57 for 9 holes* 🏌 *18 holes, 6675 yards, par 72.*

Rasmushof Golf Club

GOLF | This May-through-October golf course is also the location of the final slope of the famous Streif run of the fearsome Hahnenkamm World Cup downhill race. Part of the Rasmushof Hotel, it's also the course closest to the town center. The greens and fairways are in full view of the glorious old building's balconies, and hotel guests receive significantly discounted rates. ⊠ *Hermann-Reisch-Weg 15* ☎ *05356/65252* ⊕ *www. rasmushof.at* ✉ *€28 for 9 holes on weekdays, €34 on weekends; €38 for 18 holes on weekdays, €44 on weekends. Hotel guests: €19 per day for unlimited play* 🏌 *9 holes, 3060 yards, par 54.*

SKIING

Kitzbühel is one of Austria's leading resorts and home to the Hahnenkamm World Cup Downhill, one of the most daunting events on the ski-racing calendar. There are many easy slopes, too, and the ski network here is vast and spectacular, with 60 lovely mountain huts scattered over the slopes offering excellent food and drink to break the ski day. There are 192 km (119 miles) of slopes—106 of them blue, 66 red and 20 black—all served by 57 ski lifts throughout winter and spring (often until early May). Intersport Kitzsport has a number of shops in town with the latest equipment for rent, as does Sport 2000. There are a dozen ski schools with hundreds of instructors at peak times. The tourist office website has full information.

The Stubaital

11 km (7 miles) southwest of Innsbruck (Schönberg im Stubaital).

The delightful Stubaital is one of the most beautiful valleys in the Tyrol. Though less than 40 kilometers (25 miles) long, it has no fewer than 80 glistening glaciers (including the Stubai Glacier) and more than 40 towering peaks. The gondola lift up to the glacier is spectacular, and you can venture onto the glacier on marked walks. The higher slopes are open for skiing most of the summer, too. If you just want to look, you can see the whole Stubaital in a full day's excursion from Innsbruck.

GETTING HERE AND AROUND

The narrow-gauge electric Stubaitalbahn can take you from the center of Innsbruck (on Maria-Theresien-Strasse and in front of the main train station), as well as from the station just below the Bergisel ski jump, as far as Fulpmes, partway up the valley. You can take the bus as far as Ranalt and back to Fulpmes, to see more of the valley, then return on the quaint rail line.

Sights

★ Stubai Glacier

MOUNTAIN—SIGHT | At the southwesterly end of the valley lies Austria's biggest glacier. It's also one of the country's most popular ski resorts, with miles upon miles of snow-covered slopes open all year round, even in the height of summer. For warm-weather visitors who prefer hiking boots to ski boots, there's an extensive network of trails throughout the area. ✉ *Mutterberg 2, Innsbruck* ☎ *05226/8141* 🌐 *www.stubaier-gletscher.com/en.*

Sölden

84 km (52 miles) southwest of Innsbruck, 176 km (109 miles) southwest of Kitzbühel.

Sölden is a skier's paradise, home to the only lift system in Austria to boast skiing on three mountains more than 9,800 feet high. Its latest addition is the "Black Blade," which carries eight at a time up to the sky-high Rettenbach glacier, where panoramic mountain views await. Sölden's reputation as a wild, après-ski party town is well deserved, so if you are searching for a tranquil, romantic ski holiday, or have small children, you may want to try the quieter village of **Hochsölden** on the slopes above town instead.

GETTING HERE AND AROUND

From Innsbruck take the A12 west. Then take the B186 south to the Ötztal; after about 37 km (23 miles) you will reach the town of Sölden.

Leaving Sölden you can backtrack on the B168 north to the A12, or if you feel like some real hairpin Alpine driving, go south into Italy over the Timmelsjoch Pass.

VISITOR INFORMATION

CONTACTS Ötztal Tourismus. ✉ *Gemeindestrasse 4* ☎ *0572/00–200* 🌐 *www.soelden.com.*

Hotels

Aqua Dome Hotel and Spa

$$$$ | **HOTEL** | In the midst of breathtaking nature 15 minutes north of Sölden lies not only the finest spa in Tyrol, but also elegant guest rooms with balconies and stunning mountain views. **Pros:** incredible spa; great food; free nonalcoholic drinks in the minibar. **Cons:** spa busy on weekends; too sprawling for some; some distance from the ski slopes. [$] *Rooms from: €408* ✉ *Oberlängenfeld 140, Längenfeld* ☎ *05253/6400* 🌐 *www.aqua-dome.at* 🛏 *200 rooms* 🍴 *No meals.*

Das Central

$$$$ | **HOTEL** | Huge arches and heavy wood beams set the mood at this five-star hotel that's substantial both in size and character, and has superb spa and fitness amenities. **Pros:** wonderful personal service; on-demand shuttle to the slopes; fabulous spa. **Cons:** slopes are not within walking distance; not all rooms have great views; church bells can be an early wake-up call. [$] *Rooms from: €400* ✉ *Auweg 3* ☎ *05254/2260–0* 🌐 *www.central-soelden.at* 🛏 *125 rooms* 🍴 *Free breakfast.*

Hikers, bikers, photographers, and nature-lovers are all drawn to the Stubaital and its epic beauty in summer.

Hotel Ritzlerhof

$$$ | HOTEL | Spectacularly located in the village of Sautens, on a shelf in the hillside high above the Ötz Valley, the Ritzlerhof is single-mindedly purposed toward meditational levels of peace and relaxation. **Pros:** idyllic location; heated indoor and outdoor pools; lots of peace and quiet. **Cons:** a long way from ski lifts; evening meals are mediocre; too remote for some. $ *Rooms from: €270* ⊠ *Ritzlerhof 1, Sautens* ☎ *05252/62680* ⊕ *www.ritzlerhof.at/en* ⊅ *45 rooms* ⏏️ *Free breakfast.*

Liebe Sonne

$$ | HOTEL | Skiers will be right next to the Giggijoch chairlift to Hochsölden at this sprawling yellow complex; the famous lift is also open all summer to give hikers and mountain bikers a flying start to their day. **Pros:** spacious rooms; close to the ski slopes; on-site stables for horseback riding. **Cons:** gets extremely busy in winter; can hear après-ski revellers until late; lacking in Tyrolean tradition and decor. $ *Rooms from: €280* ⊠ *Dorfstrasse 58* ☎ *05254/2203* ⊕ *www.*

liebesonne.at ⊅ *60 rooms* ⏏️ *Free breakfast.*

★ Naturhotel Waldklause

$$$$ | HOTEL | It's hard to tell where this hotel ends and the countryside begins—floors are natural stone, rooms smell of applewood paneling, and some exterior walls are built around trees. **Pros:** environmentally friendly; guests can use the nearby Aqua Dome spa for free; beautiful natural environment. **Cons:** not close to the mountain lifts; some rooms lack mountain views; a little sterile and impersonal for some. $ *Rooms from: €350* ⊠ *Unterlängenfeld 190, Längenfeld* ☎ *05253/5455* ⊕ *www.waldklause.at* ⊅ *55 rooms* ⏏️ *Free breakfast.*

Nightlife

The nightlife here varies from wild to nonexistent, depending on the season. In winter there are more than 85 bars, discos, and pubs—and they're all packed. Many nightspots have live bands, but expect cover charges of around €5. In

You may recognize the world famous winter destination Sölden as the stunning backdrop to James Bond's *Spectre*.

summer there are far fewer options, though most Sölden hotels have on-site bars and restaurants.

Fire & Ice
BARS/PUBS | In this very popular bar, the partying lasts from 3 pm to 3 am, thanks to the great dance floor. ⊠ *Dorfstrasse 3* ☎ *05254/2203* ⊕ *www.apresskisoelden. at.*

 Activities

CLIMBING
Wildspitze
CLIMBING/MOUNTAINEERING | The Ventertal valley burrows far into the Ötztal Alps, ending in the tiny village of Vent, a popular resort center. In summer the village is transformed into a base for serious mountain climbers experienced in ice and rock climbing, who want to attempt the formidable Wildspitze (12,370 feet) or other, even more difficult neighboring peaks. Hiring a professional local guide is strongly advised. To reach Vent from Sölden, turn off at the road at Zwieselstein that's marked to Heiligenkreuz. ⊠ *Vent.*

RAFTING
Skischule Vacancia
WHITE-WATER RAFTING | As the name suggests, Vacancia is a ski school and rental shop in winter. But in the warmer months it's the best place in town to get everything you need to enjoy the area's wild waters. It even offers guided rafting trips. You can also come here to arrange other outdoors activities including canyoning, glacier walks, and special outdoor adventures for kids. ⊠ *Dorfstrasse 70* ☎ *05254/3100* ⊕ *www.vacancia.at.*

SKIING
Sölden is one of Austria's top skiing and snowboarding areas, with great snow and a long season thanks to its high-altitude slopes and two skiable glaciers. There are 150 km (93 miles) of slopes, with the top station at 10,660 feet, served by 33 lifts. The tourist office website has full information on ski instruction and equipment rental.

St. Anton am Arlberg

100 km (62 miles) west of Innsbruck, 88 km (55 miles) northwest of Sölden.

St. Anton is known as a cult destination for good skiers and boarders from around the world because of its extensive slopes full of character and challenges, and its huge amount of off-piste opportunities. But it's also a high-profile destination and attracts the wealthy, the prominent, and, occasionally, the royal. Therefore, accommodations are not cheap, but there is a wide range of options, and if you shop around you can find somewhere to stay, particularly outside the center of the action, at a bearable price.

Thanks to an amazing system of cable cars, gondolabahns, chairlifts, and T-bars, St. Anton grants skiers access to the Arlberg region's more than 300 km (186 miles) of marked runs. If you decide to take to the slopes, remember that skiing remains a serious business in St. Anton; this is a resort where skiers come in search of the steep and the deep, so choose your itinerary with care. Be aware of the different trail classifications in Europe—easy runs are marked blue on the trail map, medium is red, and difficult is black—but in places such as St. Anton, a blue might be a red elsewhere and a red might easily be a black.

St. Anton is also a particularly lovely town in summer, where visitors can enjoy hiking, mountain biking, rock-climbing, or simply soaking up the mountain views. Book a stay anywhere in town between July and mid-October and you'll get a free St. Anton Summer Card, which includes access to all cable cars, e-bike rental, a round of golf, and a whole host of other benefits.

GETTING HERE AND AROUND

If you come from Innsbruck in the east, you either take Autobahn A12, which turns into the S16, or the quieter B171. From Bregenz in the west, travel south on Autobahn A14, which at the city of Bludenz becomes the S16. Then, near the village of Klösterle, you can decide whether to continue straight on through the 14-km (8½-mile) Arlbergtunnel, or travel over the pass on the B197 1½ km (one mile) to St. Anton. If you're not in a hurry, go over the pass every time; this is high Alpine country and the surrounding views are fabulous.

VISTOR INFORMATION

CONTACTS St. Anton am Arlberg. ⊠ *Dorfstrasse 8* ☎ *05446/2269–0* ⊕ *www. stantonamarlberg.com.*

Sights

★ Galzigbahn

MOUNTAIN—SIGHT | The state-of-the-art Galzigbahn cable car rises from the heart of St. Anton up to the Galzig mountain, where it connects with the two-part Vallugabahn and climbs even higher, crossing from the province of Tirol into neighboring Vorarlberg. As well as offering spectacular mountain vistas all along the way—the panoramic mountain views from the platform at 9,222 feet are simply breathtaking—there's also a great selection of hiking and biking trails, as well as restaurants and refreshment huts along the way. It's open in the summer from July through early September, and in winter as part of the St. Anton ski resort. ⊠ *Kandaharweg 9* ☎ *05446/23520* ⊕ *www.arlbergerbergbahnen.com.*

🛏 Hotels

Anton Aparthotel

$$$ | HOTEL | If you're not looking for a quaint Tyrolean hotel, this wood-and-glass house—modern, casual, and almost Zen-like in its simplicity—could be the answer, thanks to its location in front of the slopes and steps from the main ski lifts. **Pros:** refreshing contemporary architecture; hip vibe; central location. **Cons:** not for devotees of the traditional; draws a party crowd and accompanying

noise; need to book far in advance. $ *Rooms from: €260* ⊠ *Kandaharweg 4* ☎ *05446/2408* ⊕ *www.hotelanton. at* ⇝ *14 rooms, 3 apartments* ⟨Ol *Free breakfast.*

Raffl's St. Antonerhof

$$$$ | HOTEL | The Raffl family has created a distinctive and memorable hotel filled with antiques and art of all kinds. **Pros:** great location for skiers; fabulous cuisine; supreme luxury. **Cons:** closed in summer; very expensive; early booking is essential. $ *Rooms from: €680* ⊠ *Arlbergstrasse 69* ☎ *05446/29100* ⊕ *www. antonerhof.at* ۝ *Closed Apr.–mid-Dec.* ⇝ *36 rooms* ⟨Ol *Free breakfast.*

★ Schwarzer Adler

$$$$ | HOTEL | The beautifully frescoed façade of this ancient inn, which has been offering hospitality for nearly 450 years, hints at what you'll find inside: open fireplaces, Tyrolean antiques, and colorful Oriental carpets. **Pros:** gorgeous skypool with panoramic views; best bar in St. Anton; lovely building. **Cons:** the pool area can get very busy; no minibar or hot drinks in rooms; not cheap. $ *Rooms from: €400* ⊠ *Dorfstrasse 35* ☎ *05446/22440* ⊕ *www.schwarzeradler. com* ۝ *Closed mid-Apr.–May and mid-Sep.–Nov.* ⇝ *77 rooms* ⟨Ol *No meals.*

Ⓨ Nightlife

For some visitors to St. Anton the show, not the snow, is the thing. The vast majority of the bars are in the pedestrian zone, though some of the most famous are up on the slopes.

Horny B

BARS/PUBS | Yes, it's a terrible name. But it's also one of the area's best nightclubs, with live music and guest DJs. The popular après-ski spot opens at 9 pm and closes between 3 and 4 am. ⊠ *Dorfstrasse 50* ⊕ *www.hornyb.com.*

Krazy Kanguruh

DANCE CLUBS | A favorite après-ski gathering spot, the Krazy Kanguruh is located right on the slopes: that means you'll have to ski down to get back to town, which could be tricky after a few drinks. Skiers have been partying here since 1965, and a trip to St. Anton is not complete without at least one visit here. ⊠ *Mooserweg 19* ☎ *05446/2633* ⊕ *www. krazykanguruh.com.*

Mooserwirt

BARS/PUBS | Raucous, mind-boggling, and legendary, the Mooserwirt, on the piste side above St. Anton, has carved a reputation as one of skiing's most famous—or notorious—nightlife spots. By all acounts, owner Eugen Scalet decided to "kill the cows and milk the tourists" by turning his parents' farmhouse into one of the world's rowdiest après-ski bars. It's said to sell the second-largest amount of beer annually of any bar in Austria. It has a boutique (soundproofed) hotel next door—the ultimate ski-in, ski-out destination. ⊠ *Unterer Mooserweg 2* ☎ *05446/3588* ⊕ *www.mooserwirt.at.*

Murrmel Bar

BARS/PUBS | This popular live-music bar in the heart of St. Anton opens early and closes late, making it equally appealing for a post-slopes beer or a big night out. Try to catch a set from regular Gunar Franzoi, whose sublime guitar shredding has patrons dancing on the tables. ⊠ *Dorfstrasse 64* ☎ *05446/2300* ⊕ *www. murrmel.at.*

Activities

SKIING

The *Skihaserl,* or ski bunny, as the beginner is called, usually joins a class on St. Anton's nursery slopes, where he or she will have plenty of often-distinguished company. Once past the Skihaserl stage, skiers go higher in the Arlberg mountains to the superlative runs at Galzig and the 9,100-foot Valluga above it. Check with your hotel or the ski-pass desks at the base of the Galzigbahn gondola about an **Arlberg Skipass,** which is good on cable cars and lifts in St. Anton and St. Christoph on the Tyrol side and on those in Zürs, Lech, Oberlech, and Stuben in Vorarlberg (as well as the resorts of Warth and Schrecken, to which Lech is now linked via a gondolabahn). For complete details on St. Anton's skiing facilities, contact the town's tourist office.

Skischule Arlberg

SKIING/SNOWBOARDING | This is considered by some to be the Harvard of ski schools and its location is certainly fitting, since Arlberg is known as the cradle of skiing. The world's first properly organized ski school was opened here by ski pioneer Hannes Schneider. ⊠ *St. Christoph 8* ☎ *05446/2151* ⊕ *www.skischool-arlberg. com.*

Ischgl and Galtür

105 km (65 miles) southwest of Innsbruck, 43 km (27 miles) south of St. Anton am Arlberg.

Ischgl, the best-known resort in the Paznaun Valley, has become as renowned for its party scene as for its excellent skiing—it links with the Swiss resort of Samnaun and has a wealth of high-altitude runs. In summer it's a popular health resort, with activities including hiking, climbing, and mountain biking. There are many high-profile events here, both in summer and winter, including big-name rock concerts, mountain biking, and culinary events, and one of Europe's leading snow sculpture (as opposed to ice sculpture) competitions.

Slightly higher up the valley is **Galtür,** equally popular as a winter-sports area, summer resort, and a base for mountain climbing. Although Galtür is a starting point for practiced mountaineers, many of the climbs up the Blue Silvretta are easy and lead to the half-dozen mountain

huts belonging to the Alpenverein. Galtür and the Silvretta region inspired Ernest Hemingway's novella *Alpine Idyll*; the author spent the winter of 1925 here, and the town still remembers him fondly.

You can get to Idalp, at 7,500-feet, via the four-kilometer-long (2½-mile-long) Silvretta gondolabahn. The enchanting Paznaun Valley follows the course of the Trisanna River for more than 40 km (25 miles). The valley runs into the heart of the Blue Silvretta mountains, named for the shimmering ice-blue effect created by the great peaks and glaciers, dominated by the Fluchthorn (10,462 feet) at the head of the valley.

GETTING HERE AND AROUND

From Innsbruck, follow the A12 west to Landeck. Just beyond here, take the B188 southwest into the Paznauntal (Paznaun Valley); after about 40 km (25 miles) you'll reach Ischgl, while Galtür is a farther 13 km (eight miles) on the same road. Returning to Innsbruck (or to St. Anton am Arlberg), you can either double back, or, if it's nice weather and you feel like some serious Alpine driving, head to the Silvretta-Hochalpenstrasse (Silvretta High Alpine Road). It takes you on many hairpin curves up to 7,000 feet and then down into the Montafon Valley in Vorarlberg. The cost for driving on the pass is €16.50 per car.

VISITOR INFORMATION

CONTACTS Tourismusverband Paznaun. ⊠ *Dorfstrasse 43, Ischgl* ☎ *05444/52660* ⊕ *www.ischgl.com/en.*

 Sights

Alpinarium

MUSEUM | Following an avalanche of catastrophic proportions on February 23, 1999, which took 31 lives and destroyed many centuries-old homes and guesthouses, the community of Galtür undertook a massive building project. The result? The Alpinarium; a memorial, museum, conference center, café, indoor climbing hall, library, and, most significantly, a 1,132-foot-long wall built of steel and concrete designed to prevent such an accident from occurring again. On summer Saturdays, 10–4, the *Bauernmarkt* (farmers' market) sets up in front of the Alpinarium, bringing produce, cheese, meat, and specialty products. ⊠ *Hauptstrasse 29c, Galtür* ☎ *05443/20000* ⊕ *www.alpinarium.at* ⊡ *€9* ⊗ *Museum closed Mon.*

Hotels

Hotel Madlein
$$$$ | **HOTEL** | Quirkiness reigns supreme at this luxurious design hotel, from the minimalist lobby to the Zen-influenced guest rooms (although some retain Tyrolean wood paneling), and the two nightclubs. **Pros:** unique atmosphere; exclusive celebrity vibe; escalator access to ski lift. **Cons:** expensive; lacking in Tyrolean feel; can feel very busy. $ *Rooms from: €440* ⊠ *Madleinweg 2, Ischgl* ☎ *05444/5226* ⊕ *www.madlein.com* ⮡ *79 rooms* ⋓ *No meals.*

Hotel Rössle
$$$ | **HOTEL** | The oldest guesthouse in Galtür (as shown by a tax return record from 1600), the centrally located Rössle hotel overflows with Tyrolean charm. **Pros:** plenty of atmosphere; top-notch dining; quiet village surroundings. **Cons:** the lifts are a short ski-bus ride away; no nightlife nearby; church bells can be intrusive. $ *Rooms from: €250* ⊠ *Galtür 47, Galtür* ☎ *05443/8232* ⊕ *roessle-galtuer.at/hotel-roessle* ⮡ *40 rooms* ⋓ *Free breakfast.*

Post Ischgl
$$$$ | **HOTEL** | In the middle of the town's pedestrian area, an imposing facade fronts this 200-year-old haven of luxury, with attractive rooms and a highly rated restaurant serving international and local cuisine. **Pros:** close to shops, bars, and restaurants; a luxurious atmosphere; excellent food and cocktails. **Cons:** noisy

in ski season; minimum one-week bookings in winter; smoking still seems to be tolerated in the bar. $ *Rooms from: €370* ⊠ *Dorfstrasse 47, Ischgl* ☎ *05444/5232* ⊕ *www.post-ischgl.com* ⮡ *83 rooms* ⋓ *Free breakfast.*

★ Trofana Royal
$$$$ | **HOTEL** | This is Ischgl's flagship hotel, elegant and romantic, and the only five-star property in town. **Pros:** great location; large and impressive nightclub; fabulous food. **Cons:** expensive; the popular après-ski bar can get noisy; smoking is common in the lounge. $ *Rooms from: €640* ⊠ *Dorfstrasse 95, Ischgl* ☎ *05444/600* ⊕ *www.trofana-royal.at* ⮡ *111 rooms* ⋓ *Free breakfast.*

Nightlife

Ischgl has such a rousing nightlife that during the ski season it would be difficult not to find the après-ski and nightlife action.

Kuhstall
BARS/PUBS | In the center of town, Kuhstall (meaning cowshed) in the winter is a rocking, ultrapopular après-ski bar with a rustic theme. ⊠ *Sporthotel Silvretta, Dorfstrasse 74, Ischgl* ☎ *05444/5223* ⊕ *www.kuhstall.at.*

Niki's Stadl
DANCE CLUBS | An Ischgl après-ski institution, this place is traditional, raucous, bizarre, and a must-visit. It regularly provides a mix of Europop and Tyrolean après-ski cheesy oompah-rock. ⊠ *Hotel Piz Buin, Dorfstrasse 16, Ischgl* ☎ *05444/5300* ⊕ *www.nikis-stadl.com.*

Trofana Alm
BARS/PUBS | It might feel like an ancient timbered converted barn, but Trofana Alm is actually one of the most successful and slick après-ski bars in the Alps. Open from 3 pm, it switches at 7 pm from dance venue to romantic candlelit restaurant, then at 11 it's back to full-on nightclub and disco. ⊠ *Trofana Royal Hotel,*

Dorfstrasse 91, Ischgl ☎ *05444/602* 🌐 *www.trofana-alm.at.*

Zürs

112 km (70 miles) west of Innsbruck, 12 km (7½ miles) northwest of St. Anton am Arlberg.

The chosen resort of the rich and fashionable on this side of the Arlberg, Zürs is little more than a collection of large and seriously plush hotels. Perched at 5,600 feet, it's strictly a winter-sports community; when the season is over, the hotels close. But Zürs is more exclusive than nearby Lech and even more fabulous, in an ultradiscreet fashion, than Gstaad or St. Moritz in Switzerland. Royalty and celebrities don't come here to promenade or to be seen. They come to enjoy a hedonistic lifestyle behind the often anodyne facade of their five-star hotel, and to ski on perfectly groomed slopes, anonymous in helmets and sunglasses. Full board is required in most hotels, so there are relatively few "public" restaurants in town and little chance to dine around. But the hotel dining rooms are elegant; in some, jacket and tie are required in the evening. High standards were always part of the history of Zürs—the hotel Zürserhof was built by the aristocratic hotelier Count Tattenbach in the 1920s, and the first ski lift in Austria was constructed here in 1937.

GETTING HERE AND AROUND

From Innsbruck, follow the A12 and S16 to St. Anton am Arlberg. From here, take the B197 toward the Arlberg Pass (do not go into the Arlberg Tunnel) and, shortly after Rauz, follow signs to Zürs/Lech on the B198. The Arlberg Pass is sometimes closed in winter after heavy snowfall, but the road to Zürs/Lech is rarely closed, with sections protected by avalanche balconies.

Champagne on the Slopes 🍴

Accessible by the Trittkopf cable car, at the highest point of the Flexen Pass, you'll find the Flexenhäsl (Little Flexen House), a very special little hut that can seat only 20. Here you can order mouthwatering tidbits such as scampi with garlic butter and *Hirschwürstel* (venison sausage) with fresh horseradish sauce, washed down with a bottle of chilled Dom Pérignon. In the evening join in for piping-hot fondue *chinoise*. Reservations are essential (☎ 05583/4143).

VISTOR INFORMATION

CONTACTS Lech-Zürs. ✉ *Lechtal Strasse 76* ☎ *05583/2161–251* 🌐 *www.lechzuers.com.*

🛏 Hotels

Edelweiss

$$$$ | HOTEL | Housed in a 19th-century building, the Edelweiss has become a Zürs institution. **Pros:** rooms gorgeously decorated; gourmet restaurant; stylish luxury. **Cons:** can get very lively; room decoration too busy for some; very expensive. [$] *Rooms from: €430* ✉ *Lechtal Strasse 79* ☎ *05583/2662* 🌐 *www.edelweiss-arlberg.at* ⏲ *Closed mid-Apr.–Nov.* 🛏 *63 rooms, 3 apartments* 🍴 *No meals.*

Sporthotel Lorünser

$$$$ | HOTEL | The hospitable elegance of this hotel draws royalty, including Princess Caroline of Monaco and Princess (formerly Queen) Beatrix of the Netherlands. **Pros:** discreet elegance; continued top quality; right by the slopes for skiing. **Cons:** closed in summer; extremely expensive; a little over-the-top for some. [$] *Rooms from: €714* ✉ *Zürs*

112 ☎ *05583/22540* 🌐 *www.loruenser.at* 🕒 *Closed mid-Apr.–mid-Dec.* 🛏 *74 rooms* 🍴 *All-inclusive.*

Zürserhof

$$$$ | **HOTEL** | When celebrities seek privacy, they ensconce themselves in this world-famous hostelry resembling five huge interlinked chalets, a family-run house that has managed to preserve a certain intimacy. **Pros:** exclusivity and privacy; top luxury fit for a royal; wonderful food. **Cons:** high prices; too formal for some; smoking allowed in one area of the bar. [$] *Rooms from: €620* ✉ *Zürs 75* ☎ *05583/2513–0* 🌐 *www.zuerserhof.at* 🕒 *Closed mid-Apr.–Nov.* 🛏 *104 rooms* 🍴 *Free breakfast.*

Activities

SKIING

There are four main lifts out of the village: take the chairlift to Hexenboden (7,600 feet) or the cable car to Trittkopf (7,800 feet), with a restaurant and sun terrace; two chairlifts head up to Seekopf (7,000 feet) and the Zürzersee, where there is another restaurant. This mountain often gets huge snowfalls. **■ TIP→ Skiers need to be particularly aware of avalanche conditions—check with the tourist office or your hotel before you hit the off-piste slopes.**

Lech

120 km (75 miles) west of Innsbruck, 4 km (2½ miles) north of Zürs.

Just down (literally) the road from Zürs, Lech is a fully-fledged community—and one of the most fashionable in the Alps. But there are more hotels in Lech than in Zürs, better tourist facilities, bigger ski schools, more shops, and more nightlife. Hotel prices are nearly as high. Celebrities, captains of industry, and royalty are often found in this very pretty Alpine village. Be sure to check with the hotel of your choice about meal arrangements; some hotels recommend that you take half-board, which is usually a good deal.

GETTING HERE AND AROUND

From Zürs go north on the B198 for five minutes and you're in Lech. In summer you can continue north on the B198 down to the town of Warth and Reutte in Tyrol, near the German border. You can't get to Zürs or Lech via rail; take the train to Langen am Arlberg station, then transfer to a bus or taxi.

VISITOR INFORMATION

CONTACTS Lech-Zürs. ✉ *Dorf 2* ☎ *05583/2161–0* 🌐 *www.lechzuers.com.*

Hotels

★ Post Lech

$$$$ | **HOTEL** | A gemütlich atmosphere enfolds in this family-owned Relais & Chateaux chalet hotel, with murals, flower boxes, and a wood-paneled interior of extravagant luxury. **Pros:** refined luxury in a historic setting; antiques artfully displayed throughout; huge spa with indoor and outdoor pools. **Cons:** very expensive; need to reserve well in advance; minimum one-week stay in winter. [$] *Rooms from: €530* ✉ *Dorf 11* ☎ *05583/22060* 🌐 *www.postlech.com* 🕒 *Closed mid-Apr.–mid-Jun and Oct.–Nov.* 🛏 *46 rooms* 🍴 *Free breakfast.*

Pfefferkorn's Hotel

$$$$ | **HOTEL** | A cozy yet spacious wood-paneled lobby makes you feel welcome the minute you enter the Pfefferkorn, and this warm-wood Alpine style continues into many of the guest rooms. **Pros:** warm atmosphere; very attentive staff; great location close to the main lifts. **Cons:** rooms near the street can be noisy; decor a little dated in places; lots of people coming and going. [$] *Rooms from: €526* ✉ *Dorf 138* ☎ *05583/25250* 🌐 *www.pfefferkorns.net* 🕒 *Closed May–Jun. and Oct.–Nov.* 🛏 *29 rooms* 🍴 *No meals.*

Romantik Hotel Krone

$$$$ | HOTEL | Across the street from two of the main lifts, this family-managed five-star hotel started life as a tavern in 1741 and is now providing hospitality of an altogether more luxurious variety. **Pros:** ski-in ski-out in winter; excellent cuisine; impressive spa. **Cons:** nighttime revellers can be heard; morning deliveries can be noisy too; smoking is allowed in the Krone Bar. $ *Rooms from: €480* ✉ *Dorf 13* ☎ *05583/2551* ⊕ *www.krone-lech.at* ⊗ *Closed mid-Apr.–mid-Jun. and Oct.–Nov.* ⊷ *53 rooms* ⊙ *Free breakfast.*

Nightlife

Lech has a lively après-ski and nightlife scene—not nearly as overt as in nearby St. Anton or Ischgl, but partying is important to most Austrian ski villages, even ones as upscale as Lech. Prices vary from place to place, but in general a mixed drink will cost in the region of €15.

Après Ski Ice Bar

BARS/PUBS | The tradition of tea dancing (literally a dance at teatime, popular since Victorian times, especially at smart ski resorts) carries on après-ski at the ice-bar of the Tannbergerhof—but nowadays it's more disco than foxtrot. ✉ *Dorf 111* ☎ *05583/2202* ⊕ *www.tannbergerhof. com.*

Burg

BARS/PUBS | The bar in the Burg hotel in Oberlech features live music most nights. ✉ *Burg Hotel, Oberlech 266* ☎ *05583/22910* ⊕ *www.burghotel-lech. com.*

Goldener Berg

BARS/PUBS | The bar at the Goldener Berg is usually a hot après-ski spot, often with live music. ✉ *Goldener Berg, Oberlech 117* ☎ *05583/22050* ⊕ *www.goldener-berg.at/en.*

Krone Bar

BARS/PUBS | The bar in the Romantik Hotel Krone is open, and remains quite lively,

Say Käse, Please

In the last two decades, cheese making has undergone a magnificent revival in the region. Farmers produce more than 30 varieties of *Käse*—from Emmental to beer cheese, Tilsit to red-wine cheese, and *Bergkäse* (mountain cheese) in dozens of varieties. Look for discreet *KäseStrasse* signs along the road, pointing you toward the region's elite cheese makers, or for the word *Sennerei*, which means Alpine dairy (⊕ *www.kaesestrasse. at*).

until 2 or 3 am. ✉ *Dorf 13* ☎ *05583/2551* ⊕ *www.kronelech.at/cuisine/hotel-bar-lounge-arlberg.html.*

Activities

SKIING

Lech is linked with Oberlech and Zürs, with more than 30 ski lifts and cable cars, all accessed by the regional ski pass. This also allows skiers to take in the entire region, including Stuben, St. Christoph, and St. Anton, as well as Warth and Schröcken, newly linked by lift to Lech. The St. Anton area is also now linked to Zürs thanks to a gondola system, negating the need to take a ski-bus. The area as a whole includes more than 90 cable cars and lifts (many of them with heated seats) and 300 km (186 miles) of groomed pistes. In addition, there is a large network of cross-country trails.

The slopes in Lech are spread between 4,757 feet and 9,186 feet above sea level, including the runs of Rüfikopf, Madloch, and Mohnenfluh. Some 400 skiing instructors can help you master the craft here. Snowboarders have their own Fun

Park, and there is a floodlit toboggan run and horse-drawn sleigh rides.

For more information on skiing facilities, contact the tourist office in Lech.

Schruns-Tschagguns

140 km (87 miles) west of Innsbruck, 48 km (30 miles) southwest of Lech.

Author Ernest Hemingway spent many winters at the Schruns–Tschagguns skiing area in the Montafon Valley. Today neither of the towns—across the Ill River from each other—is as fashionable as the resorts on the Arlberg, but the views over the Ferwall Alps to the east and the mighty Rätikon on the western side of the valley are unsurpassed anywhere in Austria. In winter the heavy snowfalls here provide wonderful skiing. In fact, many believe the fully integrated ski area to be seriously underrated. The snow record is good, the runs are interesting, and a renaissance of the area's winter status is on the horizon. Many skiers head for Hochjoch-Zamang—the main peak at **Schruns**—to have lunch on the spectacularly sited sun terrace of the Kapell restaurant. Then it's on to Grabs-Golm over the river in **Tschagguns**. Others prefer the Silvretta-Nova run at Gaschurn and St. Gallenkirch. In summer, the heights are given over to climbers and hikers, the mountain streams to trout anglers, and the lowlands to tennis players.

GETTING HERE AND AROUND

From Innsbruck, take the A12/S16 west to the edge of Bludenz, then turn south onto the B188 to the Montafoner Tal (Montafon Valley). After about eight km (five miles) you will reach Schruns–Tschagguns. From Bregenz take the A14 south to join the B188. If you want to experience Alpine driving after your visit to town, continue south on the B188 to the Silvretta-Hochalpenstrasse (Silvretta High Alpine Road) to the Bielerhöhe at 7,000 feet, and then over many hairpin curves into Tyrol and the Paznaun Valley. The cost of using the pass is €16.50 per car. Attempt the drive only in ideal weather conditions and if you have good brakes; in winter the pass is closed.

VISITOR INFORMATION

CONTACTS Montafon Valley. ✉ *Montafoner Strasse 21, Schruns* ☎ *050/6686* 🌐 *www.montafon.at.*

🍴 Restaurants

Gasthof Löwen

$$ | AUSTRIAN | Guests started eating here more than 500 years ago, and they've been coming back ever since. The old dining room has wood-paneled walls and is the perfect setting in which to enjoy a *Zwiebelrostbraten* (steak with onions) and a good red wine. Unfortunately, the historic tables with the beautiful inlay work are not for sale. Ernest Hemingway certainly enjoyed his stays in "the old inn with the antlers in Tschagguns." There's also folk music performed here regularly. You can ask the staff if one of the five guest rooms is available. The reception is in the Montafoner Hof, just across the street, which belongs to the same family. **Known for:** traditional atmosphere; live folk music; solid Austrian fare. [$] *Average main: €17* ✉ *Kreuzgasse 4, Tschagguns* ☎ *05556/72247* 🌐 *www.loewen-tschagguns.at* 🕒 *Closed Mon.*

🛏 Hotels

Löwen Hotel

$$$$ | HOTEL | This enormous hotel looms over the heart of Schruns, but step inside and you'll find a welcoming (if not exactly intimate) place; a modern take on a traditional Austrian abode, with the rustic dark-wood theme carried elegantly through into the comfortable rooms. **Pros:** spacious and luxurious; enormous spa including a women-only section; glorious scenic setting. **Cons:** atmosphere can feel a bit formal; large size means no sense of intimacy; some

feel it lacks Austrian tradition. $ *Rooms from: €350* ✉ *Silvrettastrasse 8, Schruns* ☎ *05556/7141* ⊕ *www.loewen-hotel.com* ⊘ *Closed mid-Apr.–mid-May* ⇆ *85 rooms* ⦿❘ *Free breakfast.*

Montafoner Hof

$$$ | **HOTEL** | There's a lot of local flavor in this popular and welcoming family-run hotel in Tschagguns, where the owner's hunting credentials are reflected in the delicious traditional food in the restaurant. **Pros:** Austrian hospitality at its finest; indoor-outdoor swimming pool; wonderful food. **Cons:** restaurant not great for vegetarians; some rooms not renovated; no air conditioning. $ *Rooms from: €300* ✉ *Kreuzgasse 9, Tschagguns* ☎ *05556/7100* ⊕ *www.montafonerhof. com* ⊘ *Closed May and end of mid-Oct.– mid-Dec.* ⇆ *48 rooms* ⦿❘ *Free breakfast.*

🏃 Activities

FISHING

The local mountain streams and rivers are full of fish. Licenses are available; ask the regional tourist office in Bregenz for detailed information on seasons and locations.

SKIING

Schruns is one of the skiing centers of the Montafon region, which also includes the Bartholomäberg, Gargellen, Gaschurn-Partenen, St. Gallenkirch-Gortipohl, Silbertal, and Vandans ski areas. They are together covered with a Montafon Ski Pass and comprise 65 lifts and 208 kilometers (129 miles) of groomed runs. Ski pass prices are attractive here, €109 for a two-day adult pass, for example, with discounts for seniors and children. For details and to book passes, visit ⊕ *www.montafon.at/en.*

Bregenz

189 km (117 miles) west of Innsbruck, 65 km (40 miles) northwest of Schruns-Tschagguns.

Lying along the southeastern shore of the Bodensee (Lake Constance) with the majestic Pfänder as its backdrop, Bregenz is where Vorarlbergers themselves come to make merry, especially in summer. The waterfront promenade is lined with inviting tree-shaded cafes, hip beach bar hangouts, and pier-end champagne pavilions, while an enormous floating stage is the open-air site for performances of grand opera and orchestral works (Verdi, Puccini, and Mozart are just some of the composers who have been featured). Bregenz is the capital of Vorarlberg, and has been the seat of the provincial government since 1819. The upper town has maintained a charming old-world character, while the lower city is packed with pedestrianized streets, shops, restaurants, museums, and galleries.

GETTING HERE AND AROUND

Bregenz is right at the northwestern tip of Austria, around 2½ hours by car or train from Innsbruck, via the Arlberg tunnel. It is actually quicker—around 1½ hours—to fly into Zurich Flughafen in neighboring Switzerland and then drive or train from there. You can also reach Bregenz from Munich in Germany in around 2½ hours by car, though train connections are poor.

For travel within Europe, there are also some small airports like St. Gallen–Altenrhein and Friedrichshafen that are within easy reach of Bregenz (by car or taxi) and offer seasonal flights.

Taxi fares in Bregenz start at about €8, so taking one even a short distance can be expensive. Call to order a radio cab. The city of Bregenz also runs a very efficient public bus line.

BUS INFORMATION Bus. ⊕ *www.bregenz.travel/bregenz-by-city-bus.*

FERRY COMPANIES Vorarlberg Lines.
✉ *VL Bodenseeschiffahrt, Seestrasse 4* ☎ *05574/42868* ⊕ *www.vorarlberg-lines. at/en.*

TAXI COMPANIES City Taxi.
☎ *05574/65400* ⊕ *www.citytaxi-bregenz. at.*

FESTIVALS
★ **Bregenzer Festspiele**
MUSIC FESTIVALS | Bregenz is pleasant at any time of year, but a great time to visit is during the Bregenzer Festspiele (Bregenz Music Festival) in July and August. Acclaimed artists from around the world perform operas, operettas, and musical comedies on the festival's floating stage, part of the Festspiel und Kongresshaus (Festival Hall and Congress Center) complex. In front of the stage, the orchestra pit is built on a jetty, while the audience of 6,800 is safely accommodated on the 30-tier amphitheater on dry land—a unique and memorable setting for a concert. Reserve your tickets and hotels in advance, as performances and rooms sell out early. In the event of rain, the concert performance is moved indoors to the adjacent Festspielhaus. ✉ *Platz der Wiener Symphoniker 1* ☎ *05574/4076* ⊕ *www.bregenzerfestspiele.com/en.*

Bregenzer Frühling
DANCE | The Bregenz Spring dance festival takes place between March and May each year in the city's iconic Festspielhaus. A springtime staple since 1987, the popular festival showcases high-quality ballet and modern dance performances from renowned ensembles all over the world. ✉ *Platz der Wiener Symphoniker 1* ☎ *05574/410–1511* ⊕ *www.bregenzerfruehling.com.*

VISITOR INFORMATION
CONTACTS Tourist Information Vorarlberg. ✉ *Poststrasse 11, Dornbirn* ☎ *05572/3770330* ⊕ *www.vorarlberg.at.*

 Sights

Herz-Jesu Kirche (*Sacred Heart Church*)
RELIGIOUS SITE | Located at the top end of Bergmannstrasse, the twin red-brick towers of the neo-Gothic Herz-Jesu Kirche are visible from far and wide. Built between 1905 and 1908 and entirely funded by the people of Bregenz, it is particularly notable for its bright and colorful stained-glass windows by Martin Hausle. ✉ *Kolpingplatz 1* ⊕ *www. pfarre-herzjesu.at.*

Kunsthaus
MUSEUM | Vorarlberg has had its own modern art museum since 1997, and it sits right in the heart of Bregenz. This eye-catching, steel-and-concrete building with etched-glass panels was designed by Swiss architect Peter Zumtho, and is now used to showcase a series of ever-changing contemporary art exhibitions, with a big focus on video and multimedia (there's no permanent exhibition). The design is striking, with each room/floor lit by sunlight that enters through the translucent glass all around, but is not always easy to navigate; good luck finding the staircase on your first visit. ✉ *Karl-Tizian-Platz* ☎ *05574/485940* ⊕ *www.kunsthaus-bregenz.at* ⦂ *€11 (free on first Friday of month)* ⊙ *Closed Mon.*

Künstlerhaus Thurn und Taxis
MUSEUM | Owned by the princely Thurn und Taxis family until 1915, this building, erected in 1848, now contains a modern art gallery. The park surrounding the house is one of the largest public gardens on the Bodensee, with a host of rare trees and plants from around the world. ✉ *Gallusstrasse 10* ☎ *05574/42751* ⊕ *www.kuenstlerhaus-bregenz.at.*

Nepomuk-Kapelle
RELIGIOUS SITE | Stroll along the Kornmarktstrasse and you can't fail to notice this distinctive circular chapel. Built in 1757 to serve the city's fishermen and sailors, the Chapel of St. John of

The Pfänder cable car affords a breathtaking panorama of the Bodensee as it whizzes to the peak of the Pfänder mountain.

Nepomuk has a richly decorated high altar and several paintings in the rococo style. ⊠ *Kornmarktstrasse 7.*

Parish Church of St. Gallus

RELIGIOUS SITE | Just around the corner from the foot of the **Meissnerstiege** (Meissner steps) lies the parish church of St. Gallus, the oldest in the lower part of Vorarlberg, which combines Romanesque, Gothic, and Rococo elements. The interior is decorated simply but beautifully with pastel coloring and subtle stuccos and paintings, instead of the usual excessive gilding. Look out for the multiple depictions of legendary Irish monk St. Gallus with his bear companion, particularly on the remarkable silver altar in the left side chapel. Empress Maria Theresa donated the money for the main altarpiece; see if you can spot the monarch's features on one of the shepherdesses depicted there. ⊠ *Kirchplatz 3* ⊕ *www.pfarre-st-gallus.at.*

★ Pfänder

VIEWPOINT | FAMILY | The Pfänderbahn cable car takes you up to this 3,491-foot peak overlooking Bregenz, one of the most famous lookout points in the region. From here, you can see four countries—Austria, Germany, Liechtenstein, and Switzerland—and almost 240 Alpine peaks. It's a breathtaking view, with the city directly below on the shores of the Bodensee and the lake stretching for 64 kilometers (40 miles) into the hazy distance. On your left lies the Rhine valley, and you can see the hills of Liechtenstein and Switzerland in the distance. Just across the water from Bregenz you'll notice the ancient and fascinating German island-city of Lindau in Bavaria, once a free state (a status it lost in 1802). The restaurant at the top is open throughout the summer, while children will enjoy the **Alpenwildpark**, a small outdoor zoo with Alpine ibex, mouflon, and wild boar that's open year-round. ⊠ *Pfänderbahn - Bergstation, Pfänder 3, Lochau* ☎ *05574/421600* ⊕ *www.pfaenderbahn. at/en* 🎫 *Cable-car round-trip €13.60.*

Seekapelle (*Lake Chapel*)

RELIGIOUS SITE | Next door to the current Rathaus (town hall), on the corner of Anton-Schneider-Strasse, is this beautiful old Lake Chapel, topped with an onion dome. The chapel was erected over the graves of a band of Swiss citizens, whose 1408 attempt to incorporate Bregenz into Switzerland was rejected. ⊠ *Rathausstrasse 4* ⊕ *www.kath-kirche-vorarlberg.at/bregenz.*

★ Seepromenade

TRAIL | Sweeping along the southeastern shore of the Bodensee, this peaceful lakeside promenade is the perfect place for a stroll any time of year. It runs all the way from the Festspielhaus to the harbor and is lined with charming cafes, hip bars, and tree-shaded benches all the way. As well as enjoying sweeping lake views in one direction, there are also city landmarks to see in the other, from the Neoclassical **Post Office,** to the glass-cube **Kunsthaus,** to the local mountain **Pfänder.** If you want to wander even farther, the Pipeline promenade continues northward from the harbor all the way to Lochau, near the German border. Or, in the other direction, the lakeside gets more natural with some lovely picnic and swimming spots. ⊠ *Seepromenade.*

★ Upper Town (*Oberstadt*)

HISTORIC SITE | Just a short walk but a whole world away from the lakeside, Bregenz's Upper Town is its historical heart. Walk all the way up Maurachgasse to the **Stadttor**, complete with a scary mummified shark (supposedly caught in the Bodensee). Through the gate is Ehregutaplatz, a pretty market square flanked by remains of the ancient city wall and overlooked by **Martinsturm**, a tower with an enormous onion dome. Built in 1601, it was the first Baroque construction on the Bodensee, though the chapel below dates back even further; step inside to see 14th-century frescoes. From here, amble along Martinsgasse to Graf-Wilhelm-Strasse and the **Altes Rathaus,**

the old town hall. This ornate, brightly shuttered, half-timber construction was completed in 1622. Behind here, on Eponastrasse, are the remnants of a **wall fresco** that depicts St. Christopher, St. Peter, and a kneeling abbot. Around the corner lies the 400-year-old castle **Deuring Schlössle**. This is now a private residence, but you can still admire its beautiful whitewashed facade. Better yet, head down the nearby **Meissnerstiege** passageway for a wider view of its majestic southwestern side. From here, you can also see the 16th century **Beckenturm**, named for bakers who were imprisoned here after short-changing their customers. ⊠ *Ehregutaplatz 1.*

Vorarlberg Museum

MUSEUM | Looming over Kornmarktplatz, this state-of-the-art museum with its facade of concrete flowers (look closely and you'll see they are molds of plastic bottle bottoms) has roots dating back 150 years. Today, it's home to four floors of exhibitions on the history, culture, and day-to-day life of Vorarlbergers. Expect everything from relics of Brigantium, the Roman administrative city that once stood where Bregenz is today, to Gothic and Romanesque ecclesiastical works, to videoed interviews with current residents. Information in English can be limited, but it's worth the entrance fee alone for the extraordinary top-floor blackout room with an expansive view over the lake. The exhibits in the atrium are free to view. ⊠ *Kornmarktplatz 1* ☎ *05574/46050* ⊕ *www.vorarlbergmuseum.at* ⊠ *€9 (free for under 19s)* ⊘ *Closed Mon.*

🍴 Restaurants

Café Götze

$ | CAFÉ | Locals frequent this small, unpretentious café and bakery as it's known to have the best pastries in town. The location halfway between the waterfront and the Upper Town is convenient. **Known for:** gorgeous displays of cakes; wonderful chocolates;

elegant gift-wrapping for souvenirs. [$] *Average main: €8* ✉ *Kaiserstrasse 9* ☎ *05574/44523* 🌐 *www.conditorei-goetze.com* 💳 *No credit cards* 🕒 *Closed weekends.*

Gasthof Goldener Hirschen

$$ | **ECLECTIC** | Allegedly the oldest tavern in Bregenz and close to the Upper Town, this rustic restaurant offers delicious traditional food and drinks in lively surroundings. Many say it's the most authentic Austrian eatery in town, great for *tafelspitz* (slow-cooked beef with horseradish). It also has tasty pasta dishes, including spicy spaghetti in a tomato, onion, bacon, and red pepper sauce. In spring, local asparagus is featured and later in the year the menu focuses on game. You won't go wrong with the apricot dumplings for dessert. **Known for:** lots of history; traditional seasonal specialities; reasonable prices. [$] *Average main: €14* ✉ *Kirchstrasse 8* ☎ *05574/42815* 🌐 *www.hotelweisseskreuz.at/golden-er-hirschen* 🕒 *Closed Sun.*

Gasthof Kornmesser

$$ | **AUSTRIAN** | This gorgeous Baroque townhouse, built in 1720 beside the iconic Nepomuk-Kapelle, is today a restaurant serving hearty Austrian dishes at very reasonable prices. Try the Wienerschnitzel, the tafelspitz, or the zander fish. Not ready for a full meal? Kornmesser also offers traditional beer snacks, like Bavarian veal sausages, as well as tasty sweet treats like apple strudel. **Known for:** excellent schnitzel; nice outdoor seating area; service can be slow when busy. [$] *Average main: €17* ✉ *Kornmarktstrasse 5* ☎ *05574/54854* 🌐 *www.kornmesser.at* 🕒 *Closed Mon.*

★ Weiss

$$ | **AUSTRIAN** | Since it opened in summer 2020, Weiss has quickly become one of the city's top dining draws, with young owner-chefs Milena and Erik bringing their burgeoning international reputations to the heart of Bregenz. Billing itself as a restaurant-bar-café, Weiss offers everything from coffee and snacks to special five-course menus of equally-sized dishes, making it an imaginative, unfussy, and surprisingly affordable dining experience. Along with neighbouring establishments like Petrus and Cafesito, Weiss has helped transform Anton-Schneider-Strasse into Bregenz's foremost foodie drag. **Known for:** delicious krautspätzle (cheese dumplings); extensive Austrian wine list; stays open late. [$] *Average main: €13* ✉ *Anton-Schneider-Strasse 5* ☎ *05574/90859* 🌐 *www.weiss-bregenz.at/en* 🕒 *Closed Tues.–Wed. No lunch.*

Wirtshaus am See

$$$ | **AUSTRIAN** | This striking half-timber house with a steep gabled roof is in an idyllic position right on the shore of the Bodensee, next to the floating stage used for the Bregenz Festival. With a fabulous lake view, diners can watch the steamers from the nearby harbor go by while enjoying classic Austrian dishes with an accent on fresh fish. Some dishes from Germany and Switzerland are also offered. The wine list is noteworthy, and in the winter the Chimney Room, with an open fire, is popular. **Known for:** terrace dining with a view; fresh fish right from the lake; excellent breakfast. [$] *Average main: €20* ✉ *Seepromenade 2* ☎ *05574/42210* 🌐 *www.wirtshausamsee.at* 🕒 *Closed Jan. and Feb.*

Hotels

Grand Hotel Bregenz

$$ | **HOTEL** | Adjacent to the Festspielhaus at the western end of the Seepromenade, the Grand Hotel has the look and atmosphere of a typical Mgallery chain property: functionally modern with every comfort. **Pros:** lovely waterside location and lake views; excellent breakfast; conveniently close to the train station. **Cons:** chain-hotel feel; surrounded by parking lots; can get busy due to casino next door. [$] *Rooms from: €170* ✉ *Platz der Wiener Symphoniker 2* ☎ *05574/461000* 🌐 *www.all.accor.com* 🛏 *105 rooms* 🍴 *Free breakfast.*

Hotel Schwärzler
$$ | HOTEL | Bregenz's most upmarket accommodation option is right on the edge of town, with guest rooms that offer clean, crisp, modern lines and muted colors (and, occasionally, balconies overlooking the serene garden). **Pros:** big and varied breakfast buffet; good gym and sauna facilities; bicycles available for use by guests. **Cons:** a bit of a trek from town center; Wi-Fi is patchy in some areas; street-side rooms can be noisy. [$] *Rooms from: €165* ✉ *Landstrasse 9* ☎ *05574/4990* 🌐 *www.schwaerzler.s-hotels.com* 🛏 *61 rooms* 🍴 *Free breakfast.*

Weisses Kreuz
$$ | HOTEL | This traditional, family-run, turn-of-the-20th-century house is in a great central location, on the edge of the pedestrian zone, and is noted for its friendly staff and comfortable, modern rooms; those overlooking the private park out back are quieter. **Pros:** traditional hospitality hub in Bregenz; handy central location; delicious breakfast. **Cons:** bar music can be heard until late; creaky floorboards; some rooms lack views. [$] *Rooms from: €140* ✉ *Römerstrasse 5* ☎ *05574/4988* 🌐 *www.hotel-weisseskreuz.at* 🛏 *44 rooms* 🍴 *Free breakfast.*

Performing Arts

Theater am Kornmarkt
CONCERTS | Constructed in 1838 as a grain storehouse, back when Bregenz was still an important commercial hub, this listed building was converted into a 700-seat theater in 1954. Today, it is part of the Vorarlberg Landestheater, showing a roster of contemporary and classic plays, along with many family-friendly productions and live music concerts. ✉ *Kornmarktstrasse 2* ☎ *05574/42018* 🌐 *www.landestheater.org.*

Activities

BICYCLING

It's possible to cycle around the Bodensee in two to four days, traveling all the while on well-marked and-maintained paths (don't forget your passport). If this sounds too strenuous, parts of the route can be covered by boat. Rental bikes can be hired at local sports shops or at the train station in Bregenz; the tourist office can provide you with maps and details. Another cycling path, popular with families, follows the Rhine—a 70-kilometer (43-mile) stretch from Bregenz south to Bludenz. Parts of the route are possible by train.

SKIING

Pfänder
SKIING/SNOWBOARDING | There is some modest skiing on the Pfänder mountain, in Bregenz's backyard, which has a cable tramway and two drag lifts. The views are stunning from atop the peak, stretching as far as the Black Forest and the Swiss Alps. ✉ *Pfänderbahn (Talstation), Steinbruchgasse 4* ☎ *05574/421600* 🌐 *www.pfaenderbahn.at.*

WATER SPORTS

With the vast lake at its doorstep, Bregenz offers a variety of water sports, from swimming to fishing to windsurfing.

Ländle SUP
WATER SPORTS | Try your hand at paddle-boarding at this watersports center north of Bregenz. Certified instructors offer a series of courses for all levels, including intensive one-on-ones, as well as sunset tours of the lake. ✉ *Am Kaiserstrand, Lochau* ☎ *0664/7388–3029* 🌐 *www.laendle-sup.at.*

Sporer-Yachting
SAILING | You can learn to sail at this segelschule in Lochau, three kilometers (two miles) north of Bregenz, although a minimum of two weeks is required for a full course. ✉ *Alte Fähre 1, Lochau* ☎ *05574/52247* 🌐 *www.sporer-yachting.com.*

Index

Photo Credits

Front Cover: stockex / Alamy [Description: A view of the Mirabell Gardens and Hohensalzburg fortress in summer.]. **Back cover, from left to right:** Alexey Fedorenko/Shutterstock, Tatiana Popova/Shutterstock, Rasto SK/Shutterstock. **Spine:** Nataliya Peregudova / Shutterstock. **Interior, from left to right:** Nok Lek/Shutterstock (1). Sina Ettmer Photography/Shutterstock (2). **Chapter 1: Experience Vienna and the Best of Austria:** VitalyEdush (6-7).S.Borisov / Shutterstock (8). Macsim | Dreamstime.com (9). R&R Publications Mark / age fotostock (9). canadastock / Shutterstock (10). Gunter LenzimageBROKER / age fotostock (10). Martin SiepmannimageBROKER / age fotostock (10). Sylvain Grandadam / age fotostock (11). Icononiac | Dreamstime.com (11). millionhope/iStockphoto (12). MAK/Katrin Wisskirchen (12). B.O'Kane / Alamy (12). S.Borisov / Shutterstock (13). Maryna Iaroshenko/iStockphoto (16). WienTourismus/Paul Bauer (17). Photosounds | Dreamstime.com (18). WienTourismus/Peter Rigaud (18). WienTourismus/Paul Bauer (18). sedmak/iStockphoto (19). Radub85 | Dreamstime.com (19). Third Man Museum, Vienna (20). Tanzschule Rueff (20). Credit: volkerpreusser / Alamy Stock Photo (20). FooTToo/Shutterstock (20). Romanple | Dreamstime.com (21). Kronsteiner/PID (21). Graphiapl | Dreamstime.com (21). Meinzahn | Dreamstime.com (21). frantic00/Shutterstock (22). WienTourismus/Peter Rigaud (22). Thomas Steinlechner/Swarovski Kristallwelten (22). Stefan Liewehr/Leschanz (22). WienTourismus/Christian Stemper (23). **Chapter 3: Innere Stadt, District 1:** cristianoalessandro/iStockphoto (53). Marcobrivio6/Dreamstime (66). Paveldeminrus | Dreamstime.com (70). Video Media Studio Europe/Shutterstock (77). Efesenko | Dreamstime.com (82). **Chapter 4: Leopoldstadt and Alsergrund, Districts 2 and 9:** Romanple | Dreamstime.com (97). Industryandtravel | Dreamstime.com (101). Plam Petrov/Shutterstock (109). **Chapter 5: Landstrasse and Wieden, Districts 3 and 4:** MarcQuebec/iStockphoto (111). travelview/Shutterstock (114). **Chapter 6: Neubau, Mariahilf, and Josefstadt, Districts 6, 7, and 8:** Fotokon/Shutterstock (123). Milangonda | Dreamstime.com (126). JJFarquitectos/iStockphoto (133). **Chapter 7: Greater Vienna, Districts 10, 11, 13, 14, 15, 16, 19, 20, 21, 22:** Preisler | Dreamstime.com (139). Dreamframer/iStockphoto (144). woolver/Shutterstock (149). **Chapter 8: Day Trips from Vienna:** Lugmayer | Dreamstime.com (153). Leobrix | Dreamstime.com (162). TTstudio/Shutterstock (167). Bence Bezeredy/iStockphoto (178). saiko3p/iStockphoto (192). **Chapter 9: Salzburg:** rsndetre/iStockphoto (199). Anibaltrojo | Dreamstime.com (209). Anibaltrejo | Dreamstime.com (213). canadastock/Sutterstock (226). Izabela23/Shutterstock (228). saiko3p/iStockphoto (236). **Chapter 10: Eastern Alps:** trabantos/Shutterstock (239). Efesenko | Dreamstime.com (247). Johnypan | Dreamstime.com (250). Bernd Thaller/Flickr (254). Damian Kania/Flickr (257). **Chapter 11: Salzkammergut:** Shaiith | Dreamstime.com (259). Brendan Riley/Shutterstock (273). Vera_Petrunina/iStockphoto (274). **Chapter 12: Carinthia and Graz:** pkazmierczak/iStockphoto (277). Iciakprzemek | Dreamstime.com (297). Spectral-Design/iStockphoto (299). **Chapter 13: Innsbruck, Tyrol, and Vorarlberg:** Alexey Oblov/Shutterstock (303). gowithstock/Shutterstock (315). Alizada Studios/Shutterstock (337). SBWorldphotography/Shutterstock (338). Angela Cini/Shutterstock (351). **About Our Writers:** All photos are courtesy of the writers.

Every effort has been made to trace the copyright holders, and we apologize in advance for any accidental errors. We would be happy to apply the corrections in the following edition of this publication.

Notes

Notes

Notes

Notes

Notes

Fodor's VIENNA & THE BEST OF AUSTRIA

Publisher: Stephen Horowitz, *General Manager*

Editorial: Douglas Stallings, *Editorial Director*; Jill Fergus, Jacinta O'Halloran, Amanda Sadlowski, *Senior Editors*; Kayla Becker, Alexis Kelly, Rachael Roth, *Editors*

Design: Tina Malaney, *Director of Design and Production*; Jessica Gonzalez, *Graphic Designer*; Mariana Tabares, *Design & Production Intern*

Production: Jennifer DePrima, *Editorial Production Manager*; Elyse Rozelle, *Senior Production Editor*; Monica White, *Production Editor*;

Maps: Rebecca Baer, *Senior Map Editor*; David Lindroth, Mark Stroud (Moon Street Cartography), *Cartographers*

Photography: Viviane Teles, *Senior Photo Editor*; Namrata Aggarwal, Ashok Kumar, Carl Yu, *Photo Editors*; Rebecca Rimmer, *Photo Intern*

Business & Operations: Chuck Hoover, *Chief Marketing Officer*; Robert Ames, *Group General Manager*; Devin Duckworth, *Director of Print Publishing*; Victor Bernal, *Business Analyst*

Public Relations and Marketing: Joe Ewaskiw, *Senior Director Communications & Public Relations*

Fodors.com: Jeremy Tarr, *Editorial Director*; Rachael Levitt, *Managing Editor*

Technology: Jon Atkinson, *Director of Technology*; Rudresh Teotia, *Lead Developer*; Jacob Ashpis, *Content Operations Manager*

Writers: Patti McCracken, Jacy Meyer, Joseph Reaney, Caroline Sieg

Editor: Jacinta O'Halloran

Production Editor: Elyse Rozelle

4th Edition

ISBN 978-1-64097-348-0

ISSN 2372–689X

SPECIAL SALES
This book is available at special discounts for bulk purchases for sales promotions or premiums. For more information, e-mail SpecialMarkets@fodors.com.

PRINTED IN CANADA

10 9 8 7 6 5 4 3 2 1

About Our Writers

Patti McCracken is a journalist and educator who has lived and worked in more than 25 countries accross Central and Eastern Europe, the Balkans, the Caucasus, North Africa, and Southeast Asia. She is a former Knight International Press Fellow whose articles have appearing in *The Wall Street Journal*, the *San Francisco Chronicle*, the *Chicago Tribune*, *Smithsonian Magazine*, and *Afar*, among other publications. She divides her time between Austria and Martha's Vineyard. Patti updated the Travel Smart chapter this edition.

Jacy Meyer has lived in Central Europe since 2004, splitting her time between Prague, Vienna, Berlin, and all points in-between. A freelance journalist, blogger, and copywriter, her work can be found in multiple print publications, on travel websites, and hidden in company's "About Us" pages. She most enjoys exploring Central Europe on either her bike or feet, having logged many kilometers of terrain over the years. In town, you'll find her in a museum, a café, or a park. For this edition, she updated the Salzkammergut and Carinthia and Graz chapters.

Joseph Reaney is an experienced British travel writer and editor specializing in Central and Eastern Europe. After living in Feldkirch, Vorarlberg for several years, he now resides across the Czech border in Prague. As well as writing for international publications like *National Geographic* and *The Guardian*, he also runs his own travel content writing agency, World Words. When he has the time, Joseph also writes and directs comedy productions, from short films to live sketch shows. For this edition, he updated the Day Trips from Vienna; Salzburg; and Innsbruck, Tyrol & Vorarlberg chapters.

Caroline Sieg is your typical lifelong nomad and third-culture kid. She carries two passports: Swiss and American and has lived in eight countries across three continents. She speaks English and German, conversational French and some Spanish. Caroline is an experienced writer, editor, and content marketer focusing on travel, food, art, design, and the outdoors. She updated Innere Stadt; Leopoldstadt and Alsergrund; Landstrasse and Wieden; Neubau, Mariahilf, and Josefstadt; Greater Vienna; and the Eastern Alps chapters for this edition. Caroline's least favorite question is "Where are you from?" Her favorite question is "Where are you going next?"